Preface

About AICPA Audit and Accounting Guides

This AICPA Audit and Accounting Guide has been developed by the AICPA Health Care Committee and the AICPA Health Care Audit and Accounting Guide Overhaul Task Force to assist management in the preparation of their financial statements in conformity with U.S. generally accepted accounting principles (GAAP) and to assist auditors in auditing and reporting on such financial statements.

The financial and reporting guidance contained in this guide was approved by the affirmative vote of at least two-thirds of the members of the Accounting Standards Executive Committee, now the Financial Reporting Executive Committee (FinREC). FinREC is the senior technical body of the AICPA authorized to speak for the AICPA in the areas of financial accounting and reporting. This guide does the following:

- Identifies certain requirements set forth in Financial Accounting Standards Board (FASB) *Accounting Standards Codification*™ (ASC).
- Describes FinREC's understanding of prevalent or sole industry practice concerning certain issues. In addition, this guide may indicate that FinREC expresses a preference for the prevalent or sole industry practice, or it may indicate that FinREC expresses a preference for another practice that is not the prevalent or sole industry practice; alternatively, FinREC may express no view on the matter.
- Identifies certain other, but not necessarily all, industry practices concerning certain accounting issues without expressing FinREC's views on them.
- Provides guidance that has been supported by FinREC on the accounting, reporting, or disclosure treatment of transactions or events that are not set forth in FASB ASC.

Accounting guidance for nongovernmental entities included in an AICPA Audit and Accounting Guide is a source of nonauthoritative accounting guidance. As discussed later in this preface, FASB ASC is the authoritative source of U.S. accounting and reporting standards for nongovernmental entities, in addition to guidance issued by the Securities and Exchange Commission (SEC) for public entities.

Accounting guidance for governmental entities included in an AICPA Audit and Accounting Guide is a source of authoritative accounting guidance, as described in category (b) of the hierarchy of GAAP for state and local governmental entities. This guide has been cleared by the Governmental Accounting Standards Board (GASB). AICPA members should be prepared to justify departures from GAAP, as discussed in Rule 203, *Accounting Principles* (AICPA, *Professional Standards*, ET sec. 203 par. .01).

Auditing guidance included in an AICPA Audit and Accounting Guide is recognized as an interpretive publication, pursuant to AU section 150, *Generally Accepted Auditing Standards* (AICPA, *Professional Standards*). Interpretive publications are recommendations on the application of Statements on Auditing

Standards (SASs) in specific circumstances, including engagements for entities in specialized industries. An interpretive publication is issued under the authority of the Auditing Standards Board (ASB) after all ASB members have been provided an opportunity to consider and comment on whether the proposed interpretive publication is consistent with the SASs. The members of the ASB have found this guide to be consistent with existing SASs.

The auditor should be aware of and consider interpretive publications applicable to his or her audit. If an auditor does not apply the auditing guidance included in an applicable interpretive publication, the auditor should be prepared to explain how he or she complied with the SAS provisions addressed by such auditing guidance.

Recognition

Jay Hanson
Former Chair, FinREC

Rich Paul
Chair, FinREC

Darrel R. Schubert
Chair, ASB

Financial Reporting Executive Committee (2010–2011)

Jay Hanson
Former Chair

Rich Paul
Chair

David Alexander

Robert Axel

Kimber Bascom

Adam Brown

Jim Dolinar

Lawrence Gray

Bruce Johnson

Mary Kane

Jack Markey

Joseph D. McGrath

Rebecca Mihalko

Angela Newell

Jonathon Nus

Brad Sparks

Terry Spidell

Richard K. Stuart

Dan Zwarn

Health Care Expert Panel (2010–2011)

Rick R. Corcoran
Chair

Robert D. Beard

Brent Beaulieu

Nicole Blythe

Cline Comer

Paul J. Drogosch

Gordon T. Edwards

Martha Garner

Kimberly K. McKay

Norman C. Mosrie

Mark Ross

Robert A. Wright

AUDIT & ACCOUNTING GUIDE

Health Care Entities

NEW EDITION AS OF
JULY 1, 2011

1 2 3 4 5 6 7 8 9 0 AAP 1 9 8 7 6 5 4 3 2 1

ISBN 978-0-87051-994-9

Health Care Audit and Accounting Guide Overhaul Task Force (2010–2011)

William R. Titera
Chair

Robert D. Beard

Brent Beaulieu

Nicole Blythe

Cline Comer

Rick R. Corcoran

Paul J. Drogosch

Gordon T. Edwards

Martha Garner

Kimberly K. McKay

Craig L. McKnight

Norman C. Mosrie

Susan L. Paulsen

Barbara L. Potts

Mark Ross

Robert A. Wright

AICPA Staff

Dan Noll
Director
Accounting Standards

Anne M. Mundinger
Technical Manager
Accounting and Auditing Publications

Acknowledgments

FinREC, the Health Care Audit and Accounting Guide Overhaul Task Force, and the AICPA thank the following former FinREC members for their contribution to this project: John Althoff, Rick Arpin, Glenn Bradley, Neri Bukspan, Brett Cohen, Pascal Desroches, Chuck Evans, Faye Feger, Richard Jones, Carl Kampel, Lisa Kelley, Peter Knutson, James Kroeker, Steve Lilien, Andrew Mintzer, David Morris, Holly Nelson, Benjamin S. Neuhausen, Richard Petersen, Roy Rendino, Coleman Ross, Randall Sogoloff, Enrique Tejerina, Robert Uhl, Dan Weaver, and Brent Woodford.

The Health Care Audit and Accounting Guide Overhaul Task Force and the AICPA thank the following former Health Care Audit and Accounting Guide Overhaul Task Force members for their contribution to this project: William T. Cuppett; Mark O. Dietrich; Paul Rathbun; and Merlin C. Tousant.

The Health Care Audit and Accounting Guide Overhaul Task Force and the AICPA would also like to acknowledge and thank Susan E. Budak for her assistance in the development of this guide.

Guidance Considered in This Edition

Authoritative guidance issued through July 1, 2011, has been considered in the development of this edition of the guide. Authoritative guidance discussed in the text of the guide (as differentiated from the temporary footnotes, which are denoted by a symbol rather than a number) is effective for entities with fiscal years ending on or before July 1, 2011. Authoritative guidance discussed only in temporary footnotes is not yet effective as of July 1, 2011, for entities with fiscal years ending after that same date. However, chapter 15, "Unique Considerations of State and Local Government Health Care Entities," of this guide has been updated to reflect the issuance of GASB Statement No. 62, *Codification of Accounting and Financial Reporting Guidance Contained in Pre-November 30, 1989 FASB and AICPA Pronouncements*, as discussed later in this preface.

This includes relevant guidance issued up to and including the following:

- FASB Accounting Standards Update (ASU) No. 2011-07, *Health Care Entities (Topic 954): Presentation and Disclosure of Patient Service Revenue, Provisions for Bad Debts, and the Allowance for Doubtful Accounts for Certain Health Care Entities (a consensus of the FASB Emerging Issues Task Force)*
- GASB Statements, Interpretations, and Technical Bulletins issued through July 1, 2011
- GASB *Comprehensive Implementation Guide 2010* as of June 30, 2010
- SAS No. 120, *Required Supplementary Information* (AICPA, *Professional Standards*, AU sec. 558)
- Interpretation No. 19, "Financial Statements Prepared in Conformity With International Financial Reporting Standards as Issued by the International Accounting Standards Board," of AU section 508, *Reports on Audited Financial Statements* (AICPA, *Professional Standards*, AU sec. 9508 par. .93–.97)
- Revised interpretations issued through July 1, 2011, including Interpretation Nos. 1–4 of AU section 325, *Communicating Internal Control Related Matters Identified in an Audit* (AICPA, *Professional Standards*, AU sec. 9325 par. .01–.13)
- Statement of Position (SOP) 09-1, *Performing Agreed-Upon Procedures Engagements That Address the Completeness, Accuracy, or Consistency of XBRL-Tagged Data* (AICPA, *Technical Practice Aids*, AUD sec. 14,440)
- Statement on Standards for Attestation Engagements No. 16, *Reporting on Controls at a Service Organization* (AICPA, *Professional Standards*, AT sec. 801)
- Interpretation No. 7, "Reporting on the Design of Internal Control," of AT section 101, *Attest Engagements* (AICPA, *Professional Standards*, AT sec. 9101 par. .59–.69)
- Public Company Accounting Oversight Board (PCAOB) Auditing Standard No. 15, *Audit Evidence* (AICPA, *PCAOB Standards and Related Rules*, Auditing Standards)

Users of this guide should consider guidance issued subsequent to those items in the preceding list to determine its effect on entities covered by this guide. In determining the applicability of recently-issued guidance, its effective date should also be considered.

Users may be able to obtain information about such subsequent pronouncements on FASB's website at www.fasb.org, GASB's website at www.gasb.org, and the AICPA's website at www.aicpa.org. In addition, the AICPA's annual Audit Risk Alert *Health Care Industry Developments* summarizes the provisions of selected pronouncements.

Applicability of U.S. Generally Accepted Auditing Standards and PCAOB Standards

Audits of the financial statements of *nonissuers* (those entities not subject to the Sarbanes-Oxley Act of 2002 or the rules of the SEC—that is, private entities, generally speaking) are conducted in accordance with U.S. generally accepted auditing standards (GAAS), as issued by the ASB, the senior technical committee of the AICPA with the authority to promulgate auditing standards for nonissuers. The ASB develops and issues standards in the form of SASs through a due process that includes deliberation in meetings open to the public, public exposure of proposed SASs, and a formal vote. The SASs and their related interpretations are codified in the AICPA's *Professional Standards*. Paragraph .03 of AU section 150 establishes that an AICPA member's failure to follow ASB standards for audits of nonissuers is a violation of Rule 202, *Compliance With Standards* (AICPA, *Professional Standards*, ET sec. 202 par. .01).

Audits of the financial statements of *issuers*, as defined by the SEC (those entities subject to the Sarbanes-Oxley Act of 2002 or the rules of the SEC—that is, public entities, generally speaking), are conducted in accordance with standards established by the PCAOB, a private sector, nonprofit corporation created by the Sarbanes-Oxley Act of 2002 to oversee the audits of issuers. The SEC has oversight authority over the PCAOB, including the approval of its rules, standards, and budget.

For audits of a nonissuer, in accordance with both GAAS and PCAOB standards, Interpretation No. 18, "Reference to PCAOB Standards in an Audit Report on a Nonissuer," of AU section 508 (AICPA, *Professional Standards*, AU sec. 9508 par. .89–.92), provides reporting guidance applicable to such engagements.

References to Professional Standards

In citing GAAS and their related interpretations, references use section numbers within the codification of currently effective SASs, not the original statement number, as appropriate. For example, SAS No. 54, *Illegal Acts by Clients* (AICPA, *Professional Standards*), is referred to as AU section 317, *Illegal Acts by Clients* (AICPA, *Professional Standards*). In those sections of the guides that refer to specific auditing standards of the PCAOB, references are made to the AICPA's *PCAOB Standards and Related Rules* publication. This edition includes SOP 99-1, *Guidance to Practitioners in Conducting and Reporting on an Agreed-Upon Procedures Engagement to Assist Management in Evaluating the Effectiveness of Its Corporate Compliance Program* (AICPA, *Technical Practice Aids*, AUD sec. 14,350), as appendix A, "Statement of Position 99-1, *Guidance to Practitioners in Conducting and Reporting on an Agreed-Upon Procedures Engagement to Assist Management in Evaluating the Effectiveness of Its Corporate Compliance Program*," and SOP 00-1, *Auditing Health Care Third-Party Revenues and Related Receivables* (AICPA, *Technical Practice Aids*, AUD sec. 14,360), as appendix B, "Statement of Position 00-1, *Auditing Health Care Third-Party Revenues and Related Receivables*." In using this guide, readers should refer to the material in these SOPs.

FASB ASC

Overview

Released on July 1, 2009, FASB ASC is a major restructuring of accounting and reporting standards designed to simplify user access to all authoritative U.S. GAAP by topically organizing the authoritative literature. FASB ASC disassembled and reassembled thousands of nongovernmental accounting pronouncements, including those of the FASB Emerging Issues Task Force and the AICPA, to organize them under approximately 90 topics.

FASB ASC also includes relevant portions of authoritative content issued by the SEC, as well as selected SEC staff interpretations, and administrative guidance issued by the SEC; however, FASB ASC is not the official source of SEC guidance and does not contain the entire population of SEC rules, regulations, interpretive releases, and staff guidance. Moreover, FASB ASC does not include governmental accounting standards.

FASB published a notice to constituents (NTC) that explains the scope, structure, and usage of consistent terminology of FASB ASC. Constituents are encouraged to read this NTC because it answers many common questions about FASB ASC. FASB ASC and its related NTC can be accessed at http://asc.fasb.org/home and are also offered by certain third-party licensees, including the AICPA. FASB ASC is offered by FASB at no charge in a Basic View and for an annual fee in a Professional View.

Issuance of Amendments to FASB ASC

FASB ASC is amended through ASUs, which serve only to update FASB ASC. FASB does not consider the ASUs authoritative in their own right; such amendments become authoritative when they are incorporated into FASB ASC.

The ASUs issued are in the form of "ASU No. 20YY-XX," in which "YY" is the last two digits of the year and "XX" is the sequential number for each update. For example, ASU No. 2011-01 is the first update in calendar year 2011. The ASUs will include the amendments to FASB ASC and an appendix of FASB ASC update instructions. ASUs also provide background information about the amendments and explain the basis for FASB's decisions.

Pending Content in FASB ASC

Amendments to FASB ASC issued in the form of ASUs that are not fully effective for all entities or transactions within their scope or that became effective within the last six months are reflected as "Pending Content" in FASB ASC. This pending content is shown in text boxes below the paragraphs being amended in FASB ASC and includes links to the transition information. The pending content boxes are meant to provide users with information about how a paragraph will change when new guidance becomes authoritative. After an amended paragraph has been fully effective for six months, the outdated guidance will be removed, and the amended paragraph will remain without the pending content box. FASB will keep any outdated guidance in the applicable archive section of FASB ASC for historical purposes.

Because not all entities have the same fiscal year-ends, and certain guidance may be effective on different dates for public and nonpublic entities, the pending content will apply to different entities at different times. As such, pending content will remain in place within FASB ASC until the roll-off date. Generally, the roll-off date is six months following the latest fiscal year-end for which the original guidance being amended or superseded by the pending content could be applied, as specified by the transition guidance. For example, assume an ASU has an effective date for fiscal years beginning after November 15, 2010. The latest possible fiscal year-end of an entity still eligible to apply the original guidance being amended or superseded by the pending content would begin November 15, 2010, and end November 14, 2011. Accordingly, the roll-off date would be May 14, 2012.

Entities cannot disregard the pending content boxes in FASB ASC. Instead, all entities must review the transition guidance to determine when the pending content is applicable to them. This guide identifies pending content, when applicable. As explained in the "Guidance Considered in This Edition" section, pending content discussed in the text of the guide (as differentiated from the temporary footnotes, which are denoted by a symbol rather than a number) is effective for entities with fiscal years ending on or before July 1, 2011. Pending content discussed only in temporary footnotes is not yet effective as of July 1, 2011, for entities with fiscal years ending after that same date.

Limitations and Relationships to Other Authoritative Literature

This guide does not discuss the application of all GAAP and GAAS that are relevant to the preparation and audit of financial statements of health care entities. The guide is directed primarily to those aspects of the preparation and audit of health care entities' financial statements that may be unique to those entities or that are considered particularly significant to them.

This guide incorporates certain provisions of FASB ASC 954, *Health Care Entities*; FASB ASC 958, *Not-for-Profit Entities*; GASB Statement No. 33, *Accounting and Financial Reporting for Nonexchange Transactions*, as amended; and GASB Statement No. 34, *Basic Financial Statements—and Management's Discussion and Analysis—for State and Local Governments*, as well as other authoritative accounting and auditing literature. Not all guidance included in that literature, however, is incorporated, repeated, or summarized in this guide. Accordingly, FASB ASC, GASB statements and interpretations, AICPA *Professional Standards*, and all authoritative guidance should be read in conjunction with this guide.

This guide is not the only industry-specific AICPA Audit and Accounting Guide that auditors should consider when performing an audit of a governmental health care entity. The Audit and Accounting Guide *State and Local Governments* includes governmental health care entities in its scope and was cleared by GASB. Therefore, certain accounting and financial reporting guidance in that guide constitutes category (b) of the hierarchy of GAAP for governmental health care entities. The auditing guidance in that guide should also be considered during an audit of a governmental health care entity that is included in the scope of this guide. In practice, auditors of governmental health care entities that issue separate financial statements as special-purpose governments engaged only in business-type activities[1] may use this guide as the primary source of guidance because this guide addresses transactions that are unique to, or prevalent in, the health care industry. However, the Audit and Accounting Guide *State and Local Governments* contains information about

---

[1] Governmental Accounting Standards Board (GASB) Statement No. 34, *Basic Financial Statements—and Management's Discussion and Analysis—for State and Local Governments*, does not provide guidance on separate reporting by individual enterprise funds of a government. Although this discussion of the guidance in GASB Statement No. 34 is written in terms of special-purpose business-type activities that are governmental health care entities, the accounting, financial reporting, and auditing considerations are usually equally applicable when the health care activity is conducted as a function or program of a general-purpose government and reported in an enterprise fund (see footnote 7 in chapter 12, "Special Purpose and State Governments," of the Audit and Accounting Guide *State and Local Governments*). Reporting guidance on separate reporting by individual enterprise funds of a government is provided in the Audit and Accounting Guide *State and Local Governments*.

governmental accounting and financial reporting standards and other matters that are unique to, or prevalent in, government and not included in this guide.[2]

Special-purpose governments are *legally separate entities*, as that term is described in paragraph 15 of GASB Statement No. 14, *The Financial Reporting Entity*. They may be component units of another governmental entity, or they may be other stand-alone governments (*component units* and *other stand-alone governments* are also defined in GASB Statement No. 14.). Because GASB Statement No. 34 is written from the perspective of general-purpose governments, paragraph 138 of GASB Statement No. 34 discusses how those requirements apply to special-purpose governments engaged only in business-type activities, such as certain governmental health care entities. Governmental health care entities that are special-purpose governments engaged only in business-type activities should present only the financial statements required for enterprise funds. These financial statements are discussed further in chapter 15 of this guide.

Office of Management and Budget (OMB) Circular A-133, *Audits of States, Local Governments and Non-Profit Organizations*, sets forth audit requirements for health care entities expending federal awards. Institutions covered by OMB Circular A-133 include not-for-profit hospitals, public hospitals, institutions of higher education and their affiliated hospitals, voluntary health and welfare entities, and other community-based organizations.[3] Auditors of health care entities who perform audits under *Government Auditing Standards*, the Single Audit Act Amendments of 1996, and OMB Circular A-133 should also refer to the Audit Guide Government Auditing Standards *and Circular A-133 Audits*.

New AICPA.org Website

The AICPA encourages you to visit its new website at www.aicpa.org. The website was launched in 2010 and provides significantly enhanced functionality and content critical to the success of AICPA members and other constituents. Certain content on the AICPA's website referenced in this guide may be restricted to AICPA members only.

Select Recent Developments Significant to This Guide

GASB Statement No. 62

In December 2010, GASB issued GASB Statement No. 62, which directly incorporates into GASB's authoritative literature certain pronouncements issued by FASB and its predecessors on or before November 30, 1989. FASB statements and interpretations, Accounting Principles Board Opinions, Accounting Research Bulletins of the AICPA Committee on Accounting Procedure, and AICPA accounting interpretations issued on or before November 30, 1989, have

---

[2] See paragraphs 1.21 and 12.11–.13 of the Audit and Accounting Guide *State and Local Governments*.

[3] Office of Management and Budget (OMB) Circular A-133, *Audits of States, Local Governments and Non-Profit Organizations*, also includes audit requirements for commercial organizations, including for-profit hospitals, that receive federal awards under Department of Health & Human Services programs. Generally, the organization has two options regarding audits: a financial-related audit of a particular award, in accordance with *Government Auditing Standards*, or an audit that meets the requirements of OMB Circular A-133. See Title 45, *Public Welfare*, U.S. *Code of Federal Regulations* Part 74.26(d) for further information.

been included in GASB Statement No. 62 to the extent that they do not conflict with or contradict GASB pronouncements. In that manner, GASB Statement No. 62 eliminates the need for financial statement preparers and auditors to determine which FASB and AICPA pronouncement provisions apply to state and local governments. When the guidance from the pre-November 30, 1989, pronouncements was included as part of GASB Statement No. 62, it was modified as necessary to appropriately recognize the governmental environment and needs of governmental financial statement users.

In addition, GASB Statement No. 62 supersedes GASB Statement No. 20, *Accounting and Financial Reporting for Proprietary Funds and Other Governmental Entities That Use Proprietary Fund Accounting*, thereby eliminating the election provided in paragraph 7 of that statement. That election permitted enterprise funds and business-type activities to apply post-November 30, 1989, FASB Statements and Interpretations that do not conflict with or contradict GASB pronouncements on an-all-or none basis. However, those entities can continue to apply post-November 30, 1989, FASB pronouncements as other accounting literature, provided that those prouncements do not conflict with or contradict GASB pronouncements, including GASB Statement No. 62.

The requirements of GASB Statement No. 62 are effective for financial statements for periods beginning after December 15, 2011. Although GASB Statement No. 62 is not effective immediately, GASB encourages early implementation, given that GASB does not anticipate that this standard will lead to substantial changes in practice. When governmental health care entities implement the provisions of GASB Statement No. 62, they will need to remove general or specific references, or both, to FASB and AICPA pronouncements issued on or before November 30, 1989, from the financial statements and notes thereto.

This guide reflects the issuance of GASB Statement No. 62 by including references to paragraphs in that statement, rather than the FASB and AICPA pronouncements that it codifies. To assist preparers and auditors in the transition, appendix A, "Cross-Reference Table for Predecessor Guidance," of chapter 15 provides cross-references to the predecessor pronouncements for all paragraphs from GASB Statement No. 62 that are included in chapter 15. Appendix B, "Interim Guidance for Entities That Elect Paragraph 7 of Governmental Accounting Standards Board Statement No. 20," of chapter 15 provides interim guidance for entities that elect paragraph 7 of GASB Statement No. 20 and have not yet implemented GASB Statement No. 62. In addition to helping identify which FASB statements and interpretations may be applied as other accounting literature, appendix B will compensate for the fact that upon the effective date of GASB Statement No. 62, GASB intends to remove from its website its chart that provides nonauthoritative guidance regarding the applicability of post-November 30, 1989, FASB pronouncements (www.gasb.org/jsp/GASB/Page/GASBSectionPage&cid=1175804837176).

As described in paragraphs 521–523 of the nonauthoritative basis for conclusions of GASB Statement No. 62, GASB excluded certain FASB and AICPA pronouncements from codification because those pronouncements conflict with or contradict GASB pronouncements in their entirety. As described in paragraphs 524–525, other FASB and AICPA pronouncements were omitted from codification because they rarely apply to state and local governments. Readers of this guide can find more information regarding GASB Statement No. 62 at www.gasb.org.

Summary of Significant Differences Between the PCAOB and AICPA Risk Assessment Standards

On August 5, 2010, the PCAOB issued Release No. 2010-004, *Auditing Standards Related to the Auditor's Assessment of and Response to Risk and Related Amendments to PCAOB Standards* (AICPA, *PCAOB Standards and Related Rules*, Select PCAOB Releases). This release includes eight auditing standards (collectively referred to as the PCAOB risk assessment standards), as adopted by the PCAOB. The eight standards, which were approved by the SEC on December 23, 2010, are as follows:

1. Auditing Standard No. 8, *Audit Risk*
2. Auditing Standard No. 9, *Audit Planning*
3. Auditing Standard No. 10, *Supervision of the Audit Engagement*
4. Auditing Standard No. 11, *Consideration of Materiality in Planning and Performing an Audit*
5. Auditing Standard No. 12, *Identifying and Assessing Risks of Material Misstatement*
6. Auditing Standard No. 13, *The Auditor's Responses to the Risks of Material Misstatement*
7. Auditing Standard No. 14, *Evaluating Audit Results*
8. Auditing Standard No. 15

The release also includes conforming amendments to other interim standards related to the PCAOB risk assessment standards. The effective date of the PCAOB risk assessment standards is for audits of financial statements of issuers with fiscal periods beginning on or after December 15, 2010.

In general, the PCAOB risk assessment standards are consistent with the AICPA SASs related to risk assessment (the AICPA risk assessment standards). When differences exist, they are due to the PCAOB

a. addressing audits of financial statements in conjunction with audits of effectiveness of internal control (often referred to as integrated audits). The AICPA risk assessment standards only address audits of financial statements.

b. presenting content in standards different than the AICPA risk assessment standards. For example, the PCAOB

   i. incorporated fraud risk assessment procedures into the PCAOB risk assessment standards.

   ii. created Auditing Standard No. 10 to separately address supervision of the audit engagement.

   iii. created Auditing Standard No. 14 to separately address the evaluation of audit results.

   iv. moved content related to other audit areas, such as analytical review procedures and audits of group financial statements.

The PCAOB risk assessment standards are not as voluminous as the AICPA risk assessment standards because the PCAOB risk assessment standards do not contain as much application guidance as the AICPA risk assessment standards. Appendix 11 of the release contains a more detailed comparison of the differences between the PCAOB risk assessment standards and AICPA risk assessment standards.

ASB Clarity Project

To address concerns over the clarity, length, and complexity of its standards, the ASB has made a significant effort to clarify the SAS. In order to address practice issues timely, SAS Nos. 117–120 have already been issued in the clarity format and are already effective. The majority of the clarified standards will be issued as one SAS, SAS No. 122. SAS No. 122 will contain 39 clarified SASs and will recodify and supersede all outstanding SASs through No. 121 except

- SAS No. 51, *Reporting on Financial Statements Prepared for Use in Other Countries*
- SAS No. 59, *The Auditor's Consideration of an Entity's Ability to Continue as a Going Concern*, as amended
- SAS No. 65, *The Auditor's Consideration of the Internal Audit Function in an Audit of Financial Statements*
- SAS No. 87, *Restricting the Use of an Auditor's Report*
- SAS Nos. 117–120

SAS No. 122 will also withdraw SAS No. 26, *Association With Financial Statements*, as amended.

This statement will initially be codified in *Professional Standards* as "AU-C" section numbers instead of "AU" section numbers and includes AU-C section numbers in its original release.

"AU-C" is a temporary identifier to avoid confusion with references to existing "AU" sections, which remain effective through 2013, in AICPA *Professional Standards*. The "AU-C" identifier will revert to "AU" in 2014, by which time this statement becomes fully effective for all engagements.

SAS No. 122 will be effective for audits of financial statements for periods ending on or after December 15, 2012. Refer to individual AU-C sections for specific effective date language.

The ASB established clarity drafting conventions and undertook to redraft all of its SASs in accordance with those conventions, which include the following:

- Establishing objectives for each clarified SAS
- Including a definitions section, where relevant, in each clarified SAS
- Separating requirements from application and other explanatory material
- Numbering application and other explanatory material paragraphs using an A- prefix and presenting them in a separate section that follows the requirements section
- Using formatting techniques, such as bulleted lists, to enhance readability
- Including, when appropriate, special considerations relevant to audits of smaller, less complex entities within the text of the clarified SAS

- Including, when appropriate, special considerations relevant to audits of governmental entities within the text of the clarified SAS

The project also has an international convergence component. AU-C section numbers for clarified SASs based on equivalent International Standards on Auditing (ISAs) are the same as the equivalent ISA numbers. AU-C section numbers for clarified SASs with no equivalent ISAs have been assigned new numbers. The ASB believes that this recodification structure will aid firms and practitioners that use both ISAs and GAAS.

Consistent with the ASB's strategy to converge its SASs with ISAs promulgated by the International Auditing and Assurance Standard Board while avoiding unnecessary conflict with standards of the PCAOB, clarified SASs have been developed using equivalent ISAs as a base, when applicable. Substantive differences in objectives, definitions, or requirements between a clarified SAS and the equivalent ISA are identified in an exhibit to each applicable clarified SAS.

International Financial Reporting Standards

International Financial Reporting Standards (IFRSs) consist of accounting standards and interpretations developed and issued by the International Accounting Standards Board (IASB), a London-based, independent accounting standard-setting body. The IASB began operations in 2001 when it succeeded the International Accounting Standards Committee (IASC). The IASC was formed in 1973, soon after the formation of FASB. In 2001, when the IASB replaced the IASC, a new, independent oversight body—the IASC Foundation—was created to appoint the members of the IASB and oversee its due process. The IASC Foundation's oversight role is very similar to that of the Financial Accounting Foundation (FAF) in its capacity as the oversight body of FASB.

The term *IFRSs* has both a narrow and broad meaning. Narrowly, IFRSs refer to the new numbered series of pronouncements issued by the IASB, as differentiated from International Accounting Standards (IASs) issued by its predecessor, the IASC. More broadly, however, IFRSs refer to the entire body of authoritative IASB pronouncements, including those issued by the IASC and their respective interpretive bodies. Therefore, the authoritative IFRSs literature, in its broadest sense, includes the following:

- Standards, whether labeled IFRSs or IASs
- Interpretations of the International Financial Reporting Interpretations Committee (IFRIC); interpretations issued by the IFRS Interpretations Committee, the interpretive body of the IASC Foundation; or interpretations of the Standing Interpretations Committee, the predecessor to IFRIC and former interpretive body of the IASC
- IFRS framework

As of March 31, 2010, IFRIC formally changed its name to the IFRS Interpretations Committee, and on July 1, 2010, the IASC Foundation formally changed its name to the IFRS Foundation.

The preface to the *IFRS 2010* bound volume states that IFRSs are designed to apply to the general-purpose financial statements and other financial reporting of all profit-oriented entities, including commercial, industrial, and financial entities, regardless of legal form or organization. Included within the scope of profit-oriented entities are mutual insurance companies and other mutual cooperative entities providing dividends or other economic benefits to their owners, members, or participants.

IFRSs are not designed to apply to not-for-profit entities or those in the public sector, but these entities may find IFRSs appropriate in accounting for their activities. In contrast, U.S. GAAP is designed to apply to all nongovernmental entities, including not-for-profit entities, and includes specific guidance for not-for-profit entities, development stage entities, limited liability entities, and personal financial statements.

The AICPA governing council voted in May 2008 to recognize the IASB as an accounting body for purposes of establishing international financial accounting and reporting principles. This amendment to appendix A of Rules 202 and 203 gives AICPA members the option to use IFRSs as an alternative to U.S. GAAP. As a result, private entities in the United States can prepare their financial statements in accordance with U.S. GAAP, as promulgated by FASB; an other comprehensive basis of accounting, such as cash or tax-basis; or IFRSs, among others. However, domestic issuers are currently required to follow U.S. GAAP and rules and regulations of the SEC. In contrast, foreign private issuers may present their financial statements in accordance with IFRSs, as issued by the IASB, without a reconciliation to U.S. GAAP or in accordance with non-IFRS home-country GAAP reconciled to U.S. GAAP, as permitted by Form 20-F.

The growing acceptance of IFRSs as a basis for U.S. financial reporting could represent a fundamental change for the U.S. accounting profession. Acceptance of a single set of high quality accounting standards for worldwide use by public companies has been gaining momentum around the globe for the past few years.

Blue Ribbon Panel on Private Company Financial Reporting

The Blue Ribbon Panel on Private Company Financial Reporting was established in December 2009 and is sponsored by the AICPA, FAF, and the National Association of State Boards of Accountancy. This panel was formed to consider how U.S. accounting standards can best meet the needs of users of private company financial statements. Members of the panel represent a cross-section of financial reporting constituencies, including lenders, investors, owners, preparers, and auditors.

In late 2010, the Blue Ribbon Panel voted to recommend that FAF accept a new standard-setting model for private companies and the creation of a separate board to set those standards. Work is continuing related to changes being considered for private company financial reporting. For more information, visit www.accountingfoundation.org/home.

TABLE OF CONTENTS

Chapter 1

Overview and Unique Considerations of Health Care Entities

Purpose

1.01 This guide has been prepared to assist health care entities[1] in preparing financial statements in conformity with generally accepted accounting principles in the United States of America and to assist independent auditors in auditing and reporting on those financial statements. This guide focuses on accounting and auditing issues that are pervasive in, or unique to, health care entities.

Applicability

1.02 This guide applies to the following types of health care entities:

- Investor-owned businesses.
- Not-for-profit entities that have no ownership interest and are essentially self-sustaining from fees charged for goods and services (the term *not-for-profit entity* is used as defined in the Financial Accounting Standards Board [FASB] *Accounting Standards Codification* [ASC] glossary).
- Governmental entities. See paragraph 1.08 and chapter 15, "Unique Considerations of State and Local Government Health Care Entities," of this guide for further discussion regarding governmental health care entities.

This guide applies to entities whose principal operations consist of providing or agreeing to provide health care services and that derive all or almost all of their revenues from the sale of goods or services; it also applies to entities whose primary activities are the planning, organization, and oversight of such entities, such as parent or holding companies of health care entities.

1.03 This guide does not apply to *voluntary health and welfare entities*, as defined in the FASB ASC glossary. It also does not apply to not-for-profit entities that are fund-raising foundations, even if those foundations are included in the consolidated financial statements of a health care entity. Voluntary health and welfare entities and fund-raising foundations follow the AICPA Audit and Accounting Guide *Not-for-Profit Entities*, rather than this guide.

1.04 Thus, this guide applies to the following entities, among others:

- Clinics, medical group practices, individual practice associations, individual practitioners, emergency care providers, laboratories, surgery centers, imaging centers, and other ambulatory care organizations
- Continuing care retirement communities

---

[1] Refer to the glossary for definitions of certain terms used throughout this guide.

- Drug and alcohol rehabilitation centers and other rehabilitation facilities
- HMOs and similar prepaid health care plans
- Home health agencies
- Hospice care providers
- Hospitals
- Institutional facilities that provide skilled nursing, intermediate, or less-intensive levels of health care
- Integrated health care delivery systems that include one or more of these entities
- Providers of durable medical equipment and related medical services

1.05 Some entities may have health care as a component of a larger, more diversified operation. For example, some senior independent living facilities are primarily real estate operations with a health care component. The Financial Reporting Executive Committee believes that to the extent such entities have unique transactions of the type covered by this guide, the recognition and measurement guidance of this guide would be applicable. Professional judgment should be exercised in determining the applicability of this guide to transactions entered into by such entities.

1.06 A health care entity may be part of another entity, such as a medical school or university, or a subsidiary of a corporation. The recommendations in this guide apply to the separate financial statements of the health care entity.

Classification of Health Care Entities

1.07 The nature of the entity and its operating structure have a significant effect on the needs of financial statement users. According to paragraph 8 of FASB Concepts Statement No. 4, *Objectives of Financial Reporting by Nonbusiness Organizations*

> [s]ome organizations have no ownership interests but are essentially self-sustaining from fees they charge for goods and services. Examples are those private nonprofit hospitals... that may receive relatively small amounts of contributions and grants but finance their capital needs largely from the proceeds of debt issues and their operating needs largely from service charges rather than from private philanthropy or governmental grants. As a result, assessment of amounts, timing, and uncertainty of cash flows becomes the dominant interest of their creditors and other resource providers and profitability becomes an important indicator of performance. Consequently, the objectives of Concepts Statement No. 1 may be more appropriate for those organizations.

1.08 Health care entities usually can be classified into the following categories on the basis of their operating characteristics:

a. *Investor-owned health care entities.* According to FASB ASC 954-10-05-2, these entities are owned by investors or others with a private equity interest and provide goods or services with the objective of making a profit.

b. *Not-for-profit business-oriented entities.* According to FASB ASC 954-10-05-2, these entities are characterized by no ownership interests and are essentially self-sustaining from fees charged for goods and services. The fees charged by such entities generally are intended to help the entity maintain its self-sustaining status, rather than maximize profits for the owner's benefit. Such entities often are exempt from federal income taxes and may receive contributions of relatively small amounts from resource providers that do not expect commensurate or proportionate pecuniary return.

c. *Governmental health care entities.* These are public corporations and bodies corporate and politic. Other entities are governmental entities if they have one or more of the following characteristics:

   i. Popular election of officers or appointment or approval of a controlling majority of the members of the entity's governing body by officials of one or more state or local governments

   ii. The potential for unilateral dissolution by a government, with the net assets reverting to a government

   iii. The power to enact and enforce a tax levy.

   Furthermore, entities are presumed to be governmental if they have the ability to directly issue (rather than through a state or municipal authority) debt that pays interest that is exempt from federal taxation. However, entities possessing only that ability (to issue tax-exempt debt) and none of the other governmental characteristics may rebut the presumption that they are governmental if their determination is supported by compelling, relevant evidence.

d. *Not-for-profit nonbusiness-oriented entities.* According to FASB ASC 954-10-15-3, these are *voluntary health and welfare entities*, as defined in the FASB ASC glossary. Such entities are within the scope of FASB ASC 958, *Not-for-Profit Entities*. Additional accounting guidance may be obtained in the AICPA Audit and Accounting Guide *Not-for-Profit Entities*, rather than this guide, as discussed in paragraph 1.03.

Regulatory Environment

1.09 Health care entities operate in a highly regulated environment. These regulations affect the provider's operations, as well as certain estimates in the financial statements, such as patient service revenue, third-party payor settlements, and general and professional liabilities. The Department of Health & Human Services (HHS) is the government's principal agency for protecting the health of all Americans and providing essential human services. The following agencies operate under the HHS:

- Administration on Aging
- Centers for Medicare & Medicaid Services
- Food and Drug Administration
- Health Resources and Services Administration
- National Institutes of Health
- Office of Inspector General

1.10 Other important agencies include the Civil and Criminal Divisions of the Department of Justice, each state's Office of the Attorney General, Medicaid, and insurance agencies or departments.

1.11 Some significant regulations affecting health care are the following:

- False Claims Act
- The antikickback statute of the Medicare and Medicaid Patient and Program Protection Act of 1987
- Stark I, II, and III
- Emergency Medical Treatment and Active Labor Act
- The Privacy Rule of the Health Insurance Portability and Accountability Act of 1996
- Health Information Technology for Economic and Clinical Health Act enacted as part of the American Recovery and Reinvestment Act of 2009
- Patient Protection and Affordable Care Act
- Health Care and Education Reconciliation Act of 2010

Health Care Reform

1.12 In March 2010, Congress passed two pieces of legislation designed to reform the U.S. health care system. The Patient Protection and Affordable Care Act was enacted on March 23 and was quickly followed by the Health Care and Education Reconciliation Act of 2010, which amended several portions of the first act and added new provisions of its own. One of the goals of the legislation is to reform the health care delivery system to improve its quality while lowering its overall cost.

1.13 Much uncertainty exists about how health reform measures will affect the way health care entities will deliver services to their patients in the future and how they will be compensated for those services. The general consensus seems to be that health reform is far-reaching and not yet finalized; as a result, the ultimate outcome is uncertain. The AICPA has dedicated a section on its website to health care reform legislation and its implementation; see www.aicpa.org/Research/HCR/Pages/HealthCareReform.aspx.

1.14 The IRS has issued proposed guidance (IRS Notice 2010-39) for tax-exempt hospitals to implement Internal Revenue Code (IRC) Section 501(r), which was added by health care legislation. IRC Section 501(r) imposes four new requirements on hospitals that want to qualify for tax exemption under IRC Section 501(c)(3). Those four requirements are as follows:

- Conduct a community health-needs assessment every 2 years, and adopt an implementation strategy to meet the community needs identified through the assessment. Noncompliance carries with it a $50,000 penalty.
- Establish policies for financial assistance and emergency care that are consistent with IRC Section 501(r)(4).
- Limit amounts charged for emergency or other medically necessary care provided to individuals eligible for financial assistance to the amounts generally charged to individuals with insurance covering such care.

- Forego aggressive collection efforts until the hospital has made reasonable efforts to determine whether the individual receiving the services is eligible for financial assistance.

Tax-exempt hospitals must comply with most of the new rules in tax years beginning after March 23, 2010. Hospitals have two additional years to comply with the community health-needs assessment requirement, which takes effect for tax years beginning after March 23, 2012. Tax-exempt hospitals will also be required to submit their audited financial statements along with Form 990.

1.15 This guide will be updated as further regulations are issued.

Chapter 2

General Auditing Considerations

2.01 In accordance with AU section 150, *Generally Accepted Auditing Standards* (AICPA, *Professional Standards*), an independent auditor plans, conducts, and reports the results of an audit in accordance with generally accepted auditing standards (GAAS). Auditing standards provide a measure of audit quality and the objectives to be achieved in an audit. This section of the guide provides guidance to health care entities primarily on the unique application of the standards of fieldwork.

Audit Planning

2.02 The objective of an audit of a health care entity's financial statements is to express an opinion about whether its financial statements present fairly, in all material respects and in conformity with generally accepted accounting principles (GAAP) or an other comprehensive basis of accounting (OCBOA), the financial position, results of operations, changes in net assets, and cash flows for the specified period just ended. To accomplish that objective, the independent auditor's responsibility is to plan and perform the audit to obtain reasonable assurance (a high but not absolute level of assurance) that material misstatements, whether caused by error or fraud, are detected.

2.03 Auditors of health care entities should refer to auditing standards, including AU section 311, *Planning and Supervision* (AICPA, *Professional Standards*), for general planning considerations. This section addresses planning considerations and other auditing considerations that are relevant to audits of health care entities.

2.04 Planning procedures usually include reviewing the independent auditor's files relating to the entity and holding discussions with audit personnel and the personnel of the entity. Industry-specific examples of these procedures include the following:

- Review the relationship of affiliated entities to the health care entity, and determine the extent to which their financial information will be included in the financial statements of the entity. See the related discussion in chapter 12, "The Reporting Entity and Related Entities," of this guide.
- Review the status of unsettled cost (reimbursement) reports for prior periods filed with third-party payors.
- Identify situations for which accounting estimates, such as third-party contractual allowances and medical malpractice liabilities, are required, and identify relevant factors that may affect those estimates.
- Review periodic reports from and to third-party payors or other regulatory bodies.
- Establish materiality and tolerable misstatement levels, which are set based on industry-specific factors, including the organizational structure of the entity.

2.05 The independent auditor may find it helpful to maintain a permanent file that includes copies of the following documents specifically relating to the health care entity:

- Specific documents concerning restrictions on donor gifts and bequests
- Contracts and agreements, including leases, agreements with physicians, agreements with third-party payors, and agreements with affiliated entities
- Loan agreements, bond indentures, and other debt instruments
- IRS determination letter (for tax-exempt entities)

Scope of the Engagement

2.06 AU section 311 states that the auditor should establish an understanding with the client regarding the services to be performed for each engagement. This understanding should be documented through a written communication with the client in the form of an engagement letter. The understanding includes the objectives of the engagement, management's responsibilities, the auditor's responsibilities, and the limitations of the engagement.

> *Considerations for Audits Performed in Accordance With Public Company Accounting Oversight Board Standards*
>
> Paragraph .06 of AU section 310, *Appointment of the Independent Auditor* (AICPA, *PCAOB Standards and Related Rules*, Interim Standards), includes requirements related to an auditor's understanding when performing an integrated audit of financial statements and internal control over financial reporting and requirements related to an audit of the financial statements in accordance with Public Company Accounting Oversight Board (PCAOB) standards.

2.07 The auditor may consider certain health-care-specific matters in establishing the terms of the engagement. For example, with respect to third-party payment matters, language such as the following might be included:

> An audit conducted in accordance with auditing standards generally accepted in the United States of America does not include audit procedures specifically designed to detect illegal acts that have only an indirect effect on the financial statements (for example, violations of fraud and abuse statutes that result in fines or penalties being imposed on the company). The auditors' procedures do not include testing compliance with laws and regulations in any jurisdiction related to Medicare and Medicaid antifraud and abuse. Management of the company is responsible for the identification of, and the company's compliance with, laws and regulations applicable to its activities, including, but not limited to, those related to Medicare and Medicaid antifraud and abuse statutes.
>
> With respect to cost reports that may be filed with a third party (such as federal and state regulatory agencies), the auditors have not been engaged to test in any way, or render any form of assurance on, the propriety or allowability of the specific costs to be claimed on, or charges to be reported in, a cost report. Management is responsible for the accuracy and propriety of all cost reports filed with Medicare, Medicaid, or other third parties.

The auditors have not been engaged to provide any services with respect to confirming the tax-exempt status of any outstanding bond issue, including testing in any way or rendering any form of assurance that the bonds are in compliance with the requirements as specified in the Internal Revenue Code (IRC) and regulations thereunder. Management is responsible for monitoring the postissuance compliance with these requirements.

2.08 In addition to reporting on the entity's basic financial statements, the independent auditor may be engaged to report on the following special reports: (*a*) cost reports for third-party payors;[1] (*b*) cost reports related to research grants; (*c*) reports for contributors; (*d*) reports for local, state, or federal authorities; (*e*) reports related to bond indentures and other debt instruments; and (*f*) other special-purpose reports. The nature, timing, and extent of procedures to be performed and the type of reports to be issued are based on the scope of services required by the entity and applicable professional standards. AU section 600, *Other Types of Reports* (AICPA, *Professional Standards*), and Statements on Standards for Attestation Engagements are useful for these engagements.

2.09 The auditor and client may consider including a provision in the engagement letter requiring the client to obtain consent from the auditor before including the auditor's report in an official statement. If the auditor and client agree not to include such a provision, the auditor considers including in the engagement letter a requirement that if the client issues any official statement, and the auditor is not associated with that statement, the client will include therein a comment that the auditor is not associated with the contents of such official statement. For example, the official statement might include a comment such as the following: "[*Name of firm*], our independent auditor, has not been engaged to perform and has not performed, since the date of its report included herein, any procedures on the financial statements addressed in that report. [*Name of firm*] also has not performed any procedures relating to this official statement."

Business Associates Agreements

2.10 The Privacy Standards of the Health Insurance Portability and Accountability Act of 1996 (HIPAA), as amended by the Health Information Technology for Economic and Clinical Health (HITECH) Act, require a covered entity to have written agreements with business associates in place. Many health care entities, including health care providers and payors and certain not-for-profit and governmental entities, are considered covered entities under HIPAA. A *business associate* is a person or an entity who performs or assists in the performance of a function or an activity on behalf of a covered entity that involves access to, or use or disclosure of, protected health information (PHI). Independent auditors and advisory and tax professionals may be considered business associates. The HITECH Act also requires business associates to comply with the HIPAA Security Rule's administrative, technical, and physical safeguard requirements and to implement security policies and procedures in the same manner as a covered entity. This will require a business associate

---

[1] See Technical Questions and Answers section 9110.15, "Reporting on Medicaid/Medicare Cost Reports" (AICPA, *Technical Practice Aids*), for additional guidance regarding auditor association with cost reports in certain jurisdictions.

to implement written policies and procedures that address each Security Rule standard; implement a security awareness and training program for workforce members; designate a security official; and conduct an accurate and thorough security risk analysis, along with a security management process. Business associates are subject to potentially significant civil and criminal penalties for violation of data privacy and security rules governing the protection of PHI. Business associates' agreements generally are an addendum to, or incorporated into, the audit engagement letter. Auditors may need to work with management to tailor the form of the business associates' agreement, so that it is consistent with the requirements of the privacy regulations of HIPAA and the HITECH Act while recognizing the various rules and regulations applicable to CPAs.

Audit Risk

2.11 AU section 312, *Audit Risk and Materiality in Conducting an Audit* (AICPA, *Professional Standards*), states that *audit risk* is a function of the risk that the financial statements prepared by management are materially misstated and the risk that the auditor will not detect such material misstatement. The auditor should consider audit risk in relation to the relevant assertions related to individual account balances, classes of transactions, and disclosures at the overall financial statement level.

2.12 At the account balance, class of transactions, relevant assertion, or disclosure level, audit risk consists of (*a*) the risks of material misstatement (consisting of inherent risk and control risk) and (*b*) detection risk (see the following for additional discussion of these components). Paragraph .23 of AU section 312 states that auditors should assess the risk of material misstatement at the relevant assertion level as a basis to design and perform further audit procedures (tests of controls or substantive procedures). Defaulting to a maximum inherent or control risk assessment is not permitted.

2.13 In considering audit risk at the overall financial statement level, the auditor should consider risks of material misstatement that relate pervasively to the financial statements as a whole and potentially affect many relevant assertions. Risks of this nature often relate to the entity's control environment and are not necessarily identifiable with specific, relevant assertions at the class of transactions, account balance, or disclosure level. Such risks may be especially relevant to the auditor's consideration of the risks of material misstatement arising from fraud (for example, through management override of internal control).

2.14 In many health care entities, certain accounts typically (*a*) will have a low volume of transactions, (*b*) will consist of transactions that are not complex, and (*c*) do not require the use of significant accounting estimates. Accounts such as inventories, marketable securities, assets whose use is limited, property and equipment, long-term debt, and net assets (equity) frequently have these characteristics and may allow the auditor to assess inherent risk as being at a relatively low level. However, in certain circumstances, such as investments in complex investments and derivative financial instruments, inherent risk may be higher.

Planning Materiality

2.15 *Materiality* is defined as the magnitude of an omission or a misstatement of accounting information that, in light of the surrounding circumstances, makes it probable that the judgment of a reasonable person relying on the information would have been changed or influenced by the omission or misstatement.

2.16 The auditor's consideration of materiality is a matter of professional judgment and is influenced by the auditor's perception of the needs of users of the financial statements. Materiality judgments necessarily take into account qualitative considerations, as well as quantitative considerations. See the following for additional discussion about the qualitative aspects of materiality.

2.17 In accordance with paragraph .27 of AU section 312, the auditor should determine a materiality level for the financial statements as a whole when establishing the overall audit strategy. The auditor often may apply a percentage to a chosen benchmark as a step in determining materiality for the financial statements as a whole. In determining an appropriate benchmark, the auditor may consider what might be important to the anticipated users of the financial statements (for example, operating results, earnings per share, compliance with restrictive debt covenants, and so on). For a for-profit entity, net income and earnings per share are the major concern of financial statement users, and operating results may be the most relevant measurement basis for materiality. On the other hand, for most not-for-profit entities, financial statement users are typically concerned primarily with the company's liquidity and ability to repay its debt, and unrestricted net assets may be the most relevant starting point for establishing planning materiality. However, other factors also may be relevant, such as the entity's overall size (for example, total revenues, total assets, and so on); compliance with its debt covenants (for example, a debt service coverage ratio); and the stability of its operating results (for example, as measured by operating income or the performance indicator).

> *Considerations for Audits Performed in Accordance With PCAOB Standards*
>
> When performing an integrated audit of financial statements and internal control over financial reporting, refer to paragraph 20 of Auditing Standard No. 5, *An Audit of Internal Control Over Financial Reporting That Is Integrated with An Audit of Financial Statements* (AICPA, *PCAOB Standards and Related Rules*, Auditing Standards), regarding materiality considerations.

Qualitative Aspects of Materiality

2.18 As previously indicated, judgments about materiality include both quantitative and qualitative information. Qualitative considerations include the following:

- The nature of the client's business and industry sector (for example, hospital, managed care, assisted living, and so on)
- Operating results (for example, stable earnings, consistently near break-even, low-margin industry, or volatile results)

- Financial position (for example, concerns regarding liquidity, debt covenants, and capital adequacy)

As a result of the interaction of quantitative and qualitative considerations in materiality judgments, misstatements of relatively small amounts that come to the auditor's attention could have a material effect on the financial statements. For example, an error of an otherwise immaterial amount could be material if a reasonable possibility exists that it could lead to a violation of the entity's debt covenants that would cause the debt to be classified as current.

2.19 Qualitative considerations also influence the auditor in reaching a conclusion about whether misstatements are material. Paragraph .60 of AU section 312 provides qualitative factors that the auditor may consider relevant in determining whether misstatements are material.

Use of Assertions in Obtaining Audit Evidence

2.20 Paragraphs .14–.19 of AU section 326, *Audit Evidence* (AICPA, *Professional Standards*), discuss the use of assertions in obtaining audit evidence. In representing that the financial statements are fairly presented in accordance with GAAP, management implicitly or explicitly makes assertions regarding the recognition, measurement, and disclosure of information in the financial statements and related disclosures. Assertions used by the auditor fall into the following categories:

Categories of Assertions

	Description of Assertions		
	Classes of Transactions and Events During the Period	*Account Balances at the End of the Period*	*Presentation and Disclosure*
Occurrence or existence	Transactions and events that have been recorded have occurred and pertain to the entity.	Assets, liabilities, and equity interests exist.	Disclosed events and transactions have occurred.
Rights and obligations	—	The entity holds or controls the rights to assets, and liabilities are the obligations of the entity.	Disclosed events and transactions pertain to the entity.
Completeness	All transactions and events that should have been recorded have been recorded.	All assets, liabilities, and equity interests that should have been recorded have been recorded.	All disclosures that should have been included in the financial statements have been included.

Description of Assertions

	Classes of Transactions and Events During the Period	*Account Balances at the End of the Period*	*Presentation and Disclosure*
Accuracy or valuation and allocation	Amounts and other data relating to recorded transactions and events have been recorded appropriately.	Assets, liabilities, and equity interests are included in the financial statements at appropriate amounts, and any resulting valuation or allocation adjustments are recorded appropriately.	Financial and other information is disclosed fairly and at appropriate amounts.
Cut-off	Transactions and events have been recorded in the correct accounting period.	—	—
Classification and understandability	Transactions and events have been recorded in the proper accounts.	—	Financial information is appropriately presented and described, and information in disclosures is expressed clearly.

2.21 Examples of industry-specific assertions for classes of transactions, account balances, and presentation and disclosures are reflected in the individual chapters of this guide.

Understanding the Entity, Its Environment, and Its Internal Control

2.22 AU section 314, *Understanding the Entity and Its Environment and Assessing the Risks of Material Misstatement* (AICPA, *Professional Standards*), requires auditors to obtain an understanding of the entity and its environment, including its internal control. In accordance with paragraph .04 of AU section 314, the auditor should use professional judgment to determine the extent of the understanding required of the entity and its environment, including its internal control. The auditor's primary consideration is whether the understanding that has been obtained is sufficient to (*a*) assess risks of material misstatement of the financial statements and (*b*) design and perform further audit procedures (tests of controls and substantive tests).

2.23 The auditor's understanding of the entity and its environment consists of an understanding of the following aspects:

- Industry, regulatory, and other external factors
- Nature of the entity
- Objectives and strategies and the related business risks that may result in a material misstatement of the financial statements
- Measurement and review of the entity's financial performance
- Internal control, which includes the selection and application of accounting policies

2.24 This section addresses unique aspects of health care entities that may be helpful in developing the required understanding of the entity, its environment, and its internal control.

Risk Assessment Procedures

2.25 As described in AU section 326, audit procedures performed to obtain an understanding of the entity and its environment, including its internal control, to assess the risks of material misstatement at the financial statement and relevant assertion levels are referred to as risk assessment procedures. Paragraph .21 of AU section 326 states that the auditor must perform risk assessment procedures to provide a satisfactory basis for the assessment of risks at the financial statement and relevant assertion levels. Risk assessment procedures by themselves do not provide sufficient appropriate audit evidence on which to base the audit opinion and must be supplemented by further audit procedures in the form of tests of controls, when relevant or necessary, and substantive procedures.

2.26 In accordance with paragraph .06 of AU section 314, the auditor should perform the following risk assessment procedures to obtain an understanding of the entity and its environment, including its internal control:

- Inquiries of management and others within the entity
- Analytical procedures
- Observation and inspection

See paragraphs .06–.13 of AU section 314 for additional guidance on risk assessment procedures.

Analytical Procedures

2.27 AU section 329, *Analytical Procedures* (AICPA, *Professional Standards*), provides guidance on the use of analytical procedures and requires their use in the planning and overall review stages of all audits. Paragraphs .04 and .06 of AU section 329 specify that the auditor should apply analytical procedures in planning the audit to assist in understanding the entity and its environment and to identify areas that may represent specific risks relevant to the audit. For example, analytical procedures may be helpful in identifying the existence of unusual transactions or events and amounts, ratios, and trends that might indicate matters that have financial statement and audit implications. Per paragraph .09 of AU section 314, in performing analytical procedures as risk assessment procedures, the auditor should develop expectations about plausible relationships that are reasonably expected to exist. When comparison of those expectations with recorded amounts or ratios developed from recorded amounts yields unusual or unexpected relationships, the auditor should consider those results in identifying risks of material misstatement. However, if such analytical procedures use data aggregated at a high level, generally, the results of those analytical procedures provide only a broad initial indication about whether a material misstatement may exist. Accordingly, the results of analytical procedures performed during planning may be considered along with other information gathered by the auditor in identifying the risks of material misstatement due to fraud.

2.28 Examples of sources of information for developing expectations include prior-period financial information, budgets, and health care financial and statistical ratios. Additional information is available from various health care industry associations.

2.29 The following are examples of analytical procedures that the independent auditor may find useful:

- Comparison of account balances with budget and prior-period amounts
- Analysis of changes in revenues during the current period based on statistical data (for example, admissions, patient days, visits, and professional service procedure counts for laboratory, radiology, and surgery) and information concerning price changes
- Comparison between periods of the number of days of revenue in receivables
- Relationship between periods of the allowance for uncollectible accounts to the balance of patient accounts receivable in the aggregate, based on known changes in the accounts receivable's aging and composition by payor
- Relationship between periods of the liability for claims incurred but not reported (IBNR) to the related expense

Discussion Among the Audit Team

2.30 In obtaining an understanding of the entity and its environment, including its internal control, AU section 314 states that there should be discussion among the audit team. In accordance with paragraph .14 of AU section 314, the members of the audit team, including the auditor with final responsibility for the audit, should discuss the susceptibility of the entity's financial statements to material misstatements. This discussion could be held concurrently with the discussion among the audit team that is specified by AU section 316, *Consideration of Fraud in a Financial Statement Audit* (AICPA, *Professional Standards*), to discuss the susceptibility of the entity's financial statements to fraud.

Understanding of the Entity and Its Environment[2]

2.31 Appendix A, "Understanding the Entity and Its Environment," of AU section 314 includes examples of matters that the auditor may consider in obtaining an understanding of the entity and its environment. The following table includes some unique characteristics of health care entities that the auditor may consider, in addition to the factors listed in appendix A of AU section 314, when obtaining an understanding of the entity and its environment in order to assess the risks of material misstatement. Some of these factors are discussed in more detail following the table.

---

[2] The Patient Protection and Affordable Care Act and the Health Care and Education Reconciliation Act of 2010 will likely create regulations that will affect health care entities in many significant ways. This section and table will be updated as those regulations are issued.

Aspects of the Auditor's Understanding of the Entity and Its Environment	*Considerations for Health Care Entities*
Industry, regulatory, and other external factors	• Regulatory requirements unique to entities receiving Medicare; Medicaid; or other federal payments, including federal financial assistance. • Service delivery regulations (for example, antidumping, Emergency Medical Treatment and Active Labor Act, use of devices approved by the Food and Drug Administration, Hill-Burton charity care, and so on). • Billing and coding regulations, including being subject to peer reviews and governmental intermediary audits. • Factors arising from an entity's tax-exempt status (for example, prohibited activities, unrelated business income, bond arbitrage rules, and so on). • Insurance-related industry regulations (for example, minimum capital requirements, statutory reporting requirements, and so on).
Nature of the entity	• The existence of related-party transactions. • The entity's experience with payment denials and other matters subject to review by medical review entities. • The nature of reports expected to be rendered. Examples include reports on consolidated or consolidating financial statements, reports on financial statements filed with the Securities and Exchange Commission, reports filed with third-party payors or other regulatory bodies, reports on compliance with debt covenants, and other special reports. • Recognition of liabilities for costs incurred by providers of prepaid health care services (see paragraph 2.32). • Contingencies for medical malpractice losses (see paragraph 2.33). • Obligations under continuing care contracts. • Revenue recognition practices (see paragraphs 2.34–.43). • Minimum loss issues.
Objectives and strategies and related business risks	• Limitations on the initiation of new services or construction (for example, certificate of need). • Required federal certification prior to billing (for example, Medicare certification). • Recognition of retrospective billing adjustments from third-party payors. • Limitations on physician arrangements, such as ones related to patient referrals.
Measurement and review of the entity's financial performance	• Risk-based capital requirements (see the "Statutory Reporting Considerations for Health Plans" section).

Cost of Prepaid Health Care Services

2.32 Risks are associated with recognizing the liability for costs incurred by providers of prepaid health care services (for example, HMOs) because such costs may have been incurred but not yet reported to the providers. Therefore, it is necessary to estimate the liability for those costs. These estimates often necessitate a high degree of management judgment. Management considers historical experience, as well as the effects of any changes in conditions, such as seasonality trends and changes in subscriber population and the services and benefits provided. Costs of prepaid health care services are discussed further in chapter 13, "Financial Accounting and Reporting for Managed Care Services," of this guide.

Medical Malpractice Losses and Obligations

2.33 Risks also are associated with contingencies for medical malpractice losses and obligations under continuing care contracts. A high degree of management judgment and complex analyses usually are involved in evaluating the related financial statement assertions. The measurement of estimates is inherently uncertain and depends on the outcome of future events. Because no one accounting estimate that involves a degree of management judgment can be considered accurate with certainty, material changes in such estimates do not indicate that the audit was not performed in accordance with professional standards. Medical malpractice losses and obligations are discussed further in chapter 8, "Contingencies and Other Liabilities," of this guide.

Revenue Recognition

2.34 Because of the large monetary amounts and complexity of determining health care service revenue and receivables, risks are associated with health care service revenue recognition and the valuation of the related receivables. A significant portion of services is usually paid by third parties, such as Medicare, Medicaid, and various health insurance carriers, under statutory provisions or other arrangements in amounts that can be significantly different from, and frequently less than, the entity's established rates. Statement of Position (SOP) 00-1, *Auditing Health Care Third-Party Revenues and Related Receivables* (AICPA, *Technical Practice Aids*, AUD sec. 14,360), provides guidance to auditors regarding uncertainties inherent in health care third-party revenue recognition. SOP 00-1 is included as appendix B, "Statement of Position 00-1, *Auditing Health Care Third-Party Revenues and Related Receivables*," of this guide.

2.35 Typically, a number of clinicians (for example, the attending physician, consulting physicians, radiologists, pathologists, therapists, and nurses) add documentation to a patient's medical record. Provider personnel generally review the medical record and assign a code (ICD-9-CM or CPT-4)* to the record. The provider prepares and submits a bill that includes, among other things, the assigned ICD-9-CM or CPT-4 code. The Medicare fiscal intermediary or other third-party payor typically reviews the bill and assigns a specific payment code, such as a diagnosis related group (DRG) number. Payment is based on the assigned DRG number or other payment code. The provider may

---

* On January 16, 2009, the Department of Health & Human Services (HHS) published a final rule adopting ICD-10-CM to replace ICD-9-CM in Health Insurance Portability and Accountability Act of 1996 transactions, with an effective implementation date of October 1, 2013. Early implementation of the codes in ICD-10-CM is not valid for any use or purpose.

check the assigned payment code and follow up on any identified discrepancies. However, the final assignment of the payment code is generally determined by the third-party payor.

2.36 Misstatements can occur throughout this process. Physicians or other clinicians may not document the appropriate procedure. Coding personnel may not notice or correctly interpret certain items in the medical record. Accordingly, an incorrect code may be assigned, and an erroneous amount may be paid.

2.37 The auditor's expertise is in accounting and auditing matters, rather than operational, clinical, or legal matters. Accordingly, the auditor's procedures focus on areas that normally are subject to internal controls relevant to financial reporting. However, the further that a potential misstatement is removed from the events and transactions ordinarily reflected in the financial statements, the less likely the auditor is to become aware of the misstatement and evaluate the effect on the financial statements. For example, determining whether a service was medically necessary; obtained through a legally appropriate referral; properly performed (including using only approved devices, rendered in a quality manner from a clinical perspective, and so on); adequately supervised; accurately documented and classified; or rendered and billed by nonsanctioned individuals typically is not within the auditor's professional expertise. As a result, an audit in accordance with GAAS is not designed to detect such matters.

2.38 Further, an audit conducted in accordance with GAAS does not include rendering an opinion or any form of assurance on an entity's compliance with laws and regulations.[3] Nor does an audit under GAAS include providing any assurance on an entity's billings or cost report. In fact, cost reports typically are not prepared and submitted until after the financial statement audit has been completed.

2.39 Due to the higher inherent risk associated with revenue recognition, including the clinical coding process, the independent auditor may consider obtaining an understanding of internal controls over documentation of the services rendered; clinical coding, including the use of groupers and supervisory reviews; and billing procedures (for example, admission, payor verification, and discharge). The auditor also may consider the results of the internal compliance program; the internal audit; and external reviews (consulting or regulator or payor), including denials.

2.40 For reasons previously discussed, an auditor would not find it necessary to consider the process of assigning codes in planning and performing an audit of the provider's financial statements. However, the auditor should investigate matters coming to his or her attention that suggest potential material misstatements of the financial statements resulting indirectly from such matters due to potential illegal acts. For example, after being informed about a special regulatory review that was performed, the auditor inquires about the results and considers whether performance of additional substantive audit procedures is necessary to evaluate the contingency, including the need for

---

[3] Even when auditors undertake a special engagement designed to attest to compliance with certain provisions of laws, regulations, contracts, and grants (for example, an audit in accordance with Office of Management and Budget [OMB] Circular A-133, *Audits of States, Local Governments and Non-Profit Organizations*), the auditor's procedures do not extend to testing compliance with laws and regulations related to Medicare and Medicaid fraud and abuse.

possible recognition or disclosure pursuant to Financial Accounting Standards Board (FASB) *Accounting Standards Codification* (ASC) 450, *Contingencies.*

2.41 The independent auditor should obtain an understanding of the specific cost-finding or other rate-setting methods used by third-party payors to determine final amounts reimbursable to the health care entity. These payment methods may require that a health care entity accumulate and report various statistical data, such as admissions, discharges, patient days, visits, beds, square footage, and pounds of laundry.

2.42 Among other duties, the Medicare fiscal intermediary is responsible for evaluating the propriety of submitted claims before processing them for payment. Absent the client committing an illegal act, the payment of a claim provides evidence that billed amounts were correct. As a result, the auditor should obtain an understanding of the entity's billing and collection history, paying particular attention to the entity's historical denial rate or the significance of coding changes.

2.43 The auditor should consider the adequacy of the financial statement disclosures regarding the inherent risk relating to revenue recognition. Generally, the notes to the financial statements disclose that amounts recognized as revenues are subject to retrospective review and laws and regulations that are extremely complex and subject to interpretation; as a result, a reasonable possibility exists that recorded estimates will change by a material amount in the near term.

Additional Audit Considerations

Accounting Estimates

2.44 Certain areas of a health care entity's operations include accounting estimates that may be material in the preparation and presentation of financial statements. FASB ASC 275, *Risks and Uncertainties*, requires entities to include in their financial statements information about the use of estimates in the preparation of financial statements. In addition, if specified disclosure criteria in FASB ASC 275-10-50-8 are met, entities are required to include the disclosures about certain significant estimates described in paragraphs 6–15 of FASB ASC 275-10-50 in their financial statements. AU section 342, *Auditing Accounting Estimates* (AICPA, *Professional Standards*), provides guidance on obtaining and evaluating sufficient appropriate audit evidence to support significant accounting estimates in an audit of financial statements conducted in accordance with GAAS.

> *Considerations for Audits Performed in Accordance With PCAOB Standards*
>
> Paragraph .10 of AU section 342, *Auditing Accounting Estimates* (AICPA, *PCAOB Standards and Related Rules*, Interim Standards), provides that for an integrated audit, auditors are required to obtain an understanding of the process that management used to develop estimates and to test controls over all relevant assertions related to the estimate.

2.45 SOP 00-1 provides guidance for auditors regarding the sufficiency of audit evidence supporting accounting estimates recorded for the proper valuation of health care third-party revenues and related receivables.

2.46 Although significant accounting estimates may affect many elements of a health care entity's financial statements, they most often affect the following:

- The provision for third-party payor contractual adjustments and allowances and the provision for estimated receivables and payables for final settlements with those payors and any other valuation allowances for revenue recognition matters, as discussed further in chapter 10, "Health Care Service Revenue and Related Receivables," of this guide
- The valuation of investments
- The accruals for taxes
- The provision for uncollectible accounts
- Accruals for medical malpractice liabilities and other similar liabilities
- Accruals for obligations under continuing care contracts
- Accruals by providers of prepaid health care services for IBNR costs
- Accruals for loss contracts

Transactions Processed by Service Organizations

2.47 Health care entities may engage outside service organizations to perform services that are part of the health care provider's information system.

2.48 Examples of service organizations used by health care entities include the following:

- Investment managers that invest and service assets for health care entities
- Service organizations that process payroll, IT, and other administrative functions
- Billing entities that prepare reimbursement claims to insurers and other third parties
- Administrators of employee benefit plans who process and pay benefit claims and maintain participant records

2.49 AU section 314 states that the auditor should obtain an understanding of each of the five components of an entity's internal control sufficient to assess the risks of material misstatement and design the nature, timing, and extent of further audit procedures. This understanding may encompass controls placed in operation by the health care entity and service organizations whose services are part of the health care entity's information system.

2.50 AU section 324, *Service Organizations* (AICPA, *Professional Standards*),[†] explains the considerations that an auditor makes in obtaining

---

[†] The guidance contained in AU section 324, *Service Organizations* (AICPA, *Professional Standards*), is in the process of being split into an attest standard and an auditing standard to better reflect the nature of the work being performed. As part of this process, the Auditing Standards Board issued Statement on Standards for Attestation Engagements (SSAE) No. 16, *Reporting on Controls at a Service Organization* (AICPA, *Professional Standards*, AT sec. 801), in April 2010. SSAE No. 16 addresses examination engagements undertaken by a service auditor to report on controls at

(continued)

an understanding of internal control and assessing control risk for entities that use a service organization to process transactions.

Considerations for Audits Performed in Accordance With PCAOB Standards

Auditing Standard No. 5 provides guidance regarding the use of service organizations for an integrated audit.

Illegal Acts

2.51 The Social Security Act provides for criminal penalties for individuals or entities that offer, pay, solicit, or receive remuneration to induce business that is reimbursed under Medicare or state health care programs. The types of remuneration covered by the antikickback statute of the Medicare and Medicaid Patient and Program Protection Act of 1987 include, with certain exceptions, kickbacks, bribes, and rebates made directly or indirectly, overtly or covertly, and in cash or in kind. In addition, prohibited conduct includes not only remuneration intended to induce referrals or patients but also remuneration intended to induce the purchasing, leasing, ordering, or arranging for any good, facility, service, or item paid for by Medicare or state health care programs. In addition, fraudulent activities may exist that are unrelated to Medicare or state programs, such as fraudulent billing and admitting practices.

2.52 The auditor's procedures will vary based on his or her assessment of the risk of material misstatement resulting from such illegal acts. AU section 317, *Illegal Acts by Clients* (AICPA, *Professional Standards*), states that the auditor should plan and perform the audit to provide reasonable assurance of detecting illegal acts having a direct and material effect on the determination of financial statement amounts. AU section 317 also notes that an audit conducted in accordance with GAAS does not include audit procedures specifically designed to detect illegal acts that have only an indirect effect on the financial statements (for example, illegal acts that have a material effect as the result of fines or penalties that may be imposed on the entity). Finally, AU section 317 provides guidance on the auditor's responsibilities when specific information concerning the possible existence of this type of illegal act comes to the auditor's attention.

2.53 Examples of laws and regulations that are generally recognized by auditors to have a direct and material effect on the determination of amounts in financial statements of health care entities include tax laws affecting tax accruals and tax expense, as well as Medicare and Medicaid laws directly affecting the amount of revenue recognized during the accounting period, such as those concerning the submission of bills for fictitious patients.

(footnote continued)

organizations that provide services to user entities when those controls are likely to be relevant to user entities' internal control over financial reporting. It is effective for service auditors' reports for periods ending on or after June 15, 2011. Early implementation is permitted. This standard supersedes the guidance for service auditors in AU section 324.

AU-C section 402, *Audit Considerations Relating to an Entity Using a Service Organization* (AICPA, *Professional Standards*), will supersede AU section 324 and addresses the user auditor's responsibility for obtaining sufficient appropriate audit evidence in an audit of the financial statements of a user entity that uses one or more service organizations. It will be effective for audits of financial statements for periods ending on or after December 15, 2012, and early adoption is prohibited.

2.54 Health care entities also may be affected by many other laws and regulations, such as those related to Medicare and Medicaid fraud and abuse, discrimination related to patients or residents, violation of patient or resident rights, securities trading, occupational safety and health, food and drug administration, environmental protection, equal employment opportunities, and price-fixing or other antitrust violations. Generally, these laws and regulations relate more to an entity's operating aspects than its financial and accounting aspects, and their financial statement effect is only indirect. An auditor ordinarily does not have a sufficient basis for recognizing possible violations of such laws and regulations. Their indirect effect is normally the result of the need to disclose a contingent liability because of the allegation or determination of illegality. For example, patients may be obtained based on illegal arrangements with physicians or other providers. Although the direct effects of the services rendered may be appropriately recorded, their indirect effects, such as the possible contingent liability for violating Medicare and Medicaid fraud and abuse statutes, may not be appropriately disclosed. Even when violations of such laws and regulations can have material consequences to the financial statements, auditors may not become aware of the existence of the illegal act, unless they are informed by the client or evidence exists of a governmental agency investigation or enforcement proceeding in the records, documents, or other information normally inspected in an audit of financial statements.

2.55 Whether an act is, in fact, illegal is a determination that is normally beyond the auditor's professional competence. The auditor's training, experience, and understanding of the client and industry may provide a basis for recognizing that some acts coming to the auditor's attention may be illegal. However, determining whether a particular client act is illegal generally would be based on the advice of an informed expert qualified to practice law or may have to await final determination by a court of law. For example, determining whether admitting a patient or providing a service is medically necessary or whether a particular procedure or device was properly approved is not within the auditor's professional competence.

Management Representations

2.56 AU section 333, *Management Representations* (AICPA, *Professional Standards*), establishes a requirement that an auditor performing an audit in accordance with GAAS obtain written representations from management for all financial statements and periods covered by the auditor's report. The specific written representations to be obtained depend on the circumstances of the engagement and the nature and basis of presentation of the financial statements.

2.57 The auditor may consider the following examples of specific representations for receivables, cost reports filed with third parties, and contingencies related to health care third-party revenue recognition:

- For receivables, consider the following:
  - — Adequate consideration has been given to, and appropriate provision made for, estimated adjustments to revenue, such as for denied claims and changes to home health resource group, resource utilization group, ambulatory payment classification, and DRG assignments.

- — Recorded valuation allowances are necessary, appropriate, and properly supported.
- — All peer review organizations, fiscal intermediary, and third-party payor reports and information have been made available.

- For cost reports filed with third parties, consider the following:
  - — All required Medicare, Medicaid, and similar reports have been properly filed.
  - — Management is responsible for the accuracy and propriety of all filed cost reports.
  - — All costs reflected on such reports are appropriate and allowable under applicable reimbursement rules and regulations and are patient-related and properly allocated to applicable payors.
  - — The employed reimbursement methodologies and principles are in accordance with applicable rules and regulations.
  - — Adequate consideration has been given to, and appropriate provision made for, audit adjustments by intermediaries, third-party payors, or other regulatory agencies.
  - — All items required to be disclosed, including disputed costs that are being claimed to establish a basis for a subsequent appeal, have been fully disclosed in the cost report.
  - — Recorded third-party settlements include differences between filed (and to-be-filed) cost reports and calculated settlements, which are necessary based on historical experience or new or ambiguous regulations that may be subject to differing interpretations. Although management believes that the entity is entitled to all amounts claimed on the cost reports, management also believes the amounts of these differences are appropriate.

- For contingencies, consider the following:
  - — No violations or possible violations of laws or regulations exist, such as those related to Medicare and Medicaid antifraud and abuse statutes, in any jurisdiction, whose effects are considered for disclosure in the financial statements or as a basis for recording a loss contingency other than those disclosed or accrued in the financial statements. This is including, but not limited to, the antikickback statute of the Medicare and Medicaid Patient and Program Protection Act of 1987, limitations on certain physician referrals (the Stark law), and the False Claims Act.
  - — Billings to third-party payors comply in all material respects with applicable coding guidelines (for example,

ICD-9-CM[‡] and CPT-4) and laws and regulations, including those dealing with Medicare and Medicaid antifraud and abuse, and billings reflect only charges for goods and services that were medically necessary; properly approved by regulatory bodies (for example, the FDA), if required; and properly rendered.

— There have been no internal or external investigations relating to compliance with applicable laws and regulations, including investigations in progress, that would have an effect on the amounts reported in the financial statements or on the disclosure in the notes to the financial statements.

— There have been no oral or written communications from regulatory agencies, governmental representatives, employees, or others concerning investigations or allegations of noncompliance with laws and regulations in any jurisdiction, including those related to Medicare and Medicaid antifraud and abuse statutes; deficiencies in financial reporting practices; or other matters that could have a material adverse effect on the financial statements.

— Adequate consideration has been given to, and appropriate provision made for, a continuing care retirement community's obligation to provide future services and the use of facilities to current residents.

— Adequate consideration has been given to, and appropriate provision made for, a prepaid health care provider's obligation to provide future health care services.

— Guarantees, whether written or oral, under which the health care entity is contingently liable, including guarantee contracts and indemnification agreements pursuant to FASB ASC 460, *Guarantees*, have been properly recorded or disclosed in the (consolidated) financial statements.

2.58 The auditor of the health care entity also might obtain specific representations, if applicable, of the following items that are unique or pervasive in the health care industry:

- The health care entity is in compliance with the provisions of IRC Section 501(c)(3) and is exempt from federal income tax under IRC Section 501(a), as evidenced by a determination letter, and from state income tax.
- Information returns (Form 990) have been filed on a timely basis.
- Provision has been made, when material, for estimated retroactive adjustments by third-party payors under reimbursement agreements.
- The health care organization is in compliance with bond indentures or other debt instruments.

[‡] See footnote †.

- For each of its outstanding bond issues, the health care entity is in compliance with postissuance requirements, as specified in the IRC, including, but not limited to, the areas of arbitrage and private business use.
- Pending changes in the organizational structure, financing arrangements, or other matters that could have a material effect on the financial statements of the entity are properly disclosed.
- The health care entity is in compliance with contractual agreements, grants, and donor restrictions.
- The health care entity has maintained an appropriate composition of net assets in amounts needed to comply with all donor restrictions.
- The internal controls over the receipt and recording of received contributions are adequate.
- The allocation of expenses reported in the notes to the financial statements is reasonable based on the health care entity's current operations.
- The health care entity has properly classified equity securities with readily determinable fair values and all debt securities as either trading or other-than-trading securities and reported these investments at fair value.
- The health care entity has reported to its risk management department all known asserted and unasserted claims and incidents. Adequate and reasonable provision has been made for losses related to asserted and unasserted malpractice, health insurance, worker's compensation, and any other claims.
- The health care entity is (or is not) subject to the requirements of Office of Management and Budget (OMB) Circular A-133, *Audits of States, Local Governments and Non-Profit Organizations*, or Title 45 U.S. *Code of Federal Regulations* (CFR) Part 74.26 because it expended (or did not expend) more than $500,000 in federal awards during the year.
- The health care entity has classified net assets as unrestricted, temporarily restricted, or permanently restricted based on its assessment of the donor's intention, as specified in original donor correspondence, when available. When not available, the entity used other corroborating evidential matter, including minutes of the board, accounting records, and financial statements. To the extent that it was unable to review original donor correspondence to determine the amount of the original gift and donor additions, its determination of such amount was based on its best estimate considering the relevant facts and circumstances. Amounts classified as temporarily restricted are subject to donor-imposed purpose or time restrictions that precluded the health care entity from expending such amounts or recognizing such amounts as unrestricted as of the balance sheet date. Amounts classified as permanently restricted are subject to donor-imposed or statutory restrictions that require these amounts to be held in perpetuity. In addition, the health care entity has classified appreciation and income related to such donations in accordance with relevant donor or statutory restrictions. Losses on investments of a

donor-restricted endowment fund have been classified in accordance with FASB ASC 958-205-45. Reclassifications between net asset classes are proper.

Single Audit Act and Related Audit Considerations

2.59 An independent auditor may be engaged to audit the financial statements of a health care entity that expends federal awards from a governmental agency in accordance with the Single Audit Act Amendments of 1996 and OMB Circular A-133. Federal awards may take the form of grants, contracts, loans, loan guarantees, property, cooperative agreements, interest subsidies, and insurance or direct appropriations.

2.60 OMB Circular A-133 prescribes policies, procedures, and guidelines to implement the Single Audit Act Amendments of 1996 and requires state and local governments and not-for-profit entities that expend total federal awards equal to, or in excess of, $500,000 in a fiscal year to have an audit performed in accordance with the Single Audit Act Amendments of 1996 and OMB Circular A-133.

2.61 Institutions covered by OMB Circular A-133 include not-for-profit hospitals, public hospitals, institutions of higher education and their affiliated hospitals, voluntary health and welfare entities, and other community-based entities.[4] Medicare payments to a nonfederal entity for providing patient care services to Medicare-eligible individuals are not considered expended federal awards under OMB Circular A-133. Medicaid payments to a subrecipient for providing patient care services to Medicaid-eligible individuals are not considered expended federal awards under OMB Circular A-133, unless a state requires the funds to be treated as expended federal awards because reimbursement is on a cost-reimbursement basis.

2.62 OMB Circular A-110, *Uniform Administrative Requirements for Grants and Other Agreements with Institutions of Higher Education, Hospitals and Other Non-Profit Organizations*, establishes standard requirements. such as insurance, record retention, and banking, for obtaining consistency and uniformity among federal agencies in the administration of grants to, and agreements with, public and private hospitals and other entities. OMB Circular A-87, *Cost Principles for State, Local and Indian Tribal Governments*, establishes principles and standards for determining allowable costs incurred by state and local governments under grants, contracts, and other agreements. OMB Circular A-21, *Cost Principles for Educational Institutions*, and A-122, *Cost Principles for Non-Profit Organizations*, establish principles and standards for determining allowable costs incurred by educational institutions and not-for-profit entities under grants, contracts, and other agreements. Federal research and development awards under grants and contracts administered by hospitals are exempt from OMB Circulars A-87, A-21, and A-122 but are subject to the requirements provided in appendix E, "Principles for Determining

---

[4] The codification of OMB Circular A-133 by the HHS also includes audit requirements for commercial entities, including for-profit hospitals, that receive federal awards under HHS programs. Generally, the entity has two options regarding audits: a financial-related audit of a particular award, in accordance with *Government Auditing Standards* (GAS), or an audit that meets the requirements of OMB Circular A-133. See Title 45 U.S. *Code of Federal Regulations* Part 74.26(d) for further information.

Costs Applicable to Research and Development Under Grants and Contracts With Hospitals," of 45 CFR 74.

2.63 AU section 801, *Compliance Audits* (AICPA, *Professional Standards*), provides general guidance for audits of governmental entities and entities that receive federal awards. AU section 801 explains the requirements of the financial audit standards contained in *Government Auditing Standards* (GAS), as amended and issued by the Comptroller General of the United States, and their relationship to GAAS.[5] It also provides general guidance on testing compliance with requirements applicable to federal awards. AU section 801 clarifies that the entity, rather than the independent auditor, is responsible for arranging for audits that meet all applicable requirements and provides guidance on communications that the auditor makes upon becoming aware that the entity may be subject to an audit requirement that may not be satisfied by the auditor's engagement.

2.64 The Audit Guide Government Auditing Standards *and Circular A-133 Audits* provides guidance on the auditor's responsibilities when conducting a single audit or program-specific audit in accordance with the Single Audit Act Amendments of 1996 and OMB Circular A-133. It discusses the auditor's responsibility for considering internal control and performing tests of compliance with applicable laws, regulations, and program compliance requirements. Further, it provides reporting guidance, including examples of the reports required by GAS and OMB Circular A-133.

2.65 In *Guidance on Complying with* Government Auditing Standards *Reporting Requirements for the Report on Internal Control for Audits of Certain Entities Subject to the Requirements of the Sarbanes-Oxley Act of 2002 and* Government Auditing Standards, which is available at www.gao.gov/govaud/ybpcaob.pdf, the Government Accountability Office (GAO) provided guidance to entities that are subject to audits conducted in accordance with GAS and the standards issued by the PCAOB. The notice states that GAS may be used in conjunction with professional standards issued by other authoritative bodies, such as the PCAOB, even though those standards are not incorporated into GAS. This GAO guidance states that it recognizes that the use of the PCAOB's framework for assessing deficiencies in internal control could result in inconsistencies in reporting on internal control under GAS. Guidance is available to facilitate the reporting of deficiencies in internal control identified during audits conducted under both PCAOB standards and GAS to ensure the consistency of information included in the GAS report on internal control and to assist auditors in complying with GAS. In November 2008, the GAO issued *Interim Guidance on Reporting Deficiencies in Internal Control for GAGAS Financial Audits and Attestation Engagements*, which states that auditors may satisfy the internal control reporting requirements in GAS by including in the GAS report all identified significant deficiencies and material weaknesses, following the definitions and requirements from AU section 325, *Communicating Internal Control Related Matters Identified in an Audit* (AICPA, *Professional Standards*). Because the definitions of *significant deficiencies* and *material weaknesses* are uniform between the PCAOB and AU section 325, this interim guidance is relevant for those entities that are

[5] In August 2010, the Government Accountability Office issued *Government Auditing Standards 2010 Exposure Draft*, a draft of proposed changes to GAS. The exposure draft is available at www.gao.gov/new.items/d10853g.pdf.

expected to apply both PCAOB standards and GAS. See the GAO website at www.gao.gov for further information.

Statutory Reporting Considerations for Health Plans

2.66 Most health plans that provide insurance coverage and bear financial risk are regulated. Generally speaking, regulated insurers are required by their state of domicile to annually submit a set of audited financial statements that are prepared using that state's prescribed or permitted statutory accounting practices (statutory financial statements).

2.67 The National Association of Insurance Commissioners (NAIC) codified the statutory accounting practices for certain insurance entities, including regulated health plans. Annually, in March of each year, the NAIC issues a revised *Accounting Practices and Procedures Manual* (manual) reflecting revisions or additions to Statements of Statutory Accounting Principles (SSAPs) and interpretations of SSAPs. States generally require health plans to comply with the provisions of the NAIC manual, unless the provisions are preempted by state statutes or regulations, or both. If the requirements of state laws, regulations, and administrative rules differ from the guidance provided in the NAIC manual, such state laws, regulations, and administrative rules take precedence. Preparers and auditors of statutory financial statements might find it useful to monitor the status of the NAIC manual, as well as all the prescribed and permitted practices of an insurer's domiciliary state. Any permitted practices granted by the domiciliary state to the health plan must be reconfirmed annually.

2.68 Statutory financial statements prepared in accordance with the NAIC manual, as well as other prescribed and permitted statutory accounting practices, are considered to be prepared in accordance with an OCBOA under AU section 623, *Special Reports* (AICPA, *Professional Standards*). Interpretation No. 12, "Evaluation of the Appropriateness of Informative Disclosures in Insurance Enterprises' Financial Statements Prepared on a Statutory Basis," of AU section 623 (AICPA, *Professional Standards*, AU sec. 9623 par. .60–.81), provides guidance in evaluating the adequacy and appropriateness of informative disclosures in financial statements prepared on a statutory basis.

2.69 Various SSAPs included in the NAIC manual specifically address issues related to health plans. These include SSAP No. 25, *Accounting for and Disclosures about Transactions with Affiliates and Other Related Parties*; No. 35, *Guaranty Fund and Other Assessments*; No. 47, *Uninsured Plans*; No. 50, *Classifications and Definitions of Insurance or Managed Care Contracts in Force*; No. 54, *Individual and Group Accident and Health Contracts*; No. 55, *Unpaid Claims, Losses and Loss Adjustment Expenses*; No. 61, *Life, Deposit-Type and Accident and Health Reinsurance*; No. 66, *Retrospectively Rated Contracts*; No. 73, *Health Care Delivery Assets—Supplies, Pharmaceutical and Surgical Supplies, Durable Medical Equipment, Furniture, Medical Equipment and Fixtures, and Leasehold Improvements in Health Care Facilities*; No. 84, *Certain Health Care Receivables and Receivables Under Government Insured Plans*; No. 85, *Claim Adjustment Expenses, Amendments to SSAP No. 55—Unpaid Claims, Losses and Loss Adjustment Expenses*; No. 87, *Capitalization Policy, An Amendment to SSAP Nos. 4, 19, 29, 73, 79 and 82*; and No. 96, *Settlement requirements for Intercompany Transactions, An Amendment to SSAP No. 25—Accounting for and Disclosures about Transactions with Affiliates and Other*

Related Parties. Preparers and auditors should consider the applicability of all the SSAPs and apply the SSAPs to the insurer, as appropriate.

RBC Requirements

2.70 The risk-based capital (RBC) formula is one of the tools used by regulators to evaluate the financial health of regulated entities. The RBC formula generally consists of the following principal risk elements: (*a*) affiliated investment risk, (*b*) asset risk, (*c*) underwriting risk, (*d*) credit risk, and (*e*) general business risk. Based on the outcome of the RBC formula, an insurer may be classified into one of four regulatory action levels. In order of increasingly stringent level of regulatory response, the action levels are company action level, regulatory action level, authorized control level, and mandatory control level. At a minimum, the company action level classification requires the filing of an RBC plan with the respective state insurance commissioner that details conditions leading to the classification event and the insurer's proposals of corrective action. State laws vary regarding compliance with the RBC formula and required actions to be taken by the health plan. Additional information can be found on the NAIC website at www.naic.org.

2.71 When assessing the risks of material misstatement, an auditor might consider the RBC formula and the impact that the RBC formula might have on the health plan's accounting and reporting.

Communications With Regulators and the Annual Financial Reporting Model Regulation

2.72 AU section 325 requires the auditor to communicate control deficiencies that are significant deficiencies or material weaknesses in internal control. The definitions in AU section 325 are consistent with PCAOB Auditing Standards in AU section 325, *Communications About Control Deficiencies in an Audit of Financial Statements* (AICPA, *PCAOB Standards and Related Rules*, Interim Standards).

2.73 The NAIC Annual Financial Reporting Model Regulation, commonly referred to as the Model Audit Rule (MAR), has incorporated the provisions of AU section 325 (AICPA, *Professional Standards*). MAR establishes new requirements related to management reporting on the effectiveness of internal controls over statutory financial reporting, audit committees, auditor independence, and other statutory filing matters.[||] A health plan will be required to file a written communication to its domiciliary state on the effectiveness of its internal control, similar to the requirements under Section 404 of the Sarbanes-Oxley Act of 2002. The NAIC developed a companion publication, *Implementation Guide for the Annual Financial Reporting Model Regulation*. The MAR implementation guide is intended to supplement MAR, not create additional requirements, by providing interpretative guidance and clarifying the meaning of terms used in MAR. The MAR implementation guide will be updated in the future, as necessary, and is included in the NAIC manual.

|| The revised National Association of Insurance Commissioners Annual Financial Reporting Model Regulation, commonly referred to as the Model Audit Rule, is effective in most states on January 1, 2010. The requirement for a Management's Report of Internal Control over Financial Reporting is for health plans that have more than $500 million in written and assumed premiums in their most recent fiscal year.

Chapter 3

Unique Financial Statement Considerations for Not-for-Profit Health Care Entities

3.01 Not-for-profit health care entities must apply the not-for-profit financial reporting model described in Financial Accounting Standards Board (FASB) *Accounting Standards Codification* (ASC) 958, *Not-for-Profit Entities*, subject to, and in accordance with, additional financial reporting guidance provided in FASB ASC 954, *Health Care Entities*. The incremental financial reporting guidance in FASB ASC 954 tailors the not-for-profit financial reporting model to better serve the needs of users of financial statements of health care entities.[1]

Complete Set of Financial Statements

3.02 In accordance with FASB ASC 958-205-45-5, a set of financial statements of a not-for-profit health care entity should include (either in the body of the statements or accompanying notes) information required by generally accepted accounting principles (GAAP) that does not specifically exempt not-for-profit entities and information required by applicable, specialized accounting and reporting principles and practices.

3.03 The financial reporting for not-for-profit business-oriented health care entities and investor-owned health care entities generally is consistent, except for transactions that clearly are not applicable. For example, not-for-profit business-oriented health care entities would have nothing to report for shareholders' equity. On the other hand, investor-owned health care entities typically would not have anything to report for contributions.

3.04 According to FASB ASC 954-205-45-1, the basic financial statements of health care entities consist of a balance sheet, a statement of operations, a statement of changes in net assets (or equity), a statement of cash flows, and notes to the financial statements.[2]

3.05 Some not-for-profit health care entities may use fund accounting for purposes of internal recordkeeping and managerial control. As noted in FASB ASC 958-205-45-3, reporting by fund groups is not a necessary part of external financial reporting; however, FASB ASC 958-205 does not preclude providing disaggregated information by fund groups. In accordance with FASB ASC 958-210-45-2, because receivables and payables between fund groups are not entity assets or liabilities, a statement of financial position should clearly label and arrange those interfund items to eliminate their amounts when displaying total assets or liabilities.

---

[1] See paragraph 1.07 of this guide for a discussion of the financial reporting objectives of not-for-profit entities that are essentially self-sustaining from fees they charge for goods and services.

[2] As noted in Financial Accounting Standards Board *Accounting Standards Codification* 958-205-45-2, the terms *balance sheet* and *statement of operations* indicate the content and purpose of the respective statements and serve as possible titles for those statements. Other appropriately descriptive titles may also be used. For example, a statement reporting financial position could be called a statement of financial position, as well as a balance sheet Current practice and purpose suggest, however, that a statement of cash flows only be titled "Statement of Cash Flows."

Balance Sheet

3.06 Not-for-profit health care entities are subject to the unique balance sheet reporting requirements for not-for-profit entities set forth in FASB ASC 958-210. That guidance is subject to the more specific reporting requirements for health care entities contained in FASB ASC 954-210. In addition, not-for-profit health care entities also should apply the requirements of FASB ASC 210, *Balance Sheet*, that are not in conflict with the more specific industry requirements.

3.07 FASB ASC 958-210-45-1 requires that a statement of financial position focus on the not-for-profit entity as a whole and report all of the following amounts: total assets; total liabilities; total net assets; and the amount of each of the three classes of net assets (permanently restricted, temporarily restricted, and unrestricted). FASB ASC 958-810-45-1 describes how to report noncontrolling interests in the equity (net assets) of consolidated subsidiaries within the appropriate class(es) of net assets.

3.08 FASB ASC 954-210-45-1 requires not-for-profit health care entities to classify assets and liabilities as current and noncurrent, as discussed in FASB ASC 210-10-45. However, rather than presenting a classified balance sheet, a continuing care retirement community may instead sequence assets according to their nearness of conversion to cash and may sequence liabilities according to the nearness of the maturity and resulting use of cash.

Statement of Operations

3.09 FASB ASC 958-225 describes the unique standards relating to the income statement (statement of activities) of a not-for-profit entity. FASB ASC 954-225 modifies the requirements of FASB ASC 958-225 as they pertain to not-for-profit health care entities.

3.10 Health care entities present the information included within the statement of activities in two separate statements: a statement of operations, which reports all changes in unrestricted net assets for the period, and a statement of changes in net assets. Alternatively, in accordance with FASB ASC 954-225-45-1, these may be combined into a single statement of operations and changes in net assets.

3.11 Revenues, expenses, gains, and losses increase or decrease net assets and are classified as provided in paragraphs 4–8 of FASB ASC 958-225-45 and are briefly discussed subsequently. Reclassifications, equity transfers, and equity transactions should be reported as separate items. A *reclassification* is the simultaneous increase of one class of net assets and decrease of another, usually as a result of the release or lapsing of restrictions. Paragraphs 12.70–.73 of this guide describe equity transfers, and paragraphs 12.74–.77 of this guide describe equity transactions.

Performance Indicator

3.12 FASB ASC 954-225-45-4 requires that the statement of operations for a not-for-profit business-oriented health care entity include a performance indicator. The FASB ASC glossary states that a performance indicator reports results of operations. A performance indicator and the income from continuing operations reported by for-profit health care entities generally are consistent, except for transactions that clearly are not applicable to one kind of entity (for example, for-profit health care entities typically would not receive contributions, and not-for-profit health care entities would not award stock compensation). The performance indicator is analogous to income from continuing operations of a for-profit entity.

3.13 FASB ASC 954-225-45-4 also states that because of the importance of the performance indicator, it should be clearly labeled with a descriptive term, such as revenues over expenses, revenues and gains over expenses and losses, earned income, or performance earnings. Not-for-profit business-oriented health care entities should report the performance indicator in a statement that also presents the total changes in unrestricted net assets.

3.14 The performance indicator reports results of operations and represents an earnings measure for the entity.[3] The section of the statement of operations below the performance indicator (referred to as "Other Changes in Unrestricted Net Assets") generally should be regarded as the functional equivalent of other comprehensive income in an investor-owned entity.

3.15 FASB ASC 954-225-50-1 requires that the notes to the financial statements include a description of the nature and composition of the performance indicator.

3.16 In accordance with FASB ASC 954-225-45-7, the following items are excluded from the performance indicator:

a. Transactions with owners acting in that capacity.

b. Equity transfers involving other entities that control the reporting entity, are controlled by the reporting entity, or are under common control with the reporting entity.

c. Receipt of restricted contributions, including temporary restrictions, such as time or purpose, or permanent restrictions.

d. Contributions of, and assets released from donor restrictions related to, long-lived assets.

e. Items that are required to be reported in, or reclassified from, other comprehensive income, such as gains or losses, prior service costs or credits, and transition assets or obligations recognized in accordance with FASB ASC 715, *Compensation—Retirement Benefits*; foreign currency translation adjustments; and the effective portion of the gain or loss on derivative instruments designated and qualifying as cash flow hedging instruments.

f. Items that are required to be reported separately under specialized not-for-profit standards. These include extraordinary items and the effect of discontinued operations. See paragraph 3.21.

g. Unrealized gains and losses on investments other than trading securities, in accordance with FASB ASC 954-320-45-1(b).

h. Investment returns restricted by donors or law. See also FASB ASC 954-320-45-2.

---

[3] Investor-owned entities are required by generally accepted accounting principles to include discontinued operations within their net income measure. Not-for-profit entities are required to report discontinued operations just before the change in net assets, preceded by a subtotal. See paragraph 3.19. Accordingly, the performance indicator is considered to be analogous to income from continuing operations, rather than net income, of an investor-owned health care entity. Further, the term *net income* is not an appropriate caption for describing the earnings measure of a not-for-profit entity.

i. Investment losses that decrease unrestricted net assets if those losses reduce the assets of a donor-restricted endowment fund below the required level, as described in FASB ASC 958-205-45-22.

j. Investment gains that increase unrestricted net assets if those gains restore the fair value of the assets of a donor-restricted endowment fund to the required level, as described in FASB ASC 958-205-45-22.

k. An inherent contribution (see FASB ASC 958-805-25-31) received in a not-for-profit acquisition transaction that increases temporarily-restricted or permanently-restricted net assets, as described in FASB ASC 954-805-45-2.

3.17 The preceding items that reflect increases or decreases in unrestricted net assets are reported below the performance indicator in the statement of operations. Items that reflect increases or decreases in temporarily-restricted or permanently-restricted net assets are reported in the statement of changes in net assets, rather than the statement of operations.

Other Intermediate Subtotals

3.18 As noted in paragraphs 5–6 of FASB ASC 954-225-45, classifying revenues, expenses, gains, and losses within classes of net assets does not preclude incorporating additional classifications within the performance indicator. For example, within a class or classes of changes in net assets, a not-for-profit health care entity may classify items as operating and nonoperating, expendable and nonexpendable, earned and unearned, recurring and nonrecurring, or in other ways. The guidance neither requires nor precludes reporting such intermediate measures or subtotals. As discussed in paragraphs 9–12 of FASB ASC 958-225-45, not-for-profit entities have the flexibility to choose whether to report an operating measure.

3.19 FASB ASC 958-225-45-11 states that if an intermediate measure of operations is reported, other subtopics within FASB ASC impose limitations on an entity's use of that measure. If a subtotal is presented, such as income from operations, it should include the amounts of the following items:

a. An impairment loss recognized for a long-lived asset (asset group) that is to be held and used, pursuant to FASB ASC 360-10-45-4

b. Costs associated with an exit or a disposal activity that does not involve a discontinued operation, pursuant to FASB ASC 420-10-45-3

c. A gain or loss recognized on the sale of a long-lived asset (disposal group) that is not a component of an entity, pursuant to FASB ASC 360-10-45-5

d. Amortization expense and impairment losses for intangible assets, pursuant to FASB ASC 350-30-45-2

3.20 As required by FASB ASC 958-225-50-1, if a not-for-profit health care entity's use of the term *operations* is not apparent from the details provided on the face of the statement, a note to the financial statements should describe the nature of the reported measure of operations or the items excluded from operations.

Extraordinary Items, Discontinued Operations, and Accounting Changes

3.21 As illustrated in FASB ASC 958-225-55-6, GAAP requires a not-for-profit entity to appropriately report labeled subtotals for changes in classes of net assets before the effects of discontinued operating segments or extraordinary items, if any.

3.22 Normally, a FASB Accounting Standards Update will provide specific transition requirements. If a newly-issued standard requires that the effect of an accounting change be reported as a cumulative-effect adjustment to the change in net assets of the period of the change, rather than by retrospective application, that amount would also be displayed with extraordinary items and discontinued operations, unless the transition requirements provided otherwise.

Revenues

3.23 FASB ASC 958-225-45-5 requires that revenues be reported as increases in unrestricted net assets, unless the use of the received assets is limited by donor-imposed restrictions.

3.24 The financial statement display requirements for patient service revenue and capitation revenue are discussed in chapter 10, "Health Care Service Revenue and Related Receivables," of this guide, and display of managed care revenue is discussed in chapter 13, "Financial Accounting and Reporting for Managed Care Services," of this guide.

3.25 As discussed in FASB ASC 954-605-05-4, other revenue, gains, or losses are derived from services other than providing health care services to patients, residents, or enrollees. These typically include the following:

- Interest and dividends from all funds held by a trustee, malpractice funds, or other miscellaneous investment activities
- Certain realized changes in fair values of marketable securities
- Fees from educational programs, which include tuition for schools, such as nursing, or laboratory and X-ray technology
- Rental of health care facility space
- Sales of medical and pharmaceutical supplies to employees, physicians, and others
- Fees charged for transcripts for lawyers, insurance companies, and others
- Proceeds from the sale of cafeteria meals and guest trays to employees, medical staff, and visitors
- Proceeds from the sale of scrap, used X-ray film, and so on
- Proceeds from sales at gift shops, snack bars, newsstands, parking lots, vending machines, or other service facilities operated by the health care entity

Expenses

3.26 FASB ASC 958-225-45-7 requires a not-for-profit entity to report all expenses as decreases in unrestricted net assets. FASB ASC 958-720-45 provides standards for the presentation of expenses in the financial statements of a not-for-profit entity.

3.27 Expenses may be reported on the face of the statement of operations using either a natural classification (for example, salaries and wages, supplies, and so on) or functional presentation (a method of grouping expenses according to the purpose for which costs are incurred). Pursuant to FASB ASC 958-205-55-11, not-for-profit entities that report using a natural classification of expenses on the face of the statement of operations are required to disclose expenses by functional classification in the notes to the financial statements.

3.28 According to FASB ASC 954-225-45-3, the primary functional classifications are program services and supporting activities. The extent of classification and subclassification of expenses depends on many factors, such as the nature and complexity of the health care entity. For example, in complying with the functional reporting requirements of FASB ASC 958-205-45-6, 958-720-05-4, and 958-720-45-2, some health care entities may present only two categories: health services, including inpatient services, outpatient procedures, home health services, and so forth, and general and administrative. Others may present additional distinctions, such as physician services, research, and teaching. Functional allocations should be based on full cost allocations.

Statement of Changes in Net Assets (or Equity)

3.29 The statement of changes in net assets (or equity) reports all changes that have occurred during the reporting period in each classification of net assets (unrestricted, temporarily restricted, and permanently restricted). As discussed in paragraph 3.10, this statement may be combined with the statement of operations or presented separately.

3.30 The statement of changes in net assets displays the four measures required by FASB ASC 958-225-45-1: the change in permanently-restricted net assets, the change in temporarily-restricted net assets, the change in unrestricted net assets, and the change in net assets for the entity as a whole. As illustrated in FASB ASC 958-205-55-16, typically, the information presented for the unrestricted net asset category in the statement of changes in net assets is highly aggregated.

3.31 Restricted contributions and restricted investment return, which are excluded from the performance indicator, are reported as increases or decreases in temporarily-restricted or permanently-restricted net assets in the statement of changes in net assets. Restricted contributions are discussed in chapter 11, "Contributions Received and Made," of this guide, and restricted investment return is discussed in paragraphs 4.32–.34 of this guide.

3.32 Because all expenses must be reported as decreases in unrestricted net assets, as discussed in paragraph 3.26, no expenses should be reported in the temporarily-restricted or permanently-restricted net asset categories. However, certain losses may be reported within those categories, as discussed in FASB ASC 958-225-45-8.

Statement of Cash Flows

3.33 The general standards for reporting cash flows are provided in FASB ASC 230, *Statement of Cash Flows*. FASB ASC 958-230 provides incremental guidance related to reporting not-for-profit-specific transactions within this statement. According to FASB ASC 230-10-45, the statement of cash flows may be prepared using the direct or indirect method of reporting cash flows.

3.34 FASB ASC 230-10-45-28 requires a not-for-profit entity to reconcile the change in net assets to net cash flows from operating activities. FASB ASC 958-205-55-20 provides an example of this reconciliation.

3.35 The reconciliation will need to accommodate certain items that are not included in cash flow statements prepared for investor-owned health care entities, such as equity transfers, contributions of long-lived assets, other contributions restricted for long-term purposes, unrealized gains and losses on certain investments, investment returns restricted for long-term purposes by donor or law, and the effective portion of fair value changes of cash flow hedging derivatives.

3.36 FASB ASC 958-230 expands the description of financing activities in FASB ASC 230 to encompass receipts of resources that are donor-restricted for long-term purposes. As discussed in FASB ASC 958-210-45-6, cash or other assets received with a donor-imposed restriction that limits their use to long term should not be classified on a statement of financial position with cash or other assets that are unrestricted and available for current use. Therefore, as discussed in FASB ASC 958-230-55-3, when a not-for-profit entity reports cash received with a donor-imposed restriction that limits its use to long-term purposes, in conformity with FASB ASC 958-210-45-6, an adjustment is necessary for the statement of cash flows to reconcile beginning and ending cash and cash equivalents. To report in conformity with FASB ASC 230, the receipt of a cash contribution that is restricted for the purchase of equipment should be reported as a cash flow from financing activities (using a caption such as "Contributions Restricted for Purchasing Equipment"), and it should be simultaneously reported as a cash outflow from investing activities (using a caption such as "Purchase of Assets Restricted to Investment in Property and Equipment" or, if the equipment was purchased in the same period, "Purchase of Equipment"). An adjustment to reconcile the change in net assets to net cash used or provided by operating activities would also be needed if the contributed asset is not classified as cash or cash equivalents on the statement of financial position. When the equipment is purchased in a subsequent period, both the proceeds from the sale of assets restricted to investment in the equipment and the purchase of the equipment should be reported as cash flows from investing activities.

Notes to the Financial Statements

3.37 The individual chapters of this guide discuss the notes to the financial statements that are unique to, or prevalent for, health care entities.

Subsequent Events

3.38 FASB ASC 855, *Subsequent Events*, establishes standards for accounting for, and disclosure of, events that occur after the balance sheet date but before financial statements are issued or available to be issued. In accordance with FASB ASC 855-10-25, an entity should recognize in the financial statements the effects of all subsequent events that provide additional evidence about conditions that existed at the date of the balance sheet, including the estimates inherent in the process of preparing financial statements. An entity should not recognize subsequent events that provide evidence about conditions that did not exist at the date of the balance sheet but arose after the balance sheet date but before financial statements are issued or available to be issued. Instead, nonrecognized subsequent events are disclosed if they are of such a nature that they must be disclosed to keep the financial statements from being misleading.

3.39 As discussed in paragraphs 7.06–.08 of this guide, because of their use of conduit debt that trades in public markets, many not-for-profit health care entities fall into the class of entities that are required to evaluate subsequent events through the issuance date of their financial statements. However, if a not-for-profit health care entity issued tax-exempt debt in a private placement, and the debt has not subsequently begun trading in a public market, the entity is not a conduit bond obligor for the purpose of FASB ASC 855 because its debt does not trade in a public market.

3.40 If a not-for-profit health care entity does not have conduit debt that trades in a public market, it is required to evaluate subsequent events up through the date that the financial statements are available to be issued. The FASB ASC glossary definition of *financial statements are available to be issued* states that "[f]inancial statements are considered available to be issued when they are complete in a form and format that complies with GAAP and all approvals necessary for issuance have been obtained, for example, from management, the board of directors, and/or significant shareholders."

Example Financial Statements

3.41 Some health care entities choose to present very detailed financial statements; others present highly condensed statements, providing only summary totals of major classifications of revenue and expense. Each entity should use the presentation that it considers to be most informative given its own facts and circumstances, provided that the statements comply with the reporting parameters of GAAP.

3.42 Examples of financial statements of health care entities are not included in this guide. Examples may be found in the following places:

- The website for Electronic Municipal Market Access (EMMA), (http://emma.msrb.org) for financial statements of not-for-profit health care entities. EMMA is the official source for municipal disclosures and market data maintained by the Municipal Securities Rulemaking Board. EMMA contains official statements and continuing disclosures for not-for-profit entities with tax-exempt bonds.
- The website for the Electronic Data Gathering, Analysis, and Retrieval (EDGAR) system (www.sec.gov/edgar/aboutedgar.htm) for financial statements of investor-owned health care entities that are required to file forms with the Securities and Exchange Commission (SEC). EDGAR is the system for the automated collection, validation, indexing, acceptance, and forwarding of submissions by companies and others that are required by law to file forms with the SEC.

- The websites of health care entities that are considered peers of the reporting entity.
- The websites of regulatory agencies, such as the secretary of state or departments of health or insurance.
- The AICPA publications *Accounting Trends and Techniques—Not-for-Profit Entities* and *Accounting Trends and Techniques* (www.cpa2biz.com), which are useful for the disclosure examples, even though they do not contain example financial statements of health care entities.
- The AICPA publications *Health Care Entities: Checklist and Illustrative Financial Statements* (www.cpa2biz.com).

Chapter 4

Cash, Cash Equivalents, and Investments

Cash and Cash Equivalents

4.01 Health care entities, both investor-owned and not for profit, hold cash balances to meet payments arising in the ordinary course of operations and unanticipated contingencies. These balances may be held as cash or cash equivalents. This chapter discusses the following industry-pervasive matters about accounting for cash and cash equivalents:

- Centralized cash management arrangements (see paragraphs 4.03–.06)
- Cash from restricted donations (see paragraph 4.07)
- Other restricted or designated cash amounts (see paragraphs 4.08–.11)

4.02 The Financial Accounting Standards Board (FASB) *Accounting Standards Codification* (ASC) glossary defines a *cash equivalent* as

> short-term, highly liquid investments that have both of the following characteristics:
>
> a. Readily convertible to known amounts of cash
>
> b. So near their maturity that they present insignificant risk of changes in value because of changes in interest rates.
>
> Generally, only investments with original maturities of three months or less qualify under that definition. Original maturity means original maturity to the entity holding the investment. For example, both a three-month U.S. Treasury bill and a three-year U.S. Treasury note purchased three months from maturity qualify as cash equivalents. However, a Treasury note purchased three years ago does not become a cash equivalent when its remaining maturity is three months. Examples of items commonly considered to be cash equivalents are Treasury bills, commercial paper, money market funds, and federal funds sold (for an entity with banking operations).

Centralized Cash Management Arrangements

4.03 Many health care entities have centralized cash management arrangements whereby excess cash is swept into a cash pool. Subsidiary cash requirements are met through withdrawals or borrowings from the cash pool. The cash pool is invested in assets, such as deposits at banks, that are in the parent company's name. Under this type of arrangement, the parent company and its subsidiaries have sweep arrangements with their respective banks whereby cash is transferred daily between the bank accounts of the entities (the parent and its subsidiaries). These arrangements serve to reduce lending costs and provide a higher rate of return on invested cash. Careful review of centralized cash management arrangements is necessary to determine the appropriate accounting and reporting of a subsidiary's deposit in the cash pool.

4.04 The FASB ASC glossary states that *cash* "includes not only currency on hand but demand deposits with banks or other financial institutions. Cash also includes other kinds of accounts that have the general characteristics of demand deposits in that the customer may deposit additional funds at any time and also effectively may withdraw funds at any time without prior notice or penalty."

4.05 Funds deposited by a subsidiary in a parent company's cash account under a centralized cash management arrangement generally would not be classified as cash and cash equivalents in the subsidiary's financial statements if the subsidiary does not have legal title to the cash on deposit. Generally, legal title in a cash account is evidenced by the cash or cash equivalent being deposited in a demand deposit account at a bank or other financial institution in the subsidiary's name. A subsidiary's deposit in a cash pool generally is not a short-term highly-liquid investment, as contemplated in the definition of a *cash equivalent* in paragraph 4.02; rather, the deposit is considered a loan, and the subsidiary would classify the deposit in the cash pool as a receivable from an affiliated entity.

4.06 If the indirect method is used to prepare the statement of cash flows, changes in the subsidiary's receivable relating to a centralized cash management program are presented as investing activities—as such, balances are generally considered loans. Payments to, and receipts from, the cash pool would be presented on a gross or net basis, in accordance with the guidance in paragraphs 7–9 of FASB ASC 230-10-45.

Cash From Restricted Donations

4.07 FASB ASC 954-305-45-3 states that for fiduciary purposes, not-for-profit business-oriented health care entities may maintain separate checking or savings accounts for restricted donations. However, unless required by FASB ASC 954-305-45-1, as discussed in paragraph 4.08, such accounts are not reported on a line separate from other cash and cash equivalents because donor restrictions generally relate to limitations on the use of net assets, rather than the use of specific assets.[1]

Other Restricted or Designated Cash Amounts

4.08 FASB ASC 954-305-45-1 states that cash and claims to cash that meet any of the following conditions should be reported separately and excluded from current assets:

a. They are restricted regarding withdrawal or use for other-than-current operations.

b. They are designated for expenditure in the acquisition or construction of noncurrent assets.

c. They are required to be segregated for the liquidation of long-term debt.

d. They are required by a donor-imposed restriction that limits their use to long-term purposes (see paragraph 11.05 of this guide.).

Further, according to FASB ASC 954-210-45-4, internally designated funds should be reported separately from externally designated funds either on the face of the balance sheet or in the notes to the financial statements.

---

[1] Per Financial Accounting Standards Board (FASB) *Accounting Standards Codification* (ASC) 954-305-45-3, a columnar presentation that highlights the three classes of net assets (permanently restricted, temporarily restricted, and unrestricted) is not precluded if the totals for the reporting entity as a whole are displayed.

4.09 For example, such amounts could be reported on a separate line and described as assets whose use has been limited or whose use is restricted, such as designated for construction, limited by donor-imposed restrictions, held by the trustee for liquidation of long-term debt, and so on.

4.10 FASB ASC 958-210-45-6 states that the asset whose use is limited should be described in the notes to the financial statements if its nature is not clear from the description on the face of the balance sheet.

4.11 Restricted cash is similar to investments in that the holder's ability to withdraw restricted cash amounts is contractually limited. As a result, deposits and withdrawals of principal balances in restricted cash accounts would be reported as investing activities in the statement of cash flows.

Investments

4.12 Health care entities can maintain and manage significant investment portfolios. The nature of such investments held by health care entities is dependent upon various factors, such as an entity's investment policies and strategies, donor and other external restrictions, and regulations. The legal structure, term, and features specific to an instrument, such as restrictions on disposing of the investment or other internal and external restrictions, can affect both the accounting and reporting of an investment and the valuation of the investment.

4.13 This chapter discusses the following industry-pervasive matters about accounting for investments:

- The fair value option to measure financial assets (see paragraphs 4.17–.22)
- Investments in equity securities that have readily determinable fair values and all investments in debt securities for which an entity has not elected to apply the fair value option (see paragraphs 4.23–.35)
- Investments for which a readily determinable fair value does not exist and for which an entity has not elected to apply the fair value option, including alternative investments, such as collective trusts, funds of funds, or hedge funds (see paragraphs 4.36–.38)
- Investment pools (see paragraphs 4.39–.47)
- Fair value measurement (see paragraph 4.48)
- Impairment of investments (see paragraphs 4.49–.59)
- Securities lending arrangements (see paragraph 4.60)
- Transfers of assets to a not-for-profit entity or charitable trust for investment (see paragraphs 4.61–.63)
- Regulation (see paragraph 4.64)
- Other financial statement presentation matters (see paragraphs 4.65–.73)

4.14 The following investments are discussed elsewhere in this guide:

- Chapter 5, "Derivatives," discusses investments in derivative instruments that are accounted for in accordance with FASB ASC 815, *Derivatives and Hedging*.

- Chapter 12, "The Reporting Entity and Related Entities," discusses investments accounted for under the equity method if the investees are an integral part of the entity's operations, such as a physician hospital organization or joint venture.[2]
- Chapter 12 also discusses investments in consolidated or combined entities.

4.15 According to FASB ASC 954-325-35-1, other types of investments that are not financial instruments, such as real estate or certain oil and gas interests, are reported at amortized cost and subject to impairment considerations consistent with the "Impairment or Disposal of Long-lived Assets" sections of FASB ASC 360-10.

4.16 Health care entities can use this chapter, not-for-profit health care entities can use exhibit 12-1, and investor-owned health care entities can use paragraph 12.55 to assist with the determination of which investments are required to be consolidated and which are accounted for using the equity method if the entity has not elected to apply the fair value option, as discussed in paragraph 4.17.

Fair Value Option

4.17 Most investments owned by health care entities are *financial assets*, as defined in FASB ASC 825-10-20. The "Fair Value Option" sections of FASB ASC 825-10 permit all entities to choose to measure eligible items at fair value (the fair value option) at specified election dates. Paragraphs 4–5 of FASB ASC 825-10-15 describe which financial assets are eligible items.

4.18 The decision about whether to elect the fair value option should be (*a*) applied instrument by instrument, except as discussed in FASB ASC 825-10-25-7; (*b*) irrevocable, unless a new election date occurs, as discussed in FASB ASC 825-10-25-4; and (*c*) applied only to an entire instrument, not specific risks, specific cash flows, or portions of that instrument.

4.19 Health care entities should follow the guidance in FASB ASC 820, *Fair Value Measurements and Disclosures*,* to determine and report an investment's fair value. FASB ASC 825-1-25-3 requires that upfront costs and fees related to items for which the fair value option is elected be recognized in earnings as incurred and not deferred. Health care entities that elect to apply

---

[2] This chapter discusses the accounting and reporting for equity investments accounted for under the equity method if such investment's purpose is investment income or return, such as collective trusts, funds of funds, hedge funds, or other alternative investments, versus an equity investment that represents an integral part of the reporting entity's operations, such as a physician hospital organization or joint venture.

* In May 2011, FASB issued Accounting Standards Update (ASU) No. 2011-04, *Fair Value Measurement (Topic 820): Amendments to Achieve Common Fair Value Measurement and Disclosure Requirements in U.S. GAAP and IFRSs*. According to FASB, the objective of this update is to improve the comparability of fair value measurements presented and disclosed in financial statements prepared in accordance with U.S. generally accepted accounting principles (GAAP) and International Financial Reporting Standards by changing the wording used to describe many of the requirements in U.S. GAAP for measuring fair value and disclosing information about fair value measurements. The amendments include those that clarify FASB's intent about the application of existing fair value measurement and disclosure requirements and those that change a particular principle or requirement for measuring fair value or disclosing information about fair value measurements. This ASU, which is to be applied prospectively, is effective for public entities during interim and annual periods beginning after December 15, 2011 (early application is not permitted). For nonpublic entities, the amendments are effective for annual periods beginning after December 15, 2011. Nonpublic entities may early implement during interim periods beginning after December 15, 2011.

the fair value option to an instrument should refer to the guidance in FASB ASC 825-10-50 and 820-10-50 for the required financial statement disclosures. FASB ASC 825-10-45-3 requires that entities classify cash receipts and payments related to items measured at fair value according to their nature and purpose, as required by FASB ASC 230, *Statement of Cash Flows*.

4.20 In accordance with FASB ASC 825-10-35-4, investor-owned health care entities should report unrealized gains and losses on items for which the fair value option has been elected in earnings.

4.21 In accordance with FASB ASC 825-10-15-7, not-for-profit health care entities should report unrealized gains and losses on items for which the fair value option has been elected within the performance indicator or as part of discontinued operations, as appropriate. Consistent with the provisions of FASB ASC 958-10 and 954-225-45-5, a not-for-profit health care entity may present such gains and losses either within or outside an intermediate measure of operations, unless such gains or losses are part of discontinued operations; however, that intermediate measure must be within the performance indicator. For not-for-profit entities, the disclosure requirements of FASB ASC 825-10-50-30 apply not only with respect to the effect on performance indicators or other intermediate measures of operations, if presented, but also on the change in each of the net asset classes (unrestricted, temporarily restricted, and permanently restricted), if applicable.

4.22 Per FASB ASC 825-10-50-28(f), for investments that would have been accounted for under the equity method if the health care entity had not chosen to apply the fair value option, the health care entity should disclose the information required by FASB ASC 323-10-50-3, excluding the disclosures in FASB ASC 323-10-50-3(a)(3), (b), and (d).

Investments in Debt Securities and Certain Equity Securities With a Readily Determinable Fair Value That Are Not Recorded Under the Fair Value Option

4.23 This section discusses the accounting and reporting for investments in equity securities that have readily determinable fair values and all investments in debt securities held by investor-owned and not-for-profit entities for which the health care entity has not elected to apply the fair value option to the instrument, as discussed in paragraph 4.17.

Investor-Owned Entities

4.24 Investor-owned health care entities are subject to the accounting and reporting requirements of FASB ASC 320, *Investments—Debt and Equity Securities*. FASB ASC 320 does not apply to (*a*) instruments for which the health care entity elected to apply the fair value option, as discussed in paragraphs 4.17–.22; (*b*) equity securities that, absent the election of the fair value option under FASB ASC 825-10-25-1, would be required to be accounted for under the equity method; (*c*) investments in consolidated entities; (*d*) investments in derivative instruments that are accounted for in accordance with FASB ASC 815, and *(e)* except with respect to impairment guidance in FASB ASC 320-10-35, equity securities within the scope of FASB ASC 325-20 (that is, cost-method investments). FASB ASC 320-10-15 provides a more complete description of the scope of FASB ASC 320.

4.25 FASB ASC 320-10-25-1 states that at acquisition, an entity shall classify its debt and equity securities into one of three categories:

a. *Trading securities*. If a security is acquired with the intent of selling it within hours or days, the security should be classified as trading. However, at acquisition, an entity is not precluded from classifying as trading a security it plans to hold for a longer period. Classification of a security as trading should not be precluded simply because the entity does not intend to sell it in the near term.

b. *Available-for-sale securities*. Investments in debt securities and equity securities that have readily determinable fair values and are not classified as trading securities or held-to-maturity securities should be classified as available-for-sale securities.

c. *Held-to-maturity securities*. Investments in debt securities should be classified as held to maturity only if the reporting entity has the positive intent and ability to hold those securities to maturity.

4.26 Per FASB ASC 320-10-35-1, investments in debt securities that are classified as held to maturity should be measured subsequently at amortized cost in the balance sheet. Investments that are classified as trading should be measured subsequently at fair value in the balance sheet, and unrealized holding gains and losses for trading securities should be included in earnings. Investments that are classified as available for sale should be measured subsequently at fair value in the balance sheet, and unrealized holding gains and losses for available-for-sale securities, including those classified as current assets, should be excluded from earnings and reported in other comprehensive income until realized, except as indicated in the following sentence. All or a portion of the unrealized holding gain and loss of an available-for-sale security that is designated as being hedged in a fair value hedge should be recognized in earnings during the period of the hedge, pursuant to paragraphs 1–4 of FASB ASC 815-25-35.

4.27 For investments within the scope of FASB ASC 320, investor-owned health care entities should follow the disclosure requirements of FASB ASC 320-10-50.

Not-for-Profit Entities

4.28 Not-for-profit health care entities are subject to the accounting and reporting requirements of FASB ASC 958-320 and 954-320. FASB ASC 958-320 does not apply to (*a*) instruments for which the health care entity elected to apply the fair value option, as discussed in paragraphs 4.17–.22; (*b*) equity investments accounted for under the equity method; (*c*) investments in consolidated subsidiaries; (*d*) investments in derivative instruments that are accounted for in accordance with FASB ASC 815; (*e*) investments held by a financially interrelated entity, as discussed in paragraph 12.75 of this guide; and (*f*) short sales of securities. FASB ASC 958-320-15 provides a more complete description of the scope of FASB ASC 958-320.

4.29 Not-for-profit health care entities can designate investment portfolios or portions of investment portfolios as trading. Investment returns from investments, inclusive of those securities designated as trading, accounted for under FASB ASC 958-320 should be included as changes in net assets, consistent with paragraphs 4.30–.34.

4.30 FASB ASC 958-320-35 requires investments in equity securities with readily determinable fair values and all debt securities to be measured at fair value in the balance sheet. According to FASB ASC 954-320-45-1, investment returns, including realized and unrealized gains and losses, not restricted by donors or law should be classified as changes in unrestricted net assets as follows:

a. The following are included in the performance indicator (see paragraphs 3.12–.17 of this guide):

   i. Dividend, interest, and other similar investment income

   ii. Realized gains and losses

   iii. Unrealized gains and losses on trading securities

   iv. Other-than-temporary impairment losses

b. The following is excluded from the performance indicator:

   i. Unrealized gains and losses on other-than-trading securities

4.31 Because the performance indicator is analogous to income from continuing operations of an investor-owned health care entity, as discussed in paragraph 3.12 of this guide, the performance indicator would also include unrealized gains and losses on investments recorded under the fair value option and equity earnings from investments in entities, such as investment companies and other alternative investments, accounted for under the equity method. The performance indicator would exclude the portion of other-than-temporary impairment losses on debt securities that is related to factors other than credit losses, as discussed in paragraph 4.55.

4.32 Pursuant to paragraphs 1–2 of FASB ASC 958-320-45, except as described in paragraphs 4.33–.34, dividend, interest, and other investment income and gains and losses should be reported as increases or decreases in unrestricted net assets, unless their use is temporarily or permanently restricted by explicit donor stipulations or law. Donor-restricted investment income should be reported as an increase in temporarily or permanently restricted net assets, depending on the type of restriction.

4.33 FASB ASC 958-320-45-3 states that gains and investment income that are limited to specific uses by donor-imposed restrictions may be reported as increases in unrestricted net assets if the restrictions are met in the same reporting period as the gains and income are recognized, provided that the not-for-profit entity has a similar policy for reporting received contributions, as discussed in paragraphs 3–5 of FASB ASC 958-605-45; reports consistently from period to period; and discloses its accounting policy. The classification of these gains and investment income within unrestricted net assets should be consistent with paragraph 4.30.

4.34 Paragraphs 16–35 of FASB ASC 958-205-45 describe the accounting for gains and losses on investments of donor-restricted endowment funds. FASB ASC 958-205-45-22 states that in the absence of donor stipulations or law to the contrary, losses on the investments of a donor-restricted endowment fund should temporarily reduce restricted net assets to the extent that donor-imposed temporary restrictions on net appreciation of the fund have not been met before the loss occurs. Any remaining loss should reduce unrestricted net assets. FASB ASC 954-225-45-7 requires that the portion of the loss that reduces the assets of a donor-restricted endowment fund below the required level[3] be excluded from the determination of the performance indicator. FASB ASC 958-205-45-24 states that if losses reduce the assets of a donor-restricted endowment fund below the level required by the donor stipulations or law, gains that restore the fair value of the assets of the endowment fund to the required level should be classified as increases in unrestricted net assets. FASB ASC 954-225-45-7 requires that those gains be excluded from the determination of the performance indicator.

4.35 Not-for-profit health care entities should follow the disclosure requirements included in FASB ASC 954-320 and 958-320-50.

Investments in Certain Other Financial Instruments Without a Readily Determinable Fair Value That Are Not Recorded Under the Fair Value Option

4.36 In an effort to improve investment returns, health care entities may invest in investment companies structured as limited liability companies, limited partnerships, institutional trusts, common and collective trusts, or financial instruments that do not have a readily determinable fair value. These types of investments are commonly referred to as alternative investments. Assuming that the health care entity has not elected to apply the fair value option to account for these investments, the accounting for these types of investments can vary depending upon the legal structure of the investment, as well as the investment's terms and features. An alternative investment may have a formal notification period that requires the investor to provide the investee 60, 90, or 360 day's notification prior to redeeming the investment for cash. Additionally, the legal structure of certain alternative investments provides the investor ownership rights and responsibilities similar to a limited partnership whereas others do not provide such ownership rights to the investor. The terms and features of each alternative investment must be carefully considered before concluding on the appropriate method of accounting. Exhibit 12-1 and paragraph 12.51 of this guide provide helpful guidance for determining the appropriate method of accounting for not-for-profit health care entities and investor-owned health care entities, respectively. Paragraphs 4.39–.47 provide additional discussion for investment pools.

4.37 Determining the fair value of alternative investments may be necessary for recognition or disclosure purposes. Many of these investees provide their investors with a net asset value (NAV) per share or its equivalent that has been calculated in a manner consistent with FASB ASC 946, *Financial Services—Investment Companies*. If those investments do not have readily determinable fair values, FASB ASC 820-10-35-59 permits a reporting entity, as a practical expedient, to estimate the fair value of an investment within the scope of paragraphs 4–5 of FASB ASC 820-10-15 using the NAV per share of the investment or its equivalent, such as member units or an ownership interest in partners' capital to which a proportionate share of net assets is attributed, if the NAV per share of the investment or its equivalent is calculated

---

[3] Donors that create endowment funds can require that their gifts be invested in perpetuity or for a specified term. Some donors may require that a portion of income, gains, or both be added to the gift and invested, subject to similar restrictions. Not-for-profit health care entities in states that have adopted the Uniform Prudent Management of Institutional Funds Act should refer to paragraphs 28–32 of FASB ASC 958-205-45 for additional information about the classification of net assets of donor-restricted endowment funds. Not-for-profit health care entities in other states should refer to paragraphs 33–35 of FASB ASC 958-205-45.

in a manner consistent with the measurement principles of FASB ASC 946 as of the reporting entity's measurement date. FASB ASC 820-10-50-6A requires certain disclosures for alternative investments, regardless of whether NAV is used as a practical expedient for fair value.

4.38 Sections .18–.26 of Technical Questions and Answers (TIS) section 2220, *Long-Term Investments* (AICPA, *Technical Practice Aids*), are intended to assist reporting entities in applying the provisions of FASB ASC 820, which are discussed in the preceding paragraph. TIS section 2220.27, "Determining Fair Value of Investments When the Practical Expedient Is Not Used or Is Not Available" (AICPA, *Technical Practice Aids*), assists reporting entities in determining the fair value of investments in circumstances in which the practical expedient NAV is not used or available.

Investment Pools

4.39 In order to effectively manage investments and improve total investment returns, many not-for-profit health care entities pool part or all of their investments with other not-for-profit health care entities. The not-for-profit entities may or may not be financially-interrelated entities, as discussed in FASB ASC 958-20-15-2 and paragraph 12.75 of this guide. The pooled investments are generally managed by a sponsoring entity's treasury department (for example, a parent treasury division) in a manner similar to a mutual fund arrangement. When a pool is established, ownership interests are initially assigned (typically through unitization) to the various pool investors (sometimes referred to as participants) based on the fair value of the cash and securities placed in the pool by each investor (participant). Current fair value is generally used to determine the number of units allocated to additional assets placed in the pool and to value withdrawals from the pool (for example, the sponsor calculates a NAV per unit, and the investor's [participant's] purchases and sales are based on the NAV unit value). Investment income, realized gains and losses, and any recognized unrealized gains and losses are allocated equitably based on the number of units assigned to each investor (participant). Generally the investor's (participant's) ownership interest in the pool is due on demand; however, in certain arrangements, investors (participants) may be required to provide notification to the pool sponsor prior to divesting, or further limitations on withdrawal may be imposed on the investors (participants). The investors (participants) generally do not have rights or interests in specific assets or investments held in the pool but, instead, own a beneficial-type interest in the pool. These pools typically do not have a formal legal structure, and no security, as defined by either FASB ASC 825, *Financial Instruments*, or FASB ASC 958-320, is created. Paragraphs 4.40–.47 provide the Financial Reporting Executive Committee's (FinREC's) recommendation on how to implement the standards in FASB ASC 958-20 and the "Transfers of Assets to a Not-for-Profit Entity or Charitable Trust that Raises or Holds Contributions for Others" sections of FASB ASC 958-605 when they are applied to investment pools.

4.40 The underlying investments are owned by the sponsor and included in the sponsor's assets. The investor's (participant's) recognition of its beneficial-type interest in the pool depends upon the relationship of the sponsor and investor (participant), as follows:

- If the investor (participant) and sponsor are neither affiliates nor financially interrelated entities (see paragraph 12.75 of this guide), the investor (participant) should recognize its beneficial-type interest as described in paragraphs 4.41–.42.

- If the investor (participant) and sponsor are affiliates or otherwise financially interrelated entities, the investor (participant) should recognize its beneficial-type interest as described in paragraphs 4.43–.45.

4.41 If the investor (participant) (beneficiary) and sponsor (recipient entity) are neither affiliates nor financially interrelated entities, the investor (participant) would recognize its rights to the assets held by the sponsor as a beneficial interest in an identifiable pool of assets, as described in FASB ASC 958-605-25-33(d). FASB ASC 958-605-30-14 and 958-605-35-3 state that if a beneficiary has an unconditional right to receive all or a portion of the specified cash flows from a charitable trust or other identifiable pool of assets, the beneficiary should measure and subsequently remeasure that beneficial interest at fair value.

4.42 Changes in fair value of the beneficial interest in the investment pool are reported above (included in) the performance indicator in the statement of operations if the investment return was unrestricted. In the investor's (participant's) balance sheet, the interest in the pool might be reported using a caption such as "Beneficial Interest in Investment Pool" or "Interest in Investment Pool." If the investor's (participant's) balances are due on demand, the change in value of the beneficial interest that related to purchases and sales of pool units would be reported net in the "Investing" section of the cash flow statement. However, if the balances are not due on demand, the purchases and sales of pool units would be recorded gross in the investor's (participant's) "Investing" section of the cash flow statement, unless the cash flows qualified for net reporting, as discussed in paragraphs 7–9 of FASB ASC 230-10-45. The change in value of the beneficial interest related to unrealized gains and losses would be reported in the cash flow statement in the same manner as unrealized gains and losses on investments are reported.

4.43 If the investor (participant) and sponsor are financially-interrelated entities, as discussed in FASB ASC 958-20-15-2 and paragraph 12.75 of this guide, the investor (participant) (beneficiary) would account for its investment in the pool as part of its interest in the sponsor (recipient entity). FASB ASC 958-20-25-2 requires that if a beneficiary and recipient entity are financially-interrelated entities, the beneficiary should recognize its interest in the net assets of the recipient entity. Recognizing an interest in the net assets of the recipient entity and adjusting that interest for a share of the change in net assets of the recipient entity is similar to the equity method, which is described in FASB ASC 323-10. Alternatively, the investor (participant) may elect the fair value option described in the "Fair Value Option" sections of FASB ASC 825-10.

4.44 Sections .36–.43 of TIS section 6400, *Health Care Entities* (AICPA, *Technical Practice Aids*), which are reproduced in appendix A, "TIS Section 6400, *Health Care Entities*," of chapter 11, "Contributions Received and Made," of this guide, discuss how a beneficiary should report and classify its interest in the net assets of a recipient entity and changes in that interest. In the investor's (participant's) balance sheet, the interest in the pool might be reported using a caption such as "Beneficial Interest in Investment Pool" or "Interest in Investment Pool." If the investor's (participant's) balances are due on demand, the change in value of the beneficial interest that related to purchases and sales of pool units would be reported net in the "Investing" section of the cash flow statement. However, if the balances are not due on demand, the purchases and sales of pool units would be recorded gross in the investor's (participant's) "Investing" section of the cash flow statement, unless the cash flows qualified for net reporting, as discussed in paragraphs 7–9 of FASB ASC 230-10-45. The change in value of the beneficial interest related to unrealized gains and losses would be reported in the cash flow statement in the same manner as all unrealized gains and losses on investments are reported.

4.45 TIS section 6400.42, "Application of FASB ASC 958—Classification of a Beneficiary's Interest in the Net Assets of a Financially Interrelated Fund-Raising Foundation (Recipient Entity)—Accounting for Unrealized Gains and Losses on Investments Held by the Foundation" (AICPA, *Technical Practice Aids*), discusses how a beneficiary should display unrealized gains and losses related to investments held for its benefit by a financially interrelated entity. It states that in circumstances in which the beneficiary (investor or participant) can influence the financial decisions of the recipient entity (pool sponsor) to such an extent that the beneficiary can determine the timing and amount of distributions from the recipient entity to the beneficiary, changes in a beneficiary's interest in the net assets of the recipient entity should be included in, or excluded from, the beneficiary's performance indicator in the same manner that they would have been had the beneficiary held the investments directly. Thus, the beneficiary should include in the performance indicator the portion of the change attributable to unrealized gains and losses on trading securities that are not restricted by donors or law and should exclude from the performance indicator the portion of the change attributable to all other unrealized gains and losses. This manner of reporting is similar to the reporting by an investor that combines its proportionate share of an investee's other comprehensive income amounts with its own other comprehensive income items, as described in FASB ASC 323-10-45-3.[†] TIS section 6400.42 also discusses how to report unrealized gains and losses in circumstances in which the beneficiary cannot influence the financial decisions of the recipient organization to such an extent that it can determine the timing and amount of distributions that it receives from the recipient entity.

4.46 As noted in FASB ASC 958-20-45-3, if the beneficiary and recipient entity are included in consolidated financial statements, the beneficiary's interest in the net assets of the recipient entity should be eliminated, in accordance with FASB ASC 810-10-45-1. Therefore, if the investor (participant) and sponsor were both included in consolidated financial statements, the interest in the investment pool and changes in that interest would be eliminated.

4.47 To determine the sponsor's accounting, the pooling arrangement would be carefully reviewed to determine if the sponsor has legal ownership

---

[†] In June 2011, FASB issued ASU No. 2011-05, *Comprehensive Income (Topic 220): Presentation of Comprehensive Income*. This ASU is intended to increase the prominence of other comprehensive income in financial statements. This ASU requires that an entity that reports items of other comprehensive income present comprehensive income in either a single statement with net income or in an income statement that is followed consecutively by a statement of comprehensive income. The current option to present other comprehensive income in the statement of changes in equity has been eliminated. The amendments in the ASU should be applied retrospectively. For public entities, the amendments are effective for fiscal years, and interim periods within those years, beginning after December 15, 2011. For nonpublic entities, the amendments are effective for fiscal years ending after December 15, 2012, and interim and annual periods thereafter. Early adoption is permitted.

and rights to the underlying investments (for example, would the pool sponsor's creditors have claim against the investments in the pool in bankruptcy) or if the sponsor is merely acting as an agent for the investors (participants). If the investments in the pool are legally owned by the sponsor, then the sponsor would report the pool of investments and related activities in its financial statements on a gross basis. At each reporting period, the sponsor would record 100 percent of the pooled investments in its balance sheet, along with a corresponding liability to the respective pool investor (participant). The sponsor would report the pool's investment returns gross in its statement of operations. If the sponsor is a not-for-profit entity that is acting as an agent, FASB ASC 958-320 and 958-325 require investments held as agent and investment return to be reported as assets and liabilities, rather than changes in net assets. However, if the sponsor is an investor-owned entity merely acting as an agent, it may be appropriate for the sponsor to record the investments and related liability to the investors (participants) on a net basis in the sponsor's financial statements.

Fair Value Measurements

4.48 FASB ASC 820 defines *fair value*, establishes a framework for measuring fair value, and requires extensive disclosures about fair value measurements. Health care entities that are required to apply fair value measures and that provide fair value disclosures are advised to read FASB ASC 820 in its entirety.

Impairment of Investments

4.49 The following guidance should be considered when determining and evaluating whether an investment's impairment is other than temporary:

- Paragraphs 17–35 of FASB ASC 320-10-35
- Paragraphs 1A–2 of FASB ASC 325-20-35
- Paragraphs 8–13 of FASB ASC 958-325-35

Paragraphs 4.50–.58 summarize some of the more significant matters included in those paragraphs. The list is not meant to be all-inclusive. Health care entities should refer to the aforementioned guidance for comprehensive guidance of matters to consider.

4.50 According to FASB ASC 320-10-35-20, impairment is assessed at the individual security level (referred to as an investment). *Individual security level* means the level and method of aggregation used by the reporting entity to measure realized and unrealized gains and losses on its debt and equity securities. FASB ASC 320-10-35-21 states that an investment is impaired if the fair value of the investment is less than its cost.

4.51 Per FASB ASC 320-10-35-25, because the fair value of cost-method investments is not readily determinable, the evaluation of whether an investment is impaired should be determined as follows:

a. If an entity has estimated the fair value of a cost-method investment (for example, for disclosure under FASB ASC 825-10-50), that estimate should be used to determine if the investment is impaired for the reporting periods in which the entity estimates fair value.

b. For reporting periods in which an entity has not estimated the fair value of a cost-method investment, the entity should evaluate whether an event or a change in circumstances has occurred in that period that may have a significant adverse effect on the fair value of the investment (an impairment indicator, examples of which are provided in paragraphs 27–28 of FASB ASC 320-10-35).

4.52 Per FASB ASC 320-10-35-30, if the fair value of an investment is less than its amortized cost basis at the balance sheet date of the reporting period for which impairment is assessed, the impairment is either temporary or other than temporary. Other than temporary does not mean permanent. The standards for measuring other-than-temporary impairment are dependent upon the type of investment: equity securities or debt securities. Per FASB ASC 320-10-35-17, entities should not look through the form of their investment to the nature of the securities held by an investee. For example, an investment in shares of a mutual fund that invests primarily in debt securities would be assessed for impairment as an equity security under FASB ASC 320-10-35.

4.53 For equity securities, FASB ASC 320-10-35-32A states that an entity should apply guidance that is pertinent to the determination of whether an impairment is other than temporary, such as FASB ASC 325-40-35. Additionally, FASB ASC 320-10-35-33 states that when an entity has decided to sell an impaired available-for-sale security, and the entity does not expect the fair value of the security to fully recover before the expected time of sale, the security should be deemed other-than-temporarily impaired in the period in which the decision to sell is made, not the period in which the sale occurs. However, an entity should recognize an impairment loss when the impairment is deemed other than temporary, even if a decision to sell has not been made. Further, FASB ASC 325-20-35-2 states that a series of operating losses of an investee or other factors may indicate that a decrease in value of the investment has occurred that is other than temporary and that should be recognized. FASB ASC 320-10-S99-1 provides guidance in the form of Topic No. 5(M), "Other Than Temporary Impairment of Certain Investments in Equity Securities," of the Securities and Exchange Commission's *Codification of Staff Accounting Bulletins*.

4.54 For a debt security, an other-than-temporary impairment should be considered to have occurred if an entity (*a*) has decided to sell the debt security, as discussed in FASB ASC 320-10-35-33A, or (*b*) has not decided to sell the debt security, but the entity more likely than not will be required to sell the security before recovery of its amortized cost basis, as discussed in FASB ASC 320-10-35-33B. Paragraphs 33C–33I of FASB ASC 320-10-35 provide additional guidance for making an assessment of whether an impairment of a debt security is other than temporary, including guidance for determining whether the entire amortized cost basis of the debt security will be recovered.

4.55 In accordance with FASB ASC 320-10-35-34C, if the health care entity does not intend to sell the debt security, and it is not more likely than not that the health care entity will be required to sell the security before recovery of its amortized cost basis less any current-period credit loss, the other-than-temporary impairment should be separated into both of the following:

a. Amounts representing the credit loss

b. Amounts related to all other factors

4.56 In accordance with FASB ASC 320-10-45-8A, in periods in which an investor-owned health care entity determines that a security's decline in fair value below its amortized cost basis is other than temporary, the entity should present the total other-than-temporary impairment in the statement of earnings, with an offset for the amount of the total other-than-temporary impairment, if any, that is recognized in other comprehensive income, in accordance with FASB ASC 320-10-35-34D (for example, the portion of the loss on a debt security that is due to factors other than the credit loss). The amount of the total other-than-temporary impairment on a debt security that is related to the other factors should be recognized in other comprehensive income net of applicable taxes. A not-for-profit health care entity would report the total other-than-temporary impairment within the performance indicator, with an offset for the portion of the loss on a debt security that is due to factors other than the credit loss, in accordance with FASB ASC 320-10-35-34D, as modified by FASB ASC 320-10-35-17. The amount of the total other-than-temporary impairment on a debt security that is related to the other factors should be recognized outside of the performance indicator.

4.57 FASB ASC 320-10-35-34 states that the measurement of the impairment of an equity security should not include partial recoveries subsequent to the balance sheet date. The fair value of the investment would then become the new amortized cost basis of the investment and should not be adjusted for subsequent recoveries in fair value.

4.58 FASB ASC 320-10-35-34E states that for debt securities, the previous amortized cost basis less the other-than-temporary impairment recognized in earnings becomes the new amortized cost basis of the debt security. That new amortized cost basis should not be adjusted for subsequent recoveries in fair value. However, the amortized cost basis should be adjusted for accretion and amortization, as prescribed in FASB ASC 320-10-35-35.

4.59 FinREC believes that if a health care entity engages an external investment manager and grants the manager broad discretion to purchase and sell investments to achieve a stated portfolio objective, the health care entity may not be able to assert that it has both the intent and ability to hold equity investments that have unrealized losses until those unrealized losses can be recovered. Further, if a debt security was sold shortly after year-end, the health care entity may not be able to assert that there was not the intent to sell the debt security at the balance sheet date. If the health care entity cannot make the necessary assertions, then the entity should recognize an other-than-temporary impairment loss. If a health care entity develops procedures to determine whether the manager has made a decision at the balance sheet date to sell any debt securities, it will be able to document when the decision was made, by whom, the factors that drove the decision to sell, and when the health care entity became aware of those factors.

Securities Lending Activities

4.60 A health care entity that has a significant investment portfolio may enter into securities lending arrangements. These arrangements allow the health care entity to increase the overall yield from the investment activity. Depending on the terms of the security lending agreements, collateral received may be required to be shown separately on the transferor's balance sheet, with a corresponding liability to show the obligation to return the collateral. Each agreement should be carefully reviewed, and the guidance in FASB ASC 860-30 would be considered to determine the appropriate accounting and reporting.

Transfers of Assets to a Not-for-Profit Entity or Charitable Trust for Investment

4.61 Sometimes, a health care entity transfers assets, including investments, to a not-for-profit entity or charitable trust (the recipient entity) that accepts those assets and agrees to use them on behalf of the health care entity or transfer them or their investment return, or both, back to the health care entity or its affiliate. Examples of this type of reciprocal transfer include (*a*) a health care entity that transfers assets to a community foundation to establish an endowment for the benefit of the health care entity or its affiliate and (*b*) a health care entity that transfers assets to a foundation that it creates to hold those assets.

4.62 FASB ASC 958-605-25-33 states that a transfer of assets to a recipient entity is not a contribution if the resource provider (the health care entity) specifies itself or its affiliate as the beneficiary of the transfer. Paragraphs 4–7 of FASB ASC 958-20-25 describe the following two types of reciprocal transfers:

- An *equity transaction*, which is a transfer of assets to a recipient entity that meets all of the following conditions: (*a*) the resource provider (health care entity) specifies itself or its affiliate as the beneficiary; (*b*) the resource provider (health care entity) and the recipient entity are financially interrelated entities; and (*c*) neither the resource provider (health care entity) nor its affiliate expects payment of the transferred assets, although payment of investment return on the transferred assets may be expected. Paragraph 12.75 of this guide discusses financially interrelated entities.
- The resource provider (health care entity) specifies itself or its affiliate as the beneficiary, and the transfer is not an equity transaction (one or both of criteria (*b*) and (*c*) in the previous bullet are not met).

4.63 According to FASB ASC 958-605-25-33, if the transfer in which the resource provider specifies itself or its affiliate as the beneficiary is not an equity transaction, the resource provider (health care entity) should report an asset, and the recipient entity should report a liability. Accounting for equity transactions is discussed in paragraphs 12.70–.73 of this guide. If the resource provider (the health care entity) transfers assets to a recipient entity and specifies itself or its affiliate as the beneficiary, it should disclose the following information for each period for which a statement of financial position is presented, in accordance with FASB ASC 958-605-50-6:

- The identity of the recipient entity to which the transfer was made.
- Whether variance power was granted to the recipient entity and, if so, a description of the terms of the variance power. Because of their reciprocal nature, such transfers are presumed not to be contributions received or made, even if the health care entity granted variance power at the time of transfer.
- The terms under which amounts will be distributed to the health care entity or its affiliate.
- The aggregate amount recognized in the statement of financial position for those transfers and whether that amount is recorded

as an interest in the net assets of the recipient entity or as another asset (for example, as a beneficial interest in assets held by others or a refundable advance).

Regulation

4.64 Because health plans have a public responsibility to be able to meet their obligations to policy holders, state statutes and regulations prescribe standards and limitations on investment activities. Regulatory requirements and restrictions vary by state. Most states require health plans to invest a certain percentage of policy reserves in specified classes of investments. Once the state regulatory agency's minimum standards are met, the health plan may invest in other types of investments. However, many states specify a maximum percentage of assets that may be invested in particular classes of investments. State regulations may also prescribe methods for reporting investments, set requirements regarding matters such as the location and safeguarding of assets, and set limitations on investing in derivatives. For example, a regulatory authority may require some investments to be deposited with the state insurance department as a condition of writing business in that state. Insurance statutes and regulations vary by state, but the regulations of the state of domicile have precedence; however, compliance provisions in states in which the plan does business also must be followed. An understanding of the statutory requirements to be followed by a health plan concerning investments is advisable, so that their impact on investment strategy, as well as accounting and reporting, are appropriately considered.

Other Financial Statement Presentation Matters

Classification

4.65 Securities should be reported as either current or noncurrent, as appropriate, under the provisions of FASB ASC 210-10-45. According to the FASB ASC glossary, the term *current assets* is used to designate cash and other assets or resources commonly identified as those that are reasonably expected to be realized in cash or sold or consumed during the normal operating cycle of the business. According to FASB ASC 210-10-45-1, current assets include marketable securities representing the investment of cash available for current operations, including investments in debt and equity securities classified as trading securities under FASB ASC 320-10. FASB ASC 210-10-45-3 indicates that a one-year time period should be used as a basis for the segregation of current assets in cases when several operating cycles occur within a year. FASB ASC 210-10-45-4 states that the concept of the nature of current assets contemplates the exclusion from that classification cash and claims to cash that are restricted regarding withdrawal or use for other-than-current operations, designated for expenditure in the acquisition or construction of noncurrent assets, or segregated for the liquidation of long-term debts. Even though not actually set aside in special accounts, funds that are clearly to be used in the near future for the liquidation of long-term debts, payments to sinking funds, or similar purposes should also, under this concept, be excluded from current assets. However, if such funds are considered to offset maturing debt that has been set up properly as a current liability, they may be included within the current asset classification. FASB ASC 958-205-55-7 explains that when a statement of financial position that sequences assets and liabilities based on their relative liquidity is presented, cash and cash equivalents of permanent endowment funds held temporarily until suitable long-term investment opportunities are identified are included in the long-term investments classification.

4.66 According to FASB ASC 230-10-45-19, cash receipts and payments resulting from purchases, sales, and maturities of trading securities, as discussed in FASB ASC 320, should be classified as investing or operating cash flows based on the nature and purpose for which the securities were acquired. According to FASB ASC 230-10-45-11, cash flows from purchases, sales, and maturities of available-for-sale securities should be classified as cash flows from investing activities and reported gross in the statement of cash flows. FASB ASC 320-10-45-13 states that if entities report certain investments in debt securities as cash equivalents, in accordance with the provisions of FASB ASC 230, the notes to the financial statements should reconcile the reporting classifications used in the statement of financial position.

4.67 Paragraphs 4.28–.34 discuss the classification of investment income, realized and unrealized gains and losses on investments, and equity earnings from investments in investment companies accounted for under the equity method by a not-for-profit health care entity.

Disclosure

4.68 All health care entities with investments that meet the definition of *financial instruments* set forth in the FASB ASC glossary are subject to the disclosure requirements of FASB ASC 825-10-50.[4] Investor-owned health care entities with investments in equity and debt securities should refer to the disclosure requirements of FASB ASC 320-10-50 and 325-50. Not-for-profit health care entities should refer to the disclosure requirements of FASB ASC 958-320-50 and 958-325-50.

4.69 If the health care entity has concentrations of credit risk related to financial instruments, the disclosure requirements of paragraphs 20–22 of FASB ASC 825-10-50 should be followed. Examples of potential exposure to credit risk include funds deposited with a single financial institution in excess of Federal Deposit Insurance Corporation limits and investments in obligations that are not insured or guaranteed by the government.

4.70 Health care entities that are accounting for investments under the equity method, including alternative investments held for investment-return purposes, should consider the disclosure requirements of FASB ASC 323-10-50.

4.71 FASB ASC 860-30-50 requires entities that enter into securities lending transactions or repurchase agreements to disclose their policies for requiring collateral or other security. FASB ASC 860-30-50 also requires the disclosure of (*a*) the fair value of collateral at the reporting date and (*b*) the portion of the collateral that has been sold or repledged if an entity accepts collateral that is permitted by contract or custom to be sold or repledged. Health care entities that are public entities should also consider the disclosure requirements of FASB ASC 860-10-50.

4.72 Health care entities should consider the fair value disclosure requirements in FASB ASC 820-10-50.

---

[4] Disclosures about the fair value of financial instruments prescribed in FASB ASC 825-10-50 are optional for an entity that meets the criteria in FASB ASC 825-10-50-3.

4.73 Not-for-profit health care entities that have investments held in donor-restricted endowment funds should consider the disclosure requirements of FASB ASC 958-205-50.

Auditing

4.74 Auditing objectives and procedures for investments of health care entities generally are similar to those of other entities. AU section 332, *Auditing Derivative Instruments, Hedging Activities, and Investments in Securities* (AICPA, *Professional Standards*), among other matters, provides guidance to auditors in planning and performing auditing procedures for assertions about investments in securities that are made in an entity's financial statements. The guidance in AU section 332 applies to all debt and equity securities. AU section 332 uses the definitions of *debt security* and *equity security* that are in included in the FASB ASC glossary. However, those definitions apply to debt and equity securities without regard to whether they are subject to the requirements of FASB ASC 320-10, such as assertions about securities accounted for under the equity method following the requirements of FASB ASC 323, *Investments—Equity Method and Joint Ventures*. A companion Audit Guide, *Auditing Derivative Instruments, Hedging Activities, and Investments in Securities*, provides practical guidance for implementing AU section 332.

> *Considerations for Audits Performed in Accordance With Public Company Accounting Oversight Board (PCAOB) Standards*
>
> Paragraph .11 of AU section 332, *Auditing Derivative Instruments, Hedging Activities, and Investments in Securities* (AICPA, *PCAOB Standards and Related Rules*, Interim Standards), states that when performing an integrated audit of financial statements and internal control over financial reporting, paragraph 39 of PCAOB Auditing Standard No. 5, *An Audit of Internal Control Over Financial Reporting That Is Integrated with An Audit of Financial Statements* (AICPA, *PCAOB Standards and Related Rules*, Auditing Standards), states that "[t]he auditor should test those controls that are important to the auditor's conclusion about whether the company's controls sufficiently address the assessed risk of material misstatement to each relevant assertion." Therefore, in an integrated audit of financial statements and internal control over financial reporting, if relevant assertions exist that are related to the company's investments in derivatives and securities, the auditor's understanding of controls should include controls over derivatives and securities transactions from their initiation to their inclusion in the financial statements and should encompass controls placed in operation by the entity and service organizations whose services are part of the entity's information system.
>
> PCAOB Staff Audit Practice Alert No. 2, *Matters Related to Auditing Fair Value Measurements of Financial Instruments and the Use of Specialists* (AICPA, *PCAOB Standards and Related Rules*, PCAOB Staff Guidance, sec. 400.02), provides guidance on auditors' responsibilities for auditing fair value measurements of financial instruments and when using the work of specialists under the existing standards of the PCAOB. PCAOB Staff Audit Practice Alerts are not rules of the PCAOB nor have they been approved by the PCAOB.

4.75 Interpretation No. 1, "Auditing Investments in Securities Where a Readily Determinable Fair Value Does Not Exist" of AU section 332 (AICPA, *Professional Standards*, AU sec. 9332 par. .01–.04), provides guidance for auditors of nonissuers regarding the adequacy of audit evidence, with respect to the existence and valuation assertions in AU section 332 (AICPA, *Professional Standards*), in confirmations received from third parties when auditing investments in securities when a readily determinable fair value does not exist, and the auditor determines that auditing procedures include verifying the existence and testing the measurement of the investments. Further guidance for auditors of nonissuers is provided in the AICPA Practice Aid *Alternative Investments—Audit Considerations*. The guidance focuses on the existence and valuation assertions associated with auditing investments for which a readily determinable fair value does not exist (collectively referred to in the practice aid as alternative investments).[5] The auditing portion of that practice aid is an *other auditing publication*, as defined in AU section 150, *Generally Accepted Auditing Standards* (AICPA, *Professional Standards*). Other auditing publications have no authoritative status; however, they may help the auditor understand and apply Statements on Auditing Standards.

4.76 In addition, the independent auditor may need to consider the examples of specific auditing objectives, selected control activities, and auditing procedures that are presented in exhibit 4-1.

---

[5] The AICPA Practice Aid *Alternative Investments—Audit Considerations* can be found at www.aicpa.org/InterestAreas/FRC/AuditAttest/Fieldwork/DownloadableDocuments/Alternative_Investments_Practice_Aid.pdf.

Exhibit 4-1

The following table illustrates the use of assertions in developing audit objectives and designing substantive tests. The examples are not intended to be all-inclusive nor is it expected that all the procedures would necessarily be applied in an audit. The auditor should design and perform substantive procedures for all relevant assertions related to each material class of transactions, account balance, and disclosure to obtain sufficient appropriate audit evidence. The use of assertions in assessing risks and designing appropriate audit procedures to obtain audit evidence is described in paragraphs .14–.26 of AU section 326, *Audit Evidence* (AICPA, *Professional Standards*). Various audit procedures and the purposes for which they may be performed are described in paragraphs .27–.41 of AU section 326.

Auditing Considerations

Financial Statement Assertions	*Specific Auditing Objectives*	*Selected Control Activities*	*Auditing Procedures*
Account Balances			
Existence, completeness, rights and obligations, and valuation and allocation	Marketable securities are fairly stated and properly classified, described, and disclosed.	An independent trustee manages the investments. The trustee's reports are reviewed by a responsible employee.	Verify existence through confirmation. Test the valuation of equity and debt securities not intended to be held to maturity by comparing the recorded values with the fair values reported by the trustee or another independent source. For fair value estimates obtained from third-party sources, the auditor should consider the applicability of the guidance in AU section 336, *Using the Work of a Specialist* (AICPA, *Professional Standards*); AU section 324, *Service Organizations* (AICPA, *Professional Standards*); or AU section 324, *Service Organizations* (AICPA, *PCAOB Standards and Related Rules*, Interim Standards).[1]

Financial Statement Assertions	*Specific Auditing Objectives*	*Selected Control Activities*	*Auditing Procedures*
Valuation and allocation, rights and obligations	Endowment funds are properly stated at their required value, and related gains and losses are properly classified.	Value of endowment funds are reviewed periodically to ensure that the balance is at its required level.	Verified that values of endowments are at required levels through confirmation. Review treatment of gains and losses on endowment funds to ensure that they are properly classified.
Transactions			
Accuracy and completeness	Investment income and gains or losses, or both, are recorded in accordance with donor restrictions.	Review investment transactions to ensure that they are recorded in compliance with donor restrictions.	Test the recording of selected transactions to ensure that amounts are properly classified in accordance with donor restrictions.
Presentation and Disclosure			
Classification and understand-ability	Securities are properly classified.	Classification is monitored periodically and is based on management's intent or ability to dispose of excess funds that are available for operations within an operating cycle.	Test the classification of investments as trading, available for sale, or held to maturity to determine whether gains and losses are properly classified within or outside the performance indicator (for not-for-profit health care entities) or within the income statement or statement of other comprehensive income (for investor-owned health care entities).

[1] Paragraphs .35–.46 of AU section 332, *Auditing Derivative Instruments, Hedging Activities, and Investments in Securities* (AICPA, *Professional Standards*), establish requirements and provide guidance to auditors on audit evidence that may be used to support assertions about the fair value of securities. Paragraphs 6.15–.37 in the companion Audit Guide *Auditing Derivative Instruments, Hedging Activities, and Investments in Securities* also provide guidance on that topic. That guidance should be considered in context of specific accounting requirements. AU section 328, *Auditing Fair Value Measurements and Disclosures* (AICPA, *Professional Standards*), establishes requirements and provides guidance on auditing fair value measurements and disclosures contained in financial statements. AU section 328 does not address specific types of assets, liabilities, components of equity, transactions, or industry-specific practices.

Chapter 5

Derivatives

Introduction

5.01 Health care entities use a wide range of derivative products,[1] with the objective of more effectively managing their financial risks related to debt, investments, and other assets and liabilities and transactions. Financial Accounting Standards Board (FASB) *Accounting Standards Codification* (ASC) 815-10-15-83 describes a *derivative instrument* as

> a financial instrument or other contract with all of the following characteristics:
>
> a. Underlying, notional amount, payment provision. The contract has both of the following terms, which determine the amount of the settlement or settlements, and, in some cases, whether or not a settlement is required:
>   1. One or more underlyings
>   2. One or more notional amounts or payment provisions or both.
>
> b. Initial net investment. The contract requires no initial net investment or an initial net investment that is smaller than would be required for other types of contracts that would be expected to have a similar response to changes in market factors.
>
> c. Net settlement. The contract can be settled net by any of the following means:
>   1. Its terms implicitly or explicitly require or permit net settlement.
>   2. It can readily be settled net by a means outside the contract.
>   3. It provides for delivery of an asset that puts the recipient in a position not substantially different from net settlement.

5.02 FASB ASC 815-10-15-88 states that an *underlying* is a variable that, along with either a notional amount or payment provision, determines the settlement of a derivative instrument. FASB ASC 815-10-15-88 provides examples of underlyings, which include a security price or security price index, a commodity price or commodity price index, and an interest rate or interest rate index. As explained in FASB ASC 815-10-15-92, a notional amount is a number of currency units, shares, bushels, pounds, or other units specified in the contract. FASB ASC 815-10-93 states that a payment provision specifies a fixed or determinable settlement to be made if the underlying behaves in a

---

[1] Chapter 18, "Derivative Instruments: Futures, Forwards, Options, Swaps, and Other Derivative Instruments," of the AICPA Audit and Accounting Guide *Depository and Lending Institutions: Banks and Savings Institutions, Credit Unions, Finance Companies, and Mortgage Companies* provides useful background information on various types of derivative instruments and hedging activities and the risks associated with various forms of contracts and transactions.

specified manner. Paragraphs 83–139 of FASB ASC 815-10-15 provide a more complete definition of a *derivative instrument*.

5.03 One of the most common uses of derivatives by health care entities is in conjunction with borrowings. The objective is that the combined cash flows of the derivative and the debt will effectively create long-term fixed-rate or variable-rate debt at an aggregate cost lower than traditional fixed- or variable-rate debt. Common examples include the following:

- An interest rate swap that is intended to effectively convert variable-rate debt to fixed-rate debt.
- An interest rate swap that is intended to effectively convert fixed-rate debt to variable-rate debt.
- A basis swap in which counterparties exchange payments based on the changes of two variable rates.
- An option on an interest rate swap—a swaption—that gives the purchaser the right but not the obligation to enter into an interest rate swap. The purchaser pays a premium to the issuer or writer.
- An interest rate cap specifically purchased to give the purchaser protection against rates rising above a given level.

5.04 Derivative instruments also might be used to

- lock in the interest rate for an anticipated future borrowing. At times, a health care entity may need to borrow money in the near term and wish to fix the interest rate on the borrowing at the current rate, even though the money will not be needed until sometime in the future. Derivative instruments, such as interest-rate options or forward contracts, can accomplish this objective.
- lock in the current price of a commodity, such as electricity, for anticipated purchases. This hedging strategy often involves the use of forward contracts or option combinations that can be settled net. A derivative instrument that is used to fix the price of anticipated future purchases could be a cash flow hedge if the derivative instrument does not meet the conditions for the normal purchase exception.

5.05 FASB ASC 815-10-55-2 contains a diagram that depicts the process for determining whether a freestanding contract is within the scope of FASB ASC 815, *Derivatives and Hedging*. The diagram is a visual supplement to the written standards. It should not be interpreted to alter any requirements of FASB ASC 815 nor should it be considered a substitute for the requirements. In addition, FASB ASC 815-15 excludes certain contracts from being accounted for using the guidance in FASB ASC 815, even though, technically, the contract may meet the definition of a *derivative instrument*.

General Guidance

5.06 FASB ASC 815 establishes accounting and reporting standards for derivative instruments and hedging activities. FASB ASC 815-10-05-4 explains that FASB ASC 815 requires that an entity recognize derivative instruments, including certain derivative instruments embedded in other contracts, as either assets or liabilities in the statement of financial position and measure them at fair value. If certain conditions are met, an entity may elect to designate a derivative instrument in any one of the following ways: (*a*) a hedge of the exposure to changes in the fair value of a recognized asset or liability or of an unrecognized firm commitment that is attributable to a particular risk (referred to as a fair value hedge), (*b*) a hedge of the exposure to variability in the cash flows of a recognized asset or liability or of a forecasted transaction that is attributable to a particular risk (referred to as a cash flow hedge), or (*c*) a hedge of foreign currency exposure.[2]

5.07 FASB ASC 954-815-25-2 states that except as provided in FASB ASC 954-815-50-1 and as discussed in paragraph 5.44, not-for-profit health care entities should apply the provisions of FASB ASC 815, including the provisions pertaining to cash flow hedge accounting, in the same manner as for-profit entities. The gain or loss items that affect a for-profit entity's income from continuing operations similarly should affect the not-for-profit health care entity's performance indicator, and the gain or loss items that are excluded from a for-profit entity's income from continuing operations, such as items reported in other comprehensive income, similarly should be excluded from the performance indicator by the not-for-profit health care entity. As explained in FASB ASC 954-815-45-1, the absence of a requirement to report a separate component of equity in the balance sheet of a not-for-profit business-oriented health care entity should not preclude those entities from using comprehensive income reporting for qualifying gains and losses on cash flow hedges. Although accumulated other comprehensive income will inherently be carried forward in a not-for-profit health care entity's net assets, no compelling need exists for it to be reported separately in the balance sheet.

5.08 FASB ASC 815-10-35-2 states that the accounting for changes in the fair value (that is, gains and losses) of a derivative instrument depends on whether it has been designated and qualifies as part of a hedging relationship and, if so, the reason for holding it.

Fair Value Hedges

5.09 FASB ASC 815-20-35-1(b) states that the gain or loss on a derivative instrument designated and qualifying as a fair value hedging instrument, as well as the offsetting loss or gain on the hedged item attributable to the hedged risk, should be recognized currently in earnings in the same accounting period, as provided in paragraphs 1–6 of FASB ASC 815-25-35-1.

5.10 Thus, investor-owned health care entities recognize the gain or loss on the derivative in earnings in the period of change, together with the offsetting loss or gain on the hedged item attributable to the risk being hedged. Similarly, not-for-profit health care entities report the derivative gains and losses, together with the offsetting loss or gain on the hedged item, in the performance indicator in the period of change.

Cash Flow Hedges

5.11 FASB ASC 815-20-35-1(c) states that the effective portion of the gain or loss on a derivative instrument designated and qualifying as a cash flow hedging instrument should be reported as a component of other comprehensive income (outside earnings) and reclassified into earnings in the same period(s)

---

[2] Health care entities do not frequently enter into foreign currency hedges; therefore, this chapter focuses on matters pertaining to fair value and cash flow hedges.

during which the hedged forecasted transaction affects earnings, as provided in FASB ASC 815-30-35-3 and paragraphs 38–41 of FASB ASC 815-30-35. The remaining gain or loss on the derivative instrument, if any, should be recognized currently in earnings, as provided in FASB ASC 815-30-35-3. If an entity's defined risk management strategy for a particular hedging relationship excludes a specific component of the gain or loss (or related cash flows) on the hedging derivative from the assessment of hedge effectiveness, as explained in paragraphs 81–83 of FASB ASC 815-20-25, that excluded component of the gain or loss should be recognized currently in earnings.

5.12 FASB ASC 815-30-35-39 states that if the hedged transaction results in the acquisition of an asset or the incurrence of a liability, the gains and losses in accumulated other comprehensive income should be reclassified into earnings in the same period(s) during which the acquired asset or incurred liability affects earnings, such as in the periods that depreciation expense, interest expense, or cost of sales is recognized.

5.13 Thus, for an investor-owned health care entity, the effective portion of the derivative's gain or loss is initially reported as a component of other comprehensive income (outside earnings) and subsequently reclassified into earnings when the forecasted transaction affects earnings. For a not-for-profit health care entity, the effective portion of the derivative's gain or loss is initially excluded from the performance indicator and subsequently reclassified into the performance indicator when the forecasted transaction affects earnings. For example, the accumulated gain or loss of a derivative instrument that hedges the variability of the cash flows of long-term debt is amortized into earnings or the performance indicator over the remaining term of the debt instrument (that is, as long as the debt remains outstanding), even if the cash flow hedge itself is terminated. Any ineffective portion of the gain or loss is immediately reported in earnings or the performance indicator.

Derivatives Not Designated as a Hedging Instrument

5.14 The gain or loss on a derivative instrument not designated as a hedging instrument should be recognized in current earnings or, in the case of a not-for-profit health care entity, the performance indicator.

Hedge Accounting[3]

5.15 A primary purpose of hedge accounting is to link items or transactions whose changes in fair values or cash flows are expected to offset each other.

5.16 To qualify for hedge accounting, at inception of the hedge, there must be formal documentation of all the information identified in FASB ASC 815-20-25-3. Specific documentation requirements include identifying the hedging relationship, the hedging instrument, the hedged item or transaction, the nature of the risk being hedged, the method that will be used to retrospectively

---

[3] On May 26, 2010, the Financial Accounting Standards Board (FASB) issued a proposed Accounting Standards Update (ASU) *Accounting for Financial Instruments and Revisions to the Accounting for Derivative Instruments and Hedging Activities—Financial Instruments (Topic 825) and Derivatives and Hedging (Topic 815)*. This proposed ASU would create a consistent, comprehensive framework for the recognition and measurement of financial instruments. It also includes changes to standards for hedge accounting and recognizing impairments. Its far-reaching scope would include most receivables, investments, payables, long-term debt, and derivative instruments. Readers should be alert to the issuance of a final standard.

and prospectively assess hedge effectiveness, and the method that will be used to measure hedge ineffectiveness, among others.

5.17 To qualify for hedge accounting, the hedging relationship, both at inception of the hedge and on an ongoing basis, should be expected to be highly effective. An entity should consider hedge effectiveness in two different ways: in prospective considerations and retrospective evaluations. Paragraphs 74–117 of FASB ASC 815-20-25 provide the criteria for assessing hedge effectiveness that are applicable to both fair value hedges and cash flow hedges.

5.18 FASB ASC 815-20-35-2 states that at least quarterly, the hedging entity should determine whether the hedging relationship has been highly effective in having achieved offsetting changes in fair value or cash flows through the date of the periodic assessment. If the hedge fails the effectiveness test at any time (that is, if the entity does not expect the hedge to be highly effective at achieving offsetting changes in fair values or cash flows), the hedge ceases to qualify for hedge accounting.[4] The shortcut method for hedges of interest rate risk, which is described in paragraphs 5.21–.29, assumes no hedge ineffectiveness.

5.19 FASB ASC 815-25-40-1 and 815-30-40-1 state that an entity must discontinue prospectively specialized hedge accounting for an existing hedge if any one of the following occurs: (*a*) any criteria in FASB ASC 815-20-25 is no longer met; (*b*) the derivative instrument expires or is sold, terminated, or exercised; or (*c*) the entity removes the designation of the hedge.

5.20 Documentation that the criteria described in FASB ASC 815-20-25 are met for the entire period to which hedge accounting is being applied is critical. Derivative instruments are designated as hedges only if appropriate, contemporaneous documentation of both the election and periodic assessment of effectiveness has been executed in conformity with FASB ASC 815.

Shortcut Method

5.21 As noted in paragraph 5.03, one of the most common uses of derivatives by health care entities is entering into interest rate swaps in connection with borrowings. If an entity enters into transactions to hedge interest rate risk related to a recognized liability, a shortcut method for determining effectiveness is available if certain conditions are met.

5.22 Paragraphs 102–117 of FASB ASC 815-20-25 describe a set of conditions that determine which hedging relationships qualify for a shortcut version of hedge accounting, which does not immediately recognize hedge ineffectiveness. If all of the applicable conditions in the list in FASB ASC 815-20-25-104 are met, an entity may assume no ineffectiveness in a relationship hedging interest rate risk that involves a recognized interest-bearing asset or liability and an interest rate swap. In addition, FASB ASC 815-20-25-105 provides incremental conditions that apply to fair value hedges only, and FASB ASC 815-20-25-106 provides incremental conditions that apply to cash flow hedges only. Special rules apply to a firm commitment arising on the trade (pricing) date to purchase or issue an interest-bearing asset or liability. The set of conditions and resulting assumption of ineffectiveness are known as the shortcut

---

[4] The requirement to assess hedge effectiveness at least every three months applies to health care entities that issue financial statements only on an annual basis, as well as entities that issue quarterly financial statements.

method. FASB ASC 815-20-25-103 notes that implicit in the conditions for the shortcut method is the requirement that a basis exist for concluding on an ongoing basis that the hedging relationship is expected to be highly effective in achieving offsetting changes in fair values or cash flows. If a hedging relationship qualifies for use of the shortcut method, the effectiveness of the hedge does not have to be proven in order to qualify for hedge accounting.

5.23 FASB ASC 815-20-25-102 states that given the potential for not recognizing hedge ineffectiveness in earnings under the shortcut method, its application should be limited to hedging relationships that meet each and every applicable condition. All the conditions applicable to fair value hedges must be met to apply the shortcut method to a fair value hedge, and all the conditions applicable to cash flow hedges must be met to apply the shortcut method to a cash flow hedge. A hedging relationship cannot qualify for application of the shortcut method based on an assumption of no ineffectiveness justified by applying other criteria.

5.24 If an interest rate swap does not qualify for use of the shortcut method, the entity must prove (initially and on an ongoing basis, as discussed in FASB ASC 815-20-25) that the hedging relationship between the hedging instrument and hedged item (the liability being hedged) is highly effective in achieving the offset of changes in those fair values or cash flows that are attributable to the hedged risk.

5.25 As a condition for using the shortcut method, FASB ASC 815-20-25-104(f) requires that the index on which the variable leg of the interest rate swap is based match the benchmark interest rate designated as the interest rate risk being hedged for that hedging relationship. FASB ASC 815-20-25-6A states that in the United States, currently, only the interest rates on direct Treasury obligations of the U.S. government and, for practical reasons, the London Interbank Offered Rate (LIBOR) swap rate are considered to be benchmark interest rates. In each financial market, only the one or two most widely used and quoted rates that meet these criteria may be considered benchmark interest rates. The federal funds rate, the prime rate, the Federal National Mortgage Association (Fannie Mae) par mortgage rate, and the Securities Industry and Financial Markets Association (SIFMA) Municipal Swap Index (formerly called the Bond Market Association/PSA Municipal Swap Index) should not be used as the benchmark interest rate in the United States.

5.26 Many health care entities use swaps whose underlying is the SIFMA Municipal Swap Index as hedges of interest rate risk associated with variable-rate tax-exempt debt. Because the SIFMA Municipal Swap Index does not constitute a benchmark interest rate for purposes of applying the shortcut method, if the variable leg of a swap is indexed to the SIFMA Municipal Swap Index (or any rate other than Treasury obligations or LIBOR), the hedging relationship does not qualify for the shortcut method. Similarly, if a bond's variable coupon references the SIFMA Municipal Swap Index or any rate other than Treasury obligations or LIBOR, the hedging relationship does not qualify for use of the shortcut method, even if the variable leg of the interest rate swap is indexed to Treasury obligations or LIBOR.

5.27 Paragraphs 71–79 and FASB ASC 815-20-55, paragraphs 40–52 of FASB ASC 815-25-55, and paragraphs 24–33 of FASB 815-30-55 contain implementation guidance and examples for use of the shortcut method.

5.28 In cash flow hedges of variable-rate debt, interest rate risk cannot be hedged, unless the cash flows of the hedged transaction are explicitly based on the same benchmark interest rate. Many not-for-profit health care entities have issued a form of variable-rate debt referred to as auction-rate debt. The interest rate is reset through a Dutch auction process.[5]

5.29 FASB ASC 815-20-55-42 states that a variable-rate financial asset or liability that is reset through an auction process is not based on a benchmark interest rate. Although the interest rate may be described as a designated benchmark interest rate plus or minus an adjustment specified by the bidder, the clearing rate is effectively established by a bidding process that does not provide for transparent separation of interest rate risk and credit risk. Thus, the designated risk being hedged in an auction rate note cannot be interest rate risk. However, health care entities wishing to hedge auction rate debt may be able to do so as a cash flow hedge of a risk of overall changes in the hedged cash flows, as described in FASB ASC 815-20-55-43.

Hybrid Instruments, Host Contracts, and Embedded Derivatives

5.30 FASB ASC 815-15-05-1 explains that contracts that do not meet the definition of a *derivative instrument* in their entirety, such as bonds, insurance policies, and leases, may contain embedded derivatives. *Embedded derivatives*, as defined in the FASB ASC glossary, are "[i]mplicit or explicit terms that affect some or all of the cash flows or the value of other exchanges required by a contract in a manner similar to a derivative instrument." The effect of embedding a derivative instrument in another type of contract (the host contract) is that some or all of the cash flows or other exchanges that otherwise would be required by the host contract, whether unconditional or contingent on the occurrence of a specified event, will be modified based on one or more underlyings. FASB ASC 815-15 applies to embedded derivatives. A contract that embodies both an embedded derivative and a host contract is referred to as a hybrid instrument.

5.31 If an embedded derivative is within the scope of FASB ASC 815-15, as defined in FASB ASC 815-15-15, and all of the criteria in FASB ASC 815-15-25-1 are met, the embedded derivative instrument must be separated from the host contract and accounted for separately as a derivative instrument pursuant to FASB ASC 815-10. However, if a hybrid instrument is a financial instrument, paragraphs 4–6 of FASB ASC 815-15-25 allow an entity to irrevocably elect to initially and subsequently measure the hybrid financial instrument in its entirety at fair value, with changes in fair value recognized in earnings, instead of requiring bifurcation. Alternatively, the entity may elect to measure the hybrid financial instrument at fair value, as described in the "Fair Value Option" sections of FASB ASC 825-10.

5.32 Although the requirement to separate an embedded derivative from a host contract applies to both parties to a contract, application of the requirements of FASB ASC 815-15 may result in different conclusions regarding the need for bifurcation based on whether the reporting entity is the holder or issuer of the hybrid instrument.

---

[5] In a Dutch auction, investors bid for the bonds, which are sold at the lowest yield necessary to sell the entire issue.

5.33 The most common host for an embedded derivative is a debt instrument that pays a fixed-rate, floating-rate, or zero-coupon rate of interest. When applying the clearly- and closely-related criteria in FASB ASC 815-15-25-1 to debt hosts, the focus is on determining whether the economic characteristics and risks of the embedded derivative have features unrelated to interest rates, such as equitylike or commoditylike features, or, if the characteristics of the derivative are related to interest rates, whether the features involve leverage or do not change in the same direction as interest rates (an inverse floater). Host contracts with debt characteristics are discussed in paragraphs 23–51 of FASB ASC 815-15-25.

Calls and Puts in Debt

5.34 Bonds and other forms of long-term debt often are structured with call and put options. An entity applies paragraphs 26–27 and 40–43 of FASB ASC 815-15-25 to determine whether embedded calls and puts are derivatives that must be accounted for separately from the debt host contract. Additional guidance is provided by the table in FASB ASC 815-15-55-13.

5.35 Issuance of convertible debt securities when the conversion feature is a written call option may involve a host of potential embedded derivatives. In such case, the need for bifurcation of embedded derivatives may differ for the holder of the debt instrument than for the issuer, particularly if the conversion is contingent on the occurrence of a specified event.

Derivatives Embedded in Split-Interest Agreements

5.36 The FASB ASC glossary defines a *split-interest agreement* as "[a]n agreement in which a donor enters into a trust or other arrangement under which a not-for-profit entity ... receives benefits that are shared with other beneficiaries."[6] The amount of benefit to each beneficiary often is a function of the fair value of the donated assets over the term of the agreement. Not-for-profit entities that are trustees or fiscal agents for a split-interest agreement report a liability for the obligation to make future payments to the other beneficiaries of the agreement. Although that liability is initially measured at its fair value, it will not reflect fair value in future periods because the discount rate used in remeasuring the liability each period is not revised to reflect current interest rates, unless a fair value election is made. Because the liability is not measured at fair value, the potential for an embedded derivative exists.

5.37 Paragraphs 7–14 of FASB ASC 958-30-25 and FASB ASC 958-30-55 provide guidance for determining whether a split-interest agreement includes an embedded derivative and, if so, whether the embedded derivative must be separated from its debt host contract and accounted for separately. As explained in FASB ASC 958-30-25-8, if the obligation is solely life contingent (that is, contingent upon the survival of an identified individual, in which case the payments are made only if the individual is alive when the payments are due), that obligation would qualify for the exception from bifurcation in paragraphs 52–57 of FASB ASC 815-10-15. If the payments are variable, and the agreement is period certain rather than life contingent, FASB ASC 958-30-25-12 states that, generally, the liability representing an obligation under a split-interest

---

[6] See FASB *Accounting Standards Codification* 958-30 and chapter 6, "Split-Interest Agreements," of the AICPA Audit and Accounting Guide *Not-for-Profit Entities* for a detailed discussion of split-interest agreements.

agreement contains an embedded derivative. The embedded derivative should be bifurcated and accounted for as a derivative instrument pursuant to the requirements of FASB ASC 815-15-25-1, unless a fair value election is made pursuant to FASB ASC 815-15-25 or the "Fair Value Option" sections of FASB ASC 825-10.

5.38 Irrevocable split-interest agreements held by an independent third-party trustee generally do not give rise to embedded derivatives. Neither do (*a*) revocable split-interest agreements or (*b*) situations in which a not-for-profit entity holds a split-interest agreement in the capacity of an independent trustee without having any beneficial interest in the arrangements (that is, acting similar to a financial institution or fiscal agent).

Financial Statement Presentation and Disclosure

5.39 FASB ASC 815 provides guidance for evaluating financial statement presentation and disclosure requirements related to derivative instruments and hedging activities. Certain aspects of presentation and disclosure relative to classification of derivative gains and losses are highlighted subsequently.

Qualifying Hedges

5.40 Paragraphs 5.09–.13 describe how to report the gains and losses on cash flow hedges and fair value hedges. FASC ASC 815-10-50-4G states that for purposes of the disclosure requirements beginning in FASB ASC 815-10-50-4A, not-for-profit health care entities should present a similarly formatted table. They should refer to amounts within their performance indicator, instead of in income, and amounts outside their performance indicator, instead of in other comprehensive income. All not-for-profit entities also would indicate which class or classes of net assets (unrestricted, temporarily restricted, or permanently restricted) are affected.

5.41 Paragraphs 8–9 of FASB ASC 815-25-35 provide standards for the changes in fair value of the hedged item. The adjustment of the carrying amount of a hedged asset or liability required by FASB ASC 815-25-35-1(b) (for a fair value hedge) should be accounted for in the same manner as other components of the carrying amount of that asset or liability. An adjustment of the carrying amount of a hedged interest-bearing financial instrument should be amortized to earnings. Amortization should begin no later than when the hedged item ceases to be adjusted for changes in its fair value that are attributable to the risk being hedged.

5.42 FASB ASC 815-30-35-44 states that if a reclassification to earnings of the amount in accumulated comprehensive income resulting from a cash flow hedge of debt is required when debt is extinguished, the amount reclassified from accumulated comprehensive income to earnings should be excluded from extinguishment gain or loss.

Nonhedging Derivatives

5.43 Some derivatives may represent hedges for risk management purposes (entered into to hedge a specific exposure) that do not receive special hedge accounting either because the hedge relationship does not qualify for hedge accounting under the criteria in FASB ASC 815 or because an entity does not elect hedge accounting. Alternatively, nonhedging derivatives may be entered into for speculative purposes. Gains and losses related to nonhedging derivatives are reported in earnings (that is, included in the performance indicator) in the period of change.

Additional Requirements for Not-for-Profit Health Care Entities

5.44 FASB ASC 954-815-50-1 requires not-for-profit health care entities to separately disclose the beginning and ending accumulated derivative gain or loss that has been excluded from the performance indicator, as discussed in paragraph 5.07; the related net change associated with current-period hedging transactions; and the net amount of any reclassifications into the performance indicator in a manner similar to that described in FASB ASC 815-30-50-2. Similarly, FASB ASC 954-815 requires not-for-profit health care entities to provide disclosures that are analogous to those required by paragraphs 1–3 of FASB ASC 815-30-50 and FASB ASC 815-35-50-2 for for-profit enterprises, including the disclosure of anticipated reclassifications into the performance indicator of gains and losses that have been excluded from that measure and reported in accumulated derivative gain or loss as of the reporting date.

5.45 In accordance with FASB ASC 958-225-45-8, the changes in fair value of derivative instruments or hedged items are classified as increases or decreases in unrestricted net assets, unless their use is temporarily or permanently restricted by explicit donor stipulations or law.

Auditing

5.46 AU section 332, *Auditing Derivative Instruments, Hedging Activities, and Investments in Securities* (AICPA, *Professional Standards*), provides guidance on auditing procedures for assertions that are made in an entity's financial statements about derivative instruments and hedging activities. A companion Audit Guide, *Auditing Derivative Instruments, Hedging Activities, and Investments in Securities*, provides practical guidance to clarify and illustrate the application of the requirements of AU section 332.

Chapter 6

Property and Equipment and Other Assets

Overview

6.01 Health care entities use various kinds of property and equipment. Those assets are generally significant to the financial position of institutional health care entities, such as hospitals and nursing homes. Typical accounts used to record property and equipment transactions are land, land improvements, buildings and improvements, leasehold improvements, fixed and movable equipment, leased property and equipment, accumulated depreciation and amortization, and construction in progress.

6.02 Health care entities also have intangible assets, which may be acquired in connection with business combinations or purchases or developed from other resources of the entity. Intangibles with finite lives are amortized according to their useful life. Examples of intangibles include the following:

- Health plans, which include the following:
  - — Customer relationships, such as employer groups or members
  - — Provider networks
  - — Trademarks
  - — Trade names
  - — Software
  - — Licenses
  - — Favorable leases
  - — Noncompete agreements
  - — Goodwill
- Hospitals and other health care facilities, which include the following:
  - — Licenses
  - — Certificates of need
  - — Managed care contracts
  - — Goodwill
- Physician practices, which include the following:
  - — Medical charts
  - — Noncompete agreements
  - — Managed care contracts
  - — Goodwill

6.03 Supplies inventories are generally not very significant to the financial position of health care entities. However, because of the volume and cost of supplies used, they may be much more significant to operating expenses and the statement of operations. Supplies typically include medical and surgical supplies; pharmaceuticals; linens, uniforms, and garments; food and other commodities; and housekeeping, maintenance, and office supplies.

6.04 Health care entities, whether investor owned or not for profit, may receive donations in the form of property, equipment, or supplies. Donations of property, equipment, and supplies are measured at fair value at the date of donation, which then becomes the cost basis for the assets, and are recorded as an increase to fixed assets, inventory, or supply expense, as appropriate.

6.05 Accounting policies and disclosure requirements for property and equipment, supplies, and certain other assets of health care entities are similar to those used by other business entities. Health care entities should apply the guidance in Financial Accounting Standards Board (FASB) *Accounting Standards Codification* (ASC) 360, *Property, Plant, and Equipment*, and FASB ASC 340, *Other Assets and Deferred Costs*, except when the guidance conflicts with the specialized guidance in FASB ASC 954, *Health Care Entities*.

Capitalized Interest

6.06 Many not-for-profit health care entities finance acquisitions, additions, and renovations of facilities by issuing tax-exempt debt, as discussed in chapter 7, "Municipal Bond Funding," of this guide. If the proceeds of tax-exempt borrowings are externally restricted to finance the acquisition of specified qualifying assets or to service the related debt, the amount of interest cost to be capitalized is determined in accordance with paragraphs 8–12 of FASB ASC 835-20-25. If the health care entity uses taxable debt or otherwise does not qualify for interest capitalization under those paragraphs, then the amount of interest cost to be capitalized is determined pursuant to paragraphs 2–7 of FASB ASC 835-20-35. Frequently, not-for-profit health care entities are required to capitalize interest under paragraphs 2–7 of FASB ASC 835-20-35 for some projects and paragraphs 8–12 of FASB ASC 835-20-35 for others.

6.07 Among the differences between the two sets of guidance are the interest cost to be capitalized and the capitalization period. For interest costs on qualifying assets acquired with proceeds of tax-exempt borrowings that are externally restricted, FASB ASC 835-20-30-11 requires that the amount of capitalized interest be all interest cost of the borrowing less any interest earned on related interest-bearing investments acquired with proceeds of the related tax-exempt borrowings from the date of the borrowing until the assets are ready for their intended use. For other borrowings, paragraphs 2–7 of FASB ASC 835-20-30 use a weighted average construction expenditures concept that is applied during the period for which the three criteria in FASB ASC 835-20-25-3 are present. Those criteria are (*a*) expenditures for the asset have been made, (*b*) activities that are necessary to get the asset ready for its intended use are in progress, and (*c*) interest cost is being incurred.

6.08 In accordance with FASB ASC 835-20-30-12, the interest cost of a tax-exempt borrowing should be eligible for capitalization on other qualifying assets of the entity when the specified qualifying assets are no longer eligible for interest capitalization. The entire interest cost on that portion of the proceeds that is available for other uses, such as refunding an existing debt issue other than a construction loan related to those assets, also is eligible for capitalization on other qualifying assets. Example 1 in FASB ASC 835-20-55-4 illustrates this guidance.

6.09 In certain circumstances in which an entity has an investment (equity, loans, and advances) accounted for by the equity method, and the investee has not begun its planned principal operations, FASB ASC 835-20-35-2 requires capitalization of interest cost. As explained in FASB ASC 835-20-15-5(c), the investor's investment in the investee, not the individual assets or projects of the investee, is the qualifying asset for purposes of interest capitalization. Interest is capitalized while the investee has activities in progress necessary to commence its planned principal operations, provided that the investee's activities include the use of funds to acquire qualifying assets for operations.

6.10 FASB ASC 835-20-15 specifies the types of assets for which interest is not capitalized. Among the listed items are assets acquired with gifts and grants that are restricted by the donor or grantor to acquisition of those assets, to the extent that funds are available from such gifts and grants; interest earned from the temporary investment of those funds that is similarly restricted should be considered an addition to the gift or grant for this purpose. Other items include assets not included in the consolidated balance sheet of the parent company and consolidated subsidiaries and assets that are not being used in the earning activities of the entity and not undergoing the activities necessary to get them ready for use.

6.11 Some health care entities finance construction projects with municipal securities that have both taxable and tax-exempt components. The aggregate proceeds are to finance a specific construction project and are restricted by a common indenture or trust agreement to use only for construction of the project, repayment of the debt, or both. In such situations, the interest to be capitalized on the taxable portion of the issue is accounted for separate from the interest on the tax-exempt portion, based on paragraphs 2–7 of FASB ASC 835-20-30.

Supplies, Rebates, and Discounts

6.12 Many health care entities receive rebates and discounts from purchase agreements or other arrangements with vendors. Time may pass between the purchase of supplies and receipt of the rebate. Rebates and discounts are credited to the related expense or asset account. Paragraphs 10–12 of FASB ASC 605-50-25 and paragraphs 12–15 of FASB ASC 605-50-45 provide guidance when a health care entity is given cash considerations, rebates, refunds, or other up-front considerations by vendors.

6.13 Supply purchase contracts or other arrangements that include the use of vendor equipment may be considered to include a lease, as discussed in FASB ASC 440-10-25.

Lessee Involvement in Fixed Asset Construction[1]

6.14 Frequently, health care entities, such as hospitals and the hospital's employed physicians, enter into agreements with real estate developers for the

---

[1] On August 17, 2010, the Financial Accounting Standards Board (FASB) issued a proposed Accounting Standards Update (ASU), *Leases (Topic 840)*, which would make significant changes to the accounting requirements for both lessees and lessors. Readers should be alert to the issuance of a final standard.

construction of satellite buildings (for example, ambulatory surgery centers and medical office buildings). If the health care entity agrees to lease space in the building, the transaction is referred to as a build-to-suit transaction.

6.15 In these situations, FASB ASC 840-40-15-5 states that the health care entity (lessee) should be considered the owner of an asset during the construction period and, thus, be subject to FASB ASC 840-40 if it bears substantially all of the construction period risks; effectively, a sale and leaseback of the asset occurs when construction of the asset is complete, and the lease term begins. Paragraphs 2–16 of FASB ASC 840-40-55 provide specific criteria to apply in order to determine whether the health care entity (lessee) should be considered the owner of the asset during the construction period. If deemed to be the owner, the health care entity (lessee) should account for the arrangement as a sale-leaseback, in accordance with FASB ASC 840-40.

6.16 Thus, if the health care entity (lessee) bears substantially all of the construction-period risks, it should recognize construction in progress and a related financing obligation during the construction period. When the construction of the asset is complete, the health care entity (lessee) determines if it has met the requirements of sale-leaseback accounting, and if so, the deemed sale is recognized.

6.17 Additional guidance for build-to-suit transactions is found in the following standards:

- Paragraphs 42–47 of FASB ASC 840-40-55 provide guidance for costs incurred by a lessee before entering into a lease agreement with the developer-lessor.
- Paragraphs 7–16 of FASB ASC 958-810-55 provide guidance if a not-for-profit health care entity is engaged in leasing transactions with a special-purpose-entity lessor.

Asset Retirement and Environmental Remediation Obligations

6.18 Many health care entities operate facilities that were originally constructed prior to the existence of modern building codes. FASB ASC 410, *Asset Retirement and Environmental Obligations*, provides guidance for a facility that, upon disposal or abandonment, would be required by current regulations to remove, treat, or dispose of items such as asbestos; hazardous chemicals; test equipment; and building improvements, such as lead shielding or underground storage tanks, and to remediate environmental liabilities.

6.19 FASB ASC 410-20 addresses financial accounting and reporting for obligations associated with the retirement, sale, abandonment, recycling, disposal, or other-than-temporary idling of tangible long-lived assets and the associated asset retirement costs. It applies to legal obligations associated with the retirement of long-lived assets that result from the acquisition, construction, development, or normal operation of a long-lived asset, except for certain obligations. Paragraphs 8.59–.61 of this guide provide additional information about asset retirement obligations.

6.20 FASB ASC 410-30 requires that an entity recognize a liability for obligations associated with environmental remediation liabilities that relate to pollution arising from some past act, generally as a result of the provisions of

Superfund, the corrective-action provisions of the Resource Conservation and Recovery Act, or analogous state and non-U.S. laws and regulations. Generally, an environmental remediation liability results from the improper operation of a long-lived asset; an environmental remediation liability that results from the normal operation of a long-lived asset and is associated with the retirement of that asset is an asset retirement liability, as discussed in paragraph 6.19. FASB ASC 410-30 provides a brief overview of environmental laws and regulations, which may be helpful in understanding potential remediation liabilities.

Impairment or Disposal

6.21 The "Impairment or Disposal of Long-Lived Assets" sections of FASB ASC 360-10 provide guidance whenever events or changes in circumstances indicate that the carrying amount of a long-lived asset (asset group[2]) may not be recoverable. FASB ASC 360-10-35-17 states that an impairment loss should be recognized only if the carrying amount of the long-lived asset or asset group is not recoverable and exceeds its fair value.

6.22 Some of the following changes in circumstances of health care providers may indicate that the carrying amount of a long-lived asset group is not recoverable:

- There has been an adverse change in the use of the assets, such as the loss of certain core services to a specialty hospital.
- Patient volumes have significantly declined.
- Market conditions, such as the payment rates being received, increased competition, declining market demographics, or other conditions, have changed in such a manner that operating cash flow losses have been incurred or are projected to occur.
- The provider has lost its eligibility to be paid for services by a major payor, such as Medicare.
- The provider has lost its federal or state tax exemption.

6.23 FASB ASC 360-10-35-23 requires that for purposes of recognition and measurement of an impairment loss, a long-lived asset or assets be grouped with other assets and liabilities at the lowest level for which identifiable cash flows are largely independent of the cash flows of other assets and liabilities. Further, because FASB ASC 205-20 requires discontinued operations to be reported separately from continuing operations at the level of a component of an entity, a health care entity needs to determine whether a disposal group is a component of an entity. The FASB ASC glossary states that a *component of an entity* "comprises operations and cash flows that can be clearly distinguished, operationally and for financial reporting purposes, from the rest of the entity."

6.24 It may be difficult for health care systems to apply those guidelines due to arrangements that affect numerous entities under common control, such as multientity managed care contracts, centralized billing offices, and

---

[2] The FASB *Accounting Standards Codification* (ASC) glossary defines an *asset group* as "the unit of accounting for a long-lived asset or assets to be held and used, which represents the lowest level for which identifiable cash flows are largely independent of the cash flows of other groups of assets and liabilities." The FASB ASC glossary states that "[a] *disposal group* for a long-lived asset or assets to be disposed of by sale or otherwise represents assets to be disposed of together as a group in a single transaction and liabilities directly associated with those assets that will be transferred in the transaction."

shared purchasing operations and arrangements with physicians involved in providing services at multiple locations. Additionally, it is not uncommon for health care entities that operate multiple entities to support a service or facility that generates ongoing negative cash flows because the related services may be either (*a*) central to the furtherance of the overall entity's mission or (*b*) offered in order to reach a market segment that management believes will ultimately utilize other services within the entity to generate positive cash flows.

6.25 If a health care entity commits to a plan to abandon a long-lived asset before the end of its previously estimated useful life, FASB ASC 350-10-35-47 requires depreciation estimates to be revised, in accordance with paragraphs 17–20 of FASB ASC 250-10-45 and FASB ASC 250-10-50-4, to reflect the use of the asset over the shortened useful life.

6.26 Paragraphs 9–11 of FASB ASC 360-10-45 provide the criteria for classifying a long-lived asset group as held for sale. Consideration of those criteria by not-for-profit health care entities may be complicated by multiple levels of corporate governance and the interests of other authorities, such as the state attorney general, in the use of the assets. Large health care systems may be organized in such a way that the sale of certain assets must be approved by the governing board of the entity that owns the assets; any parent corporations; and, potentially, appointed representatives of groups that sponsor the system, such as religious congregations. Additionally, many transactions require approval by the state attorney general. These factors will affect the assessment of whether management has the authority to approve a sale and may also affect the timing of the completion of the transaction and, thus, the probability that the sale will be completed within one year.

6.27 In accordance with FASB ASC 360-10-35-44, if the health care entity decides not to sell a long-lived asset (disposal group) previously classified as held for sale, the asset (disposal group) should be reclassified as held and used. A long-lived asset that is reclassified should be measured individually at the lower of (*a*) its carrying amount before the asset (disposal group) was classified as held for sale, adjusted for any depreciation (amortization) expense that would have been recognized had the asset (disposal group) been continuously classified as held and used, or (*b*) its fair value at the date of the subsequent decision not to sell.

6.28 Per FASB ASC 205-20-45-1, the results of operations of a component of a health care entity that either has been disposed of or is classified as held for sale under the requirements of FASB ASC 360-10-45-9 should be reported in discontinued operations, in accordance with FASB ASC 205-20-45-3, if both of the following conditions are met: (*a*) the operations and cash flows of the component have been or will be eliminated from the ongoing operations of the health care entity as a result of the disposal transaction, and (*b*) the health care entity will not have any significant continuing involvement in the operations of the component after the disposal transaction. FASB ASC 205-20-55 provides implementation guidance to help an entity determine whether the two conditions are met.

6.29 In evaluating those criteria, consideration may be given to the geographic proximity of similar facilities operated by the health care entity, the existence of plans to relocate services to facilities under common control, whether the medical staff utilizing the disposed facility will be utilizing a facility within the same health care entity, and whether the health care entity will be continuing to utilize any of the long-lived assets previously included in the disposed component.

6.30 Per FASB ASC 205-20-45-3, the results of discontinued operations less applicable income taxes (benefit) should be reported as a separate component of income before extraordinary items. For not-for-profit health care entities, FASB ASC 954-225-45-7 requires that discontinued operations be reported separately from the performance indicator.

Nonreciprocal Transfers

6.31 A health care entity may transfer ownership of its long-lived assets, either individual pieces of equipment or an entire facility, to another health care entity in a nonreciprocal transaction.

6.32 FASB ASC 720-25 applies if such transactions are *contributions*, as defined in the FASB ASC glossary. Accounting for contributions made is discussed in paragraph 11.39 of this guide.

6.33 Similar to the recording of an impairment of long-lived assets, a gain or loss recognized to adjust to fair value would be included in income from continuing operations before income taxes in the income statement of an investor-owned health care entity or in the performance indicator in the statement of operations of a not-for-profit entity. If a subtotal, such as "Income From Operations," is presented, it would include the amounts of those gains or losses.

Other Long-Lived Assets

6.34 Health care entities that incur costs for upgrading or improving computer systems should follow the guidance in FASB ASC 350-40 for costs of computer software developed or obtained for internal use and FASB ASC 720-45 for business and technology reengineering. Business and technology reengineering may include software development, software acquisition, software implementation, training, and ongoing support.

6.35 Many health care entities have other long-lived or intangible assets, such as goodwill, trademarks, prepaid benefits, patents, and costs associated with certificates of need. These assets may be acquired by purchase, through internal development, or through research and development efforts, among other activities.

6.36 The cost of an intangible asset acquired other than in an acquisition by a not-for-profit entity or business combination is capitalized in accordance with FASB ASC 350, *Intangibles—Goodwill and Other*. Costs of start-up activities, including organization costs, should be expensed as incurred, as discussed in FASB ASC 720-15.

6.37 In accordance with FASB ASC 350-20, goodwill that is not written off on the acquisition date, as discussed in paragraph 12.99 of this guide, should not be amortized. Instead, it should be tested for impairment at a level of reporting referred to as a reporting unit. Paragraphs 33–46 of FASB ASC 350-20-35 provide guidance on determining reporting units. *Impairment* is the condition that exists when the carrying amount of goodwill exceeds its implied fair value. The fair value of goodwill can be measured only as a residual and cannot be measured directly. Therefore, FASB ASC 350-20 includes a methodology to determine an amount that achieves a reasonable estimate of the value of goodwill for purposes of measuring an impairment loss. That estimate is referred to as the implied fair value of goodwill. The two-step impairment test discussed in paragraphs 4–19 of FASB ASC 350-20-35 should be used to identify potential goodwill impairment and measure the amount of a goodwill impairment loss to be recognized, if any.*

6.38 Under the requirements of FASB ASC 350-30, accounting for a recognized intangible asset is based on its useful life to the reporting entity. An intangible asset with a finite useful life should be amortized; an intangible asset with an indefinite useful life should not be amortized. If an intangible asset has a finite useful life, but the precise length of that life is not known, that intangible asset should be amortized over the best estimate of its useful life. The method of amortization should reflect the pattern in which the economic benefits of the intangible asset are consumed or otherwise used up. If that pattern cannot be reliably determined, a straight-line amortization method should be used. An intangible asset that is subject to amortization should be reviewed for impairment in accordance with the "Impairment or Disposal of Long-Lived Assets" sections of FASB ASC 360-10 by applying the recognition and measurement provisions in paragraphs 17–35 of FASB ASC 360-10-35.

6.39 If an intangible asset is determined to have an indefinite useful life, it should not be amortized until its useful life is determined to be no longer indefinite. Instead, an intangible asset that is not subject to amortization should be tested for impairment annually or more frequently if events or changes in circumstances indicate that the asset might be impaired, as described in paragraphs 15–20 of FASB ASC 350-30-35. FASB ASC 360-10-35-21 includes examples of impairment indicators. The impairment test should consist of a comparison of the fair value of an intangible asset with its carrying amount. If the carrying amount of an intangible asset exceeds its fair value, an impairment loss should be recognized in an amount equal to that excess.

Financial Statement Presentation

6.40 Financial statement presentation of property and equipment, supplies, and other assets of health care entities is similar to that of other business entities.

6.41 FASB ASC 954-205-45-9 states that the expiration of donor-imposed restrictions on long-lived assets should be recognized when the asset is placed in service, rather than as depreciated, as permitted by FASB ASC 958-205-45-12. Thus, if contributions of long-lived assets with explicit donor restrictions are reported as temporarily-restricted support, a health care entity reports expirations of those donor restrictions when the stipulation is fulfilled, and the assets are placed in service. Similarly, donations of cash or other assets that

---

* In December 2010, FASB issued ASU No. 2010-28, *Intangibles—Goodwill and Other (Topic 350): When to Perform Step 2 of the Goodwill Impairment Test for Reporting Units with Zero or Negative Carrying Amounts (a consensus of the FASB Emerging Issues Task Force)*. This ASU simplifies how an entity is required to test goodwill for impairment. For public entities, this ASU is effective for fiscal years, and interim periods within those years, beginning after December 15, 2010. For nonpublic entities, it is effective for fiscal years, and interim periods within those years, beginning after December 15, 2011. Early adoption is not permitted for public entities, but nonpublic entities may adopt the amendments using the effective date for public entities.

must be used to acquire long-lived assets are reported as temporarily-restricted support in the period received, and expirations of those donor restrictions are reported when the acquired long-lived assets are placed in service, and donor-imposed restrictions are satisfied.

6.42 According to FASB ASC 954-360-45-1, property held for investment purposes is presented as part of investments.

6.43 FASB ASC 958-360-50-4 requires that donor or legal restrictions on the use of, or proceeds from, the disposition of donated property and equipment or property and equipment purchased with cash restricted for the acquisition of long-lived assets be disclosed.

Auditing

6.44 Auditing objectives for property and equipment, supplies, and other assets of health care entities are similar to those in audits of other business entities. The auditor may be able to assess the risks of material misstatement for these accounts as being relatively low because the transactions therein are generally small in number, relatively simple in nature, and do not involve the use of complex estimates. The auditor must obtain a sufficient understanding of the entity and its environment, including its internal control, to assess the risk of material misstatement for these accounts.

6.45 A health care entity may have access to the use of property and equipment under a variety of arrangements. It may (*a*) own property and equipment; (*b*) rent property and equipment from an independent or related entity; (*c*) use property and equipment provided by a related entity, such as a religious order, or an unrelated entity under an affiliation program; or (*d*) use property and equipment provided by a government agency or unit or government-related hospital district. The independent auditor may inquire into, and the financial statements might disclose, the nature of any relationship between the health care entity and lessors, bailors, or other owners of property.

6.46 In evaluating the entity's capitalization policies, the independent auditor should consider whether interest has been capitalized in accordance with the provisions of FASB ASC 835-20.

6.47 In evaluating the entity's depreciation policies, the auditor may wish to refer to the American Hospital Association's *Estimated Useful Lives of Depreciable Hospital Assets*, which is revised periodically and sets forth plant asset classifications and the estimated useful lives of depreciable assets. Additionally, social, economic, and scientific advances in the health care industry make obsolescence an important factor to be considered when evaluating depreciation policies and methods.

6.48 In considering a health care entity's application of the "Impairment or Disposal of Long-Lived Assets" sections of FASB ASC 360-10, auditors may obtain an understanding of the policies and procedures used by management to determine whether all impaired assets have been properly identified. In addition to evaluating the entity's procedures for identifying indicators of impairment, the auditor may consider information obtained during the audit in determining whether the health care entity has identified appropriate indicators of impairment. For example, a change in the use of a facility from an acute-care hospital to an ambulatory surgery center may require that the asset be reviewed for impairment.

6.49 In obtaining sufficient appropriate audit evidence with respect to property and equipment, supplies, and other assets, the auditor may consider the examples of specific auditing objectives, selected control activities, and auditing procedures that are presented in exhibit 6-1.

Exhibit 6-1

The following table illustrates the use of assertions in developing audit objectives and designing substantive tests. The examples are not intended to be all-inclusive nor is it expected that all the procedures would necessarily be applied in an audit. The auditor should design and perform substantive procedures for all relevant assertions related to each material class of transactions, account balance, and disclosure to obtain sufficient appropriate audit evidence. The use of assertions in assessing risks and designing appropriate audit procedures to obtain audit evidence is described in paragraphs .14–.26 of AU section 326, *Audit Evidence* (AICPA, *Professional Standards*). Various audit procedures and the purposes for which they may be performed are described in paragraphs .27–.41 of AU section 326.

Auditing Considerations

Financial Statement Assertions	*Specific Auditing Objectives*	*Selected Control Activities*	*Auditing Procedures*
Donated Property Equipment			
Account Balances			
Valuation and allocation	Donated property and equipment is reported at fair value at the date of donation.[1]	Procedures ensure that the donation of property and equipment is known and recorded and that documentation supports the determination of the fair value.	Review the documentation supporting the determination of the fair value.[2]
Presentation and Disclosure			
Classification and understandability	The receipt of donated property and equipment is properly reported.		Review material donated property and equipment transactions to ensure the propriety of the reporting.
Property and Equipment Not Held for Use in Operations			
Presentation and Disclosure			
Classification and understandability	Property and equipment not used for operations is reported separately.	Property records segregate property and equipment not used for operating purposes.	Determine that property held for nonoperating purposes is reported separately.

(continued)

Auditing Considerations—continued

Financial Statement Assertions	*Specific Auditing Objectives*	*Selected Control Activities*	*Auditing Procedures*
Property and Equipment Additions			
Rights and obligations	The appropriate health care planning agency or other regulatory agency approvals, if required, have been obtained for property and equipment additions.	Management regularly monitors compliance with health care planning agency regulations related to additions of property and equipment.	For material new construction, determine compliance with health care planning agency or other regulatory agency requirements.
		Additions are authorized in the capital budget.	
Existence and valuation and allocation	Recorded property and equipment are owned by the entity and carried at the appropriate amounts.	Inventory of property and equipment is taken periodically. Detailed property records are periodically reconciled to the recorded amounts.	Review a summary of property and equipment (cost and accumulated depreciation), including additions, deletions, and transfers.

[1] For additional discussion on fair value measurements, refer to chapter 4, "Cash, Cash Equivalents, and Investments," of this guide.

[2] AU section 328, *Auditing Fair Value Measurements and Disclosures* (AICPA, *Professional Standards*), provides guidance on auditing fair value measurements and disclosures contained in financial statements. AU section 328 does not address specific types of assets, liabilities, components of equity, transactions, or industry-specific practices. *Considerations for Audits Performed in Accordance With Public Company Accounting Oversight Board (PCAOB) Standards* PCAOB Staff Audit Practice Alert No. 2, *Matters Related to Auditing Fair Value Measurements of Financial Instruments and the Use of Specialists* (AICPA, *PCAOB Standards and Related Rules*, PCAOB Staff Guidance, sec. 400.02), provides guidance on auditors' responsibilities for auditing fair value measurements of financial instruments and when using the work of specialists under the existing standards of the PCAOB. This practice alert is focused on specific matters that are likely to increase audit risk related to the fair value of financial instruments in a rapidly changing economic environment. This practice alert also highlights certain requirements in the auditing standards related to fair value measurements and disclosures in the financial statements and certain aspects of generally accepted accounting principles that are particularly relevant to the current economic environment. PCAOB Staff Audit Practice Alerts are not rules of the PCAOB nor have they been approved by the PCAOB.

Chapter 7

Municipal Bond Financing

Introduction

7.01 Although health care entities utilize many forms of debt financing, this chapter focuses on municipal bonds issued on behalf of not-for-profit health care entities. Because of its capital-intensive nature, health care is among the largest industry sectors that raise funds through the municipal securities market.

7.02 Typically, a qualified governmental agency, such as a health care financing authority (the issuer), issues the securities and then lends the proceeds to the health care entity (the obligor). In these conduit financings, although the securities bear the name of the issuing government, the issuer has no obligation for repayment of the debt; the bondholders' principal and interest will be paid solely from resources of the obligor.

7.03 Most municipal bonds issued on behalf of health care entities are revenue bonds. For revenue bond issues, the health care entity pledges a specific revenue stream, typically revenue derived from the project or enterprise being funded. There may also be a mortgage on the financed property and other restrictive covenants. To obtain project financing, a financing authority may require a health care entity to enter into a lease arrangement, a sublease arrangement, or both. It is also common practice for a health care system to create an obligated group of affiliated entities, the assets and revenues of which serve as collateral for the debt.

7.04 Municipal bonds are issued with either a variable or fixed interest rate. A fixed-rate bond bears interest at a specified, constant rate. Variable-rate (floating-rate) bonds bear interest at a rate that is reset from time to time. Some documents provide the ability to change the interest mode (for example, from auction rate[1] to variable rate). In addition, financing strategies have emerged that convert a variable-rate obligation into a fixed-rate obligation, or vice versa, using derivative instruments. For example, a common financing structure involves creating fixed-rate debt by initially issuing lower cost variable-rate debt coupled with a floating-to-fixed interest rate swap. Additional considerations related to interest rate swaps are discussed in chapter 5, "Derivatives," of this guide.

7.05 The type of project(s) that is funded with municipal bond proceeds affects the taxability of income received by the bond holders and, thus, whether the bonds are characterized as tax exempt or taxable. Generally, tax-exempt bonds are issued to finance services or facilities that are for the public good. Interest paid to holders of tax-exempt bonds is often exempt from all federal income taxes and sometimes state or local taxes, as well. Taxable bonds may be issued for uses not qualifying for tax-exempt financing (for example, medical office buildings). Tax considerations are discussed in paragraphs 7.39–.43.

---

[1] In a Dutch auction, investors bid for the bonds, which are sold at the lowest yield necessary to sell the entire issue.

Conduit Bonds That Trade in Public Markets

7.06 Certain accounting standards require entities that have securities that trade in public markets to provide more extensive disclosures than is required for entities that do not have securities trading in public markets. Generally, the rationale behind these requirements is that the entity's financial statements are being utilized in public markets for making decisions about whether to buy, sell, or hold that entity's securities.

7.07 The Financial Accounting Standards Board (FASB) *Accounting Standards Codification* (ASC) glossary has multiple definitions for the term *public entity*. Generally, these are entities that have debt or equity securities that trade in public markets. When applying accounting standards that refer to public entities, careful attention should be paid to the requirements to determine which definition applies and whether the definition includes conduit bond obligors within its scope. If within its scope, it is also necessary to determine whether the obligor's securities trade in public markets (for example, over-the-counter markets). As discussed in paragraph 7.12, if conduit bonds have been issued on behalf of a health care entity in a competitive or negotiated offering, they are deemed to trade in public markets. Bonds issued in a private placement would not be deemed to trade in public markets for as long as the bonds are privately held.

7.08 The fact that a not-for-profit health care entity with conduit bonds that trade in public markets is considered a public entity does not change that entity's status for purposes of applying accounting standards with requirements that are specific to not-for-profit entities or that explicitly exclude not-for-profit entities. If the scope of an accounting standard that contains expanded disclosure requirements or additional accounting requirements for public entities explicitly excludes not-for-profit entities, not-for-profit health care entities would not apply that standard. Additionally, classification as a public entity under generally accepted accounting principles (GAAP) does not impose Securities and Exchange Commission (SEC) or other regulatory filing requirements (such as Regulations S-X or S-K) on not-for-profit health care conduit debt obligors. It also does not result in a not-for-profit health care entity being required to comply with the portions of the Sarbanes-Oxley Act of 2002 that apply only to *issuers*, as defined by the Securities Exchange Act of 1934.

Credit Enhancement[2]

7.09 Health care entities may utilize credit enhancements to make their bonds more attractive to investors or to allow them to access the market at more favorable rates. Credit enhancement involves the use of the credit standing of an entity, other than the issuer or obligor, to provide additional security in a bond or note financing. Credit enhancement typically refers to bond insurance, bank letters of credit, and similar facilities but also may refer more broadly to the use of any form of guaranty; secondary source of payment; or similar, additional credit-improving instruments.

7.10 When credit enhancement is provided through a bank letter of credit, the bonds bear the rating of the issuing bank that commits to pay the principal and interest on the securities in the event that the obligor is unable to do so.

---

[2] Paragraph 7.67 discusses the fair value of bonds with third-party credit enhancements, whether measured for purposes of disclosure or reporting under the "Fair Value Option" sections of Financial Accounting Standards Board (FASB) *Accounting Standards Codification* 825-10.

Letters of credit cover a specified time period. *Bond insurance* is an unconditional and irrevocable commitment from a municipal bond insurance company to make scheduled bond debt service payments in the event of nonpayment by the obligor. Bonds secured by a municipal bond insurance policy carry the rating of the municipal bond insurer. Once acquired, a bond insurance policy generally is in place for the life of the bonds. Government programs, such as the Federal Housing Administration Section 242 mortgage insurance program, enable some obligors to enhance their credit using the creditworthiness of the federal government.

7.11 Because credit-enhanced bonds are rated based on the credit standing of another entity, downgrades of the other entity's ratings can have implications for the obligor's own credit ratings, as well as potentially triggering defaults under debt agreements and derivative contracts. See related discussion in paragraph 7.82.

Issuance of Municipal Bonds

7.12 Municipal bonds are issued through negotiated sales, competitive bids, or private placements. In a negotiated sale, the issuer or obligor negotiates a price with one or more underwriters. In a competitive bid sale, the securities are sold to one or more underwriters who submitted the best acceptable bid(s). The underwriters then resell the securities to the general investing public. Municipal bonds issued in negotiated sales or competitive bids are deemed to be traded in public markets; thus, conduit borrowers under those arrangements are considered public entities for purposes of providing certain disclosures under accounting standards, as discussed in paragraph 7.06. In addition, when underwriters sell municipal securities to the general investing public, the SEC imposes certain requirements on the underwriters, who in turn require the obligors to file certain disclosure documents. An overview of SEC considerations related to municipal bonds is provided in appendix A, "Municipal Securities Regulation," of this chapter. In a private placement, the securities generally are sold directly to qualified investors (for example, an institutional investor), rather than through an offering to the general investing public. Municipal bonds issued in private placements are not deemed to trade in public markets because the investors typically are subject to restrictions on resale.

7.13 A health care entity that is issuing municipal bonds through a financing authority prepares an official statement that offers the securities for sale and provides appropriate financial and other information about the offering, the health care entity, and any guarantors or credit-enhancement providers. Financial advisers; bond counsel; and, frequently, engineers and appraisers assist the health care entity in preparing information for the official statement. Professional requirements related to auditor association with municipal securities offerings are discussed in paragraph 7.86. The following are important stages in a municipal securities offering (the time periods between these stages may vary):

- The preliminary official statement is issued to all prospective buyers of the securities.
- The financing authority, health care entity, and underwriters execute the bond purchase agreement.
- The official statement is issued at the time of sale (sometimes referred to as the effective date) and identifies the actual debt service requirements of the securities.

- The closing date is the date that the transaction is finalized, and the proceeds are transferred from the buyers to the health care entity.

Extinguishment and Modification Transactions

7.14 Not-for-profit health care entities generally follow the same accounting and financial reporting standards for extinguishment and modification of debt as investor-owned entities. Those standards are found in FASB ASC 405-20 and 470-50.

7.15 FASB ASC 405-20-40 states that a liability is extinguished either when the debtor pays the creditor and is relieved of its obligation for the liability or when the debtor is legally released from being the primary obligor under the liability, either judicially or by the creditor. FASB ASC 405-20-40-1(a)(4) states that paying the creditor includes reacquisition by the debtor of its outstanding debt securities, regardless of whether the securities are cancelled or held as Treasury bonds.

7.16 Thus, a debt obligation is derecognized if a health care entity reacquires its bonds through open market purchases, regardless of whether the reacquired securities are then held by the debtor as Treasury bonds or retired. Treasury bonds that are held should never be reported as an asset of the health care entity, even if the entity intends to remarket the bonds at a future date or hold and manage them as part of its investment portfolio.

7.17 Another way that a health care entity may extinguish its debt is by issuing new bonds whose proceeds are used to repay the previously-issued bonds (a refunding transaction). If the new bonds are held by the same creditor as the old bonds, the refunding may be a modification of debt terms, rather than an extinguishment, as discussed in paragraphs 6–12 of FASB ASC 470-50-40. See also paragraphs 7.27–.31. Three types of refunding transactions exist: current refunding, advance refunding, and crossover refunding. In a current refunding, the new debt proceeds may be used to repay the old bonds within 90 days of the first call date or maturity of the bonds to be refunded. In an advance refunding, the new debt proceeds are placed with an escrow agent and invested until they are used to pay principal and interest of the old debt at a future time; outstanding securities are refinanced more than 90 days prior to their call or maturity date.[3] In a crossover refunding, bonds referred to as crossover bonds are issued for the purpose of paying off an existing bond issue (referred to as the refunded bonds). The crossover bonds are initially collateralized by an escrow of investments purchased with the crossover bond proceeds, and the refunded bonds continue to be secured by their original collateral or revenue stream. On a specified date, the investments held in escrow are sold, and the refunded bonds are redeemed. Then, the crossover bonds become collateralized by the original collateral or payable from the original revenue stream. In refunding transactions, the entity must either call the bonds (if allowed) to redeem them early or irrevocably set aside the funds to pay them off in a defeasance. These situations are discussed subsequently.

---

[3] Per the Tax Reform Act of 1986, new money bonds issued prior to January 1, 1986, can be advance refunded twice, but bonds issued on or after that date can only be advance refunded once.

Calls and Mode Conversions

7.18 Some bond contracts allow a health care entity to repay the bonds prior to their scheduled maturity date, which is referred to as a call option. Typically, new bonds are issued to pay off the outstanding bonds (a refunding).

7.19 Some bonds are structured as multimodal, which permits the health care entity to exercise an interest mode conversion. A multimodal feature provides the health care entity with a contractual right to change the interest feature of the bond from one form to another (for example, an auction-based interest rate to a fixed-rate or index-based variable interest rate). In most cases, a mode conversion involves a call (referred to as a mandatory tender) of the old bonds and marketing of new bonds to new investors, as well as existing bondholders. Thus, the mode conversion is similar to a traditional refunding, and the same accounting considerations apply to mode conversions as refunding.

Defeasance

7.20 If the health care entity would like to retire the debt early but does not have a call option, defeasance is a financing tool that allows it to obtain some or all of the benefits of repaying bondholders prior to actually retiring the debt. In a defeasance, the health care entity purchases government securities for deposit into an escrow account and irrevocably pledges the securities to the payment of the outstanding bonds. The securities and their related earnings are sufficient to pay the principal and interest on the bonds when they come due. In essence, the health care entity is substituting collateral on the debt. Often, some or all of the funds deposited into the escrow account arise from an advance refunding. Generally, the revenues originally pledged as security on the outstanding securities switch over to become security for payment of the refunding bonds (the new issue) on the date that the advance refunding bonds are issued.

7.21 Defeasances are categorized as legal or economic. The terms of some bond contracts allow for *legal defeasance*, which is the termination of the rights and interests of the bondholders and their lien on the pledged revenues or other security. When the conditions specified in the bond contract for legal defeasance are met, the health care entity's obligation for repayment of the bonds is satisfied in full, and the debt is extinguished.

7.22 In other situations, sometimes referred to as an in-substance or economic defeasance, establishing a defeasance escrow account makes the revenues pledged as collateral available for other purposes without actually effecting a legal defeasance. This might be used if, for example, the bond contract does not provide a procedure for termination of the bondholders' rights and interests other than through redemption of the bonds. In an economic defeasance, if for some reason the escrowed funds prove insufficient to make future payments on the old debt, the health care entity is still legally obligated to make payment on such debt from the pledged revenues.

7.23 FASB ASC 405-20-55 provides implementation guidance on the extinguishment of liabilities, including in-substance and legal defeasances.

7.24 When a defeasance occurs, the debtor has not paid the creditor. Therefore, liabilities are considered extinguished for accounting purposes only if the debtor is legally released from being the primary obligor under the liability, either judicially or by the creditor. In a legal defeasance, generally, the creditor legally releases the debtor from being the primary obligor under the liability; however, the question of whether the debtor has in fact been legally released is a matter of law, not an accounting determination. A legal opinion may be required. An in-substance defeasance transaction normally does not meet the derecognition criteria for either the liability or escrowed assets, unless a legal release is obtained.

7.25 Paragraphs 4–6 of FASB ASC 860-10-40 provide standards for determining whether financial assets should be derecognized.

7.26 Derecognition of the assets in the defeasance trust may need to be separately evaluated, even if the defeased debt has met the criteria for derecognition. Because the obligor must surrender control over the assets transferred to the trust, and the transferred assets must be legally isolated from the obligor (for example, presumptively put beyond the reach of the obligor and its creditors, even in bankruptcy or other receivership), if the obligor has any type of continuing involvement with the transferred assets (for example, if the obligor has the ability to direct the investment of trust assets or is entitled to residual assets upon termination of the trust), a separate legal isolation opinion may be required in order to conclude that the conditions for derecognition have been met.

Modifications

7.27 When one debt instrument is replaced with another, such as occurs in refundings or interest mode conversions, and the new debt instrument is held by the same creditor(s) as the old, questions may arise about whether the transaction is considered a debt modification or debt extinguishment.

7.28 Paragraphs 6–12 of FASB ASC 470-50-40 provide guidance for determining whether a replacement of one debt instrument with another is a modification of the original debt terms or the extinguishment of one obligation and issuance of another. FASB ASC 470-50-40-6 states that an exchange of debt instruments with substantially different terms is a *debt extinguishment* and should be accounted for in accordance with FASB ASC 405-20-40-1 by derecognizing the liability. FASB ASC 470-50-40-10 states that from the debtor's perspective, an exchange of debt instruments between a debtor and creditor in a nontroubled debt situation is deemed to have been accomplished with debt instruments that are substantially different if the present value of the cash flows under the terms of the new debt instrument is at least 10 percent different from the present value of the remaining cash flows under the terms of the original instrument. However, if the debt modification is considered a troubled debt restructuring, the guidance in FASB ASC 760-60 would apply.

7.29 When evaluating whether a modification or an exchange has occurred with a public debt issuance, the debt instrument is the individual security held by an investor, and the creditor is the security holder. Thus, the unit of account is not for the bond issue in total but on a bondholder-by-bondholder basis. As a practical matter, if the bonds are widely held, it may be reasonable to conclude that the issuance of new bonds to pay off old bonds is not a refinancing of debt with the same creditors; thus, it is an extinguishment, rather than a modification. If the bonds are not widely held, and the transaction is in essence a refinancing of debt with the same creditor(s), it is necessary to determine whether the difference between the present value of the remaining cash flows associated with the original obligation and the present value of the cash flows associated with the new obligation is less than 10 percent. If the difference is less than 10 percent, the transaction is a modification.

7.30 For a conduit bond offering involving a governmental financing agency, a health care entity should determine whether the financing agency is acting as a principal or an agent of the obligor in order to determine whether the transaction is an extinguishment or a modification.

7.31 Paragraphs 19–20 of FASB ASC 470-50-40 and paragraphs 4–7 of FASB ASC 470-50-55 provide guidance and indicators to consider in making such a determination.

Gain or Loss on Debt Extinguishment

7.32 FASB ASC 470-50 addresses how a gain or loss on a debt extinguishment should be measured. It applies to all extinguishments of debt, regardless of whether the extinguishment is early, except debt that is extinguished through a troubled debt restructuring or convertible debt. Per FASB ASC 470-50-40-2, the difference between the reacquisition price and net carrying amount of the extinguished debt should be recognized currently in income of the period of extinguishment as losses or gains and identified as a separate item. Gains and losses should not be amortized to future periods. Classification of the gain or loss is discussed in FASB ASC 470-50-45. See paragraph 7.64 for additional discussion.

7.33 The *reacquisition price* of debt is the amount paid on extinguishment, including a call premium and miscellaneous costs of reacquisition. If extinguishment is achieved by a direct exchange of new securities, the reacquisition price is the fair value of the new securities. The net carrying amount of the extinguished debt is the amount due at maturity, adjusted for unamortized premium, discount, and cost of issuance.

Debt Issuance Costs

7.34 Paragraphs 17–18 of FASB ASC 470-50-40 provide guidance for reporting costs incurred by the debtor in connection with an exchange or a modification of debt instruments. The accounting treatment depends on whether the fees are paid to the creditor or other third parties. The following paragraph summarizes that guidance but is not a substitute for reading the referenced paragraphs.

7.35 If the exchange or modification is to be accounted for in the same manner as a debt extinguishment, and the new debt instrument is initially recorded at fair value, then (*a*) the fees between the debtor and creditor are included in determining the debt extinguishment gain or loss to be recognized, and (*b*) the third-party costs are amortized over the term of the new debt instrument using the interest method in a manner similar to debt issue costs. If the exchange or modification is not accounted for in the same manner as a debt extinguishment, then (*a*) the fees between the debtor and creditor, along with any existing unamortized premium or discount, are amortized as an adjustment of interest expense over the remaining term of the replacement or modified debt instrument using the interest method, and (*b*) the third-party costs are expensed as incurred.

7.36 As discussed in FASB ASC 470-50-40, in the event of a mode conversion, modification, or extinguishment of debt, there may be effects on the related prepaid bond issuance costs or deferred issuance costs, such as writing off all or a portion of these costs or revised amortization periods.

Puts or Tender Options

7.37 Some bond contracts allow the bonds to be repaid prior to their stated maturity at the option of the bondholder. The bondholder's right to request earlier payment is referred to as a tender option (or sometimes a put option). Some health care entities utilize bank agreements, such as letters of credit or standby bond purchase agreements (a liquidity facility), to provide liquidity for the put or tender feature. If a bondholder exercises its put option, the health care entity generally will seek to sell the put bonds to another investor through its remarketing agent. If another investor is found who accepts the same terms as the original bondholder, the transaction occurs between the bondholders and does not affect the accounting by the health care entity. The proceeds of the resale are used to pay the original bondholder. If another investor cannot be found (for example, a failed remarketing), the health care entity is required to pay the bondholder. If the health care entity has a liquidity facility, then the liquidity provider generally advances the funds needed to pay the bondholder. At that point, ownership of the bonds transfers to the liquidity provider, and they become bank bonds. The interest rate payable on bank bonds converts to the rate stipulated in the liquidity facility agreement. Efforts continue to remarket the bank bonds for the period of time stipulated in the liquidity facility agreement. If another bondholder is found within that period, the proceeds generally are used to pay off the liquidity facility; the interest rate returns to the terms in the original bond agreement; and the bonds revert to their normal status, with the one exception discussed in paragraph 7.15.

7.38 If another buyer cannot be found after a certain period, the liquidity facility generally ceases to be interest only and converts to a term loan. The health care entity repays the debt over a relatively short period of time, rather than over the original stated maturity of the bonds. In effect, the bank (the liquidity facility) exchanges the term loan for the bond, and the bond is derecognized because its terms are substantially different from those of the term loan.

7.39 In some cases, health care entities may forego using an external liquidity facility. If a failed remarketing occurs, the health care entity pays the holder of the put bonds using its own cash and liquid investments (self-liquidity). In these situations, the bonds are considered extinguished when the failed remarketing occurs, regardless of whether the put bonds are retained by the health care entity as Treasury bonds or retired.

IRS Considerations

7.40 As discussed in paragraph 7.05, interest paid to holders of tax-exempt bonds is often exempt from all federal income taxes and sometimes state or local taxes, as well. In order to maintain the bonds' tax-exempt status, health care entities must comply with all applicable federal tax laws and Treasury regulations, including, but not limited to, the use of bond-financed property and arbitrage requirements. The IRS encourages Internal Revenue Code (IRC) Section 501(c)(3) organizations to implement procedures that will enable them to adequately safeguard against postissuance violations that could result in the loss of the tax-exempt status of the bonds. IRS Publication 4078, *Tax-Exempt Private Activity Bonds* (available for download at www.irs.gov/pub/irs-pdf/p4078.pdf) is a helpful source of information regarding the requirements. Requirements related to arbitrage and the qualified use of proceeds are briefly summarized subsequently.

7.41 Tax-exempt bonds bear interest at lower rates than taxable bonds due to the inherent federal tax subsidy. Safeguards exist, so that entities do not attempt to inappropriately benefit from this subsidy by issuing tax-exempt bonds and then investing the proceeds to earn *arbitrage*, which is the difference between the interest earned on the invested funds and the interest rate that the health care entity must pay to the bondholders. Specific IRS requirements control arbitrage and dictate which bond issues are subject to rebate (for example, remitting excess earnings to the federal government) and when the yield on investments must be restricted. Certain exceptions apply to these provisions based on the nature and timing of the expenditures paid by the bond proceeds.

7.42 FASB ASC 954-470-25-2 states that IRS regulations concerning tax-exempt debt prohibit the yield realized from the investment of the proceeds of tax-exempt debt from exceeding the interest rate to be paid on such debt. Whenever a health care entity invests tax-exempt bond proceeds, and the ultimate yield is higher than the interest rate on the bonds, the entity may be subject to an arbitrage rebate liability. The arbitrage determination is made as of the date of the issue; however, intentional acts undertaken after the date of the issue can retroactively disqualify the issue. The earnings in excess of interest expense represent a liability that must be paid to the Department of the Treasury in order for the bonds to maintain their tax-exempt status. The arbitrage rebate liability may be a substantial amount if the bond proceeds are not spent as quickly as planned. For example, this may occur if a provider encounters a delay in a major construction project.

7.43 The type of project(s) that is funded by a bond affects the taxability of income received by the bondholders. Conduit bonds issued for projects that only benefit private parties (private activity bonds) normally are taxable. Conduit bonds issued to finance facilities owned and utilized by IRC Section 501(c)(3) nonprofit organizations are exempt from federal income tax if they are qualified 501(c)(3) bonds. To qualify for tax exemption, at least 95 percent of the net bond proceeds must be used for exempt activities. Thus, no more than 5 percent of the net proceeds may be used in any private business use or by the not-for-profit entity in an unrelated trade or business activity. Bond issuance costs are considered part of the 5 percent private use and reduce the available net proceeds for other types of private use. IRC Section 501(c)(3) borrowers must ensure that the IRS rules on private use are met both at the time that the bonds are issued and throughout the life of the bonds.

7.44 Treasury regulations provide for certain remedial actions to cure uses of proceeds that would otherwise cause the qualified 501(c)(3) bonds to lose their exempt status. Those remedial actions can include redemption or defeasance of bonds, alternative qualified use of disposition proceeds, or alternative use of the bond-financed facilities. Entities may also be eligible to enter into a closing agreement under IRS Notice 2008-31, *Voluntary Closing Agreement Program For Tax-Exempt Bonds and Tax Credit Bonds*, which is available at www.irs.gov/pub/irs-drop/n-08-31.pdf.

Financial Statement Presentation and Disclosure

Balance Sheet

7.45 According to FASB ASC 954-470-25-1, when a financing authority issues tax-exempt bonds or similar debt instruments and uses the proceeds for the benefit of a health care entity, the obligation should be reported as a liability in the entity's balance sheet if the health care entity is responsible for repayment. In some cases, this obligation may take the form of a liability arising from a capital lease.* If a health care entity has no obligation to make payments of principal and interest on the debt or capital or operating lease payments on related buildings or equipment, the entity should not reflect the liability on its balance sheet. In such circumstances, proceeds from the bond issue shall be reported as contributions from the sponsoring entity.

7.46 Although bonds typically have a stated maturity of many years, careful consideration should be given to classification of the liability as current or noncurrent based on the features of the debt. Debt that appears to be long term based on its legal maturity might not be considered long term for financial reporting purposes because of subjective acceleration clauses or due-on-demand (put) provisions. Careful consideration of the bond agreements and related documents (for example, bond indenture, loan and trust agreement, liquidity facility, and so on) may be required in order to make a determination of whether debt is properly classified.

7.47 The principal guidance for evaluating the appropriate balance sheet classification of debt obligations is found in FASB ASC 210-10-45, 470-10-45, and 470-10-55.

Classification of Debt With Due-on-Demand or Put Provisions

7.48 FASB ASC 470-10-45-10 states that the current liability classification should include obligations that, by their terms, are due on demand or will be due on demand within one year (or operating cycle, if longer) from the balance sheet date, even though liquidation may not be expected within that period.

7.49 For example, some variable-rate bonds have a demand feature (a put or tender option) whereby the bondholder may require the health care entity or its remarketing agent to repurchase the bonds, often on short notice. Demand obligations normally are classified as current liabilities, despite the fact that the bond's stated maturities cover many years. However, such obligations often are supported by a liquidity facility, such as a standby bond purchase agreement or letter of credit from a financial institution, that provides the health care entity with the ability to refinance, on a long-term basis, any obligation that may arise if tendered bonds cannot immediately be remarketed to another investor, as discussed in paragraph 7.37.

7.50 FASB ASC 470-10-55-8 states that debt agreements that allow a debt holder to redeem (or put) a debt instrument on demand (or within one year) should be classified as short-term liabilities despite the existence of a best-efforts remarketing agreement. Unless the issuer (health care entity) of the redeemable debt instrument has the ability and intent to refinance the debt on a long-term basis, as provided for in FASB ASC 470-10-45-14, the debt should be classified as a current liability.

7.51 FASB ASC 470-10-45-14 requires that the intent to refinance the short-term obligation on a long-term basis be supported by an ability to consummate the refinancing that is demonstrated in either of the following ways:

---

* On August 17, 2010, FASB issued proposed Accounting Standards Update *Leases (Topic 840)*, which would make significant changes to the accounting requirements for both lessees and lessors. Readers should be alert to the issuance of a final standard.

(*a*) postbalance sheet date issuance of a long-term obligation or equity securities or (*b*) a financing agreement. If a financing agreement is used to justify noncurrent classification of the bonds, FASB ASC 470-10-45-14(b) requires that before the balance sheet is issued or available to be issued, the entity must have entered into a financing agreement that clearly permits the entity to refinance the short-term obligation on a long-term basis on terms that are readily determinable, and all three conditions in FASB ASC 470-10-45-14(b) must be met.

7.52 In summary, those three conditions are as follows:

a. The agreement does not expire within one year from the date of the entity's balance sheet, and during that period, the agreement is not cancelable by the lender, except for violation of a provision with which compliance is objectively determinable or measurable. Further, any obligations incurred under the agreement are not callable during that period.

b. No violation of any provision in the financing agreement exists at the balance sheet date, and no available information indicates that a violation has occurred thereafter, or if a violation has occurred thereafter, a waiver has been obtained.

c. The lender is expected to be financially capable of honoring the agreement.

However, the conditions are very complex, and the preceding summary is not intended as a substitute for reading paragraphs 14–20 of FASB ASC 470-10-45.

7.53 If the liquidity facility, which is the financing agreement, contains a subjective acceleration clause, the liquidity facility does not meet the first condition in the previous paragraph because compliance with that clause is not objectively determinable or measureable. The health care entity is not deemed to have the ability and intent to finance on a long-term basis and, thus, cannot classify the debt as noncurrent, even if the repayment terms of the liquidity facility would otherwise support such classification. See paragraph 7.55 for the definition of a *subjective acceleration clause*. The probability of the subjective acceleration clause being exercised is irrelevant when attempting to demonstrate the ability to refinance a short-term obligation on a long-term basis. See related discussion in paragraph 7.56.

7.54 Rather than utilizing a liquidity facility issued by an external third party, some health care entities choose to utilize their own funds for satisfying puts or tenders. Health care entities that do so have no basis for excluding those put and tender obligations from current liabilities because no third party provides liquidity that would effectively allow the entity to refinance the debt on a long-term basis.

Classification of Debt With a Subjective Acceleration Clause

7.55 The FASB ASC glossary defines a *subjective acceleration clause* as "a provision in a debt agreement that states that the creditor may accelerate the scheduled maturities of the obligation under conditions that are not objectively determinable (for example, if the debtor fails to maintain satisfactory operations or if a material adverse change occurs)." For long-term obligations, the effect of a subjective acceleration clause on balance sheet classification is determined by FASB ASC 470-10-45-2. That paragraph states that in some situations, the circumstances (for example, recurring losses or liquidity problems) would indicate that long-term debt subject to a subjective acceleration clause should be classified as a current liability. Other situations would indicate only disclosure of the existence of such clauses. Neither reclassification nor disclosure would be required if the likelihood of the acceleration of the due date was remote, such as if the lender historically has not accelerated due dates of loans containing similar clauses and the financial condition of the borrower is strong and its prospects are bright.

7.56 In other words, a long-term obligation could continue to be classified as noncurrent, unless it was probable it would be called. For an obligation that by its terms is short term, FASB ASC 470-10-55-1 states that a higher standard is required for a financing agreement that permits an entity to refinance a short-term obligation on a long-term basis than is required for an existing long-term loan for which early repayment might be requested. As discussed in paragraph 7.53, if a financing agreement that permits an entity to refinance a short-term obligation on a long-term basis contains a subjective acceleration clause, its mere presence is enough to preclude long-term classification.

Classification of Long-Term Debt With a Covenant Violation

7.57 Violations of covenants could cause termination of the financing agreement or demand for immediate repayment. Thus, debt covenant violations can affect the balance sheet classification.

7.58 Paragraphs 11–12 of FASB ASC 470-10-45 discuss the classification of long-term obligations that are callable by the creditor because the debtor's violation of a provision of the debt agreement at the balance sheet date either makes the obligation callable or may become callable because the violation, if not cured within a specified grace period, will make the obligation callable. Those paragraphs require that such callable obligations be classified as current liabilities, unless either of the two conditions in FASB ASC 470-10-45-11 is met.

7.59 In summary, those two conditions are as follows:

a. The creditor has waived or subsequently lost the right to demand repayment more than one year from the balance sheet date.

b. The long-term obligation contains a grace period within which the debtor may cure the violation, and it is probable that the violation will be cured within that period.

However, the conditions are complex, and the preceding summary is not intended as a substitute for reading paragraphs 11–12 of FASB ASC 470-10-45.

7.60 If neither of those two conditions is met, the debt is classified as short term, regardless of the fact that the creditor has not demanded repayment, and no indication exists that the creditor intends to do so within the next year. Further, no distinction between significant and insignificant violations should be drawn. That is the right of the creditor, and if the violation is considered insignificant by the creditor, the debtor should be able to obtain a waiver.

7.61 Paragraphs 2–6 of FASB ASC 470-10-55 provide examples of classification of long-term debt when a debt covenant violation at the balance sheet date is waived by a lender for a period greater than one year, but the entity must meet the covenant on a quarterly or semiannual basis.

Subsequent Events

7.62 Events occurring subsequent to the balance sheet date but before the financial statements are issued or available to be issued may need to be reflected in the financial statements, either by changing the balance sheet classification of the debt or by disclosure. For example, bond restructuring transactions occurring after the balance sheet date may have an effect on the debtor's current or noncurrent balance sheet classifications as of that balance sheet date, and extinguishing or modifying the terms of a bond issue may require disclosure. Chapter 3, "Unique Financial Statement Considerations for Not-for-Profit Health Care Entities," of this guide includes additional information about subsequent events, including a discussion of whether a health care entity evaluates subsequent events through the issuance date of the financial statements or the date that the financial statements are available to be issued.

Assets Limited as to Use

7.63 Debt-financing instruments may require either cash or investments, or both, to be set aside in special accounts that can only be used for debt-related purposes, such as unexpended proceeds of debt issues and funds deposited with a trustee and limited to use in accordance with the requirements of a bond indenture or similar document (for example, sinking funds, debt reserve funds, or defeasance-related escrows). Such assets are usually reported in the balance sheet caption "Assets Limited as to Use." The portion of assets whose use is limited (that is, required for liquidation of current liabilities) is reported as current assets, with the remainder reported as noncurrent assets.

Statement of Operations

7.64 If the proceeds of tax-exempt borrowings are externally restricted to the acquisition of specified qualifying assets or to service the related debt, the amount of interest cost capitalized should be determined in accordance with paragraphs 10–12 of FASB ASC 835-20-30. Those considerations are discussed in chapter 6, "Property and Equipment and Other Assets," of this guide.

7.65 Pursuant to FASB ASC 470-50-40-2, gains or losses on the extinguishment of debt should be recognized currently in income of the period of extinguishment and identified as a separate item. Paragraphs 2–7 of FASB ASC 225-20-45 provide the criteria that must be met for gains and losses from the extinguishment of debt to be classified as extraordinary items.

Disclosures

7.66 General disclosure requirements for debt, such as description of the debt, collateral, interest rate, covenants, and guarantees, are set forth in FASB ASC 470-10-50. If debt was considered to be extinguished by in-substance defeasance under the provisions of FASB Statement No. 76, *Extinguishment of Debt—an amendment of APB Opinion No. 26*, before the effective date of FASB Statement No. 125, *Accounting for Transfers and Servicing of Financial Assets and Extinguishments of Liabilities* (that is, before December 31, 1996), FASB ASC 470-40-50-1 requires disclosure of the amount of the debt and a description of the transaction as long as the debt remains outstanding. FASB ASC 860-30-50-2 provides disclosure requirements for assets that are set aside solely for the purpose of satisfying scheduled payments of a specific obligation.

7.67 If short-term obligations are classified in the balance sheet as a long-term liability because the health care entity has the ability and intent to refinance the debt on a long-term basis, as discussed in paragraph 7.51, those obligations need to be included in the disclosure of the combined aggregate amount of maturities and sinking fund requirements for all long-term borrowings that is required by FASB ASC 470-10-50-1. In those situations, the health care entity must ensure that disclosure is made of both the debt repayment schedule of the liquidity facility and the stated maturity of the bonds. This can be done by either (*a*) including one repayment schedule in the table and providing a narrative disclosure related to the other or (*b*) providing two tabular schedules (one for the liquidity facility payment schedule and the other based on the stated maturity of the bonds).

7.68 As discussed in paragraphs 7.06–.08, additional disclosures are required for entities defined as *public entities*. Generally, *public entities* are those that have debt or equity securities that trade in public markets. Because FASB ASC has multiple definitions for the term *public entity*, careful attention should be paid to such disclosure requirements to determine if their scope includes conduit bond obligors whose bonds trade in public markets.

7.69 Paragraphs 10–19 of FASB ASC 825-10-50 require that public entities disclose the fair value of all financial instruments, whether recognized or not recognized in the statement of financial position, for which it is practicable to estimate that value. The disclosure is also required of nonpublic entities if their assets are $100 million or more on the date of the financial statements or if they have derivative instruments.

7.70 As discussed in paragraphs 7.09–.11, some health care entities may utilize a credit enhancement to make their bonds more attractive to investors or to allow them to access the market at more favorable rates. FASB ASC 820-10-35-18A states that an entity should not include the effect of an inseparable third-party credit enhancement in the fair value measurement of the liability. For the issuer (obligor), the unit of accounting for a liability measured or disclosed at fair value does not include the third-party credit enhancement. Thus, when disclosing the fair value of debt obligations that have a third-party credit enhancement that is inseparable from the liability, such as bond insurance, the fair value measurement should consider only the credit standing of the health care entity, rather than the credit standing of the guarantor. If fair value is determined based on the prices at which the bonds are trading in markets, an adjustment needs to be made for the difference between the credit standing of the guarantor (on which the market trades are based) and the credit standing of the health care entity.

7.71 FASB ASC 855-10-55-2 cites the sale of a bond after the balance sheet date but before financial statements are issued or available to be issued as an example of an event that requires disclosure in the notes to the financial statements.

7.72 Other events occurring after the balance sheet date, such as failed auctions, potential or actual cancellation of a liquidity facility, defaults, or a mandatory tender of bonds may also need to be disclosed in the financial statements as subsequent events.

Obligated Group Reporting

7.73 Many debt agreements involving obligated groups require audited financial statements for the obligated group to use in the bond offering document and thereafter to the underwriters or bond repositories, or both, on an annual, on-going basis. Often, this special financial statement presentation will exclude entities otherwise required to be consolidated in a health care entity's general-purpose financial statements. Financial statements that exclude these entities are no longer a GAAP presentation, and AU section 623, *Special Reports* (AICPA, *Professional Standards*), requires that a special-purpose report must be issued that is restricted to use by specified parties.

7.74 Many obligated groups are required to annually submit audited financial statements to the Municipal Securities Rulemaking Board's (MSRB's) Electronic Municipal Market Access (EMMA) system, which is a system for disseminating the information to investors in municipal securities and other interested parties. See appendix A of this chapter for additional information. Because this system would make the obligated group financial statements broadly available, it is not appropriate to submit statements containing a restricted-use report. Paragraph .25 of AU section 623 states that a separate paragraph in a special-purpose report is not appropriate if the report and related financial presentation are to be filed with a regulatory agency, such as the SEC, and are to be included in a document, such as a prospectus, that is distributed to the general public. Instead, consolidating schedules presenting the obligated group as supplemental information to the consolidated financial statements may meet the requirements within the bond contract.

Interim Financial Reporting

7.75 Often, continuing disclosure agreements entered into by a health care entity in connection with municipal bond financings will require the entity to provide financial information to investors on both a quarterly and an annual basis. In such situations, the entity should consider the requirements of FASB ASC 270, *Interim Reporting*, which provides guidance on accounting and disclosure issues peculiar to interim reporting and sets forth minimum disclosure requirements for interim financial reports of publicly-traded companies. FASB ASC 270-10-50-3 states that it is presumed that users of summarized interim financial data will have read the latest published annual report, including the financial disclosures required by GAAP and management's commentary concerning the annual financial results, and that the summarized interim data will be viewed in that context.

7.76 FASB ASC 270-10-50-1 provides the minimum requirements for summarized financial information at interim dates, including reports on fourth quarters, presented by publicly-traded companies. In addition, FASB ASC 270-10-50-4 encourages publicly-traded companies to publish balance sheet and cash flow data at interim dates because this data often assists users of the interim financial information in their understanding and interpretation of the reported income data. If condensed interim balance sheet information or cash flow data is not presented at interim reporting dates, significant changes since the last reporting period with respect to liquid assets, net working capital, long-term liabilities, and stockholders' equity (net assets) should be disclosed.

Auditing

General

7.77 Auditing objectives and procedures for long-term debt issued by health care entities generally are similar to those of other entities. In obtaining sufficient appropriate audit evidence with respect to long-term debt, the auditor may consider the examples of specific auditing objectives, selected control activities, and auditing procedures that are presented in exhibit 7-1.

7.78 The amount, type, and classification of bonds in the financial statements is of interest to investors, bond rating agencies, and others who influence the supply of financial resources, such as financial guarantors. As discussed in the accounting sections of this chapter, many bond-related transactions and accounts involve special accounting measurement, presentation, and disclosure principles that require particular audit attention. The auditor should read financing instruments carefully to be sure that the financing is properly classified and described in the financial statements. Determining whether debt is considered long term or short term for accounting purposes has pervasive implications for financial reporting and compliance with debt covenants. Audit implications of certain other matters are highlighted subsequently, including compliance with debt covenants, credit-related triggers in debt agreements, and implications of transactions related to the issuance, remarketing, and refinancing of debt.

Covenants

7.79 The auditor should consider reviewing restrictive covenants of the various bond-related agreements to evaluate the health care entity's compliance with covenants and the appropriateness of the presentation and disclosure of covenants in the financial statements. A borrower's failure to comply with financial covenants may be a signal that the borrower is facing financial troubles and that the debt may become callable, changing the historical classification and disclosure requirements associated with its debt. If a default on a bond covenant has occurred, the auditor should evaluate the appropriateness of classification of debt as long term. If several types of financing are outstanding, the auditor should compare transactions in each type with the restrictions and provisions of the others. For example, some debt obligations contain a cross-default provision, which could result in acceleration of the lender's right of repayment because of default under, or violation of, other agreements. The existence of certain types of covenants can have implications for classification of the bonds, even in the absence of a covenant violation.

7.80 The auditor should obtain written waivers of conditions of noncompliance of debt covenants directly from the responsible lending officers or trustees. It is not appropriate for the auditor to rely solely on management's written or oral representations or representations from the client's legal counsel that lenders or trustees have waived the violations. In reviewing a waiver of debt covenant violations to determine whether the liability should be classified as current or long term, the auditor should obtain assurance that the waiver is unconditional for a period greater than one year from the balance sheet date and that it specifically and appropriately addresses each event of noncompliance.

7.81 Some covenants take the form of a subjective acceleration clause in which the creditor may accelerate the scheduled maturities of the obligation under conditions that are not objectively determinable (for example, if the debtor fails to maintain satisfactory operations or a material adverse change occurs). The mere presence of a subjective acceleration clause in a lending document has implications for balance sheet classification, even if it is not in danger of being triggered. In evaluating those implications, the auditor will need to carefully consider whether the underlying debt is considered long term or short term (see paragraphs 7.53 and 7.55–.56).

Credit Ratings

7.82 Credit rating downgrades of material counterparties to debt-related transactions of the health care entity can have implications for the entity's own credit standing. For example, if bonds are credit enhanced, the credit rating on the health care entity's bonds is based on the credit rating of the guarantor or letter of credit provider, rather than the financial stability of the health care entity itself. A downgrade in the credit rating of the credit enhancer will automatically trigger a downgrade of the rating on the health care entity's bonds, even if the health care entity's financial health has not deteriorated. Credit rating downgrades of others may trigger clauses in derivative agreements that result in the automatic termination of a swap, a demand presented to a health care entity for immediate payment of a swap liability, or a requirement for a health care entity to post collateral based on the downgrade of either the derivative counterparty (or its guarantor) or the health care entity.

Debt Restructuring

7.83 Changes in market conditions may cause health care entities to restructure their bonds in various ways. Some may seek to issue new bonds, to change the interest mode on existing bonds, or buy back their own bonds. In such situations, the auditor may be required to evaluate management's analysis of whether the transaction represented a modification of debt or an extinguishment. In addition, such actions may affect the balance sheet classification of the liabilities. A refinancing from long-term debt to short-term debt (for example, from fixed-rate or auction-rate bonds to variable-rate demand obligations) can potentially cause changes in the balance sheet classification and potentially trigger liquidity covenants. Debt restructuring may result in the discontinuation of hedge accounting for related interest rate swaps, which can also have bond covenant compliance implications.

7.84 An advance refunding transaction that results in defeasance may trigger the need for audit evidence supporting assertions of legal release from liabilities or legal isolation of escrowed assets. Although no direct auditing guidance regarding the form and content of a typical legal letter governing a legal defeasance exists, the principles outlined in Interpretation No. 1, "The Use of Legal Interpretations as Audit Evidence to Support Management's Assertion That a Transfer of Financial Assets Has Met the Isolation Criterion in Paragraphs 7–14 of Financial Accounting Standards Board *Accounting Standards Codification* 860-10-40," of AU section 336, *Using the Work of a Specialist* (AICPA, *Professional Standards*, AU sec. 9336 par. .01–.21), may be helpful in determining whether documentation obtained by the health care entity is adequate audit evidence that the debtor has been legally released as the primary obligor of the bonds. Based on the facts and circumstances of a particular defeasance transaction, in the auditor's judgment, a legal opinion obtained by the health care entity may be needed as audit evidence to support the assertion that the assets transferred to the defeasance escrow trust have met the isolation criterion discussed in paragraph 7.26.

7.85 Some bonds (for example, variable-rate demand obligations) may involve the use of remarketing agreements and backup liquidity facilities. Failed remarketings and resulting draws upon liquidity facilities may create or exacerbate liquidity problems for a health care entity. As discussed in paragraph 7.37, if a significant amount of bonds are tendered and ultimately become bank bonds, the health care entity must repay those obligations based on the much shorter debt repayment schedule of the liquidity facility, rather than the expected maturity of the bonds. In some cases, the financial viability of the liquidity provider may be in question. The implications of such matters should be considered when assessing debt covenant compliance, liquidity, and going concern.

Auditor Association With Disclosure Documents

7.86 Because no SEC requirement exists for auditor association with official statements in municipal securities offerings, an auditor generally is not required to participate in, or undertake any procedures with respect to, a client's official statement.[4] However, when an auditor becomes associated with the official statement, as discussed subsequently, AU section 550A, *Other Information in Documents Containing Audited Financial Statements* (AICPA, *Professional Standards*), provides requirements and guidance on the auditor's responsibilities for information in those official statements other than the financial statements covered by the auditor's opinion[†] (see the overview of the provisions of AU section 550A in paragraph 7.89). The following are the situations in which the auditor becomes associated with the official statement:

- Assisting in preparing the financial information[5] included in the official statement
- Reviewing a draft of the official statement at the client's request
- Manually or electronically signing the independent auditor's report for inclusion in a specific official statement[6]
- Providing written agreement (for example, through a consent letter or signed authorization form) for the use of the independent auditor's report in a specific official statement (see paragraphs 7.92–.96)
- Providing a revised independent auditor's report[7] for inclusion in a specific official statement

---

[4] Some auditors require that they become associated with a health care entity's official statements, even though the conditions described in this paragraph establishing association would not otherwise exist. See the discussion in paragraph 7.87.

[†] In February 2010, the Auditing Standards Board issued Statement on Auditing Standards (SAS) No. 118, *Other Information in Documents Containing Audited Financial Statements* (AICPA, *Professional Standards*, AU sec. 550). This SAS will supersede AU section 550A, *Other Information in Documents Containing Audited Financial Statements* (AICPA, *Professional Standards*). SAS No. 118 is effective for audits of financial statements for periods beginning on or after December 15, 2010. Early application is permitted. Appendix E, "Other Information, Supplementary Information, and Required Supplementary Information," of this guide provides additional information on SAS No. 118.

[5] For the purpose of this requirement, financial information does not include the financial statements covered by the auditor's opinion or, for governmental health care entities, the required supplementary information (RSI) or supplementary information, other than RSI accompanying those financial statements that the auditor has already considered during the audit of the financial statements.

[6] This situation involves an original manual or electronic signature on the auditor's report, not a reproduction of an auditor's report that was manually or electronically signed. For example, the underwriter or bond counsel may require a copy of the auditor's report with an original manual or electronic signature to file with the official closing documents for the offering.

[7] A revised report would, for example, eliminate the references made by the auditor in the original report to audits and reports required by *Government Auditing Standards* (GAS), which is issued by the Comptroller General of the United States. See the discussion in paragraph 7.96.

- Issuing a comfort letter, as described in paragraph .09 of AU section 634, *Letters for Underwriters and Certain Other Requesting Parties* (AICPA, *Professional Standards*), or an attestation engagement report in lieu of a comfort or similar letter on information included in the official statement (see paragraphs 7.98–.101)
- Issuing a report on an attestation engagement relating to the debt offering (see paragraph 7.103)

7.87 Although an auditor is not required to become associated with a client's official statements, except in the situations described in paragraph 7.86, some auditors include a provision in the terms of the engagement requiring the client to obtain permission from the auditor before using the independent auditor's report in the official statement. Such a provision may be used by the auditor to establish a requirement that the auditor become associated with the client's official statements when the client requests the required permission from the auditor.

7.88 When the auditor and client agree not to include a provision in the terms of the engagement that would require auditor association, as discussed in paragraph 7.86, the auditor may include in the terms of the engagement a requirement that any official statements issued by the client with which the auditor is not associated clearly indicate that the auditor is not associated with the contents of such official statements. Such a disclosure could read as follows: "[*Name of firm*], our independent auditor, has not been engaged to perform and has not performed, since the date of its report included herein, any procedures on the financial statements addressed in that report. [*Name of firm*] also has not performed any procedures relating to this official statement."

7.89 If the auditor is associated with an official statement, the guidance in paragraphs .04–.06 of AU section 550A provides that the auditor has no obligation to perform any procedures to corroborate other information[8] contained in those documents. However, the auditor should read the other information and consider whether that information or the manner of its presentation is materially inconsistent with information or the manner of its presentation appearing in the financial statements. AU section 550A provides guidance if the auditor concludes that a material inconsistency or material misstatement of fact exists that is not a material inconsistency.[‡]

7.90 AU section 380, *The Auditor's Communication With Those Charged With Governance* (AICPA, *Professional Standards*), states that the auditor should determine that certain significant and relevant financial statement audit-related matters are communicated orally or in writing to those charged with governance of the entity. AU section 380 states that the auditor should discuss his or her responsibility for other information in documents containing audited financial statements, any procedures performed, and the results. That requirement pertains to the financial statements currently being issued and, thus, would not apply retroactively to official statements. However, that communication could supply that information for official statements issued during the current audit period and through the auditor's report date, regardless of whether the auditor was associated with those official statements.

---

[8] *Other information* is a term used in AU section 550, *Other Information in Documents Containing Audited Financial Statements* (AICPA, *Professional Standards*), and is defined therein as information in addition to audited financial statements and the independent auditor's report thereon.

[‡] See footnote †.

7.91 The auditor is not required to participate in, or undertake any procedures with respect to, a client's continuing disclosure documents, even though they may include audited financial statements. A client's continuing disclosures are not required to be submitted to, or disseminated from, the distributing organizations as a single document. Thus, an auditor's association with other information encompassed by such disclosures cannot be clearly established. Therefore, the provisions of AU section 550A do not apply to documents that contain those disclosures.[||] Any attention that the auditor devotes to other information included with audited financial statements in continuing disclosure documents at the client's request should be considered a consulting engagement under the provisions of Statement on Standards for Consulting Services No. 1, *Consulting Services: Definitions and Standards* (AICPA, *Professional Standards*, CS sec. 100).

7.92 The AICPA has issued interpretations to AU section 711, *Filings Under Federal Securities Statutes* (AICPA, *Professional Standards*), that address the auditor's agreement[9] to (*a*) being named and (*b*) the use of an auditor's report in an offering document other than one registered under the Securities Act of 1933 (the 1933 Act).[10]

7.93 Interpretation No. 2, "Consenting to Be Named as an Expert in an Offering Document in Connection With Securities Offerings Other Than Those Registered Under the Securities Act of 1933," of AU section 711 (AICPA, *Professional Standards*, AU sec. 9711 par. .12–.15), states that when a client wishes to make reference to the auditor's role in an offering document in connection with a securities offering that is not registered under the 1933 Act, the caption "Independent Auditors" should be used to title that section of the document; the caption "Experts" should not be used nor should the auditor be referred to as an expert anywhere in the document. The following paragraph should be used to describe the auditor's role:[11]

Independent Auditors

> The financial statements as of December 31, 20XX, and for the year then ended, included in this [*name of document*], have been audited by ABC, independent auditor, as stated in its report(s) appearing herein.

If the client refuses to delete from the offering document the reference to the auditor as an expert, then the auditor should not permit inclusion of the auditor's report in the offering document.

7.94 Interpretation No. 3, "Consenting to the Use of an Audit Report in an Offering Document Other Than One Registered Under the Securities Act of 1933," of AU section 711 (AICPA, *Professional Standards*, AU sec. 9711 par. .16–.17), states that the auditor is not required to but may provide an agreement to the inclusion of the auditor's report in an offering document

---

|| See footnote †.

9 The term *consent* is a Securities and Exchange Commission (SEC) term that relates to registered securities, and municipal securities are not registered securities. Therefore, this guide uses the term *agreement*, even though the AICPA interpretations refer to *consent*.

10 As discussed in the glossary, an official statement is not considered to be an offering document registered under the Securities Act of 1933.

11 As discussed in paragraph 7.88, if the auditor is not associated with the offering document, and the terms of the engagement require disclosure of this fact, additional disclosure similar to that illustrated in paragraph 7.88 should be included here.

other than one registered under the 1933 Act. The interpretation provides the following example language that the auditor may use:

> We agree to the inclusion in this [*name of document*] of our report, dated February 5, 20XX, on our audit of the financial statements of [*name of entity*].

7.95 When the auditor is asked to issue a letter agreeing to the inclusion of the auditor's report in the offering document, the effective date of the letter can be the preliminary official statement date or the official statement date, as defined in paragraph 7.13.

Independent Accountants' Reports Included in an Official Statement

7.96 If the auditor is associated with a client's official statement, he or she should consider which auditors' reports the client presents in the official statement. The official statement should not include the reports required by *Government Auditing Standards* (GAS), which is issued by the Comptroller General of the United States, because those reports are restricted-use reports under the provisions of AU section 532, *Restricting the Use of an Auditor's Report* (AICPA, *Professional Standards*). Further, it generally is advisable for the official statements to use an auditor's report on the financial statements that does not refer to the GAS audit or those reports because those references, without the presentation of the reports in the official statements, could confuse the users of the official statement.

Independent Accountants' Reports Included on a Continuing Disclosure Website

7.97 Many obligated groups are required to annually submit audited financial statements to the MSRB's EMMA system. When obligated group financial statements exclude entities that are required under GAAP to be consolidated, the accountants' reports should restrict the use of the financial statements to specified parties. Because inclusion in the EMMA system of financial statements for such an obligated group would make those financial statements broadly available, it is not appropriate to submit financial statements containing a restricted-use report (see paragraph 7.74). Instead, consolidating schedules presenting the obligated group as supplemental information to the consolidated financial statements may meet the requirements within the bond contract.

Letters for Underwriters[#]

7.98 Underwriting agreements between a health care entity and its underwriters may require the auditor to prepare a comfort letter addressed to the underwriters. AU section 634 defines the term *underwriters* and gives guidance to auditors[12] in providing letters to underwriters and certain other requesting parties in connection with the offering or placement of securities. An auditor may provide a comfort letter to a broker-dealer or other financial intermediary acting as principal or agent in offerings of securities that are exempt from

[#] In July 2010, the AICPA issued an exposure draft of a proposed SAS, *Letters for Underwriters and Certain Other Requesting Parties* (Redrafted), which would supersede the guidance in AU section 634, *Letters for Underwriters and Certain Other Requesting Parties* (AICPA, *Professional Standards*). This guide will be revised as necessary upon issuance of a final standard.

[12] Because of its use in SEC literature, certain auditing literature uses the term *accountant* to refer to the auditor; however, this chapter replaces the term *accountant* with the term *auditor*.

registration under the 1933 Act only if the broker-dealer or other financial intermediary provides the required representation letter described in paragraph .06 of AU section 634.

7.99 When a party requesting a comfort letter has provided the auditor with the required representation letter, the auditor should refer to the requesting party's representations in the comfort letter. See example P in paragraph .64 of AU section 634, which is a typical comfort letter in a non-1933 Act offering, including the required underwriter representations. If the required representation letter is not provided by the broker-dealer or other financial intermediary, paragraph .09 of AU section 634 provides requirements and guidance for auditors.

7.100 As discussed in paragraph .10 of AU section 634, when a comfort letter is requested by a party other than the underwriter, broker-dealer, or other financial intermediary, the auditor should not provide that party with a comfort letter or the letter described in paragraph .09 of AU section 634. Instead, the auditor may provide the party with a report on agreed-upon procedures and should refer to AT section 201, *Agreed-Upon Procedures Engagements* (AICPA, *Professional Standards*), for additional specific guidance. See paragraphs .06–.10 of AU section 634 for further discussion.

7.101 Auditors may be asked to comment upon information other than audited financial statements. Guidance for the procedures to be performed and the form of the comments is provided by the following paragraphs of AU section 634:

a. Unaudited condensed interim financial information (paragraphs .36–.38)

b. Capsule financial information (paragraphs .36 and .39–.41)

c. Pro forma financial information (paragraphs .42–.43)

d. Financial forecasts (paragraphs .36 and .44)

e. Changes in capital stock, increases in long-term debt, and decreases in other specified financial statement items (paragraphs .36 and .45–.53)

f. Tables and statistics (paragraphs .54–.60)

7.102 When the auditor is asked to prepare a letter for the underwriter, the letter can be as of the preliminary official statement date or the official statement date, as defined in paragraph 7.13, with updating letters issued as of the official statement date, if applicable, and the closing date. Paragraph .23 of AU section 634 states that the underwriting agreement ordinarily specifies the date, often referred to as the cutoff date, to which certain procedures described in the letter are to relate (for example, a date five days before the date of the letter). The letter should state that the inquiries and other procedures described in the letter did not cover the period from the cutoff date to the date of the letter. The five-day cutoff period in AU section 634 is illustrative only and does not set a standard, but practice generally does not exceed a five-day cutoff period.

Attestation Engagements Related to Securities Issuance

7.103 During the process of issuing municipal securities, health care entities or other involved parties often engage practitioners to provide certain needed information. For example, a health care entity or its bond counsel may engage an auditor to review the health care entity's compliance with the revenue coverage requirements on outstanding bonds or to verify the calculation of escrow account requirements for an advance refunding of bonds. Those engagements should be conducted in accordance with AT section 201.[13] If the auditor of the financial statements included in the official statement also provides an attestation engagement report relating to a debt offering, that establishes an association with the official statement, as indicated in paragraph 7.86. An attestation engagement report relating to a debt offering need not be referred to or included in the official statement to associate the auditor of the financial statements with the official statement. Sometimes, the attestation engagement report may only be included in the official closing documents for the offering. Also, if the practitioner providing the attestation engagement report is not the auditor of the financial statements included in the official statements, the issuance of the attestation engagement report does not, by itself, associate either the auditor of the financial statements or the practitioner who issued the attestation report with the official statement.

---

[13] Generally, these attestation engagements are performed only in accordance with the AICPA's Statements on Standards for Attestation Engagements. However, if the auditor is performing the engagement in accordance with GAS, the auditor should apply the guidance of GAS, including chapter 6, "General, Field Work, and Reporting Standards for Attestation Engagements." The auditor also should consider the guidance in Interpretation No. 6, "Reporting on Attestation Engagements Performed in Accordance With *Government Auditing Standards*," of AT section 101, *Attest Engagements* (AICPA, *Professional Standards*, AT sec. 9101 par. .56–.58), which explains how an attestation report should be modified when the engagement is performed in accordance with GAS and provides an illustrative attestation report.

Exhibit 7-1

The following table illustrates the use of assertions in developing audit objectives and designing substantive tests. The examples are not intended to be all-inclusive nor is it expected that all the procedures would necessarily be applied in an audit. The auditor should design and perform substantive procedures for all relevant assertions related to each material class of transactions, account balance, and disclosure to obtain sufficient appropriate audit evidence. The use of assertions in assessing risks and designing appropriate audit procedures to obtain audit evidence is described in paragraphs .14–.26 of AU section 326, *Audit Evidence* (AICPA, *Professional Standards*). Various audit procedures and the purposes for which they may be performed are described in paragraphs .27–.41 of AU section 326.

Auditing Considerations

Financial Statement Assertions	*Specific Auditing Objectives*	*Selected Control Activities*	*Auditing Procedures*
Bonds Payable			
Presentation and disclosure	Bond liabilities are properly classified in the financial statements, and related disclosures are adequate.	Procedures ensure that the health care entity appropriately classifies debt based on its terms and monitors its compliance with restrictive debt covenants.	Review the terms of the bond indenture for the presence of any put options. Review the terms of lines of credit or other liquidity facilities underlying puttable bonds. Review the debt instruments for the presence of any restrictive debt covenants, including subjective acceleration clauses and cross-default provisions. Test compliance with restrictive debt covenants.

7.104

Appendix A—Municipal Securities Regulation

A-1 Currently, municipal securities are exempt from all the provisions of the Securities Act of 1933 (the 1933 Act) and the Securities Exchange Act of 1934 (the 1934 Act), except the antifraud provisions of Section 17(a) of the 1933 Act and Section 10(b) of the 1934 Act and the associated Securities and Exchange Commission (SEC) Rule 10b-5. Those antifraud provisions prohibit any person from misrepresenting or omitting material facts in the offering or sale of securities. Instances of the application of the antifraud provisions in SEC enforcement actions offer guidance within the context of actual transactions.

A-2 The SEC published its views with respect to the disclosure obligations of participants in the municipal securities markets under the antifraud provisions of the federal securities laws in its 1994 Release No. 33-7049, *Statement of the Commission Regarding Disclosure Obligations of Municipal Securities Issuers and Others*. In it, the SEC reviews numerous municipal disclosure practices needing improvement in light of the antifraud provisions.

A-3 SEC Rule 15c2-12 and associated SEC releases impose certain requirements on the underwriters of municipal securities.[1] Because of Rule 15c2-12, obligors of most municipal securities offerings over set dollar amounts must provide certain disclosure documents when issuing securities (primary market disclosures), as well as at certain times thereafter (referred to as continuing disclosures or secondary market disclosures). Primary market disclosures are made by issuing an official statement. Secondary market disclosures consist of (*a*) annual continuing disclosures as contractually established and (*b*) material events notices. Both primary and secondary market disclosure documents are available through the nationally-recognized municipal securities information repository known as the Electronic Municipal Market Access (EMMA) system and state information depositories, if one exists in the obligor's state.

SEC's Office of Municipal Securities

A-4 The Office of Municipal Securities (OMS), which is located in the Division of Trading and Markets, coordinates the SEC's municipal securities activities, advises the SEC on policy matters relating to the municipal bond market, and provides technical assistance in the development and implementation of major SEC initiatives in the municipal securities area. In addition, the OMS assists the Division of Enforcement and other SEC offices and divisions on a wide array of municipal securities matters. The OMS works closely with the municipal securities industry to educate state and local officials and conduit borrowers about risk-management issues and foster a thorough understanding of the SEC's policies. The OMS also maintains a website of helpful information specifically directed to municipal securities issues and conduit obligors (www.sec.gov/info/ municipal.shtml).

Secondary Market Disclosure Requirements

A-5 In 1994, as a condition of the issuance of debt securities, the SEC issued rules requiring that the obligor agree to implement a system of continuing disclosure that remains in effect as long as the bonds are outstanding. The core

---

[1] For the adopting release, see www.sec.gov/rules/final/adpt6.txt. For the text of Rule 15c2-12, see www.law.uc.edu/CCL/34ActRls/rule15c2-12.html.

of this system is the continuing disclosure agreement (sometimes referred to as a 15c2-12 contract or 15c2-12 agreement). This is a covenant entered into by the obligor in which the obligor agrees to provide certain specified information to bondholders and beneficial owners throughout the life of the bond issue. The terms of the obligor's continuing disclosure agreement are spelled out in the indenture or bond resolution and also are summarized in the official statement.

A-6 The system is much less prescriptive than the system of periodic reporting required of publicly-traded companies. The primary elements are (*a*) annual reporting of financial and operating information and (*b*) material events reporting. Quarterly reporting is encouraged but not required, unless agreed to in the continuing disclosure covenant for a particular issue.

A-7 Similar to Form 10-K, no prescribed reporting format exists for submission of the annual financial and operating information. The specific list of items to be included in the annual report will be agreed upon by the parties to the financing transaction and enumerated in the continuing disclosure agreement and an appendix to the official statement. Usually, it consists largely of audited financial statements and updates of specified categories of financial information and operating data or specific sections and charts in the final official statements.

A-8 Unlike Form 10-K filings, no statutory due date exists for filing annual financial information. Instead, the filing deadline is contractually agreed to in the continuing disclosure agreement. If an obligor fails to file information by the agreed-upon deadline and subsequently issues an official statement for new bonds, it must disclose its failure to file in that official statement. Failure to disclose this information constitutes a material omission in the official statement.

A-9 The annual report does not have to be submitted all at once in a single document; it may be submitted as a single document or separate documents comprising a package.

A-10 Similar to Form 8-K filings, the continuing disclosure agreement also requires the obligor to file disclosures related to significant events within 10 days of their occurrence.[*] The following events are required disclosures:

- Principal and interest payment delinquencies
- Unscheduled draws on debt service reserves reflecting financial difficulties
- Unscheduled draws on credit enhancements reflecting financial difficulties
- Substitution of credit or liquidity providers or their failure to perform
- Adverse tax opinions or events affecting the tax status of the security
- Defeasances
- Rating changes
- Tender offers
- Bankruptcy, insolvency, receivership, or similar event of the obligated person

---

[*] Readers can view Rule 15c2-12 in its entirety at www.sec.gov/rules/final/2010/34-62184afr.pdf.

- Notices of failure to provide annual financial information on or before the date specified on the continuing disclosure agreement

The following events must be disclosed, if material:

- Appointment of successor or additional trustees or the change of name of a trustee
- Nonpayment-related defaults
- Modifications to rights of security holders
- Bond calls
- Matters affecting collateral (for example, release, substitution, or sale of property securing repayment of the securities)
- Consummation of a merger, consolidation or acquisition involving an obligated person, or the sale of substantially all the assets of an obligated person, other than in the ordinary course of business; the entry into definitive agreements to undertake such an action; or the termination of an agreement as it relates to any such sale, other than pursuant to its terms

EMMA System

A-11 Effective July 1, 2009, EMMA became the nationally recognized municipal securities information repository for filing annual reports, material event notices, and voluntarily-submitted information. EMMA is an Internet-based centralized database that provides free public access to disclosure and transaction information about municipal bonds to the municipal market. EMMA also provides access to official statements, advance refunding documents, real-time trade and historical trade information, daily market information, and other educational materials about municipal bonds. Essentially, EMMA makes municipal disclosure information available to the market in a manner similar to the SEC's Electronic Data Gathering, Analysis, and Retrieval system for the disclosures of publicly-traded companies. Rule 15c2-12 requires all continuing disclosure information to be filed using EMMA. EMMA's website is www.emma.msrb.org. The SEC release concerning this amendment to Rule 15c2-12 is available at www.sec.gov/rules/sro/msrb/2008/34-59061.pdf.

Chapter 8

Contingencies and Other Liabilities

8.01 Health care entities are similar to other industries, recording liabilities associated with accounts payable; salaries and payroll taxes; deferred revenue; commitments and contingencies; and other accruals for pension or profit sharing contributions, compensated absences, and income and other taxes. This chapter considers those liabilities that are not discussed elsewhere in this guide. This chapter also discusses certain tax considerations relevant to not-for-profit entities.

Contingencies and Commitments

8.02 Self-insured obligations, other contingencies, and commitments may include the following:

a. Losses arising from medical malpractice, worker's compensation, and other self-insured claims

b. Contingencies related to risk contracting

c. Construction contract commitments

d. Commitments and guarantees that include contractual agreements with physicians, specialists, and others who perform services by agreement with health care entities

e. Losses arising from litigation and other regulatory matters, such as Medicare and Medicaid fraud and abuse settlements

The Essentials of Recognition, Measurement, and Disclosure for Contingencies

8.03 The following locations provide the primary standards for contingencies and commitments:

- Financial Accounting Standards Board (FASB) *Accounting Standards Codification* (ASC) 440, *Commitments*, which provides general guidance regarding commitments such as those for plant acquisition; unused letters of credit; and obligations to reduce debts, maintain working capital, or restrict dividends
- FASB ASC 450, *Contingencies*, which provides general guidance regarding loss contingencies
- FASB ASC 460, *Guarantees*, which provides general guidance regarding guarantees, including minimum revenue guarantees and guarantees of the indebtedness of others
- FASB ASC 275, *Risks and Uncertainties*, which provides general guidance regarding disclosure of certain significant risks and uncertainties

8.04 FASB ASC 450-20-25 states that when it is probable that a loss has been incurred, and the available information indicates that the loss is within a range of amounts, it follows that some amount of loss has occurred and can be reasonably estimated, and the loss should be recognized. According to FASB ASC 450-20-30-1, if some amount within a range of loss appears at the time to be a better estimate than any other amount within the range, that amount should be accrued. However, when no amount within the range is a better estimate than any other amount, the minimum amount in the range should be accrued. FASB ASC 450-20-50-3 requires that disclosure of the contingency be made if at least a reasonable possibility exists that a loss or an additional loss may have been incurred, and either an exposure to loss exists in excess of the accrued amount or an accrual is not made for a loss contingency because any of the conditions in FASB ASC 450-20-25-2 are not met.

8.05 According to FASB ASC 954-450-35-1, estimated losses are reviewed and changed, if necessary, at each reporting date. The amounts of the changes are recognized currently as additional expense or a reduction of expense.

8.06 Consistent with the guidance in FASB ASC 210-10-45-6, accrued unpaid claims and expenses that are expected to be paid during the normal operating cycle (generally within one year of the date of the financial statements) are classified as current liabilities. All other accrued unpaid claims and expenses are classified as noncurrent liabilities.

Recognition of Insurance Recoveries

8.07 The amount of a contingency should be determined independently from any potential claim for recovery, and an asset relating to the recovery may be recognized only when realization of the claim for recovery is deemed probable.

8.08 In accordance with FASB ASC 954-450-25-2, the liability for malpractice or similar claims should not be presented net of anticipated insurance recoveries. Per FASB ASC 954-450-25-2, to the extent that an entity is indemnified for those liabilities, the entity should recognize an insurance receivable at the same time that it recognizes the liability, measured on the same basis as the liability and subject to the need for a valuation allowance for uncollectible amounts. Per FASB ASC 720-20-25-5, if a purchased insurance contract includes coverage for legal and other costs, the accounting for those costs should be consistent between the asset and liability. If the entity's accounting policy is to accrue legal and other costs, then the insurance receivable should reflect those costs if they are covered under the terms of the insurance policy. If an entity's accounting policy is not to accrue for those costs, then the insurance receivable should not reflect those costs on an accrual basis. FASB ASC 954-720-25-1 states that insurance recoveries from a retrospectively-rated insurance policy whose ultimate premium is based primarily on the health care entity's loss experience should not be recognized until the estimated losses exceed the stipulated maximum premium.

Managing Risk of Loss

8.09 Health care entities typically use commercial insurance to manage some portion of the risk of loss from medical malpractice, workers' compensation, and employee health claims. However, as the cost of commercial insurance has continued to rise, many health care entities are managing their risk through higher deductibles, self-insured retentions, retrospective premiums, and reduced or no coverage under their insurance policies. In some cases, a health care entity will form its own insurance company, known as a captive insurance company, to manage its risk. It is important for the health care entity to identify its risk and the portion of that risk that is insured. Generally, a health care entity uses actuaries to assist in identifying and quantifying the retained risk. An assessment of the risk that is insured is necessary for the determination of anticipated insurance recoveries.

8.10 Insurance policies may be issued on either an occurrence basis or a claims-made basis. Occurrence basis policies provide coverage for insured events occurring during the contract period, regardless of the length of time that passes before the insurance company is notified of the claim. A claims-made policy only covers claims reported to the insurer during the contract period; however, in practice, claims-made policies generally cover claims reported to either the insurer or insured during the contract period. As a result, claims might be reported to the insurer after the contract expires. Even if claims have been reported to the insurer during the contract period, it may take several months for the insurer to investigate and establish a case reserve for reported claims. In practice, most claims-made insurance policies contain extended reporting clauses or endorsements that, in specified circumstances, provide for coverage of claims occurring during the contract period but reported after the expiration of the policy.

8.11 Although paragraphs 8.12–.44 provide specific guidance relating to accounting for medical malpractice, the guidance may be helpful in accounting for other self-insured liabilities, including workers' compensation and employee health insurance.

Medical Malpractice

8.12 According to FASB ASC 954-450-25-2, a health care entity should evaluate its exposure to losses arising from claims and record a liability, if appropriate. The provisions in FASB ASC 720-20-25 and 944-40 discuss the accounting for insurance claims costs, including estimates of costs relating to incurred-but-not-reported (IBNR) claims. The liability should not be presented net of anticipated insurance recoveries. See paragraph 8.08 for additional information about insurance recoveries.

8.13 In determining the best estimates of the ultimate costs of malpractice claims, health care entities should consider the guidance for contingencies in FASB ASC 450-20 and 954-450. Health care entities should take into consideration how malpractice claims develop over time (for example, the fact that some claims require a number of years before they are settled). FASB ASC 944-40 discusses accounting for claims costs, including estimates of costs relating to IBNR claims. Although health care entities are not required to apply the guidance in FASB ASC 944-40, that guidance may be helpful in estimating loss liabilities. Governmental health care entities should also consider the accounting and disclosure requirements of Governmental Accounting Standards Board Statement No. 10, *Accounting and Financial Reporting for Risk Financing and Related Insurance Issues*, as amended.

8.14 According to FASB ASC 954-450-25-2, the ultimate costs of malpractice claims, which include costs associated with litigating or settling claims, should be accrued when the incidents that give rise to the claims occur. FASB ASC 954-450-30-1 states that estimated losses from asserted and unasserted medical malpractice claims should be accrued either individually or on a group basis, based on the best estimates of the ultimate costs of the claims and the relationship of past reported incidents to eventual claims payments. The accrual includes an estimate of the losses that will result from unreported incidents, which are probable of having occurred before the end of the reporting period. All relevant information, including industry experience, the entity's own historical experience, the entity's existing asserted claims, and reported incidents should be used in estimating the expected amount of claims.

8.15 FASB ASC 954-450-30-2 states that in estimating losses from malpractice claims, a health care entity may need to modify data drawn from industry experience, so it is relevant to developing an estimate that is specific to the entity. Various factors, such as the nature of operations, size, and the entity's past experience, are considered in assessing comparability. Further, industry data that is not current may not be relevant.

8.16 According to FASB ASC 954-720-25-3, an accrual for malpractice losses should be based on estimated ultimate losses and costs associated with litigating and settling claims.

8.17 FASB ASC 954-450-25-2A indicates that accruals should not be based on recommended funding amounts, which in addition to a provision for the actuarially-determined liability may also include a provision for (*a*) credit for investment income and (*b*) an excess margin for risk of adverse deviation. FASB ASC 954-450-25-2B provides the following examples of factors to consider and adjustments that may be required to convert actuarially-determined malpractice funding amounts to an appropriate loss accrual to be reported in the financial statements:

- The risk of adverse deviation is an additional cost factor applied to bring a funding requirement to a selected confidence level. This factor does not meet the criteria for recognition as a liability in accordance with FASB ASC 450.
- An evaluation should be made of the extent and validity of industry data when the credibility factor actuarial technique is used. The lower the credibility factor, the greater the blending of industry data. This may create an unacceptable level of industry data at lower confidence levels. Further, a low credibility factor may indicate that provider-specific data is not sufficient to support the claims liability estimation process.
- A review of the discounting approach that is used is necessary to develop the required disclosure. The impact on the discounting calculation of any other adjustment made to the actuarially-determined amounts, such as risk of adverse deviation or the credibility of the risk-management system, has to be evaluated.
- A review of the expenses included in the loss estimation process should be made. Such expenses include the expense of settlement and litigation (that is, allocated loss-adjustment expenses).

8.18 Limitations on the availability of provider-specific data, lack of a sufficient patient population for claims projection purposes, a very low credibility factor, and a variety of other factors may cause the actuary's estimate of loss to be of limited value in developing an estimate of the liability under generally accepted accounting principles (GAAP).

8.19 According to FASB ASC 954-450-30-2, in estimating the probability that unreported incidents have occurred, some health care entities may develop a range of possible estimates of the number of unreported incidents, including zero. However, the greater the volume of a health care entity's operations, the greater the likelihood that the entity's minimum estimate of the number of probable unreported incidents will be greater than zero.

8.20 If a health care entity cannot estimate losses from asserted or unasserted malpractice claims, and therefore, an accrual is not made, FASB ASC 450-20-50-3 requires disclosure of the contingency if at least a reasonable possibility exists that a loss or an additional loss may have been incurred.

8.21 Further guidance about specific risk-management approaches is provided as follows:

- Policies written by captive insurance companies are discussed in paragraphs 8.27–.30.
- Claims-made insurance policies are discussed in paragraphs 8.31–.33.
- Retrospectively-rated insurance policies are discussed in paragraphs 8.34–.40.
- Self-funded trust funds are discussed in paragraphs 8.41–.44

Discounting of Medical Malpractice Liabilities

8.22 The Financial Reporting Executive Committee (FinREC) believes that the accrued liabilities for medical malpractice claims may be discounted to reflect the time value of money if all of the following are true: (*a*) the amount of the liability, individually or in the aggregate, is fixed or reliably determinable; (*b*) the amount and timing of cash payments for the liability, individually or in the aggregate, based on the health care entity's specific experience, are fixed or reliably determinable; and (*c*) expected insurance recoveries, if any, are also discounted. FASB Concepts Statement No. 7, *Using Cash Flow Information and Present Value in Accounting Measurements*, provides a useful discussion of general principles governing the use of present value and the objective of present value in accounting measurements. FASB Concepts Statements are not sources of established accounting principles; thus, they do not amend, modify, or justify a change from GAAP currently in effect.

8.23 The objective of discounting loss reserves is to account for the time value of money in a way that accurately reflects the anticipated future cash flows based on the characteristics of the obligation. Reasonable diversity exists regarding what rates should be used for discounting liabilities for unpaid claims and claim adjustment expenses and how they are applied. If an entity decides to discount, it might analogize to the following guidance in determining an appropriate discount rate:

- FASB ASC 340-30-35-6 states that for the insurer or assuming entity, the discount rate used to determine the deposit liability should be the current rate on U.S. government obligations with similar cash flow characteristics.
- FASB ASC 450-20-S99-1 states that the rate used to discount the cash payments should be the rate that will produce an amount at which the environmental or product liability could be settled in an arm's-length transaction with a third party. Statement of Position (SOP) 96-1, *Environmental Remediation Liabilities*, further states that the discount rate used to discount the cash payments should not exceed the interest rate on monetary assets that are essentially risk free, as described in FASB Concepts Statement No. 7, and have maturities comparable to that of the environmental or product liability.

- FASB ASC 944-20-S99-1 notes that pending authoritative guidance resulting from those efforts, the Securities and Exchange Commission staff will raise no objection if a registrant follows a policy for GAAP reporting purposes of discounting liabilities for unpaid claims and claim adjustment expenses at the same rate that it uses for reporting to state regulatory authorities with respect to the same claim liabilities.

8.24 Careful consideration of the facts and circumstances surrounding a change in the discount rate for the liabilities for unpaid claims is needed to determine the proper accounting for the change (change in accounting principle or change in accounting estimate). A change from not discounting loss reserves to discounting loss reserves would generally be a change in accounting principle.

8.25 FASB ASC 954-450-50-2 requires that health care entities that discount accrued malpractice claims disclose in the notes to the financial statements the carrying amount of accrued malpractice claims that are discounted in the financial statements and the interest rate(s) used to discount those claims.

8.26 FinREC recommends that a health care entity that discounts accrued malpractice claims also disclose the following information: (*a*) its policy concerning the timing of recognition of insurance recoveries; (*b*) its policy for discounting accrued malpractice claims and, if it has any, recognized insurance recoveries; (*c*) the interest rate(s) used to discount its insurance recoveries receivable; and (*d*) the undiscounted amount of accrued malpractice claims that are discounted in the financial statements.

Captive Insurance Companies

8.27 Health care entities may be insured by wholly-owned or multiprovider captive insurance companies. See chapter 12, "The Reporting Entity and Related Entities," of this guide for a discussion of considerations related to consolidation and the use of the equity method for equity interests, including equity interests in captive insurance companies.

8.28 The economic substance of the terms of an insurance policy with a captive insurance company may more closely resemble a claims-funding mechanism than an instrument that provides rights for recovery of loss from an external third party. The health care entity should consider whether the economic substance of a captive insurance company is sufficient that the health care entity can recognize anticipated insurance recoveries. For example, any anticipated insurance recoveries under a policy with a wholly-owned captive insurance company would be eliminated in the consolidation of the entities. Because the captive insurance company is part of the reporting entity, the liability for asserted and unasserted claims is assessed for both the parent and wholly-owned subsidiary at the reporting entity level.

8.29 FASB ASC 954-720-50-3 requires that a health care entity that is insured by a multiprovider captive insurance company disclose in its financial statements (*a*) that it is insured by such an entity; (*b*) its ownership percentage in the captive company; and (*c*) the method of accounting for its investment in, and the operations of, the captive entity.

8.30 Retrospectively-rated policies written by captive insurance companies are discussed in paragraphs 8.38–.40.

Claims-Made Insurance

8.31 A claims-made insurance policy provides rights for recovery of losses within the policy limits for asserted claims and incidents reported to the insurance carrier during the policy period. However, the policy does not provide rights for recovery of losses for claims and incidents not reported to the insurance carrier during the policy period. Unless the policy is continually renewed or tail coverage is purchased, the health care entity is uninsured for claims reported after the termination of the policy, even if the event occurred during the period in which the policy was in force.

8.32 As discussed in FASB ASC 720-20-25-14, a health care entity that is insured under a claims-made insurance policy recognizes the estimated cost of those IBNR claims and incidents to the insurance carrier if the loss is both probable and reasonably estimable. The "Claims-Made Contracts" sections of FASB ASC 720-20 apply if a health care entity purchases a claims-made insurance policy, subject to the measurement guidance in the following paragraph.

8.33 FASB ASC 720-20-30-2 states that the estimated cost of purchasing tail coverage is not relevant in determining the loss to be accrued because FASB ASC 210-20-45-1 prohibits netting the insurance receivable against the claim liability. However, if the insured health care entity had the unilateral option to purchase tail coverage at a premium not to exceed a specified fixed maximum, then the entity could record a receivable for expected insurance recoveries, after considering deductibles and policy limits, for the portion of the IBNR liability that is insurable under the tail coverage. In that case, the health care entity would need to record as a cost the expected premium for the coverage. The purchase of tail coverage does not eliminate the need to determine if an additional liability should be accrued because of policy limits or other factors.

Retrospectively-Rated Premium Policies

8.34 An insurance policy with a premium that is adjustable based on actual experience during the policy term is known as a retrospectively-rated premium policy. Under this type of policy, a deposit premium is generally paid to the insurer at the beginning of the coverage period. This usually consists of a minimum premium representing the insurance company's expenses and profits and an additional amount for estimated claims. The portion for estimated claims is adjusted during the term of the policy, subject to any minimums or maximum limitations specified in the policy. The economic substance of the terms of a retrospectively-rated insurance policy may more closely resemble a claims-funding mechanism.

8.35 The "Retroactive Contracts" and "Multiple-Year Retrospectively Rated Contracts" sections of FASB ASC 720-20 provide guidance for those insurance contracts, subject to the guidance in paragraphs 8.36–.37. For a multiple-year retrospectively-rated contract accounted for as insurance, FASB ASC 720-20-25-15 states that the health care entity should recognize either of the following:

- A liability to the extent that the insured has an obligation to pay cash or other considerations to the insurer that would not have been required, absent experience under the contract
- An asset to the extent that any cash or other consideration would be payable by the insurer to the insured based on experience to date under the contract

Per FASB ASC 720-20-30-3, the amount to be recognized in the current period should be computed using a with and without method as the difference between the health care entity's total contract costs before and after the experience under the contract as of the reporting date, including costs such as premium adjustments, settlement adjustments, and impairments of coverage. The amount of premium expense related to impairments of coverage should be measured in relation to the original contract terms. Future experience under the contract (that is, future losses and future premiums that would be paid regardless of past experience) should not be considered in measuring the amount to be recognized. The liability would be measured in accordance with FASB ASC 720-20-30-4 if the health care entity could terminate the contract before the end of its term and if termination would change the paid amounts.

8.36 FASB ASC 954-720-25-1 states that a health care entity with a retrospectively-rated insurance policy whose ultimate premium is based primarily on the health care entity's loss experience accounts for the minimum premium as an expense over the period of coverage under the policy.

8.37 FASB ASC 954-720-35-1 requires that a health care entity insured under a retrospectively-rated policy whose ultimate premium is based primarily on the experience of a group of health care entities amortize the initial premium to expense on a pro rata basis over the policy term. FASB ASC 954-720-25-2 states that the health care entity also should accrue additional premiums or refunds on the basis of the group's experience to date, which includes a provision for the ultimate cost of asserted and unasserted claims before the financial statement date, whether reported or unreported. FASB ASC 954-720-50-1 requires that the health care entity disclose that (*a*) it is insured under a retrospectively-rated policy, and (*b*) premiums are accrued based on the ultimate cost of the experience to date of a group of entities.

Retrospectively-Rated Policy Written by a Captive Insurance Company

8.38 A health care entity insured by an unconsolidated multiprovider captive insurance company for medical malpractice claims under a retrospectively-rated insurance policy whose ultimate premium is based primarily on the health care entity's experience up to a maximum premium, if any, accounts for such insurance as indicated in paragraph 8.36.

8.39 FASB ASC 954-720-35-2 states that a health care entity insured by an unconsolidated multiprovider captive insurance company for medical malpractice claims under a retrospectively-rated policy whose ultimate premium is based primarily on the experience of a group of health care entities accounts for such insurance as indicated in FASB ASC 954-720-25-2 and further discussed in paragraph 8.37.

8.40 According to FASB ASC 954-720-50-2, the health care entity should disclose that (*a*) it is insured under a retrospectively-rated policy of a multiprovider captive insurance company, and (*b*) the premiums are accrued based on the captive insurance company's experience to date.

Trust Funds

8.41 Some health care entities establish a medical malpractice self-funded trust fund for the purpose of paying medical malpractice claims.

8.42 FASB ASC 954-810-45-4 states that in general, a trust fund, whether legally revocable or irrevocable, should be included in the financial statements of the health care entity. A portion of the fund equal to the amount of assets expected to be liquidated to pay malpractice claims classified as current liabilities is classified as a current asset; the balance of the fund, if any, is classified as a noncurrent asset. Revenues and administrative expenses of the trust fund are included in the statement of operations. In some circumstances, the foregoing may not be possible (for example, if a common trust fund exists for a group of health care entities; if the health care entity is part of a common municipality risk-financing internal-service fund; or if the legal, regulatory, or indenture restrictions prevent the inclusion of a trust fund in a health care entity's financial statements). In those circumstances, the provisions of FASB ASC 954-450-25-3, 954-720-25-5, and 954-810-50-1 apply; those provisions are included in the following two paragraphs.

8.43 FASB ASC 954-450-25-3 states that estimated losses from asserted and unasserted claims should be accrued and reported, as indicated in paragraphs 1–2 of FASB ASC 954-450-30 (see paragraphs 8.14–.15). The estimated losses are not based on payments to the trust fund. FASB ASC 954-720-25-5 states that an entity that participates in a common trust fund and forfeits its rights to any excess funding should expense its contributions and account for its participation in the trust fund based on the type of obtained coverage (for example, occurrence basis, claims made, or retrospectively rated).

8.44 FASB ASC 954-810-50-1 requires that the existence of the trust fund and whether it is irrevocable be disclosed in the financial statements.

Disclosures for Medical Malpractice[1]

8.45 Disclosures about medical malpractice should be consistent with the requirements of FASB ASC 450-20-50. Disclosure of a contingency should be made if at least a reasonable possibility exists that a loss or an additional loss may have been incurred, and an accrual is not made for a loss contingency because any of the conditions in FASB ASC 450-20-25-2 are not met. The guidance further states that disclosure is preferable to accrual when a reasonable estimate of loss cannot be made.

8.46 In addition to the disclosures required by FASB ASC 450-20-50 and those discussed in paragraphs 8.13, 8.25–.26, 8.29, 8.37, 8.40, and 8.44, FASB ASC 954-450-50-1 requires that a health care entity disclose its program of medical malpractice insurance coverages.

8.47 FinREC recommends that those disclosures include the nature of the insurance coverage (for example, claims made or occurrence); related terms (for example, self-insured retention and excess levels); and expected insurance recoveries and the basis for any related loss accruals.

8.48 If the entity cannot estimate losses relating to a particular category of malpractice claims (for example, asserted claims, reported incidents, or unreported incidents), the potential losses related to that category of claims are

---

[1] On August 24, 2010, the Financial Accounting Standards Board issued proposed Accounting Standards Update *Health Care Entities (Topic 954): Accounting for Legal Costs Associated with Medical Malpractice and Similar Claims*, which would eliminate the requirement that health care entities accrue legal costs. Instead, health care entities would make a policy election to either expense legal costs as incurred or accrue estimated legal costs when the associated claim is incurred. Readers should be alert to the issuance of a final standard.

not accrued. However, the contingency is disclosed in the notes to the financial statements.

8.49 FinREC recommends that health care entities disclose the reasons for significant changes in the costs of incurred claims recognized in the income statement or statement of operations, including the costs associated with litigating or settling those claims. In addition to medical malpractice, this disclosure is recommended for all significant claims obligations, such as workers' compensation and employee health insurance.

8.50 FASB ASC 275-10-50 requires disclosures regarding an estimate when, based on known information available before the financial statements are issued or available to be issued, as discussed in FASB ASC 855-10-25, it is reasonably possible that the estimate will change in the near term, and the effect of the change will be material. For more information, see paragraphs 8.90–.96 of this guide.

Physician Guarantees and Other Agreements With Physicians

8.51 The physicians practicing at health care entities may be employees of the entity or affiliated entity or independent of the entity. These physicians join the entity's medical staff and agree to abide by those bylaws and govern themselves accordingly. Health care entities enter into a variety of agreements with physicians. Although this section provides accounting guidance relating to certain of these agreements, health care entities and their independent auditors also should consider the associated regulatory issues. See chapter 1, "Overview and Unique Considerations of Health Care Entities," of this guide for a discussion of those regulatory issues.

8.52 Health care entities sometimes guarantee nonemployee physicians that the revenue of the physicians' business or a specific portion of the business for a specified period of time will be at least a specified amount. Some of these guarantees are structured as minimum revenue guarantees (see paragraph 8.53); others are structured as financing transactions (see paragraph 8.54).

8.53 FASB ASC 460 applies to *minimum revenue guarantees*, which the FASB ASC glossary defines as "[a] guarantee granted to a business or its owners that the revenue of the business (or a specific portion of the business) for a specified period of time will be at least a specified minimum amount." FASB ASC 460-10-55-11 provides an example of a minimum revenue guarantee granted to a nonemployee physician by a not-for-profit health care facility. In the example, the health care facility has recruited the physician to move to the facility's geographical area to establish a practice. The health care facility, as the guarantor, has agreed to make payments to the newly arrived physician (the guaranteed party) at the end of specific periods of time if gross revenues (gross receipts) generated by the physician's new practice during that period of time do not equal or exceed a specific dollar amount. FASB ASC 460 applies to minimum revenue guarantees granted to physicians, regardless of whether the physician's practice qualifies as a *business*, as defined in the FASB ASC glossary. FASB ASC 460-10 requires that at the inception of a guarantee, the health care entity, as a guarantor, should recognize in its statement of financial position a liability for that guarantee. The liability should be initially measured at fair value.

8.54 Certain income guarantees are structured as advances whereby the physician is required to repay the outstanding balance of all advances after the end of the guarantee period, although a forgiveness clause may be included in exchange for the physician's commitment to stay in the community for a specified period of time. If the health care entity is tax exempt, the agreement is often structured as an advance to avoid potential problems associated with private inurement. See paragraphs 8.82–.83 for a discussion of private inurement. In determining the appropriate accounting for a physician income guarantee, it is important to evaluate the substance of the agreement. Such agreements may be promissory notes. In those situations, the income guarantee may be a financing arrangement. As noted in Technical Questions and Answers (TIS) section 6400.45, "Applicability of FASB Interpretation No. 45—Accounting and Disclosure Requirements for Guarantees, Including Indirect Guarantees of Indebtedness of Others" (AICPA, *Technical Practice Aids*), financing arrangements are excluded from the scope of FASB ASC 460 and, generally, would be accounted for as loans.

8.55 Another common recruitment incentive is a guarantee of a physician's personal home mortgage for his or her residence in the health care entity's service area. If the physician is not an employee, TIS section 6400.46, "Applicability of FASB ASC 460—Guarantor's Accounting and Disclosure Requirements for Guarantees, Including Indirect Guarantees of Indebtedness of Others—Mortgage Guarantees" (AICPA, *Technical Practice Aids*), notes that the agreement is considered a guarantee under FASB ASC 460. The presence of the health care entity's guarantee, obtained through a local bank, reduces the interest rate on the physician's mortgage loan. At inception, the health care entity would record an obligation to stand ready to perform in an amount equal to the fair value of the guarantee. In the preceding situation, the health care entity typically would be released from risk as the physician's outstanding mortgage obligation is reduced.

8.56 In current practice, most health care entities offset the entry recognizing the liabilities for the guarantees described in paragraphs 8.53 and 8.55 by recognizing an intangible asset. That intangible asset is then amortized over the life of the contract.

8.57 Health care entities need to ensure that they maintain adequate physician coverage to support their operations. This means that the entity needs to have certain specialties available based on the needs of the patients. For example, a patient who arrives at the emergency room may require surgery, and as a result, the entity needs to have physician coverage to provide this service. Historically and in many cases, the physicians have provided this service to the entity free of charge as part of their responsibilities of being on the medical staff; however, this practice has changed. Health care entities are routinely reimbursing physicians to provide emergency room coverage. This might be done through paying stipends, actual claims for services provided to uninsured or Medicaid patients, or through other agreements negotiated with the physicians. These agreements may include settlement provisions based on volumes or the mix of patients. In all cases, these costs should be accrued as incurred by the health care entity.

8.58 In addition, health care entities contract with certain physicians as medical directors to provide clinical oversight. These medical director agreements may be at a specific stipend, hourly rate, or even involve more complex formulas based on the services and needs of the entity. In all cases, these costs should be accrued as incurred by the entity.

Other Liabilities

Asset Retirement Obligations

8.59 An *asset retirement obligation* is an obligation associated with the other-than-temporary removal of a tangible long-lived asset from service. That term encompasses sale, abandonment, recycling, or disposal in some other manner. Chapter 6, "Property and Equipment and Other Assets," provides examples of asset retirements that may cause obligations. The FASB ASC glossary defines *conditional asset retirement obligation* as "[a] legal obligation to perform an asset retirement activity in which the timing and (or) method of settlement are conditional on a future event that may or may not be within the control of the entity." FASB ASC 410-20-25-7 states that an entity should recognize a liability for the fair value of a conditional asset retirement obligation if the fair value of the liability can be reasonably estimated. Paragraphs 4–5 of FASB ASC 410-20-25 require an entity to recognize the fair value of a liability for an asset retirement obligation in the period in which it is incurred, if a reasonable estimate of fair value can be made, and increase the carrying amount of the related long-lived asset by the same amount as the liability. An expected present value technique incorporates uncertainty about the timing and method of settlement into the fair value measurement. Uncertainty is factored into the measurement of the fair value of the liability through assignment of probabilities to cash flows.

8.60 FASB ASC 410-20-25-13 states that if current law, regulation, or contract, including the doctrine of promissory estoppel, requires an entity to perform an asset retirement activity when an asset is sold, abandoned, recycled, dismantled, demolished, or disposed of in some other manner, an unambiguous requirement exists to perform the retirement activity, even if that activity can be indefinitely deferred. At some time, deferral will no longer be possible because no tangible asset will last forever, except land. Therefore, the obligation to perform the asset retirement activity is unconditional, even though uncertainty exists about the timing or method, or both, of settlement.

8.61 The evaluation of the existence of an asset retirement obligation is generally performed on an asset-by-asset basis. The health care industry is capital intensive, and many health care entities have older physical plant facilities. Health care entities may have asset retirement obligations associated with these assets because federal, state, and local regulations typically require one or more specified activities to be performed upon abandonment, disposal, or significant renovation of long-lived assets. These activities typically relate to asbestos removal but may also relate to the disposal of medical waste, certain medical equipment, or underground storage tanks. A provision may even be included to restore a leased asset to its original condition upon termination of a lease.

Compensation and Related Benefits

8.62 Health care entities are usually labor intensive and compete for a limited number of qualified employees. The workforce at some health care entities is unionized, subjecting the entity to collective bargaining agreements that outline the compensation and benefits provided to employees. In many cases, more than one union will be present at the entity, resulting in multiple collective bargaining agreements. In addition, not-for-profit entities have additional regulatory restrictions regarding the amount and structure of compensation arrangements and benefit plans for their employees. These environmental factors have resulted in health care entities developing and maintaining multiple compensation and benefit plans.

8.63 Careful consideration of the compensation arrangements is required in order to apply the appropriate standards. FASB ASC 710-10-15 may be helpful in locating the appropriate standards. The following four FASB ASC topics provide guidance for compensation:

- FASB ASC 710, *Compensation—General*
- FASB ASC 712, *Compensation—Nonretirement Postemployment Benefits*
- FASB ASC 715, *Compensation—Retirement Benefits*
- FASB ASC 718, *Compensation—Stock Compensation*

Complex Pay Practices

8.64 For many health care entities, the majority of employees are nonexempt (subject to overtime compensation for hours worked over certain statutory limits) and compensated under complex pay practices. To attract and retain staff in many critical positions, employees may be paid multiple pay differentials, in addition to their base rate. The determination of benefit eligibility or calculation of benefit amounts may relate to only some of the pay practices of the entity. As a result, these practices require entities to develop systems to capture time worked in a manner consistent with the practice or benefit plans, or both.

Incentive and Deferred Compensation Plans

8.65 Health care entities typically maintain an incentive compensation plan for all or certain groups of employees. When compensation is based on attaining a particular goal or set of goals over a period of time, such as achieving a certain operating margin or quality score, it is accrued over the period in relation to the results achieved to date.

8.66 Due to the regulations relating to deferred compensation for not-for-profit entities, health care entities utilize a variety of structures to provide deferred compensation benefits to their employees that are competitive with other entities, including for-profit entities. These deferred compensation plans are designed for highly compensated employees and are considered nonqualified plans. Some plans are considered eligible plans by the IRS (for example, 457(b) plans); in other cases, they are considered nonqualified plans. In the simplest form, deferred compensation plans provide that an employee may defer a portion of his or her salary until a later date. That date may be after the employee has left the entity or retired. More complex deferred compensation plans provide for payments of periodic amounts or noncompete arrangements for a specified period of time, or both.

8.67 Although many scope limitations exist, and care should be taken when determining the appropriate standards, in general, guidance for deferred compensation is found in the following locations:

- FASB ASC 715-10 and 715-30 provide guidance for individual deferred compensation contracts if those contracts, taken together, are equivalent to a defined benefit pension plan.

- FASB ASC 715-10 and 715-60 provide guidance for individual deferred compensation contracts if those contracts, taken together, are equivalent to a defined benefit other postretirement benefit plan.
- FASB ASC 710-10 provides guidance for rabbi trusts.
- FASB ASC 710-10 provides guidance for individual deferred compensation arrangements that do not fall within the scope of other topics in FASB ASC.

8.68 Typically, any funding for these deferred compensation arrangements provided by the health care entity is available to its general creditors. An entity may establish a trust to fund compensation for a certain group of management or highly paid executives. In some cases, the executives or management may invest these funds in a select group of securities.

8.69 FASB ASC 710-10-25-18 requires that assets held by a rabbi trust be accounted for in accordance with GAAP for the particular asset and that the deferred compensation obligation be classified as a liability. Paragraphs 16–17 of FASB ASC 710-10-25 apply if the rabbi trust is invested in the employer's stock.

8.70 In addition, a health care entity may utilize split-dollar life insurance policies to fund its obligation under the deferred compensation agreements. The "Split-Dollar Life Insurance Arrangements" sections of FASB ASC 715-60 provide guidance for accounting for these benefits.

Sabbaticals and Other Compensated Absences

8.71 Health care entities typically provide employees with compensated absences, such as for holidays, vacations, and illness. These liabilities should be accounted for in accordance with FASB ASC 710-10. In addition to these typical compensated absences, FASB ASC 710-10 also provides guidance for health care entities that have a sabbatical program for certain employees.

Postretirement and Postemployment Benefit Plans

8.72 Similar to other industries, health care entities historically have provided pension benefits to their employees. Over the last several years, many health care entities have converted their traditional defined benefit plans to cash balance or defined contribution plans. In addition, some health care entities have agreed to provide postretirement health benefits.

8.73 Although many scope limitations exist, and care should be taken when determining the appropriate standards, in general, guidance for postretirement and postemployment benefits is found in the following locations:

- FASB ASC 715-20 and 715-30 provide guidance for pension benefits provided through defined benefit pension plans.
- FASB ASC 715-20 and 715-60 provide guidance for other postretirement benefits provided through defined benefit plans.
- FASB ASC 715-70 provides guidance for defined contribution plans.
- FASB ASC 715-80 provides guidance for multiemployer pension and other postretirement benefit plans, including those provided pursuant to one or more collective bargaining agreements.

- FASB ASC 712-10 provides guidance for special or contractual termination benefits that are payable before retirement and not payable from a pension or other postretirement plan, including guidance for health care entities that have a formal severance plan as part of their health and welfare plans.
- FASB ASC 712-10 also provides guidance for all types of other postemployment benefits provided to former or inactive employees, their beneficiaries, and covered dependents after employment but before retirement.

Agency Funds

8.74 As described in FASB ASC 954-305-45-4, health care entities may receive and hold assets owned by others under agency relationships. For example, they may perform billing and collection services for physicians. In accepting responsibility for those assets, the health care entity incurs a liability to the principal under the agency relationship to return the assets in the future or, if authorized, disburse them to another party on behalf of the principal. If held by not-for-profit business-oriented health care entities, such agency funds shall be reported as unrestricted assets.

8.75 As a result, physician fees collected by the health care entity as a conduit are reported as a liability to the physicians and not recognized in the statement of income or operations and changes in net assets.

Tax Considerations for Not-for-Profit Health Care Entities

8.76 Not-for-profit health care entities generally are exempt from taxation. Tax exemption is a privilege and not a right. At the federal level, the IRS has the authority to revoke an entity's exempt status for any one of several reasons. Furthermore, individual states have regulatory bodies that oversee not-for-profit entities and can revoke their state tax-exempt status without regard to their federal tax-exempt status and even prevent them from operating. Many potential threats exist to an entity's federal tax-exempt status, of which the following are particularly important:

- Material changes in the entity's character, purpose, or method of operation
- Private inurement
- Private benefit
- Commerciality
- Lobbying
- Political campaign activities
- Unrelated business income
- Failure of the entity to meet the commensurate test
- Violation of public policy by the entity

8.77 Not-for-profit entities should be aware of relevant federal and state tax laws and regulations and their potential impact on the entity and its financial statements. An entity's failure to maintain its tax-exempt status could have serious financial consequences. As discussed in chapter 2, "General Auditing Considerations," of this guide, failure to comply with tax laws and regulations could be an illegal act that may have either a direct and material effect on the determination of financial statement amounts (for example, the result of an incorrect accrual for taxes on unrelated business income) or a material indirect effect on the financial statements that would require appropriate disclosures (for example, the result of a potential loss of tax-exempt status).

8.78 Not-for-profit health care entities usually seek exemption from federal income tax under Internal Revenue Code (IRC) Section 501(a). Under IRC Section 501(a), entities organized and operated exclusively for religious, charitable, or educational purposes, as described in IRC Section 501(c)(3), are exempt from federal income taxes. The following are additional requirements for such entities:

- No part of the organization's net earnings, either directly or indirectly, inures to any private shareholder or individual.
- No substantial part of the organization's activities consists of carrying on propaganda or otherwise attempting to influence legislation. IRC Section 501(h) provides a limited exception to the general rule that public charities may not incur expenditures to influence legislation.
- The organization does not participate or intervene in any political campaign on behalf of, or in opposition to, any candidate for public office.

8.79 The term *charitable* is used in IRC Section 501(c)(3) in its generally accepted legal sense. Providing health care to the community is considered a charitable activity when provided by a health care organization not organized or operated for the benefit of private interests, such as designated individuals, the founder or founder's family, shareholders of the organization, or people directly or indirectly controlled by such private interests.

8.80 FASB ASC 954-740-50-1 requires that a not-for-profit health care entity disclose its tax-exempt status.

8.81 Health care entities must file annual information returns (Form 990) with the IRS. Most states also have their own registration and filing requirements, some of which include using Form 990 as part of an annual report. In 2008, the IRS issued a completely revised Form 990 with expanded reporting requirements in the areas of governance and compensation of officers, directors, and other key employees. Other changes include an increased focus on the determination of public charity status and public support, supplemental financial statement reporting, and fundraising. Separately, the *IRS Exempt Organizations (TE/GE) Hospital Compliance Project Final Report*, issued in February 2009, places increased emphasis on community benefit reporting and executive compensation. Additional changes are expected because of health care reform, which is discussed further in chapter 1 of this guide.

Private Inurement and Intermediate Sanctions

8.82 Under IRC Section 501(c)(3), no part of the net earnings of the charitable organization shall inure to the benefit of any private shareholder, individual, or insider. A private shareholder, individual, or insider refers to a person(s) having a private or personal interest in the activities of the organization. *Insiders* are individuals with a personal or private interest in the organization, such as governing board members, officers, certain employees, and substantial contributors. The IRS has stated that physicians have a personal or private interest in the activities of a health care organization and could be subject to the private inurement proscription. Transactions between insiders and not-for-profit entities are permitted, but the not-for-profit entity has the burden of proving that the transactions do not result in private inurement. The not-for-profit entity must be able to satisfy the IRS that the transaction was reasonable, was adequately documented, had independent approval, and did not violate any law or regulation. Employee compensation can create an inurement problem if it is judged to be unreasonably high.

8.83 The IRS instituted intermediate sanctions regulations that allow the IRS to penalize the individuals who received and approved the excess benefit transactions. The intermediate sanctions regulations are designed to curtail excess benefits (private inurement) provided to individuals with substantial influence over the affairs of the not-for-profit entity (organizational insiders). The intermediate sanctions regulations provide the IRS with the ability to punish those who participate in private inurement (excess benefit) transactions. An insider (generally, certain members of management, officers, physicians, and board members) is subject to a 25 percent tax or up to 200 percent if the amount of an excess benefit is not repaid within a certain period of time. However, even if an insider does not benefit from the transaction, he or she may be subject to the 10 percent tax if he or she knowingly and willfully approved a transaction subsequently determined by the IRS to be an excess benefit transaction.

Unrelated Business Income

8.84 Although not-for-profit entities may be exempt from federal income tax, they may be subject to tax on unrelated business income. The objective of the tax on unrelated business is to place such activities on the same basis as that of taxable entities. *Unrelated business income* is the income from any regularly carried on trade or business, the conduct of which is not substantially related to the exercise or performance of the organization's tax-exempt purpose or function. The fact that proceeds from an activity are used exclusively for the organization's tax-exempt purpose does not make the activity substantially related to its tax-exempt purpose or function. As is the case with most tax-related definitions, qualifications and exceptions exist.

State and Local Taxes

8.85 Tax-exempt entities may also be subject to property taxes or other state and local business and occupancy taxes. Exemptions from state and local sales, real estate, and other taxes vary from jurisdiction to jurisdiction and may be different than for federal taxes. Entities are generally subject to the laws of the state of incorporation, as well as the laws of states in which they conduct significant activities. Each state's laws govern exemption from its taxes and should be consulted for the applicable definitions and requirements.

Tax Positions

8.86 The tax considerations discussed in this chapter often result in an entity or its for-profit or not-for-profit subsidiaries making a determination about whether a transaction or event must be reported in a tax return. The term *tax position* refers to a position in a previously-filed tax return or a position expected to be taken in a future tax return that is reflected in measuring current or deferred income tax assets and liabilities for interim or annual periods. The term *tax position* encompasses, but is not limited to, the following:

- An entity's status, including its status as a tax-exempt not-for-profit entity
- A decision to classify a transaction, entity, or other position in a tax return as tax exempt or subject to a lower rate of tax
- A decision not to file a tax return, such as a decision that Form 990-T need not be filed
- The characterization of income, such as a characterization of income as passive, or a decision to exclude reporting taxable income in a tax return
- An allocation or a shift of income between jurisdictions (federal, state, local, or foreign)

8.87 The validity of a tax position is a matter of tax law. It is not controversial to recognize the benefit of a tax position in financial statements when the degree of confidence is high that that tax position will be sustained upon examination by a taxing authority. However, in some cases, the law is subject to varied interpretation, and whether a tax position will ultimately be sustained may be uncertain. FASB ASC 740-10-25-6 limits the recognition of uncertain tax positions to only those positions that are more likely that, based on the technical merits, the position will be sustained on examination.

Medicaid Voluntary Contribution or Taxation Programs

8.88 The Medicaid program is set up on a state-by-state basis to provide medical assistance to the indigent. Although state administered, the program is actually a joint federal and state program for which the federal government funds a portion of the cost. Under this arrangement, the federal government matches a percentage of the total amount paid by the state to health care entities. This matching is referred to as federal financial participation. States have attempted to increase the amount of federal matching funds for which they are eligible by increasing the amount of medical assistance they provide. In order to pay for the increased medical assistance, some states have imposed a tax on health care entities or sought donations or other voluntary payments from them, or both. As a result, the states have been able to generate additional federal matching funds without expending additional state funds.

8.89 TIS section 6400.30, "Accounting for Transactions Involving Medicaid Voluntary Contribution or Taxation Programs" (AICPA, *Technical Practice Aids*), notes that the accounting for these types of programs is dependent on the individual facts and circumstances. For example, if a guarantee exists that specific monies given to the state by the health care entity will be returned to the entity from the state, those amounts should be recorded as receivables. In addition, if the health care entity has met all the requirements to be legally entitled to additional funds from the state, the revenue or gain should be recognized. However, if the monies go into a pool with other contributions that are then disbursed based on factors over which the health care entity has little or no control, the payments should be recognized as an expense. Any subsequent reimbursements would be recognized as revenue or gain when the entity is entitled to them and payment is assured. Care should be taken to avoid delayed recognition of expenses or improperly recognizing contingent gains. Because of the complexities that are involved, it may be necessary for the health care entity to consult with legal counsel.

Risks and Uncertainties

8.90 FASB ASC 275-10-50 requires entities to include in their financial statements information about risks and uncertainties in the following areas as of the date of those statements:

- The nature of their operations
- Use of estimates in the preparation of financial estimates
- Certain significant estimates
- Current vulnerability due to certain concentrations

8.91 FASB ASC 275-10-50-6 requires discussion of estimates when, based on known information available before the financial statements are issued or available to be issued, as discussed in FASB ASC 855-10-25, it is reasonably possible that the estimate will change in the near term, and the effect of the change will be material. The estimate of the effect of a change in a condition, situation, or set of circumstances that existed at the date of the financial statements should be disclosed, and the evaluation should be based on known information available before the financial statements are issued or available to be issued.

8.92 Examples of estimates that may be included in financial statements of health care entities that are particularly sensitive to changes in the near term include, but are not limited to, the following:

- Third-party revenue and related receivables
- Provision for bad debts
- Obligation by continuing care retirement communities to provide future services and the use of facilities to current residents
- IBNR relating to medical malpractice and prepaid health care services liabilities
- Accruals for loss contracts under managed care agreements
- Assets subject to impairment (for example, goodwill)
- Environmental remediation-related obligations
- Litigation-related contingencies (for example, fraud and abuse actions by regulators)
- Estimated risk pool settlements arising from managed care contracting
- Amounts reported for long-term obligations, such as amounts reported for pensions and postemployment benefits
- Estimated net proceeds recoverable or the provisions for expected loss to be incurred, or both, on the disposition of a business or assets

8.93 In the health care environment, it almost always is reasonably possible that estimates regarding third-party payments could change in the near term as a result of one or more future confirming events (for example, regulatory action reflecting local or national audit or enforcement initiatives). Paragraph .07 of SOP 00-1, *Auditing Health Care Third-Party Revenues and Related Receivables* (AICPA, *Technical Practice Aids*, AUD sec. 14,360), provides examples of risks unique to the government-contracting environment that make it difficult to estimate net realizable third-party revenues and receivables. For most entities with significant third-party revenues, the effect of the change could be material to the financial statements. When material exposure exists, the uncertainty regarding revenue realization is disclosed in the notes to the financial statements. A sample disclosure is presented in paragraph .37 of SOP 00-1. Among other things, the sample disclosure indicates that laws and regulations governing the Medicare and Medicaid programs are extremely complex and subject to interpretation. As a result, at least a reasonable possibility exists that recorded estimates will change by a material amount in the near term.[2]

8.94 FASB ASC 275-10-50-16 requires that financial statements disclose certain concentrations (those described in the following paragraph) if, based on information known to management before the financial statements are issued or available to be issued, as discussed in FASB ASC 855-10-25, all of the following criteria are met:

- The concentration exists at the date of the financial statements.
- The concentration makes the entity vulnerable to the risk of a near-term severe impact.
- It is at least reasonably possible that the events that could cause the severe impact will occur in the near term.

8.95 Examples of concentrations that may meet those criteria and that require disclosure in the financial statements of health care entities include the following:

- Concentrations in the volume of business transacted with a particular payor, supplier, lender, grantor, or contributor
- Concentrations in revenue from particular products, services, or fund-raising events
- Concentrations in the available sources of supply of material, labor, or services or licenses or other rights used in the entity's operations
- Concentrations in the market or geographic area in which an entity conducts its operations

8.96 FASB ASC 275-10-50-20 requires health care entities to disclose the percentage of the labor force covered by a collective bargaining agreement and the percentage of labor force covered by a collective bargaining agreement that will expire within one year.

Auditing Contingencies and Other Liabilities

8.97 Auditing objectives and procedures for contingencies and other liabilities generally are similar to those of other entities. The independent auditor may need to consider the specific auditing objectives, selected control activities, and auditing procedures presented in exhibit 8-1.

---

[2] Statement of Position (SOP) 00-1, *Auditing Health Care Third-Party Revenues and Related Receivables* (AICPA, *Technical Practice Aids*, AUD sec. 14,360), provides guidance to independent auditors regarding uncertainties inherent in health care revenue recognition. SOP 00-1 is included as appendix B, "Statement of Position 00-1, *Auditing Health Care Third-Party Revenues and Related Receivables*," of this guide.

Auditing Medical Malpractice Loss Contingencies

8.98 Although this chapter focuses on medical malpractice loss contingencies, the auditing objectives and procedures that are discussed also are relevant to other self-insured obligations. The existence of an insurance policy, by itself, is no assurance that malpractice contingencies are assumed by others. The independent auditor should review the insurance contracts and determine the extent of the risk retained by the entity. Specific auditing procedures to consider include the following:

- Determine the type, such as occurrence basis or claims made, and level (per occurrence or in the aggregate) of insurance protection that the entity has obtained.
- Determine if the coverage actually provides for the recovery of losses from malpractice risks. Is the insurance with a related party (for example, a captive insurance company)? Does it provide for retrospective premiums or similar adjustments?

Once the extent of the retained risk is understood, the independent auditor will be able to determine the nature, extent, and timing of other auditing procedures.

8.99 Paragraph 8.33 discusses the conditions for which an insured health care entity can recognize a receivable for expected insurance recoveries, even though tail coverage has not been purchased at the balance sheet date. In evaluating the amount of the receivable, the independent auditor should consider the extent to which the claim liability is insurable under the coverage. The receivable cannot be recognized if the insured entity did not have the unilateral option to purchase the tail coverage at the balance sheet date and record as an expense the premium for the tail coverage. See paragraphs 8.31–.33 for a discussion of accounting for claims-made insurance policies and tail coverage.

8.100 Management's intent to renew a claims-made policy is not sufficient to recognize a receivable for expected insurance recoveries as of the balance sheet date, unless management contractually obligates itself for renewal before the issuance date of the financial statements, and the cost is expensed in the period covered by the financial statements. The requirement to renew a claims-made policy or purchase and expense tail coverage applies even if state regulations require that renewal of claims-made coverage be offered continually.

8.101 If the health care entity discounts accrued malpractice claims, the auditor should consider whether that discounting is appropriate (for example, that the conditions in paragraph 8.22 are met). The auditor should consider tests of the estimates of the amount and timing of cash payments based on the health care entity's specific experience. The auditor should also consider whether the discount rate is reasonable. Paragraph 41 of FASB Concepts Statement No. 7 and paragraphs 12–13 of FASB ASC 835-30-25 provide general principles for present value measurements and determining an appropriate discount rate. Also, see paragraph 8.23 for additional discussion on determining an appropriate discount rate.

Auditing Accounting Estimates

8.102 Management is responsible for making the accounting estimates that are included in the financial statements. Management is also responsible for providing proper disclosure of (*a*) the use of estimates in the preparation of financial statements and (*b*) certain significant estimates.[3] The independent auditor is responsible for evaluating the reasonableness of management's estimates and the adequacy of the related disclosures. AU section 342, *Auditing Accounting Estimates* (AICPA, *Professional Standards*), provides guidance to auditors on obtaining and evaluating sufficient appropriate audit evidence to support significant accounting estimates in an audit of financial statements in accordance with GAAP. The independent auditor does this using one or more of the following approaches:

- Review and test the process used by management to develop the estimate.
- Develop an independent expectation of the estimate to corroborate the reasonableness of management's estimate.
- Review subsequent events or transactions occurring prior to the date of the auditor's report.

8.103 In evaluating management's estimates of asserted and unasserted claims, the independent auditor should consider factors such as management's description and evaluation of asserted and unasserted claims arising from reported incidents; the lawyer's and, if appropriate, the outside risk manager's assessment of asserted claims and reported incidents not covered by insurers; and the actuary's evaluations of the aggregate liability covering asserted and unasserted claims arising from reported and unreported incidents.

8.104 Paragraph .06 of AU section 333, *Management Representations* (AICPA, *Professional Standards*), requires that the management representation letter include a specific representation that unasserted claims or assessments that the entity's lawyer has advised are probable of assertion have been disclosed, in accordance with FASB ASC 450.

8.105 According to AU section 337, *Inquiry of a Client's Lawyer Concerning Litigation, Claims, and Assessments* (AICPA, *Professional Standards*), a letter of audit inquiry to the lawyer handling the claims is the auditor's primary means of obtaining corroboration of the information furnished by management concerning claims made and known incidents for which claims have not been made that are either uninsured or in excess of the insurance coverage. Audit inquiry letters generally would not be required with respect to reported contingencies that were not considered to have a material potential loss. In evaluating the information provided by legal counsel, it may be necessary to supplement the written representations with inquiries if the representations are not clear regarding the probability of the litigation outcome or potential range of loss. The inability or unwillingness of counsel to evaluate asserted claims or reported incidents, or both, would give rise to a modification of the auditor's opinion.

8.106 The independent auditor should consider the frequency of losses due to unreported incidents and the magnitude of prior losses and underlying causes for the IBNR claims. If a basis for an accrual exists, the independent auditor should then determine whether the entity's prior history supports the estimation of the number of claims and probable settlement value.

---

[3] See paragraphs 8.59–.73.

Use of Actuaries and Actuarial Methods

8.107 Developing the estimate of the medical malpractice loss amount often requires special skill or knowledge. In the auditor's judgment, the work of a specialist may be required to obtain appropriate audit evidence. An actuary may be engaged by management to help prepare or review management's estimate of the medical malpractice loss amount (or range of amounts) or to assist in developing certain factors and assumptions used in estimating the malpractice liability. The decision to use an actuary should be based on a consideration of whether (*a*) the estimated claim liability is potentially material to the fair presentation of financial statements in conformity with GAAP and (*b*) special skill or knowledge is required to estimate the claim liability.

8.108 If an actuary is involved in a substantial way in determining the amount of an entity's malpractice self-insurance liability, the independent auditor should follow the requirements of AU section 336, *Using the Work of a Specialist* (AICPA, *Professional Standards*). The independent auditor should consider the actuary's professional qualifications, reputation, prior experience in estimating malpractice claim losses, and relationship to the client. There should be an understanding among the independent auditor, client, and actuary of the objectives and scope of the analysis and the methods and assumptions used.

8.109 Paragraph .12 of AU section 336 states that the appropriateness and reasonableness of methods and assumptions used and their application are the responsibility of the specialist. The auditor should (*a*) obtain an understanding of the methods and assumptions used by the specialist; (*b*) make appropriate tests of data provided to the specialist, taking into account the auditor's assessment of control risk; and (*c*) evaluate whether the specialist's findings support the related assertions in the financial statements. Ordinarily, the auditor would use the work of the specialist, unless the auditor's procedures lead him or her to believe that the findings are unreasonable in the circumstances. If the auditor believes that the findings are unreasonable, he or she should apply additional procedures, which may include obtaining the opinion of another specialist.

8.110 The independent auditor should perform an appropriate test of the accounting data provided to the actuary by the client. Such accounting data may include historical claim experience; policy terms, such as coverage, expiration, deductibles, presence of retrospectively-determined premiums, and indemnity limitations; exposure data, such as the number of beds, high-risk medical specialties, outpatient visits, and emergency room visits; and information about risk-management systems, personnel, and procedures. Other factors that might be considered include inflation rates, judicial decisions assessing liability and noneconomic damages, changes in legislation affecting payment levels and settlement practices, changes in the entity's experience or trends in loss reporting and settlements, divergence in an entity's experience relative to industry experience, reinsurance programs and changes therein, and recent catastrophic occurrences.

Evaluating Lawyers' Responses

8.111 Determining the outcome of pending or threatened litigation, claims, and assessments, including unasserted claims and assessments, normally is beyond the independent auditor's professional competence.

Accordingly, the independent auditor's evaluation of the need for disclosures or report modifications is based primarily on the opinion of the lawyer handling the matter. The American Bar Association (ABA) has adopted a *Statement of Policy Regarding Lawyers' Responses to Auditors' Requests for Information* under which lawyers accept certain responsibility for responses to independent auditors' inquiries. However, the ABA statement is not enforceable by the ABA in the same way that the AICPA is able to enforce its standards under the accounting profession's Code of Professional Conduct. As a result, lawyers' responses may vary widely.

8.112 Interpretation No. 7, "Assessment of a Lawyer's Evaluation of the Outcome of Litigation," of AU section 337 (AICPA, *Professional Standards*, AU sec. 9337 par. .18–.23), includes the following examples of evaluations of litigation, which may be considered to communicate in a sufficiently clear manner a remote likelihood of an unfavorable outcome:

- "We are of the opinion that this action will not result in any liability to the company."
- "It is our opinion that the possible liability to the company in this proceeding is nominal in amount."
- "We believe the company will be able to defend this action successfully."
- "We believe that the plaintiff's case against the company is without merit."
- "Based on the facts known to us, after a full investigation, it is our opinion that no liability will be established against the company in these suits."

8.113 On the other hand, the lawyer may use terms, such as *meritorious defenses*, that have different meanings to different lawyers. Paragraph .22 of AU section 9337 includes the following examples of lawyers' evaluations that are unclear regarding the likelihood of an unfavorable outcome:

- "This action involves unique characteristics wherein authoritative legal precedents do not seem to exist. We believe that the plaintiff will have serious problems establishing the company's liability under the act; nevertheless, if the plaintiff is successful, the award may be substantial."
- "It is our opinion that the company will be able to assert meritorious defenses to this action." (The term "meritorious defenses" indicates that the company's defenses will not be summarily dismissed by the court; it does not necessarily indicate counsel's opinion that the company will prevail.)
- "We believe the action can be settled for less than the damages claimed."
- "We are unable to express an opinion as to the merits of the litigation at this time. The company believes there is absolutely no merit to the litigation." (If client's counsel, with the benefit of all relevant information, is unable to conclude that the likelihood of an unfavorable outcome is "remote," it is unlikely that management would be able to form a judgment to that effect.)

- "In our opinion, the company has a substantial chance of prevailing in this action." (A "substantial chance," a "reasonable opportunity," and similar terms indicate more uncertainty than an opinion that the company will prevail.)

8.114 When the lawyer's response is unclear, the independent auditor may request a conference to clarify the lawyer's opinion. If the response is still unclear, or the materiality of the uncertainty cannot be determined, the independent auditor should consider the guidance in paragraphs .29–.32 of AU section 508, *Reports on Audited Financial Statements* (AICPA, *Professional Standards*).

Income Taxes

8.115 The auditor should perform procedures to determine whether the health care entity has obtained a qualifying income tax exemption from the appropriate governmental authority and whether disclosures relating to the entity's tax-exempt status are appropriate.

Auditing Considerations

8.116 The auditor may need to consider the examples of specific auditing objectives, selected control activities, and auditing procedures for contingencies and other liabilities that are presented in exhibit 8-1.

Exhibit 8-1

The following table illustrates the use of assertions in developing audit objectives and designing substantive tests. The examples are not intended to be all-inclusive nor is it expected that all the procedures would necessarily be applied in an audit. The auditor should design and perform substantive procedures for all relevant assertions related to each material class of transactions, account balance, and disclosure to obtain sufficient appropriate audit evidence. The use of assertions in assessing risks and designing appropriate audit procedures to obtain audit evidence is described in paragraphs .14–.26 of AU section 326, *Audit Evidence* (AICPA, *Professional Standards*). Various audit procedures and the purposes for which they may be performed are described in paragraphs .27–.41 of AU section 326.

Auditing Considerations

Financial Statement Assertions	*Specific Auditing Objectives*	*Selected Control Activities*	*Auditing Procedures*
Malpractice Loss Contingencies			
Existence and occurrence, completeness, rights and obligations, and valuation	The liability for malpractice claims is properly reported in the balance sheet.	Insurance coverage is reviewed regularly, including the financial viability of the insurer. The risk-management system identifies and monitors malpractice incidents and evaluates associated losses.	Review the amount of insurance coverage, the type of coverage (claims made or occurrence), the deductible provisions, and so on to determine the level of risk that is retained by the entity. Consider the financial viability of the insurance carrier.
		Outside legal counsel and insurance carriers review and monitor all claims.	Send letters of inquiry to malpractice insurance carriers and legal counsel, in accordance with AU section 337, *Inquiry of a Client's Lawyer Concerning Litigation, Claims, and Assessments* (AICPA, *Professional Standards*).

Financial Statement Assertions	*Specific Auditing Objectives*	*Selected Control Activities*	*Auditing Procedures*
		The adequacy of malpractice accruals is regularly reviewed by management, including information obtained from qualified specialists. Information supplied to specialists is reviewed for accuracy and completeness. Actuarial assumptions are reviewed for compliance with generally accepted accounting principles.	Review and test the method of estimating accruals (for example, review actuarial reports and prior historical loss experience). If the accrual is discounted, review and test the present value calculation, including the reasonableness of the inputs. Determine that additional premiums charged by insurers for retrospectively-related policies are reported as a liability.
		Changes in the risk-management system are communicated on a timely basis.	Review prior estimates and historical loss experience. Determine whether uncertainties related to medical malpractice claims need to be disclosed in the independent auditor's report.
Presentation and disclosure	The program of medical malpractice insurance coverage and the basis for any loss accruals are adequately disclosed in the financial statements.		

(continued)

Auditing Considerations—continued

Financial Statement Assertions	*Specific Auditing Objectives*	*Selected Control Activities*	*Auditing Procedures*
Income Taxes			
Rights and obligations	The not-for-profit entity has obtained a qualifying income tax exemption from the appropriate governmental authority.	Management monitors compliance with applicable tax regulations. Transactions are reviewed for their effect on the tax status and tax liabilities, including Internal Revenue Code (IRC) Section 4958.	Determine that the not-for-profit entity has obtained a determination of its tax-exempt status. Consider the effect of new, expanded, or unusual activities on the not-for-profit entity's tax status. Inquire if tax returns have been filed on a timely basis. Determine the status of the tax returns under examination. Read the prior year's tax returns. Read the minutes and accounting for evidence of significant unrelated business activities. Review for reasonableness the unrelated business income tax liability. Review transactions with *disqualified persons*, as defined in IRC Section 4958.
Presentation and disclosure	The entity's tax-exempt status and its tax contingencies are disclosed in the notes to the financial statements.		Determine that the entity's tax-exempt status is disclosed in the notes to the financial statements.

Chapter 9

Net Assets (Equity)

Investor-Owned Health Care Entities

9.01 The equity accounts of investor-owned health care entities are similar to those of other investor-owned entities.

Not-for-Profit Entities

9.02 The Financial Accounting Standards Board (FASB) *Accounting Standards Codification* (ASC) glossary defines *net assets* as "[t]he excess or deficiency of assets over liabilities of a not-for-profit entity (NFP), which is classified into three mutually exclusive classes according to the existence or absence of donor-imposed restrictions."[1]

9.03 As a residual interest, net assets cannot be measured independently of a not-for-profit entity's assets and liabilities. Changes in net assets result from transactions and other events and circumstances in which total assets and total liabilities change by different amounts. In many not-for-profit entities, such changes include nonreciprocal transfers of assets received from donors who do not expect to receive either repayment or proportionate economic benefit in return. See chapter 11, "Contributions Received and Made," of this guide for further discussion. Display of, and disclosures about, net assets and changes in them are intended to assist donors and other users in assessing an entity's efforts to provide goods and services to its constituencies, its efficiency and effectiveness in providing such services, and its continuing ability to do so.

9.04 Changes in net assets result from revenue, expenses, gains, losses, and equity transfers; those changes are discussed in other chapters of this guide. This chapter describes the principles for reporting total net assets in statements of financial position and changes in total net assets in statements of operations, as well as related disclosures.

Net Asset Classes

9.05 Paragraphs 9–11 of FASB ASC 958-210-45 provide guidance for the classification of net assets. According to FASB ASC 958-210-45-1, the statement of financial position (balance sheet) of a not-for-profit health care entity should focus on the entity as a whole and report separate amounts for each of three classes of net assets: (*a*) permanently-restricted net assets, (*b*) temporarily-restricted net assets, and (*c*) unrestricted net assets.[2] Net assets are included in one of the three classes depending on the presence and type of donor-imposed restrictions.

---

[1] Although some health care entities may use other terms, such as *equity*, this guide uses the term *net assets* to describe the residual interest.

[2] As explained in Financial Accounting Standards Board (FASB) *Accounting Standards Codification* (ASC) 958-210-55-3, FASB ASC 958, *Not-for-Profit Entities*, encourages the use of the terms *unrestricted*, *temporarily restricted*, and *permanently restricted net assets*; however, other labels exist. For example, *equity* may be used for net assets, and *other* or *not donor restricted* may be used with care to distinguish unrestricted net assets from the temporarily and permanently restricted classes of net assets.

9.06 The FASB ASC glossary defines a *donor-imposed restriction* as

> [a] donor stipulation that specifies a use for a contributed asset that is more specific than the broad limits resulting from the following:
>
> a. The nature of the not-for-profit entity (NFP)
>
> b. The environment in which it operates
>
> c. The purposes specified in its articles of incorporation or bylaws or comparable documents for an unincorporated association.
>
> A donor-imposed restriction on an NFP's use of the asset contributed may be temporary or permanent. Some donor-imposed restrictions impose limits that are permanent, for example, stipulating that resources be invested in perpetuity (not used up). Others are temporary, for example, stipulating that resources may be used only after a specified date, for particular programs or services, or to acquire buildings and equipment.

9.07 In addition to the three classes of net assets—permanently restricted, temporarily restricted, and unrestricted—further disaggregation of total net assets may also be reported. For example, unrestricted net assets may be subdivided into board-designated net assets and undesignated net assets. Donor-imposed restrictions limit a not-for-profit health care entity's ability to use or dispose of specific contributed assets or the economic benefits embodied in those assets. Donor stipulations should not be considered restrictions, unless they include limitations on the use of contributed assets that are more specific than the broad limits imposed by the not-for-profit health care entity's purpose and nature.

9.08 As explained in FASB ASC 958-210-45-3, generally, restrictions apply to net assets, not specific assets. However, assets may be restricted by donors. For example, land could be restricted to use as a public park.

Permanently-Restricted Net Assets

9.09 The FASB ASC glossary defines *permanently restricted net assets* as

> [t]he part of net assets of a not-for-profit entity (NFP) resulting from the following:
>
> a. Contributions and other inflows of assets whose use by the NFP is limited by donor-imposed stipulations that neither expire by passage of time nor can be fulfilled or otherwise removed by the actions of the NFP
>
> b. Other asset enhancements and diminishments subject to the same kinds of stipulations
>
> c. Reclassifications from or to other classes of net assets as a consequence of donor-imposed stipulations.

9.10 Permanently-restricted net assets must be maintained by the not-for-profit health care entity in perpetuity. For example, contributions of cash or securities restricted by the donor with the stipulation that they be invested in perpetuity (donor-restricted endowment funds) are recognized as increases in permanently-restricted net assets.

9.11 Permanently-restricted net assets also may change as a result of increases and decreases in assets that are subject to permanent restrictions.

FASB ASC 958-205-45-18 provides the following examples. If a donor stipulates that net gains be added to the principal of its gift until that endowed gift plus accumulated gains increases to a specified dollar level, the gains are permanently restricted. Similarly, if a donor states that a specific investment security must be held in perpetuity, the gains and losses on that security are subject to that same permanent restriction, unless the donor specifies otherwise. However, if a donor allows the not-for-profit entity to choose suitable investments, the gains are not permanently restricted, unless the donor or law requires that an amount be permanently retained.

Temporarily-Restricted Net Assets

9.12 The FASB ASC glossary defines *temporarily restricted net assets* as

> [t]he part of the net assets of a not-for-profit entity (NFP) resulting from the following:
>
> a. Contributions and other inflows of assets whose use by the NFP is limited by donor-imposed stipulations that either expire by passage of time or can be fulfilled and removed by actions of the NFP pursuant to those stipulations
>
> b. Other asset enhancements and diminishments subject to the same kinds of stipulations
>
> c. Reclassification from or to other classes of net assets as a consequence of donor-imposed stipulations, their expiration by passage of time, or their fulfillment and removal by actions of the NFP pursuant to those stipulations.

9.13 Temporarily-restricted net assets are those net assets whose use by the not-for-profit health care entity have been limited by donors to (*a*) later periods or after specified dates or (*b*) specified purposes.[3] For example, contributions restricted by the donor to be used by the entity over the next five years or support a specific future program are recognized as increases in temporarily-restricted net assets. Contributions of assets, such as equipment or buildings, that by their nature are used up over time and that the donor stipulates must be used by the entity also are recognized as increases in temporarily-restricted net assets. Paragraphs 9.25–.31 discuss the temporarily-restricted net assets of endowment funds.

9.14 Temporarily-restricted net assets also may change as a result of increases and decreases in assets or the economic benefits embodied in those assets that are subject to donor-imposed temporary restrictions. For example, as explained in paragraphs 9.28–.29, if a donor has stipulated that assets be held in perpetuity as a donor-restricted endowment fund, the net appreciation of those assets and their income are temporarily restricted until appropriated for expenditure by the not-for-profit health care entity.

Unrestricted Net Assets

9.15 The FASB ASC glossary defines *unrestricted net assets* as

> [t]he part of net assets of a not-for-profit entity (NFP) that is neither permanently restricted nor temporarily restricted by donor-imposed

---

[3] As described in paragraph 11.12 of this guide, contributions received with restrictions that are met in the same reporting period may be reported as unrestricted if the health care entity discloses its policy and consistently reports from period to period.

stipulations. The only limits on the use of unrestricted net assets are the broad limits resulting from the following:

a. The nature of the NFP

b. The environment in which the NFP operates

c. The purposes specified in the NFP's articles of incorporation or bylaws

d. Limits resulting from contractual agreements with suppliers, creditors, and others entered into by the NFP in the course of its business.

Unrestricted net assets generally result from revenues from providing services, producing and delivering goods, receiving unrestricted contributions, and receiving dividends or interest from investing in income-producing assets, less expenses incurred in providing services, producing and delivering goods, raising contributions, and performing administrative functions.

9.16 In accordance with FASB ASC 958-210-50-2, information about significant limits resulting from contractual agreements with suppliers, creditors, and others, including the existence of loan covenants, generally is provided in the notes to the financial statements. FASB ASC 958-210-45-11 states that information about self-imposed limits also may be useful, including information about voluntary resolutions by the governing board of an entity to designate a portion of its unrestricted net assets to function as an endowment (sometimes called a board-designated endowment). That information may be presented in notes to, or on the face of, the financial statements.

9.17 For example, a health care entity might include information about voluntary resolutions to designate a portion of its unrestricted net assets for funded depreciation.

9.18 FASB ASC 958-810-45-1 states that noncontrolling interests[4] in the equity (net assets) of consolidated subsidiaries should be reported as a separate component of the appropriate class of net assets in the consolidated statement of financial position of a not-for-profit entity. That amount should be clearly identified and described (for example, as noncontrolling ownership interest in subsidiaries) to distinguish it from the components of net assets of the parent, which includes the parent's controlling financial interest in its subsidiaries. The effects of donor-imposed restrictions, if any, on a partially-owned subsidiary's net assets should be reported in accordance with FASB ASC 958-205 and 958-320. Paragraphs 17–25 of FASB ASC 958-810-55 illustrate one way in which the consolidated financial statements of a hospital might satisfy the presentation and disclosure requirements for noncontrolling interests in a consolidated subsidiary and subsequent changes in ownership interests of that subsidiary.

Reclassifications

9.19 FASB ASC 958-225-45-13 states that reclassifications of net assets (that is, simultaneous increases in one net asset class and decreases in another) should be made if any of the following events occur: (*a*) the not-for-profit

---

[4] A *noncontrolling interest* is the portion of equity in a subsidiary that is not directly or indirectly attributable to a parent.

entity fulfills the purposes for which the net assets were restricted, (*b*) donor-imposed restrictions expire with the passage of time or death of a split-interest agreement beneficiary[5] (if the net assets are not otherwise restricted), (*c*) a donor withdraws or court action removes previously-imposed restrictions, or (*d*) donors impose restrictions on otherwise unrestricted net assets.

9.20 For example, the amount of a donor's contribution that must be used by the health care entity for a specified program would be reclassified from temporarily-restricted to unrestricted net assets in the period in which the health care entity conducts the program. A purpose restriction is often fulfilled when the entity incurs an expense or recognizes a liability to a vendor to acquire goods or services that satisfies the restriction.

9.21 FASB ASC 958-205-45-9 states that if two or more temporary restrictions are imposed on a contribution, the effect of the expiration of those restrictions should be recognized in the period in which the last remaining restriction has expired. Expirations of donor-imposed restrictions are reported as reclassifications, decreasing temporarily-restricted net assets and increasing unrestricted net assets. In accordance with FASB ASC 958-225-45-3, reclassifications of amounts between net asset classes are reported separately from other transactions in the statement of operations.

9.22 As explained in FASB ASC 958-205-45-11, if an expense is incurred for a purpose for which both unrestricted and temporarily-restricted net assets are available, a donor-imposed restriction is fulfilled to the extent of the incurred expense, unless the expense is for a purpose that is directly attributable to another specific external source of revenue. Temporarily-restricted net assets with time restrictions are not available to support expenses until the time restrictions have expired.

9.23 For example, an employee's salary may meet donor-imposed restrictions to support the activity on which the employee is working. In that situation, the restriction is met to the extent of the incurred salary expense, unless incurring the salary will lead to inflows of revenue from a specific external source, such as revenue from a cost reimbursement contract or a conditional promise to give that becomes unconditional when the health care entity incurs the salary expense.

9.24 As explained in FASB ASC 954-210-50-1 and 954-205-45-9, health care entities are prohibited from implying a time restriction that expires over the useful life of a donated long-lived asset. Thus, if contributions of long-lived assets with explicit donor restrictions are reported as temporarily-restricted support, a health care entity reports expirations of those donor restrictions when the stipulation is fulfilled, and the assets are placed in service. Similarly, donations of cash or other assets that must be used to acquire long-lived assets are reported as temporarily-restricted support in the period that they are received, and expirations of those donor restrictions are reported when the

---

[5] FASB ASC 958-30 provides guidance for reporting arrangements under which a not-for-profit entity shares the benefits of assets with other beneficiaries (a split-interest agreement). Those other beneficiaries generally are not not-for-profit entities. For example, a donor may give a not-for-profit entity the right to receive all or a portion of the specified cash flows from a charitable trust or other identifiable pool of assets that is held either by the not-for-profit entity or an unrelated third party, such as a bank, trust company, foundation, or private individual. Chapter 6, "Split Interest Agreements," of the Audit and Accounting Guide *Not-for-Profit Entities* provides additional guidance on split-interest gifts.

acquired long-lived assets are placed in service, and donor-imposed restrictions are satisfied.

Classification of Donor-Restricted Endowment Funds

9.25 The FASB ASC glossary defines a *donor-restricted endowment fund* as "[a]n endowment fund that is created by a donor stipulation requiring investment of the gift in perpetuity or for a specified term. Some donors may require that a portion of income, gains, or both be added to the gift and invested subject to similar restrictions." FASB ASC 958-205-45-14 states that when classifying an endowment fund, each source—original gift, gains and losses, and interest and dividends—must be evaluated separately. Each source is unrestricted, unless its use is temporarily or permanently restricted by explicit donor stipulations or law. Thus, an endowment fund that is created by a governing board from unrestricted net assets is classified as unrestricted because all three sources are free of donor restrictions. If an endowment fund is created by a donor, the donor may have placed different restrictions on each of the three sources. Classification of the original gifts and the income earned by endowments generally is straightforward because, usually, donors explicitly state any time or purpose restrictions on those two sources. Determining how to classify gains on endowments may not be as easy because agreements with donors often are silent on how gains should be used and whether losses must be restored immediately from future gains or not at all.

9.26 FASB ASC 958-205-05-9 notes that because donor stipulations and laws vary, not-for-profit entities must assess the relevant facts and circumstances for their endowment gifts and relevant laws to determine if net appreciation on endowments is available for spending or permanently restricted. Paragraphs 13–35 of FASB ASC 958-205-45 provide guidance for reporting the net assets of endowment funds and the changes in those net assets. The guidance for states that have enacted a version of the Uniform Prudent Management of Institutional Funds Act (UPMIFA) is summarized in the following four paragraphs, but it is not intended as a substitute for reading the standards themselves.

9.27 A not-for-profit entity that is subject to an enacted version of UPMIFA should classify a portion of a donor-restricted endowment fund of perpetual duration as permanently-restricted net assets. The amount classified as permanently restricted should be either (*a*) the amount of the fund that must be permanently retained in accordance with explicit donor stipulations, as explained in paragraphs 3–4 of FASB ASC 958-605-45, or (*b*) the amount of the fund that, in the absence of explicit donor stipulations, the not-for-profit entity's governing board determines must be permanently retained (preserved), consistent with the relevant law, as explained in FASB ASC 958-205-45-21.

9.28 The relevant law of a state that has enacted a version of UPMIFA may include the limitation "[u]nless stated otherwise in the gift instrument, the assets in an endowment fund are donor-restricted assets until appropriated for expenditure by the institution," which is from subsection 4(a) of UPMIFA. For each donor-restricted endowment fund for which the restriction described in subsection 4(a) of UPMIFA applies, a not-for-profit entity should classify the portion of the fund that is not classified as permanently-restricted net assets as temporarily-restricted net assets (time restricted) until appropriated for expenditure by the not-for-profit entity.

9.29 Upon appropriation for expenditure, the time restriction expires to the extent of the amount appropriated and, in the absence of any purpose restrictions, results in a reclassification of that amount to unrestricted net assets. If the fund is also subject to a purpose restriction, the reclassification of the appropriated amount to unrestricted net assets would not occur until that purpose restriction also has been met, in accordance with the guidance beginning in FASB ASC 958-205-45-9. Pursuant to FASB ASC 958-205-45-11, temporarily-restricted net assets with time restrictions are not available to support expenses until the time restrictions have expired.

9.30 In the absence of donor stipulations or law to the contrary, losses on the investments of a donor-restricted endowment fund should reduce temporarily-restricted net assets to the extent that donor-imposed temporary restrictions on net appreciation of the fund have not been met before a loss occurs. Any remaining loss should reduce unrestricted net assets. The amount of permanently-restricted net assets is not reduced by losses on the investments of the fund or a not-for-profit entity's appropriations from the fund. If losses or, as UPMIFA states, appropriations reduce the assets of a donor-restricted endowment fund below the level required by the donor stipulations or law, gains that restore the fair value of the assets of the endowment fund to the required level should be classified as increases in unrestricted net assets. After the fair value of the assets of the endowment fund equals the required level, gains that are restricted by the donor should be classified as increases in temporarily-restricted or permanently-restricted net assets, depending on the donor's restrictions on the endowment fund.

9.31 Paragraphs 3.16, 4.21, and 4.30 of this guide provide information about whether the income, gains, and losses of donor-restricted endowment funds are included or excluded from the performance indicator.

Disclosure

9.32 FASB ASC 958-210-45-9 requires that information about the nature and amounts of different types of permanent or temporary restrictions be provided either by reporting their amounts on the face of the financial statements or including relative details in the notes to financial statements.

9.33 For example, information about the following would be shown on the face of the financial statements or in the notes:

- Different kinds of permanent restrictions, such as specific assets to be held in perpetuity and assets that have been contributed by donors with stipulations that they be invested in perpetuity
- Different kinds of temporary restrictions, such as those concerning the support of specific operating activities, use in specific future periods, or acquisition of long-term assets

9.34 Separate disclosures of significant limitations other than those imposed by donors, such as those imposed by governing boards or regulatory bodies, are permitted to be made on the face of the financial statements or in the notes to the financial statements.

9.35 Paragraphs 1A–2A of FASB ASC 958-205-50 require disclosures for both donor-restricted and board-designated endowment funds. A health care entity should disclose information about net asset classification, net asset composition, changes in net asset composition, spending policies, and related investment policies.

9.36 FASB ASC 958-810-50-1 requires that if consolidated financial statements are presented, the reporting entity (parent) should disclose any restrictions made by entities outside of the reporting entity on distributions from the controlled not-for-profit entity (subsidiary) to the parent and any resulting unavailability of the net assets of the subsidiary for use by the parent.

Auditing

9.37 The independent auditor may need to consider the examples of specific auditing objectives, selected control activities, and auditing procedures relating to net assets (equity) that are presented in exhibit 9-1.

Exhibit 9-1

The following table illustrates the use of assertions in developing audit objectives and designing substantive tests. The examples are not intended to be all-inclusive nor is it expected that all the procedures would necessarily be applied in an audit. The auditor should design and perform substantive procedures for all relevant assertions related to each material class of transactions, account balance, and disclosure to obtain sufficient appropriate audit evidence. The use of assertions in assessing risks and designing appropriate audit procedures to obtain audit evidence is described in paragraphs .14–.26 of AU section 326, *Audit Evidence* (AICPA, *Professional Standards*). Various audit procedures and the purposes for which they may be performed are described in paragraphs .27–.41 of AU section 326.

Auditing Considerations

Financial Statement Assertions	*Specific Auditing Objectives*	*Selected Control Activities*	*Auditing Procedures*
Net Assets (Equity)			
Account Balances			
Rights and obligations	Resources are used and accounted for in accordance with donor and grantor restrictions.	Management monitors compliance with these restrictions.	Review the minutes of board and board committee meetings for evidence of donor restrictions.
Presentation and Disclosure			
Classification and understandability	Net assets are presented and disclosed properly in the financial statements.	Procedures ensure proper authorization, recording, and presentation.	Test significant net asset transactions to determine that they are properly authorized and recorded.
	Temporarily-restricted net assets are reclassified as unrestricted net assets when donor-imposed restrictions have been fulfilled.	Controls ensure that reclassification of temporarily-restricted net assets occurs when donor-imposed restrictions have been fulfilled.	Determine compliance with donor and grantor restrictions. Test expenditures to determine that restricted net assets are used for their restricted purposes.
			Determine that appropriate reclassifications are reported in the statement of activities when donor-imposed restrictions have been fulfilled.

Chapter 10

Health Care Service Revenue and Related Receivables[*]

Overview of the Health Care Environment

10.01 A unique aspect of the health care industry is the involvement of multiple parties in the provision of, and payment for, health care services. As many as four parties may be involved in a health care service transaction, including the following:

- The patient who receives the care
- The physician who orders the services on behalf of the patient
- The health care entity that provides the setting or administers the treatment (for example, hospital, home health company, and so on)
- The third-party payor(s) that provides payment to the health care entity on behalf of the patient

10.02 The third-party payor may be a government program, such as Medicare or Medicaid; a commercial insurer, such as a managed care plan; a commercial insurance company; a preferred provider organization (PPO); or a self-funded employer plan. In managed care entities, the physician, health care entity, and third-party payor may all be part of the same reporting entity.

10.03 The extent to which third-party payors are involved in paying for services varies by type of health care facility. For hospitals, rehabilitation facilities, and home health companies, third-party payors typically pay for the majority of provided services. In the nursing home sector, a certain portion of the patients are considered private pay (that is, the patient or his or her family pays for the care); for the remainder, Medicaid is the dominant third-party payor for care provided to low-income individuals. Minimal commercial insurance coverage presently exists for nursing home care, and Medicare provides limited nursing home benefits for short stays. In continuing care retirement communities (CCRCs), the residents themselves typically pay entrance and monthly service fees, and third-party payor involvement is limited to the payment of some services that may be provided in the nursing care portion of the facility.

10.04 Revenue recognition and the valuation of related receivables of health care entities are subject to inherent uncertainties and complexities, including the following:

---

[*] On June 24, 2010, the Financial Accounting Standards Board (FASB) issued proposed Accounting Standards Update (ASU) *Revenue Recognition (Topic 605): Revenue from Contracts with Customers*, to improve and align with International Financial Reporting Standards the financial reporting of revenue from contracts with customers and related costs. The core principle of the draft standard is that an entity should recognize revenue from contracts with customers when it transfers goods or services to the customer in the amount of consideration that the entity receives or expects to receive from the customer. The proposed standard would replace most of the guidance in FASB *Accounting Standards Codification* 605, *Revenue Recognition*. Readers should be alert for the issuance of a final standard.

- Rate setting with third-party payors, including settlements that are not known with certainty until after a considerable period of time has elapsed after the related services were rendered
- The regulations and laws on which governmental third-party payments are based
- The determination of what constitutes charity care

Rate Setting With Third-Party Payors

10.05 Third-party payors typically do not pay the health care entity's full established rates. The paid amount may be based on government regulations for Medicare, Medicaid, and other government programs or contractual arrangements for PPOs, health maintenance organizations, or HMOs, workers' compensation insurers, and commercial insurers. When multiple third-party payors are involved, payment rates and coverages often vary by payor.

10.06 As noted in Financial Accounting Standards Board (FASB) *Accounting Standards Codification* (ASC) 954-605-05-5, payment rates established by regulations or contractual agreements may be determined either prospectively or retrospectively. Some rate-setting methods described as prospective, such as the Medicare Prospective Payment System (PPS), may include provisions for retrospective adjustments (for example, billing denials, coding changes, and settlements with third-party payors). Some third parties pay prospective rates for certain services and retrospective rates for other services.

10.07 Prospective rate setting is a method used to set payment rates in advance of the delivery of health care services. Such payment rates determine what third parties will pay for health care services during the rate period (generally one year). Prospective rate setting may result from a contractual agreement with a third party, or it may be mandated through legislation. The intent of prospective rate setting is to establish payment rates before the period to which they will apply and that are not subject to change.

10.08 Under retrospective rate setting, third parties usually determine an interim payment rate and, during the rate period (generally one year), pay the health care entity for rendered services using that rate. After the rate period has ended, a final settlement is made in accordance with federal or state regulations or contractual agreements.

10.09 When rates are subject to retrospective adjustments, the amounts of the final settlements may not be known with certainty until a considerable period of time has elapsed from when the related services were rendered. Reasonable estimates of such settlements are central to the revenue recognition process in health care in order to avoid recognizing revenue that the health care entity will not ultimately realize or failing to recognize revenues that will ultimately be realized. The basis for such estimates may range from relatively straightforward calculations using information that is readily available to highly complex judgments based on assumptions about future decisions. The estimation process is further complicated by the complexities of billing and reimbursement regulations. Estimating revenues from third-party payors is discussed in paragraphs 10.20–.24.

10.10 FASB ASC 954-605-25-9 requires that rate-setting methods that are described as prospective but provide for retrospective adjustments should be accounted for as retrospective rate-setting systems for the services to which they apply.

The Government-Contracting Environment

10.11 The largest third-party payor in the United States is the federal government, which purchases health care services through its Medicare, Medicaid, TRICARE, and Federal Employees Health Benefits programs. Most institutional health care providers and many managed care plans serve Medicare or Medicaid beneficiaries, or both, to some extent. Consequently, most health care entities are considered to be government contractors. The contractual relationship is defined by regulations written by government agencies and enforced by an elaborate oversight network of government auditors and contract administrators. For example, Medicare administers its own contracts and subcontracts audits and claims processing functions to private-sector Medicare Administrative Contractors (MAC). The regulations and laws on which they are based are inherently political and subject to frequent change and differing interpretations.

10.12 Health care entities doing business with governmental payors (for example, Medicare and Medicaid) are subject to the following risks that are unique to the government-contracting environment, that are hard to anticipate and quantify, and that may vary from entity to entity:

- A health care entity's revenues and allowable costs may be subject to adjustment as a result of examination by government agencies or contractors. The audit process and resolution of significant related matters, including disputes based on differing interpretations of the regulations, often are not finalized until several years after the services were rendered.
- Different MACs (entities that contract with the federal government to assist in the administration of the Medicare program) may interpret governmental regulations differently.
- Differing opinions on a patient's principal medical diagnosis, including the appropriate sequencing of codes used to submit claims for payment, can have a significant effect on the payment amount.
- Otherwise valid claims may be determined to be nonallowable after the fact due to differing opinions on medical necessity.
- Claims for rendered services may be nonallowable if they are later determined to have been based on inappropriate referrals.
- Government agencies may make changes in program interpretations, requirements, or conditions of participation, some of which may have implications for previously-estimated amounts.
- Certain states determine rates of payment for Medicare or Medicaid payments, or both, in accordance with the statewide rate-setting method, which is different from the method used by the federal government.
- Government agencies have the right to withhold or reduce contract payments for an extended period of time.
- Health care entities may receive add-on payments for serving a disproportionately high percentage of low-income patients.
- Extensive and complex reimbursement methodologies exist for teaching institutions.

10.13 As a result of such risks, retrospective adjustments can be particularly difficult to estimate with respect to governmental payors. The delay between rendering services and reaching final settlement, as well as the complexities and ambiguities of billing and reimbursement regulations, makes it difficult to estimate net patient service revenue associated with government programs. However, despite the difficulty, health care entities paid through programs that are subject to retrospective adjustments need to estimate amounts that ultimately will be realizable in order for revenues associated with those payment systems to be fairly stated in accordance with generally accepted accounting principles (GAAP). Estimating revenues from government programs is discussed in paragraphs 10.20–.24.

10.14 In addition, risks may result from the applicability of certain laws that provide for potentially significant penalties to be assessed if the contractor violates them. For example, a contractor that submits a false claim to the government may be subject to penalties ranging from a monetary penalty for each submitted false claim to suspension or exclusion from the program. Thus, noncompliance could result in a material contingent liability, a material loss of future revenue, or cause the health care entity to be unable to continue as a going concern.

Charity Care

10.15 The FASB ASC glossary states that "[c]harity care represents health care services that are provided but are never expected to result in cash flows. Charity care is provided to a patient with demonstrated inability to pay. Each entity establishes its own criteria for charity care consistent with its mission statement and financial ability." Distinguishing charity care from bad-debt expense requires the exercise of judgment. Charity care is discussed further in paragraphs 10.25–.28.

Types of Health Care Revenue

10.16 In accordance with FASB ASC 954-605-45-1, health care revenue should be classified based on the type of services rendered or contracted to be rendered. Examples include the following:

- Patient service revenue, which is derived from fees earned in exchange for providing services to patients
- Resident service revenue, which is derived from fees charged to residents of a long-term care facility, such as a skilled nursing facility or CCRC[1]
- Capitation revenue, which is derived from capitation-type arrangements with third-party payors by which fees are earned by agreeing to provide services to qualified beneficiaries, not necessarily as a result of actually providing the care[2]
- Premium revenue, which is the primary source of revenue of prepaid health care plans[3]

---

[1] Refer to chapter 14, "Financial Accounting and Reporting by Continuing Care Retirement Communities," of this guide for additional information.

[2] Refer to chapter 13, "Financial Accounting and Reporting for Managed Care Services," of this guide for additional information.

[3] See footnote 2.

- Refundable and nonrefundable advance fees received by certain types of CCRCs[4]

Types of Payment Methodologies

10.17 Common payment methodologies utilized by third-party payors include the following:

- *Fee-for-service.* Under fee-for-service arrangements, payment is based on the specific services that are provided to the patient; therefore, the health care entity earns revenue as a result of providing those services. Payment may be at the health care entity's full established rates, with a predetermined discounted rate (for example, percent of charges), or based on a fee schedule agreed to by the health care entity and third-party payor.
- *Per diem.* Under a per diem arrangement, the health care entity is paid a flat rate per day of inpatient care, regardless of the level of intensity of the provided care. Therefore, revenue is earned as a result of the patient occupying an inpatient bed for a particular day. The Medicare PPS for skilled nursing facility services is an example of a per diem methodology. The contract specifies the manner in which partial days of care, such as the day of admission or discharge, will be paid, and revenue for those days is recognized accordingly. A prorated payment may be made for a partial day of care. Alternatively, the terms of the payor's policy may provide for a full payment for the day of admission and pay nothing for the day of discharge.
- *Per case.* When payment is made on a per-case basis, the health care entity is paid a predetermined amount based on the patient's discharge category. The Medicare PPS for hospital inpatient services is an example of a per-case payment methodology. Under per-case payment, revenue is earned as a result of the patient receiving treatment from the health care entity. If the contract calls for payment on a per-case basis, and the patient is hospitalized at the end of the accounting period, a portion of the total revenue for the case will be earned in one period, with the balance earned in the next period. In such situations, the total revenue for the case is allocated between the two accounting periods using an allocation method that fairly apportions the revenue between periods.
- *Episodic.* Under an episodic payment methodology, the health care entity is paid a predetermined amount for services provided to patients during an episode of care (for example, a stipulated period of time). Revenue normally is earned based on the passage of time. Medicare's PPS for home health services is an example of an episodic payment methodology.
- *Capitation.* Generally, capitation payments are received at the beginning of each month and obligate the health care entity to stand ready to render covered services during the month. Capitation revenue is earned as a result of agreeing to provide services

---

[4] See footnote 1.

to qualified beneficiaries, not as a result of actually providing the care. If the health care entity's accounting system records patient charges and establishes patient receivables as services are rendered, appropriate valuation allowances or adjustments are recorded, so only the amount of contract revenue is reported.

Patient (or Resident) Service Revenue

Revenue Recognition

10.18 Paragraph 83 of FASB Concepts Statement No. 5, *Recognition and Measurement in Financial Statements of Business Enterprises*, provides a general rule that revenue is earned when an entity has substantially accomplished what it must do to be entitled to those revenues.

10.19 With respect to third-party payor arrangements, governmental regulations or contractual terms will specify the performance requirements or conditions that the health care entity must meet in order to be entitled to revenue under the contract or provider agreement. Regulations or contracts also will address payment terms and the degree of risk that is to be assumed by the health care entity. Consequently, a thorough understanding of the terms of the health care entity's arrangements with significant third-party payors is important for appropriate revenue recognition.

Estimating Revenue Related to Government Programs and Other Third-Party Payors

10.20 The amount of revenue earned under arrangements with government programs is determined under complex rules and regulations that subject the health care entity to the potential for retrospective adjustments in future years. Several years may elapse before all potential adjustments related to a particular fiscal year are known and before the amount of revenue to which the health care entity is entitled is known with certainty. As noted in paragraph .10 of Statement of Position (SOP) 00-1, *Auditing Health Care Third-Party Revenues and Related Receivables* (AICPA, *Technical Practice Aids*, AUD sec. 14,360), management makes a reasonable estimate of amounts that ultimately will be realized, considering, among other things, adjustments associated with regulatory reviews, future program audits, billing reviews, investigations, or other proceedings. In making these estimates, management also considers the potential for regulatory investigations that may result in the denial of otherwise valid claims for payment. These matters are discussed in SOP 00-1, which, among other matters, provides guidance to auditors regarding uncertainties inherent in third-party revenue recognition.[5]

10.21 As noted in paragraph .06 of SOP 00-1, health care entities need to estimate amounts that ultimately will be realizable in order for revenues to be fairly stated in accordance with GAAP. Thus, in the period in which services are rendered, health care entities estimate the amount to which they ultimately will be entitled for providing those services and report that amount as revenue. The difference between that estimated amount and the amount of payments received prior to the balance sheet date is reflected as a receivable or payable in

[5] Statement of Position 00-1, *Auditing Health Care Third-Party Revenues and Related Receivables* (AICPA, *Technical Practice Aids*, AUD sec. 14,360), is included as appendix B, "Statement of Position 00-1, *Auditing Health Care Third-Party Revenues and Related Receivables*," of this guide.

the balance sheet. The difference between gross patient service revenues and the estimated amount is a contractual adjustment that, along with courtesy and policy discounts and other adjustments and deductions, adjusts gross service revenues, which excludes charity care, to arrive at net service revenues in the statement of operations. The relationship between various amounts can be depicted as follows:

Gross charges	XXX,XXX
Less charges associated with charity patients	(XX,XXX)
Gross patient service revenue	XXX,XXX
Less deductions from revenue:	
Contractual allowances	(XXX,XXX)
Courtesy/policy/other discounts	(XX,XXX)
Net patient service revenue	XXX,XXX

10.22 Management's estimates relating to third-party contractual adjustments are based on subjective, as well as objective, factors. This requires judgment that normally is based on management's knowledge of, and experience with, past and current events and its assumptions about conditions that it expects to exist and courses of action that it expects to take.

10.23 Approaches for making estimates of third-party contractual adjustments vary from entity to entity, depending on individual facts and circumstances. Some entities with significant prior experience may attempt to quantify the effects of individual potential intermediary or other governmental (for example, Office of Inspector General or Department of Justice) or private payor adjustments based on detailed calculations and assumptions regarding potential future adjustments. Some entities may prepare cost report analyses[6] to estimate the effect of potential adjustments. Other entities may base their estimates on an analysis of potential adjustments in the aggregate, in light of the payors involved; the nature of the payment mechanism; the risks associated with future audits; and other relevant factors.

10.24 In some situations (for example, Medicare or Medicaid provider agreements), payments received under contracts with third-party payors are subject to adjustment after the contract term is completed, based on findings of audits, reviews, or investigations. In such cases, net service revenue also includes a provision for estimated future retroactive adjustments. Such provisions are accrued on an estimated basis in the period that the related services are rendered and adjusted in future periods as additional information is obtained or adjustments become known, or both. That accrual is subsequently adjusted as events occur that change the estimate of earned revenue. Such adjustments have the potential to materially affect the health care entity's financial position and results of operations. Accounting for the subsequent adjustments is discussed beginning at paragraph 10.43.

[6] Medicare cost reimbursement is based on the application of highly complex technical rules, some of which are ambiguous and subject to different interpretations, even among Medicare's Administrative Contractors. To estimate the effects of potential adjustments, some health care entities will prepare a cost report based on alternative assumptions.

Charity Care

10.25 Each health care entity establishes its own criteria for charity care consistent with its mission statement, its financial ability, the current economy, and other circumstances. In some instances, prior to any care being provided, a health care entity is able to obtain information regarding a patient's financial status and determine whether that patient meets the criteria for uncompensated care. If so, the patient would be classified as charity prior to receiving treatment. In other cases, such as trauma care, patient financial information may not be available at the time that treatment is provided to the patient. A health care entity may provide care because it either is required to do so by law (for example, emergency care) or chooses to do so, with the understanding that a charity care application will be completed in the future.

10.26 FASB ASC 954-605-25-10 states that charity care does not qualify for recognition as revenue in the financial statements. Distinguishing charity care from bad-debt expense requires the exercise of judgment. Only the portion of a patient's account that meets the health care entity's charity care criteria is recognized as charity. As noted in FASB ASC 954-605-25-11, although it is not necessary for the entity to make this determination upon admission or registration of an individual, the entity determines at some point whether the individual meets the established criteria for charity care.

10.27 This determination is made as quickly as practicably possible, generally before any substantial collection effort is initiated. Charity care does not include contractual adjustments that result from third-party arrangements, such as Medicare, Medicaid, government funding programs, or other third-party arrangements, because the health care entity has accepted the payment terms for the services provided by agreement. In addition, charity care does not include discounts given to uninsured or underinsured patients if those patients do not qualify under the health care entity's charity care policy.

10.28 Pursuant to FASB ASC 954-605-50-3, management's policy for providing charity care, as well as the level of charity care provided, should be disclosed in the financial statements. Such disclosure should be measured based on the health care entity's direct and indirect costs of providing charity care services. If costs cannot be specifically attributed to services provided to charity care patients (for example, based on a cost accounting system), management may estimate the costs of those services using reasonable techniques. For example, one such estimation technique might involve calculating a ratio of cost to gross charges and then multiplying that ratio by the gross uncompensated charges associated with providing care to charity patients. Other reasonable techniques also are permitted. The method used to identify or estimate such costs should be disclosed. Funds received to offset or subsidize provided charity services (for example, from gifts or grants restricted for charity care or from an uncompensated care fund) also should be separately disclosed.

Estimating Revenue Related to Care Not Covered by Third-Party Payors

10.29 A portion of a health care entity's charges typically will not be paid by third-party payors, and the patient will be responsible. This self-pay portion of revenue comprises revenue for services provided to uninsured patients; insurance copays and deductibles; as well as noncovered services (for example, cosmetic surgery). Estimating revenue for the self-pay portion also may be challenging, but as noted in paragraph .06 of SOP 00-1, health care entities need to estimate amounts that ultimately will be realizable in order for revenues to be fairly stated in accordance with GAAP. The predominant industry practice for reporting revenue from self-pay patients is to recognize gross service revenue for those patients at the health care entity's gross charges (that is, full established billing rates) when the services are provided and adjust for bad debts (an operating expense) based on collection assessments. No revenues are recognized for patients identified as receiving charity care services. If the health care entity offers a discount to uninsured patients, those discounts are recorded as a reduction to gross service revenues, so that the resulting net service revenue is recorded in the statement of operations. Bad debt expense is then recognized as an operating expense based on collection assessments.[†]

Accounting and Financial Reporting Requirements

10.30 Per FASB ASC 954-605-25-3, in general, gross service revenue is recorded in the accounting records on an accrual basis at the health care entity's established rates, regardless of whether the health care entity expects to collect that amount.

10.31 That amount that is used for internal record-keeping purposes is referred to as gross service revenues. The revenues are recorded as services are rendered. Any difference between the established rates for provided services and amounts agreed to under agreements with third parties is accounted for as a contractual adjustment. An estimate of the contractual adjustment is recorded in the same period that the services were provided. In addition, some health care entities offer discounts (for example, courtesy, prompt pay, or employee discounts). The discount also is recorded in the same period that the services were provided. Thus, internal records will generally reflect the gross patient service revenues offset by the contractual adjustments and discounts.

10.32 Per FASB ASC 954-605-25-4, the provision for contractual adjustments (that is, the difference between established rates and third-party payors' payments) and discounts (that is, the difference between established rates and the collectible amount) are recognized on an accrual basis and deducted from gross services revenue to determine net service revenue. For financial reporting purposes, FASB ASC 954-605-45 requires that revenue be classified based on the type of rendered service and that service revenue, including patient service revenue, be reported net of contractual and other adjustments in the statement of operations.

10.33 In accordance with FASB ASC 954-605-25-6, estimates of contractual adjustments, other adjustments, and the allowance for uncollectibles should be reported in the period during which the services are provided, even

---

[†] In July 2011, FASB issued ASU No. 2011-07, *Health Care Entities (Topic 954): Presentation and Disclosure of Patient Service Revenue, Provision for Bad Debts, and the Allowance for Doubtful Accounts for Certain Health Care Entities (a consensus of the FASB Emerging Issues Task Force)*, which would require certain health care entities to change the presentation of their statement of operations by reclassifying the provision for bad debts associated with patient service revenue from an operating expense to a deduction from patient service revenue (net of contractual allowances and discounts). Additionally, those health care entities are required to provide enhanced disclosures about their policies for recognizing revenue and assessing bad debts. The amendments also require disclosures of patient service revenue (net of contractual services), as well as qualitative and quantitative information about changes in the allowance for doubtful accounts. The amendments in this ASU will be effective for fiscal years beginning after December 15, 2011, for public entities, and for the first annual period ending after December 15, 2012, for nonpublic entities.

though the actual amounts may become known at a later date. This later date may be any one of the following: (*a*) when the patient is discharged, (*b*) subsequent to discharge or completion of service, (*c*) when the third party is billed, or (*d*) when payment or partial payment is received. Also, as discussed in paragraph 10.26, charity care does not qualify for recognition as revenue in the financial statements.

Premium and Capitation Revenues

10.34 As noted in FASB ASC 954-605-05-6, in many cases, revenues are generated as a result of an agreement to provide health care, rather than from the actual provision of services. For example, an integrated delivery system may agree to provide all health-related services for a specified group residing within its primary service area for an agreed-upon amount per member per month. These revenues are premium revenues, not patient service revenues, because they are earned by agreeing to provide care, regardless of whether services are rendered.

10.35 FASB ASC 954-405-25-1 states that if a capitation contract obligates the health care entity to assume the risk of physician referrals and other outside services, a liability for unpaid claims, including incurred but not reported claims, should be established. A lag analysis may be helpful in estimating the liability.

10.36 In addition to the capitation payments, the amount of contract revenue may be affected by factors such as reinsurance recoveries, deductibles, coinsurance, and risk pool adjustments. Risk pool adjustments may be based on factors such as utilization or cost targets.

10.37 In accordance with FASB ASC 954-605-45-3, significant revenue earned under capitation arrangements should be reported separately.

Patient Receivables

10.38 Patient receivables may include amounts due (*a*) from patients, third-party payors, and employers for provided health care services and (*b*) for premiums and stop-loss insurance recoveries. Premiums and stop-loss insurance recoveries are discussed in chapter 13, "Financial Accounting and Reporting for Managed Care Services," of this guide.

10.39 In accordance with FASB ASC 954-310-30-1, contractual adjustments, discounts, and an allowance for uncollectibles should be recorded to initially measure the receivables for health care services at net realizable value. FASB ASC 954-605-25-6 explains that estimates of contractual adjustments, other adjustments, and the allowance for uncollectibles should be reported in the period during which the services are provided, even though the actual amounts may become known at a later date. FASB ASC 954-310-45-1 states that although the aggregate amount of receivables may include balances due from patients and third-party payors, including final settlements and appeals, the amounts due from third-party payors for retroactive adjustments of items such as final settlements or appeals should be reported separately in the financial statements.

10.40 Accounts receivable of health care entities generally are subject to the same financial disclosure requirements as those of other business entities.

Health care entities with loans and trade receivables follow the presentation and disclosure guidance in FASB ASC 310-10 to the extent that guidance is applicable.

10.41 Paragraphs 20–22 of FASB ASC 825-10-50 set forth disclosure requirements concerning significant concentrations of credit risk arising from all financial instruments, including trade accounts receivable. Concentration of credit risk frequently is an issue because most health care entities tend to treat patients from their local or surrounding communities. Accordingly, disclosure is made of the primary service area of patients. It should be noted that concentration of credit risk may be a significant issue in stand-alone financial statements issued for a member hospital of a large, national multihospital system but may not be an issue for financial statements prepared for the hospital system. When the individual facilities' financial statements are consolidated into statements prepared for the entire system, the credit risk is dispersed over a much larger base of health plans, patients, and geographies and, therefore, is not as concentrated.

10.42 Off-balance-sheet risk exists when the potential accounting loss from a financial instrument is not reflected on the balance sheet. Health care entities (most notably hospitals) may enter into arrangements in which they will factor or securitize their patient accounts receivable as a cash flow management strategy or to manage their concentrations of customer credit risk. These arrangements may not qualify for sale transactions under the criteria of FASB ASC 860, *Transfers and Servicing*. Consequently, the patient accounts receivable and the corresponding financing obligation would be reflected on the balance sheet of the health care entity. Health care entities should follow the presentation and disclosure guidance in paragraphs 9–10 of FASB ASC 310-10-50 regarding credit losses on off-balance-sheet instruments to the extent that guidance is applicable.

Estimated Final Settlements

10.43 Under a retrospective rate-setting system, a health care entity may be entitled to receive additional payments or required to refund amounts received in excess of amounts earned under the system. Although final settlements are not made until a subsequent period, as discussed in paragraphs 10.20–.24, they are usually subject to reasonable estimation and reported in the financial statements in the period in which services are rendered.

10.44 For example, as noted in FASB ASC 954-310-05-3, some third-party payors retrospectively determine final amounts that are reimbursable for services rendered to their beneficiaries based on allowable costs. These payors reimburse the health care entity on the basis of interim payment rates until the retrospective determination of allowable costs can be made. In most instances, the accumulation and allocation of allowable costs and other factors result in final settlements that are different from the interim payment rates. Final settlements are determined after the close of the fiscal periods to which they apply.

10.45 The balance sheet accounts "Settlements Due to Third-Party Payors" and "Settlements Due From Third-Party Payors" reflect management's best estimate of amounts expected to be payable or receivable. As a result of the complex nature of government reimbursement rules and the fact that settlements may occur years after the services are provided, it is not unusual for actual settlement amounts to differ significantly from estimated amounts.

10.46 FASB ASC 954-605-35-1 requires that differences between original estimates and subsequent revisions, including final settlements, be included in the period in which the revisions are made. FASB ASC 954-605-50-2 states that those differences should be disclosed. Those differences are not treated as restatements of prior periods, unless they meet the definition of an *error in previously issued financial statements*, as defined in FASB ASC 250, *Accounting Changes and Error Corrections*.

10.47 As explained in paragraphs .15 and .17 of SOP 00-1, the fairness or reasonableness of the financial statement presentation of estimates is not dependent on the outcome of the uncertainty (for example, management's ability to predict the future with accuracy) but, rather, on the quality and nature of the evidence supporting management's assertions at the time that the estimate is made. The fact that future events may differ materially from management's assumptions or estimates does not necessarily mean that management's estimates were not reasonable or valid at the time that they were made.

10.48 The likelihood for subsequent revisions of estimates, coupled with their potential material effect on the financial statements, generally requires disclosure in accordance with FASB ASC 275-10-50. Such disclosures might include the significance of government program revenues to the entity's overall revenues and a description of the complex nature of applicable laws and regulations indicating that the possibility of future government review and interpretation exists. Paragraph .37 of SOP 00-1 provides a sample disclosure for the possibility of material differences between an original estimate and subsequent revisions.

10.49 FASB ASC 275-10-50-6 states that a discussion of estimates is required when, based on known information available before the financial statements are issued or available to be issued, it is reasonably possible that the estimate will change in the near term, and the effect of the change will be material. The estimate of the effect of a change in a condition, situation, or set of circumstances that existed at the date of the financial statements should be disclosed, and the evaluation should be based on known information available before the financial statements are issued or available to be issued. In addition, FASB ASC 954-405-50-1 requires that, with regard to contractual adjustments and third-party settlements, identification and explanation of the estimated amounts that are payable by the entity should be disclosed.

10.50 The Financial Reporting Executive Committee recommends that the following additional disclosures also be included in the financial statements:

- Disclose settlement amounts due to and from each significant third-party payor.
- For each significant third-party payor, provide a summary of activity for each operating period. The summary would distinguish settlements relating to prior years from those relating to the current year's activity and would identify current-year changes to settlement amounts estimated in prior periods.
- Disclose the status of third-party settlement claims.

10.51 In accordance with FASB ASC 210-10-45, settlements due to or from third-party payors should be classified as current or noncurrent, depending on the expected timing of the settlements. Settlements can be netted only if a right of setoff exists, as described in FASB ASC 210-20-45.

Auditing

> ***Note:*** This guide presents auditing guidance to help you implement auditing standards included in both AICPA *Professional Standards* and Public Company Accounting Oversight Board (PCAOB) professional standards. In citing the professional standards, references are made to the AICPA's *Professional Standards* publication and the AICPA's *PCAOB Standards and Related Rules* publication, depending upon the applicable professional standards. Additionally, when referencing professional standards, this guide cites section numbers, not the original statement number, as appropriate. For example, Statement on Auditing Standards No. 54, *Illegal Acts by Clients* (AICPA, *Professional Standards*), is referred to as AU section 317.

10.52 In general, receivables, particularly those arising from health care services, are material to the financial position of health care entities. Examples of specific auditing objectives, selected control activities, and auditing procedures that may be considered by the independent auditor as they relate to the major components of receivables of health care entities are presented in exhibit 10-1.

10.53 SOP 00-1 provides guidance to auditors in evaluating the reasonableness of management's estimates regarding the proper valuation of health care third-party revenues and receivables embodied in the financial statements. SOP 00-1 is included as appendix B, "Statement of Position 00-1, *Auditing Health Care Third-Party Revenues and Related Receivables*," of this guide.

10.54 Paragraphs .17–.18 of SOP 00-1 state that the auditor's judgment regarding the sufficiency and appropriateness of the evidence is based on the evidence that is available or can reasonably be expected to be available in the circumstances. If after considering the existing conditions and available evidence, the auditor concludes that the evidence is sufficient and appropriate and supports management's assertions about the valuation of revenues and receivables and their presentation and disclosure in the financial statements, ordinarily, an unqualified opinion is appropriate. The inability to obtain relevant evidence that the auditor needs may require the auditor to express a qualified opinion or disclaim an opinion because of a scope limitation.

Accounts Receivable Confirmations

10.55 Generally, the amount receivable for a patient's care is not determinable until the medical coding process is complete; thus, alternative procedures, rather than confirmation, are performed for receivables from patients for whom care is continuing. Further, many patients whose accounts are expected to be paid by a third-party payor may not have received bills, and many third-party payors may be unable to respond to confirmation requests on specific account balances. In addition, obtaining confirmation of receivables from patients who are not discharged or final billed may be impracticable because those patients may not yet know the amount of their indebtedness. However, there may be instances when direct confirmation may be an appropriate audit procedure to be considered to obtain evidence about the existence and accuracy of amounts that are due.

10.56 If confirmation of amounts that are due from patients and third-party payors is impracticable or determined not to be effective, the independent auditor should document this decision in accordance with AU section 330, *The Confirmation Process* (AICPA, *Professional Standards*), and should use alternative procedures such as the following:

- Performing an analytical procedure or testing the details of subsequent cash receipts
- Reviewing third-party contracts or payment agreements
- Comparing billings with documentation in medical records and census data
- Reviewing the results of third-party payor audits and, if available, independent review or internal audit reports
- Examining or confirming interim payments with third-party payors

Exhibit 10-1

The following table illustrates the use of assertions in developing audit objectives and designing substantive tests. The examples are not intended to be all-inclusive nor is it expected that all the procedures would necessarily be applied in an audit. The auditor should design and perform substantive procedures for all relevant assertions related to each material class of transactions, account balance, and disclosure to obtain sufficient appropriate audit evidence. The use of assertions in assessing risks and designing appropriate audit procedures to obtain audit evidence is described in paragraphs .14–.26 of AU section 326, *Audit Evidence* (AICPA, *Professional Standards*). Various audit procedures and the purposes for which they may be performed are described in paragraphs .27–.41 of AU section 326.

Auditing Considerations[1]

Financial Statement Assertions	*Specific Auditing Objectives*	*Selected Control Activities*	*Auditing Procedures*
Receivables for Health Care Services			
Account Balances			
Existence	Amounts reported in the financial statements represent valid receivables, which do not include charity care balances.	Charges are generated automatically when services are performed.	Review and test subsequent cash receipts.
		A medical record is prepared.	Compare billing information to the documentation contained in the medical records or census records.

(continued)

[1] Statement of Position (SOP) 00-1, *Auditing Health Care Third-Party Revenues and Related Receivables* (AICPA, *Technical Practice Aids*, AUD sec. 14,360), discusses matters for auditors to consider in testing third-party revenues and related receivables and provides guidance to auditors regarding the sufficiency of evidential matter and reporting on financial statements of health care entities exposed to material uncertainties. SOP 00-1 is included as appendix B, "Statement of Position 00-1, *Auditing Health Care Third-Party Revenues and Related Receivables*," of this guide.

Auditing Considerations—continued

Financial Statement Assertions	*Specific Auditing Objectives*	*Selected Control Activities*	*Auditing Procedures*
		Procedures ensure that amounts due from third-party payors for individual accounts are properly supported.	Review the independent review or internal audit, if any, and insurance company reviews for evidence that might indicate receivables may not be realized.
		Procedures ensure the proper recording of cash receipts.	Trace the receipts applicable to patient accounts to the accounts receivable records.
		Procedures ensure that charity care balances are identified and excluded from gross receivables.	Review the management policy for determining charity care. Review the reasonableness of charity care measurement.
Completeness	Amounts reported in the financial statements are complete and properly calculated and accumulated.	Procedures ensure that (*a*) detailed accounts receivable records are routinely compared with control accounts and third-party payor logs; (*b*) differences are investigated and reconciled; and (*c*) adjustments, if necessary, are promptly made.	Compare detailed accounts receivable records with control accounts and third-party payor logs, and investigate reconciling items.

Financial Statement Assertions	*Specific Auditing Objectives*	*Selected Control Activities*	*Auditing Procedures*
Valuation and allocation	Receivables are reported in the financial statements at net realizable value.	Allowances for uncollectibles and contractual adjustments are periodically reviewed by management to ensure that receivables are reported at estimated net realizable value.	Review third-party contracts, and recompute patient receivables. Examine contracts or confirm interim third-party payments with third-party payors.
		Write-offs and allowances for uncollectibles are identified and approved in accordance with the entity's established policy.	Review and test the method used to determine the allowances for uncollectible accounts.
			Determine that patient accounts are appropriately classified by payor (for example, Medicare or self-pay) to evaluate collectibility.
			Test Medicare logs for accuracy and completeness.
			Test and analyze aged accounts receivable trial balances, collection trends, delinquent accounts, subsequent period write-offs, and economic or other factors used to determine the allowance for uncollectible accounts.

(continued)

Auditing Considerations—continued

Financial Statement Assertions	*Specific Auditing Objectives*	*Selected Control Activities*	*Auditing Procedures*
Presentation and Disclosure			
Classification and understandability	Significant contractual arrangements with third parties are disclosed.		Determine that significant contractual arrangements with third parties are disclosed.
Estimated Third-Party Settlements			
Account Balances			
Existence	Amounts reported in the financial statements represent valid receivables or payables, or both.	Procedures ensure that estimated third-party settlements are determined in accordance with the reimbursement and rate-setting methodologies applicable to the entity.	Review correspondence from significant third-party payors related to (*a*) interim payment rates applicable to periods for which final settlements have not been made and (*b*) the amount of interim or final settlements made during the period.
Transactions			
Completeness and accuracy and valuation and allocation	Amounts included in the financial statements are accurate and complete.	Procedures ensure that estimated third-party settlements are reasonably calculated and reported.	Test the reasonableness of settlement amounts, including specific and unallocated reserves, in light of the involved payors, the nature of the payment mechanism, the risks associated with future audits, and other relevant factors.

Financial Statement Assertions	*Specific Auditing Objectives*	*Selected Control Activities*	*Auditing Procedures*
			Review third-party payor audit reports and adjustments for prior years' cost reports or settlements to consider whether (*a*) the effect of such adjustments has been properly reported in the financial statements and (*b*) adjustments of a similar nature apply to the current period.
			Obtain a representation from management that provisions for estimated retroactive adjustments by third-party payors under reimbursement agreements for open years are adequate.
Presentation and Disclosure			
Classification and understandability	Amounts reported in the financial statements are properly presented, and all required disclosures are made.		Determine that the tentative nature of third-party settlement amounts is properly disclosed.

(continued)

Auditing Considerations—continued

Financial Statement Assertions	*Specific Auditing Objectives*	*Selected Control Activities*	*Auditing Procedures*
			Determine that differences between original estimates and subsequent revisions, including final settlements, are included in the statement of operations in the period in which the revisions are made and disclosed, if material.
Revenue and Gains for Health Care Services			
Transactions, Account Balances, Presentation, and Disclosure			
Existence and occurrence, completeness, and classification and understandability	Revenue and gains are reported in the proper period using the accrual basis of accounting and are properly classified by the type of service rendered.	Procedures help ensure that revenue is accrued as services are performed or contractual obligations are satisfied.	Perform a walk-through of the revenue system. Compare the current period's revenue with prior periods' revenue or budgets, or both, and obtain explanations for large or unusual variances.
		Management establishes and monitors controls over the recognition of revenue.	Consider the adequacy of the controls over the revenue recognition process.

Financial Statement Assertions	*Specific Auditing Objectives*	*Selected Control Activities*	*Auditing Procedures*
	In the statement of operations, revenue from health care services is reported net of contractual adjustments and other adjustments in the proper period and is properly classified.	Controls ensure that deductions from revenue are recorded in the proper period and properly classified. Contractual and other adjustments are authorized, controlled, and properly recorded. Charity care, bad-debt write-offs, and courtesy and policy discounts are authorized, controlled, and properly recorded.	Review the financial statements to determine that revenue is reported net of contractual adjustments and other adjustments. Test contractual adjustments, other adjustments, and bad debts to determine that they are accounted for both in accordance with the respective contracts and the entity's policy. Review third-party payor contracts and methods of payment, and test the entity's computation of estimated adjustments to revenue as required under such contracts.

Chapter 11

Contributions Received and Made

11.01 Health care entities that receive contributions are subject to the requirements of the "Contributions Received" sections of Financial Accounting Standards Board (FASB) *Accounting Standards Codification* (ASC) 958-605. Health care entities that make contributions are subject to the requirements of FASB ASC 720-25.

Contributions Received

11.02 FASB ASC 958-605-25-2 states that except as provided for contributed services and art collections, contributions received should be recognized as revenues or gains in the period received and as assets, decreases of liabilities, or expenses depending on the form of the benefits received. FASB ASC 958-605-55-26 observes that contributions are received in several different forms. Most often, the contributed item is an asset, but it also can be forgiveness of a liability. The types of assets commonly contributed include cash, marketable securities, land, buildings, the use of facilities or utilities, materials and supplies, intangible assets, other goods or services, and unconditional promises to give those items in the future. FASB ASC 958-605-30-2 requires that contributions received be measured at their fair values. FASB ASC 820, *Fair Value Measurements and Disclosures*, establishes a framework for measuring fair value.[*]

11.03 Accounting for contributions depends on whether the transfer of assets is received by the not-for-profit entity with donor-imposed conditions, donor-imposed restrictions, or both. Donor-imposed conditions create a barrier that must be overcome before a contribution can be recognized; by definition, a contribution is unconditional. Donor-imposed restrictions do not affect recognition; instead, they affect the classification of the contribution revenue.

11.04 Donations received without restrictions attached are reported as unrestricted support in the statement of operations within the performance indicator. Donations with explicit donor restrictions attached are reported as restricted support. Some restrictions permanently limit the not-for-profit entity's use of contributed assets (for example, permanent endowments). Other restrictions are temporary in nature, limiting the not-for-profit entity's use of contributed assets to (*a*) later periods or after specific dates (time restrictions),

---

[*] In May 2011, the Financial Accounting Standards Board (FASB) issued Accounting Standards Update (ASU) No. 2011-04, *Fair Value Measurement (Topic 820): Amendments to Achieve Common Fair Value Measurement and Disclosure Requirements in U.S. GAAP and IFRSs*. According to FASB, the objective of this update is to improve the comparability of fair value measurements presented and disclosed in financial statements prepared in accordance with U.S. generally accepted accounting principles (GAAP) and International Financial Reporting Standards (IFRSs) by changing the wording used to describe many of the requirements in U.S. GAAP for measuring fair value and disclosing information about fair value measurements. The amendments include those that clarify FASB's intent about the application of existing fair value measurement and disclosure requirements and those that change a particular principle or requirement for measuring fair value or disclosing information about fair value measurements. This ASU, which is to be applied prospectively, is effective for public entities during interim and annual periods beginning after December 15, 2011 (early application is not permitted). For nonpublic entities, the amendments are effective for annual periods beginning after December 15, 2011. Nonpublic entities may early implement during interim periods beginning after December 15, 2011.

(*b*) specific purposes (purpose restrictions), or (*c*) both. As noted in paragraph 3.17 of this guide, items that reflect increases or decreases in temporarily-restricted or permanently-restricted net assets are reported in the statement of changes in net assets, rather than the statement of operations.

Contributions of Long-Lived Assets, the Use of Long-Lived Assets, or Resources to Acquire Them

11.05 Contributions of long-lived assets, including the use of long-lived assets such as land, buildings, and equipment, are reported as support or gains in the period received. The donation is measured at its fair value. In accordance with FASB ASC 958-605-45-6, in the absence of donor-imposed restrictions on the use of the asset, gifts of long-lived assets should be reported as unrestricted support. Contributions of long-lived assets with explicit donor restrictions are reported as temporarily- or permanently-restricted support.

11.06 Donations of cash or other assets that must be used to acquire long-lived assets are reported as temporarily-restricted support in the period received. In accordance with FASB ASC 958-210-45-6, cash or other assets received with a donor-imposed restriction that limits their use to long-term purposes should not be classified with cash or other assets that are unrestricted and available for current use. Consistent with FASB ASC 958-205-55-7, those items are reported as assets restricted to investment in land, buildings, and equipment and are sequenced closer to land, buildings, and equipment. See paragraph 4.08 of this guide for additional discussion of restricted assets. Pursuant to FASB ASC 958-210-50-3, when the title "Assets Whose Use Is Limited" is used on the face of the statement of financial position, the kind of asset (that is, cash, receivables, investments, and so forth) is required to be described in the notes to the financial statements because its nature is not clear from the description on the face of the statement of financial position.

11.07 FASB ASC 954-205-45-9 states that the expiration of donor-imposed restrictions on long-lived assets should be recognized when the asset is placed in service, rather than as depreciated, as permitted by FASB ASC 958-205-45-12. Thus, if contributions of long-lived assets with explicit donor restrictions are reported as temporarily-restricted support, a not-for-profit health care provider reports expirations of those donor restrictions when the stipulation is fulfilled, and the assets are placed in service. Similarly, donations of cash or other assets that must be used to acquire long-lived assets are reported as temporarily-restricted support in the period received, and expirations of those donor restrictions are reported when the acquired long-lived assets are placed in service, and donor-imposed restrictions are satisfied.

Contributed Services

11.08 The nature and extent of donated services received by health care entities varies and can range from the limited participation of many people in fund-raising activities to active participation in the entity's service programs.

11.09 FASB ASC 958-605-25-16 requires that contributions of services be recognized if the services received meet any of the following criteria:

a. They create or enhance a nonfinancial asset. The FASB ASC glossary defines a *nonfinancial asset* as "[a]n asset that is not a financial asset. Nonfinancial assets include land, buildings, use of facilities or utilities, materials and supplies, intangible assets, or services."

b. They require specialized skills, are provided by individuals possessing those skills, and would typically need to be purchased if they are not provided by donation. Services requiring specialized skills are provided by accountants, architects, carpenters, doctors, electricians, lawyers, nurses, plumbers, teachers, and other professionals and craftspeople.

11.10 FASB ASC 958-605-25-16 states that contributed services and promises to give services that do not meet these criteria should not be recognized. Additional guidance with regard to the accounting for, and reporting of, contributed services is provided in paragraphs 52–68 of FASB ASC 958-605-55.

Expiration of Donor-Imposed Restrictions

11.11 Paragraphs 9–12 of FASB ASC 958-205-45 and FASB ASC 958-225-45-13 provide guidance for reporting reclassifications for the expiration of donor-imposed restrictions. A restriction expires when the stipulated time has elapsed, when the stipulated purpose for which the resource was restricted has been fulfilled, or both. If two or more temporary restrictions are imposed on a contribution, the effect of the expiration of those restrictions should be recognized in the period in which the last remaining restriction has expired. When the restriction expires, the temporarily-restricted net assets are reclassified to unrestricted net assets and reported in the statement of operations as "Net Assets Released From Restriction." In accordance with FASB ASC 958-225-45-3, reclassifications are presented as separate items.

11.12 FASB ASC 958-605-45-4 states that donor-restricted contributions whose restrictions are met in the same reporting period may be reported as unrestricted support, provided that a not-for-profit health care entity has a similar policy for reporting investment gains and income, as explained in FASB ASC 958-320-45-3; reports consistently from period to period; and discloses its accounting policy.

11.13 Paragraph 11.26 provides guidance for the expiration of restrictions on unconditional promises to give. Paragraphs 9.19–.24 of this guide provide guidance for the expiration of other donor-imposed restrictions.

Distinguishing Contributions From Exchange Transactions

11.14 FASB ASC 958-605-55-4 states that foundations, business entities, and other types of entities may provide resources to health care entities under programs referred to as grants, awards, or sponsorships. Those asset transfers are contributions if the resource providers receive no value in exchange for the transferred assets or if the value received by the resource provider is incidental to the potential public benefit from using the transferred assets.

11.15 Because some exchange transactions may appear to be much like contributions, a careful assessment of the characteristics of the transaction from the perspectives of both the resource provider and recipient is required to determine whether the recipient of a transfer of assets has given up an asset or incurred a liability of commensurate value. Additional guidance can be found in FASB ASC 958-605-55-8.

11.16 For example, a research grant made by a foundation to a hospital would likely be a contribution if the research program is to be planned and carried out by the hospital, and the hospital has the right to publish the results. However, if the grant is made by a pharmaceutical manufacturer that provides potential new medications to be tested in the hospital's research facilities and retains the right to any patents or other results, the grant would likely be an exchange transaction.

11.17 As noted in FASB ASC 958-605-55-6, a single transaction may be in part an exchange and in part a contribution. For example, if a donor transfers a building to an entity at a price significantly lower than its market value, and no unstated rights or privileges are involved, the transaction is in part an exchange of assets and in part a contribution to be accounted for as required by the "Contributions Received" sections of FASB ASC 958-605.

Reporting the Cost of Special Events and Other Fund-Raising Activities

11.18 Some health care entities conduct fund-raising or joint activities, including special social and educational events, such as symposia, dinners, dances, and theater parties, in which the attendee receives a direct benefit (for example, a meal or theater ticket).

11.19 FASB ASC 958-225-45-17 states that a not-for-profit health care entity may report net amounts for its special events if they result from peripheral or incidental transactions. However, so-called special events often are ongoing and major activities; if so, a not-for-profit health care entity should report the gross amounts of revenues and expenses of those activities. Costs netted against receipts from peripheral or incidental special events should be limited to direct costs.

11.20 Paragraphs 11–15 of FASB ASC 958-225-55 illustrate three possible methods to display a special event that is an ongoing and major activity. Health care entities may report the gross revenues of special events and other fund-raising activities, with the cost of direct benefits to donors (for example, meals and facilities rental) displayed either (*a*) as a line item deducted from the special event revenues or (*b*) in the same section of the statement of operations as other programs or supporting services, allocated, if necessary, among those various functions. Alternatively, the health care entity could consider revenue from special events and other fund-raising activities as part exchange (for the fair value the participant received) and part contribution (for the excess of the payment over that fair value) and report the two parts separately.

Promises to Give in Future Periods (Pledges)

11.21 Health care entities involved in fund-raising campaigns frequently are the recipients of promises to give, with payments due in future periods. Pledge drives are a common example. Health care entities may also be the beneficiaries of fund-raising campaigns conducted by others.

11.22 FASB ASC 958-310 and 958-605 establish the accounting and financial reporting guidance for promises to give (contributions receivable). A general summary of those standards is presented subsequently but is not intended as a substitute for reading the standards themselves. Additional guidance is provided in chapter 5, "Contributions Received and Agency Transactions," of the Audit and Accounting Guide *Not-for-Profit Entities*.

11.23 The recognition guidance in paragraphs 7–15 of FASB ASC 958-605-25 depends on whether the promise to give is unconditional or conditional. That guidance is summarized in the next two paragraphs but is not intended as a substitute for reading the standards themselves.

11.24 Conditional promises to give, which depend on the occurrence of a specified future and uncertain event to bind the promisor, should be recognized when the conditions on which they depend are substantially met (that is, when the conditional promise becomes unconditional). Imposing a condition creates a barrier that must be overcome before the recipient of the transferred assets has an unconditional right to retain those promised assets. For example, a transfer of cash with a promise to contribute that cash if a like amount of new gifts is raised from others within 30 days and a provision that the cash be returned if the gifts are not raised imposes a condition on which a promised gift depends. A transfer of assets with a conditional promise to contribute them should be accounted for as a refundable advance (that is, a liability) until the conditions have been substantially met or explicitly waived by the donor.[1]

11.25 An unconditional promise to give should be recognized when it is received. However, to be recognized, there must be sufficient evidence in the form of verifiable documentation that a promise was made and received. According to FASB 958-605-45-5, contributions of unconditional promises to give, with payments due in future periods, should be reported as restricted support, unless explicit donor stipulations or circumstances surrounding the receipt of a promise make clear that the donor intended it to be used to support activities of the current period. It is reasonable to assume that by specifying future payment dates, donors indicate that their gift is to support activities in each period in which a payment is scheduled. For example, receipts of unconditional promises to give cash in future years generally increase temporarily-restricted net assets.

11.26 The expiration of those restrictions or the expiration of a portion of the restriction is recognized as the donor makes the future payment(s). If the promise is to be paid in one future payment, the related temporarily-restricted net assets will be transferred to unrestricted net assets in the period in which that payment is due. If the donor sets forth a schedule of future payments, a reclassification from temporarily-restricted net assets to unrestricted net assets is made in each period that a payment is due. If other explicit donor restrictions are attached to the promise, such as that the gift be used for a specific purpose, the expiration of the restriction is recognized in the time period in which the purpose restriction has been fulfilled because, as noted in FASB ASC 958-205-45-11, temporarily-restricted net assets with time restrictions are not available to support expenses until the time restrictions have expired. In the period(s) in which the restrictions expire, temporarily-restricted net assets or the portion of the temporarily-restricted net assets that relate to the

---

[1] According to FASB *Accounting Standards Codification* (ASC) 958-605-25-12, a conditional promise to give is considered unconditional if the possibility that the condition will not be met is remote. FASB ASC 958-605-25-14 states that in cases of ambiguous donor stipulations, a promise containing stipulations that are not clearly unconditional should be presumed to be a conditional promise. Additional guidance on distinguishing conditional promises from unconditional promises is provided in paragraphs 14–15 of FASB ASC 958-605-25 and paragraphs 15–17 of FASB ASC 958-605-55.

particular payment installment are reclassified to unrestricted net assets and reported in the statement of operations as net assets released from restriction.

11.27 Paragraphs 4–7 of FASB ASC 958-605-30 provide guidance for initially measuring unconditional promises to give. If present value techniques are used to measure the fair value of unconditional promises to give, a not-for-profit entity should determine the amount and timing of the future cash flows of unconditional promises to give cash or, for promises to give noncash assets, the quantity and nature of assets expected to be received. In determining the estimated future cash flows of unconditional promises to give cash, not-for-profit entities should consider all the elements in FASB ASC 820-10-55-5, including the following: (*a*) when the receivable is expected to be collected; (*b*) the creditworthiness of the other parties; (*c*) the entity's past collection experience and its policies concerning the enforcement of promises to give; (*d*) expectations about possible variations in the amount or timing of the cash flows (that is, the uncertainty inherent in the cash flows); and (*e*) other factors concerning the receivable's collectability. Unconditional promises to give that are expected to be collected in less than one year may be measured at their net realizable value because that amount results in a reasonable estimate of fair value.

11.28 Paragraphs 4–13 of FASB 958-310-35 discuss the subsequent measurement of contributions receivable. According to FASB ASC 958-310-35-7, if the fair value of a contribution receivable decreases because of changes in the quantity or nature of assets expected to be received, the decrease should be recognized in the period(s) in which the expectation changes. That decrease should be reported as an expense or a loss (bad debt), in accordance with FASB ASC 958-310-45-3.[2] According to FASB ASC 958-310-35-6, if an unconditional promise to give cash is initially measured using a present value technique, subsequent accruals of the interest element should be accounted for as contribution revenue by donees, pursuant to FASB ASC 835-30-35.

11.29 If a health care entity routinely conducts fund drives, an estimate of the future cash flows of a portfolio of short-term unconditional promises to give resulting from a mass fund-raising appeal may be made based on experience gained from similar appeals in prior years.

Investments Gain or Loss Related to Donor-Restricted Contributions

11.30 Chapter 4, "Cash, Cash Equivalents, and Investments," of this guide discusses the classification of dividend, interest and other investment income, and gains and losses. Chapter 9, "Net Assets (Equity)," of this guide discusses the classification of the net assets of donor-restricted endowment funds.

Transfers of Assets to a Not-for-Profit Organization or Charitable Trust That Raises or Holds Contributions for Others

11.31 The "Transfers of Assets to a Not-for-Profit Entity or Charitable Trust That Raises or Holds Contributions for Others" sections of FASB ASC 958-605 establish standards for transactions in which an entity (donor) makes a contribution by transferring assets to a not-for-profit entity or charitable

---

[2] According to FASB ASC 958-310-45-3, because all expenses are reported as decreases in the unrestricted net asset class, those decreases should be reported as losses if they are decreases in temporarily-restricted or permanently-restricted net assets.

trust (recipient entity) that accepts the assets from the donor and agrees to use the assets on behalf of another entity or transfer those assets, the return on investment of those assets, or both to another entity (the beneficiary) that is specified by the donor.[3]

11.32 Federated fund-raising organizations, community foundations, and institutionally-related entities are examples of not-for-profit entities that commonly serve as recipient entities, such as agents, trustees, or intermediaries, but any not-for-profit entity or charitable trust can function in that capacity. Not-for-profit health care entities often are the ultimate recipients (for example, specified beneficiaries of the contribution or grant).

11.33 Paragraphs 28–30 of FASB ASC 958-605-25 provide guidance for recognition by the specified beneficiary of the transfer of assets from the donor. A specified beneficiary should recognize its rights to the financial or nonfinancial assets held by a recipient entity as an asset, unless the recipient entity is explicitly granted variance power, as discussed in paragraph 11.34. Those rights are any one of the following:

a. An interest in the net assets of the recipient entity, as discussed in paragraph 11.35

b. A beneficial interest, as discussed in paragraph 11.36

c. A receivable, as discussed in paragraph 11.37

11.34 The FASB ASC glossary defines *variance power* as

> [t]he unilateral power to redirect the use of the transferred assets to another beneficiary. A donor explicitly grants variance power if the recipient entity's unilateral power to redirect the use of the assets is explicitly referred to in the instrument transferring the assets. Unilateral power means that the recipient entity can override the donor's instructions without approval from the donor, the specified beneficiary, or any other interested party.

As discussed in FASB ASC 958-605-25-31, if the donor explicitly grants a recipient entity variance power, and the specified beneficiary is not an affiliate of the recipient entity or the donor, the specified beneficiary (not-for-profit health care entity) should not recognize its potential for future distributions from the assets held by the recipient entity. Those future distributions, if they occur, should be recognized as contributions by the specified beneficiary (health care organization) when received or unconditionally promised.

11.35 If a recipient entity and specified beneficiary are financially interrelated entities (see paragraph 12.75 of this guide), and the recipient entity is not a trustee, FASB ASC 958-605-25-27 states that the recipient entity should recognize a contribution received when it receives assets (financial or nonfinancial) from the donor that are specified for the beneficiary. FASB ASC 958-20-25 provides the following example. A foundation that exists to raise, hold, and invest assets for the specified beneficiary or a group of affiliates of which the

---

[3] The "Transfers of Assets to a Not-for-Profit Entity or Charitable Trust that Raises or Holds Contributions for Others" sections of FASB ASC 958-605 also establish standards for transactions that take place in a similar manner but are not contributions because the transfers are revocable, repayable, or reciprocal. For example, if a resource provider transfers assets to a recipient organization and names itself or its affiliate as beneficiary, that transaction is reciprocal, even if the resource provider grants variance power. Those reciprocal transactions are discussed in chapters 4, "Cash, Cash Equivalents, and Investments," and 12, "The Reporting Entity and Related Entities," of this guide.

specified beneficiary is a member generally is financially interrelated with the not-for-profit entity(ies) it supports. The foundation should recognize contribution revenue when it receives assets from the donor. Pursuant to FASB ASC 958-20-25-2, the beneficiary should recognize its interest in the net assets of the recipient entity and adjust that interest for its share of the change in net assets of the recipient entity using a method similar to the equity method of accounting for investments in common stock.[4] Examples 1–3 in paragraphs 3–17 of FASB ASC 958-20-55 provide examples of this guidance. Appendix A, "TIS Section 6400, *Health Care Entities*," of this chapter provides guidance for the classification of a beneficiary's interest in the net assets of a financially-interrelated fund-raising foundation.

11.36 If the beneficiary has an unconditional right to receive all or a portion of the specified cash flows from a charitable trust or other identifiable pool of assets, the beneficiary should recognize that beneficial interest. Pursuant to FASB ASC 958-605-30-14 and 958-605-45-35-3, the beneficiary recognizes that beneficial interest as an asset and a contribution received, measuring and subsequently remeasuring it at fair value.

11.37 FASB ASC 958-605-25-30 states that if the beneficiary's rights are neither an interest in the net assets of the recipient entity nor a beneficial interest, the beneficiary should recognize its rights to the assets held by a recipient entity as a receivable and contribution revenue, in accordance with paragraphs 8–10 of FASB ASC 958-605-25 and FASB ASC 958-605-45-5 for unconditional promises to give. Paragraphs 11.21–.29 discuss the recognition of promises to give.

11.38 Additional information about transfers of assets to a not-for-profit entity or charitable trust that raises or holds contributions for others is found in chapters 4, "Cash and Cash Equivalents" (for investments held by others) and 5 (for accounting and reporting by the recipient entity) of the Audit and Accounting Guide *Not-for-Profit Entities*.

Contributions Made

11.39 FASB ASC 720-25 states that contributions made should be recognized as expenses in the period made and decreases of assets or increases of liabilities, depending on the form of the benefits given. For example, gifts of items from inventory held for sale are recognized as decreases of inventory and contribution expenses, and unconditional promises to give cash are recognized as payables and contribution expenses. For guidance on conditional promises to give and determining whether a promise is conditional or unconditional, see paragraphs 11–15 of FASB ASC 958-605-25 and FASB ASC 958-605-25-33. See paragraphs 45–48 of FASB ASC 958-605-55 for an example that illustrates a donor's accounting for an unconditional promise to give. Contributions made are measured at fair value. If the fair value of a transferred asset differs from its carrying amount, a gain or loss should be recognized on the disposition of the asset, as discussed in paragraphs 1–2 of FASB 845-10-30.

Other Considerations

11.40 A *split-interest agreement* is a form of contribution in which a not-for-profit entity receives benefits that are shared with other beneficiaries

[4] FASB ASC 958-20-55-11 states that an interest in the net assets of an affiliate would be eliminated if that affiliate was included in consolidated financial statements of the interest holder.

designated by the donor. Common kinds of such agreements include charitable lead and remainder trusts, charitable gift annuities, and pooled (life) income funds. The special accounting for split-interest agreements is discussed in FASB ASC 958-30 and chapter 6, "Split-Interest Agreements," of the Audit and Accounting Guide *Not-for-Profit Entities*.

11.41 The majority of the disclosures for contributions receivable and transfers of assets to a not-for-profit entity that raises or holds contributions for others are located in FASB ASC 958-310-50 and 958-605-50. The following paragraphs discuss the more common of those disclosures but are not intended as a substitute for the "Disclosures" sections of FASB ASC 958, *Not-for-Profit Entities*.

11.42 Contributions receivable should be reported net of an allowance for uncollectible amounts. That allowance may be based on the receivable's age, the creditworthiness of the parties, the entity's past collection experience and its policies concerning the enforcement of promises to give, and other factors concerning the receivable's collectability. After the date of initial measurement, bad debt expense should be reported for the amount of promises to give that are expected to be uncollectible.

11.43 In accordance with FASB ASC 958-310-45-1, contributions receivable should be reported net of the discount that arises if measuring a promise to give at present value. The discount should be separately disclosed by reporting it as a deduction from contributions receivable either on the face of the statement of financial position or in the notes to financial statements.

11.44 FASB ASC 958-310-50-1 requires that a health care entity that is the recipient of unconditional pledges (promises to give in future periods) disclose the following:

a. The amounts of promises receivable in less than one year, in one to five years, and in more than five years

b. The amount of the allowance for uncollectible promises receivable

c. The discount that arises if measuring a promise to give at present value, if that discount is not separately disclosed by reporting it as a deduction from contributions receivable on the face of the statement of financial position, pursuant to FASB ASC 958-310-45-1

11.45 FASB ASC 958-310-50-4 requires that a health care entity that is the recipient of conditional pledges (promises to give in future periods) disclose both of the following:

a. The total of the amounts promised

b. A description and amount for each group of promises having similar characteristics, such as amounts of promises conditioned on establishing new programs, completing a new building, or raising matching gifts by a specified date

11.46 Pursuant to FASB ASC 958-205-50-3, if a not-for-profit health care entity discloses in its financial statements a ratio of fund-raising expenses to amounts raised, it also should disclose how it computes that ratio.

11.47 When reporting unrestricted contributions, not-for-profit health care entities should apply the standards in paragraphs 4–7 of FASB ASC

954-225-45 to determine whether contributions are reported within or outside the performance indicator.

Auditing

11.48 Because investor-owned entities do not usually receive contributions or enter into agency transactions, the specific audit objectives; selected controls; and auditing procedures related to contributions, contributions receivable, and agency transactions are unique to not-for-profit entities and presented in the following paragraphs.

11.49 A not-for-profit health care entity that receives a significant amount of contributions may have an increased risk of material misstatement if it does not have proper internal controls in place. Paragraph .54 of AU section 314, *Understanding the Entity and Its Environment and Assessing the Risks of Material Misstatement* (AICPA, *Professional Standards*), states that obtaining an understanding of internal control involves evaluating the design of a control and determining whether it has been implemented. Evaluating the design of a control involves considering whether the control, individually or in combination with other controls, is capable of effectively preventing or detecting and correcting material misstatements. Implementation of a control means that the control exists, and the entity is using it. An improperly designed control may represent a significant deficiency or material weakness in the entity's internal control, and the auditor should consider whether to communicate this to those charged with governance and management.

11.50 In order to have an effective system of internal control, a not-for-profit health care entity that receives significant amounts of contributions should have an internal control system that provides effective controls to ensure that all contributions received are recorded, and suitable collection efforts are pursued for unconditional promises to give. The internal control system also should provide effective controls to ensure that revenues arising from conditional promises to give are recognized when the conditions have been substantially met, and restrictions on contributions are recognized in the appropriate net asset class.

11.51 Contributions received are measured at fair value. AU section 328, *Auditing Fair Value Measurements and Disclosures* (AICPA, *Professional Standards*), addresses audit considerations relating to the measurement and disclosure of assets, liabilities, and specific components of equity presented or disclosed at fair value in financial statements. Interpretation No. 1, "Auditing Interests in Trusts Held by a Third-Party Trustee and Reported at Fair Value," of AU section 328 (AICPA, *Professional Standards*, AU sec. 9328 par. .01–.04), provides guidance for auditing interests in trusts held by a third-party trustee.

11.52 Paragraph .34 of AU section 330, *The Confirmation Process* (AICPA, *Professional Standards*), states that confirmation of accounts receivable is a generally accepted auditing procedure and that a presumption exists that the auditor will request the confirmation of accounts receivable, except under certain specified circumstances. That paragraph defines *accounts receivable* as (*a*) the entity's claims against customers that have arisen from the sale of goods or services in the normal course of business and (*b*) a financial institution's loans. Although under that definition contributions receivable are not accounts receivable to which that presumption would apply, the auditor may nevertheless decide to request confirmation of contributions receivable.

11.53 Receivables are usually principally confirmed to provide evidence about the existence assertion. FASB ASC 958-605-25-8 specifies that for a promise to give to be recognized in financial statements, there must be sufficient evidence in the form of verifiable documentation that a promise was made and received. If the documentation is not present, an asset should not be recognized. The verifiable documentation for recognition of promises to give may not be sufficient evidence concerning the existence assertion. Confirming recorded promises to give (contributions receivable) may provide additional evidence about the existence of promises to give, the existence or absence of restrictions or conditions, and the periods over which the promises to give become due. If the auditor confirms promises to give, AU section 330 provides requirements and guidance concerning the confirmation process.

11.54 The following table illustrates the use of assertions in developing audit objectives and designing substantive tests. The examples are not intended to be all-inclusive nor is it expected that all the procedures would necessarily be applied in an audit. The auditor should design and perform substantive procedures for all relevant assertions related to each material class of transactions, account balance, and disclosure to obtain sufficient appropriate audit evidence. The use of assertions in assessing risks and designing appropriate audit procedures to obtain audit evidence is described in paragraphs .14–.26 of AU section 326, *Audit Evidence* (AICPA, *Professional Standards*). Various audit procedures and the purposes for which they may be performed are described in paragraphs .27–.41 of AU section 326.

Exhibit 11-1

The following table illustrates the use of assertions in developing audit objectives and designing substantive tests. The examples are not intended to be all-inclusive nor is it expected that all the procedures would necessarily be applied in an audit. The auditor should design and perform substantive procedures for all relevant assertions related to each material class of transactions, account balance, and disclosure to obtain sufficient appropriate audit evidence. The use of assertions in assessing risks and designing appropriate audit procedures to obtain audit evidence is described in paragraphs .14–.26 of AU section 326, *Audit Evidence* (AICPA, *Professional Standards*). Various audit procedures and the purposes for which they may be performed are described in paragraphs .27–.41 of AU section 326.

Auditing Considerations

Financial Statement Assertions	*Specific Audit Objectives*	*Selected Controls Activities*	*Auditing Procedures*
Transactions			
Contributions Received			
Occurrence	Amounts recognized as contribution revenues represent valid unconditional contributions.	Controls ensure that only unconditional contributions are recognized in the financial statements.	Examine documentation supporting the recognition of contribution revenues, noting information such as the absence of conditions.
Completeness	All unconditional contributions are recognized.	Controls ensure that all unconditional contributions are recognized in the financial statements. Controls ensure that revenue is recognized when the conditions on conditional promises to give have been substantially met.	Select from data accumulated and maintained by the fund-raising function, and determine whether a contribution should have been recognized and, if so, vouch it to a recognized contribution, investigating reconciling items.

Financial Statement Assertions	*Specific Audit Objectives*	*Selected Controls Activities*	*Auditing Procedures*
Valuation and allocation	Contribution revenues are appropriately valued.	Controls ensure the appropriate valuation of contribution revenue at the time of initial recognition.	Review and test the methods and assumptions used to measure contribution revenue at the time of initial recognition.
Cut-off	Contributions are reported in the period in which they were given.	Controls ensure that contributions occurring near fiscal period-end are recorded in the proper period.	Examine contributions reported before and after fiscal period-end to determine if they are reported in the appropriate period.
Contributed Services, Utilities, Facilities, and Use of Long-Lived Assets			
Occurrence, completeness, valuation and allocation	Assets, expenses, and revenues from contributed services, utilities, facilities, and use of long-lived assets meet the appropriate recognition criteria; all such contributions that meet the recognition criteria are recognized and appropriately measured.	Controls ensure that only contributed services, utilities, facilities, and use of long-lived assets that meet the appropriate recognition criteria are recognized; controls ensure that all such contributions that meet the recognition criteria are recognized and appropriately measured.	Review the documentation underlying the recognition of contributed services, utilities, facilities, and use of long-lived assets for completeness and propriety of recognized amounts.
Contributions Made			
Occurrence	Amounts recognized as contributions made are properly authorized and reported in the period in which they become unconditional.	Controls ensure that only unconditional contributions made and promises to give are recognized in the financial statements.	Examine documentation supporting the recognition of contributions made, including notification of the donee and whether the contribution is conditional or unconditional.

(continued)

Auditing Considerations—continued

Financial Statement Assertions	*Specific Audit Objectives*	*Selected Controls Activities*	*Auditing Procedures*
Completeness	All unconditional contributions made are recognized.	Controls ensure that all unconditional contributions made are recognized in the financial statements.	Review minutes of governing board and governing board committee meetings for information about contributions.
Valuation and allocation	Contributions made are measured at fair value at initial recognition.	Controls ensure the appropriate valuation of contributions made, including promises to give, at the time of initial recognition.	Review and test the method used for valuing contributions made, including promises to give.
Account Balances			
Contributions Receivable			
Occurrence	Amounts recognized as contributions receivable represent valid unconditional promises to give.	Controls ensure that only unconditional promises to give are recognized in the financial statements.	Examine documentation supporting the recognition of promises to give, noting information such as the absence of conditions and the periods over which the promises to give become due.
Completeness	All unconditional promises to give are recognized.	Controls ensure that all unconditional promises to give are recognized in the financial statements. Controls ensure that conditional promises to give are recognized when the conditions have been substantially met.	Compare the detail of contributions receivable with data accumulated and maintained by the fund-raising function, and investigate reconciling items.

Financial Statement Assertions	*Specific Audit Objectives*	*Selected Controls Activities*	*Auditing Procedures*
Valuation and Allocation	Contributions receivable are appropriately valued.	Controls ensure the appropriate valuation of promises to give at the time of initial recognition.	Review and test the methods and assumptions used to measure promises to give at the time of initial recognition.
		The valuation of promises to give is periodically reviewed by management.	Review promises to give for collectability and, if appropriate, changes in fair value of the underlying asset.
		Write-offs of uncollectible promises to give are identified and approved in accordance with the entity's established policy.	
Promises to Give			
Occurrence	Amounts recognized as contributions payable represent valid unconditional promises to give.	Controls ensure that only unconditional promises to give are recognized in the financial statements.	Examine documentation supporting recognition of contributions payable, including information such as the absence of conditions and the periods over which the promises to give become due.
Completeness	All unconditional promises to give are recognized.	Controls ensure that all unconditional promises to give are recognized in the financial statements.	Review minutes of governing board and governing board committee meetings for information about promises to give.

(continued)

Auditing Considerations—continued

Financial Statement Assertions	*Specific Audit Objectives*	*Selected Controls Activities*	*Auditing Procedures*
Cut-off	All unconditional promises to give are recognized in the proper period.	Controls ensure that contributions made near fiscal period-end are recorded in the appropriate period.	Review cash disbursements subsequent to year-end to ascertain that contributions made were recorded in the proper period.
Valuation and allocation	Contributions made and related liabilities expected to be paid beyond one year are measured using the method elected by the not-for-profit entity.	Controls ensure the appropriate valuation of promises to give at the end of the fiscal period.	Review and test the method used for valuing promises to give that are payable more than one year from the date of the financial statements.
Agency Transactions			
Occurrence and completeness	Assets and liabilities from agency transactions meet the criteria for classification and recognition as agency transactions.	Controls ensure that (*a*) only resources received and paid in agency transactions are recognized as agency transactions, and (*b*) all such transactions are recognized.	Review the documentation underlying the receipt of assets from resource providers for propriety of classification and recognition as resources that are to be transferred to others.
	All agency transactions are recognized.		Review the documentation underlying the distribution of assets to others for propriety of classification and recognition.
			Review the historical patterns of the distribution of gifts in kind and other assets to determine the extent of the entity's discretion over those distributions.

Financial Statement Assertions	*Specific Audit Objectives*	*Selected Controls Activities*	*Auditing Procedures*
Presentation and Disclosures			
Contribution Revenues and Contributions Receivable			
Classification and understandability	Restricted contributions are reported in the proper net asset class.	Contributions are reviewed for restrictions and other limitations.	Review the documentation underlying contributions and promises to give, including donor correspondence and governing board minutes, for propriety of classification, including classification within or outside the performance indicator.
	Disclosures related to contributions are clear and understandable.	Controls ensure that contributions are appropriately presented and disclosed.	Determine the appropriateness of disclosures for conditional and unconditional promises to give.
Agency Transactions			
Rights and obligations	Intermediary or agent transactions or transactions for which the health care entity acts as a recipient are not included in reported amounts of contributions.	Controls ensure that those transactions are identified and not included in contribution totals.	Determine whether agency transactions are excluded from the statement of operations and the statement of changes in net assets. If they are not, determine that the transactions are reported as described in the "Transfers of Assets to a Not-for-Profit Entity or Charitable Trust that Raises or Holds Contributions for Others" sections of Financial Accounting Standards Board *Accounting Standards Codification* 958-605.

11.55

Appendix A—TIS Section 6400, *Health Care Entities*

.35 Note to Sections 6400.36–.42—Implementation of FASB ASC 958—Classification of a Beneficiary's Interest in the Net Assets of a Financially Interrelated Fund-Raising Foundation (in the Beneficiary's Financial Statements)

Some not-for-profit entities have separate fund-raising foundations (commonly referred to as "institutionally related foundations") that solicit contributions on their behalf. FASB ASC 958 provides guidance on (among other things) the accounting that should be followed by such in-stitutionally related foundations and their related beneficiary entity(ies) with respect to contributions received by the foundation.

Some institutionally related foundations and their beneficiary entities meet the characteristics of financially interrelated entities provided in FASB ASC 958-20-15-2. If entities are financially interrelated, FASB ASC 958 provides that the balance sheet of the beneficiary entity(ies) should reflect that entity's interest in the net assets of the foundation, and that interest should be periodically adjusted to reflect the beneficiary's share of the changes in the net assets of the foundation. This accounting is similar to the equity method of accounting, which is described in FASB ASC 323.

FASB ASC 323-10-35-5 requires that the periodic adjustment of the investment be included in the determination of the investor's net income. The purpose of sections 6140.14–.18 (applicable to not-for-profit entities [NPEs] other than health care [HC] entities) and sections 6400.36–.42 (applicable to not-for-profit health care entities) is to clarify that in circumstances in which the recipient and the beneficiary are financially interrelated:

- Beneficiary entities should segregate the adjustment into changes in restricted and unrestricted net assets. (NPE TPA [sections 6140.14–.16]; HC TPA [sections 6400.36–.37 and .39])
- In circumstances in which the beneficiary can influence the financial decisions of the recipient entity to such an extent that the beneficiary can determine the timing and amount of distributions from the recipient to the beneficiary, the existence of the recipient entity should be transparent in determining the net asset classifications in the beneficiary's financial statements. In other words, the recipient cannot impose time or purpose restrictions beyond those imposed by the donor. (NPE TPA [section 6140.14 and .16]; HC TPA [sections 6400.36 and .39])
- In circumstances in which the beneficiary cannot influence the financial decisions of the recipient entity to such an extent that the beneficiary can determine the timing and amount of distributions from the recipient to the beneficiary, the existence of the recipient entity creates an implied time restriction on the beneficiary's net assets attributable to the beneficiary's interest in the net assets of the recipient (in addition to any other restrictions that may exist). Accordingly, in recognizing its interest in the net assets of the recipient entity and the

changes in that interest, the beneficiary should classify the resulting net assets and changes in those net assets as temporarily restricted (unless donors placed permanent restrictions on their contributions). (NPE TPA [section 6140.15]; HC TPA [section 6400.37])

- In circumstances in which the beneficiary can influence the financial decisions of the recipient entity to such an extent that the beneficiary can determine the timing and amount of distributions from the recipient to the beneficiary and some net assets held by the recipient for the benefit of the beneficiary are subject to purpose restrictions [for example, net assets of the recipient restricted to the beneficiary's purchase of property, plant, and equipment (PPE)], expenditures by the beneficiary that meet those purpose restrictions result in the beneficiary (and recipient) reporting reclassifications from temporarily restricted to unrestricted net assets (assuming that the beneficiary has no other net assets subject to similar purpose restrictions), unless those net assets are subject to time restrictions that have not expired, including time restrictions that are implied on contributed long-lived assets as a result of the beneficiary's accounting policy pursuant to FASB ASC 958-605-45-6. (If those net assets are subject to time restrictions that have not expired and the beneficiary has other net assets with similar purpose restrictions, the restrictions on those other net assets would expire in accordance with FASB ASC 958. These TPAs do not, however, establish a hierarchy pertaining to which restrictions are released first—restrictions on net assets held by the recipient or purpose restrictions on net assets held by the beneficiary.) (NPE TPA [section 6140.17]; HC TPA [section 6400.40])
- In circumstances in which the beneficiary cannot influence the financial decisions of the recipient entity to such an extent that the beneficiary can determine the timing and amount of distributions from the recipient to the beneficiary and some net assets held by the recipient for the benefit of the beneficiary are subject to purpose restrictions, though not subject to time restrictions other than the implied time restrictions that exist because the beneficiary cannot determine the timing and amount of distributions from the recipient to the beneficiary, expenditures by the beneficiary that are consistent with those purpose restrictions should not result in the beneficiary reporting a reclassification from temporarily restricted to unrestricted net assets, subject to the exceptions in the following sentence. Expenditures by the beneficiary that are consistent with those purpose restrictions should result in the beneficiary reporting a reclassification from temporarily restricted to unrestricted net assets if (*a*) the recipient has no discretion in deciding whether the purpose restriction is met[1] or (*b*) the recipient distributes or obligates itself to distribute to the beneficiary amounts attributable to net assets restricted for the particular

---

[1] In some circumstances, the purpose restrictions may be so broad that the recipient entity has discretion in deciding whether expenditures by the beneficiary that are consistent with those purpose restrictions actually meet those purpose restrictions. For example, the recipient's net assets may have arisen from a contribution that was restricted for the beneficiary's purchase of research equipment, with no particular research equipment specified. Purchasing an XYZ microscope, which is consistent with that purpose restriction, may or may not meet that purpose restriction, depending on the decision of the recipient. In contrast, the net assets may have arisen from a contribution that was restricted for an XYZ microscope. Purchasing an XYZ microscope, which also is consistent with that purpose restriction, would result in the recipient having no discretion in determining whether that purpose restriction is met.

purpose, or otherwise indicates that the recipient intends for those net assets to be used to support the particular purpose as an activity of the current period. In all other circumstances, (*a*) purpose restrictions and (*b*) implied time restrictions on the net assets attributable to the interest in the recipient entity exist and have not yet expired. (However, if the beneficiary has other net assets with similar purpose restrictions, those restrictions would expire in accordance with FASB ASC 958. These TPAs do not establish a hierarchy pertaining to which restrictions are released first—restrictions on net assets held by the recipient or restrictions on net assets held by the beneficiary.) (NPE TPA [section 6140.18]; HC TPA [section 6400.41])

- *For HC NPEs Only.* In circumstances in which the beneficiary can influence the financial decisions of the recipient to such an extent that the beneficiary can determine the timing and amount of distributions from the recipient to the beneficiary, changes in the beneficiary's interest in the net assets of a recipient entity attributable to unrealized gains and losses on investments should be included or excluded from the performance indicator in accordance with FASB ASC 954-10, FASB ASC 954-205-45, FASB ASC 954-320-45, FASB ASC 954-320-55, and FASB ASC 954-605, in the same manner that they would have been had the beneficiary had the transactions itself. Similarly, in applying this guidance, the determination of whether amounts are included or excluded from the performance measure should comprehend that if the beneficiary cannot influence the financial decisions of the recipient entity to such an extent that the beneficiary can determine the timing and amount of distributions from the recipient to the beneficiary, an implied time restriction exists on the beneficiary's net assets attributable to the beneficiary's interest in the net assets of the recipient (in addition to any other restrictions that may exist). Accordingly, in circumstances in which the beneficiary cannot influence the financial decisions of the recipient entity to such an extent that the beneficiary can determine the timing and amount of distributions from the recipient to the beneficiary, the beneficiary should classify the resulting net assets and changes in those net assets as temporarily restricted (unless donors placed permanent restrictions on their contributions) and therefore exclude those changes from the performance indicator. (HC TPA [section 6400.42])
- *For HC NPEs Only.* In circumstances in which the recipient entity and the beneficiary are both controlled by the same entity, entities should consider the specific facts and circumstances to determine whether the beneficiary can influence the financial decisions of the recipient entity to such an extent that the beneficiary can determine the timing and amount of distributions from the recipient to the beneficiary. (HC TPA [section 6400.38])

**Technical Practice Aids for Not-for-Profit Entities
Implementation of FASB ASC 958—Classification of a Beneficiary's Interest in the
Net Assets of a Financially Interrelated Fund-Raising Foundation (in the Beneficiary's Financial Statements)**

HC NPEs			
NPEs that are not HC NPEs			
Can the beneficiary determine the timing and amount of distributions from the recipient to the beneficiary? [Not-for-profit health care entities (HC NPEs) under common control consider HC Technical Practice Aid (TPA) section 6400.38]	**How does the existence of the recipient affect the beneficiary's reporting of its interest?**	**Are any net assets held by the recipient for the benefit of the beneficiary subject to donor-imposed purpose restrictions and has the beneficiary made expenditures that meet those purpose restrictions (in circumstances in which the beneficiary can determine the timing and amount of distributions from the recipient to the beneficiary) or that are consistent with those purpose restrictions (in circumstances in which the beneficiary cannot determine the timing and amount of distributions from the recipient to the beneficiary)?**	**Are any changes in the beneficiary's interest in the net assets of the recipient attributable to unrealized gains and losses on investments?**

(continued)

HC NPEs			
NPEs that are not HC NPEs			
Yes	Existence of recipient is transparent in determining net asset clas-sifications. (NPE TPA [sections 6140.14 and .16]; HC TPA [sections 6400.36 and .39])	Reclass the applicable net assets from temporarily restricted (TR) to unrestricted (UR) unless those net assets are subject to time restrictions that have not expired. (NPE TPA [section 6140.17]; HC TPA [section 6400.40])	Changes in the beneficiary's interest in the net assets of a recipient entity attributable to unrealized gains and losses on investments should be included or excluded from the per-formance indicator in accordance with FASB ASC 954-10, FASB ASC 954-205-45, FASB ASC 954-320-45, FASB ASC 954-320-55, and FASB ASC 954-605, in the same manner that they would have been had the benefici-ary had the transactions itself. (HC TPA [section 6400.42])
No	Existence of the recipient creates an implied time restriction on the beneficiary's net assets attributable to the beneficiary's interest in the net assets of the recipient. (NPE TPA [section 6140.15]; HC TPA [section 6400.37])	Reclass the applicable net assets from TR to UR only if the purpose restriction and the implied time restriction are met. Whether the purpose restriction is met depends in part on (1) whether the recipient has discretion in determining whether the purpose restriction is met and (2) the recipient's decision in exercising that discretion, if any. (NPE TPA [section 6140.18]; HC TPA [section 6400.41])	An implied time restriction exists on the beneficiary's net assets attributable to the beneficiary's interest in the net assets of the recipient. The beneficiary should classify the resulting net assets and changes in those net assets as temporarily restricted (unless donors placed permanent restrictions on their contributions) and therefore exclude those changes from the performance indicator. (HC TPA [section 6400.42])

[Revised, June 2009, to reflect conforming changes necessary due to the issuance of FASB ASC.]

.36 Application of FASB ASC 958—Classification of a Beneficiary's Interest in the Net Assets of a Financially Interrelated Fund-Raising Foundation (The beneficiary can influence the operating and financial decisions of the foundation to such an extent that the beneficiary can determine the timing and amount of distributions from the foundation.)

Inquiry—ABC Hospital, a not-for-profit health care entity subject to FASB ASC 954[2] and ABC Foundation are financially interrelated entities as described in FASB ASC 958-20-15-2. ABC Foundation's bylaws state that it is organized for the purpose of stimulating voluntary financial support from donors for the sole benefit of ABC Hospital. Assume that ABC Hospital can influence the operating and financial decisions of ABC Foundation to such an extent that ABC Hospital can determine the timing and amount of distributions from ABC Foundation to ABC Hospital.

During its most recent fiscal year, ABC Foundation's activities resulted in an increase in net assets (before distributions) of $3,200, comprised of $2,000 in unrestricted contributions, $1,000 in temporarily restricted contributions (purpose restrictions), $500 in unrestricted dividend and interest income, and $300 in expenses. In addition, ABC Foundation distributed $2,500 in cash representing unrestricted net assets to ABC Hospital. How should this activity be reported in ABC Hospital's financial statements?

Reply—Because ABC Foundation (the recipient entity) and ABC Hospital (the beneficiary) are financially interrelated, FASB ASC 958-20-25-2 requires ABC Hospital to recognize its interest in the net assets of ABC Foundation and periodically adjust that interest for its share of the change in net assets of ABC Foundation. This is similar to the equity method of accounting described in FASB ASC 323.

In recognizing its interest in the net assets of ABC Foundation and the changes in that interest, ABC Hospital should classify the resulting net assets as if contributions were received by ABC Hospital directly from the donor, because ABC Hospital can influence the operating and financial decisions of ABC Foundation to such an extent that ABC Hospital can determine the timing and amount of distributions from ABC Foundation to ABC Hospital. In other words, the existence of ABC Foundation should be transparent in determining the net asset classifications in ABC Hospital's financial statements because ABC Foundation cannot impose time or purpose restrictions beyond those imposed by the donor. (Any instructions given by ABC Foundation are designations, rather than restrictions.)

In the circumstances described previously, ABC Hospital would initially increase its asset, "Interest in Net Assets of ABC Foundation" for the change in ABC Foundation's net assets ($3,200). ABC Hospital's Statement of Operations would include "Change in Unrestricted Interest in ABC Foundation" of $2,200

---

[2] This section addresses not-for-profit health care entities subject to Financial Accounting Standards Board (FASB) *Accounting Standards Codification* (ASC) 954, *Health Care Entities*. Section 6140.14, "Application of FASB ASC 958—Classification of a Beneficiary's Interest in the Net Assets of a Financially Interrelated Fund-Raising Foundation (The beneficiary can influence the operating and financial decisions of the foundation to such an extent that the beneficiary can determine the timing and amount of distributions from the foundation.)," addresses a similar issue for not-for-profit entities subject to FASB ASC 958, *Not-for-Profit Entities*.

(which would be included in the performance indicator in accordance with FASB ASC 954-10, FASB ASC 954-205, FASB ASC 954-310, 954-405, and FASB ASC 954-605) and "Change in Temporarily Restricted Interest in ABC Foundation" of $1,000 which would be reported in the Statement of Changes in Net Assets.

The $2,500 distribution from ABC Foundation to ABC Hospital would not be reported as an increase in net assets on ABC Hospital's Statement of Operations or its Statement of Changes in Net Assets. By analogy to equity method accounting, the $2,500 would be reported in a manner similar to a distribution from a subsidiary to its parent (for example, a dividend). ABC Hospital should report the distribution by increasing cash and decreasing its interest in the net assets of ABC Foundation.

If the distribution represented restricted net assets, ABC Hospital would not reclassify the net assets from temporarily restricted to unrestricted at the time of the distribution. Instead, ABC Hospital would reclassify the net assets from temporarily restricted to unrestricted when those restrictions were met.

[Revised, June 2009, to reflect conforming changes necessary due to the issuance of FASB ASC.]

.37 Application of FASB ASC 958—Classification of a Beneficiary's Interest in the Net Assets of a Financially Interrelated Fund-Raising Foundation (The beneficiary cannot influence the operating and financial decisions of the foundation to such an extent that the beneficiary can determine the timing and amount of distributions from the foundation.)

Inquiry—ABC Hospital, a not-for-profit health care entity subject to FASB ASC 954[3] and ABC Foundation are financially interrelated entities described in FASB ASC 958-20-15-2. ABC Foundation's bylaws state that it is organized for the purpose of stimulating voluntary financial support from donors for the sole benefit of ABC Hospital. Assume that ABC Hospital cannot, however, influence the operating and financial decisions of ABC Foundation to such an extent that ABC Hospital can determine the timing and amount of distributions from ABC Foundation to ABC Hospital.

During its most recent fiscal year, ABC Foundation's activities resulted in an increase in net assets (before distributions) of $3,200, comprised of $2,000 in unrestricted contributions, $1,000 in temporarily restricted contributions (purpose restrictions), $500 in unrestricted dividend and interest income, and $300 in expenses. In addition, ABC Foundation elected to distribute $2,500 in cash representing unrestricted net assets to ABC Hospital. How should this activity be reported in ABC Hospital's financial statements?

Reply—Because ABC Foundation (the recipient entity) and ABC Hospital (the beneficiary) are financially interrelated, FASB ASC 958-20-25-2 requires

---

[3] This section addresses not-for-profit health care entities subject to FASB ASC 954. Section 6140.15, "Application of FASB ASC 958—Classification of a Beneficiary's Interest in the Net Assets of a Financially Interrelated Fund-Raising Foundation (The beneficiary cannot influence the operating and financial decisions of the foundation to such an extent that the beneficiary can determine the timing and amount of distributions from the foundation.)," addresses a similar issue for not-for-profit entities subject to FASB ASC 958.

ABC Hospital to recognize its interest in the net assets of ABC Foundation and periodically adjust that interest for its share of the change in net assets of ABC Foundation. This is similar to the equity method of accounting described in FASB ASC 323.

ABC Hospital cannot influence the operating and financial decisions of ABC Foundation to such an extent that ABC Hospital can determine the timing and amount of distributions from ABC Foundation. Therefore, an implied time restriction exists on ABC Hospital's interest in the net assets of ABC Foundation (in addition to any other restrictions that may exist). Accordingly, in recognizing its interest in the net assets of ABC Foundation and the changes in that interest, ABC Hospital should classify the resulting net assets as changes in temporarily restricted net assets (unless donors placed permanent restrictions on their contributions).

In the circumstances previously described, ABC Hospital would initially increase its asset, "Interest in Net Assets of ABC Foundation" for the change in ABC Foundation's net assets ($3,200). ABC Hospital's Statement of Changes in Net Assets would include "Change in Temporarily Restricted Interest in ABC Foundation" of $3,200 as an increase in temporarily restricted net assets.

The $2,500 distribution from ABC Foundation to ABC Hospital would not be reported as an increase in net assets on ABC Hospital's Statement of Operations or its Statement of Changes in Net Assets. By analogy to equity method accounting, the $2,500 would be treated similar to a distribution from a subsidiary to its parent (for example, a dividend). ABC Hospital should report the distribution by increasing cash and decreasing its interest in the net assets of ABC Foundation.

ABC Hospital would reclassify the net assets from temporarily restricted to unrestricted at the time of the distribution, because the time restriction would expire at the time of the distribution. The reclassification would be reported as "net assets released from restrictions" and included in the performance indicator in the statement of operations. (If those net assets were subject to purpose or time restrictions that remained even after the net assets had been distributed to ABC Hospital, ABC Hospital would not reclassify the net assets from temporarily restricted to unrestricted at the time of the distribution. Instead, ABC Hospital would reclassify the net assets from temporarily restricted to unrestricted when those restrictions were met and the reclassification would be included in or excluded from the performance indicator in accordance with FASB ASC 954-10, FASB ASC 954-205, FASB ASC 954-310, FASB ASC 954-405, and FASB ASC 954-605.)

[Revised, June 2009, to reflect conforming changes necessary due to the issuance of FASB ASC.]

.38 Application of FASB ASC 958—Classification of a Beneficiary's Interest in the Net Assets of a Financially Interrelated Fund-Raising Foundation—Does Common Control Lead to the Conclusion That the Beneficiary Can Determine the Timing and Amount of Distributions from the Recipient?

Inquiry—ABC Holding Company (a not-for-profit entity) has two not-for-profit subsidiaries (ABC Hospital and ABC Foundation) that it controls and consolidates in accordance with the guidance in FASB ASC 954-10, FASB ASC

954-205, FASB ASC 954-605, and FASB ASC 954-810. ABC Hospital and ABC Foundation are brother-sister entities that are financially interrelated entities as described in FASB ASC 958-20-15-2. ABC Hospital issues separate financial statements in connection with a loan agreement. ABC Foundation's bylaws state that it is organized for the purpose of stimulating voluntary financial support from donors for the sole benefit of ABC Hospital.

Because ABC Hospital and ABC Foundation are under common control, does that lead to the conclusion that ABC Hospital can influence the financial decisions of ABC Foundation (either directly or indirectly) to such an extent that ABC Hospital can determine the timing and amount of distributions from ABC Foundation to ABC Hospital?

Reply—In some circumstances ABC Hospital, though a subsidiary of ABC Holding Company, may be able to influence the financial decisions of ABC Foundation (either directly or indirectly) to such an extent that ABC Hospital can determine the timing and amount of distributions from ABC Foundation to ABC Hospital. For example, if ABC Hospital formed ABC Holding Company as a nominally-capitalized shell with no real operating powers, a rebuttable presumption exists that ABC Hospital can influence the financial decisions of ABC Foundation (either directly or indirectly) to such an extent that ABC Hospital can determine the timing and amount of distributions from ABC Foundation to ABC Hospital. On the other hand if, for example, ABC Hospital formed ABC Holding Company to be an operating entity with substance, other factors would need to be considered in determining whether ABC Hospital can influence the financial decisions of ABC Foundation (either directly or indirectly) to such an extent that ABC Hospital can determine the timing and amount of distributions from ABC Foundation to ABC Hospital. Therefore, it is necessary to consider the facts and circumstances surrounding the relationships between ABC Holding Company and ABC Hospital, and ABC Hospital and ABC Foundation, to determine whether ABC Hospital exerts enough influence over ABC Foundation to determine the timing and amount of distributions from ABC Foundation to ABC Hospital. Indicators to consider may include, but are not limited to, the following:

- What is the extent of overlap among the boards of ABC Hospital, ABC Holding Company, and ABC Foundation (for example, do a majority of the individuals who govern ABC Hospital also govern ABC Foundation; do a majority of the individuals who govern ABC Hospital also govern ABC Holding Company; are the boards of ABC Hospital, ABC Foundation and ABC Holding Company substantially independent of one another)? The greater the overlap among the boards of ABC Hospital and either ABC Holding Company or ABC Foundation, the more likely that ABC Hospital can influence the financial decisions of ABC Foundation (either directly or indirectly) to such an extent that ABC Hospital can determine the timing and amount of distributions from ABC Foundation to ABC Hospital.

- What is the extent of overlap among management teams of ABC Hospital, ABC Holding Company, and ABC Foundation (for example, do the individuals who manage ABC Hospital also manage ABC Foundation; do the individuals who manage ABC Hospital also manage ABC Holding Company; does ABC Holding Company have a separate management team that exercises significant authority over both ABC Hospital and ABC Foundation)? The greater the overlap between

ABC Hospital's management and management of either ABC Holding Company or ABC Foundation, the more likely that ABC Hospital can influence the financial decisions of ABC Foundation (either directly or indirectly) to such an extent that ABC Hospital can determine the timing and amount of distributions from ABC Foundation to ABC Hospital.

- What are the origins of the parent/holding company structure? For example, were ABC Holding Company and ABC Foundation created by ABC Hospital through a corporate restructuring, which may indicate that ABC Hospital, as the original entity, can influence the financial decisions of ABC Foundation (either directly or indirectly) to such an extent that ABC Hospital can determine the timing and amount of distributions from ABC Foundation to ABC Hospital. Alternatively, were ABC Hospital and ABC Foundation independent entities that merged and created ABC Holding Company to govern the combined entity, which may indicate that ABC Hospital cannot influence the financial decisions of ABC Foundation (either directly or indirectly) to such an extent that ABC Hospital can determine the timing and amount of distributions from ABC Foundation to ABC Hospital.
- What is the number of entities under common control? The greater the number of entities under ABC Holding Company's control, the less likely it is that any one subsidiary, such as ABC Hospital, can influence the financial decisions of another brother-sister subsidiary, such as ABC Foundation, (either directly or indirectly) to such an extent that ABC Hospital can determine the timing and amount of distributions from ABC Foundation to ABC Hospital

Other relevant facts and circumstances should also be considered.

[Revised, June 2009, to reflect conforming changes necessary due to the issuance of FASB ASC.]

.39 Application of FASB ASC 958—Classification of a Beneficiary's Interest in the Net Assets of a Financially Interrelated Fund-Raising Foundation (More Than One Beneficiary—Some Contributions Are Designated)

Inquiry—DEF Health Entity is the parent company of three brother-sister not-for-profit entities: Health A, a not-for-profit health care entity subject to FASB ASC 954[4] Health B, and Foundation. Foundation is organized for the purpose of raising contributions for the benefit of both Health A and Health B. The four entities are legally separate not-for-profit entities that are financially interrelated pursuant to the guidance in FASB ASC 958-20-15-2. Assume that Health A can influence the financial decisions of Foundation to such an extent that Health A can determine the timing and amount of distributions from Foundation to Health A.

A donor contributes $5,000 cash to Foundation and stipulates that the contribution is for the benefit of Health A. Foundation would record the

[4] This section addresses not-for-profit health care entities subject to FASB ASC 954. Section 6140.16, "Application of FASB ASC 958—Classification of a Beneficiary's Interest in the Net Assets of a Financially Interrelated Fund-Raising Foundation (More Than One Beneficiary—Some Contributions Are Designated)," addresses a similar issue for not-for-profit entities subject to FASB ASC 958.

contribution as temporarily restricted revenue because Foundation must use the contribution for the benefit of Health A. In its separately issued financial statements, Health A would recognize its interest in the net assets attributable to that contribution by debiting "Interest in Net Assets of Foundation" for $5,000. Would the offsetting credit be reported as temporarily restricted revenue (because the net assets attributable to the contribution are restricted on Foundation's Balance Sheet) or unrestricted revenue (because there are no donor-imposed time restrictions or purpose restrictions on how Health A must use the contribution)?

Reply—Health A should report the offsetting credit as unrestricted revenue. Because Health A can influence the financial decisions of Foundation to such an extent that Health A can determine the timing and amount of distributions from Foundation to Health A, no implied time restriction exists on Health A's net assets attributable to its interest in the net assets of Foundation. Accordingly, in recognizing its interest in the net assets of Foundation and the changes in that interest, Health A should classify the resulting net assets as if contributions were received by Health A directly from the donor. In other words, the existence of Foundation should be transparent in determining the net asset classifications in Health A's separately issued financial statements because Foundation cannot impose time or purpose restrictions beyond those imposed by the donor. (Any instructions given by Foundation are designations, rather than restrictions.)

Because no donor-imposed restrictions exist on how Health A must use the contribution, Health A should report the change in its interest in the net assets attributable to the contribution as an increase in unrestricted net assets that is included in its performance indicator (in accordance with FASB ASC 954-10, FASB ASC 954-205, FASB ASC 954-310, FASB ASC 954-405, and FASB ASC 954-605) in its separately issued Statement of Operations. When Foundation actually distributes the funds, Health A should increase cash and decrease its interest in net assets of Foundation; the distributions would have no effect on Health A's Statement of Operations or its Statement of Changes in Net Assets.

[Revised, June 2009, to reflect conforming changes necessary due to the issuance of FASB ASC.]

.40 Application of FASB ASC 958—Classification of a Beneficiary's Interest in the Net Assets of a Financially Interrelated Fund-Raising Foundation (The beneficiary makes an expenditure that meets a purpose restriction on net assets held for its benefit by the recipient entity—The beneficiary can influence the operating and financial decisions of the recipient to such an extent that the beneficiary can determine the timing and amount of distributions from the recipient.)

Inquiry—ABC Hospital, a not-for-profit health care entity subject to FASB ASC 954[5] and ABC Foundation are financially interrelated entities as described

[5] This section addresses not-for-profit health care entities subject to FASB ASC 954. Section 6140.17, "Application of FASB ASC 958—Classification of a Beneficiary's Interest in the Net Assets of a Financially Interrelated Fund-Raising Foundation (The beneficiary makes an expenditure that

(continued)

in FASB ASC 958-20-15-2. ABC Foundation's bylaws state that it is organized for the purpose of stimulating voluntary financial support from donors for the sole benefit of ABC Hospital. Assume that ABC Hospital can influence the operating and financial decisions of ABC Foundation to such an extent that ABC Hospital can determine the timing and amount of distributions from ABC Foundation to ABC Hospital.

ABC Foundation's net assets consist of $3,000,000 resulting from cash contributions restricted for the purchase of property, plant, and equipment (PPE) by ABC Hospital. ABC Hospital has recorded its interest in those net assets by debiting "Interest in net assets of ABC Foundation" and crediting "Change in interest in ABC Foundation," which is reported as an increase in temporarily restricted net assets. ABC Hospital's accounting policy is to not imply a time restriction that expires over the useful life of the donated long-lived assets pursuant to FASB ASC 958-605-45-6 and it has no other net assets restricted for the purchase of PPE.[6] ABC Hospital subsequently purchased and placed into service $3,000,000 of PPE that meets those donor restrictions prior to receiving a distribution from ABC Foundation. Should ABC Hospital reclassify $3,000,000 from temporarily-restricted net assets as a result of building and placing into service the $3,000,000 of PPE?

Reply—Because ABC Foundation (the recipient entity) and ABC Hospital (the beneficiary) are financially interrelated, FASB ASC 958-20-25-2 requires ABC Hospital to recognize its interest in the net assets of ABC Foundation and periodically adjust that interest for its share of the change in net assets of ABC Foundation. This is similar to the equity method of accounting described in FASB ASC 323.

In recognizing its interest in the net assets of ABC Foundation and the changes in that interest, ABC Hospital should classify the resulting net assets as if contributions were received by ABC Hospital directly from the donor, because ABC Hospital can influence the operating and financial decisions of ABC Foundation to such an extent that ABC Hospital can determine the timing and amount of distributions from ABC Foundation to ABC Hospital. Accordingly, the net assets representing contributions restricted for the purchase of PPE should be reported as temporarily restricted net assets (purpose restricted) in ABC Hospital's financial statements. Upon purchasing and placing into service the PPE, ABC Hospital (and ABC Foundation) should reclassify $3,000,000 from temporarily restricted to unrestricted net assets,[7] reported separately from the performance indicator in the statement of operations in

---

(footnote continued)

meets a purpose restriction on net assets held for its benefit by the recipient entity—The beneficiary can influence the operating and financial decisions of the recipient to such an extent that the beneficiary can determine the timing and amount of distributions from the recipient.)," addresses a similar issue for not-for-profit entities subject to FASB ASC 958.

[6] The assumption that ABC Hospital has no other net assets restricted for the purchase of PPE is intended to avoid establishing a hierarchy pertaining to which restrictions are released first—restrictions on net assets held by the recipient or restrictions on net assets held by the beneficiary. That issue is not addressed in this TPA.

[7] In this fact pattern, ABC Research Institute's interest in the net assets of ABC Foundation is subject to only purpose restrictions because the net assets arose from cash contributions with no time restrictions. If instead the net assets arose from promises to give rather than from cash contributions, the net assets might be subject to time restrictions in addition to the purpose restrictions. In determining whether net assets that arose from promises to give are subject to time restrictions, NPEs should consider the guidance in section 6140.04, *Lapsing of Restrictions on Receivables if Purpose*

(continued)

accordance with the guidance in FASB ASC 954-10, FASB ASC 954-205, FASB ASC 954-310, FASB AC 954-405, and FASB ASC 954-605. In other words, the existence of ABC Foundation should be transparent in determining the net asset classifications in ABC Hospital's financial statements because ABC Foundation cannot impose time or purpose restrictions beyond those imposed by the donor. (Any instructions given by ABC Foundation are designations, rather than restrictions.)

[Revised, June 2009, to reflect conforming changes necessary due to the issuance of FASB ASC.]

.41 Application of FASB ASC 958—Classification of a Beneficiary's Interest in the Net Assets of a Financially Interrelated Fund-Raising Foundation (The beneficiary makes an expenditure that is consistent with a purpose restriction on net assets held for its benefit by the recipient entity—The beneficiary cannot influence the operating and financial decisions of the recipient to such an extent that the beneficiary can determine the timing and amount of distributions from the recipient.)

Inquiry—ABC Hospital, a not-for-profit health care entity subject to FASB ASC 954[8] and ABC Foundation are financially interrelated entities as described in FASB ASC 958-20-15-2. ABC Foundation's bylaws state that it is organized for the purpose of stimulating voluntary financial support from donors for the sole benefit of ABC Hospital. Assume that ABC Hospital cannot, however, influence the operating and financial decisions of ABC Foundation to such an extent that ABC Hospital can determine the timing and amount of distributions from ABC Foundation to ABC Hospital.

ABC Foundation's net assets consist of $3,000,000 resulting from cash contributions restricted for the purchase of property, plant, and equipment (PPE) by ABC Hospital. ABC Hospital has recorded its interest in those net assets by debiting "Interest in net assets of ABC Foundation" and crediting "Change in interest in ABC Foundation," which is reported as an increase in temporarily restricted net assets. ABC Hospital has no other net assets restricted for the purchase of PPE.[9]

(footnote continued)

Restrictions Pertaining to Long-Lived Assets are Met Before the Receivables are Due, which discusses whether restrictions on net assets arising from promises to give that are restricted by donors for investments in long-lived assets are met when the assets are placed in service or when the receivables are due.

[8] This section addresses not-for-profit health care entities subject to FASB ASC 954. Section 6140.18, "Application of FASB ASC 958—Classification of a Beneficiary's Interest in the Net Assets of a Financially Interrelated Fund-Raising Foundation (The beneficiary makes an expenditure that is consistent with a purpose restriction on net assets held for its benefit by the recipient entity—The beneficiary cannot influence the operating and financial decisions of the recipient to such an extent that the beneficiary can determine the timing and amount of distributions from the recipient.)," addresses a similar issue for not-for-profit entities subject to FASB ASC 958.

[9] The assumption that ABC Hospital has no other net assets restricted for the purchase of PPE is intended to avoid establishing a hierarchy pertaining to which restrictions are released first—restrictions on net assets held by the recipient or restrictions on net assets held by the beneficiary. That issue is not addressed in this TPA.

ABC Hospital subsequently built and placed into service the New Modern Hospital Wing (at a cost of $3,000,000) prior to receiving a distribution from ABC Foundation or any indication from ABC Foundation that it intends to support building and placing into service the New Modern Hospital Wing. Should ABC Hospital reclassify $3,000,000 from temporarily-restricted net assets to unrestricted net assets as a result of building and placing into service the New Modern Hospital Wing?

Reply—From ABC Hospital's perspective, its interest in the net assets of ABC Foundation has two restrictions—a purpose restriction (the purchase of the PPE) and an implied time restriction. (ABC Hospital cannot influence the operating and financial decisions of ABC Foundation to such an extent that ABC Hospital can determine the timing and amount of distributions from ABC Foundation to ABC Hospital, including distributions pertaining to expenditures by ABC Hospital that meet the donor-imposed purpose restrictions. Therefore, an implied time restriction exists on ABC Hospital's interest in the net assets of ABC Foundation.) FASB ASC 958-205-45-9 provides, in part, as follows:

> If two or more temporary restrictions are imposed on a contribution, the effect of the expiration of those restrictions is recognized in the period in which the last remaining restriction has expired.

FASB ASC 958-205-45-11 further provides, in part:

> Temporarily restricted net assets with time restrictions are not available to support expenses until the time restrictions have expired.

In considering whether the purpose restriction on ABC Hospital's interest in the net assets of ABC Foundation is met, ABC Hospital should determine whether ABC Foundation has discretion in deciding whether an expenditure by ABC Hospital that is consistent with the purpose restriction satisfies that purpose restriction. For example, if the restricted net assets arose from a contribution that was restricted for "building projects of ABC Hospital," with no particular building project specified, purchasing and placing into service the New Modern Hospital Wing is consistent with the purpose restriction but may or may not meet it, because ABC Foundation has some discretion in deciding which building project releases the purpose restriction. In other words, ABC Foundation may, at its discretion, either release restricted net assets in support of building the New Modern Hospital Wing or not, because the purpose restriction imposed by the donor was broad enough to give ABC Foundation discretion in deciding which building projects meet the purpose restriction. If ABC Foundation has such discretion, a purpose restriction and an implied time restriction on ABC Hospital's interest in the net assets of ABC Foundation exist. Therefore, ABC Hospital should not reclassify $3,000,000 from temporarily-restricted net assets to unrestricted net assets as a result of building and placing into service the New Modern Hospital Wing unless ABC Foundation distributes or obligates itself to distribute to ABC Hospital amounts attributable to net assets restricted for the purchase of PPE by ABC Hospital, or ABC Foundation otherwise indicates that it intends for those net assets to be used to support the building and placing into service the New Modern Hospital Wing as an activity of the current period (assuming that

ABC Hospital had no other net assets that were restricted for the purchase of PPE).[10,11]

In contrast to the example in the previous paragraph, if the restricted net assets arose from a contribution that was restricted for "building and placing into service the New Modern Hospital Wing," ABC Foundation has no discretion in deciding whether that purpose restriction is met by building and placing into service the New Modern Hospital Wing. Therefore, if ABC Hospital builds and places into service the New Modern Hospital Wing, the purpose restriction is met (assuming that ABC Hospital had no other net assets that were restricted for building and placing into service the New Modern Hospital Wing). In addition, the implied time restriction is met because ABC Foundation is required to distribute the funds to ABC Hospital in order to meet the donor's stipulation. Therefore, ABC Hospital (and ABC Foundation) should reclassify $3,000,000 from temporarily-restricted net assets as a result of building and placing into service the New Modern Hospital Wing.

In summary, ABC Hospital should not reclassify $3,000,000 from temporarily-restricted net assets to unrestricted net assets as a result of building and placing into service the New Modern Hospital Wing until both the purpose restriction and the implied time restriction are met. If both the purpose restriction and the implied time restriction are met, ABC Hospital should decrease its interest in the net assets of ABC Foundation and increase cash

---

[10] In this fact pattern, the expenditure is made prior to meeting the purpose restriction and the implied time restriction that exists because ABC Hospital cannot determine the timing and amount of distributions from ABC Foundation to ABC Hospital. FASB ASC 958-205-45-11 provides that in circumstances in which both purpose and time restrictions exist, expenditures meeting the purpose restriction must be made simultaneous with or after the time restriction has expired in order to satisfy both the purpose and time restriction and result in a reclassification of net assets from temporarily restricted to unrestricted. In other words, time restrictions, if any, must be met before expenditures can result in purpose restrictions being met. In this fact pattern, however, the time restriction is an implied time restriction that exists because the beneficiary cannot determine the timing and amount of distributions from the recipient to the beneficiary, rather than an implied time restriction that exists because a promise to give is due in a future period or because of an explicit donor stipulation. Accordingly, in this fact pattern, temporarily restricted net assets with implied time restrictions are available to support expenditures made before the expiration of the time restrictions and the net assets should be reclassified from temporarily restricted to unrestricted in the period in which the last remaining restriction has expired. In other words, in this fact pattern, if the expenditure that meets the purpose restriction is made before meeting the implied time restriction that exists because the beneficiary cannot determine the timing and amount of distributions from the recipient to the beneficiary, all the restrictions should be considered met once the implied time restriction is met.

[11] In this fact pattern, ABC Hospital's interest in the net assets of ABC Foundation is subject to an implied time restriction that exists because ABC Hospital cannot determine the timing and amount of distributions from ABC Foundation to ABC Hospital and a purpose restriction. Because the net assets arose from cash contributions with no other donor-imposed time restrictions, no time restrictions other than those imposed by ABC Foundation exist. If instead the net assets arose from promises to give rather than from cash contributions, the net assets might be subject to donor-imposed time restrictions in addition to the time restriction imposed by ABC Foundation and the purpose restriction. In determining whether net assets that arose from promises to give are subject to donor-imposed time restrictions in addition to the time restrictions imposed by ABC Foundation, NPEs should consider the guidance in section 6140.04, *Lapsing of Restrictions on Receivables if Purpose Restrictions Pertaining to Long-Lived Assets are Met Before the Receivables are Due*, which discusses whether restrictions on net assets arising from promises to give that are restricted by donors for investments in long-lived assets are met when the assets are placed in service or when the receivables are due. In circumstances in which the net assets are subject to (*a*) donor-imposed time restrictions in addition to the (*b*) implied time restrictions that exist because ABC Hospital cannot determine the timing and amount of distributions from ABC Foundation to ABC Hospital and (*c*) purpose restrictions, the last remaining time restriction should be considered in applying the guidance in FASB ASC 958-205-45-11 that provides that temporarily restricted net assets with time restrictions are not available to support expenses until the time restrictions have expired.

(or a receivable, if the Foundation has merely obligated itself to make the distribution) by the amount of the distribution, and simultaneously reclassify the same amount from temporarily restricted net assets to unrestricted net assets. The reclassification should be reported separately from the performance indicator in the statement of operations in accordance with the guidance in FASB ASC 954-10, FASB ASC 954-205, FASB ASC 954-310, FASB ASC 954-405, and FASB ASC 954-605.

[Revised, June 2009, to reflect conforming changes necessary due to the issuance of FASB ASC.]

.42 Application of FASB ASC 958—Classification of a Beneficiary's Interest in the Net Assets of a Financially Interrelated Fund-Raising Foundation (Recipient Entity)—Accounting for Unrealized Gains and Losses on Investments Held by the Foundation

Inquiry—FASB ASC 958 provides that if entities are financially interrelated, the balance sheet of the beneficiary entity should reflect that entity's beneficial interest in the net assets of the recipient entity, and that that interest should be adjusted periodically to reflect the changes in the net assets of the recipient entity. This accounting is similar to the equity method of accounting. FASB ASC 954-10, FASB ASC 954-205-45, FASB ASC 954-320-45, FASB ASC 954-320-55, and FASB ASC 954-605 provide guidance pertaining to the classification of investment returns in the financial statements of health care entities.

ABC Hospital and ABC Foundation are financially interrelated entities. How should changes in ABC Hospital's interest in the net assets of ABC Foundation attributable to unrealized gains and losses on Foundation's investments be classified in ABC Hospital's financial statements?

Reply—In circumstances in which ABC Hospital can influence the financial decisions of ABC Foundation to such an extent that ABC Hospital can determine the timing and amount of distributions from Foundation to ABC Hospital, changes in ABC Hospital's interest in the net assets of ABC Foundation attributable to unrealized gains and losses on investments should be classified in the same manner that they would have been had ABC Hospital held the investments and had the transactions itself. In accordance with the guidance in FASB ASC 954-10, FASB ASC 954-205-45, FASB ASC 954-320-45, FASB ASC 954-320-55, and FASB ASC 954-605, ABC Hospital should include in the performance indicator the portion of the change attributable to unrealized gains and losses on trading securities that are not restricted by donors or by law, and should exclude from the performance indicator the portion of the change attributable to all other unrealized gains and losses.

In circumstances in which ABC Hospital cannot influence the financial decisions of Foundation to such an extent that ABC Hospital can determine the timing and amount of distributions ABC Hospital receives from Foundation, an implied time restriction exists on ABC Hospital's net assets attributable to its interest in the net assets of Foundation (in addition to any other restrictions that many exist). Accordingly, ABC Hospital should classify all changes in that interest, including the portion of the change attributable to unrealized gains and losses on investments, as changes in temporarily restricted net assets (unless donors placed permanent restrictions on investment gains and losses pertaining to their contributions) and therefore should exclude those changes from the performance indicator.

[Revised, June 2009, to reflect conforming changes necessary due to the issuance of FASB ASC.]

.43 Application of FASB ASC 958—Classification of Distributions From a Financially Interrelated Fund-Raising Foundation (Recipient Entity) to a Health Care Beneficiary

Inquiry—How should a fund-raising foundation (recipient), a not-for-profit entity subject to FASB ASC 958 report (in its separately issued financial statements) distributions to a financially interrelated beneficiary that is a health care entity? In other words, should such distributions be reported following (*a*) the guidance on reporting transfers among affiliated health care entities in FASB ASC 954-10, FASB ASC 954-205, FASB ASC 954-605, and FASB ASC 954-810 or (*b*) the guidance in FASB ASC 958.

Reply—FASB ASC 958 applies to all not-for-profit entities, except those that are providers of health care services (FASB ASC 958-10-15-3). Therefore, the guidance in FASB ASC 954 generally does not apply to financial statements of recipient entities that are financially interrelated fund-raising foundations. The foundation should follow the accounting and reporting requirements of FASB ASC 958 rather than FASB ASC 954 in the foundation's separately issued financial statements. The foundation should report distributions to beneficiary entities as expenses or distributions to related entities. The guidance in the previous sentence applies regardless of whether the recipient entity and the beneficiary are under common control or whether one controls the other in a parent-subsidiary relationship.

[Revised, June 2009, to reflect conforming changes necessary due to the issuance of FASB ASC.]

Chapter 12

The Reporting Entity and Related Entities

Overview

12.01 Health systems are complex operations made up of various business lines and subsidiaries. Not-for-profit systems are likely to operate through a combination of for-profit and not-for-profit entities. Various for-profit entities, such as health maintenance organizations (HMOs) or insurance entities, may be organized as stock corporations, partnerships, or limited liability entities. Fund-raising typically is accomplished through a separate foundation. There may be financial transfers of cash or assets among related entities either to fund capital needs or start-up costs or to provide operating subsidies. Certain entities within the system may be obligated for repayment of the system's municipal bonds, but others are not. The system may also be involved in joint ventures or joint operating agreements. This chapter addresses accounting and financial reporting considerations associated with these issues, including consolidation and combinations of entities (that is, mergers and acquisitions).

12.02 This chapter discusses the accounting and reporting for equity investments accounted for under the equity method if the investee is an integral part of the reporting entity's operations, such as a physician hospital organization or joint venture. Chapter 4, "Cash, Cash Equivalents, and Investments," of this guide discusses accounting and reporting if the investment's purpose is investment income or return (for example, collective trusts, funds of funds, hedge funds, or other alternative investments).

Reporting by Not-for-Profit Health Care Entities

12.03 The guidance that follows in this section of the guide discusses a not-for-profit health care entity's relationships with for-profit and not-for-profit entities that result in either consolidation of parent-subsidiary relationships, whether through stock ownership or other means of control, or equity method accounting. Other circumstances may exist in the health care industry in which combined financial statements involving commonly controlled entities are more meaningful than their separate financial statements. More specific guidance related to combined financial statements can be found in paragraphs 12.67–.68.

12.04 Per Financial Accounting Standard Board (FASB) *Accounting Standards Codification* (ASC) 954-810-45-1, whether the financial statements of a reporting health care entity and those of one or more other for-profit or not-for-profit entities should be consolidated; whether those other entities should be reported using the equity method; and the extent of disclosure that should be required, if any, if consolidated financial statements are not presented should be based on the nature of the relationship between the entities.

12.05 Health care organizations may be related to one or more other entities in numerous ways, including ownership, control, or economic interests. Exhibit 12-1, "Relationships of a Not-for-Profit Reporting Entity," describes some common relationships with other entities and identifies where those relationships are discussed in this chapter and FASB ASC. Exhibit 12-1 and this chapter summarize certain guidance in FASB ASC but are not intended as a substitute for reading the guidance itself.

Exhibit 12-1

Relationships of a Not-for-Profit Reporting Entity

Relationship	Financial Accounting Standards Board *Accounting Standards Codification* Reference	*Discussion in This Chapter*
Relationships With Not-for-Profit Entities		
The reporting entity is the sole corporate member of a not-for-profit entity.	Use the guidance in Financial Accounting Standards Board (FASB) *Accounting Standards Codification* (ASC) 958-810-25-2 and 954-810-45-3A.	Paragraphs 12.09–.10
The reporting entity has a controlling financial interest through a direct or indirect ownership of a majority voting interest in the other not-for-profit entity.	Use the guidance in FASB ASC 958-810-25-2.	Paragraph 12.09
The reporting entity controls another not-for-profit entity through a majority voting interest in its board and has an economic interest in that other entity.	Use the guidance in FASB ASC 958-810-25-3.	Paragraph 12.11
The reporting entity controls a not-for-profit entity through a form other than majority ownership, sole corporate membership, or majority voting interest in its board and has an economic interest in that other entity.	Use the guidance in FASB ASC 958-810-25-4.	Paragraphs 12.12–.14
The reporting entity has control over another not-for-profit entity or an economic interest in the other but not both.	Use the guidance in FASB ASC 958-810-25-5.	Paragraph 12.15

Relationship	Financial Accounting Standards Board *Accounting Standards Codification* Reference	*Discussion in This Chapter*
The reporting entity receives distributions from a related fund-raising foundation, but it does not control that foundation.	Use the guidance in the "Transfers of Assets to a Not-for-Profit Entity or Charitable Trust that Raises or Holds Contributions for Others" sections of FASB ASC 958-605.	Paragraphs 12.16–.24
Relationships With For-Profit Entities		
The reporting entity owns a majority of a for-profit entity's common voting stock.	Use the guidance in the "General" sections of FASB ASC 810-10 to determine whether that interest constitutes a controlling financial interest.	Paragraphs 12.28–.30
The reporting entity owns 50 percent or less of the common voting stock of an investee and can exercise significant influence over operating and financial policies.	Except when the reporting entity elects to report such interests at fair value, in accordance with the "Fair Value Option" sections of FASB ASC 825-10, use the equity method of accounting, in accordance with FASB ASC 323-10.	Paragraphs 12.33–.35
The reporting entity has an interest in a general partnership.	Except when the reporting entity elects to report such interests at fair value, in accordance with the "Fair Value Option" sections of FASB ASC 825-10, entities typically use by analogy the guidance in FASB ASC 970-810.	Paragraph 12.36
The reporting entity is the general partner of a for-profit limited partnership or similar entity, such as a limited liability company that has governing provisions that are the functional equivalent of a limited partnership.	Use the guidance in FASB ASC 810-20 to determine whether the general partner within the group controls and, therefore, should consolidate the limited partnership or similar entity.	Paragraphs 12.37–.38

(continued)

Relationships of a Not-for-Profit Reporting Entity—continued

Relationship	Financial Accounting Standards Board *Accounting Standards Codification* Reference	*Discussion in This Chapter*
The reporting entity has an investment in a limited liability company that has governing provisions that are the functional equivalent of a regular corporation.	Use the guidance in FASB ASC 810-10 to determine whether the reporting entity has a majority voting interest that provides it with a controlling financial interest.	Paragraph 12.29
The reporting entity has a noncontrolling interest that constitutes more than a minor interest in a for-profit partnership, limited liability entity, or similar entity engaged in real estate activities.	Except when the reporting entity elects to report such interests at fair value, in accordance with the "Fair Value Option" sections of FASB ASC 825-10, use the equity method, in accordance with the guidance in FASB ASC 970-323.	Paragraphs 12.40–.42
The reporting entity has a noncontrolling interest that constitutes more than a minor interest in a for-profit partnership, limited liability entity, or similar entity other than one engaged in real estate activities.	Except when the reporting entity elects to report such interests at fair value, in accordance with the "Fair Value Option" sections of FASB ASC 825-10, entities typically use by analogy the equity method, in accordance with the guidance in FASB ASC 970-323.	Paragraph 12.39
The reporting entity has a contractual management relationship with another entity in which it does not have an investment (for example, a physician practice).	Use the guidance in the "Consolidation of Entities Controlled by Contract" sections of FASB ASC 810-10 to determine whether the arrangement constitutes a controlling financial interest.	Paragraphs 12.30–.32

Relationship	Financial Accounting Standards Board *Accounting Standards Codification* Reference	*Discussion in This Chapter*
Relationships With Special Entities		
The reporting entity has a relationship with a variable interest entity (VIE), as described in the "Variable Interest Entities" sections of FASB ASC 810-10.	Pursuant to FASB ASC 810-10-15-17, not-for-profit health care entities are not subject to the "Variable Interest Entities" sections of FASB ASC 810-10, unless the not-for-profit entity is used by a business entity in a manner similar to a VIE in an effort to circumvent the provisions of those standards.	
The reporting entity is engaged in a leasing transaction with a special-purpose entity lessor.	Use the guidance in paragraphs 8–10 of FASB ASC 958-810-25 and paragraphs 7–16 of FASB ASC 958-810-55 to determine whether to consolidate the lessor.	Paragraphs 12.46–.50
The reporting entity has entered into a joint operating agreement with another entity. They agree to jointly conduct an activity while sharing the operating results and a residual interest upon dissolution.	If housed in a separate legal entity, use the equity method of accounting in FASB ASC 323-10, except when the reporting entity elects to report such interests at fair value, in accordance with the "Fair Value Option" sections of FASB ASC 825-10; otherwise, use the guidance in FASB ASC 808, *Collaborative Arrangements*.	Paragraphs 12.51–.53
The reporting entity is a sponsor in a research and development arrangement.	Use the guidance in FASB ASC 810-30.	Uncommon; not discussed in this chapter.
The reporting entity has another type of relationship with a special-purpose entity.	In practice, entities analogize to the guidance in paragraphs 8–10 of FASB ASC 958-810-25 and paragraphs 7–16 of FASB ASC 958-810-55.	Paragraph 12.54

Relationships With Another Not-for-Profit Entity

12.06 FASB ASC 958-810-05-3 states that ownership of not-for-profit entities may be evidenced in various ways because not-for-profit entities may exist in various legal forms, such as corporations issuing stock, corporations issuing ownership certificates, membership corporations issuing membership certificates, joint ventures, partnerships, and other forms. As discussed in FASB ASC 954-810-05-3, the rights and powers of the controlling entity may vary depending on the legal structure of the controlled entity and the nature of control.

12.07 As a result, whether the financial statements of a controlled not-for-profit entity should be consolidated with those of the reporting entity depends on the nature of control and whether an economic interest exists, as follows:

- Certain kinds of control, such as controlling financial interests, require consolidation (see paragraphs 12.09–.10).
- Other kinds of control (for example, a majority voting interest in the board of the other not-for-profit entity) result in consolidation only if coupled with an economic interest (see paragraph 12.11).
- Still other kinds of control, if coupled with an economic interest, result in consolidation being permitted but not required (see paragraphs 12.12–.14).
- The existence of either control or an economic interest, but not both, precludes consolidation but may trigger disclosure requirements (see paragraph 12.15).

12.08 The FASB ASC glossary defines *control* as "[t]he direct or indirect ability to determine the direction of management and policies through ownership, contract, or otherwise." The FASB ASC glossary states that an *economic interest* is

> [a] not-for-profit entity's (NFP's) interest in another entity that exists if any of the following criteria are met:
>
> a. The other entity holds or utilizes significant resources that must be used for the unrestricted or restricted purposes of the NFP, either directly or indirectly by producing income or providing services.
>
> b. The NFP is responsible for the liabilities of the other entity.

FASB ASC 958-810-55-6 provides the following examples of economic interests:

a. Other entities solicit funds in the name of and with the expressed or implied approval of the not-for-profit entity, and substantially all the solicited funds are intended by the contributor or are otherwise required to be transferred to the not-for-profit entity or used at its discretion or direction.

b. The not-for-profit entity transfers significant resources to another entity whose resources are held for the benefit of the not-for-profit entity.

c. The not-for-profit entity assigns certain significant functions to another entity.

d. The not-for-profit entity provides or is committed to provide funds for another entity, or the not-for-profit entity guarantees significant debt of another entity.

e. The not-for-profit entity has a right to, or the responsibility for, the operating results of another entity, or upon dissolution, the not-for-profit entity is entitled to the net assets or is responsible for any deficit of another entity.

Consolidation Required if a Controlling Financial Interest Exists

12.09 FASB ASC 958-810-25-2 states that a not-for-profit entity with a controlling financial interest in another not-for-profit entity through direct or indirect ownership of a majority voting interest or through sole corporate membership in that other not-for-profit entity should consolidate that other not-for-profit entity, unless control does not rest with the majority owner or sole corporate member (for instance, if the other not-for-profit entity is in legal reorganization or bankruptcy), in which case consolidation is prohibited, as discussed in FASB ASC 810-10-15-8. In addition, FASB ASC 958-810-25-2A states that if certain actions require approval by a supermajority vote of the board, such voting requirements might overcome the presumption of control by the owner or holder of a majority voting interest. Paragraphs 12.28–.32 provide additional information about controlling financial interests.

12.10 FASB ASC 954-810-45-3A states that a parent corporation typically owns stock in a for-profit entity whereas a sole corporate member holds membership rights in a not-for-profit entity. Sole corporate membership in a not-for-profit entity, such as ownership of a majority voting interest in a for-profit entity, should be considered a controlling financial interest, unless control does not rest with the sole corporate member, as discussed in the previous paragraph.

Majority Voting Interest in the Board Coupled With an Economic Interest

12.11 According to FASB ASC 958-810-25-3, in the case of control of a related but separate not-for-profit entity through (*a*) a majority voting interest in the board of the other not-for-profit entity by means other than ownership or sole corporate membership[1] and (*b*) an economic interest in the other such entity, consolidation is required, unless control does not rest with the holder of the majority voting interest, in which case consolidation is prohibited. A not-for-profit health care entity has a majority voting interest in the board of another health care entity if it has the direct or indirect ability to appoint individuals that together constitute a majority of the votes of the fully constituted board (that is, including any vacant board positions). See paragraph 12.29 for discussion about when control does not rest with a majority owner.

---

[1] A majority voting interest in the board of another entity by means other than ownership or sole corporate membership is illustrated by the following example from Financial Accounting Standards Board (FASB) *Accounting Standards Codification* (ASC) 958-810-55-5. Entity B has a five-member board, and a simple voting majority is required to approve board actions. Entity A will have a majority voting interest in the board of Entity B if Entity A has the ability to appoint three or more of Entity B's board members. If three of Entity A's board members, employees, or officers serve on the board of Entity B, but Entity A does not have the ability to require that those members serve on Entity B's board, Entity A does not have a majority voting interest in the board of Entity B.

Control Through Other Means Coupled With an Economic Interest

12.12 FASB ASC 958-810-25-4 states that control of a related but separate not-for-profit entity in which the reporting entity has an economic interest may take forms other than majority ownership interest, sole corporate membership, or majority voting interest in the board of the other entity (for example, control may be through contract or affiliation agreement). In circumstances such as these, consolidation is permitted but not required.[2] Consolidation is encouraged for these entities if it would be meaningful.

12.13 Evidence of control, as discussed in the preceding paragraph, may include authority to amend articles of incorporation and bylaws or authority to approve operating, capital, and construction budgets; capital acquisitions; strategic plans, goals, and objectives; authority to select, terminate, and set the compensation of management responsible for implementing the policies and procedures; and mergers or dissolutions.

12.14 According to FASB ASC 958-810-50-2, if a not-for-profit entity (the reporting entity) controls a related but separate not-for-profit entity through a form other than majority ownership, sole corporate membership, or majority voting interest in the board of the other entity and has an economic interest in that other not-for-profit entity, the reporting entity should disclose all of the following information if it does not present consolidated financial statements:

a. Identification of the other not-for-profit entity and the nature of its relationship with the reporting entity that results in control

b. Summarized financial data of the other not-for-profit entity, which should include the following information: total assets, liabilities, net assets, revenue, and expenses and resources that are held for the benefit of the reporting entity or under its control

c. The related-party disclosures set forth in paragraphs 1–6 of FASB ASC 850-10-50.

Consolidation Precluded if Either Control or an Economic Interest (but Not Both) Are Present

12.15 FASB ASC 958-810-25-5 states that the existence of control or an economic interest, but not both, precludes consolidation. Pursuant to FASB ASC 958-810-50-3, the reporting entity should disclose the information required by paragraphs 1–6 of FASB ASC 850-10-50 for these relationships.[3]

Related Fund-Raising Organizations

12.16 A common situation in which a health care entity may have an economic interest in another entity but may not control it is the fund-raising entity described in paragraph 12.08(a). In such situations, the related not-for-profit entity acts as a recipient entity (an agent, a trustee, or an intermediary) for contributions made to the health care entity.

12.17 The "Transfers of Assets to a Not-for-Profit Entity or Charitable Trust that Raises or Holds Contributions for Others" sections of FASB

---

[2] Additional information about the consolidation of entities controlled by contract can be found in paragraphs 12.30–.32.

[3] FASB ASC 958-810-50-3 states that the existence of an economic interest does not necessarily cause the entities to be *related parties*, as defined in the FASB ASC glossary. However, the disclosures required by paragraphs 1–6 of FASB ASC 850-10-50 are required if an economic interest exists.

ASC 958-605 apply if contributions intended to benefit a specific not-for-profit entity (the beneficiary) are made through another not-for-profit entity acting as an agent, a trustee, or an intermediary. In such transactions, a donor makes a contribution by transferring assets to a not-for-profit entity or charitable trust (the recipient entity) that accepts the assets from the donor and agrees to use those assets on behalf of an unaffiliated entity (beneficiary) or transfer those assets, the return on investment of those assets, or both to an unaffiliated entity (the beneficiary) that is specified by the donor.[4] FASB ASC 958-605-55-78 states that a donor may specify the beneficiary by (*a*) name; (*b*) stating that all entities that meet a set of donor-defined criteria are beneficiaries; or (*c*) actions surrounding the transfer that make clear the identity of the beneficiary, such as by responding to a request from a recipient entity to raise assets for the beneficiary. Paragraphs 80–115 of FASB ASC 958-605-55 provide examples of donor stipulations and discuss whether those stipulations specify a beneficiary.

12.18 According to FASB ASC 958-20-25-1, if a recipient entity and specified health care entity (beneficiary) are *financially-interrelated entities*, as defined in FASB ASC 958-20-15-2 and described in paragraph 12.75, and the recipient entity is not a trustee, the recipient entity should recognize a received contribution when it receives financial or nonfinancial assets from the donor that are specified for the beneficiary. For example, a foundation that exists to raise, hold, and invest assets for the specified health care entity (beneficiary) or a group of affiliates of which the specified health care entity is a member generally is financially interrelated with the not-for-profit entity(ies) it supports and recognizes contribution revenue when it receives assets from the donor.[5] According to FASB ASC 958-20-25-2 and 958-20-35-1, the specified health care entity (beneficiary) should recognize its interest in the net assets of the foundation (the recipient entity) and adjust that interest for its share of the change in net assets of the recipient entity. Recognizing an interest in the net assets of the recipient entity and adjusting that interest for a share of the change in net assets of the recipient entity is similar to the equity method, which is described in FASB ASC 323-10.[6]

12.19 According to FASB ASC 958-20-55-11, when measuring its interest in the foundation (recipient entity), the health care entity (specified beneficiary) would include only the net assets of the recipient entity that are restricted to that health care entity's use. According to FASB ASC 958-20-55-12, if the recipient entity supports more than one beneficiary, and an agreement with the recipient entity specifies how unrestricted gifts to the recipient entity should be divided between the supported entities, the specified health care entity would also include its share of the recipient entity's unrestricted assets, computed in

---

[4] The "Transfers of Assets to a Not-for-Profit Entity or Charitable Trust that Raises or Holds Contributions for Others" sections of FASB ASC 958-605 also establish standards for transactions that take place in a similar manner but are not contributions because the transfers are revocable, repayable, or reciprocal. For example, FASB ASC 958-605-55-110 states that if a resource provider transfers assets to a recipient entity and specifies itself or its affiliate as the beneficiary, a presumption that the transfer is reciprocal and, therefore, not a contribution is necessary, even if the resource provider explicitly grants the recipient entity variance power. Those standards and transactions are discussed in paragraphs 4.61–.63 and 12.74–.77 of this guide. FASB ASC 958-605 and this guide do not use the word *donor* in discussing those transactions because they are not contributions.

[5] Foundations that are not providers of health care services are not covered by this guide and should follow the Audit and Accounting Guide *Not-for-Profit Entities*.

[6] FASB ASC 958-20-45-3 states if the beneficiary and recipient entity are included in consolidated financial statements, the beneficiary's interest in the net assets of the recipient entity should be eliminated, in accordance with FASB ASC 810-10-45-1.

accordance with that agreement, when it measures its interest in the recipient entity. Similarly, if a parent entity controls both the recipient entity and specified health care entity, and the parent directed that unrestricted gifts would be distributed to affiliates in accordance with a specified formula, each affiliate would include its share of unrestricted net assets, computed in accordance with that formula, when it measures its interest in the recipient entity.

12.20 According to FASB ASC 954-605-25-12, distributions from a financially-interrelated recipient entity to a nongovernmental health care entity that it supports should generally be reported by the health care entity as a reduction of its interest in the recipient entity. However, if the distribution is made from net assets that are not includable in that interest because the health care entity does not have rights to them (that is, the recipient entity can determine to whom the assets will be distributed), the health care entity should report a contribution from the related recipient entity.

12.21 For example, assume a foundation's mission is to raise contributions for 2 financially interrelated health care entities: Hospital A and Hospital B. The foundation receives $10,000 in contributions from donors who do not specify which of the 2 hospitals should benefit from their gifts. No agreement exists between the foundation and Hospitals A and B that specifies how gifts to the foundation should be divided between the hospitals if the donor does not specify a beneficiary. Hospital A would report contribution revenue for any portion of the $10,000 that it receives from the foundation. Likewise, Hospital B would report contribution revenue for any portion of the $10,000 that it receives, but neither Hospital A nor Hospital B would record an interest in those assets before the foundation either distributes them or unconditionally promises them.

12.22 As discussed in FASB ASC 958-605-25-24, if the recipient entity and specified health care entity are not *financially-interrelated entities*, as defined in FASB ASC 958-20-15-2 (see paragraph 12.75), a recipient entity that accepts assets from a donor and agrees to use those assets on behalf of the specified health care entity (beneficiary) or transfer those assets, the return on investment of those assets, or both to the specified health care entity (beneficiary) should recognize its liability to the specified health care entity (beneficiary) concurrent with its recognition of cash or other financial assets received from the donor, unless the recipient entity is explicitly granted variance power (see the discussion of variance power in paragraph 11.34 of this guide). Except in cases when the donor grants variance power, or the entities are financially interrelated, as described in paragraphs 25–26 of FASB ASC 958-605-25 and FASB ASC 958-605-25-27, respectively, a recipient entity that receives nonfinancial assets is permitted, but not required, to recognize its liability and those assets, provided that the recipient entity consistently reports from period to period and discloses its accounting policy. The FASB ASC glossary defines *nonfinancial asset* as "[a]n asset that is not a financial asset. Nonfinancial assets include land, buildings, use of facilities or utilities, materials and supplies, intangible assets, or services." According to FASB ASC 968-605-25-28, a specified health care entity (beneficiary) should recognize its rights to the financial or nonfinancial assets held by a recipient entity as an asset, unless the recipient entity is explicitly granted variance power (see further discussion in paragraph 11.34 of this guide).

12.23 In contrast, if the donor does not specify a beneficiary (see further discussion in paragraph 12.17, and the foundation and a hospital are under common control, but they are not financially interrelated, the recipient entity should recognize contribution revenue when it receives the gift. At a later date, when the foundation transfers assets to the hospital, the gift should be accounted for as contributions received by the hospital, consistent with the "Contributions Received" sections of FASB ASC 958-605, provided that the foundation is acting other than as an owner.

12.24 Additional guidance regarding accounting for contributions received by agents, trustees, and intermediaries can be found in sections .35–.43 of Technical Questions and Answers section 6400, *Health Care Entities* (AICPA, *Technical Practice Aids*) (appendix A, "TIS Section 6400, *Health Care Entities*," of chapter 11, "Contributions Received and Made," of this guide) and chapter 5, "Contributions Received and Agency Transactions," of the Audit and Accounting Guide *Not-for-Profit Entities*.

Relationships With a For-Profit Entity

12.25 A not-for-profit health care system may own stock, partnership interests, or other ownership interests in for-profit entities, such as HMOs or insurance entities, that may or may not provide patient care. Whether the financial statements of a for-profit entity should be consolidated with the reporting entity depends on the nature of control. Certain types of control require consolidation; other relationships require the equity method of accounting to be used. Chapter 4 of this guide discusses the reporting of an interest in a for-profit entity if it is neither consolidated nor reported using the equity method.

12.26 When applying the guidance in FASB ASC 810-10, not-for-profit health care entities do not apply tests to determine whether the other entity is a variable interest entity (VIE). According to FASB ASC 810-10-15-17, not-for-profit entities are not subject to the "Variable Interest Entities" sections of FASB ASC 810-10, except that they may be related parties for purposes of applying paragraphs 42–44 of FASB ASC 810-10-25.

12.27 Guidance in this section is organized as follows:

- Consolidation required by a controlling financial interest
- Equity method of accounting for noncontrolling interests in corporations
- Interests in general partnerships
- Interests in limited partnerships and similar entities

Consolidation Required by a Controlling Financial Interest

12.28 Pursuant to FASB ASC 810-10-15-10(a), all majority-owned subsidiaries (that is, all entities in which a parent has a controlling financial interest) should be consolidated. However, exceptions exist to this general rule.

12.29 FASB ASC 810-10-15-10(a)(1) provides an exception if control does not rest with the majority owner. For instance, a majority-owned subsidiary should not be consolidated if any of the following are present: (*a*) the subsidiary is in legal reorganization; (*b*) the subsidiary is in bankruptcy; (*c*) the subsidiary operates under foreign exchange restrictions, controls, or other governmentally-imposed uncertainties that are so severe that they cast significant doubt on the parent's ability to control the subsidiary; and (*d*) the rights of noncontrolling shareholder(s) are so restrictive that it is questioned whether control rests with the majority owner. The guidance in paragraphs 2–14 of FASB ASC 810-10-25 should be applied in assessing the impact of consolidation on noncontrolling shareholder approval or veto rights. That guidance is also applied to determine the impact of consolidation on investments in which the investor has a majority voting interest in a limited liability company that has governing provisions that are the functional equivalent of a regular corporation.

12.30 FASB ASC 810-10-15-8 states that the usual condition for a controlling financial interest is ownership of a majority voting interest; therefore, as a general rule, direct or indirect ownership by one reporting entity of more than 50 percent of the outstanding voting shares of another entity is a condition pointing toward consolidation. The power to control may also exist with a lesser percentage of ownership (for example, by contract, lease, agreement with other stockholders, or court decree).

12.31 Legal or business reasons often preclude a physician practice management entity from acquiring the outstanding equity instruments of the physician practice. Per FASB ASC 810-10-15-21, a physician practice management entity can establish a controlling financial interest in a physician practice through contractual management arrangements. Specifically, a controlling financial interest exists if, for a requisite period of time, the physician practice management entity has control over the physician practice and a financial interest in the physician practice that meets all six of the requirements listed in FASB ASC 810-10-15-22. That paragraph contains guidance that describes how those six requirements are to be applied. FASB ASC 810-10-55-206 contains a decision tree illustrating the basic analysis called for by both the six requirements and presumptive, but not other, interpretive guidance.

12.32 The "Consolidation of Entities Controlled by Contract" sections of FASB ASC 810-10 provide additional guidance about consolidation by physician practice management entities and other situations in which one entity manages another under similar circumstances and arrangements.

Equity Method of Accounting for Noncontrolling Interests in Corporations

12.33 Investments in common stock of for-profit entities in which the reporting entity has 50 percent or less of the voting stock in the investee should be reported under the guidance in FASB ASC 323, *Investments—Equity Method and Joint Ventures*, unless the reporting entity elects to report that investment at fair value, in accordance with the "Fair Value Option" sections of FASB ASC 825-10. FASB ASC 323-10-15-3 requires that the equity method of accounting should be used if investments in common stock or in-substance common stock give the investor the ability to exercise significant influence over operating and financial policies of an investee, even though the investor holds 50 percent or less of the common stock or in-substance common stock or both common stock and in-substance common stock.

12.34 *Significant influence* is defined in paragraphs 6–11 of FASB ASC 323-10-15. Determining the ability of an investor to exercise significant influence is not always clear, and applying judgment is necessary to assess the status of each investment. A direct or indirect investment of 20 percent or more of the voting stock of an investee should lead to a presumption that in the absence of predominant evidence to the contrary, an investor has the ability to exercise significant influence over an investee. However, this presumption can be overcome in certain instances. Paragraphs 10–11 of FASB ASC 323-10-15 provide examples of indications that an investor may be unable to exercise significant influence. Conversely, an investment of less than 20 percent of the voting stock of an investee should lead to a presumption that an investor does not have the ability to exercise significant influence, unless such ability can be demonstrated. According to FASB ASC 323-10-25-2, the limitations under which a majority-owned subsidiary should not be consolidated, as discussed in FASB ASC 810-10-15-8 and 810-10-15-10, should also be applied as limitations to the use of the equity method. Health care entities that report investments on the equity method should make the financial statement disclosures required by FASB ASC 323-10-50.

12.35 Paragraphs 37–39 of FASB ASC 323-10-35 provide guidance on how an investor should account for its proportionate share of an investee's equity adjustments for other comprehensive income (below the performance indicator) in all of the following circumstances: (*a*) a loss of significant influence, (*b*) a loss of control that results in the retention of a cost method investment, and (*c*) discontinuation of the equity method for an investment in a limited partnership because the conditions in FASB ASC 970-323-25-6 are met for applying the cost method. Those paragraphs do not provide guidance for entities that have not historically recorded their proportionate share of an investee's equity adjustments for other comprehensive income. In accordance with FASB ASC 954-225-45-7(e), a not-for-profit health care entity should report items that are required to be reported in, or reclassified from, other comprehensive income separately from (below) the performance indicator.

Interests in General Partnerships

12.36 FASB ASC 970-810 provides consolidation guidance for the real estate industry and partners in general partnerships. Although health care entities are not required to apply that guidance, in current practice, they often apply it for their interests in general partnerships. FASB ASC 970-810-25-1 states that a general partnership that is directly or indirectly controlled by an investor is, in substance, a subsidiary of the investor. FASB ASC 970-810-25-2 states that a noncontrolling investor in a general partnership should account for its investment by the equity method and be guided by the provisions of FASB ASC 323. Alternatively, the reporting entity may elect to report that investment at fair value, in accordance with the "Fair Value Option" sections of FASB ASC 825-10.

Interests in Limited Partnerships and Similar Entities

12.37 FASB ASC 810-20 discusses the potential consolidation of partnerships and similar entities. It provides a framework for the determination of which, if any, general partner within the group controls and, therefore, should consolidate a limited partnership or limited liability company that has governing provisions that are the functional equivalent of a limited partnership. See paragraph 12.29 for a limited liability company that is the functional equivalent of a regular corporation.

12.38 FASB ASC 810-20-25-3 states that the general partners in a limited partnership are presumed to control a limited partnership, regardless of the extent of the general partners' ownership interest in the limited partnership. Paragraphs 4–20 of FASB ASC 810-20-25 provide guidance for purposes of assessing whether the limited partners' rights might preclude a general partner from controlling a limited partnership. Paragraphs 10–11 of FASB

ASC 810-20-25 state that if the presumption of control by the general partners is overcome, each of the general partners would account for its investment in the limited partnership using the equity method of accounting.

12.39 FASB ASC 970-323 provides guidance for the real estate industry and limited partners in limited partnerships, noncontrolling interests in corporate joint ventures, and undivided interests in real property. Although health care entities are not required to apply that guidance, except as indicated in the following paragraph, in current practice, not-for-profit health care entities often apply it for their noncontrolling interests in all limited partnerships, limited liability companies, corporate joint ventures, and similar entities. Alternatively, the reporting entity may elect to report that investment at fair value, in accordance with the "Fair Value Option" sections of FASB ASC 825-10.

12.40 FASB ASC 954-810-15-3(i) states that noncontrolling interests in for-profit real estate partnerships, limited liability entities, and similar entities over which the reporting entity has more than a minor interest should be reported under the equity method, in accordance with the guidance in the "General" sections of FASB ASC 970-323, unless the reporting entity elects to report that investment at fair value, in accordance with the "Fair Value Option" sections of FASB ASC 825-10. Those sections state that the equity method of accounting is generally appropriate for accounting by limited partners for their investments in limited partnerships. Alternatively, a not-for-profit health care entity can irrevocably elect fair value as the initial and subsequent measure for noncontrolling interests in partnerships under the "Fair Value Option" sections of FASB ASC 825-10. Paragraph 12.44 provides additional information about distinguishing a minor interest from a more than a minor interest.

12.41 FASB ASC 954-810-15-3(i) also states that a not-for-profit health care entity should apply the guidance in FASB ASC 970-323-25-2 to determine whether its interest in a for-profit real estate partnership, limited liability entity, or similar entity is a controlling or noncontrolling interest. FASB ASC 970-323-25-2 refers to FASB ASC 970-810-25-2, which states that a majority interest holder may not control the entity if one or more of the other partners have substantive participating rights that permit those other partners to effectively participate in significant decisions that would be expected to be made in the ordinary course of business. The determination of whether the rights of the other partners are substantive participating rights should be evaluated in accordance with the guidance for substantive participating rights in FASB ASC 810-20. If the other partners have substantive participating rights, the presumption of control by the majority interest holder is overcome.

12.42 A not-for-profit health care entity should apply the guidance in FASB ASC 323-30-35-3 to determine whether a limited liability company should be viewed as similar to a partnership, as opposed to a corporation, for purposes of determining whether a noncontrolling interest in a limited liability entity or similar entity should be accounted for in accordance with FASB ASC 970-323 or 323-10. FASB ASC 323-30-35-3 states that an investment in a limited liability company should be viewed as similar to an investment in a limited partnership if the limited liability company maintains a specific ownership account for each investor—similar to a partnership capital account structure.

12.43 A limited partner's interest may be so minor that the limited partner may have virtually no influence over partnership operating and financial policies. FASB ASC 970-323-25-6 states that such a limited partner is, in substance, in the same position (with respect to the investment) as an investor that owns a minor common stock interest in a corporation; accordingly, accounting for the investment using the cost method may be appropriate.

12.44 Although not registrants, many not-for-profit health care entities analogize to the guidance in FASB ASC 323-30-S99-1 to determine what is more than a minor interest. FASB ASC 323-30-S99-1 states that the Securities and Exchange Commission (SEC) staff understands that practice generally has viewed investments of more than 3 percent to 5 percent to be more than minor.

Special Entities

12.45 This section discusses relationships with three types of special entities, as follows:

- Special-purpose leasing entities
- Joint operating agreements
- Other special-purpose entities

Consolidation of a Special-Purpose Leasing Entity

12.46 FASB ASC 954-810-15-3(g) states that if a not-for-profit business-oriented health care entity is engaged in leasing transactions with a special-purpose-entity (SPE) lessor, it should consider whether it should consolidate the lessor, in accordance with the guidance in paragraphs 8–10 of FASB ASC 958-810-25.

12.47 FASB ASC 958-810-25-8 states that a not-for-profit entity should consolidate such a lessor if all of the following conditions exist:

a. Substantially all of the activities of the SPE involve assets that are to be leased to a single lessee.

b. The expected substantive residual risks, substantially all the residual rewards of the leased asset(s), and the obligation imposed by the underlying debt of the SPE directly or indirectly reside with the lessee through means such as any of the following:

   i. The lease agreement

   ii. A residual value guarantee through, for example, the assumption of first-dollar-of-loss provisions

   iii. A guarantee of the SPE's debt

   iv. An option granting the lessee a right to do either of the following:

      (1) Purchase the leased asset at a fixed price or a defined price other than fair value determined at the date of the exercise

      (2) Receive any of the lessor's sales proceeds in excess of a stipulated amount

c. The owner(s) of record of the SPE has not made an initial, substantive, residual equity capital investment that is at risk during the entire term of the lease. This criteria should be considered met if the majority owner(s) of the lessor is not an independent third party, regardless of the level of capital investment.

12.48 According to FASB ASC 958-810-25-9, to satisfy the at-risk requirement in FASB ASC 958-810-25-8(c) (see paragraph 12.47), an initial, substantive, residual equity capital investment should meet all of the following conditions:

a. It represents an equity interest in legal form.

b. It is subordinate to all debt interests.

c. It represents the residual equity interest during the entire lease term.

12.49 FASB ASC 958-810-25-10 states that if all the conditions in FASB ASC 958-810-25-8 (see paragraph 12.47) exist, the assets, liabilities, results of operations, and cash flows of the SPE should be consolidated in the lessee's financial statements. This conclusion should be applied to SPEs that are established for both the construction and subsequent lease of an asset for which the lease would meet all the conditions in FASB ASC 958-810-25-8 (see paragraph 12.47). In those cases, the consolidation by the lessee should begin at the lease inception, rather than the beginning of the lease term. Implementation guidance may be found in FASB ASC 958-810-55-4A and 958-840-55-1.

12.50 The Financial Reporting Executive Committee believes that 3 percent is the minimum acceptable investment to qualify as an initial, substantive, residual equity capital investment. A greater investment may be necessary depending on the facts and circumstances, including the credit risk associated with the lessee and market risk factors associated with the leased property. For example, the cost of borrowed funds for the transaction might be indicative of the risk associated with the transaction and whether an equity investment greater than 3 percent is needed.

Agreements to Jointly Operate a Facility or Other Activity

12.51 Health care systems may enter into an agreement in which two or more entities agree to jointly operate and control a certain endeavor, such as a hospital or treatment center, while sharing in the operating results and residual interest upon dissolution, based upon an agreed-upon ratio. Those agreements are similar to joint ventures and, typically, are characterized by factors such as the following:

- *Common purpose.* For example, to share risks and rewards; develop a new market, health service, or program; or pool resources.
- *Joint funding.* All parties contribute resources toward the accomplishment.
- *Defined relationship.* Typically governed by an agreement.
- *Joint control.* No one entity controls the joint operating activity.

12.52 If the endeavor is housed in a separate legal entity, such as a corporation or partnership, it would be accounted for similar to a corporate joint venture using the equity method of accounting described in FASB ASC 323-10. Alternatively, the reporting entity may elect to report such interests at fair value, in accordance with the "Fair Value Option" sections of FASB ASC 825-10.

12.53 If the endeavor is not conducted within a separate legal entity, it would be accounted for based on the guidance in FASB ASC 808, *Collaborative Arrangements.* FASB ASC 808-10-45-1 states that participants in a collaborative arrangement should report costs incurred and revenue generated from transactions with third parties (that is, parties that do not participate in the arrangement) in each entity's respective income statement, pursuant to the guidance in FASB ASC 605-45 for principal agents. An entity should not apply the equity method of accounting to the activities of a collaborative arrangement.

Other Special-Purpose Entities

12.54 A not-for-profit business-oriented health care entity may be engaged in transactions with an SPE that are other than leasing transactions or transactions of a collaborative arrangement. In practice, entities analogize to the guidance in paragraphs 8–10 of FASB ASC 958-810-25 and paragraphs 7–16 of FASB ASC 958-810-55 to determine whether to consolidate the SPE.

Reporting by Investor-Owned Health Care Entities

12.55 FASB ASC 954-810-15-2 provides a summary of the locations of standards that an investor-owned health care entity uses for reporting relationships with other entities, as follows:

a. Pursuant to FASB ASC 810-10-15-3(a), an investor-owned health care entity should first apply the guidance in the "Variable Interest Entities" sections of FASB ASC 810-10 if it is within the scope of those sections.

b. Pursuant to FASB ASC 810-10-15-3(b), if the investor-owned health care entity has an investment in another entity that is not determined to be a VIE, it should use the guidance in the "General" sections of FASB ASC 810-10 to determine whether that interest constitutes a controlling financial interest. That guidance also is used to determine if a not-for-profit health care entity has a controlling financial interest in a for-profit entity, and it is discussed in paragraphs 12.28–.32.

c. Pursuant to FASB ASC 810-10-15-3(c), if the investor-owned health care entity has a contractual management relationship with another entity (for example, a physician practice), and that other entity is not determined to be a VIE, it shall use the guidance in the "Consolidation of Entities Controlled by Contract" sections of FASB ASC 810-10 to determine whether the arrangement constitutes a controlling financial interest. That guidance also is used to determine if a not-for-profit health care entity has a controlling financial interest in a for-profit entity, and it is discussed in paragraphs 12.30–.32.

d. Pursuant to FASB ASC 810-20-15, if the investor-owned health care entity is the general partner of a limited partnership or similar entity, such as a limited liability entity that has governing provisions that are the functional equivalent of a limited partnership, it should apply the guidance in FASB ASC 810-20. That guidance also is used by a not-for-profit health care entity that has an interest in a for-profit partnership, and it is discussed in paragraph 12.38.

e. Pursuant to FASB ASC 810-30-15, if the investor-owned health care entity is a sponsor in a research and development arrangement, it shall apply the guidance in FASB ASC 810-30.

12.56 In addition, the SEC staff's position is that health care entities that are registrants should follow applicable SEC guidance and the guidance in paragraphs 6–7 of FASB ASC 970-323-25 for their noncontrolling interests in non-real estate limited partnerships. Although investor-owned health care entities that are not registrants are not required to apply that guidance, in current practice, they often apply it for their noncontrolling interests in general partnerships, limited partnerships, limited liability companies, corporate joint ventures, and similar entities.

12.57 The "Variable Interest Entities" sections of FASB ASC 810-10 address consolidation by business entities of VIEs. An investor-owned health care entity should follow the guidance in the "Variable Interest Entities" sections if, by design, any of the conditions in FASB ASC 810-10-15-14 exist. The phrase *by design* refers to entities that meet the conditions in that paragraph because of the way they are structured. For example, a legal entity under the control of its equity investors that originally was not a VIE does not become one because of operating losses. The design of the legal entity is important in the application of these provisions. Although according to FASB ASC 810-10-15-17, not-for-profit entities are not subject to the "Variable Interest Entities" sections of FASB ASC 810-10, if a not-for-profit entity is used by a business reporting entity in a manner similar to a VIE in an effort to circumvent the provisions of the "Variable Interest Entities" sections, that not-for-profit entity is subject to the guidance in the "Variable Interest Entities" sections.

Presentation of Consolidated and Combined Financial Statements

12.58 Some accounting standards, including some for reporting relationships with other entities, specify the display of certain financial statement elements or items without considering the reporting model used by not-for-profit health care entities. Therefore, FASB ASC 958-10-45-1 states that preparers of financial statements of not-for-profit entities should follow the guidance in an analogous manner that is appropriate for their method of reporting financial performance and financial position and should consider the reporting objectives of the guidance when exercising judgment about how best to display elements, such as in which net asset class.

12.59 FASB ASC 810-10-10-1 states that the purpose of consolidated financial statements is to present, primarily for the benefit of the shareholders and creditors of the parent entity, the results of operations and financial position of a parent entity and its subsidiaries essentially as if the group was a single entity with one or more branches or divisions. A presumption exists that consolidated financial statements are more meaningful than separate financial statements and that they are usually necessary for a fair presentation when one of the entities in the group has a direct or indirect controlling financial interest in the other entities.

12.60 FASB ASC 810-10-25-15 states that application of guidance of an industry-specific topic to a subsidiary within the scope of that industry-specific topic should be retained in consolidation of that subsidiary.

12.61 For example, if a not-for-profit health care entity has a controlling financial interest in an investor-owned entity, and that entity in turn has a controlling financial interest in a VIE, the consolidation of the VIE is retained in the consolidated financial statements. Similarly, if a not-for-profit health care entity has a controlling financial interest in an investor-owned entity, the debt and equity securities owned by the investor-owned entity are measured and reported using the standards in FASB ASC 320, *Investments—Debt and Equity Securities*, rather than being remeasured using the standards in FASB ASC 958-320.

12.62 FASB ASC 958-810-45-1 states that noncontrolling interests in the equity (net assets) of consolidated subsidiaries should be reported as a separate component of the appropriate class of net assets in the consolidated statement of financial position of a not-for-profit health care entity. That amount shall be clearly identified and described (for example, as noncontrolling ownership interest in subsidiaries) to distinguish it from the components of net assets of the parent, which includes the parent's controlling financial interest in its subsidiaries. The effects of donor-imposed restrictions, if any, on a partially-owned subsidiary's net assets should be reported in accordance with FASB ASC 958-205 and 958-320. Paragraphs 4–6 of FASB ASC 958-810-50 require certain disclosures about noncontrolling interests. Paragraph 9.18 of this guide provides additional information about noncontrolling interests.

12.63 According to FASB ASC 954-810-45-3B, when consolidated financial statements are required or permitted by FASB ASC 958-810-25, a noncontrolling interest in the other not-for-profit entity should be provided if such interest is represented by an economic interest whereby the noncontrolling interest would share in the operating results or residual interest upon dissolution.

12.64 According to FASB ASC 958-810-50-1, if consolidated financial statements are presented by a not-for-profit entity (parent), the parent should disclose any restrictions made by entities outside the reporting entity on distributions from the controlled not-for-profit entity (subsidiary) to the parent and any resulting unavailability of the net assets of the subsidiary for use by the parent.

12.65 FASB ASC 810-10-45-11 states that in some cases, parent-entity financial statements may be needed, in addition to consolidated financial statements, to adequately indicate the position of bondholders and other creditors or preferred shareholders of the parent. Consolidating financial statements, in which one column is used for the parent and other columns for particular subsidiaries or groups of subsidiaries, often are an effective means of presenting the pertinent information. However, consolidated financial statements are the general-purpose financial statements of a parent having one or more subsidiaries; thus, parent-entity financial statements are not a valid substitute for consolidated financial statements.

12.66 However, neither generally accepted accounting principles (GAAP) nor this guide discuss the use of the parent entity's financial statements as other than the general-purpose financial statements for the primary reporting entity.[7] GAAP does not preclude the issuance of financial statements for the subsidiary only. However, care should be taken to include all disclosures required by FASB ASC 850, *Related Party Disclosures*, and other relevant pronouncements.

---

[7] Contractual agreements or regulatory provisions may require parent company-only financial statements. AU section 623, *Special Reports* (AICPA, *Professional Standards*), provides guidance for reporting on financial presentations to comply with contractual agreements or regulatory provisions.

12.67 FASB ASC 810-10-55-1B states that in some circumstances, combined financial statements, as distinguished from consolidated financial statements, of commonly controlled entities are likely to be more meaningful than their separate statements. Combined statements would be useful if one individual owns a controlling financial interest in several entities that are related in their operations. Combined financial statements might also be useful to present the financial position and results of operations of entities under common management. Pursuant to FASB ASC 810-10-45-10, both consolidation and combination require elimination of intraentity transactions and profits and losses.

12.68 In some situations, debt agreements may require the combined financial statements of affiliated entities, the assets or revenues of which serve as collateral for the related debt (sometimes called an obligated group). However, if debt or other agreements prescribe a financial presentation that varies from GAAP (for example, exclusion of entities otherwise required to be consolidated), AU section 623, *Special Reports* (AICPA, *Professional Standards*), establishes requirements and provides guidance regarding auditor's reports.

Accounting for Transfers Between Related Entities

12.69 Transfers from a foundation that acts as an agent, a trustee, or an intermediary (that is, a recipient entity) for contributions to a related nongovernmental health care entity are discussed in paragraphs 12.16–.24. This section discusses equity transfers, equity transactions, and other transfers between related entities.

Equity Transfers

12.70 The FASB ASC glossary defines an *equity transfer* as follows:

> An equity transfer is nonreciprocal. An equity transfer is a transaction directly between a transferor and a transferee. Equity transfers are similar to ownership transactions between a for-profit parent and its owned subsidiary (for example, additional paid-in capital or dividends). However, equity transfers can occur only between related not-for-profit entities (NFPs) if one controls the other or both are under common control. An equity transfer embodies no expectation of repayment, nor does the transferor receive anything of immediate economic value (such as a financial interest or ownership).

Per FASB ASC 954-225-45-2, equity transfers are reported separately as changes in net assets, are excluded from the performance indicator, and do not result in any step-up in the basis of the transferred underlying assets.

12.71 The "Transactions Between Entities Under Common Control" sections of FASB ASC 805-50 provide guidance when accounting for a transfer of assets or exchange of shares between entities under common control. The entity that receives the net assets or equity interests should recognize the transferred assets and liabilities at the date of transfer, initially measuring them at their carrying amounts in the accounts of the transferring entity. If the carrying amounts of the transferred assets and liabilities differ from the historical cost of the parent of the entities under common control (for example, because push-down accounting had not been applied), then the financial statements of the receiving entity should reflect the transferred assets and liabilities at the historical cost of the parent of the entities under common control. FASB

ASC 805-50-45 provides guidance on the presentation of financial statements for the period of transfer and comparative financial statements for prior years, and disclosures are required by FASB ASC 805-50-50.

12.72 FASB ASC 805-50-30-6 notes that in some instances, the entity that receives the net assets or equity interests (the receiving entity) and the entity that transferred the net assets or equity interests (the transferring entity) may account for similar assets and liabilities using different accounting methods. In such circumstances, the carrying amounts of the transferred assets and liabilities may be adjusted to the basis of accounting used by the receiving entity if the change would be preferable. Any such change in accounting method should be applied retrospectively, and financial statements presented for prior periods should be adjusted, unless it is impracticable to do so. FASB ASC 250-10-45 provides guidance if retrospective application is impracticable.

12.73 In most situations, transfers are recorded at the time they are formally obligated to occur (formal board resolutions, legal notes, passage of title to real estate, and so on), as would be the case when each of the entities have independent governance, and the timing of the transfer is controlled by the governing board of the transferor. Yet, in situations of clear, common control of the related entities, it would be appropriate to record transfers at the time when both the transfer amount is known, and the receiving entity is given control over the timing of the transfer.

Equity Transactions

12.74 According to FASB ASC 958-20-25-4, a transfer from a nongovernmental health care entity to a not-for-profit entity or charitable trust (referred to as a recipient entity) is an equity transaction if all of the following conditions are present:

- A nongovernmental health care entity transfers assets to a not-for-profit entity or charitable trust (called a recipient entity) that accepts those assets and agrees to use them on behalf of the nongovernmental health care entity or transfer them, their investment return, or both back to the nongovernmental health care entity or its affiliate (that is, the nongovernmental health care entity specifies itself or its affiliate as the beneficiary of the transfer).
- The nongovernmental health care entity and recipient entity are financially-interrelated entities.
- Neither the nongovernmental health care entity nor its affiliate expects payment of the transferred assets, although payment of investment return on the transferred assets may be expected.

12.75 FASB ASC 958-20-15-2 provides that a recipient entity and specified beneficiary are financially-interrelated entities if the relationship between them has both of the following characteristics: one entity has the ability to influence the operating and financial decisions of the other, and one entity has an ongoing economic interest in the net assets of the other. The ability to exercise that influence can be demonstrated in several ways, including the following:

a. The entities are *affiliates*, as defined in the FASB ASC glossary.

b. One entity has considerable representation on the governing board of the other entity.

c. The charter or bylaws of one entity limits its activities to those that are beneficial to the other entity.

d. An agreement between the entities allows one entity to actively participate in the policy-making processes of the other, such as setting organizational priorities, budgets, and management compensation.

The FASB ASC glossary defines an *ongoing economic interest in the net assets of another* as "[a] residual right to another not-for-profit entity's (NFP's) net assets that results from an ongoing relationship. The value of those rights increases or decreases as a result of the investment, fundraising, operating, and other activities of the other entity."

12.76 Per FASB ASC 954-225-55-1, an equity transaction differs from an equity transfer in that an equity transaction, as described in FASB ASC 958-20-25-4, involves a financially-interrelated party either as a third party in a transfer from an entity to one of its affiliates or a counterparty in a transfer from an entity to itself. An *equity transfer*, as described in the guide, is a transaction directly between a transferor and transferee. In addition, an equity transaction is reciprocal; the health care entity or its affiliate named as the beneficiary receives an ongoing economic interest in the assets held by the recipient entity. As noted in the FASB ASC glossary definition of *equity transfer*, an equity transfer is nonreciprocal; no expectation of repayment exists, and the transferor does not receive a financial interest or ownership (see paragraphs 12.70–.73).

12.77 The reporting of an equity transaction depends upon whether the resource provider or its affiliate is the specified beneficiary. As discussed in FASB ASC 958-20-25-5, if the resource provider specifies itself as beneficiary, it should report an equity transaction as an asset—an interest in the net assets of the recipient entity or an increase in a previously-recognized interest.[8] According to FASB ASC 958-20-25-6, if a resource provider specifies an affiliate as beneficiary of an equity transaction, the resource provider should report an equity transaction as a separate line in its statement of activities, and the affiliate named as beneficiary should report an interest in the net assets of the recipient entity.[9] In accordance with FASB ASC 958-20-45-1, the recipient entity should report an equity transaction as a separate line in its statement of activities. The resource provider should disclose the information described in FASB ASC 958-605-50-6 (see paragraph 4.63 of this guide) for each period for which a statement of financial position is presented.

Other Transfers

12.78 Other transfers may occur among related entities. If the entities are consolidated or combined, such transfers are eliminated in consolidation or combination, or both. If the entities are not consolidated or combined (for example, in separate subsidiaries or obligated group financial statements),[10] the method of accounting for such transfers is dictated by the substance of

[8] According to FASB ASC 958-20-45-3, if the beneficiary (resource provider) and recipient entity are included in consolidated financial statements, the beneficiary's interest in the net assets of the recipient entity should be eliminated, in accordance with FASB ASC 810-10-45-1.

[9] According to FASB ASC 958-20-45-3, if the beneficiary (affiliate) and recipient entity are included in consolidated financial statements, the beneficiary's interest in the net assets of the recipient entity should be eliminated, in accordance with FASB ASC 810-10-45-1.

[10] See paragraphs 7.72–.74 of this guide for additional discussion regarding obligated group financial statements.

the transaction, as well as the legal form. For example, certain transfers by a foundation to a related not-for-profit health care entity are reported as contributions, as discussed in paragraphs 12.16–.24. In other situations, payments may be made for services provided between not-for-profit entities under common control, which should be accounted for as revenues and expenses depending on the types of provided services. Transfers that result in changes in ownership interest are accounted for as investments, in accordance with FASB ASC 323 and 810.

12.79 Assets transferred from one commonly controlled entity to another should be recorded by the transferee at the carrying value of the transferring entity. This treatment is consistent with the guidance prescribed in the "Transactions Between Entities Under Common Control" sections of FASB ASC 805-50. For additional information, see paragraphs 12.71–.73.

12.80 According to FASB ASC 954-310-25-3, a health care entity may loan or advance resources to a related entity. If repayment is reasonably assured, a receivable or payable should be recorded by the entities.

12.81 Subsequent to the time that a receivable is recorded, the ability of the receiving entity to repay the receivable should be considered.

12.82 According to FASB ASC 954-310-40-1, if the receivable from a related entity is not to be repaid, or the related entity is perceived as unable to repay, the write-off of the receivable is recognized as an equity transfer, as discussed in FASB ASC 954-225-45-2, with the transferor reducing net assets and the transferee increasing net assets at the date such determination is made. See paragraphs 12.70–.73 for additional discussion.

Disclosure

12.83 Significant relationships and transactions not in the ordinary course of business with directors; management; medical staff; or other related parties, including unconsolidated related entities, should be disclosed in accordance with FASB ASC 850. AU section 334, *Related Parties* (AICPA, *Professional Standards*), establishes requirements and provides guidance for the auditor when determining the existence of transactions with related parties and identifying them.

12.84 Hospital boards may contract with management companies to operate their facilities. Frequently, the management company will employ the administrator, as well as other key personnel. Further, services may be acquired from entities related to the management company. The auditor should evaluate the impact of these arrangements on the hospital's internal controls and disclose related-party transactions, as required by FASB ASC 850.

Mergers and Acquisitions

12.85 The reporting entity is changed by mergers and acquisitions (referred to jointly as combinations) entered into by the health care entity. Standards for financial accounting and reporting for combinations differ depending upon whether the combining entities are investor-owned entities, not-for-profit entities, or one of each. Paragraphs 12.86–.108 summarize some of the guidance in FASB ASC 958-805 and FASB ASC 805, *Business Combinations*, but are not intended as a substitute for reading those standards.

12.86 FASB ASC 805 provides guidance on accounting and reporting for transactions or other events in which an acquirer obtains control of one or more businesses in a combination to be accounted for under the acquisition method. FASB ASC 958-805 provides guidance on a transaction or other event in which a not-for-profit entity that is the reporting entity combines with one or more other not-for-profit entities, businesses, or nonprofit activities.

12.87 If the reporting entity is an investor-owned health care entity, all combinations are accounted for using the acquisition method, including transactions or events referred to as true mergers or mergers of equals.

12.88 If the reporting entity is a not-for-profit health care entity, FASB ASC 958-805-25-1 requires that it determine whether the combination transaction or event is a merger of not-for-profit entities or an acquisition by a not-for-profit entity by applying the definitions of those combinations. FASB ASC 958-805-55-1 states that ceding control to a new not-for-profit entity is the sole definitive criteria for identifying a merger, and one entity obtaining control over the other is the sole definitive criteria for an acquisition. Paragraphs 1–31 of FASB ASC 958-805-55 provide guidance on distinguishing between a merger and an acquisition.

12.89 The guidance for combinations of entities in this section is organized as follows:

- Mergers of not-for-profit entities
- Acquisitions by a not-for-profit entity
- Acquisitions by an investor-owned entity, including a for-profit subsidiary of a not-for-profit health care entity
- Disclosures about combinations

Merger of Not-for-Profit Entities

12.90 The FASB ASC glossary defines *merger of not-for-profit entities* as "[a] transaction or other event in which the governing bodies of two or more not-for-profit entities cede control of those entities to create a new not-for-profit entity." FASB ASC 958-805-25-3 requires that the not-for-profit entity resulting from a merger (the new entity) account for the merger by applying the carryover method described in the "Merger of Not-for-Profit Entities" sections of FASB ASC 958-805.

12.91 Applying the carryover method requires combining the assets and liabilities recognized in the separate financial statements of the merging entities as of the merger date (or that would be recognized if the entities issued financial statements as of that date), with certain adjustments. The new not-for-profit entity does not recognize additional assets or liabilities, such as internally-developed intangible assets, that GAAP did not require or permit the merging entities to recognize. However, if a merging entity's separate financial statements are not prepared in accordance with GAAP, those statements should be adjusted to GAAP before the new entity recognizes the assets and liabilities. The new not-for-profit health care entity should carry forward at the merger date the merging entities' classifications and designations of their assets and liabilities, unless one of the exceptions in FASB ASC 958-805-25-9 applies. Those exceptions are for certain modifications in contracts as a result of the merger and for conforming accounting policies to reflect a consistent method of accounting.

Acquisition by a Not-for-Profit Entity

12.92 The FASB ASC glossary defines *acquisition by a not-for-profit entity* as "[a] transaction or other event in which a not-for-profit acquirer obtains control of one or more nonprofit activities or businesses and initially recognizes their assets and liabilities in the acquirer's financial statements." A not-for-profit health care entity should account for each acquisition of a business or nonprofit activity by applying the acquisition method described in the "Acquisition by a Not-for-Profit Entity" sections of FASB ASC 958-805. That acquisition method is the same as the acquisition method described in FASB ASC 805; however, FASB ASC 958-805 includes guidance on aspects of the items that are unique or especially significant to a not-for-profit entity.

12.93 Pursuant to FASB ASC 805-10-05-4, as modified by FASB ASC 958-805-25-13, the steps for applying the acquisition method are as follows:

a. Identifying the acquirer

b. Identifying the acquisition date

c. Recognizing the identifiable acquired assets, the assumed liabilities, and any noncontrolling interest in the acquiree

d. Recognizing acquired goodwill or a contribution received, including transferred consideration

e. Determining what is part of the acquisition transaction

12.94 FASB ASC 805-10-25-4 requires that one of the combining entities be identified as the acquirer. The guidance on control and consolidation of not-for-profit entities should be used to identify the acquirer. For a not-for-profit entity acquirer other than a health care entity, the guidance to be used is the guidance in FASB ASC 958-810, including the guidance referenced in FASB ASC 958-810-15-4. Consolidation of not-for-profit entities is discussed beginning at paragraph 12.03. If that guidance does not clearly indicate which of the combining entities is the acquirer, the factors in paragraphs 42–46 of FASB ASC 958-805-55 should be considered in making that determination.

12.95 Paragraphs 6–7 of FASB ASC 805-10-25 require that the acquirer identify the *acquisition date*, which is the date on which it obtains control of the acquiree. The date on which the acquirer obtains control of the acquiree generally is the date on which the acquirer legally transfers the consideration, if any; acquires the assets; and assumes the liabilities of the acquire (the closing date). In addition, FASB ASC 958-805-25-17 states that the date on which a not-for-profit acquirer obtains control of a not-for-profit entity with sole corporate membership generally is also the date on which the acquirer becomes the sole corporate member of that entity.

12.96 FASB ASB ASC 805-20 requires that as of the acquisition date, the acquirer recognize separately from goodwill the identifiable acquired assets, the assumed liabilities, and any noncontrolling interest in the acquiree.

12.97 In conformity with FASB ASC 958-805-30-6(b), a not-for-profit acquirer determines the net of the acquisition date amounts of the identifiable acquired assets and assumed liabilities, measured in accordance with FASB ASC 805-20 and 958-805. Most assets and liabilities are measured at fair value. However, FASB ASC 805-20-25-16 notes that limited exceptions exist to the recognition and measurement principles applicable to business combinations, including acquisitions by a not-for-profit entity. The limited exceptions are specified in paragraphs 16–28 of FASB ASC 805-20-25, paragraphs 12–23 of FASB ASC 805-20-30, and paragraphs 21–26 of FASB ASC 958-805-25. Examples of items that are either not recognized or are measured at an amount other than their acquisition date fair values include income taxes, employee benefits, assets held for sale, collections, conditional promises to give, donor relationships, and certain assets and liabilities arising from contingencies.

12.98 Next, in conformity with FASB ASC 958-805-30-6(a), a not-for-profit acquirer determines the aggregate of the following:

a. The transferred consideration, measured at its acquisition date fair value, as discussed in paragraphs 10–13 of FASB ASC 958-805-30

b. The fair value of any noncontrolling interest in the acquire

c. In an acquisition by a not-for-profit entity achieved in stages, the acquisition date fair value of the acquirer's previously-held equity interest in the acquire

12.99 If the amount in FASB ASC 958-805-30-6(a) is greater than the amount in FASB 958-805-30-6(b), a not-for-profit acquirer should determine whether the operations of the acquiree as part of the combined entity are expected to be predominantly supported by contributions and returns on investments. If the operations of the acquiree are not expected to be predominantly supported by contributions and returns on investments, in conformity with FASB ASC 958-805-25-28, a not-for-profit acquirer should recognize goodwill as of the acquisition date, measured as of the acquisition date as the excess of FASB ASC 958-805-30-6(a) over FASB ASC 958-805-30-6(b). *Predominantly supported by* means that contributions and returns on investments are expected to be significantly more than the total of all other sources of revenues.

12.100 In rare cases, the operations of the acquiree as part of the combined not-for-profit health care entity are expected to be predominantly supported by contributions and returns on investments. If so, FASB ASC 958-805-25-29 requires a not-for-profit acquirer to recognize a separate charge in its statement of activities as of the acquisition date, measured as the excess of FASB ASC 958-805-30-6(a) over FASB 958-805-30-6(b), rather than goodwill.

12.101 If the amount in FASB ASC 958-805-30-6(b) is greater than the amount in FASB 958-805-30-6(a), FASB ASC 958-805-25-31 requires a not-for-profit acquirer to recognize an inherent contribution received, measured as the excess of FASB ASC 958-805-30-6(b) over FASB ASC 958-805-30-6(a). The inherent contribution is reported as a separate credit in the statement of activities as of the acquisition date and, in accordance with FASB ASC 958-805-45-6, is classified on the basis of the type of restrictions imposed on the related net assets. FASB ASC 958-805-45-6 states that those restrictions include restrictions imposed on the net assets of the acquiree by a donor before the acquisition and those imposed by the donor of the acquired business or nonprofit activity, if any. Donor-restricted contributions are reported as restricted support, even if the restrictions are met in the same reporting period in which the acquisition occurs. The acquirer should not apply the reporting exception in FASB ASC 958-605-45-4, as discussed in paragraph 11.12 of this guide, to restricted net assets acquired in an acquisition.

Performance Indicator

12.102 FASB ASC 954-805 provides standards for reporting amounts related to an acquisition by a not-for-profit health care entity within or outside of the performance indicator. The following amounts are reported within the performance indicator:

- The changes in the fair value of a contingent consideration recognized in accordance with FASB ASC 958-805-35-3, unless the arrangement is a hedging instrument for which FASB ASC 954-815 requires the entity to recognize the changes outside the performance indicator
- The separate charge that is recognized in accordance with FASB ASC 958-805-25-29 (that is, the immediate write-off of the goodwill amount)
- The gain or loss resulting from remeasuring a previously-held equity interest in the acquiree in an acquisition achieved in stages, as discussed in paragraphs 9–10 of FASB ASC 805-10-25 and FASB ASC 954-805-45-3

12.103 Per FASB ASC 954-805-45-2, whether the inherent contribution received, recognized in accordance with FASB ASC 958-805-25-31, is presented within or outside the performance indicator depends on whether the contribution is unrestricted or restricted. An unrestricted contribution should be presented within the performance indicator. A contribution that is either temporarily restricted or permanently restricted should be presented outside the performance indicator.

12.104 FASB ASC 954-805-50 requires disclosures about the performance indicator in periods in which mergers or acquisitions occur.

Acquisition by an Investor-Owned Entity, Including a For-Profit Subsidiary of a Not-for-Profit Health Care Entity

12.105 FASB ASC 805-10-25-1 requires that an investor-owned health care entity determine whether a transaction or other event is a business combination by applying the definition of a *business combination*, which requires that the acquired assets and assumed liabilities constitute a *business*, as defined. If the acquired assets are not a business, the reporting entity should account for the transaction or other event as an asset acquisition. An entity should account for each business combination by applying the acquisition method.

12.106 FASB ASC 805-10-05-4 states that the acquisition method requires all of the following steps:

a. Identifying the acquirer, which is discussed in FASB ASC 805-10

b. Determining the acquisition date, which is discussed in FASB ASC 805-10

c. Recognizing and measuring the identifiable acquired assets, the assumed liabilities, and any noncontrolling interest in the acquiree, as discussed in FASB ASC 805-20

d. Recognizing and measuring goodwill or a gain from a bargain purchase, as discussed in FASB ASC 805-30

12.107 FASB ASC 958-805-25-14 identifies the differences in the application of the acquisition method by a not-for-profit acquirer from the application of the acquisition method by a business entity. Those differences include all of the following:

a. An investor-owned health care entity identifies the acquirer in accordance with FASB ASC 805-10-25-5 instead of the guidance in paragraphs 15–16 of FASB ASC 958-805-25.

b. An investor-owned health care entity recognizes and measures goodwill in accordance with FASB ASC 805-30-25-1 and paragraphs 1–3 of FASB ASC 805-30-30-3 instead of the guidance in paragraphs 27–30 of FASB ASC 958-805-25. Only a not-for-profit acquirer may recognize the immediate charge to the statement of activities.

c. An investor-owned health care entity recognizes and measures a gain from a bargain purchase in accordance with paragraphs 2–4 of FASB ASC 805-30-25 and paragraphs 4–6 of FASB ASC 805-30-30 instead of the guidance for an inherent contribution received in FASB ASC 958-805-25-31 and paragraphs 8–9 of FASB ASC 958-805-30.

Disclosures About Combinations*

12.108 FASB ASC 958-805-50 requires a not-for-profit health care entity to disclose information that enables users of its financial statements to evaluate the nature and financial effect of a merger of not-for-profit entities or an acquisition by a not-for-profit entity. Similarly, FASB ASC 805-10-50, 805-20-50, and 805-30-50 require an investor-owned health care entity to disclose information that enables users of its financial statements to evaluate the nature and financial effect of a business combination. If acquisitions are individually immaterial but collectively material, the entity should disclose the required information in the aggregate. Disclosures are also required if an acquisition date is after the reporting date but before the financial statements are issued or available for issue. If the initial accounting for an acquisition by an entity is incomplete, the entity should disclose information that enables users of its financial statements to evaluate the financial effects of adjustments recognized in the current reporting period that relate to acquisitions that occurred in the current or previous reporting periods.

Auditing

12.109 The independent auditor may consider the examples of specific auditing objectives, selected control activities, and auditing procedures for related parties, balances, and transactions that are presented in exhibit 12-2.

---

* In December 2010, FASB issued Accounting Standards Update (ASU) No. 2010-29, *Business Combinations (Topic 805): Disclosure of Supplementary Pro Forma Information for Business Combinations (a consensus of the FASB Emerging Issues Task Force)*. This ASU is intended to clarify requirements for reporting pro forma revenue and earnings disclosures in business combinations. This ASU is effective for business combinations with acquisition dates on or after the beginning of the first annual reporting period beginning on or after December 15, 2010.

Exhibit 12-2

The following table illustrates the use of assertions in developing audit objectives and designing substantive tests. The examples are not intended to be all-inclusive nor is it expected that all the procedures would necessarily be applied in an audit. The auditor should design and perform substantive procedures for all relevant assertions related to each material class of transactions, account balance, and disclosure to obtain sufficient appropriate audit evidence. The use of assertions in assessing risks and designing appropriate audit procedures to obtain audit evidence is described in paragraphs .14–.26 of AU section 326, *Audit Evidence* (AICPA, *Professional Standards*). Various audit procedures and the purposes for which they may be performed are described in paragraphs .27–.41 of AU section 326.

Auditing Considerations

Financial Statement Assertions	*Specific Auditing Objectives*	*Selected Control Activities*	*Auditing Procedures*
Reporting Entity and Related Entities			
Transactions/Account Balances/Presentation and Disclosure			
Existence and occurrence, completeness, and presentation and disclosure	The reporting entity is appropriate.	Procedures ensure that investees, affiliates, and other related entities are accounted for appropriately.	Review the articles of incorporation, bylaws, and minutes of directors' meetings; shareholder lists; and filings with regulatory authorities to determine the existence of related parties. Obtain representations from management about whether all investees, affiliates, and related entities have been accounted for properly or disclosed.

(continued)

Auditing Considerations—continued

Financial Statement Assertions	*Specific Auditing Objectives*	*Selected Control Activities*	*Auditing Procedures*
			Review transactions with investees, affiliates, and other related entities to determine that they are properly reported and clearly expressed.
	Relationships and transactions with related entities are identified and disclosed, if appropriate, because of economic dependence of the entity.	Procedures ensure that conflict-of-interest policies, procedures, and disclosure requirements are met.	Test significant related-party transactions as follows: • Determine substance. • Examine documents (invoices, contracts, and agreements). • Determine the basis of pricing. • Determine the collectibility of receivables and advances.
			Review related-party transactions for completeness by • considering previously identified transactions or relationships. • reviewing the minutes of directors' and other meetings. • discussing related-party transactions with entity personnel.

Financial Statement Assertions	Specific Auditing Objectives	Selected Control Activities	Auditing Procedures
			• reviewing unusual transactions. • reviewing the responses to related-party (conflict-of-interest) questionnaires.
Presentation and Disclosure			
Classification and understandability	Related-party transactions and entities are properly reported.		Review the presentation and disclosure of related-party information for completeness and understandability.

Chapter 13

Financial Accounting and Reporting for Managed Care Services

Overview

13.01 Managed care entities, health maintenance organizations (HMOs), physicians, hospitals, and other health care providers and managers have organized into integrated delivery systems and networks that combine inpatient, outpatient, pharmacy, and physician services into single contracting entities. These systems and networks may be formed by merger, joint venture, affiliation, or contractual risk sharing. Services may be provided under predetermined, fixed-fee capitation arrangements, such as per member per month, or other risk-based arrangements, rather than charging fees for provided services (fee for service). As health care providers and managed care entities adopt new structures and commence new operations in response to the demands of the market, many activities that were traditionally performed by insurance entities, such as assuming medical insurance risk, are being performed by health care entities. Conversely, many activities that were performed by health care entities, such as arranging for the provision of medical services, are being performed by managed care entities.

13.02 This chapter provides guidance for transactions in which an entity assumes or transfers the medical insurance risk or administers the costs of health care services for a predetermined amount. Examples of entities that enter into such transactions include HMOs, hospitals, nursing homes, specialty care managers, managed care entities, physician entities, preferred provider organizations (PPOs), public entity risk pools, and third-party administrators. This chapter covers various kinds of managed care arrangements, including group health managed care, capitation arrangements, and administrative services only (ASO) arrangements. Paragraphs 2.66–.73 of this guide provide additional guidance on statutory reporting and other regulatory considerations.

Recognition and Classification of Revenue

13.03 Revenue from managed care arrangements is classified based on the assumed risk and type of service provided, as follows:

- Revenue received in exchange for assuming full medical risk is recognized as premium revenue.
- Revenue received in exchange for performing administrative services is recognized as administrative fees. See paragraphs 13.25–.29.

Under arrangements in which administrative services are typically an integral part of providing or arranging medical care, revenue from those administrative services is included in premium revenue.

13.04 Premium revenue is recognized in income in the period that members are entitled to receive services, as specified by the provisions of the arrangement. Premiums billed or received in advance are reported as deferred revenue (unearned premiums).

13.05 Administrative fees are recognized in income in the period that the related services are performed. Administrative fees billed or received in advance are reported as deferred revenue.

13.06 Under arrangements that include performing administrative services, such as third-party administrator, cost-plus, and minimum premium contracts, entities (*a*) act as administrators or network managers between employers or other obligated entities and providers of health care services and (*b*) handle cash inflows and outflows in connection with amounts due from obligated entities to providers of health care services. The inflows and outflows associated with the health care payments from obligated entities to providers of health care services are not revenue and expenses of the entity providing the administrative services.

Capitation Arrangements

13.07 Costs of capitation arrangements are reported as health care expenses. The Financial Reporting Executive Committee (FinREC) recommends that amounts received under capitation arrangements be reported as premium revenue. The recognition of premium revenue from capitation arrangements is discussed in paragraphs 10.34–.37 of this guide.

Accounting for Health Care Costs

13.08 According to Financial Accounting Standards Board (FASB) *Accounting Standards Codification* (ASC) 954-405-25-2, health care costs should be accrued as services are rendered, including estimates of the costs of services rendered but not yet reported. Furthermore, if a provider of prepaid health care services is obligated to render services to specific members beyond the premium period due to provisions in the contract or regulatory requirements, the costs of such services to be incurred also should be currently accrued. Costs that will be incurred after a contract is terminated, such as guaranteed salaries, rent, and depreciation, net of any anticipated revenue, should be accrued when it is determined that a contract with a sponsoring employer or other group will be terminated.

13.09 FASB ASC 954-405-25-2 also requires that amounts payable to hospitals, physicians, or other health care providers under risk-retention, bonus, or similar programs be accrued during the contract period based on relevant factors, such as experience to date.

13.10 According to FASB ASC 954-405-50-2, providers of prepaid health care services should disclose the basis for accruing health care costs and the nature of significant business and contractual arrangements (for example, capitation arrangements) with hospitals, physicians, or other associated entities in the notes to the financial statements.

13.11 The following health care costs are accrued:

- Estimated costs of services rendered but not reported. Typically, health care entities utilize actuaries to assist in determining estimated costs of services rendered but not reported. Auditors often also use actuaries to assist in auditing the recorded liability. See paragraphs 8.107–.110 of this guide for additional discussion on the use of actuaries and actuarial methods. Paragraph 2.32 of this guide discusses the risks associated with costs of services rendered but not reported.

- Estimated costs of future health care services to be rendered that the entity is presently obligated to provide, with or without receiving future premiums, according to the terms of the arrangement, regulatory requirements, or other requirements.

13.12 The effects of reinsurance and stop-loss insurance recoveries are considered in calculating those estimated costs. See paragraphs 13.18–.19 for additional information.

Accounting for Loss Contracts

13.13 FASB ASC 954-450-25-4 states that a prepaid health care provider enters into contracts to provide members with specified health care services for specified periods in return for fixed periodic premiums. The premium revenue is expected to cover health care costs and other costs over the terms of the contracts. Only in unusual circumstances would a provider be able to increase premiums on contracts in force to cover expected losses. A provider may be able to control or reduce future health care delivery costs to avoid anticipated losses, but the ability to avoid losses under existing contracts may be difficult to measure or demonstrate. Associated entities, such as hospitals, medical groups, and individual practice associations, may enter into similar contracts with prepaid health care providers in which they agree to deliver identified health care services to the providers' members for specified periods in return for fixed fees.

13.14 In accordance with FASB ASC 954-450-30-4, losses under prepaid health care services contracts should be recognized when it is probable that expected future health care costs and maintenance costs under a group of existing contracts will exceed anticipated future premiums and stop-loss insurance recoveries on those contracts. Contracts should be grouped in a manner consistent with the provider's method of establishing premium rates (for example, by community rating practices, geographical area, or statutory requirements) to determine whether a loss has been incurred. FASB ASC 954-450-30-3 states that the estimated future health care costs and maintenance costs to be considered in determining whether a loss has been incurred should include fixed and variable, direct, and allocable indirect costs.

13.15 For example, for purposes of determining whether a loss (premium deficiency) will occur over the remaining terms of existing contracts for which premiums will be received, managed care arrangements, including noncancellable, executed contracts that are not yet in force, would be grouped on a basis consistent with the entity's manner of acquiring, servicing, and measuring the profitability of those arrangements. Groupings would be done on a consistent basis from year to year. A loss would be recognized if the sum of expected future fixed and variable, direct, and allocable indirect costs, including health care costs, claim adjustment expenses, maintenance costs, and other costs that are related to a group of contracts, exceeds the sum of related anticipated future premiums, other direct contract revenue, unearned premiums, reinsurance recoveries on those contracts, and investment income considered. See paragraph 13.17 for additional discussion.

13.16 The calculation of loss contracts would be made at the end of each reporting period. Changes in loss contract accruals represent changes in estimate that are reported in the current period's operations.

Consideration of Anticipated Investment Income

13.17 For purposes of determining whether a premium deficiency will occur and measuring that deficiency, FinREC recommends that entities consider investment income that is expected to be earned on premiums received in advance of health care costs incurred during the contract period for the group of contracts. Entities would disclose their accounting policy concerning whether they consider investment income in determining whether a premium deficiency exists on managed care arrangements.

Accounting for Stop-Loss Insurance

13.18 By using stop-loss insurance, prepaid health care providers or associated entities contract to recover health care costs in excess of stated amounts during the contract periods.

13.19 FASB ASC 954-720-45-1 requires that stop-loss insurance premiums be included in reported health care costs. Stop-loss insurance recoveries should be reported as reductions of related health care costs. FASB ASC 954-310-25-2 states that amounts recoverable from stop-loss insurers, reduced by appropriate valuation allowances, should be included in receivables. In addition, FASB ASC 954-720-50-4 requires that the nature, amounts, and effects of significant stop-loss insurance contracts be disclosed.

General and Administrative Expenses

13.20 General and administrative expenses are reported as gross amounts, rather than net of other items, such as fees for administering payments under Medicare and Medicaid arrangements.

Acquisition Costs

13.21 As described in FASB ASC 954-720-05-2, many prepaid providers of managed care services incur costs that vary with, and are primarily related to, the marketing of subscriber contracts and member enrollment. These costs, sometimes referred to as acquisition costs, consist mainly of commissions paid to agents or brokers and incentive compensation based on new enrollments. Commissions and incentive compensation may be paid when the contracts are written, at later dates, or over the terms of the contracts as premiums are received. Some providers incur additional costs related directly to the acquisition of specific contracts, such as the costs of specialized brochures, marketing, and advertising. Providers also incur costs that are related to the acquisition of new members but do not relate to specific contracts and are not considered acquisition costs. These costs include salaries of the marketing director and staff, general marketing brochures, and general advertising and promotion expenses.

13.22 FASB ASC 954-720-25-6 explains that although theoretical support exists for deferring certain contract or member acquisition costs, acquisition costs of providers of prepaid health care services, other than costs of advertising, should be expensed as incurred. Advertising costs should be accounted for in accordance with the guidance in FASB ASC 720-35.

Financial Statement Display Considerations

Balance Sheet

13.23 Pursuant to FASB ASC 954-210-45-1, entities whose primary business is engaging in managed care arrangements should classify assets and liabilities as current and noncurrent, as discussed in FASB ASC 210-10-45.

13.24 Receivables and payables related to ASO contracts usually are reported at gross values. An ASO arrangement involves three parties (the employer, the hospital or other provider of health care to employees, and the ASO organization); therefore, these arrangements do not meet the conditions of FASB ASC 210-20-45-1 for right of offset. Those conditions are not met in situations involving more than two parties.

Income and Cash Flow Statement

13.25 When entities act as administrators or network managers between employers or other obligated entities and providers of health care services, cash inflows and outflows associated with amounts due from obligated entities to providers of health care services are not accounted for as revenues and expenses in the income statement. Cash flow related to both ASO revenue and cash inflows and outflows through the company would be reflected in the operating cash flows in the cash flow statement.

13.26 FASB ASC 605-45 provides guidance about whether an entity should report revenue gross or net of certain amounts paid to others. The reporting depends on whether the entity functions as principal or agent. FASB ASC 605-45-45 states that it is a matter of judgment whether an entity should report revenue based on either of the following: (*a*) the gross amount billed to a customer because it has earned revenue as a principal from the sale of the goods or services or (*b*) the retained net amount (that is, the amount billed to the customer less the amount paid to a supplier) because it has earned a commission or fee as an agent. The factors or indicators set forth in FASB ASC 605-45-45 should be considered in that evaluation. Those factors are listed in paragraphs 13.28–.29 but are not intended as a substitute for reading the cited paragraphs.

13.27 Although FASB ASC 605-45-15-4(b)(3) lists insurance and reinsurance premiums as transactions to which the guidance does not apply, that exclusion pertains to transactions for which guidance is provided in other subtopics of FASB ASC, rather than the managed care arrangements addressed in this guide. Gross versus net revenue reporting is a matter of judgment that depends on each entity's relevant facts and circumstances after evaluating those facts and circumstances using the indicators.

Indicators of Gross Revenue Reporting

13.28 FASB ASC 605-45-45 describes the following eight indicators that may support reporting gross revenue:

- The entity is the primary obligor in the arrangement, as discussed in FASB ASC 605-45-45-4.

- The entity has general inventory risk before a customer order is placed or upon customer return, as discussed in paragraphs 5–7 of FASB ASC 605-45-45.
- The entity has latitude in establishing price, as discussed in FASB ASC 605-45-45-8.
- The entity changes the product or performs part of the service, as discussed in FASB ASC 605-45-45-9.
- The entity has discretion in supplier selection, as discussed in FASB ASC 605-45-45-10.
- The entity is involved in the determination of product or service specifications, as discussed in FASB ASC 605-45-45-11.
- The entity has physical loss inventory risk after a customer order or during shipping, as discussed in FASB ASC 605-45-45-12.
- The entity has credit risk, as discussed in paragraphs 13–14 of FASB ASC 605-45-45.

Indicators of Net Revenue Reporting

13.29 FASB ASC 605-45-45 describes the following three indicators that may support reporting net revenue:

- The entity's supplier is the primary obligor in the arrangement, as discussed in FASB ASC 605-45-45-16.
- The amount that the entity earns is fixed, as discussed in FASB ASC 605-45-45-17.
- The supplier has credit risk, as discussed in FASB ASC 605-45-45-18.

Disclosures

13.30 Consistent with the requirements of FASB ASC 275, *Risks and Uncertainties*, managed care entities may consider disclosing the following in the notes to the financial statements:

a. Nature of operations, such as the following:

   i. Types of rendered managed care services (for example, health maintenance, third-party administrator, and risk sharing)

   ii. Types of entity structures from which the services are rendered (for example, HMO, PPO, point of service, and indemnity)

   iii. Types of customers

b. Risk assumption and risk management profile.

c. The amount of ceded premiums and recognized reinsurance recoveries, if not reported in the income statement as separate line items or parenthetically.

d. Entities that incur health care costs pertaining only to premium revenue disclose total health care costs either in the income statement as separate line items or parenthetically or in the notes to the financial statements.

e. Entities that incur health care costs pertaining to both other revenue and premiums disclose health care costs related to premiums, if practicable.

Nature of, and amounts paid under, capitation arrangements included in health care costs.

Chapter 14

Financial Accounting and Reporting by Continuing Care Retirement Communities

Overview

14.01 Continuing care retirement communities (CCRCs) provide residents with a diversity of residential, social, and health care services, in accordance with a resident service agreement (resident agreement or contract) or other agreement specifying the obligations of the CCRC to the resident. This chapter provides guidance on applying generally accepted accounting principles (GAAP) to transactions found in CCRCs for refundable and nonrefundable advance fees, obligations to provide future services and the use of facilities to current residents, and the costs of acquiring initial care contracts.

14.02 The United States has over 1,800 CCRCs. Many CCRCs are operated by not-for-profit organizations, and many are affiliated with religious organizations. Recently, there has been an increase in the number of investor-owned entities operating CCRCs.

14.03 Financial Accounting Standards Board (FASB) *Accounting Standards Codification* (ASC) 954-605-05-7 explains that CCRC facilities may be independent, or they may be affiliated with other health care facilities. They usually provide less intensive care than hospitals.

14.04 CCRCs may provide a variety of health care services, including nursing care, home health care, physician services, and other services either directly or by agreement with other health care providers. These health care services are provided in addition to the residential services and amenities, including social, recreational, dining, and laundry services. In addition to providing services to CCRC residents, certain services, predominantly nursing services, may be provided to nonresidents. CCRCs have increased the diversity of residential, social, and health care services rendered in response to consumer demands.

14.05 Many states regulate CCRCs; however, state oversight of CCRCs and the CCRC's disclosures to residents may take various forms.

Types of Contracts

14.06 CCRCs use a variety of contracts, which are constantly undergoing change based on financial and consumer-driven considerations. These continuing-care contracts contain a number of different approaches to providing delivery of services and the fees associated with those services. The fees charged to residents generally consist of three basic components: advance fees, periodic fees, and use fees (or a combination of these fees).

14.07 The contract provisions generally stipulate the amount of the advance fee; whether periodic fees and use fees, or both, are required; whether those fees can be adjusted; and the underlying circumstances and computations for such adjustments. In addition, contracts generally detail the future services that will be provided to residents; explain how residents will be charged for services; and describe the CCRC's refund policies, if applicable, and formula for calculating the amount of the refunds, if any. Furthermore, the contract would describe the obligation of the CCRC and resident if a contract is terminated, and a residential unit is or is not reoccupied. Contracts that convey the right to use facilities may contain a lease if the arrangement conveys to the resident the right to control the use of the underlying facilities, as discussed in FASB ASC 840-10-15.[1]

Advance Fees

14.08 *Advance fees* (one-time fee typically at the time of occupancy) are those paid by the resident as a condition of admission to the CCRC for future services and use of the facilities, as specified in the resident agreement. The advance fee generally entitles the resident to the use of the residential facilities; access to amenities and social services; and the provision of, or access to, certain health care services. In addition to advance fees for admission to the CCRC, residents may also pay advance fees relating to upgraded furnishings and amenities, renovation or additions to the residential facility, or other upgrades. These additional advance fees may be nonrefundable or refundable to the resident or resident's estate, depending on the terms of the contract with the resident. The extent to which amenities, social services, and health care services are included is based on the respective resident agreement. In certain instances, the advance fee may be payment for an all-inclusive continuing-care contract that includes residential facilities, meals, and amenities. It may also provide nursing care for little or no increase in periodic fees, except to cover normal operating costs and inflation.

Periodic Fees

14.09 *Periodic fees*, sometimes referred to as service or maintenance fees, are those paid periodically (generally monthly) for services typically provided by CCRCs that are not covered by the advance fees. These periodic fees may be fixed at the time of admission, fixed with periodic modification based on increases in operating costs, or dependent on circumstances defined in the resident agreement or other agreement between the CCRC and resident.

Use Fees

14.10 *Use fees* are those that may be charged to the resident based on personal preferences or usage by the resident. These fees are paid periodically (generally monthly) for services not covered by the advance or periodic fees. Items typically provided for a separate use fee could include provision of a special parking arrangement, beauty and salon services, health care services above those included in the advance or periodic fees, excess meal or other amenity services beyond those provided through the payment of advance or periodic fees, and other items or services specified in the resident agreement or other agreement with the resident.

Types of Living Accommodations

14.11 CCRCs offer different types of living accommodations to residents, such as single or shared apartment units or individual homes. They also provide

---

[1] On August 17, 2010, the Financial Accounting Standards Board issued proposed Accounting Standards Update *Leases (Topic 840)*, which would make significant changes to the accounting requirements for both lessees and lessors. Readers should be alert to the issuance of a final standard.

a variety of amenities, including social, recreational, dining, housekeeping, and laundry services.

14.12 CCRCs may provide nursing-care services at the same location or, by agreement, with another facility. Residents are transferred to or from a nursing center as medical care is required. As the health of a resident declines, he or she may be permanently transferred to an assisted living facility; a nursing center; or a specialized long-term care facility or unit, such as a memory-care facility.

Fees and Payment Methods

14.13 As explained in FASB ASC 954-605-05-10, a CCRC may require several different payment methods for services and the use of facilities. The following are the three most prevalent methods:

- *a.* *Advance fee only*. Under this method, a resident pays an advance fee in return for future services and the use of facilities. Such services generally include CCRC housing-related services (for example, meals, laundry, housekeeping, and social services) and health care. These services usually are provided to the resident for the remainder of his or her life or until the contract is terminated. Additional periodic fees are not paid, regardless of how long a resident lives or if the resident requires more services than anticipated. Generally, the resident receives no ownership interest in the facility.
- *b.* *Advance fee with periodic fees*. Under this method, a resident pays an advance fee and periodic fees for services and the use of facilities. Such periodic fees may be fixed, or they may be subject to adjustment for increases in operating costs or inflation or other economic reasons.
- *c.* *Periodic fees only*. Under this method, a resident pays a fee at periodic intervals for services and the use of the facilities provided by the CCRC. Such fees may be either fixed or adjustable.

14.14 According to FASB ASC 954-605-05-11, an advance fee may be met by transferring a resident's personal assets, which may include rights to future income or paying a lump sum of cash to the CCRC. Some contracts allow the advance fee to be paid by installment payments. Advance fees received for future services may be refunded at the occurrence of some future event, such as death, withdrawal from the CCRC, termination of the contract, or reoccupancy of a residential unit. The amount and timing of the refund generally is based on contractual provisions or statutory requirements.

14.15 As explained in FASB ASC 954-605-05-9, many continuing-care contracts are similar to annuity contracts. Under those contracts, the CCRC assumes the risks associated with both of the following: (*a*) estimating the amount of the advance fee and other fees to be paid by a resident and (*b*) determining whether such fees will be sufficient to cover the cost of providing a resident's required services and the use of facilities. For some contracts, residents may share the future costs without limit. The CCRC has an obligation to provide future services for the length of the contract or life of the resident. In certain circumstances, this obligation continues regardless of whether advance or periodic fees are sufficient to meet the costs of providing services to a resident.

Accounting for Refundable Advance Fees

14.16 As explained in FASB ASC 954-605-05-12, payment of an advance fee generally is required before a resident acquires a right to reside in an apartment or a residential unit for life. A portion of advance fees may be refundable by rescission within a legally or contractually set time period or if a certain future event occurs, such as the death or withdrawal of a resident or termination of the contract. Some refunds are paid only if a residential unit is reoccupied.

14.17 FASB ASC 954-605-05-13 states that CCRC refund policies vary either by region or according to statutory requirements, but generally, the amount of the refund is based on provisions specified in a contract. For example, some contracts require a refund of the advance fee less a reasonable processing fee. Refunded amounts may be based on a fixed amount or percentage, an amount that declines to a fixed amount over time (see paragraph 14.19), an amount that declines to zero (see paragraph 14.19), or an amount based on the resale amount. Refunds may be contingent on vacating the unit, resale of the unit, or passage of a fixed period of time if the unit is not resold.

14.18 For some contracts, the refundable amount is determinable because the contract is fully refundable, the refund amount is fixed, or the refund amount is a percentage. Contracts that provide for fully-refundable advance fees are accounted for and reported as liabilities. If contracts provide for amounts to be refunded based on a fixed amount or percentage, the portion of the advance fee attributable to the fixed amount or percentage is accounted for and reported as a liability, with the balance accounted for as deferred revenue within the "Liability" section of the balance sheet and amortized as discussed in paragraph 14.20. In situations in which the refundable amount declines over time to a fixed amount or zero, the guidance in paragraph 14.19 is applied.

14.19 For other contracts, the refundable amount must be estimated. FASB ASC 954-430-25-1 states that the estimated amount of advance fees that is expected to be refunded to current residents under the terms of the contracts should be accounted for and reported as a liability. The remaining amount of refundable advance fees should be accounted for as deferred revenue within the "Liability" section of the balance sheet. According to FASB ASC 954-430-30-1, the estimated amount of advance fees that are expected to be refunded to current residents under the terms of contracts should be based on the individual facility's own experience or, if records are not available, the experience of comparable facilities. FASB ASC 954-430-35-3 states that adjustments to the estimated liability should be accounted for as deferred revenue and amortized together with nonrefundable advance fees, as discussed in FASB ASC 954-430-35-1 (see paragraph 14.20).

14.20 In accordance with FASB ASC 954-430-35-1, deferred revenue from advance fees from a resident should be amortized to income over future periods based on the estimated life of the resident or the contract term, if shorter. The period of amortization should be adjusted annually based on the actuarially determined, estimated remaining life expectancy of each individual or the joint and last survivor life expectancy of each pair of residents occupying the same unit. The straight-line method is used to amortize deferred revenue, except in certain circumstances when costs are expected to increase at a significantly higher rate than future revenues in the later years of residence. In those situations, deferred revenue may be amortized to income using a method that reflects the disproportionate ratio between the costs of the expected services and expected revenues. The amortized amount should not exceed the amount available to the CCRC under state regulations, contract provisions, or management policy. According to FASB ASC 954-430-40-1, unamortized deferred revenue from nonrefundable advance fees should be recorded as revenue upon a resident's death or termination of the contract.

Accounting for Fees Refundable to Residents Only From Reoccupancy Proceeds of a Contract Holder's Unit

14.21 As explained in FASB ASC 954-605-05-14, some contracts between a CCRC and resident stipulate that all or a portion of the advance fee may be refundable if the contract holder's unit is reoccupied by another person. The source of money for the payment is from the proceeds of the advance fees collected by the CCRC from the next resident of the reoccupied unit. The terms governing how the proceeds from the next resident are to be paid to the previous resident vary from contract to contract. In effect, the CCRC acts as if it were an agent for present and future residents.

14.22 According to FASB ASC 954-430-25-1, the portion of the fees that will be paid to current residents or their designees, only to the extent of the proceeds of reoccupancy of a contract holder's unit, should be accounted for as deferred revenue, provided that legal and management policy and practice support the withholding of refunds under this condition. Similar amounts received from new residents in excess of the amount to be paid to previous residents or their designees also should be deferred. According to FASB ASC 954-430-35-4, the resulting deferred revenue should be amortized to income over future periods based on the remaining useful life of the facility. The basis and method of amortization should be consistent with the method for calculating depreciation and should be disclosed in the notes to the financial statements, in accordance with FASB ASC 954-430-50-4.

Accounting for Nonrefundable Advance Fees

14.23 FASB ASC 954-430-25-1 states that under provisions of continuing-care contracts entered into by a CCRC and residents, nonrefundable advance fees represent payment for future services and are accounted for as deferred revenue. According to FASB ASC 954-430-35-2, if a CCRC has sufficient historical experience and relevant statistical data about life expectancies, it should consider that information when determining the remaining life of residents. A CCRC with insufficient historical experience or reliable actuarial data may use relevant data of similar communities within that area, relevant national industry statistics, or other appropriate data. Nonrefundable advance fees are amortized in the manner discussed in FASB ASC 954-430-35-1 (see paragraph 14.21).

14.24 The application of the conclusions in paragraphs 14.22–.23 is presented in exhibit 14-1.

Classification of Refundable Advance Fees

14.25 Diversity in practice exists regarding classification of the refundable portion of the advance fee between CCRCs that are Securities and Exchange Commission (SEC) registrants and those that are not.

14.26 CCRCs that are SEC registrants are required to consider paragraphs 9–10 of FASB ASC 470-10-45 in determining the classification of the refundable portion of advance fees. Frequently, resident agreements will provide that refundable advance fees are subject to repayment if the residents elect to terminate the agreement and put the refund obligation to the CCRC. CCRC residents do not frequently exercise the option to terminate the resident agreement early; however, the resident does have the contractual right to do so. Upon the resident's election to terminate, the CCRC is then obligated to repay the refundable portion of the advance fee deposit to the resident within a short period of time, generally less than one year. In many cases, this put or on-demand provision will require that the refundable advance fees be shown as a current liability.

14.27 In practice, CCRCs that are not SEC registrants classify refundable advance fees based upon the expected timing of refunds to be made. The classification as current or noncurrent depends upon the CCRC's own history of refunds and the terms of its resident agreements.

14.28 Other contract provisions or regulations also may affect the CCRC's ability to control the timing of refund payments. For example, provisions that make refunds to a former resident dependent upon resale to, and reoccupancy by, a new resident might allow the CCRC to classify some or all of the refundable advance fees as a noncurrent liability. In addition, if contract provisions or regulations state that a portion of a nonrefundable advance fee (for example, the deferred revenue component) is repayable to the resident only if the CCRC contract is terminated in its early years, and after that period, the advance fee is nonrefundable, the specific terms of each agreement or regulation may indicate that some or all of the advance fees would be reported as a liability (see paragraph 14.19) and that some portion of that liability might be classified as current.

14.29 The Financial Reporting Executive Committee (FinREC) recommends CCRCs provide disclosure of the classification of these refundable advance fees; the key terms of the underlying agreements; and, if classified as noncurrent, the amount of the advance fees that are subject to repayment based on the residents' ability to terminate the agreement and put the refund obligation to the CCRC.

Accounting for the Obligation to Provide Future Services and the Use of Facilities to Current Residents

14.30 FASB ASC 954-440 discusses the commitments of CCRCs to provide services. This paragraph and paragraphs 14.32–.33 summarize that guidance. A CCRC expects to provide services and the use of facilities to individuals over their remaining lives under continuing-care contract agreements. The nature and extent of such services depend on such variables as the individual's age, health, sex, and economic status upon entering the CCRC. Thus, the CCRC assumes a risk in estimating the cost of future services and use of facilities.

Although many CCRCs are contractually allowed to increase periodic fees, some contracts may restrict increases in periodic fees and require continuing services without additional compensation. If the advance and periodic fees that are charged are insufficient to meet the costs of providing future services and the use of facilities, the CCRC should record a liability based on actuarial assumptions, such as mortality and morbidity rates, on estimates of future costs and revenues and on the specific CCRC's historical experience and statistical data. The liability is equal to the amount that is expected to be incurred to provide services and the use of facilities to individuals over their remaining lives under continuing-care contracts, including resident-care, dietary, health care, facility, interest, depreciation, and amortization costs, in excess of the related anticipated revenues.

14.31 In accordance with paragraphs 1 and 3 of FASB ASC 954-440-35, the obligation of a CCRC to provide future services and the use of facilities to current residents should be calculated annually in order to determine whether a liability should be reported in the financial statements. The liability related to continuing-care contracts should be the present value of future net cash flows, minus the balance of unamortized deferred revenue, plus depreciation of facilities to be charged related to the contracts, plus unamortized costs of acquiring the related initial continuing-care contracts, if applicable. The calculation should be made by grouping contracts by type, such as all contracts with a limit on annual increases in fees, contracts with unlimited fee increases, and so on.

14.32 In measuring the liability, FASB ASC 954-440-35-3 states that the cash inflows should include revenue contractually committed to support the residents and inflows resulting from monthly fees, including anticipated increases in accordance with contract terms. This measurement should include third-party payments, contractually- or statutorily-committed investment income from services related to CCRC activities, contributions pledged by donors to support CCRC activities, and the volume of deferred nonrefundable advance fees. Cash outflows should comprise operating expenses, including interest expense and excluding selling expense, and general and administrative expenses. Anticipated cost increases affecting these operating expenses should be considered in determining cash outflows. The expected inflation rate, as well as other factors, is considered in determining the discount rate. In calculating the liability, the specific CCRC's historical experience or statistical data relating to the residents' life spans should be used. The life spans that are used should be the same as those used to amortize deferred revenue (see paragraph 14.21). For a new CCRC, either relevant data of similar communities in the area or relevant national industry statistics may be used if they are deemed to be representative.

14.33 FASB Concepts Statement No. 7, *Using Cash Flow Information and Present Value in Accounting Measurements*, provides a useful discussion of general principles governing the use of present value and of the objective of present value in accounting measurements. FASB Concepts Statements are not sources of established accounting principles and, thus, do not amend, modify, or justify a change from GAAP currently in effect.

14.34 The application of the conclusions in paragraph 14.32 is presented in exhibit 14-2.

Accounting for the Costs of Acquiring Initial Continuing-Care Contracts

14.35 Advertising costs incurred in connection with acquiring initial continuing-care contracts should be accounted for in conformity with the guidance in FASB ASC 720-35. Start-up costs are expensed as incurred, in accordance with FASB ASC 720-15. However, according to FASB ASC 954-340-25-1 and 954-720-25-7, costs of acquiring initial continuing-care contracts that are within the scope of FASB ASC 970, *Real Estate—General*, should be expensed or capitalized in accordance with that guidance. FASB ASC 954-340-35-1 states that capitalized costs should be amortized to expenses on a straight-line basis over the average expected remaining lives of the residents under the contract or the contract term, if shorter. According to FASB ASC 954-720-25-7, the costs of acquiring continuing-care contracts after a CCRC is substantially occupied or one year following completion should be expensed when incurred.

Financial Statements

14.36 FASB ASC 954-210-45-1 indicates that rather than presenting a classified balance sheet, a CCRC may instead sequence assets according to their nearness of conversion to cash and may sequence liabilities according to the nearness of the maturity and resulting use of cash.

14.37 The following information about advance fees is required to be disclosed, per FASB ASC 954-430-50:

- The method of accounting for advance fees, the method of calculating the obligation to provide future services and the use of facilities, and the refund policy for refundable fees
- The gross amount of contractual refund obligations under existing contracts and the CCRC's refund policy
- The method(s) of amortization for refundable advance fees and deferred revenue for advance fees

14.38 Because the liability amount in the balance sheet is based upon the CCRC's expected refunds, the amount disclosed in the preceding paragraph will exceed the amount of the liability for entities that have sliding scale contracts.

14.39 FASB ASC 954-440-50 requires that a CCRC disclose the following in the notes to the financial statements for each year presented:

a. A description of the CCRC and the nature of the related continuing-care contracts entered into by the CCRC

b. The carrying amount of the liability to provide future services and the use of facilities related to continuing-care contracts that is presented at present value in the financial statements, if not separately disclosed in the balance sheet

c. The interest rate used to discount that liability to provide future services

d. The statutory escrow or similar requirements

e. The refund policy of the CCRC and the general amount of refund obligation under the existing contracts

14.40 In addition to the required disclosures, FinREC recommends that CCRCs disclose all of the following:

- Amounts classified as current and noncurrent for deferred revenues and liabilities under provisions of resident contracts
- Any applicable state regulatory requirements regarding refunds under existing contracts
- The carrying amount of the obligation to provide future services and the use of facilities to current residents, which is presented at present value in the financial statements, if not separately disclosed in the balance sheet
- The interest rate used to discount that liability
- The disclosures recommended in paragraph 14.29 for the classification of refundable advance fees

14.41 FASB ASC 954-430-50-2 requires that advance fees refunded be disclosed in the statement of cash flows as a financing transaction.

14.42 Paragraphs 3.41–.42 discuss locating example financial statements.

Auditing

14.43 When auditing a CCRC, the independent auditor may need to consider the examples of specific auditing objectives, selected control activities, and auditing procedures that are presented in exhibit 14-3.

14.44 A CCRC ordinarily documents the terms of its arrangements with its residents using standardized sales or residency contracts. As discussed in paragraphs 14.13–.24, the terms of those contracts may significantly affect the accounting treatment for the transactions. Reading the standardized contract(s) and analyzing the terms allows auditors to determine whether the revenue associated with the transactions is recognized in accordance with GAAP.

14.45 In determining which standardized agreements to read and analyze, audit procedures may include the following:

- Requesting copies of all standardized contract(s) currently in use
- Evaluating the standardized contracts for terms that may affect revenue recognition
- Reviewing a sample of transactions for compliance with the standardized agreement

14.46 In determining which transactions to review, the auditor should select a sufficient number and type of contracts to reduce audit risk to an acceptable level. In determining which transactions to select, the auditor might consider the following:

- *The materiality of the transaction.* An auditor may be able to reduce audit risk to an acceptable level by analyzing all material contracts entered into during the audit period, together with a selection of other contracts that, individually, were not considered material.
- *The date the contract was entered into.* To reduce the risk of revenues being recorded in the wrong period, the auditor might

consider focusing audit attention on transactions near the end of the reporting period.

- *Whether the transaction utilizes a new form of standardized contract.* To reduce the risk of misstatement of revenues due to transactions on new forms of standardized contracts, the auditor might focus attention on whether revenues and obligations were recognized in the correct amount and period.
- *Contracts relating to transactions with a relatively higher inherent risk.* For example, auditors might consider focusing audit attention on transactions that include notes receivable or that restrict or limit future revenues. If the resident has negotiated a note receivable, a risk exists that payments will not be collected in accordance with terms. Contract terms that require continuing services or provide for other services without additional compensation or with limitations of fee increases may require recognition of a liability, as discussed in paragraphs 14.31–.35.

14.47 When reviewing a transaction, the auditor might consider the following:

- Whether the contract was fully executed by both parties during the fiscal period
- The fees provided for under the contract
- The payment provisions
- The obligations of both parties under the contract
- Any other terms that affect the revenue recognition

14.48 In order to address the completeness assertion, the auditor also should determine whether any revenue recognized is subject to forfeiture, refund, or other concessions. To make this determination, the auditor may consider such factors as the terms specified in the contract(s) and management's intent to provide refunds or the historical pattern of providing refunds or other concessions that are not required under the provisions of the contract.

Exhibit 14-1

The following example is reproduced from paragraphs 1–3 of Financial Accounting Standards Board (FASB) *Accounting Standards Codification* (ASC) 954-430-55.

Continuing Care Retirement Community

Accounting for Refundable and Nonrefundable Advance Fees

This Example illustrates the guidance in Sections 954-430-25, 954-430-35, and 954-430-40. This Example has the following assumptions for a continuing care retirement community and a resident of that community:

a. The unit is occupied for 20 years.

b. The facility has an estimated 30-year life.

c. The resident is admitted on the first day of the year indicated and dies on the last day of year indicated.

d. The estimated remaining life expectancy is taken from an appropriate actuarial table.

e. The cost of providing future services is expected to be incurred equally over the remaining life.

Advance fees are accounted for as follows.

					Advance Fees		
Year Admitted	*Dies*	*Resident*	*Entry Age*	*Total*	*Nonrefundable 25%*	*Refundable 75%*	*Refunded to the Previous Occupant*[(a)]
1	4	A	68	$100,000	$25,000	$75,000	—
5	8	B	82	120,000	30,000	90,000	$75,000
9	13	C	79	150,000	37,500	112,500	90,000
14	—	D	80	130,000	32,500	97,500	97,500

(a) Per contract, the amount is limited to 75% of proceeds of reoccupancy up to amount originally paid by previous occupant.

Amortization of Advance Fees Refundable to Residents
$75,000 years = $2,500 per year for Years 1 through 4
15,000 years = $577 additional or $3,077 per year for Years 5 through 8
22,500 years = $1,023 additional or $4,100 per year for Years 9 through next change in occupancy

The following tables illustrate the amortization of nonrefundable advance fees.

Resident A	*Unamortized Deferred Revenue*	*Estimated Remaining Life (in Years)*	*Income*
Year 1	$25,000	12.1 =	$2,066
Year 2	22,934	11.5 =	1,994
Year 3	20,940	11.1 =	1,886
Year 4	19,054	10.6 =	1,798
Unamortized deferred revenue recognized upon the death of the resident			17,256
		Total	$25,000

Resident B	*Unamortized Deferred Revenue*	*Estimated Remaining Life (in Years)*	*Income*
Year 5	$30,000	6.1 =	$4,918
Year 6	25,082	5.8 =	4,324
Year 7	20,758	5.5 =	3,774
Year 8	16,984	5.3 =	3,205
Unamortized deferred revenue recognized upon the death of the resident			13,779
		Total	$30,000

Resident C	*Unamortized Deferred Revenue*	*Estimated Remaining Life (in Years)*	*Income*
Year 9	$37,500	7.0 =	$5,357
Year 10	32,143	6.7 =	4,797
Year 11	27,346	6.4 =	4,273
Year 12	23,073	6.1 =	3,783
Year 13	19,290	5.8 =	3,324
Unamortized deferred revenue recognized upon the death of the resident			15,966
		Total	$37,500

Resident D	*Unamortized Deferred Revenue*	*Estimated Remaining Life (in Years)*	*Income*
Year 14	$32,500	6.7 =	$4,851
Year 15	27,649	6.4 =	4,321
Year 16	23,328	6.1 =	3,824
Year 17	19,504	5.8 =	3,363
Year 18	16,141	5.5 =	2,935
Year 19	13,206	5.3 =	2,492
Year 20	10,714	5.1 =	2,100

Amortization continues until the death of the resident.

Exhibit 14-2

The following example is reproduced from paragraphs 1–4 of Financial Accounting Standards Board (FASB) *Accounting Standards Codification* (ASC) 954-440-55.

Continuing Care Retirement Community

Accounting for the Obligation to Provide [Future] Services and the Use of Facilities to Current Residents

This Example illustrates the guidance in Sections 954-440-25 and 954-440-35. This example has the following assumptions:

a. All residents pay a $50,000 fee, which is refundable less 2 percent per month for the first 36 months. After that period, none of the fee is refundable. The continuing care retirement community opened on 1/1/X4. (See exhibit 14-1 for an illustration of how to compute refundable and deferred revenue.)

b. An additional periodic fee of $1,000 is payable monthly with a 5 percent increase annually.

c. The unamortized (deferred) costs of acquiring related initial contracts on 12/31/X6 are assumed to be $17,000.

d. The unamortized deferred revenue on 12/31/X6 is assumed to be $27,027.

The following tables illustrate the present value of net cash flow on 12/31/X6.

Resident	*Estimated Remaining Life (in Months) on 12/31/X6*	*Estimated Cash Inflows*			
		[20]X7	*[20]X8*	*[20]X9*	*[20]X0*
A	36	$12,000	$12,600	$13,230	—
B	22	12,000	10,500	—	—
C	27	12,000	12,600	3,308	—
D	38	12,000	12,600	13,230	$2,315
Estimated cash inflows		$48,000	$48,300	$29,768	$2,315

Resident	*Estimated Remaining Life (in Months) on 12/31/X6*	*Estimated Cash Outflows*			
		[20]X7	*[20]X8*	*[20]X9*	*[20]X0*
A	36	$10,000	$12,000	$15,000	—
B	22	15,000	11,000	—	—
C	27	14,000	17,000	5,000	—
D	38	8,000	12,000	14,000	$4,000
Estimated cash outflows		$47,000	$52,000	$34,000	$4,000

Recapitulation	*[20]X7*	*[20]X8*	*[20]X9*	*[20]X0*
Cash inflows	$ 48,000	$ 48,300	$29,768	$ 2,315
Cash outflows	(47,000)	(52,000)	(34,000)	(4,000)
	$1,000	$(3,700)	$(4,232)	$(1,685)
Present value of net cash flows discounted at 10 percent				$(7,137)

The following tables illustrate the depreciation of facilities to be charged to current residents.

Original cost of facility		$17,000,000
Cost of facility allocable to revenue-producing service areas		$(2,000,000)
Cost of facility to be allocated to residents (including common areas)		$15,000,000
Useful life	40 years	
Annual depreciation using straight-line method		$375,000
Number of residents expected to occupy the facility	200	
Annual depreciation per resident		$1,875
Monthly depreciation per resident		$156

Resident	*Estimated Remaining Life (in Months) on 12/31/X6*	*[20]X7*	*[20]X8*	*[20]X9*	*[20]X0*
A	36	$1,875	$1,875	$1,875	—
B	22	1,875	1,560	—	—
C	27	1,875	1,875	468	—
D	38	1,875	1,875	1,875	$ 312
Yearly estimated depreciation of facilities to be charged to current residents		$7,500	$7,185	$4,218	$ 312
Total estimated depreciation of the use of facilities to be charged to the current residents					$19,215

The following table illustrates the liability for providing future services and the use of facilities to current residents.

Present value of future net cash outflows	$7,137
Minus:	
Unamortized deferred revenue on 12/31/X6	(27,027)
Plus:	
Depreciation to be charged to current residents	19,215
Unamortized costs of acquiring initial contracts—see paragraph 954-440-55-1(c)	17,000[a]
Liability for providing future services and the use of facilities to current residents on 12/31/X6	$16,325

[a] These numbers are for illustrative purposes only and no inference has been made as to the recoverability of the $17,000.

Exhibit 14-3

The following table illustrates the use of assertions in developing audit objectives and designing substantive tests. The examples are not intended to be all-inclusive nor is it expected that all the procedures would necessarily be applied in an audit. The auditor should design and perform substantive procedures for all relevant assertions related to each material class of transactions, account balance, and disclosure to obtain sufficient appropriate audit evidence. The use of assertions in assessing risks and designing appropriate audit procedures to obtain audit evidence is described in paragraphs .14–.26 of AU section 326, *Audit Evidence* (AICPA, *Professional Standards*). Various audit procedures and the purposes for which they may be performed are described in paragraphs .27–.41 of AU section 326.

Auditing Considerations

Financial Statement Assertions	*Specific Auditing Objectives*	*Selected Control Activities*	*Auditing Procedures*
Transactions, Account Balances, and Presentation and Disclosures			
Existence, completeness, and presentation and maturity	Liabilities relating to refundable fee arrangements are accounted for and properly reported.	Written documentation is prepared for refundable fee arrangements.	Review the refundable fee arrangements regarding stipulations for repayments, and determine that such arrangements are properly classified and disclosed in the financial statements.
	Liabilities are accounted for and properly reported.	All liabilities are classified, described, and properly disclosed in the financial statements.	Compare the account balances with the prior periods' balance and amortization schedules.
		Management monitors compliance with restrictive covenants.	Confirm any significant new obligations.
Deferred Revenue			
Transactions, Account Balances, and Presentation and Disclosures			
Completeness, rights and obligations, and presentation and disclosure	Deferred revenue and the obligation to provide future services to, and the use of	Procedures ensure that amounts received as advance fees are recognized in the proper period and that the	Test the procedures related to the recognition of advance fees, and determine that the obligation to provide

Financial Statement Assertions	*Specific Auditing Objectives*	*Selected Control Activities*	*Auditing Procedures*
	facilities by, current residents of continuing care retirement communities are recognized and properly reported.	future services and the use of facilities is reported.	obligation to provide future services and the use of facilities is properly reported.
	Deferred revenues are appropriately classified on the balance sheet.	Appropriate consideration is given to those factors influencing classification of deferred revenues relating to refunds based on reoccupancy proceeds.	Review and document any applicable state requirements relating to the timing and other factors relating to making refunds to residents.
Long-Term Obligations			
Transactions, Account Balances, and Presentation and Disclosures			
Existence, completeness, and presentation and maturity	Liabilities relating to refundable fee arrangements are accounted for and properly reported.	Written documentation is prepared for refundable fee arrangements.	Review the refundable fee arrangements regarding stipulations for repayments, and determine that such arrangements are properly classified and disclosed in the financial statements.
Obligations to Provide Future Services			
Existence, completeness, and presentation and maturity	Liabilities relating to any obligations to provide future services appropriately consider contractual rate constraints.	Written documentation is maintained and used in future cash flow considerations based on existing resident agreements.	Review the resident agreements for appropriate consideration in the determination of future cash flows.
Revenues From Periodic Service Fees			
Transactions, Account Balances, and Presentation and Disclosures			
Existence and completeness	Propriety of revenue from periodic service fees	Written documentation and monitoring of service fees established and charged to residents.	Review resident agreements and charges, including changes in charges to residents, for consistency.

Chapter 15

Unique Considerations of State and Local[1] Government Health Care Entities

Introduction

15.01 This chapter discusses the accounting, financial reporting, and auditing requirements of this guide as they apply to governmental health care entities. The topics covered in this chapter are organized in a manner similar to the organization of topics by chapter in this guide. This chapter is intended to be the primary source of guidance for governmental health care entities; content in the other chapters of this guide is referenced, if applicable. This chapter addresses transactions that are unique to, or prevalent in, the health care industry. However, the Audit and Accounting Guide *State and Local Governments* contains information about governmental accounting and financial reporting standards and other matters that are unique to, or prevalent in, governmental entities that are not comprehensively addressed in this guide.

15.02 The Governmental Accounting Standards Board (GASB) is the primary accounting and financial reporting standard setter for governmental entities. This chapter references provisions of certain GASB statements, as well as the Audit and Accounting Guide *State and Local Governments*. However, not all guidance included in the GASB statements and that guide is incorporated, repeated, or summarized in this chapter. Accordingly, the GASB statements, that guide, and all other relevant authoritative guidance should be read in conjunction with this chapter.

Applicability of this Chapter

15.03 The definition of a *governmental health care entity* (see paragraph 1.08(c) of this guide) must be applied to determine whether a health care entity is subject to the governmental generally accepted accounting principles (GAAP) hierarchy or private-sector GAAP (for example, Financial Accounting Standards Board [FASB] *Accounting Standards Codification*™ [ASC]). Entities are governmental or nongovernmental for accounting and financial reporting purposes based solely on the application of that definition.

15.04 The provisions of this chapter apply to governmental health care entities that report as special-purpose governments engaged only in business-type activities (that is, whose financial statements are prepared using enterprise fund accounting and reporting).[2] Accounting, financial reporting, and auditing matters associated with other types of governmental health care entities (that is, those that use governmental fund accounting and financial reporting) are

---

[1] Paragraph 1.08 of this guide defines a *governmental health care entity*. This guide is not applicable to federal government health care entities.

[2] Paragraph 15 of Governmental Accounting Standards Board (GASB) Statement No. 34, *Basic Financial Statements—and Management's Discussion and Analysis—for State and Local Governments*, as amended, describes *business-type activities* as those financed in whole or part by fees charged to external parties for goods or services. Paragraphs 91–105 and 138 of GASB Statement No. 34 describe the financial statements of enterprise funds.

not within the scope of this chapter or guide.[3] A governmental health care entity that uses enterprise fund accounting and reporting may be part of a larger entity, such as a general-purpose government, medical school, or university. In those situations, the recommendations in this chapter apply to the health care entity's separately-issued financial statements.

GAAP Hierarchy for Governmental Health Care Entities

15.05 GASB Statement No. 55, *The Hierarchy of Generally Accepted Accounting Principles for State and Local Governments*, identifies the framework for the GAAP hierarchy for state and local governmental entities. For financial statements of state and local governmental entities, the hierarchy is summarized as follows (in descending order of authority):

- Category (a) consists of officially established accounting principles, which are GASB Statements and Interpretations. GASB Statements and Interpretations are periodically incorporated in the *Codification of Governmental Accounting and Financial Reporting Standards*. Category (a) standards are the subject of Rule 203, *Accounting Principles* (AICPA, *Professional Standards*, ET sec. 203 par. .01).
- Category (b) consists of GASB Technical Bulletins and, if specifically made applicable to state and local governmental entities by the AICPA and cleared[4] by GASB, AICPA Audit and Accounting Guides and AICPA Statements of Position (SOPs).
- Category (c) consists of AICPA Practice Bulletins, if specifically made applicable to state and local governmental entities and cleared[5] by GASB, as well as consensus positions of a group of accountants organized by GASB that attempts to reach consensus positions on accounting issues applicable to state and local governmental entities.[6]
- Category (d) consists of implementation guides published by the GASB staff, as well as practices that are widely recognized and prevalent in state and local government.

15.06 If the accounting treatment for a transaction or other event is not specified by a pronouncement in category (a), a governmental health care entity should consider whether the accounting treatment is specified by an accounting principle from a source in another category. In such cases, if categories (b)–(d) contain accounting principles that specify accounting treatments for

---

[3] Often, governments will use governmental funds, rather than enterprise funds, to report activities relating to long-term institutional care, which includes health care, of the elderly; children; and mentally impaired when user fees (for example, fees for services) are not a principal revenue source for the activity. Although activities that are reported in governmental funds are not within the scope of this guide, chapter 12, "Special Purpose and State Governments," of the Audit and Accounting Guide *State and Local Governments* indicates that auditors of such entities should consider referring to this guide for specific auditing considerations unique to health care entities, such as audit procedures relating to amounts due from discharged patients and third-party payors, to the extent they are relevant.

[4] Auditors should assume that such pronouncements specifically made applicable to state and local governments have been cleared by GASB, unless the pronouncement indicates otherwise.

[5] See footnote 4.

[6] As of the date of this guide, GASB had not organized such a group.

a transaction or other event, the governmental entity should follow the accounting treatment specified by the accounting principle from the source in the highest category—for example, follow category (b) treatment over category (c) treatment. If the accounting treatment for a transaction or other event is not specified by a pronouncement or established in practice, as described in categories (a)–(d), a governmental entity should consider accounting principles for similar transactions or other events within categories (a)–(d) and may consider other accounting literature. A governmental health care entity should not follow the accounting treatment specified in accounting principles for similar transactions or other events in cases in which those accounting principles either prohibit the application of the accounting treatment to the particular transaction or other event or indicate that the accounting treatment should not be applied by analogy.

15.07 Other accounting literature includes, for example, GASB Concepts Statements; the pronouncements referred to in categories (a)–(d) of the GAAP hierarchy for nongovernmental entities if not specifically made applicable to state and local governmental entities by GASB; FASB ASC and Concepts Statements; Federal Accounting Standards Advisory Board Statements, Interpretations, Technical Bulletins, and Concepts Statements; AICPA issues papers; International Public Sector Accounting Standards of the International Public Sector Accounting Standards Board; International Financial Reporting Standards of the International Accounting Standards Board; pronouncements of other professional associations or regulatory agencies; Technical Questions and Answers included in AICPA *Technical Practice Aids*; and accounting textbooks, handbooks, and articles. The appropriateness of other accounting literature depends on its relevance to particular circumstances, the specificity of the guidance, and the general recognition of the issuer or author as an authority. For example, GASB Concepts Statements would normally be more influential than other sources in this category. **Inclusion in this guide of other accounting literature does not elevate that guidance to category (b) guidance.**

15.08 This chapter makes various references to implementation guidance published in the GASB staff document *Comprehensive Implementation Guide* (hereafter referred to as GASB Q&A). That implementation guidance is category (d) guidance in the governmental GAAP hierarchy. ***References to the guidance in the GASB Q&A in this chapter do not elevate that guidance to category (b) guidance. Further, GASB's clearance of this guide does not elevate the guidance it contains from the implementation guides to category (b) guidance. Similarly, references in this chapter to discussions or examples in the nonauthoritative appendixes of GASB pronouncements do not elevate that guidance from other accounting literature.***

Applicability of FASB and AICPA Pronouncements

15.09 GASB Statement No. 62, *Codification of Accounting and Financial Reporting Guidance Contained in Pre-November 30, 1989 FASB and AICPA Pronouncements*,[*] directly incorporates into GASB's authoritative literature certain pronouncements issued by FASB and its predecessors on or before

[*] The requirements of GASB Statement No. 62, *Codification of Accounting and Financial Reporting Guidance Contained in Pre-November 30, 1989 FASB and AICPA Pronouncements*, are effective for financial statements for periods beginning after December 15, 2011. Earlier application is

(continued)

November 30, 1989. Governmental entities, including health care entities, were required by paragraph 17 of GASB Statement No. 34, *Basic Financial Statements—and Management's Discussion and Analysis—for State and Local Governments*, to apply those pronouncements to the extent that they do not conflict with or contradict GASB pronouncements. FASB Statements and Interpretations, Accounting Principles Board (APB) Opinions, Accounting Research Bulletins of the AICPA Committee on Accounting Procedure, and AICPA accounting interpretations issued on or before November 30, 1989, have been included in GASB Statement No. 62 to the extent that they do not conflict with or contradict GASB pronouncements. In that manner, GASB Statement No. 62 eliminates the need for financial statement preparers and auditors to determine which FASB and AICPA pronouncement provisions apply to state and local governments. When the guidance from the pre-November 30, 1989, pronouncements was included as part of GASB Statement No. 62, it was modified as necessary to appropriately recognize the governmental environment and needs of governmental financial statement users.

15.10 GASB Statement No. 62 also eliminates the election provided in paragraph 7, as amended, of GASB Statement No. 20, *Accounting and Financial Reporting for Proprietary Funds and Other Governmental Entities That Use Proprietary Fund Accounting*.[†] That election permitted governmental entities engaged in business-type activities to elect to apply all FASB statements and interpretations issued after November 30, 1989, that are applicable to private-sector business enterprises and do not conflict with or contradict GASB pronouncements. However, those governmental entities can continue to apply as other accounting literature post-November 30, 1989, FASB pronouncements that do not conflict with or contradict GASB pronouncements, as discussed in paragraph 15.07.

15.11 As governmental health care entities and their auditors consider the applicability of private-sector standards discussed in the other chapters of this guide, they must be mindful that governmental health care entities were prohibited by GASB Statement No. 29[‡] from applying FASB Statement No. 116, *Accounting for Contributions Received and Contributions Made*; No. 117, *Financial Statements of Not-for-Profit Organizations*; No. 124, *Accounting for Certain Investments Held by Not-for-Profit Organizations*; No. 136, *Transfers of Assets to a Not-for-Profit Organization or Charitable Trust That Raises or Holds Contributions for Others*; and No. 164, *Not-for-Profit Entities: Mergers and Acquisitions—Including an amendment of FASB Statement No. 142*, as level (a) GAAP. (Those FASB Statements are included in FASB ASC 958, *Not-for-Profit Entities*.) For governmental health care entities that have implemented GASB Statement No. 62, those FASB statements cannot be applied as

---

(footnote continued)

encouraged. The provisions of GASB Statement No. 62 generally are required to be applied retroactively for all periods that are presented. Appendix A, "Cross-Reference Table for Predecessor Guidance," of this chapter cross-references the GASB Statement No. 62 paragraphs used in the chapter to their predecessor guidance in Financial Accounting Standards Board (FASB) Statements and Interpretations.

[†] See footnote * and appendix B, "Interim Guidance for Entities That Elect Paragraph 7 of Governmental Accounting Standards Board Statement No. 20," of this chapter. Appendix B provides interim guidance for entities that have not yet implemented GASB Statement No. 62.

[‡] GASB Statement No. 29, *The Use of Not-for-Profit Accounting and Financial Reporting Principles by Governmental Entities*, is superseded by GASB Statement No. 62, which is effective for periods beginning after December 15, 2011.

other accounting literature if they are in conflict with GASB pronouncements, including the guidance in GASB Statement No. 31, *Accounting and Financial Reporting for Certain Investments and for External Investment Pools*; No. 33, *Accounting and Financial Reporting for Nonexchange Transactions*; No. 34; and No. 39, *Determining Whether Certain Organizations Are Component Units—an amendment of GASB Statement No. 14*. FASB Statement No. 164 cannot be applied even as other accounting literature because it is not part of current practice, as further discussed in paragraphs 15.139–.140.

Basic Financial Statements

15.12 Governmental health care entities covered by this chapter use a financial reporting model established by GASB Statement No. 34, as amended, for special-purpose governments engaged only in business-type activities. GASB Statement No. 34 requires the following statements and information to be provided in separately-issued, general-purpose external financial statements of special-purpose governments engaged only in business-type activities:[7,8]

a. Statement of net assets or balance sheet[||]

b. Statement of revenues, expenses, and changes in net assets or equity

c. Statement of cash flows

d. Notes to financial statements

e. Management's discussion and analysis (MD&A) as required supplementary information (RSI)

f. If applicable, other RSI established by GAAP

The statements must be prepared using the accrual basis of accounting and economic resources measurement focus.[9]

---

[7] Paragraph 138 of GASB Statement No. 34.

[8] Although this discussion of the guidance in GASB Statement No. 34 is written from the perspective of legally-separate governmental health care entities, the accounting, financial reporting, and auditing considerations are usually equally applicable when the health care activity is conducted as a function or program of a general-purpose government and reported within an enterprise fund of that government. In developing an opinion on financial statements for one or more individual funds, the auditor considers generally accepted accounting principles (GAAP) to the extent those principles apply to the fund financial statements. Although GASB standards do not address the accounting and financial reporting for separately-issued, GAAP-based financial statements for one or more individual funds, and accordingly, GASB did not clear the provisions set forth in this footnote, paragraph 14.65 of the Audit and Accounting Guide *State and Local Governments* states that in auditing financial statements of such activities, auditors should consider long-established practice dictating that those presentations should apply all relevant GAAP. Thus, in developing an opinion on the separately-issued, GAAP-based financial statements for one or more individual funds, the auditor considers whether the financial statements include all relevant GAAP financial statements, note disclosures, management's discussion and analysis topics, and other required supplementary information (RSI).

[||] In June 2011, GASB issued GASB Statement No. 63, *Financial Reporting of Deferred Outflows of Resources, Deferred Inflows of Resources, and Net Position*. Among other changes, the statement amends the net asset reporting requirement of GASB Statement No. 34 by incorporating deferred outflows of resources and deferred inflows of resources into the definitions of the required components of the residual measure and by renaming that measure as net position, rather than net assets. Readers should be alert to the issuance of a final standard. The provisions of this statement are effective for financial statements for periods beginning after December 15, 2011. Earlier application is encouraged.

[9] See paragraph 92 of GASB Statement No. 34.

Statement of Net Assets or Balance Sheet[10]

15.13 Governmental health care entities may report their financial position using either a balance sheet format (assets equal liabilities plus net assets or equity) or a net assets format (assets less liabilities equal net assets or equity). The difference between assets and liabilities is referred to as either net assets or equity (use of either term is acceptable).

15.14 Assets and liabilities must be presented in a classified format that distinguishes between current and long-term assets and liabilities, as discussed in paragraphs 29–44 of GASB Statement No. 62.[11] Paragraph 99 of GASB Statement No. 34 states that restricted assets should be reported when *restrictions*, as defined in paragraph 34 of GASB Statement No. 34, on asset use change the nature or normal understanding of the availability of the asset. Restrictions[12] or constraints may require assets that normally would be reported as current, such as cash and cash equivalents, short-term investments, and certain receivables, to be classified as noncurrent for financial reporting purposes. Paragraph 31(a) of GASB Statement No. 62 states that current assets should exclude cash and claims to cash that are restricted regarding withdrawal or use for other than current operations, designated for disbursement in the acquisition or construction of noncurrent assets, or segregated for the liquidation of long-term debt. When such constraints exists (for example, when cash or short-term investments are held as collateral on debt obligations, set aside within debt sinking funds and debt service reserve funds, donor restricted for the construction or purchase of property and equipment, or donor restricted for permanent or term endowment), the assets should be reported as noncurrent. Item 7.71.1 of the GASB Q&A discusses the reporting of restricted assets in a classified balance sheet. GASB Statement No. 34 does not otherwise require restricted assets to be displayed separately from unrestricted assets on the face of the balance sheet.

15.15 Either the term *net assets* or *equity* may be used to refer to the difference between assets and liabilities. Net assets or equity is required to be reported in three broad components: invested in capital assets, net of related debt; restricted; and unrestricted. When a portion of restricted net assets is required to be retained in perpetuity, restricted net assets should be displayed in two additional components: expendable and nonexpendable.[13] The individual components of net assets are discussed in more detail in paragraphs 15.107–.108.

15.16 Some governmental health care entities may be organized and operated on a fund basis (for example, they use several separate enterprise funds for the purpose of carrying on specific activities or attaining certain objectives

---

[10] See paragraphs 97–99 GASB Statement No. 34.

[11] The requirements of GASB Statement No. 62 related to the classification of items as current or noncurrent are similar to those applied by nongovernmental entities. To the extent that other chapters of this guide discuss the balance sheet classification of certain specific assets or liabilities (for example, investments and long-term debt) as current or noncurrent, that information may be helpful to governmental health care entities, provided that it does not conflict with or contradict GASB pronouncements.

[12] The term *restricted* is defined by paragraphs 34, as amended, and 99 of GASB Statement No. 34. As discussed in paragraph 15.102, a *restriction* is a constraint placed on the use of assets or net assets that is either externally imposed, such as by creditors through debt covenants, or imposed by law through constitutional provisions or enabling legislation.

[13] See paragraph 35 of GASB Statement No. 34.

in accordance with regulatory restrictions or limitations). Interfund receivable and payable balances are eliminated in the "Total Primary Government" column. Paragraph 14 of GASB Statement No. 38, *Certain Financial Statement Note Disclosures*, requires disclosure of certain information pertaining to interfund balances.

Statement of Revenues, Expenses, and Changes in Net Assets

15.17 A governmental health care entity's statement of revenues, expenses, and changes in net assets[14] presents the same types of activities and transactions that are reported in a not-for-profit health care entity's statement of operations and statement of changes in net assets. The required format for this statement is illustrated in paragraph 101 of GASB Statement No. 34, as follows:

Operating revenues (detailed)

Total operating revenues

Operating expenses (detailed)

Total operating expenses

Operating income (loss)

Nonoperating revenues and expenses (detailed)

Income before other revenues, expenses, gains, losses, and transfers

Capital contributions (grant, developer, and other); additions to permanent and term endowments; special and extraordinary items (detailed); and transfers

Increase (decrease) in net assets

Net assets—beginning of period

Net assets—end of period

Although this prescribed sequence, including the provision of required subtotals, must be adhered to, paragraph 434 of the nonauthoritative basis for conclusions of GASB Statement No. 34 indicates that it does not preclude governments from presenting additional subtotals before the comprehensive performance measure, such as the increase (decrease) in net assets.

15.18 The format of the governmental statement of revenues, expenses, and changes in net assets does not disaggregate transactions by components of net assets (for example, it does not segregate transactions that increase restricted net assets from those that increase unrestricted net assets). The statement does not require disaggregated reporting of transactions based on the types of restrictions that may exist, such as unrestricted, restricted expendable, or restricted nonexpendable. For example, restricted contributions are not reported separately from unrestricted contributions, except for those that are restricted for capital acquisition or endowments, as discussed subsequently. Because of this all-inclusive focus, reclassifications of net assets representing the expiration of restrictions are not reported. Therefore, reclassifications and subtotals, such as net assets released from restrictions, changes in temporarily-restricted net assets, and changes in permanently-restricted net assets, that

---

[14] As discussed in paragraph 15.13, it is equally appropriate to refer to equity, rather than net assets, in the title of this statement.

are customarily seen in not-for-profit health care entities' statements of activities are not displayed in a governmental health care entity's statement of revenues, expenses, and changes in net assets.

15.19 Governmental health care entities must distinguish between operating revenues and expenses and nonoperating revenues and expenses and provide an intermediate subtotal for operating income or loss. This is a difference from the not-for-profit model in which entities are permitted, but not required, to classify transactions as operating or nonoperating. GASB requires entities to establish a policy for defining operating revenues and expenses that is appropriate to the nature of the activities being reported; however, the determination of which revenues and expenses should be classified as operating should consider how the underlying transactions would be classified in the statement of cash flows.[15] Using this approach, transactions that are considered investing, capital and related financing, and noncapital financing activities in the statement of cash flows (for example, investment revenues and interest expense, as well as most nonexchange transactions, including taxes and noncapital grants and contributions) would be classified as nonoperating, rather than operating. Once established, this policy should be consistently applied and must be disclosed in the notes to the financial statements.

15.20 Contributions of capital assets or financial resources required to be used to acquire capital assets, contributions of term and permanent endowments, special and extraordinary items, and transfers are reported separately after nonoperating revenues and expenses. The determination of whether a transaction is an extraordinary item is made based on the guidance in paragraphs 45–50 of GASB Statement No. 62. Special items should be reported separately after capital contributions and contributions to permanent and term endowments but before extraordinary items, if any. Paragraph 56 of GASB Statement No. 34 defines a *special item* as a significant transaction or other event that is within the control of management and that meets one, but not both, of the criteria for classification as an extraordinary item (that is, it is either unusual in nature or infrequent in occurrence). Similar transactions that are beyond the control of management are not special items but should be disclosed in accordance with paragraph 56 of GASB Statement No. 34.

15.21 As discussed in paragraph 15.16, some governmental health care entities may be organized and operated on a fund basis. Those entities should display interfund transfers, if any, after special and extraordinary items. Interfund transfers include capital contributions received from other funds of the same financial reporting entity, as discussed in item 7.74.4 of the GASB Q&A. Paragraph 15 of GASB Statement No. 38 requires disclosure of certain information pertaining to interfund transfers.

15.22 If a governmental health care entity has a change in accounting principle during a reporting period, as described in paragraphs 63–89 of GASB Statement No. 62, the effect of the change should be reported as a restatement of net assets at the beginning of the period, not a separately identified cumulative effect in the current-period statement of revenues, expenses, and changes in net assets.[16] If a governmental health care entity must correct a prior-period's error, item 7.22.16 of the GASB Q&A states that the entity should report the correction by displaying either (*a*) the amount of the change as an

---

[15] See paragraph 102 of GASB Statement No. 34.

[16] See footnote 13 to paragraph 17 of GASB Statement No. 34.

adjustment to beginning net assets on the face of the statement of revenues, expenses, and changes in net assets, as previously reported, or (*b*) beginning net assets restated on the face of the statement of revenues, expenses, and changes in net assets, with the details of the restatement provided in the notes to the financial statements.

15.23 APB Opinion No. 30, *Reporting the Results of Operations—Reporting the Effects of Disposal of a Segment of a Business, and Extraordinary, Unusual and Infrequently Occurring Events and Transactions*, addresses the accounting for a segment of a business (discontinued operations). As explained in paragraph 535 of the nonauthoritative basis for conclusions of GASB Statement No. 62, the provisions of APB Opinion No. 30 pertaining to accounting for the disposal of a segment of a business were not incorporated into GASB Statement No. 62 because GASB intends to address these matters in its project on government combinations. However, the separate reporting of discontinued operations described in APB Opinion No. 30 conflicts with the reporting format required for the statement of revenues, expenses, and changes in net assets under GASB Statement No. 34.

15.24 FASB ASC 220, *Comprehensive Income*, conflicts with the all-inclusive format required by GASB Statement No. 34, as discussed in item 7.72.1 of the GASB Q&A, and should not be applied by governmental health care entities. Gains and losses that private-sector standards classify as elements of other comprehensive income should be reported no differently than other gains and losses. As previously described, they are classified by governmental health care entities as operating, nonoperating, special, or extraordinary.

Statement of Cash Flows

15.25 GASB Statement No. 9, *Reporting Cash Flows of Proprietary and Nonexpendable Trust Funds and Governmental Entities That Use Proprietary Fund Accounting*, as amended, establishes standards for cash flow reporting for governmental entities. The requirements of GASB Statement No. 9 differ from those of FASB ASC 230, *Statement of Cash Flows*, as described in item 2.2.1 of the GASB Q&A. Those differences are as follows:

- GASB Statement No. 9, as amended, requires the use of the direct method of presenting operating cash flows,[17] with a reconciliation provided of operating cash flows to operating income (loss).
- GASB Statement No. 9 requires two categories of financing activities—noncapital financing and capital and related financing—for a total of four categories in the statement of cash flows. The capital and related financing category is used for acquiring and disposing of capital assets, borrowing money for acquiring capital assets, and repaying the borrowed amounts. All other financing is classified as noncapital.[18]
- Some transactions are classified differently by GASB and FASB. For example, under GASB Statement No. 9, unrestricted contributions are classified as noncapital financing, interest expense is

---

[17] See paragraph 105 of GASB Statement No. 34.

[18] Paragraph 29 of GASB Statement No. 9, *Reporting Cash Flows of Proprietary and Nonexpendable Trust Funds and Governmental Entities That Use Proprietary Fund Accounting*, provides criteria for distinguishing between capital and noncapital financing activities.

classified as either capital and related financing or noncapital financing, and investment income is classified as investing. Under FASB ASC 220, unrestricted contributions, interest expense, and investment income are all operating cash flows. Similarly, capital asset purchases are classified under GASB Statement No. 9 as capital and related financing activities. Under FASB ASC 220, they are investing activities.

- Paragraph 8 of GASB Statement No. 9 provides that a statement of cash flows should explain the change in all cash and cash equivalents, regardless of any restrictions on their use. This would include any cash and cash equivalents classified as noncurrent, as discussed in paragraph 15.14. The total amount of cash and cash equivalents in the statement of cash flows should be easily traceable to similarly-titled line items in the statement of net assets. If it is not, a reconciliation should be provided on the face of the statement or in the notes.

Chapter 2 of the GASB Q&A discusses implementation issues regarding GASB Statement No. 9.

Segment Reporting

15.26 If applicable, governmental health care entities must comply with the segment reporting requirements of GASB Statement No. 34.[19] GASB's definition of *segment* differs from that in FASB ASC 280, *Segment Reporting*. GASB's definition focuses solely on information about activities financed by revenue-backed debt. GASB Statement No. 34 defines a *segment* as an identifiable activity or grouping of activities reported as or within an enterprise fund or another stand-alone entity that (*a*) has one or more outstanding bonds or other debt instruments, such as certificates of participation, with a revenue stream pledged in support of that debt and (*b*) is required by an external party, such as through a bond indenture, to separately account for that activity's assets, liabilities, revenues, and expenses. Segment disclosures are not required if the activity is not financed with revenue-backed debt; the requirement to separately report is not imposed by an external party; or separate reporting is required for only a portion of the activity's transactions, such as for only the revenues and expenses.

15.27 Paragraph 122 of GASB Statement No. 34, as amended, details the disclosures required for segments. Additional information on segment reporting can be found in chapter 8, "Expenses or Expenditures and Liabilities," of the Audit and Accounting Guide *State and Local Governments* and items 7.86.1–7.86.6 of the GASB Q&A.

RSI, Including MD&A

15.28 Some GASB standards require the presentation of certain specified information to accompany the basic financial statements. This RSI differs from other types of information that accompanies the basic financial statements because RSI is considered an essential part of financial reporting, and GASB has established authoritative guidelines for measuring and presenting that

---

[19] See paragraphs 122–123 of GASB Statement No. 34 and paragraph 17 of GASB Statement No. 37, *Basic Financial Statements—and Management's Discussion and Analysis—for State and Local Governments: Omnibus—an amendment of GASB Statements No. 21 and No. 34.*

information. At present, RSI applicable to governmental health care entities consists of MD&A and certain information related to employer-sponsored benefit plans. RSI other than MD&A should be presented immediately following the notes to the financial statements.[20] MD&A should precede the basic financial statements.

15.29 GASB standards require MD&A to introduce the basic financial statements by presenting certain financial information, as well as management's analytical insights on that information. That analysis should provide users with the information they need to help them assess whether the government's financial position has improved or deteriorated as a result of a given year's operations. Paragraphs 8–11 of GASB Statement No. 34, as amended, establish eight required elements of MD&A for general-purpose governments. Because certain of those elements would not apply to special-purpose governments engaged only in business-type activities, governmental health care entities should limit their MD&A to only those required elements that are applicable to their activities. The information to be presented in MD&A should be confined to the topics discussed in paragraphs 8–11 of GASB Statement No. 34.

15.30 When a governmental health care entity presents comparative financial statements, MD&A is also required to be comparative, which would include comparative, condensed financial information and related analyses for both years, as discussed in item 7.5.4 of the GASB Q&A. MD&A should provide data so that each of the two years presented in the comparative financial statements can be compared with its prior year. Therefore, there should be three years of comparative data and accompanying analyses: the current year, the prior year, and the year preceding the prior year. If only comparative financial data is presented for the prior year, as distinguished from a complete set of comparative statements, notes, and RSI, MD&A requirements apply only to the current year, with comparisons to the prior year, as discussed in item 7.5.6 of the GASB Q&A.

15.31 Paragraph 22 of GASB Statement No. 27, *Accounting for Pensions by State and Local Governmental Employers*, as amended, and paragraphs 26–27 of GASB Statement No. 45, *Accounting and Financial Reporting by Employers for Postemployment Benefits Other Than Pensions*, require employers that participate in single-employer and agent multiple-employer defined benefit pension and other postemployment benefit (OPEB) plans to report certain multiyear actuarial data as RSI.

15.32 Inclusion of information relating to discretely-presented component units in MD&A or other RSI is a matter of professional judgment. If component unit information is provided, the RSI should focus on the primary government and distinguish between information pertaining to the primary government and information pertaining to the component unit(s).

Cash, Cash Equivalents, and Investments

Cash and Cash Equivalents

15.33 In accordance with paragraph 9 of GASB Statement No. 9, cash and cash equivalents include all cash and highly liquid investments that are both (*a*)

---

[20] See paragraph 6 and footnote 5 of GASB Statement No. 34.

readily convertible to known amounts of cash and (*b*) so near to their maturity that they present an insignificant risk of changes in value because of changes in interest rates. Cash equivalents generally are limited to investments with original maturities of three months or less from the date of purchase, although paragraph 11 of GASB Statement No. 9 provides that not all investments that meet GASB's definition of *cash equivalents* are required to be accounted for as such. Paragraph 8 of GASB Statement No. 9 states that the total amounts of cash and cash equivalents at the beginning and end of the period in the statement of cash flows should be easily traceable to similarly-titled items or subtotals shown in the statement of net assets as of those dates.

15.34 Cash and cash equivalents are considered to be restricted[21] when limitations on the use of those assets change the nature or normal understanding of the availability of the asset. For example, cash normally is classified as current assets, and a normal understanding of those assets presumes that no limitations exist on the government's ability to use those resources to satisfy current liabilities. However, cash held by a trustee that can only be used to pay bond principal and interest and that cannot be used to pay other current liabilities would be considered restricted assets. See paragraph 15.102 for a discussion of classification of net assets when the use of assets is restricted. Such restrictions or constraints may require cash and cash equivalents to be classified as noncurrent for financial reporting purposes, as discussed in paragraph 15.14.

15.35 Governmental health care entities are required by GASB standards to provide disclosures related to cash and deposit accounts. For example, paragraph 8 of GASB Statement No. 40, *Deposit and Investment Risk Disclosures—an amendment of GASB Statement No. 3*, requires certain disclosures related to deposit accounts that are exposed to custodial credit risk. Deposits are exposed to custodial credit risk if they are not covered by depository insurance, and the deposits are (*a*) uncollateralized, (*b*) collateralized with securities held by the pledging financial institution, or (*c*) collateralized with securities held by the pledging financial institution's trust department or agent but not in the depositor-government's name. Paragraph 11 of GASB Statement No. 9 requires disclosure of the governmental health care entity's policy for determining which investments are treated as cash equivalents. Paragraph 113 of GASB Statement No. 62 requires disclosure of any pledge of cash and cash equivalents as security for loans. Additional GASB disclosures related to deposit accounts are discussed in paragraph 15.51.

15.36 Additional guidance related to cash and cash equivalents can be found in chapter 5, "Cash, Investments, and Derivative Instruments," of the Audit and Accounting Guide *State and Local Governments* and chapters 1–2 of the GASB Q&A.

Investments

15.37 When accounting for investments, governmental health care entities follow the accounting and financial reporting requirements of the following GASB statements:

- GASB Statement No. 3, *Deposits with Financial Institutions, Investments (including Repurchase Agreements), and Reverse Repurchase Agreements*

---

[21] See footnote 12.

- GASB Statement No. 10, *Accounting and Financial Reporting for Risk Financing and Related Insurance Issues*
- GASB Statement No. 28, *Accounting and Financial Reporting for Securities Lending Transactions*
- GASB Statement No. 31
- GASB Statement No. 40
- GASB Statement No. 52, *Land and Other Real Estate Held as Investments by Endowments*
- GASB Statement No. 53, *Accounting and Financial Reporting for Derivative Instruments*
- GASB Statement No. 59, *Financial Instruments Omnibus*
- GASB Interpretation No. 3, *Financial Reporting for Reverse Repurchase Agreements—an interpretation of GASB Statement No. 3*

Additional guidance can be found in chapter 5 of the Audit and Accounting Guide *State and Local Governments* and chapter 6 of the GASB Q&A.

15.38 For private-sector entities, the starting point in analyzing the accounting for an equity investment is determining whether the investee must be consolidated.[22] In the governmental sector, investments in for-profit companies made with the intent of generating investment return do not require evaluation for consolidation (that is, for presentation as a blended or discretely-presented component unit).[23,#] Instead, once the determination is made that the purpose is investment, the starting point is to determine if the investment must be accounted for using the equity method of accounting described in paragraphs 202–210 of GASB Statement No. 62.

15.39 Investments in equity securities must be evaluated to determine if the equity method of accounting described in paragraphs 202–210 of GASB Statement No. 62 must be applied.[24] (Note that GASB and FASB have differing definitions of a *security*, as discussed in paragraph 15.40.) If so, then the investment is within the scope of those paragraphs, rather than GASB Statement No. 31.

15.40 The scope of GASB Statement No. 31 is somewhat similar to private-sector standards in that it includes equity securities with readily-determinable fair values, debt securities, and open-ended mutual funds. The differences are as follows:

- GASB defines a security differently, focusing in part on an instrument's transferability. GASB Statement No. 31 defines a *security*

---

[22] See chapter 12, "The Reporting Entity and Related Entities," of this guide.

[23] See paragraph 55 of GASB Statement No. 14, *The Financial Reporting Entity*.

[#] In November 2010, GASB issued GASB Statement No. 61, *The Financial Reporting Entity: Omnibus—an amendment of GASB Statements No. 14 and No. 34*. The objective of the statement is to improve the financial reporting of a governmental financial reporting entity by modifying the criteria for inclusion of component units and amending the criteria for blending. The statement also clarifies the reporting of equity interests in legally-separate entities. The provisions of GASB Statement No. 61 are effective for financial statements for periods beginning after June 15, 2012. For additional information, see footnote ## to "The Reporting Entity and Related Entities" section heading.

[24] See paragraph 5 of GASB Statement No. 31 and item 6.4.3 of the GASB *Comprehensive Implementation Guide* (GASB Q&A).

as "a transferable financial instrument that evidences ownership or creditorship, whether in physical or book entry form." As a result, certain types of investments that would be considered equity securities under FASB literature (for example, certain limited partnership interests) are not considered equity securities under GASB Statement No. 31.

- Private-sector standards include certain interest-earning contracts, such as guaranteed investment contracts and certificates of deposit, in their scope but only to the extent that those investments meet FASB's definition of a *security*. GASB Statement No. 31 includes all such contracts, regardless of whether they are considered a security.
- The scope of GASB Statement No. 31 includes external investment pools, which are not included in private-sector investment standards unless they are securities.

Appendix 6-1 of the GASB Q&A provides GASB's definitions of a number of different types of investments.

15.41 Investments within the scope of GASB Statement No. 31 are reported in the balance sheet at fair value, with the exception of nonparticipating, interest-earning investment contracts and money market investments with a remaining maturity of one year or less at time of purchase, which are permitted to be reported at amortized cost. *Fair value* is the amount at which an investment could be exchanged in a current transaction between willing parties, other than in a forced or liquidation sale, as discussed in paragraph 3 of GASB Statement No. 31 and item 6.11.2 of the GASB Q&A. Paragraphs 7 and 10–11 of GASB Statement No. 31 describe how fair value is measured for various types of investments.[25]

15.42 Evaluating whether an alternative investment, as described in paragraph 4.36 of this guide, falls within the scope of GASB Statement No. 31 typically focuses on whether a particular investment vehicle meets the definition of an *equity security*, as discussed in paragraph 15.40; an *external investment pool*; or some other type of investment. Paragraph 22 of GASB Statement No. 31 defines an *external investment pool* as an arrangement that commingles (pools) the monies of more than one legally-separate entity and invests in an investment portfolio on the participants' behalf; one or more of the participants is not part of the sponsor's reporting entity.[26] Some instruments that convey an ownership interest are not *equity securities*, as defined by GASB, because they do not meet the definition of a *security*. Item 1.11.1 of the GASB Q&A states that investments without a transferable financial instrument that evidences ownership or creditorship are not securities. Item 1.48.2 of the GASB Q&A states that shares in closed-end mutual funds and unit investments trusts are securities but that open-end mutual funds are not. Item 1.11.1 of the GASB Q&A states that the term *securities* does not include investments made directly with another party (for example, a limited partnership interest). In evaluating

---

[25] FASB Statement No. 157, *Fair Value Measurement*, is not applicable to investments within the scope of GASB Statement No. 31 because GASB Statement No. 31 provides guidance for measuring the fair value of those investments. However, FASB Statement No. 157 may be applicable as other accounting literature to certain other fair value measurements of governmental health care entities (see paragraph 15.07).

[26] See also item 6.34.1 of the GASB Q&A.

the nature of an alternative investment, careful consideration should be given to the specific characteristics of the investment.

15.43 Some alternative investments, such as hedge funds, are arrangements that commingle the money of multiple investors and invest them in an investment portfolio. Based on the definitions in GASB Statement No. 31, such investments, particularly those in a limited liability corporation or those as a limited partner in a limited partnership or limited liability partnership, may appear to meet the definition of both an *external investment pool* (an arrangement that commingles the money of more than one legally-separate entity and invests in an investment portfolio on the participants' behalf) and an *equity security* (any security that represents an ownership interest in an entity). Analyzing the characteristics of the investment to determine whether it meets the definition of a *security* may be helpful in determining whether and how GASB Statement No. 31 applies to the investment. Because the definition of a *security* focuses in part on transferability, an alternative investment that cannot be transferred would not be considered a security. In addition, investments that are transacted directly with another party, such as most commingled investment vehicles in limited partnership form, are not considered securities. A commingled investment vehicle that does not meet the definition of a *security* is evaluated to determine if it is an interest in an external investment pool, which is reported at fair value, or a financial instrument that is reported at amortized cost, as discussed in paragraph 15.45.

15.44 GASB Statement No. 52 requires that certain land and other real estate held as investments by endowments be reported at fair value, with changes in fair value reported as investment income. GASB Statement No. 52 applies to permanent and term endowments and permanent funds; it does not apply to quasiendowments.

15.45 Except as provided in paragraph 15.37, GASB has not issued any standards regarding the valuation or recognition of investments by health care entities. Investments for which GASB has not issued standards and that are not financial instruments, such as real estate held by a quasiendowment or certain oil and gas interests, are required by this guide to be reported at amortized cost and subsequently evaluated for impairment, as discussed in paragraphs 15.46–.47.[27] All other investments are reported using cost-based measures, provided that there has not been an impairment in that value, as discussed in items 6.4.2 and 6.12.8 of the GASB Q&A. Evaluating cost-basis investments for impairment is discussed in paragraphs 15.46–.47. Item 6.4.1 of the GASB Q&A describes a number of different types of investments that generally would not fall within the scope of GASB Statement No. 31.

Impairment of Investments

15.46 Other-than-temporary impairment is not an issue for investments reported at fair value, in accordance with GASB Statement No. 31, because GASB does not provide for the segregation of realized gains and losses from unrealized gains and losses. For investments covered by GASB Statement No. 31 that are reported using cost-based measures, such as money market investments and certain investment contracts, paragraphs 8–9 of GASB Statement

---

[27] This requirement is established by this guide and is category (b) of the governmental GAAP hierarchy (see paragraph 15.05). This requirement is consistent with paragraph 5.24, which applies to governmental funds, of the Audit and Accounting Guide *State and Local Governments* and items 6.4.2 and 6.12.8 of the GASB Q&A.

No. 31 require the cost-based measure to be reevaluated if the fair value of the investment is significantly affected by the impairment of the credit standing of the issuer or other factors.[28] Determining the amount and timing of a write-down of those investments is a matter of professional judgment.

15.47 For all other investments reported using cost-based measures, if the fair value of investments declines, an unrealized loss may have to be recorded if the decline is not due to a temporary condition.[29] In making impairment evaluations for these investments, health care entities might consider as other accounting literature (see paragraph 15.07) the guidance in FASB ASC 320-10-35 for other-than-temporary impairments of investments and FASB ASC 360-10-35 for impairments of long-lived assets.

Investment Return

15.48 Investment income arises from interest and dividend income, sales of investments at a gain or loss, and changes in the fair value of investments during the holding period. Under the GASB Statement No. 34 reporting model, all investment income of governmental health care entities, regardless of any restrictions placed upon its use, is reported as nonoperating revenue.[30] This differs significantly from the private-sector standards described in paragraphs 4.30–.34 of this guide. GASB Statement No. 31 permits the change in fair value of investments, such as the difference between the fair value of investments at the beginning of the year and end of the year, taking into consideration investment purchases, sales, and redemptions, to be presented separately or combined with other investment income as a single amount. If the change in the fair value of investments is displayed as a separate element within investment income, it should be captioned "Net Increase (Decrease) in the Fair Value of Investments." GASB Statement No. 31 prohibits displaying realized gains and losses separately from other fair value changes on the face of the statement. However, note disclosure of realized gains and losses is permitted, provided that certain information about the nature of those amounts and their relationship to the amounts reported in the financial statements also is disclosed, as illustrated in appendix C of GASB Statement No. 31.

15.49 Cash flows from purchases, sales, maturities, and income of investments should be classified as cash flows from investing activities in the statement of cash flows.

Securities Lending and Reverse Repurchase Agreements

15.50 Governmental health care entities account for securities lending transactions in accordance with GASB Statement No. 28 and reverse repurchase agreements in accordance with GASB Statement No. 3 and GASB Interpretation No. 3. That accounting differs from the private-sector standards of FASB ASC 860, *Transfers and Servicing*.

---

[28] See paragraphs 8–9 of GASB Statement No. 31.

[29] See paragraph 5.24 of the Audit and Accounting and Guide *State and Local Governments*.

[30] As discussed in items 7.73.5 and 7.74.3 of the GASB Q&A, interest earned on endowments generally should be classified as nonoperating revenue. This includes investment income restricted to increase permanent or term endowments. It is not appropriate to report such amounts as additions to permanent or term endowments.

Financial Reporting and Disclosure

15.51 Investments held by governmental health care entities should be reported as either current or noncurrent, as appropriate, under the provisions of paragraphs 29–44 of GASB Statement No. 62. Entities are required to disclose information about their investments in accordance with the GASB Statements and Interpretation included in paragraph 15.37. Among the required disclosures are the following:

- The types of deposits or investments authorized by legal or contractual provisions. See paragraph 65 of GASB Statement No. 3, as amended.
- Deposit and investment policies related to the risks that GASB Statement No. 40 requires to be disclosed. If a government has no investment policy that addresses a specific type of risk to which it is exposed, the disclosure should indicate that fact. See paragraph 6 of GASB Statement No. 40.
- Significant violations during the period of legal or contractual provisions for deposits and investments and the actions taken to address such violations. See paragraph 66 of GASB Statement No. 3 and paragraph 9 of GASB Statement No. 38.
- The policy for determining which investments, if any, are reported at amortized cost. See paragraph 15 of GASB Statement No. 31.
- The methods and significant assumptions used to estimate the fair value of investments if that fair value is based on other than quoted market prices. See paragraph 15 of GASB Statement No. 31.
- The credit quality ratings of investments in debt securities as described by nationally-recognized statistical-rating organizations (rating agencies) as of the date of the financial statements. This disclosure does not apply to investments issued or explicitly guaranteed by the U.S. government, but it does apply to investments in external investment pools, money market funds, bond mutual funds, and other pooled investments of fixed-income securities. If a credit quality disclosure is required, and the investment is unrated, the disclosure should indicate that fact. See paragraph 7 of GASB Statement No. 40, as amended.
- For investment securities and deposits, including securities underlying repurchase agreements, at the end of the period that are exposed to custodial credit risk, the investment's type, the reported amount, and how the investments are held. This disclosure does not apply to investments in external investment pools and open-end mutual funds or securities underlying reverse repurchase agreements. See paragraph 9 of GASB Statement No. 40.
- Investments in any one issuer, by amount and issuer, that represent 5 percent or more of total investments. This disclosure does not apply to investments issued or explicitly guaranteed by the U.S. government or investments in mutual funds, external investment pools, or other pooled investments. See paragraph 11 of GASB Statement No. 40, as amended.

- Information about interest rate risk using one of the five disclosure methods listed in GASB Statement No. 40. If a method requires an assumption regarding timing of cash flows, interest rate changes, or other factors that affect interest rate information, that assumption should be disclosed. This disclosure applies to investments in debt (bond) mutual funds, external debt (bond) investment pools, or other pooled debt investments that do not meet the definition of a 2a7-like pool. See paragraphs 14–15 of GASB Statement No. 40, as amended.
- The terms of debt investments or an investment derivative instrument with fair values that are highly sensitive to changes in interest rates, such as coupon multipliers, benchmark indexes, reset dates, and embedded options, to the extent investment terms are not considered in the interest rate risk disclosure requirements of paragraph 15 of GASB Statement No. 40. See paragraphs 14 and 16 of GASB Statement No. 40, as amended.
- Certain information about investments in external investment pools. See paragraph 15 of GASB Statement No. 31.
- The U.S. dollar balances of deposits or investments exposed to foreign currency risk, organized by currency denomination and, if applicable, investment type. See paragraph 17 of GASB Statement No. 40.
- For entities with donor-restricted endowments, disclosures about the use of investment income generated by those endowments. See paragraph 121 of GASB Statement No. 34.
- For reverse repurchase agreements, whether the maturities of investments made with the proceeds of reverse repurchase agreements generally are matched to the maturities of the agreements, as well as the extent of such matching. See paragraph 6 of GASB Interpretation No. 3.
- For investments arising from securities lending activities, the authority for securities lending activities and any violations, a description of the securities lending activities, whether the maturities of investments made with invested collateral generally are matched to the maturities of the securities loans, the extent of such matching, the amount of assumed credit risk, and losses arising from securities lending. See paragraphs 12–15 of GASB Statement No. 28, as amended.

Derivatives

15.52 A *derivative instrument* is a financial instrument or other contract with all three of the characteristics in the following list:

- *Settlement factors.* It has one or more reference rates and one or more notional amounts or payment provisions, or both. Those terms determine the amount of the settlement(s) and, in some cases, whether a settlement is required.
- *Leverage.* It requires no initial net investment or an initial net investment that is smaller than would be required for other types of contracts that would be expected to have a similar response to changes in market factors.

- *Net settlement*. Its terms require or permit net settlement, it can readily be settled net by a means outside the contract, or it provides for delivery of an asset that puts the recipient in a position not substantially different from net settlement.

15.53 GASB Statement No. 53 requires that all derivatives within its scope, including certain derivative instruments embedded in a financial instrument or other contract, be reported in the statement of net assets at fair value. An exception exists to fair value measurement for fully benefit-responsive, synthetic guaranteed investment contracts; they are measured at contract value. The scope of GASB Statement No. 53 excludes derivative instruments that are normal purchases and normal sales contracts; insurance contracts accounted for under GASB Statement No. 10, as amended; certain financial guarantee contracts; certain contracts that are not exchange traded; and loan commitments. The definition of *derivative* and the scope of the statement are similar to that used by private-sector entities.

15.54 GASB Statement No. 53 divides derivative instruments into two types, which determines how changes in the fair value of a derivative instrument are reported, as follows:

- *Hedging derivative instruments* are derivative instruments associated with a hedgeable item and significantly reduce an identified financial risk by substantially offsetting changes in cash flows or fair values of that hedgeable item. Changes in fair values of hedging derivative instruments should be recognized through the application of hedge accounting, with deferred inflows and deferred outflows reported in the statement of net assets.
- *Investment derivative instruments* are derivative instruments that are entered into primarily for the purpose of obtaining income or profit or a derivative instrument that does not meet, or no longer meets, the definition of a *hedging derivative instrument*. Changes in fair values of investment derivative instruments should be reported within investment revenue (nonoperating) in the statement of revenues, expenses, and changes in net assets. See paragraph 15.48 for further discussion.

15.55 Paragraphs 36–62 of GASB Statement No. 53 provide guidance on methods to be used for evaluating the effectiveness of a potential hedging derivative instrument. Users of this guide should refer to GASB Statement No. 53, chapter 5 of the Audit and Accounting Guide *State and Local Governments*, and chapter 10 of the GASB Q&A for additional guidance related to these methods.

15.56 A health care entity that holds derivative instruments should disclose the information required by paragraphs 69–79 of GASB Statement No. 53. Those disclosures include summary information about derivative instrument activity during the reporting period, information about the objectives for entering into hedging derivative instruments, their significant terms, contingent features of the derivative instruments, and information about the entity's exposure to various types of risk that is caused by holding derivative instruments at the end of the reporting period. Disclosures are also required for the companion instrument of any embedded derivatives and about synthetic guaranteed investment contracts.

Property and Equipment and Other Assets

15.57 The accounting requirements for capital assets and intangible assets of governmental health care entities are summarized subsequently. Accounting for supplies inventories and other assets of governmental health care entities is similar to that used by nongovernmental health care entities, as described in chapter 6, "Property and Equipment and Other Assets," of this guide.

Capital Assets—General

15.58 The primary differences related to capital assets involve impairment evaluation and financial statement display and disclosure. *Capital assets* are defined in paragraph 19 of GASB Statement No. 34 as "land, improvements to land, easements, buildings, building improvements, vehicles, machinery, equipment, works of art and historical treasures, infrastructure, and all other tangible or intangible assets that are used in operations and that have initial useful lives extending beyond a single reporting period." Acquired or donated capital assets are capitalized and depreciated over their estimated useful lives. Works of art and historical treasures need not be capitalized if they are added to collections that meet the requirements of paragraph 27 of GASB Statement No. 34. Chapter 7, "Capital Assets," of the Audit and Accounting Guide *State and Local Governments* contains additional information.

15.59 If the potential exists that a capital asset has been impaired, governmental health care entities should consider the guidance in GASB Statement No. 42, *Accounting and Financial Reporting for Impairment of Capital Assets and for Insurance Recoveries*. These standards differ significantly from the model applied by private-sector entities for the impairment of tangible capital assets. FASB ASC 360-10-35 should not be applied by governmental health care entities. GASB Statement No. 42 establishes accounting and financial reporting standards for the impairment of capital assets, including standards for the assessment of the impairment of capital assets and the measurement of impairment. It requires the evaluation of prominent events or changes in circumstances affecting a capital asset's use to determine whether impairment has occurred. A capital asset generally should be considered impaired if both the decline in service utility of the capital asset is large in magnitude, and the event or change in circumstances is unexpected (for example, outside the normal life cycle of the capital asset).

15.60 If the governmental health care entity will continue to use the impaired asset, it should measure the amount of impairment by one of three methods that most appropriately reflect the decline in service utility of the asset. The three methods, which are described more fully in paragraph 12 of GASB Statement No. 42, are as follows:

- The restoration cost approach, which derives the amount of the impairment from the estimated costs to restore the service utility of the capital asset
- The service units approach, which isolates the historical cost of the service utility of the capital asset that cannot be used due to the impairment event or change in circumstances
- The deflated depreciated replacement cost approach, which replicates the historical cost of the produced service

The restoration cost approach generally should be used to measure impairments resulting from physical damage. The service units approach generally should be used to measure impairments resulting from the enactment or approval of laws or regulations or other changes in environmental factors or from technological development or obsolescence. The deflated depreciated replacement cost or the service units approach generally should be used to measure impairments identified from a change in manner or duration of use. An impairment loss recognized in accordance with GASB Statement No. 42 should not be reversed in future years, even if the events or circumstances causing the impairment have changed.

15.61 Impairment losses should be reported in the statement of revenues, expenses, and changes in net assets as an operating expense, special item, or extraordinary item, in accordance with the guidance in paragraphs 41–46, 55–56, and 101–102 of GASB Statement No. 34 and paragraphs 45–50 of GASB Statement No. 62. If not otherwise apparent from the face of the financial statements, a general description, the amount, and the financial statement classification of the impairment loss should be disclosed in the notes to the financial statements. Additional guidance related to reporting impairment losses is provided in chapter Z.42 of the GASB Q&A.

Intangible Assets Other Than Goodwill

15.62 Many governmental health care entities have goodwill and other intangible assets. GASB Statement No. 51, *Accounting and Financial Reporting for Intangible Assets*, provides guidance for accounting for intangibles other than goodwill. Accounting for goodwill is discussed in paragraph 15.65.

15.63 An intangible asset should be recognized only if it is *identifiable*, meaning that the asset either (*a*) is capable of being separated or divided from the governmental health care entity and sold, transferred, licensed, rented, or exchanged, either individually or together with a related contract, asset, or liability, or (*b*) arises from contractual or other legal rights, regardless of whether those rights are transferable or separable from the entity or other rights and obligations. Intangible assets that are internally generated are capitalized only if they meet the conditions in paragraph 8 of GASB Statement No. 51. Paragraphs 9–15 of GASB Statement No. 51 provide additional guidance for internally-generated software. GASB Statement No. 51 also provides guidance on determining the useful life of intangibles that are limited by legal or contractual provisions. Intangible assets with a finite useful life are amortized over that life. If no factors exist that indicate a limitation on the useful life of an intangible asset, the asset has an indefinite useful life. Indefinite-lived intangibles should not be amortized, unless their useful life is subsequently determined to be finite due to a change in circumstances.

15.64 GASB Statement No. 51 also considers all intangible assets within its scope to be capital assets and extends existing authoritative guidance related to the accounting and financial reporting for capital assets, such as recognition, measurement, depreciation or amortization, impairment, presentation, and disclosure, to intangible assets within its scope. Among other matters, this requires intangible assets other than goodwill to be included in the roll-forward disclosure of capital assets by major classes. See paragraph 15.69 for further discussion.

Goodwill

15.65 GASB Statement No. 51 excludes from its scope goodwill created through the combination of a government and another entity. GASB currently has on its agenda a project that is considering the financial reporting requirements for government combinations and the resulting goodwill. Until that project is complete, paragraph 534 of the nonauthoritative basis for conclusions of GASB Statement No. 62 states, "In the interim, the Board believes that state and local governments should continue their current practice of accounting and reporting of government combinations until the Board can develop specific accounting and financial reporting standards for government combinations." Thus, governmental health care entities that previously applied APB Opinion No. 17, *Intangible Assets*, continue to do so. Those entities that previously applied FASB Statement No. 142, *Goodwill and Other Intangible Assets*, in accordance with an ongoing election under paragraph 7 of GASB Statement No. 20 to apply post-November 30, 1989, FASB Statements and Interpretations that do not conflict with or contradict GASB pronouncements, should continue to apply that FASB Statement until the entity implements GASB Statement No. 62 or until GASB completes its combinations project, and the new standards are effective, whichever is earlier.

Leases

15.66 Paragraphs 211–271 of GASB Statement No. 62 provide essentially the same guidance as FASB Statement No. 13, *Accounting for Leases*, as amended and interpreted as of November 30, 1989, and they provide additional guidance on specific matters unique to governmental entities. GASB Statement No. 13, *Accounting for Operating Leases with Scheduled Rent Increases*, provides additional guidance for operating leases of governmental health care enterprises.[31]

Asset Retirement and Pollution Remediation Obligations

15.67 When evaluating asset retirement and pollution remediation obligations, such as asbestos removal, governmental health care entities consider the guidance in GASB Statement No. 49, *Accounting and Financial Reporting for Pollution Remediation Obligations*. Those standards differ significantly from the private-sector standards of FASB ASC 410, *Asset Retirement and Environmental Obligations*. GASB Statement No. 49 provides guidance on reporting the costs of, and obligations for, pollution remediation (for example, the cleanup of pollution or asbestos contamination). GASB Statement No. 49 does not require governmental entities to search for pollution remediation obligations but, instead, sets forth triggers that would signal that a governmental entity should determine if it has to report a remediation liability.

15.68 The scope of GASB Statement No. 49 includes obligations that address the current or potential detrimental effects of existing pollution by

---

[31] The provisions of GASB Statement No. 13, *Accounting for Operating Leases with Scheduled Rent Increases*, and paragraphs 211–271 of GASB Statement No. 62 should not be applied to a *service concession arrangement*, which is an arrangement between a transferor (government) and an operator (governmental or nongovernmental entity) in which (*a*) the transferor conveys to an operator the right and related obligation to provide services through the use of infrastructure or another public asset (a facility) in exchange for significant consideration, and (*b*) the operator collects and is compensated by fees from third parties. Those arrangements are within the scope of GASB Statement No. 60, *Accounting and Financial Reporting for Service Concession Arrangements*. The provisions of GASB Statement No. 60 are effective for financial statements for periods beginning after December 15, 2011.

participating in pollution remediation activities, such as obligations to clean up spills of hazardous wastes or substances and obligations to remove contamination, such as asbestos. The scope of GASB Statement No. 49 excludes pollution prevention or control obligations with respect to current operations. It also excludes future pollution remediation activities that are required upon retirement of an asset, such as landfill closure and postclosure care and nuclear power plant decommissioning. However, GASB Statement No. 49 applies to activities at the retirement of an asset if the obligating events are met, and pollution-related asset retirement obligations have not been previously recognized.

Disclosures

15.69 Governmental standards require specific disclosures pertaining to capital assets, as follows:

- The policy for capitalizing assets and estimating the useful lives of those assets in the entity's summary of significant accounting policies. See paragraph 115(e) of GASB Statement No. 34.
- A general description of the method(s) used to compute depreciation with respect to major classes of depreciable assets. See paragraph 95 of GASB Statement No. 62.
- Information about major classes of capital assets presented in a roll-forward format, including beginning and ending balances, capital acquisitions, sales or other dispositions, current period depreciation expense, and accumulated depreciation. Intangible assets, if any, must be included in this disclosure as a major class(es) of capital assets. See paragraphs 116–117 and 120 of GASB Statement No. 34 and item Z.51.29 of the GASB Q&A.
- If significant, capital assets that are not being depreciated, including construction in progress,[32] should be reported on the face of the statement of net assets separately from capital assets being depreciated. These two categories of capital assets should also be disclosed separately in the roll-forward disclosure. See paragraph 20 of GASB Statement No. 34.
- Construction commitments. See paragraph 158 of National Council on Governmental Accounting (NCGA) Statement No. 1, *Governmental Accounting and Financial Reporting Principles*, as amended, and paragraph 4 of NCGA Interpretation No. 6, *Notes to the Financial Statements Disclosure*.
- Pertinent data regarding leases. See paragraphs 223, 231, 239, 255–256, and 270 of GASB Statement No. 62.
- If not otherwise apparent from the face of the financial statements, a general description, the amount, and the financial statement classification of capital asset impairment losses. See paragraph 17 of GASB Statement No. 42.
- The carrying amount of impaired capital assets that are idle at year-end, if any, regardless of whether the impairment is considered permanent or temporary. See paragraph 20 of GASB Statement No. 42.

[32] See item 7.11.1 of the GASB Q&A.

Municipal Bond Financing and Other Long-Term Debt

15.70 Like not-for-profit health care entities, governmental health care entities typically finance their acquisitions, additions, and renovations with tax-exempt debt. Thus, many of the general considerations discussed in chapter 7, "Municipal Bond Financing," of this guide will also apply to governmental health care entities. The primary differences arise with respect to measurement and disclosure; when they exist, such differences are highlighted in the discussion that follows.

15.71 In accordance with paragraph 42 of NCGA Statement No. 1, as amended, when a financing authority issues tax-exempt bonds or similar debt instruments and uses the proceeds for the benefit of a governmental health care entity, the obligation is reported as a liability in the health care entity's balance sheet if the health care entity is responsible for repayment. In some cases, this obligation may take the form of a liability arising from a capital lease. If a health care entity has no obligation to make payments of principal and interest on the debt or capital or operating lease payments on related buildings or equipment (for example, if general obligation debt is issued on behalf of the governmental enterprise), the health care entity should not reflect the liability on its balance sheet. In those circumstances, proceeds from the bond issue are reported as contributions from the sponsoring government.[33]

15.72 Among the many provisions normally included in the bond indentures of tax-exempt issues are the requirements to annually set aside funds from operations to ensure that bond principal and interest payments and other requirements are met. Cash, cash equivalents, and investments that can only be used to pay debt principal and interest would be reported as restricted assets, as discussed in paragraph 15.34. The classification of net assets relating to assets set aside based on the requirements of debt-financing instruments is discussed in items 7.24.1, 7.24.2, 7.24.7, and 7.24.25 of the GASB Q&A and paragraphs 15.99–.106. The restricted component of net assets represents restricted assets reduced by liabilities related to those assets; thus, the net assets associated with assets restricted to debt service are restricted net assets. This differs from the financial reporting requirements applicable to not-for-profit health care entities under which such resources are part of the entity's unrestricted net assets, unless restricted by a donor for debt service, and the related assets generally are reported as assets whose use is limited.

Debt Defeasance and Extinguishment

15.73 GASB Statement No. 7, *Advance Refundings Resulting in Defeasance of Debt*, and No. 23, *Accounting and Financial Reporting for Refundings of Debt Reported by Proprietary Activities*, as amended, provide accounting and financial reporting guidance for refundings that result in the defeasance of debt. In a refunding, a government issues new debt to finance the repayment of previously-issued (old) debt. The repayment of the old debt may either be immediate (a current refunding) or at some future time (an advance refunding).

15.74 An advance refunding may defease the old debt, either legally or in substance, as described in paragraphs 3–4 of GASB Statement No. 7, as

---

[33] This requirement is established by this guide and is category (b) of the governmental GAAP hierarchy. See paragraph 15.05 for additional discussion.

amended. A legal defeasance occurs when debt is legally satisfied based on certain provisions in the debt instrument, even though the debt is not actually paid. In-substance defeasance occurs if the government irrevocably places cash or other qualifying assets with an escrow agent in a trust to be used solely to satisfy scheduled interest and principal payments of the debt, and the possibility that the government will be required to make future payments on the debt is remote.[34] When debt is defeased, neither that liability nor the escrowed assets are reported in the financial statements; only the new debt is reported. That accounting is different in the private sector. Private-sector standards require the debt to be reported as a liability until it is legally defeased.

15.75 GASB Statement No. 23 requires that the difference between the reacquisition price and net carrying amount of the old debt be deferred and amortized as a component of interest expense in a systematic and rational manner over the remaining life of the old debt or the life of the new debt, whichever is shorter. This deferred amount should be reported as a deduction from, or an addition to, the new debt liability in the statement of net assets. The deferred amount may be reported net, with either parenthetical or note disclosure of the deferred amount on refunding, or it may be reported gross, with both the debt liability and related deferred amount presented in the statement of net assets. GASB Statement No. 23 provides additional standards for debt that refunds previous refunding debt.

15.76 Paragraphs 124–127 of GASB Statement No. 62 require that a gain or loss in the period of extinguishment be recognized if debt is extinguished by means other than defeasance in a current or an advanced refunding or a troubled debt restructuring.[35] The gain or loss should be identified as a separate item in the statement of revenues, expenses, and changes in net assets. That accounting and reporting is similar to the private-sector standards of FASB ASC 470-50-40.

Capitalization of Interest Cost

15.77 Interest expense and investment income associated with tax-exempt debt are capitalized pursuant to the guidance in paragraphs 19–20 of GASB Statement No. 62. Those standards are similar to private-sector standards for capitalizing the interest on tax-exempt borrowings that are externally restricted to finance the acquisition of specified qualifying assets or to service the related debt, as discussed in chapter 6 of this guide.

Disclosures

15.78 GASB standards require certain disclosures about debt, including the following:

- Information about long-term debt, such as bonds payable, including beginning and ending balances, increases, decreases, and the portions of each item that are due within one year. See paragraphs 116 and 119–120 of GASB Statement No. 34.

---

[34] See paragraph 4 of GASB Statement No. 7, *Advance Refundings Resulting in Defeasance of Debt*.

[35] A debtor applies paragraphs 128–148 of GASB Statement No. 62 if debt is extinguished in a troubled debt restructuring. That accounting and reporting is similar to the private-sector standards of FASB *Accounting Standards Codification* (ASC) 470-60.

- Debt service requirements to maturity presented separately for each of the five subsequent years and in five-year increments thereafter. Principal and interest requirements are required to be disclosed separately. Similar requirements apply to obligations under capital leases and noncancelable operating leases. See paragraphs 10–11 of GASB Statement No. 38.
- For governmental health care entities with conduit debt obligations, a general description of the conduit debt transactions, the aggregate amount of all conduit debt obligations outstanding at the financial statement date, and a clear indication that the entity has no obligation for the debt beyond the resources provided by related leases or loans. See paragraph 3 of GASB Interpretation No. 2, *Disclosure of Conduit Debt Obligations—an interpretation of NCGA Statement 1*.
- Disclosures about short-term debt activity during the year, even if no short-term debt is outstanding at year-end. For this purpose, short-term debt consists of anticipation notes, use of lines of credit, and similar loans. Disclosures should include a schedule of changes in short-term debt, as well as a discussion of the purposes for which short-term debt was issued. See paragraph 12 of GASB Statement No. 38.
- Disclosure of actions taken to remedy significant violations of finance-related legal or contractual provisions. See paragraph 9 of GASB Statement No. 38.
- In all periods following an advance refunding during which debt that was defeased in substance remains outstanding, governments should disclose the outstanding amount of that debt, if any, at the financial statement date. See paragraph 14 of GASB Statement No. 7.
- The following disclosures are required for all defeasances in the year of refunding: (*a*) a general description of the transaction, (*b*) the difference between the cash flow required to service the old debt and the cash flow required to service the new debt and complete the refunding, and (*c*) the economic gain or loss resulting from the transaction. These are similar to disclosures required of private-sector entities. Paragraph 11 of GASB Statement No. 7 provides guidance on the various measures needed for those disclosures.

Contingencies and Other Liabilities

Insurance-Related Contingencies

15.79 Governmental health care entities are generally exposed to the same risks of loss that are described in chapter 8, "Contingencies and Other Liabilities," of this guide. The most common losses arise from medical malpractice, worker's compensation, and medical benefits provided to employees. GASB has issued standards that governmental health care entities must apply in accounting for insurance-related contingencies (primarily GASB Statement No. 10, as amended). Paragraphs 52–80 of GASB Statement No. 10 apply to health care entities and include the following standards:

- General principles for recognition, measurement, and disclosure of claims liabilities (paragraphs 52–58), which are discussed in paragraph 15.80
- Incurred but not reported losses (paragraph 56 and footnote 5), which are recognized if the loss can be reasonably estimated, and it is probable that a claim will be asserted
- Discounting of claims liabilities (paragraphs 59–60), which is neither mandated nor prohibited
- Annuity contracts purchased to satisfy a claim liability (paragraph 61)
- Investments that are separately maintained for risk financing (paragraph 62), which are accounted for in the same manner as all other investments, as discussed in paragraphs 15.37–.56
- Participation in a public-entity risk pool (paragraphs 69–71), which is discussed in paragraph 15.83
- Claims-made policies (paragraph 72), which are discussed in paragraph 15.81
- Retrospectively-rated policies and contracts (paragraph 73–74), which are discussed in paragraph 15.82
- Disclosures (paragraphs 77–80)

General Principles for Recognition, Measurement, and Disclosure of Contingencies

15.80 The recognition and measurement requirements in paragraphs 53–56 and the disclosure requirements in paragraph 58 of GASB Statement No. 10 are primarily those of FASB Statement No. 5, *Accounting for Contingencies*, and FASB Interpretation No. 14, *Reasonable Estimation of the Amount of a Loss—an interpretation of FASB Statement No. 5*, which are included in FASB ASC 450-20.[36] Therefore, much of the insurance-related guidance in chapter 8 of this guide applies to governmental health care entities. However, recognition and measurement of claims liabilities differ because GASB Statement No. 10 looks to whether risk has, in fact, been transferred when determining whether to recognize a loss. An estimated loss from a claim is reported as an expense and a liability if risk has not been transferred to an unrelated third party, and claims expenses and liabilities should be reduced by amounts expected to be recovered through insurance. Private-sector standards require that the amount of a contingency be determined independently from any potential claim for recovery and that possible insurance recoveries be reported separately as assets.

Claims-Made Policies

15.81 Paragraph 72 of GASB Statement No. 10 states that a claims-made policy represents a transfer of risk within the policy limits for incidents reported to the insurer. Consequently, a health care entity should account for the estimated cost of claims and incidents that are not reported to the insurer, unless the entity has purchased tail coverage and included the cost of the premium or required contribution as an expense for the period. This

---

[36] See paragraph 107 of GASB Statement No. 10, *Accounting and Financial Reporting for Risk Financing and Related Insurance Issues*.

accounting is similar to the private-sector standards described in paragraphs 8.31–.33 of this guide, except that amounts recoverable through insurance reduce the liability, rather than being reported as a receivable.

Retrospectively-Rated Policies and Contracts

15.82 Paragraph 73 of GASB Statement No. 10 states that an entity with a retrospectively-rated policy or contract whose ultimate premium or required contribution is based on the entity's loss experience should account for the minimum premium as an expense over the period of coverage and accrue estimated losses from reported and unreported claims in excess of the minimum premium. However, losses should not be accrued in excess of the stipulated maximum premium or contribution requirement. If the entity cannot estimate those losses, the entity should disclose the contingency, in accordance with paragraph 58 of GASB Statement No. 10. Paragraph 74 of GASB Statement No. 10 provides guidance when the premium or contribution amount is based on the experience of a group of entities.

Participation in Public-Entity Risk Pools

15.83 GASB Statement No. 10 specifically addresses situations in which governmental health care entities participate in risk-financing programs sponsored by other governments (for example, a public-entity risk pool). That guidance is summarized as follows. A governmental health care entity that participates in a public-entity risk pool in which risk is transferred or pooled with other entities should present its premium or required contribution as insurance expense, as discussed in paragraphs 69–70 of GASB Statement No. 10. Entities that participate in public-entity risk pools that do not involve transfer or pooling of risk should report payments made to pools as deposits and recognize and measure claims liabilities, in accordance with paragraphs 53–58 of GASB Statement No. 10, as discussed in paragraph 15.79. Governmental health care entities that are component units of a state or local governmental reporting entity and participate in that entity's risk-financing internal-service fund should report the charges from the internal service fund as claims expenses if those charges meet the requirements of paragraphs 65–68 of GASB Statement No. 10.

Irrevocable Self-Insurance Trusts

15.84 The risk-financing techniques of some governmental health care entities include risk retention (sometimes referred to as self-insurance). A governmental health care entity that has not transferred risk to a third party should evaluate its exposure to losses arising from all claims and incidents and recognize liabilities and expenses, in accordance with paragraphs 53–56 of GASB Statement No. 10. Assets that have been contributed to irrevocable self-insurance trusts are reported as restricted assets, such as assets limited regarding use or otherwise segregated, in its statement of net assets. This restricted classification is due to the limited use of the funds as defined in the trust fund document and the fact that the funds are not available to finance other activities of the government. A governmental health care entity would also report restricted net assets to the extent that the assets exceed the associated self-insured liability and will be used to liquidate the liability. See paragraph 15.103 for a discussion on calculating restricted net assets. Private-sector not-for-profit health care entities report the net assets related to the excess of self-insurance assets over related liabilities in unrestricted net assets because the limitations on use are not imposed by a donor.

Physician Guarantees and Other Agreements

15.85 Risk of loss due to guarantees, including guarantees of the indebtedness of others, should be evaluated by applying the loss contingency standards in paragraphs 96–113 of GASB Statement No. 62. The private-sector standards for guarantees, including indirect guarantees of indebtedness of others and minimum revenue guarantees, in FASB ASC 460-10 conflict with the requirements of NCGA Statement No. 4, *Accounting and Financial Reporting Principles for Claims and Judgments and Compensated Absences*, as amended, and, therefore, should not be applied by governmental health care entities.[**]

Other Contingencies

15.86 Governmental health care entities are also exposed to loss contingencies that are outside the scope of GASB Statement No. 10. The criteria in paragraphs 96–113 of GASB Statement No. 62 are used as guidelines for recognizing certain liabilities that arise from loss contingencies, including collectability of receivables; agreements to repurchase receivables (or the related property) that have been sold; and breach of contract or similar actions, such as claims for delays or inadequate specifications on contracts or guarantees of the indebtedness of others,[††] property tax appeals, and unemployment compensation claims.[37] Those criteria are similar to the private-sector standards in FASB ASC 450-20.

Compensation and Related Benefits

15.87 GASB pronouncements require governmental health care entities to present information related to compensation and related benefits beyond or different from that presented by not-for-profit and investor-owned entities. The primary standards related to compensation and employee benefits are highlighted subsequently. Chapter 8 of the Audit and Accounting Guide *State and Local Governments* contains more expansive discussions of these standards.

Pensions[‡‡]

15.88 Governmental health care entities follow GASB Statement No. 27, as amended; GASB Statement No. 50, *Pension Disclosures—an amendment of GASB Statements No. 25 and No. 27*; and GASB Technical Bulletin (TB) 2004-2, *Recognition of Pension and Other Postemployment Benefit Expenditures/Expense and Liabilities by Cost-Sharing Employers*, for accounting and financial reporting of pension expenses and related assets and liabilities. Chapter 5 of the GASB Q&A provides implementation guidance for pensions.

[**] GASB currently has a project on its agenda, the objective of which is to establish additional guidance regarding the recognition and disclosure of financial guarantees made by state and local governments.

[††] See footnote **.

[37] See paragraphs 9 and 14 of National Council on Governmental Accounting Statement No. 4, *Accounting and Financial Reporting Principles for Claims and Judgments and Compensated Absences*, as amended.

[‡‡] In July 2011, GASB issued an exposure draft, *Financial Reporting for Pension Plans—an amendment of GASB Statement No. 25*. GASB is considering improvements to the existing standards of accounting and financial reporting for pension benefits by state and local governmental employers and the trustees, administrators, or sponsors of pension plans.

15.89 GASB Statement No. 27, as amended, has accounting and reporting requirements for multiple-employer cost-sharing defined benefit and defined contribution plans that are similar to those for private-sector health care entities. The principal measurement differences between the standards for governmental and nongovernmental entities relate to accounting for single employer and agent multiple-employer defined benefit plans. GASB Statement No. 27, as amended, requires the measurement of employer pension expense based on funding requirements whereas private-sector standards require a standardized measure of employer net periodic pension cost. Under GASB Statement No. 27, as amended, the over- or underfunded status of a plan is disclosed in the notes to the financial statements and not recognized as a liability.

Postemployment Benefits Other Than Pensions

15.90 GASB Statement No. 45 establishes standards for the measurement, recognition, and display of other postemployment benefit expenses and related liabilities (assets), which are referred to as OPEB. OPEB includes postemployment health care benefits, such as medical, dental, vision, and hearing, even if those benefits are provided through a Public Employees Retirement System (PERS) plan or pension plan. OPEB also includes, for example, life insurance, disability income, tuition assistance, legal services, and other assistance programs, unless the benefits are provided through a PERS or pension plan.

15.91 The approach used in GASB Statement No. 45 generally is consistent with the approach used for pensions in GASB Statement No. 27, as amended, with appropriate modifications to reflect differences between OPEB and pension benefits. GASB Statement No. 45 requires systematic, accrual-basis measurement and recognition of OPEB cost over a period that approximates employees' years of service. GASB Statement No. 45 also requires information related to the funded status of the plan to be presented in the notes and RSI, not reflected on the face of the balance sheet as a liability or an asset. Chapter 8 of the GASB Q&A provides additional guidance on GASB Statement No. 45.

15.92 Employers that provide postretirement prescription drug coverage benefits may receive federal subsidy payments related to Medicare Part D prescription drug coverage. Governmental health care entities must account for those payments as a voluntary nonexchange transaction received based on the requirements of GASB TB No. 2006-1, *Accounting and Financial Reporting by Employers for Payments from the Federal Government Pursuant to the Retiree Drug Subsidy Provisions of Medicare Part D*. That accounting is different in the private sector. Private-sector health care entities net the subsidy payments against the related OPEB costs and liabilities.

Sabbaticals and Other Compensated Absences

15.93 Compensated absences, such as holidays, vacations, sick leave, and sabbaticals, should be accounted for in accordance with GASB Statement No. 16, *Accounting for Compensated Absences*. The underlying concepts of GASB Statement No. 16 are similar to those of FASB ASC 710-10 for compensated absences, with some differences, such as the following:

- GASB Statement No. 16 does not require accrual prior to the occurrence of the illness, unless it is probable that the employer will compensate the employee for unused sick leave or similar benefits with cash payment at termination or retirement. FASB ASC 710-10-25 addresses sick leave in the context of the vesting of sick leave benefits; it does not require the accrual of a liability for nonvesting rights to receive sick pay.

- GASB Statement No. 16 requires accrual of payments that an employer expects to make that will be directly and incrementally associated with payments made for compensated absences at termination or retirement, such as FICA or Medicare tax. FASB ASC 710-10 has no similar requirement.
- GASB Statement No. 16 mandates the use of certain rates of pay for calculating the liability, and it limits the liability to amounts that employers will pay at termination or retirement. FASB ASC 710-10 has no similar requirement.

Termination Benefits and Restructuring Costs

15.94 GASB Statement No. 47, *Accounting for Termination Benefits*, establishes accounting standards for the measurement, recognition, and disclosures of voluntary and involuntary termination benefits. Section Z.47 of the GASB Q&A provides additional helpful guidance. To date, this is the only guidance that GASB has issued on accounting for costs associated with exit or disposal activities. Thus, the accounting for exit and disposal activities by governmental entities differs from the accounting in FASB ASC 420, *Exit or Disposal Cost Obligations*, which is used by private-sector entities.

Tax Considerations

15.95 Health care entities owned and operated by a state or local government typically are exempt from federal income tax, pursuant to IRC Section 115, and also are exempt from the federal income tax filing requirements. Such entities are exempt not only from regular federal income tax but also from the tax on unrelated business income. If a health care entity is owned and operated by a separately-constituted authority or other legal entity, the entity's management should consider whether such authority or other legal entity is properly organized to preserve qualification of the tax exemption, pursuant to IRC Section 115.

15.96 In some cases, state or local governmental entities will secure tax-exempt status as an IRC Section 501(c)(3) organization.[38] If such an exemption is secured, the entity may become subject to federal unrelated business income tax and filing requirements on the same basis as other tax-exempt entities, as discussed in chapter 8 of this guide.

Disclosures

15.97 Paragraph 3 of GASB Statement 10 and NCGA Statement No. 4, as amended, require various disclosures related to claims and judgments. Paragraphs 116 and 119–120 of GASB Statement No. 34 require disclosure of certain information related to liabilities associated with claims and judgments. These include beginning and ending liability balances, increases, decreases, and the portion that is expected to be due within one year.

---

[38] This is sometimes done to facilitate fundraising because Internal Revenue Code Section 501(c)(3) status assures potential donors that their contributions will be tax deductible.

15.98 GASB standards require certain disclosures related to other liabilities, including the following:

- Detailed disclosures about accounts payable balances when significant components of those balances have been obscured by aggregation. See paragraph 13 of GASB Statement No. 38.
- Information about long-term operating liabilities, such as compensated absences and claims and judgments, including beginning and ending balances, increases, decreases, and the portions of each item that are due within one year. See paragraphs 116 and 119–120 of GASB Statement No. 34.
- Disclosures about pension benefits provided to employees of governmental health care entities. See paragraphs 20–22 of GASB Statement No. 27, as amended, and paragraphs 7–9 of GASB Statement No. 50.
- Disclosures about other postemployment benefits. See paragraphs 24–27 and 34 of GASB Statement No. 45.
- Disclosures about termination benefits. See paragraphs 18–21 of GASB Statement No. 47.
- Disclosure of actions taken to remedy significant violations of finance-related legal or contractual provisions. See paragraph 9 of GASB Statement No. 38.

Net Assets (Equity)

15.99 GASB Statement No. 34 establishes requirements for reporting net assets that differ in several respects from the requirements for not-for-profit health care entities. Under GASB Statement No. 34, net assets or equity are reported in three components: restricted (distinguishing between major categories of restrictions); invested in capital assets, net of related debt; and unrestricted. When a portion of restricted net assets is required to be retained in perpetuity, restricted net assets should be displayed in two additional components: expendable and nonexpendable.[39] Either the term *net assets* or *equity* may be used in referring to the difference between assets and liabilities.

15.100 The unrestricted component is the residual category of net assets. It includes all assets and liabilities that are not reported as restricted or invested in capital assets, net of related debt. Unrestricted net assets are available to finance day-to-day operations free of constraints imposed by debt covenants, donor restrictions, irrevocable trusts, and so on. Net assets that are board- or management-designated for specific purposes are reported in this component.[40]

15.101 The invested in capital assets, net of related debt component is not used by not-for-profit health care entities. As discussed in paragraph 33 of GASB Statement No. 34, this component represents the sum of capital assets shown in the balance sheet (net of accumulated depreciation) less any related debt used to finance those assets (for example, the outstanding balances of any

---

[39] See paragraph 35 of GASB Statement No. 34.

[40] However, these designations should not be displayed on the face of the balance sheet. See paragraph 15.108.

bonds, mortgages, notes, or other borrowings that are attributable to the acquisition, construction, or improvement of those assets). If capital debt exceeds the carrying value of capital assets, a negative amount should be reported, as discussed in item 7.23.9 of the GASB Q&A. Paragraph 15.103 provides additional guidance about calculating the amount of the net asset component invested in capital assets, net of related debt.

15.102 Governmental-restricted net assets differ in several respects from the restricted net assets reported by not-for-profit health care entities. First, GASB's definition of *restricted* is broader. In the not-for-profit sector, restrictions relate solely to limitations imposed by donors or grantors. In the governmental sector, restrictions arise from constraints on the use of assets that are imposed (*a*) by external parties (for example, creditors, grantors, and contributors) or laws or regulations of other governments[41] or (*b*) by law through constitutional provisions or enabling legislation.[42] Thus, in addition to resources restricted for purposes identified by donors and grantors, governmental-restricted net assets include net assets related to restricted assets, as discussed in paragraph 15.34, such as unexpended debt proceeds held by trustees, bond sinking and debt service reserve funds, assets set aside to meet statutory reserve requirements, and assets held in irrevocable malpractice self-insurance trusts. The underlying concept is that the government itself cannot unilaterally establish a restriction, except by enabling legislation, and cannot remove a restriction, except by fulfilling it. Thus, board designations on the use of assets are not restrictions. Under GASB Statement No. 34, assets and net assets are reported as restricted until the resources have been used for the specified purpose or, in the case of time requirements, as long as the resource provider requires (for example, in perpetuity).

15.103 Another difference is that GASB focuses on identifying specific assets that are restricted, along with any related liabilities; thus, restricted net assets represent restricted assets reduced by the liabilities related to those assets. In not-for-profit reporting, the concept of restriction focuses on a donor's restriction of the use of net assets versus restricting specific assets, as discussed in paragraph 9.08 of this guide. Item 7.24.7 of the GASB Q&A states that generally, a liability relates to restricted assets if the asset results from incurring the liability, or the liability will be liquidated with the restricted assets.[||||] For example, unexpended debt proceeds that must be used to acquire or construct capital assets are restricted assets, and the portion of the debt attributable to the unexpended proceeds is a related liability that should be offset, if significant, in calculating restricted net assets.[43] If a bond indenture requires a portion of the proceeds to be used to establish a reserve for the payment of principal and interest, the assets of the reserve account are restricted assets, and the portion of debt related to the establishment of the reserve is included in the calculation of restricted net assets.[44] However, some exceptions exist. If, for example, a bond sinking fund contains assets held in trust that are restricted for principal and interest payments on capital-related debt, the capital-related

---

[41] See paragraphs 34–35 of GASB Statement No. 34.

[42] See GASB Statement No. 46, *Net Assets Restricted by Enabling Legislation—an amendment of GASB Statement No. 34.*

[||||] This general rule is included in GASB Statement No. 63 *Financial Reporting of Deferred Outflows of Resources, Deferred Inflows of Resources, and Net Position*, issued in June 2011.

[43] See item 7.23.2 of the GASB Q&A.

[44] See item 7.24.25 of the GASB Q&A.

debt would not be offset against the restricted sinking fund assets in calculating restricted net assets. Instead, it is required to be netted against the capital assets that were financed with the debt in calculating the net asset component invested in capital assets, net of related debt.[45]

15.104 To determine the overall restricted net asset balance, the financial statement preparer first must compare individual restricted asset line items with their related liabilities and then aggregate the results. In comparing individual restricted asset line items with related liabilities, negative amounts should never be reported.[46] If liabilities that relate to specific restricted assets exceed those assets, the net asset balance for that line item would be zero, and the deficit would reduce the unrestricted net assets component.

15.105 Financial reporting of permanently-restricted net assets is another area where GASB and FASB standards differ. When a portion of restricted net assets is required to be retained in perpetuity, restricted net assets must be subdivided into expendable and nonexpendable components. In the governmental sector, restricted nonexpendable net assets should represent the reported amount of restricted assets (typically endowments) subject to a donor-imposed time requirement that they be invested and reinvested in perpetuity less any related liabilities. If no related liabilities exist, then the amount of restricted nonexpendable net assets equals the value of the restricted investments, even if that value has fallen below the amount of the original gift.[47] This differs from the not-for-profit reporting model that focuses on maintaining permanently-restricted net assets at the amount determined at the time of the original gift (see paragraphs 9.25–.31 of this guide). In calculating net asset balances associated with permanent endowments, care must be exercised to appropriately reflect the expendable and nonexpendable components if endowment assets include both corpus and spendable accumulated net appreciation (for example, nonexpendable restricted assets are commingled with spendable restricted assets).

15.106 GASB's guidance related to the net asset component calculations is prescriptive, and care must be employed when linking liabilities to specific restricted or capital assets for purposes of calculating the net asset components. Chapter 7 of the GASB Q&A contains guidance regarding the GASB staff's views on how the standards should be applied in various scenarios.

Financial Reporting

15.107 Restricted assets are not required to be labeled as restricted on the balance sheet, as long as the descriptions used on the face of the balance sheet make it clear that such assets cannot be used to satisfy liabilities or purposes other than those that are specifically intended to be satisfied with the restricted assets (see paragraph 15.107). The supporting details of restricted net assets (for example, major categories of restrictions) must be displayed on the face of the statement of net assets or balance sheet; note disclosure is not an acceptable alternative.[48] Not-for-profit health care entities are permitted to provide that information in either the notes to the financial statements or on the face of the balance sheet.

---

[45] See item 7.24.2 of the GASB Q&A.

[46] See item 7.24.13 of the GASB Q&A.

[47] See item 7.24.14 of the GASB Q&A.

[48] See item 7.22.8 of the GASB Q&A.

15.108 Paragraphs 37 and 98 of GASB Statement No. 34, as amended, prohibit reporting internal designations of net assets separately within unrestricted net assets on the face of the balance sheet but allow disclosure in the notes to the financial statements. Designations are management's plans for the use of resources, which should not be afforded the same status as restrictions. No prohibition exists against displaying the associated designated assets (for example, investments set aside for future expansion or quasiendowment) on the face of the balance sheet. Not-for-profit health care entities are permitted to display designations within unrestricted net assets on the face of the balance sheet or in the notes.

Health Care Service Revenue and Receivables

15.109 As discussed in chapter 10, "Health Care Service Revenue and Related Receivables," of this guide, under most third-party payor arrangements, governmental health care entities receive payment amounts that are less than their full established rates. The amount paid may be based on government regulations, such as Medicare, Medicaid, and other government programs, or contractual arrangements, such as PPOs, Blue Cross and Blue Shield plans, HMOs, and commercial insurers. Under this guide, provisions recognizing contractual and other adjustments are recorded on an accrual basis and deducted from gross service revenue to determine net service revenue. Charity care represents health care services that are provided but never expected to result in cash flows; therefore, charity care does not qualify for recognition as revenue. For financial reporting purposes, gross service revenue does not include charity care, and net service revenue is reported net of contractual and other adjustments in the statement of revenues, expenses, and changes in net assets or equity.[49]

15.110 Footnote 41 to paragraph 100 of GASB Statement No. 34 states, "Revenues should be reported net of discounts and allowances with the discount or allowance amount parenthetically disclosed on the face of the statement or in a note to the financial statements. Alternatively, revenues may be reported gross, with the related discounts and allowances reported directly beneath the revenue amount." For purposes of that display and disclosure, discounts and allowances include the difference between a health care provider's full established rates and its negotiated or contractual payment amounts previously described. However, allowances, as used in footnote 41, also include increases or decreases in the estimate of uncollectible accounts. As a result, the financial statements of governmental health care entities display changes in the estimate of uncollectible accounts differently from the display of similar amounts in financial statements of private-sector entities. Governmental health care entities report those amounts as a deduction from revenue. Private-sector entities report them as bad debt expense, as discussed in paragraph 10.29 of this guide. Paragraph 100 of GASB Statement No. 34 also requires governmental health care entities to separately identify revenues that provide security for revenue bonds.

15.111 Governmental health care entities that enter into arrangements in which they finance or sell their patient accounts receivable as a cash flow management strategy apply criteria in GASB Statement No. 48, *Sales and Pledges*

---

[49] See footnote 33.

of Receivables and Future Revenues and Intra-Entity Transfers of Assets and Future Revenues, in determining when transactions should be reported as a collateralized borrowing or sale. Determining whether a transaction should be reported as a sale, rather than a collateralized borrowing, requires an assessment of a government's continuing involvement with the receivables or future transferred revenues. A significant aspect of that assessment is the degree to which the selling or pledging government (the transferor) retains or relinquishes to the transferee control over the receivables or future transferred revenues. FASB ASC 860 should not be applied as other accounting literature by governmental health care entities because it conflicts with GASB Statement No. 48.

15.112 Governmental health care entities are required to disclose certain information about revenue and receivables, as follows:

- The accounting policies used for recognizing revenues, as discussed in paragraph 69 of NCGA Statement No. 1 and paragraphs 90–94 of GASB Statement No. 62.
- The policy for defining operating and nonoperating revenues, as discussed in paragraphs 102 and 115 of GASB Statement No. 34.
- Information about specific revenues pledged to collateralize or secure debt, as discussed in paragraph 21 of GASB Statement No. 48.
- Detailed disclosures about receivable balances when significant components of those receivables have been obscured by aggregation, as discussed in paragraph 13 of GASB Statement No. 38.
- Separate disclosure of significant receivable balances not expected to be collected within one year of the balance sheet date, as discussed in paragraph 13 of GASB Statement No. 38.
- The allowance for estimated uncollectible receivables should be disclosed on the face of the financial statement either parenthetically or as a separate line item or in the notes to the financial statements, as discussed in paragraph 33 of GASB Statement No. 62.
- Management's policy for providing charity care, as well as the level of charity care provided, measured based on the governmental health care entity's costs, units of service, or other statistical measure.[50] Private-sector health care entities disclose the information in paragraph 10.28 of this guide.

Chapter 6, "Revenues and Receivables," of the Audit and Accounting Guide *State and Local Governments* contains additional guidance on accounting, financial reporting, and auditing considerations related to revenue and receivables.

Contributions and Other Nonexchange Transactions

15.113 Governmental health care entities may receive contributions, grants, or tax support in transactions with no direct and equivalent exchange of value with the resource provider. Governmental health care entities

---

[50] See footnote 33.

follow GASB Statement No. 33, *Accounting and Financial Reporting for Nonexchange Transactions*, as amended, which establishes accounting and financial reporting standards for the recognition of nonexchange transactions involving financial or capital resources.[51]

15.114 Nonexchange transactions are classified into one of four classes based on their principal characteristics, as discussed in paragraph 7 of GASB Statement No. 33. Most contributions and grants received by governmental health care entities are classified as voluntary nonexchange transactions. Revenue from voluntary nonexchange transactions should be recognized when all applicable eligibility requirements have been met. Eligibility requirements comprise one or more of the following:

- Required characteristics of recipients
- Time requirements
- Reimbursements
- Contingencies

Detailed guidance on the application of eligibility requirements is provided in paragraphs 20–26 of GASB Statement No. 33.

15.115 Voluntary nonexchange transactions may be received with associated time or purpose restrictions. As discussed in paragraph 14 of GASB Statement No. 33, purpose restrictions imposed on nonexchange revenues, such as grants, contributions, and endowments, do not affect when revenues are recognized. Rather, resulting net assets should be reported as restricted until the resources have been used for the specified purpose or for as long as the resource provider requires (for example, for endowments).

15.116 If the transaction is a permanent or term endowment, the resource provider's stipulation that the resources should be maintained intact in perpetuity for a specified number of years or until a specific event has occurred (for example, the donor's death) is a time requirement, as described in paragraph 20(b) of GASB Statement No. 33. In such situations, the time requirement is considered met as soon as the recipient begins to honor the provider's stipulation not to sell, disburse, or consume the resources, which occurs upon receipt of the resources. Therefore, revenues from term or permanent endowments should be recognized at the time the resources are received, provided that all other eligibility requirements have been met. The associated net assets should be reported as restricted for as long as the donor's time requirements and purpose restrictions, if applicable, remain in effect.

15.117 Promises of cash or other assets that nongovernmental entities, including individuals, voluntarily make to governments may be referred to as pledges, promises to give, promised donations, or some other term. Promised assets may include permanently nonexpendable additions to endowments and

---

[51] To date, GASB has not issued any guidance related to noncapital gifts-in-kind or contributed services.

other trusts; term endowments; contributions of works of art and similar assets to capitalized collections; or other kinds of capital or financial assets, with or without purpose restrictions or time requirements. Governmental health care entities that receive promises to give should recognize receivables and revenues net of estimated uncollectible amounts only after all eligibility requirements are met, provided that the promise is verifiable, and the resources are measurable and probable of collection.[52] As noted in item Z.33.19 of the GASB Q&A, governmental standards neither require nor prohibit the discounting of promises to give that are to be received over an extended period of time. Private-sector standards require discounting of such promises. Transactions that are not recognizable because they are not measurable should be disclosed.[53] For term or permanent endowments, the health care entity cannot begin to honor a provider's stipulation that the resources not be sold, disbursed, or consumed until the resources are actually received. Therefore, promises to give term or permanent endowments are not recognized in financial statements.[54]

15.118 In some cases, it may become apparent after revenue has been recognized in the financial statements that the GASB Statement No. 33 eligibility criteria are no longer met (for example, because an audit of a particular grant program determined that certain expenses did not meet purpose restrictions). Paragraph 26 of GASB Statement No. 33 provides that if it is probable that the recipient will return all or part of the transferred resources, a liability or reduction of a receivable and an expense should be recognized for the amount that the resource provider (grantor) is expected to cancel or reclaim.

15.119 Governmental health care entities may be beneficiaries of charitable gifts structured as split-interest agreements. Common forms of split-interest agreements include charitable gift annuity contracts, pooled life income trusts, charitable remainder unitrusts, charitable remainder annuity trusts, and charitable lead annuity trusts. Item 7.72.11 of the GASB Q&A provides guidance to governmental health care entities in situations in which the health care entity is the trustee, as well as the beneficiary; thus, the trust assets are under their control. The governmental health care entity should recognize an asset for the fair value of the trust assets and a liability for the obligation to the beneficiary. The difference between the assets in the trust and the liability owed to the other beneficiary(ies) would be reported as restricted net assets that are expendable or nonexpendable based on the nature of the donor's restrictions. Changes should be reflected in the statement of revenues, expenses, and changes in net assets or equity.

15.120 Foundations, businesses, and other types of entities may provide resources to health care entities under programs referred to as grants, awards, or sponsorships. The asset transfers are likely exchange or exchangelike transactions if the potential public benefit is secondary to the resource providers' potential direct benefits. The transfers are likely contributions (voluntary

---

[52] See paragraph 25 and examples 21 and 21(a) in appendix D of GASB Statement No. 33, *Accounting and Financial Reporting for Nonexchange Transactions*.

[53] See paragraph 11 of GASB Statement No. 33.

[54] See examples 24–25 in appendix D of GASB Statement No. 33.

nonexchange transactions) if the resource providers receive no value in exchange for the transferred assets or if the value received by the resource provider is incidental to the potential public benefit from using the transferred assets. For example, a research grant made by a foundation to a governmental hospital would likely be a contribution if the research program is to be planned and carried out by the hospital, and the hospital has the right to publish the results. However, if the grant is made by a pharmaceutical manufacturer that provides potential new medications to be tested in the hospital's research facilities and retains the right to any patents or other results, the grant would likely be an exchange transaction.[55] Item Z.33.1 in the GASB Q&A also discusses considerations related to determining whether a grant is an exchange or a nonexchange transaction.

15.121 Statement of Position (SOP) 98-2, *Accounting for Costs of Activities of Not-for-Profit Organizations and State and Local Governmental Entities That Include Fund Raising* (AICPA, *Technical Practice Aids*, ACC sec. 10,730), provides guidance for state and local governmental entities, including health care entities, that conduct fund-raising activities with activities related to other functions, such as program activities or supporting services (joint activities). FASB ASC 958-720 superseded SOP 98-1, *Accounting for the Costs of Computer Software Developed or Obtained for Internal Use*, as it relates to nongovernmental entities; however, SOP 98-2 is still applicable to governmental entities. SOP 98-2 establishes financial accounting standards for accounting for costs of joint activities and requires financial statement disclosures about the nature of the activities for which joint costs have been allocated and the amounts of those joint costs.

15.122 GASB Statement No. 34 provides guidance related to the presentation of nonexchange transactions in financial statements. Contributions of capital assets or financial resources required to be used to acquire capital assets are reported separately after nonoperating revenues and expenses in the statement of revenues, expenses, and changes in net assets, as illustrated in paragraph 15.17. Contributions of term and permanent endowments should be reported in the same manner. All other contributions (both restricted and unrestricted) are reported as nonoperating revenues and expenses. As discussed in paragraph 15.18, net assets released from restriction are not reported in the statement of revenues, expenses, and changes in net assets, as is done in the not-for-profit reporting model.

15.123 In the statement of net assets, an amount equal to unexpended restricted contributions at the reporting date should be included in the restricted net assets component of net assets. GASB Statement No. 34 does not require that restricted resources be used first when an expenditure is made for a purpose for which both unrestricted and temporarily-restricted net assets are available. Instead, each entity is required to establish a policy for whether restricted or unrestricted resources will be used first when both sources are available and to disclose that policy in the notes to the financial statements.[56]

---

[55] See example 22 in appendix D of GASB Statement No. 33.

[56] See paragraph 115 of GASB Statement No. 34.

The Reporting Entity and Related Entities##

15.124 Governmental health care entities and private-sector health care entities use different definitions of the *financial reporting entity*. GASB Statement No. 14, *The Financial Reporting Entity*, as amended, establishes standards for defining and reporting the governmental financial reporting entity and addresses issues related to the display of entities included within the reporting entity, the application of the equity method of accounting, and accounting and reporting considerations for various types of joint ventures entered into by governmental entities. Unlike the private sector, which employs variable interest and voting interest models for defining the *reporting entity*, GASB's reporting entity model is based on the concept of financial accountability.[57]

15.125 Under GASB Statement No. 14, the governmental financial reporting entity consists of the primary government and any legally-separate entities that meet the definition of a *component unit*. *Component units* are (*a*) legally-separate entities for which the primary government is financially accountable, as discussed in paragraph 15.126; (*b*) certain entities that are included in the reporting entity because of the nature and significance of their relationship with the primary government, as described in GASB Statement No. 39 and paragraph 15.128; and (*c*) other legally-separate organizations for which the primary government is not financially accountable, but the nature and significance of their relationship with the primary government are such that exclusion would cause the reporting entity's financial statements to be misleading or incomplete. A nonauthoritative flowchart in appendix D of GASB Statement No. 39 aids in the evaluation of whether an entity is a component unit.

15.126 A governmental health care entity is financially accountable for another entity if it appoints a voting majority of the entity's governing body, and it is able to impose its will on that entity, or a potential exists for the entity to provide specific financial benefits to, or impose specific financial burdens

---

In November 2010, GASB issued GASB Statement No. 61. The objective of the statement is to improve the financial reporting of a governmental financial reporting entity by modifying the criteria for inclusion of component units and amending the criteria for blending. The statement modifies certain requirements for inclusion of component units in the financial reporting entity. For organizations that previously were required to be included as component units by meeting the fiscal dependency criterion, a financial benefit or burden relationship also would need to be present between the primary government and that organization for it to be included in the reporting entity as a component unit. Further, for organizations that do not meet the financial accountability criteria for inclusion as component units but that, nevertheless, should be included because the primary government's management determines that it would be misleading to exclude them, GASB Statement No. 61 clarifies the manner in which that determination should be made and the types of relationships that generally should be considered in making the determination. It also amends the criteria for reporting component units as if they were part of the primary government (that is, blending) in certain circumstances. For component units that currently are blended based on the "substantively the same governing body" criteria, it additionally requires that (*a*) the primary government and component unit have a financial benefit or burden relationship, or (*b*) management of the primary government below the level of the elected officials have operational responsibility, as defined in paragraph 8(a), for the activities of the component unit. New criteria also are added to require blending of component units whose total outstanding debt is expected to be repaid entirely or almost entirely with resources of the primary government. Additional reporting guidance is provided for blending a component unit if the primary government is a business-type activity that uses a single column presentation for financial reporting. The statement also clarifies the reporting of equity interests in legally-separate entities. It requires a primary government to report its equity interest in a component unit as an asset. The provisions of GASB Statement No. 61 are effective for financial statements for periods beginning after June 15, 2012.

[57] See paragraphs 10–11 and 21 of GASB Statement No. 14.

on, the governmental health care entity, as described in paragraphs 21–33 of GASB Statement No. 14. A governmental health care organization also may be financially accountable for an entity that is fiscally dependent on it, as described in paragraphs 34–37 of GASB Statement No. 14.

15.127 Generally, significant investments made by a governmental entity primarily for the purpose of obtaining income or profit are evaluated as investments, rather than potential component units.[58]

15.128 GASB Statement No. 39 amended GASB Statement No. 14 to provide additional guidance for determining whether certain entities (for example, institutionally-related fund-raising foundations) for which the primary government is not financially accountable should be reported as discretely-presented component units based on the nature and significance of their relationship with the primary government. Paragraph 5 of GASB Statement No. 39 requires reporting as a discretely-presented component unit an organization that meets all three of the following criteria:

- The economic resources received or held by the separate organization are entirely or almost entirely for the direct benefit of the governmental health care entity, its component units, or its constituents.
- The governmental health care entity or its component units is entitled to, or has the ability to otherwise access, a majority of the economic resources received or held by the separate organization.
- The economic resources held by the separate organization are significant to the governmental health care entity.

Additional considerations related to applying GASB Statement No. 39 are discussed in paragraphs 15.133–.138.

15.129 GASB Statement No. 14 also contains standards for displaying component units in a financial reporting entity's basic financial statements. Some component units are required by paragraph 53 of GASB Statement No. 14 to be blended with the financial information of the primary government (similar to the presentation of consolidated subsidiaries in the private sector). Those that are not required to be blended are discretely presented. In discrete presentation, the financial information of the component unit is displayed separately from the financial information of the primary government (that is, in a separate column or on a separate page).[59] Component units included as a result of meeting the criteria in GASB Statement No. 39 must always be discretely presented.

15.130 If a primary government and its component units have different fiscal year-ends, the financial reporting entity reports using the primary government's fiscal year and incorporates financial statements for the component units' fiscal years ending during the reporting entity's fiscal year. If a component unit's fiscal year ends within the first quarter of the reporting entity's

---

[58] See paragraph 55 of GASB Statement No. 14.

[59] Some governmental health care entities may be organized and operated on a fund basis (for example, they use several separate enterprise funds for the purpose of carrying on specific activities or attaining certain objectives in accordance with regulatory restrictions or limitations). Item 4.28.10 of the GASB Q&A discusses various financial statement display options for governments that have discretely-presented component units.

subsequent fiscal year, the component unit's financial statements for that subsequent year may be used if doing so does not adversely affect the timely and accurate presentation of the reporting entity's financial statements. The fiscal year of the component units included in the reporting entity should be consistent from year to year.[60] If transactions between component units that have different fiscal years result in inconsistencies in amounts reported as intraentity receivables or payables, the governmental health care entity should disclose the nature and amount of those transactions in the notes to the financial statements.[61]

15.131 Because of the separate nature of discretely-presented component units, GASB Statement No. 34 generally requires that transactions between a primary government and its discretely-presented component units (intraentity transactions) be reported as if they were transactions with external parties.[62] However, GASB Statement No. 48 requires that intraentity transfers of capital and financial assets should be reported based on the carrying value of the transferor.[63] In separately-issued financial statements of discretely-presented component units, amounts receivable from, or payable to, the primary government should be reported on a separate line from other receivables (payables). Chapter 9, "Interfund, Internal, and Intra-Entity Activity and Balances," of the Audit and Accounting Guide *State and Local Governments* contains a detailed discussion of accounting and financial reporting considerations related to intraentity activity and balances. Section Z.48 of the GASB Q&A provides implementation guidance for GASB Statement No. 48.

15.132 Additional guidance is provided in chapter 3, "The Financial Reporting Entity," of the Audit and Accounting Guide *State and Local Governments* and chapters 4 and 7 of the GASB Q&A, which provide nonauthoritative illustrations, examples, disclosures, and financial statement presentations. Appendix 4-2 of the GASB Q&A provides examples that evaluate potential component units for inclusion in the financial statements, and appendix 4-5 of the GASB Q&A provides a useful flowchart for evaluating potential component units.

Institutionally-Related Foundations

15.133 Legally-separate not-for-profit foundations may be established to raise, hold, and invest funds on behalf of a governmental health care entity. Because of its close relationship to the governmental health care entity, a foundation should be evaluated to determine whether it is included in the reporting entity because it is a component unit, as described in paragraph 15.125.

15.134 If the fundraising foundation is a component unit because it meets the three criteria in paragraph 5 of GASB Statement No. 39, as discussed in paragraph 15.128, the governmental health care entity is required to report the fundraising foundation as a discretely-presented component unit. Distributions made or promised by the foundation to the health care entity are reported as expenses by the foundation and contribution revenue by the health care entity.

---

[60] See paragraphs 59–60 of GASB Statement No. 14.

[61] See paragraph 60 of GASB Statement No. 14.

[62] See paragraph 61 of GASB Statement No. 34.

[63] See paragraph 15 of GASB Statement No. 48, *Sales and Pledges of Receivables and Future Revenues and Intra-Entity Transfers of Assets and Future Revenues.*

The nonauthoritative exhibits E-1 and E-2 of GASB Statement No. 39 illustrate discretely presenting the foundation by displaying the foundation's financial statements in their original formats on separate pages. The nonauthoritative exhibits E-3 and E-4 of GASB Statement No. 39 illustrate one way in which a discretely-presented component unit could be displayed side-by-side on the face of the health care entity's statement of net assets and statement of revenues, expenses, and changes in net assets.

15.135 If the foundation is included in the reporting entity for one of the other two reasons in paragraph 15.125 (that is, because the governmental health care entity is financially accountable or because, without it, the financial statements of the governmental health care entity are misleading or incomplete), the fundraising foundation will be either blended or discretely presented. The method to use is determined by applying the criteria in paragraph 53 of GASB Statement No. 14. If the foundation provides benefits entirely or almost entirely to the governmental health care entity, the foundation is a blended component unit of the health care entity.[64] The foundation also is a blended component unit if the governing bodies of the health care entity and foundation are substantively the same. If neither of the criteria for blending is met, the fundraising foundation is discretely presented.

15.136 In most cases, the foundation prepares its financial statements in accordance with FASB standards. If a nongovernmental foundation's stand-alone financial statements state that the foundation and governmental health care entity are financially interrelated, as described in FASB ASC 958-20, then as explained in footnote a to paragraph 40(a) of GASB Statement No. 14, the governmental health care entity is able to otherwise access the majority of the economic resources received or held by the financially-interrelated entity (the foundation). If the foundation meets the other two criteria in paragraph 5 of GASB Statement No. 39, it is a component unit. Paragraph 29 of the nonauthoritative basis for conclusions of GASB Statement No. 39 also states that in these circumstances, the health care entity's financial statements would be rendered misleading or incomplete if the financial statements of the financially-interrelated entity (foundation) were excluded, particularly if the financially-interrelated entity holds the majority of the primary government's endowments, gifts, and contributions whereby the gift or earnings thereon are restricted by donors for the activities of the primary government or its component units. A nongovernmental foundation that is financially interrelated with a health care entity reports contributions according to the guidance discussed in paragraph 11.35 of this guide. The governmental health care entity that is the specified beneficiary does not report an interest in the net assets of the foundation, as is done by private-sector health care entities; instead, a governmental health care entity recognizes contributions received from, or pledged by, the foundation, in accordance with the standards in paragraphs 19–25 of GASB Statement No. 33.

15.137 If a foundation's stand-alone FASB financial statements do not indicate whether the foundation and governmental health care entity are financially interrelated, the governmental health care entity's ability to otherwise access a majority of the economic resources received or held by the separate organization might be demonstrated in other ways. For example, historically, the health care entity may have directly or indirectly received a majority of

---

[64] See case 17 in appendix 4-2 of the GASB Q&A.

the economic resources provided by the foundation, or previously, the foundation may have received and honored requests to provide resources to the health care entity. If the ability to otherwise access the economic resources is demonstrated, and the foundation meets the other two criteria in paragraph 5 of GASB Statement No. 39, it is a component unit. If the foundation does not meet the three criteria in GASB Statement No. 39, the foundation should be evaluated for inclusion as a component unit using the remaining two tests described in paragraph 15.125. If the foundation does not meet any of those three tests, then the foundation is not a component unit of the health care entity. The health care entity recognizes contributions received from, or pledged by, the foundation, in accordance with the standards in paragraphs 19–25 of GASB Statement No. 33.[65]

15.138 Section 4.33 of the GASB Q&A describes various ways in which the financial statements of nongovernmental component units can be displayed in the financial statements of the governmental reporting entity.

Business Combinations

15.139 Governmental health care entities may participate in business combination transactions with other governmental entities or private-sector entities. GASB has a project underway that will develop accounting and reporting standards for government combinations. Paragraph 534 of the nonauthoritative basis for conclusions of GASB Statement No. 62 states that governments should continue their current practice of accounting and reporting of government combinations until GASB can develop specific accounting and financial reporting standards.

15.140 In practice, some governmental health care entities, primarily those that elected to follow post-November 30, 1989, FASB Statements and Interpretations that do not conflict with or contradict GASB pronouncements, applied FASB ASC 805, *Business Combinations*, to purchase transactions. Others accounted for purchase transactions in accordance with APB Opinion No. 16, *Business Combinations*, as amended and interpreted through November 30, 1989. For change of control transactions that did not involve an exchange of consideration, many governmental health care entities applied accounting similar to the pooling-of-interest method described in APB Opinion No. 16. Governmental health care organizations were precluded from applying the provisions of FASB ASC 958-805, which are applicable to not-for-profit health care organizations.

General Auditing Considerations for Governmental Health Care Entities

15.141 Chapter 2, "General Auditing Considerations," of this guide provides guidance on the unique application of the standards of fieldwork to health care entities, including guidance for audits conducted in accordance with financial audit standards contained in *Government Auditing Standards*,

---

[65] If the foundation prepares its financial statements in accordance with FASB standards, it uses the standards in the "Transfers of Assets to a Not-for-Profit Entity or Charitable Trust that Raises or Holds Contributions for Others" sections of FASB ASC 958-605 to determine whether to recognize contribution revenue or a liability when it receives contributions for the governmental health care entity's use or benefit. Those standards are discussed in paragraphs 11.31–.38 of this guide.

as amended, which is issued by the Comptroller General of the United States. The AICPA Audit and Accounting Guide *State and Local Governments* discusses in detail the requirements for a generally accepted auditing standards audit of financial statements prepared in accordance with the governmental GAAP hierarchy described in paragraph 15.05. It contains information about auditing considerations that are unique to the governmental financial reporting model that are not contemplated in this guide. Therefore, in performing audits of separately-issued financial statements of governmental health care entities, the auditing guidance contained in both the Audit and Accounting Guide *State and Local Governments* and this guide will be useful.

15.142 Paragraph 4.32 of the Audit and Accounting Guide *State and Local Governments* states that an auditor's consideration of whether a government's basic financial statements are presented fairly, in all material respects and in conformity with GAAP, should be based on opinion units. Auditors apply the concept of opinion units in planning, performing, evaluating the results of, and reporting on audits of governmental entities, including governmental health care entities. The concept of opinion units is unique to audits of state and local governmental entities. Chapters 4, "General Auditing Considerations"; 13, "Concluding the Audit"; and 14, "Audit Reporting," of the Audit and Accounting Guide *State and Local Governments* define *opinion units* and discuss the nature and effect of opinion units in planning, performing, evaluating the results of, and reporting on the audit of such entities' basic financial statements.

15.143 The number of opinion units will depend on whether the governmental health care entity (*a*) accounts for and reports its activities in a single enterprise fund or multiple enterprise funds[66] and (*b*) has any discretely-presented component units (see paragraphs 15.124–.138). A governmental health care entity that reports its activities in a single enterprise fund and has no discretely-presented component units will have a single opinion unit. A governmental health care entity that operates in a single enterprise fund and has one or more discretely-presented component units will have more than one opinion unit: one for the primary government (the health care entity) and another for the discretely-presented component unit. If more than one discretely-presented component unit exists, the opinion unit is referred to as aggregate discretely-presented component units. A governmental health care entity that reports its activities in multiple enterprise funds will have an opinion unit for each major enterprise fund[67] and an additional opinion unit for all nonmajor funds in the aggregate (aggregate remaining fund information). If that entity also has one or more discretely-presented component units, there will be an additional opinion unit for the aggregate discretely-presented component unit(s).[68]

15.144 Paragraphs 2.15–.19 of this guide provide general guidance on the concept of materiality. In accordance with paragraph .27 of AU section

---

[66] Some governmental health care entities may be organized and operated on a fund basis (for example, they use several separate enterprise funds for the purpose of carrying on specific activities or attaining certain objectives in accordance with regulatory restrictions or limitations).

[67] An exercise for determining major and nonmajor funds is included as exercise 5 in chapter 7 of appendix 7-3 of the GASB Q&A.

[68] As discussed in chapter 4, "General Auditing Considerations," of the Audit and Accounting Guide *State and Local Governments*, if either the aggregate discretely-presented component units opinion unit or the aggregate remaining fund information opinion unit is not quantitatively or qualitatively material to the primary government, those two units may be combined and titled the "Aggregate Discretely-Presented Component Unit and Remaining Fund Information Opinion Unit."

312, *Audit Risk and Materiality in Conducting an Audit* (AICPA, *Professional Standards*), the auditor should determine a materiality level for the financial statements as a whole, which in the context of a governmental audit means establishing materiality levels by each opinion unit. Chapter 4 of the Audit and Accounting Guide *State and Local Governments* provides detailed guidance on audit materiality determinations for governmental entities, including guidance on assessing materiality based on the concept of opinion units. The materiality evaluation for one opinion unit should not be affected by other information in the government's financial statements or, if applicable, quantitative or qualitative factors relating to other opinion units.

15.145 Paragraphs 2.56–.58 of this guide discuss management's representations for financial statements. Paragraphs 13.09–.10 of the Audit and Accounting Guide *State and Local Governments* list the types of representations that are particularly important in a governmental engagement. Paragraph .07 of AU section 558A, *Required Supplementary Information* (AICPA, *Professional Standards*), states that the auditor should consider whether representations for RSI should be included.[***]

15.146 Governmental health care entities are subject to various legal and contractual provisions (compliance requirements) that may affect their financial statements. As discussed in paragraph 12.10 of the Audit and Accounting Guide *State and Local Governments*, the auditor should consider whether it is necessary to evaluate the entity's compliance with those requirements as part of the financial statement audit.

Independent Auditor's Reports

15.147 The AICPA's fourth standard of reporting requires that the auditor's report contain either an expression of opinion regarding the financial statements as a whole or an assertion to the effect that an opinion cannot be expressed. As discussed in chapter 14 of the Audit and Accounting Guide *State and Local Governments*, auditors of governmental health care entities express or disclaim opinions on a government's financial statements as a whole by providing in the aggregate separate opinions or disclaimers of opinion on the financial statements of each opinion unit. Examples 15-1 and 15-2 are illustrative reports for a governmental health care entity that accounts for and reports its activities in a single enterprise fund. Note that in these illustrative reports, auditors do not express opinions on results of operations, as is done for private-sector health care entities. Instead, auditors of governmental health care entities opine on the change in financial position. Chapter 14 of the Audit and Accounting Guide *State and Local Governments* contains numerous additional report examples, including examples for entities that use multifund reporting and a number of situations unique to government reporting (for example, reporting on a single fund or department and reporting when a component unit is omitted).

[***] In February 2010, the Auditing Standards Board (ASB) issued Statement on Auditing Standards (SAS) No. 120, *Required Supplementary Information* (AICPA, *Professional Standards*, AU sec. 558). This SAS will supersede AU section 558A, *Required Supplementary Information* (AICPA, *Professional Standards*). SAS No. 120 is effective for audits of financial statements for periods beginning on or after December 15, 2010. Early application is permitted. Appendix E, "Other Information, Supplementary Information, and Required Supplementary Information," of this guide provides additional information on SAS No. 120. Management's representations are discussed in paragraph .09 of AU section 558.

15.148 The auditor's primary responsibility is to report on the results of his or her audit of the basic financial statements. The auditor has additional responsibilities related to RSI and, if applicable, supplementary information (SI) other than RSI. Those responsibilities, which are discussed in detail in chapter 14 of Audit and Accounting Guide *State and Local Governments*, are briefly described subsequently.

RSI

15.149 As discussed in paragraph 15.28, GASB requires that certain information accompany the basic financial statements and be presented as RSI. Unless the auditor has been engaged to examine and express an opinion on RSI, the auditor's responsibility with respect to RSI is limited to applying certain limited procedures to RSI and reporting deficiencies in, or the omission of, such information, as described in paragraphs .07–.08 of AU section 558A.[†††] If the deficiencies described in paragraph .08 of AU section 558A do not exist, and the auditor's report appears in an auditor-submitted document, the auditor's report should be expanded in accordance with paragraph .15 of AU section 551A, *Reporting on Information Accompanying the Basic Financial Statements in Auditor-Submitted Documents* (AICPA, *Professional Standards*). The following paragraph is an example that an auditor might use in the circumstances to disclaim an opinion on unaudited RSI:[69]

> The [*identify the required supplementary information, such as management's discussion and analysis*] on pages XX–XX are not a required part of the basic financial statements but is (are) supplementary information required by accounting principles generally accepted in the United States of America. We have applied certain limited procedures, which consisted principally of inquiries of management regarding the methods of measurement and presentation of the required supplementary information. However, we did not audit the information and express no opinion on it.

If instead the auditor's report appears in a client-prepared document, the auditor is not required to add an explanatory paragraph to his or her report to refer to the unaudited RSI or limited procedures, although a disclaimer paragraph may be voluntarily included, if desired.

15.150 If any of the deficiencies described in paragraph .08 of AU section 558A exist (for example, the client omits MD&A or a portion of MD&A, or the information is presented in a manner that does not meet the standards established by GAAP), this does not affect the auditor's conclusion regarding the fair presentation of the basic financial statements because RSI is not considered essential to the fair presentation of the basic financial statements. In such situations, the auditor's report should include an explanatory paragraph, such as the following, after the auditor's opinion, which is required for such situations by paragraph .08 of AU section 558A:[‡‡‡]

[†††] See footnote ***.

[69] *Unaudited RSI* is information that accompanies the basic financial statements on which the auditor is not engaged to express an opinion whether it is fairly presented in conformity with GAAP. Unless the auditor is engaged to audit the RSI, this section of this guide and the Audit and Accounting Guide *State and Local Governments* refer to the information as unaudited, even though generally accepted auditing standards require the auditor to perform specific procedures and, perhaps, report on the information. See footnote 21 to paragraph 14.54 in the Audit and Accounting Guide *State and Local Governments*.

[‡‡‡] See footnote ***.

> The management's discussion and analysis for the year ended December 31, 20X7, on pages XX–XX is not a required part of the basic financial statements as of and for the year then ended but is supplementary information required by the accounting principles generally accepted in the United States of America. We have applied certain limited procedures, which consisted principally of inquiries of management regarding the methods of measurement and presentation of the required supplementary information. However, we did not audit the information and express no opinion on it. Health Care Entity has not presented the management's discussion and analysis for the year ended December 31, 20X6, that accounting principles generally accepted in the United States of America require to supplement, although not to be part of, the basic financial statements for each year presented.

This paragraph should be included regardless of whether the auditor's report appears in a client-prepared document or an auditor-submitted document.

15.151 If an auditor is engaged to report on whether RSI is fairly stated, in all material respects, in relation to the financial statements as a whole, AU section 551A applies. For further discussion of AU section 551A, see paragraph 15.152.

SI

15.152 If SI is included in an auditor-submitted document, AU section 551A[||||||] requires that the auditor either report on whether the SI is fairly stated, in all material respects, in relation to the basic financial statements as a whole or disclaim such an opinion. The auditor also may express an opinion on a portion of SI and disclaim an opinion on the remainder. A paragraph, such as the following, should be added to the standard report[70] if the auditor expresses an unqualified opinion on the basic financial statements and SI:

> Our audit was conducted for the purpose of forming an opinion[71] on the Health Care Entity's basic financial statements. The [*identify accompanying supplementary information*] is (are) presented for purposes of additional analysis and is (are) not a required part of the basic financial statements. Such information has been subjected to the auditing procedures applied in the audit of the basic financial statements and, in our opinion, is fairly stated, in all material respects and in relation to the financial statements as a whole.

Paragraphs .13–.14 of AU section 551A provide examples for other circumstances, including those in which the opinion on the basic financial statements is other than an unqualified opinion, or the auditor disclaims an opinion on all or part of the accompanying information.

|||||| In February 2010, the ASB issued SAS No. 119, *Supplementary Information in Relation to the Financial Statements as a Whole* (AICPA, *Professional Standards*, AU sec. 551). This SAS will supersede AU section 551A, *Reporting on Information Accompanying the Basic Financial Statements in Auditor-Submitted Documents* (AICPA, *Professional Standards*). SAS No. 119 is effective for audits of financial statements for periods beginning on or after December 15, 2010. Early application is permitted. Appendix E of this guide provides additional information on SAS No. 119.

70 Alternatively, the auditor may issue a separate report that precedes the additional information.

71 If multiple opinion units exist, this would instead refer to *opinions*.

15.153 If the auditor has not been engaged to report on whether SI is fairly stated, in all material respects and in relation to the financial statements as a whole, the auditor has no obligation to perform any procedures to corroborate other information contained in a document. However, AU section 550A, *Other Information in Documents Containing Audited Financial Statements* (AICPA, *Professional Standards*), states that the auditor should read the other information and consider whether such information or the manner of its presentation is materially inconsistent with information or the manner of its presentation appearing in the financial statements.[###] The auditor is not required to reference the SI in the auditor's report on the basic financial statements. However, the auditor may include an explanatory paragraph disclaiming an opinion on the SI. For example, an auditor may choose to include a disclaimer on the SI when the auditor believes that he or she could be associated with the information, and the user may infer a level of assurance that is not intended. If the auditor chooses to include an explanatory paragraph that disclaims an opinion on SI, that paragraph could read as follows:

Our audit was conducted for the purpose of forming an opinion on the Health Care Entity's basic financial statements as a whole. The [*identify the other information*] is (are) presented for purposes of additional analysis and is (are) not a required part of the basic financial statements. Such information has not been subjected to the auditing procedures applied by us in the audit of the basic financial statements, and accordingly, we express no opinion on it.

15.154 Auditors often are engaged to report on some or all of the SI that accompanies financial statements in client-prepared documents using AU section 551A,[****] although the scope of AU section 551A does not include client-prepared documents. Chapter 14 of the Audit and Accounting Guide *State and Local Governments* provides guidelines for doing so. If the auditor has not been engaged to audit SI included in a client-prepared document, the preceding paragraph is not required. However, the auditor may choose to issue a disclaimer of opinion on the SI or ask the government to label the SI as unaudited.

[###] In February 2010, the ASB issued SAS No. 118, *Other Information in Documents Containing Audited Financial Statements* (AICPA, *Professional Standards*, AU sec. 550). This SAS will supersede AU section 550A, *Other Information in Documents Containing Audited Financial Statements* (AICPA, *Professional Standards*). SAS No. 118 is effective for audits of financial statements for periods beginning on or after December 15, 2010. Early application is permitted. Appendix E of this guide provides additional information on SAS No. 118.

[****] See footnote ||||||.

Example 15-1

Unqualified Opinion on Comparative Basic Financial Statements of a Governmental Hospital (Special-Purpose Government) That Has a Single Opinion Unit and for Which the Auditor Has Not Been Engaged to Examine and Express an Opinion on RSI

Independent Auditor's Report

To the Board of Trustees

Sample Governmental Hospital Authority

We have audited the accompanying statements of net assets of the Sample Governmental Hospital Authority (the Authority)[, *a component unit of Feeling County, State of Union,*][72] as of December 31, 20X1 and 20X0, and the related statements of revenues, expenses, and changes in net assets and statements of cash flows for the years then ended. These financial statements are the responsibility of the Authority's management. Our responsibility is to express an opinion on these financial statements based on our audits.[73]

We conducted our audits[74] in accordance with auditing standards generally accepted in the United States of America. Those standards require that we plan and perform the audit to obtain reasonable assurance about whether the financial statements are free of material misstatement. An audit includes examining, on a test basis, evidence supporting the amounts and disclosures in the financial statements. An audit also includes assessing the accounting principles used and significant estimates made by management, as well as evaluating the overall financial statement presentation. We believe that our audits[75] provide a reasonable basis for our opinion.

In our opinion, the financial statements referred to above present fairly, in all material respects, the financial position of the Authority as of December 31, 20X1 and 20X0, and the changes in its financial position and its cash flows for the years then ended in conformity with accounting principles generally accepted in the United States of America.

The management's discussion and analysis on pages XX through XX is not a required part of the basic financial statements but is supplementary information required by accounting principles generally accepted in the United States of America.

We have applied certain limited procedures, which consisted principally of inquiries of management regarding the methods of measurement and presentation of the required supplementary information. However, we did not audit the information and express no opinion on it.

[*Signature*]

[Date]

---

[72] If the entity being reported on is a component unit of a larger financial reporting entity, the auditor's report should disclose that fact, as discussed in paragraph 14.45 of the Audit and Accounting Guide State and Local Governments.

[73] Because the report is covering audits for two years, the reference is to *audits*, rather than *audit*.

[74] See footnote 73.

[75] See footnote 73.

Example 15-2

Unqualified Opinions on Single-Year Basic Financial Statements of a Governmental Hospital That Has One Opinion Unit for the Primary Government and Another Opinion Unit for Its Discretely-Presented Component Unit and for Which the Auditor Has Not Been Engaged to Examine and Express an Opinion on RSI

Independent Auditor's Report

To the Board of Trustees

University Hospital

We have audited the accompanying statements of net assets and the related statements of revenues, expenses and changes in net assets and statements of cash flows[76] of the University Hospital [*, a component unit of University, Any City and Any State*][77] and of its discretely presented component unit as of and for the year ended December 31, 20XY, which collectively comprise the Hospital's basic financial statements. These financial statements are the responsibility of the Hospital's management. Our responsibility is to express opinions[78] on these financial statements based on our audit.[79]

[*Same second paragraph as in Example A-1*]

In our opinion, the financial statements referred to above present fairly, in all material respects, the respective financial position of the University Hospital and of its discretely presented component unit as of December 31, 20XY, and the respective changes in financial position and cash flows thereof for the year then ended in conformity with accounting principles generally accepted in the United States of America.

[*Same disclaimer on MD&A as in Example A-1*]

[*Signature*]

[*Date*]

---

76 Presentation of a statement of cash flows for the discretely-presented component unit is not required.

77 See footnote 72.

78 Because two opinion units exist, the auditor is rendering two opinions (one on the Hospital and one on the discretely-presented component unit), and the report should refer to *opinions*, rather than *opinion*.

79 The opinion on a set of single-year statements refers to one audit. Even though the auditor may be expressing multiple opinions, he or she is conducting only one audit of the opinion units.

15.155

Appendix A—Cross-Reference Table for Predecessor Guidance

Governmental Accounting Standards Board (GASB) Statement No. 62, *Codification of Accounting and Financial Reporting Guidance Contained in Pre-November 30, 1989 FASB and AICPA Pronouncements*[1] directly incorporates into GASB's authoritative literature certain pronouncements issued by the Financial Accounting Standards Board (FASB) and its predecessors. Chapter 15 references those standards using the paragraph numbers in GASB Statement No. 62. As an interim measure, to facilitate the understanding of our readers, the following table includes the paragraphs from GASB Statement No. 62 that are cited in chapter 15 and the related predecessor guidance:

Topical Section of Chapter 15	*Paragraph in Chapter 15*	*Paragraph of GASB Statement No. 62*	*Predecessor Guidance*
Statement of Net Assets or Balance Sheet	15.14	29–44	Chapter 3 of Accounting Research Bulletin (ARB) No. 43, *Restatement and Revision of Accounting Research Bulletins*
Statement of Revenues, Expenses, and Changes in Net Assets	15.23	45–50	Paragraphs 19–25 of Accounting Principles Board (APB) Opinion No. 30, *Reporting the Results of Operations—Reporting the Effects of Disposal of a Segment of a Business, and Extraordinary, Unusual and Infrequently Occurring Events and Transactions*
	15.22	63–89	APB Opinion No. 20, *Accounting Changes*
Cash and Cash Equivalents	15.35	113	Paragraph 18 of FASB Statement No. 5, *Accounting for Contingencies*

[1] The requirements of Governmental Accounting Standards Board (GASB) Statement No. 62, *Codification of Accounting and Financial Reporting Guidance Contained in Pre-November 30, 1989 FASB and AICPA Pronouncements*, are effective for financial statements for periods beginning after December 15, 2011. Earlier application is encouraged. The provisions of GASB Statement No. 62 generally are required to be applied retroactively for all periods presented.

Topical Section of Chapter 15	*Paragraph in Chapter 15*	*Paragraph of GASB Statement No. 62*	*Predecessor Guidance*
Investments	15.38	202–210	APB Opinion No. 18, *The Equity Method of Accounting for Investments in Common Stock*
	15.39	202–210	APB Opinion No. 18
Financial Reporting and Disclosure	15.51	29–44	Chapter 3 of ARB No. 43
Capital Assets—General	15.61	45–50	Paragraphs 19–25 of APB Opinion No. 30
Leases	15.66	211–271	FASB Statement No. 13, *Accounting for Leases,* as amended and interpreted as of November 30, 1989
Disclosures	15.69	95	Paragraph 5 of APB Opinion No. 12, *Omnibus Opinion*
	15.69	223, 231, 239, 255–256, and 270	Paragraphs 16, 23, 29, and 47, as amended and interpreted as of November 30, 1989, of FASB Statement No. 13, *Accounting for Leases*; paragraphs 17–18 of FASB Statement 98, *Accounting for Leases: Sale-Leaseback Transactions Involving Real Estate, Sales-Type Leases of Real Estate, Definition of the Lease Term, and Initial Direct Costs of Direct Financing Leases—an amendment of FASB Statements No. 13, 66, and 91 and a rescission of FASB Statement No. 26 and Technical Bulletin No. 79-11*; and paragraph 11

(continued)

Topical Section of Chapter 15	*Paragraph in Chapter 15*	*Paragraph of GASB Statement No. 62*	*Predecessor Guidance*
			of GASB Statement No. 38, *Certain Financial Statement Note Disclosures*
Debt Defeasance and Extinguishment	15.76	124–127	Paragraphs 2–3 and 20 of APB Opinion No. 26, *Early Extinguishment of Debt*, as amended by paragraph 3 of FASB Statement No. 76, *Extinguishment of Debt—an amendment of APB Opinion No. 26*
	Footnote 35 to 15.76	128–148	FASB Statement No. 15, *Accounting by Debtors and Creditors for Troubled Debt Restructurings*
Capitalization of Interest Cost	15.77	19–20	Paragraphs 3–4 of FASB Statement No. 62, *Capitalization of Interest Cost in Situations Involving Certain Tax-Exempt Borrowings and Certain Gifts and Grants—an amendment of FASB Statement No. 34*
Retrospectively-Rated Policies and Contracts	15.82	96–113	FASB Statement No. 5 and FASB Interpretation No. 14, *Reasonable Estimation of the Amount of a Loss—an interpretation of FASB Statement No. 5*
Participation in Public-Entity Risk Pools	15.83	96–113	FASB Statement No. 5 and FASB Interpretation No. 14
Health Care Service Revenue and Receivables	15.110	90–94	APB Opinion No. 22, *Disclosure of Accounting Policies*
	15.110	33	Paragraph 15 of APB Opinion No. 12

15.156

Appendix B[1]—Interim Guidance for Entities That Elect Paragraph 7 of Governmental Accounting Standards Board Statement No. 20

Governmental Accounting Standards Board (GASB) Statement No. 62, *Codification of Accounting and Financial Reporting Guidance Contained in Pre-November 30, 1989 FASB and AICPA Pronouncements*,[2] supersedes the requirement of paragraph 17 of GASB Statement No. 34, *Basic Financial Statements—and Management's Discussion and Analysis—for State and Local Governments*. That paragraph required governmental health care entities that report as special-purpose governments engaged only in business-type activities to apply all GASB pronouncements and Financial Accounting Standards Board (FASB) Statements and Interpretations, Accounting Principles Board Opinions, Accounting Research Bulletins of the AICPA Committee on Accounting Procedure, and AICPA accounting interpretations issued on or before November 30, 1989, that do not conflict with or contradict GASB pronouncements. Until the implementation of GASB Statement No. 62, pronouncements issued on or before November 30, 1989, remain effective for governmental entities as amended to that date, even if they are superseded, amended, or interpreted by subsequent FASB pronouncements. GASB Statement No. 62 and its nonauthoritative basis for conclusions is useful in determining whether FASB pronouncements issued before November 30, 1989, conflict with or contradict GASB pronouncements.

GASB Statement No. 62 also eliminates the election provided in paragraph 7, as amended, of GASB Statement No. 20, *Accounting and Financial Reporting for Proprietary Funds and Other Governmental Entities That Use Proprietary Fund Accounting*. That election permitted governmental entities engaged in business-type activities to elect to apply all FASB Statements and Interpretations issued after November 30, 1989, that are applicable to private-sector business enterprises and that do not conflict with or contradict GASB pronouncements. Governmental entities that elect to apply post-1989 FASB pronouncements must apply them on an all or none basis (that is, they may not selectively choose certain pronouncements to apply). They also should apply superseding, amending, or interpreting FASB pronouncements, except for those that conflict with or contradict GASB pronouncements. Paragraph 115 of GASB Statement No. 34 requires disclosure in the summary of significant policies of the entity's policy for applying FASB pronouncements issued after November 30, 1989.

Although GASB Statement No. 62 is effective for financial statements for periods beginning after December 15, 2011, this guide has been updated to reflect the elimination of the election in paragraph 7 of GASB Statement No. 20. The purpose of this appendix is to assist entities that make the paragraph 7 election and have not yet implemented GASB Statement No. 62.

---

[1] The Governmental Accounting Standards Board (GASB) did not clear the guidance set forth in this appendix.

[2] The requirements of GASB Statement No. 62, *Codification of Accounting and Financial Reporting Guidance Contained in Pre-November 30, 1989 FASB and AICPA Pronouncements*, are effective for financial statements for periods beginning after December 15, 2011. Earlier application is encouraged. The provisions of GASB Statement No. 62 generally are required to be applied retroactively for all periods presented.

In addition, governmental entities can apply as other accounting literature post-November 30, 1989, FASB pronouncements that do not conflict with or contradict GASB pronouncements (see paragraph 15.09). This appendix may be useful to those entities is determining when FASB pronouncements conflict.

This appendix lists FASB pronouncements issued since November 30, 1989, and provides nonauthoritative guidance regarding the applicability of their accounting and reporting requirements to governmental health care entities that apply paragraph 7 of GASB Statement No. 20. This appendix will be removed from the guide when GASB Statement No. 62 is fully effective.

This appendix discusses the applicability of all FASB Statements and Interpretations issued after November 30, 1989. If a FASB Statement or Interpretation is not listed in this appendix, GASB has previously indicated that it contradicted or conflicted with GASB pronouncements. In addition, the FASB pronouncements on income tax, stock compensation, and earnings per share are not included in the appendix because their subject matter is typically not applicable to governmental entities.

Paragraph 33 in the nonauthoritative basis for conclusions of GASB Statement No. 20 also provided that AICPA pronouncements issued after November 30, 1989, and not specifically made applicable to governmental entities should be applied using the same logic used in the application of FASB pronouncements. Many of the AICPA pronouncements issued after November 30, 1989, provide guidance on specialized industries. Like the FASB pronouncements, they should be applied on an all or none basis. Readers should note these AICPA pronouncements in particular:

- Audit and Accounting Guide *Depository and Lending Institutions: Banks and Savings Institutions, Credit Unions, Finance Companies and Mortgage Companies*
- Statement of Position (SOP) 93-7, *Reporting on Advertising Costs*
- SOP 94-6, *Disclosure of Certain Significant Risks and Uncertainties*
- SOP 97-1, *Accounting by Participating Mortgage Loan Borrowers*
- SOP 97-3, *Accounting by Insurance and Other Enterprises for Insurance-Related Assessments*
- SOP 98-5, *Reporting on the Costs of Start-Up Activities*

FASB Pronouncements—Applicability Under Paragraph 7 of GASB Statement No. 20

FASB Statements Issued After November 30, 1989		*Apply?*
104	*Statement of Cash Flows—Net Reporting of Certain Cash Receipts and Cash Payments and Classification of Cash Flows from Hedging Transactions—an amendment of FASB Statement No. 95*	**Yes**—See paragraph 74 of GASB Statement No 9, *Reporting Cash Flows of Proprietary and Nonexpendable Trust Funds and Governmental Entities That Use Proprietary Fund Accounting.*

FASB Statements Issued After November 30, 1989		*Apply?*
107	*Disclosures about Fair Value of Financial Instruments*	**In Part**—GASB Statement No. 31, *Accounting and Financial Reporting for Certain Investments and for External Investment Pools*, requires many investments to be reported at fair value and provides related disclosures for investments within its scope. GASB Statement No. 51, *Accounting and Financial Reporting for Intangible Assets*, requires many derivatives to be reported at fair value.
111	*Rescission of FASB Statement No. 32 and Technical Corrections*	**Yes**—Except for corrections of standards that conflict with GASB standards (FASB Statement No. 14, *Financial Reporting for Segments of a Business Enterprise*, and No. 76, *Extinguishment of Debt—an amendment of APB Opinion No. 26*).
114	*Accounting by Creditors for Impairment of a Loan—an amendment of FASB Statements No. 5 and 15*	**Yes**
118	*Accounting for Creditors for Impairment of a Loan—Income Recognition and Disclosures—an amendment of FASB Statement No, 114*	**Yes**
126	*Exemption from Certain Required Disclosures about Financial Instruments for Certain Nonpublic Entities—an amendment of FASB Statement No. 107*	**In Part**—See preceding FASB Statement No. 107. The decision on whether to discontinue application of FASB Statement No. 107 should be based on the prevalent practice in the reporting entity's industry (for example, health care and so forth).
129	*Disclosure of Information about Capital Structure*	**Yes**—Paragraph 4 applies to debt issued.

(continued)

FASB Statements Issued After November 30, 1989		Apply?
135	*Rescission of FASB Statement No. 75 and Technical Corrections*	**Yes**—To the extent that it corrects currently applicable FASB pronouncements issued after November 30, 1989, that do not conflict with GASB standards and that it amends FASB Statement No. 35, *Accounting and Reporting by Defined Benefit Pension Plans*, and rescinds FASB Statement No. 75, *Deferral of the Effective Date of Certain Accounting Requirements for Pension Plans of State and Local Governmental Units—an amendment of FASB Statement No. 35*. For example, corrections to FASB Statement No. 87, *Employers' Accounting for Pensions*, and the standards noted in this table as conflicting would not apply.
139	*Rescission of FASB Statement No. 53 and amendments to FASB Statements No. 63, 89, and 121*	**Yes**
141 (revised 2007)	*Business Combinations*	**In Part**—Applies only to business combinations. (see paragraphs 3(d)–(e) of FASB Statement No. 141(R)). It does not apply to combinations of or acquisitions by not-for-profit organizations. Many governmental enterprises have similar characteristics. Applicable GASB Statements should be used in assigning amounts to assets acquired and liabilities assumed (for example, GASB Statement No. 13, *Accounting for Operating Leases with Scheduled Rent Increases*; No. 16, *Accounting for Compensated Absences*; No. 27, *Accounting for Pensions by State and Local Governmental Employers*; No. 31; and No. 45, *Accounting and Financial Reporting by Employers for Postemployment Benefits Other Than Pensions*).

FASB Statements Issued After November 30, 1989		Apply?
142	*Goodwill and Other Intangible Assets*	**In Part**—Apply GASB Statement No. 42, *Accounting and Financial Reporting for Impairment of Capital Assets and for Insurance Recoveries*, as amended by GASB Statement No. 51, *Accounting and Financial Reporting for Intangible Assets*, to impairment of tangible and intangible capital assets. Does not apply to intangibles acquired in combinations between not-for-profit organizations or arising from acquisition of a for-profit by a not-for-profit. Many governmental enterprises have similar characteristics.
143	*Accounting for Asset Retirement Obligations*	**In Part**—Does not apply to asset retirement obligations involving pollution remediation obligations within the scope of GASB Statement No. 49, *Accounting and Financial Reporting for Pollution Remediation Obligations*, such as asbestos removal obligations. Does not apply to other conditional obligations, unless probable of occurrence. (Paragraphs 9 and 14 of National Council on Governmental Accounting (NCGA) Statement No. 4, *Accounting and Financial Reporting Principles for Claims and Judgments and Compensated Absence*, as amended by GASB Statement No. 10, *Accounting and Financial Reporting for Risk Financing and Related Insurance Issues*, and No. 34, *Basic Financial Statements—and Management's Discussion and Analysis—for State and Local Governments*. Paragraph 69 of NCGA Statement No. 4 requires the application of FASB Statement No. 5, *Accounting for Contingencies*.)

(continued)

FASB Statements Issued After November 30, 1989		*Apply?*
144	*Accounting for the Impairment or Disposal of Long-Lived Assets*	**In Part**—Apply GASB Statement No. 42, as amended by GASB Statement No. 51, to the impairment of tangible and intangible capital assets. A separate display of net gain or loss from discontinued operations conflicts with GASB Statement No. 34.
145	*Rescission of FASB Statements No. 4, 44, and 64, Amendment of FASB Statement No. 13, and Technical Corrections*	**Yes**—To the extent that it amends currently applicable FASB pronouncements, except that paragraph 9(b) conflicts with paragraph 56 of GASB Statement No. 34, and paragraph 9(f)–(g) conflicts with GASB Statement Nos. 9 and 31. FASB Statement No. 4, *Reporting Gains and Losses from Extinguishment of Debt—an amendment of APB Opinion No. 30*, conflicted with paragraph 55 of GASB Statement No. 34.
146	*Accounting for Costs Associated with Exit or Disposal Activities*	**In Part**—Accounting for termination benefits should follow GASB Statement No. 47, *Accounting for Termination Benefits*. Apply nonconflicting sections, such as contract termination costs and employee relocation costs. The requirement in paragraph 18 for separate reporting of discontinued operations conflicts with the format required by GASB Statement No. 34.
147	*Acquisitions of Certain Financial Institutions—an amendment of FASB Statements No. 72 and 144 and FASB Interpretation No. 9*	**Yes**—Does not apply to transactions between mutual enterprises. Many governmental enterprises have similar characteristics. Apply GASB Statement No. 42, as amended by GASB Statement No. 51, to the impairment of tangible and intangible capital assets.
150	*Accounting for Certain Financial Instruments with Characteristics of both Liabilities and Equity*	**Yes**

FASB Statements Issued After November 30, 1989		*Apply?*
151	*Inventory Costs—an amendment of ARB No. 43, Chapter 4*	**Yes**
153	*Exchanges of Nonmonetary Assets—an amendment of APB Opinion No. 29*	**In Part**—FASB Statement No. 153 includes amendments to or related to other FASB pronouncements listed in this applicability table. Those amendments are applicable only to the extent that the related FASB pronouncement is applicable, as provided in this table.
157	*Fair Value Measurements*	**In Part**—Applies only when another applicable pronouncement requires measurement at fair value. Paragraphs 7 and 10–11 of GASB Statement No. 31 provide the primary guidance for measuring fair value for investments within its scope. Apply GASB Statement No. 53, *Accounting and Financial Reporting for Derivative Instruments*, to derivatives.
163	*Accounting for Financial Guarantee Insurance Contracts—an interpretation of FASB Statement No. 60*	**Yes**
FASB Interpretations Issued After November 30, 1989		*Apply?*
39	*Offsetting of Amounts Related to Certain Contracts—an interpretation of APB Opinion No. 10 and FASB Statement No. 105*	**In Part**—This interpretation does not apply to reinsurance transactions of public-entity risk pools, which are addressed in GASB Statement No. 10.
40	*Applicability of Generally Accepted Accounting Principles to Mutual Life Insurance and Other Enterprises—an interpretation of FASB Statements No. 12, 60, 97, and 113*	**Yes**
43	*Real Estate Sales—an interpretation of FASB Statement No. 66*	**Yes**

Appendix A

Statement of Position 99-1, Guidance to Practitioners in Conducting and Reporting on an Agreed-Upon Procedures Engagement to Assist Management in Evaluating the Effectiveness of Its Corporate Compliance Program

May 21, 1999

NOTE

This Statement of Position (SOP) is an interpretive publication and represents the recommendations of the AICPA Health Care Pilot Task Force of the AICPA Auditing Standards Board (ASB) regarding the application of Statements on Standards for Attestation Engagements to agreed-upon procedures attestation engagements performed to assist a health care provider in evaluating the effectiveness of its corporate compliance program consistent with the requirements of a Corporate Integrity Agreement entered into with the Office of Inspector General of the U.S. Department of Health and Human Services. The ASB has found the recommendations in this SOP to be consistent with existing standards covered by Rule 202, Compliance With Standards (AICPA, *Professional Standards*, vol. 2, ET sec. 202.01), of the AICPA Code of Professional Conduct.

Interpretive publications are not as authoritative as pronouncements of the ASB; however, if a practitioner does not apply the attestation guidance included in this SOP, the practitioner should be prepared to explain how he or she complied with the provisions of this SOP.

TABLE OF CONTENTS

Summary

This Statement of Position (SOP) provides guidance to practitioners in conducting and reporting on an agreed-upon procedures engagement performed pursuant to the AICPA Statements on Standards for Attestation Engagements to assist a health care provider in evaluating the effectiveness of its corporate compliance program consistent with the requirements of a Corporate Integrity Agreement (CIA) entered into with the Office of Inspector General (OIG) of the U.S. Department of Health and Human Services. CIAs are specific to the entity involved; consequently, users of this SOP should be familiar with the specific requirements of the entity's CIA.

Introduction and Background

.01 Within the past several years, the health care industry has experienced a significant increase in the number and magnitude of allegations of fraud and abuse involving federal health care programs (for example, Medicare and Medicaid) and private health care insurance. These allegations have triggered regulatory scrutiny, litigation, significant monetary settlements, and negative publicity related to—among other things—coding and billing practices, patient referrals, cost reporting, quality of care, and clinical practices. Typically, as part of the global resolution of these allegations, the entity enters into a Corporate Integrity Agreement (CIA) with the Office of Inspector General (OIG) of the U.S. Department of Health and Human Services. Such agreements require that management annually report on its compliance with the terms of the CIA and that there be an assessment of the entity's compliance with the CIA. This assessment includes a billing analysis, which may be performed by an independent review organization (such as a practitioner or consultant) or the provider (if permitted by the OIG), and an agreed-upon procedures engagement.

.02 This SOP provides guidance to practitioners in conducting and reporting on an agreed-upon procedures engagement performed pursuant to the American Institute of Certified Public Accountants (AICPA) Statements on Standards for Attestation Engagements (SSAEs) to assist an entity in evaluating the effectiveness of its corporate compliance program consistent with the requirements of a CIA.[1] The terms of a CIA are unique to the entity; consequently, users of this SOP need to be familiar with the actual CIA and its requirements.

.03 This SOP applies to agreed-upon procedures engagements to assist in evaluating an entity's compliance for a specified period. Such engagements should follow the AICPA attestation standards, including AT section 201, *Agreed-Upon Procedures Engagements* (AICPA, *Professional Standards*), and the applicable sections of AT section 101, *Attest Engagements*, and AT section 601, *Compliance Attestation* (AICPA, *Professional Standards*). The engagement should be conducted in accordance with standards established by the AICPA, including the criteria set forth in this SOP. However, this SOP is not intended to provide all the required criteria set forth in individual CIAs, nor all the applicable standards established by the AICPA. Additionally, the SOP contains some guidance that may be applied in evaluating an organization's corporate compliance program, even though the program was not imposed by a CIA.

Overview of a Typical Corporate Integrity Agreement

.04 A CIA is an agreement between a health care provider and the OIG in conjunction with a global settlement of a fraud investigation. Such an agreement typically seeks to establish a compliance program within the health care

---

[1] The practitioner also might be engaged to assist in other areas beyond an agreed-upon procedures engagement such as providing consulting services in connection with evaluating the company's billing practices, policies, and procedures as required by the CIA or in implementing, assessing, and reporting on voluntarily adopted compliance programs. In addition, the practitioner may assist in preparing an entity's self-disclosure reports to federal health agencies related to billing errors and other compliance matters. Similarly, practitioners may be involved in an entity's preparation of government-required (but not CIA-imposed) compliance reporting (for example, contract requirements for Medicare part C) beyond an agreed-upon procedures engagement.

provider (for example, hospital, clinical lab, physician group) that will promote compliance with the requirements of Medicare, Medicaid, and all other federal health care programs.

.05 CIAs are case-specific. Their terms are tailored to address the organizational and operating deficiencies related to providing and billing for health care services that have been identified by the OIG, the entity, or others. Detailed compliance requirements are imposed as a condition for continued participation in federal health care programs. A sample CIA, provided by the OIG and intended to identify potential requirements, is included in appendix A [paragraph .32], "Sample Corporate Integrity Agreement." Typical agreements cover five years and require the entity to address the following areas:

- Appointment of a compliance officer and establishment of a compliance committee
- Establishment of a code of conduct
- Establishment of policies and procedures regarding the compliance program
- Development of an information and education program as to the CIA requirements, compliance program and code of conduct
- Annual assessment of billing policies, procedures, and practices
- Establishment of a confidential disclosure program
- Prohibition of employment of excluded or convicted persons
- Notification to OIG of investigation or legal proceedings
- Reporting of credible evidence of misconduct
- Notifications to OIG of new provider locations
- Provision of implementation and annual reports
- Proper notification and submission of required reports
- Granting of OIG access to documents and individuals to conduct assessments
- Documentation of record retention requirements
- Awareness of disclosure criteria
- Agreement to comply with certain default provisions, penalties, and remedies
- Review of rights as to dispute resolution
- Review of effective and binding agreement clauses

Conditions for Engagement Performance

.06 A practitioner may perform an agreed-upon procedures engagement related to management's compliance with a CIA if all of the conditions specified in AT sections 201 and 601 are met.

.07 As discussed more fully in the AT sections identified in paragraph .06, management's assertions as to its compliance must be capable of evaluation against reasonable criteria that either have been established by a recognized body or are stated in or attached to the practitioner's report in a sufficiently clear and comprehensive manner. Generally, to avoid confusion, management's assertions, which are based on the specific terms of its CIA, should be attached to the practitioner's report. If the entity is not required to have a CIA, management may develop its assertions using the model CIA. A sample based on the model CIA, which is not meant to be all-inclusive, is included as appendix B (paragraph .33), "Sample Statement of Management's Assertions." [Revised, June 2009, to reflect conforming changes necessary due to the issuance of recent authoritative literature.]

Establishing an Understanding With the Client

.08 The practitioner should document the understanding in the working papers, preferably through a written communication with the client, such as an engagement letter. Appendix C [paragraph .34], "Sample Engagement Letter," contains a sample engagement letter that may be used for this kind of engagement.

Responsibilities of Specified Parties

.09 AT section 201 identifies the users of an agreed-upon procedures report as specified parties. The specified parties to the agreed upon procedures report described in this SOP typically would be the management of the health care provider and the OIG. Management is responsible for ensuring that the entity complies with the requirements of the CIA. That responsibility encompasses (*a*) identifying applicable compliance requirements, (*b*) establishing and maintaining internal control policies and procedures to provide reasonable assurance that the entity complies with those requirements, (*c*) evaluating and monitoring the entity's compliance, and (*d*) preparing reports that satisfy legal, regulatory, or contractual requirements. Management's evaluation may include documentation such as accounting or statistical data, policy manuals, accounting manuals, narrative memoranda, procedural write-ups, flowcharts, completed questionnaires, internal auditors' reports, and other special studies or analyses. The form and extent of documentation will vary depending on the nature of the compliance requirements and the size and complexity of the entity. Management may engage the practitioner to gather information to assist it in evaluating the entity's compliance. Regardless of the procedures performed by the practitioner, management must accept responsibility for its assertions and must not base such assertions solely on the practitioner's procedures. [Revised, June 2009, to reflect conforming changes necessary due to the issuance of recent authoritative literature.]

.10 The specified parties are responsible for the sufficiency (nature, timing, and extent) of the agreed-upon procedures because they best understand their own needs. The specified parties assume the risk that such procedures might be insufficient for their purposes. In addition, the specified parties assume the risk that they might misunderstand or otherwise inappropriately use findings properly reported by the practitioner. Use of an agreed-upon procedures report is restricted to the specified parties. [Revised, June 2009, to reflect conforming changes necessary due to the issuance of recent authoritative literature.]

Practitioner's Responsibilities

.11 The objective of the practitioner's agreed-upon procedures is to present specific findings to assist the specified parties in evaluating an entity's compliance with the requirements specified in the CIA. (See appendix D [paragraph .35], "Sample Procedures.") [Revised, June 2009, to reflect conforming changes necessary due to the issuance of recent authoritative literature.]

.12 The practitioner's procedures generally may be as limited or extensive as the specified parties desire, as long as the specified parties s agree upon the procedures performed or to be performed and take responsibility for the sufficiency of the agreed-upon procedures for their purposes. [Revised, June 2009, to reflect conforming changes necessary due to the issuance of recent authoritative literature.]

.13 To satisfy the requirements that the practitioner and the specified parties agree upon the procedures performed or to be performed and that the specified parties take responsibility for the sufficiency of the agreed-upon procedures for their purposes, ordinarily the practitioner should communicate directly with and obtain affirmative acknowledgment from each of the specified parties. For the purposes of these engagements, an effective way to obtain this agreement ordinarily is to distribute a draft of the report, detailing the procedures, that is expected to be issued to the OIG with a request for any comments it may have. [Revised, June 2009, to reflect conforming changes necessary due to the issuance of recent authoritative literature.]

.14 To avoid possible misunderstandings, the practitioner should circulate the draft with a legend stating that these are the procedures expected to be performed, and unless informed otherwise, the practitioner assumes that there are no additional procedures that he or she is expected to perform. A legend such as the following might be used.

> This draft is furnished solely for the purpose of indicating the form of report that we would expect to be able to furnish pursuant to the request by Management of [*Provider*] for our performance of limited procedures relating to [*Provider's*] compliance with the Corporate Integrity Agreement with the Office of Inspector General (OIG) of the U.S. Department of Health and Human Services. Based on our discussions with [*Provider*], it is our understanding that the procedures outlined in this draft report are those we are expected to follow. Unless informed otherwise within ninety (90) days of this transmittal, we shall assume that there are no additional procedures that we are expected to follow. The text of the definitive report will depend, of course, on the results of the procedures.

Involvement of a Specialist[2]

.15 The practitioner's education and experience enable him or her to be knowledgeable about business matters in general, but he or she is not expected to have the expertise of a person trained for or qualified to engage in the practice of another profession or occupation. In certain circumstances, it may be appropriate to involve a specialist to assist the practitioner in the performance of one or more procedures. The following are examples:

---

[2] A *specialist* is a person (or firm) possessing special skill or knowledge in a particular field other than the attest function. As used herein, a specialist does not include a person employed by the practitioner's firm who participates in the attestation engagement.

- An attorney might provide assistance concerning the application of laws, regulations, or rules to a client's situation.
- A medical specialist might provide assistance in understanding the characteristics of diagnosis codes documented in patient medical records.

.16 The practitioner and the specified parties should agree to the involvement of a specialist in assisting a practitioner in the performance of an agreed-upon procedures engagement. This agreement may be reached when obtaining agreement on the procedures performed or to be performed and acknowledgment of responsibility for the sufficiency of the procedures, as discussed previously. The practitioner's report should describe the nature of the assistance provided by the specialist. [Revised, June 2009, to reflect conforming changes necessary due to the issuance of recent authoritative literature.]

.17 A practitioner may agree to apply procedures to the report or work product of a specialist that does not constitute assistance by the specialist to the practitioner in an agreed-upon procedures engagement. For example, the practitioner may make reference to information contained in a report of a specialist in describing an agreed-upon procedure. However, it is inappropriate for the practitioner to agree to merely read the specialist's report solely to describe or repeat the findings, or to take responsibility for all or a portion of any procedures performed by a specialist or the specialist's work product.

Internal Auditors and Other Personnel[3]

.18 The agreed-upon procedures to be enumerated or referred to in the practitioner's report are to be performed entirely by the practitioner except as discussed in paragraphs .16–.18 of this SOP. However, internal auditors or other personnel may prepare schedules, accumulate data, perform an internal assessment of management's compliance, or provide other information for the practitioner's use in performing the agreed-upon procedures.

.19 A practitioner may agree to perform procedures on information documented in the working papers of internal auditors. For example, the practitioner may agree to—

- Repeat all or some of the procedures.
- Determine whether the internal auditors' working papers contain documentation of procedures performed and whether the findings documented in the working papers are presented in a report by the internal auditors.

.20 However, it is inappropriate for the practitioner to—

- Agree to merely read the internal auditor's report solely to describe or repeat its findings.
- Take responsibility for all or a portion of any procedures performed by internal auditors by reporting those findings as the practitioner's own.
- Report in any manner that implies shared responsibility for the procedures with the internal auditors.

---

[3] AU sec. 322, *The Auditor's Consideration of the Internal Audit Function in an Audit of Financial Statements* (AICPA, *Professional Standards*), does not apply to agreed-upon procedures engagements.

Planning the Engagement

.21 Planning an agreed-upon procedures engagement involves working with the specified parties to develop an overall strategy for the expected conduct and scope of the engagement. To develop such a strategy, practitioners should have adequate technical training and proficiency in the attestation standards and have adequate knowledge in health care regulatory matters to enable them to sufficiently understand the events, transactions, and practices that, in their judgment, have a significant effect on the presentation of the assertions. [Revised, June 2009, to reflect conforming changes necessary due to the issuance of recent authoritative literature.]

Documentation

.22 The practitioner should prepare and maintain attest documentation, the form and content of which should be designed to meet the circumstances of the particular attest engagement. Attest documentation is the principal record of attest procedures applied, information obtained, and conclusions or findings reached by the practitioner in the engagement. The quantity, type, and content of attest documentation are matters of the practitioner's professional judgment and are discussed in paragraphs .100–.103 of AT section 101. Paragraphs .104–.107 of AT section 101 present further requirements and guidance regarding attest documentation. [Revised, June 2009, to reflect conforming changes necessary due to the issuance of recent authoritative literature.]

.23 Concern over access to the practitioner's documentation might cause some clients to inquire about documentation requirements. In situations where the practitioner is requested to not maintain copies of certain client documentation, or to not prepare and maintain documentation similar to client documents, the practitioner may refer to the Auditing Interpretation No. 3, "The Auditor's Consideration of the Completeness Assertion," of AU section 326, Audit Evidence (AICPA, Professional Standards, AU sec. 9326.24–.27), for guidance. See Attestation Interpretation No. 4, "Providing Access to or Copies of Attest Documentation to a Regulator," of AT section 101 (AICPA, Professional Standards, AT sec. 9101.43–.46) for guidance related to providing access to or copies of attest documentation to a regulator in connection with work performed on an attestation engagement. [Revised, June 2009, to reflect conforming changes necessary due to the issuance of recent authoritative literature.]

Management's Representations

.24 The practitioner should obtain written representation from management on various matters including the following:

a. Acknowledging management's responsibility for complying with the CIA

b. Acknowledging management's responsibility for establishing and maintaining effective internal control over compliance

c. Stating that management has performed an evaluation of the entity's compliance with CIA-specified requirements *d.* Stating management's assertions about the entity's compliance with all aspects of the CIA, including the specific issues that gave rise to the CIA[4,5]

e. Stating that management has disclosed to the practitioner all known noncompliance with the CIA

f. Stating that management has made available all documentation relating to compliance with the CIA

g. Stating management's interpretation of any compliance requirements that have varying interpretations

h. Stating that management has disclosed any communication from regulatory agencies, internal auditors, legal counsel, and other parties concerning matters regarding the design, implementation, and monitoring of the policies and procedures in place, including communication received between the end of the reporting period and the date of the practitioner's report (the date of signature)

i. Stating that management has disclosed any known noncompliance occurring subsequent to the end of the reporting period

j. Describing any related material fraud or abuse, other fraud, abuse or illegal acts that, whether or not material, involve management or other employees who have a significant role in the entity's design, implementation, and monitoring of the policies and procedures in place upon which compliance is based

k. Stating that management has disclosed to the practitioners, orally or in writing, information about past noncompliance issues covered in the settlement agreement that gave rise to the CIA and the related corrective measures taken to support compliance in those areas

Management's refusal to furnish all appropriate written representations constitutes a limitation on the scope of the engagement sufficient to require withdrawal from the engagement.[6]

Reporting Considerations

.25 A practitioner should present the results of applying agreed-upon procedures to the specific subject matter in the form of findings. The practitioner

---

[4] Footnote 21 in paragraph .100 of AT section 101, *Attest Engagements* (AICPA, *Professional Standards*), indicates that attest documentation may also be referred to as working papers. [Footnote added, June 2009, to reflect conforming changes necessary due to the issuance of recent authoritative literature.]

[5] Depending on the circumstances, representations in the following areas might be appropriate.

- Violations or possible violations of laws or regulations, such as those related to the Medicare and Medicaid antifraud and abuse statutes
- Compliance of third-party billings with applicable coding guidelines (for example, ICD-9-CM, CPT) and laws and regulations (including medical necessity, proper approvals, and proper rendering of care)
- Proper filing of all required Medicare, Medicaid, and similar reports under the applicable reimbursement rules and regulations (including nature of costs—allowable, patient-related, properly allocated, in accordance with applicable rules and regulations, properly adjusted to reflect prior audit adjustments) and adequacy of disclosures (including disputed costs) [Footnote renumbered, June 2009, to reflect conforming changes necessary due to the issuance of recent authoritative literature.]

[6] See paragraph .62 of AT section 101. [Footnote added, June 2009, to reflect conforming changes necessary due to the issuance of recent authoritative literature.]

should not provide negative assurance about whether the assertion is fairly stated in accordance with established or stated criteria. For example, the practitioner should not include a statement that "nothing came to my attention that caused me to believe that the assertion is not fairly stated in accordance with (established or stated) criteria."

.26 The practitioner should report all findings from the application of the agreed-upon procedures. The concept of materiality does not apply to findings to be reported in an agreed-upon procedures engagement unless the definition of materiality is agreed to by the specified parties. Any agreed-upon materiality limits should be described in the practitioner's report. [Revised, June 2009, to reflect conforming changes necessary due to the issuance of recent authoritative literature.]

.27 The practitioner has no obligation to perform procedures beyond the agreed-upon procedures. However, if noncompliance related to management's assertion comes to the practitioner's attention by other means, such information ordinarily should be included in his or her report.

.28 The practitioner may become aware of noncompliance related to management's assertion that occurs subsequent to the reporting period but before the date of the practitioner's report. The practitioner should consider including information regarding such noncompliance in his or her report. However, the practitioner has no responsibility to perform procedures to detect such noncompliance other than obtaining management's representation about noncompliance in the subsequent period.

.29 practitioner should follow the reporting guidance in AT section 201. A sample report is included in appendix E (paragraph .36), "Sample Report."

.30 Evaluating compliance with certain requirements may require interpretation of the laws, regulations, rules, contracts, or other agreements that establish those requirements. In such situations, the practitioner should consider whether he or she is provided with the reasonable criteria required to evaluate an assertion under the third general attestation standard. If these interpretations are significant, the practitioner may include a paragraph stating the description and the source of interpretations made by the entity's management. An example of such a paragraph, which should precede the procedures and findings paragraph(s), follows:

> We have been informed that, under [*name of entity's*] interpretation of [*identify the compliance requirement*], [*explain the nature and source of the relevant interpretation*].

.31 The date of completion of the agreed-upon procedures should be used as the date of the practitioner's report.

.32

Appendix A

Sample Corporate Integrity Agreement Between the Office of Inspector General of the Department of Health and Human Services and [*Provider*]

I. Preamble

[*Provider*] ("[*Provider*]") hereby enters into this Corporate Integrity Agreement ("CIA") with the Office of Inspector General ("OIG") of the United States Department of Health and Human Services ("HHS") to ensure compliance by its employees with the requirements of Medicare, Medicaid and all other Federal health care programs (as defined in 42 U.S.C. 1320a-7b(f)) (hereinafter collectively referred to as the "Federal health care programs"). [*Provider's*] compliance with the terms and conditions in this CIA shall constitute an element of [*Provider's*] present responsibility with regard to participation in the Federal health care programs. Contemporaneously with this CIA, [*Provider*] is entering into a Settlement Agreement with the United States, and this CIA is incorporated by reference into the Settlement Agreement.

II. Term of the CIA

The period of the compliance obligations assumed by [*Provider*] under this CIA shall be 5 years from the effective date of this CIA (unless otherwise specified). The effective date of this CIA will be the date on which the final signatory of this CIA executes this CIA (the "effective date").*

III. Corporate Integrity Obligations

[*Provider*] shall establish a compliance program that includes the following elements:

A. *Compliance Officer*

Within ninety (90) days after the effective date of this CIA, [*Provider*] shall appoint an individual to serve as Compliance Officer, who shall be responsible for developing and implementing policies, procedures, and practices designed to ensure compliance with the requirements set forth in this CIA and with the requirements of the Federal health care programs. The Compliance Officer shall be a member of senior management of [*Provider*], shall make regular (at least quarterly) reports regarding compliance matters directly to the CEO and/or to the Board of Directors of [*Provider*] and shall be authorized to report to the Board of Directors at any time. The Compliance Officer shall be responsible for monitoring the day-to-day activities engaged in by [*Provider*] to further its compliance objectives as well as any reporting obligations created under this CIA. In the event a new Compliance Officer is appointed during the term of this CIA, [*Provider*] shall notify the OIG, in writing, within fifteen (15) days of such a change.

[*Provider*] shall also appoint a Compliance Committee within ninety (90) days after the effective date of this CIA. The Compliance Committee shall, at a minimum, include the Compliance Officer and any other

---

* *Source:* Office of the Inspector General of the United States Department of Health and Human Services.

appropriate officers as necessary to meet the requirements of this CIA within the provider's corporate structure (e.g., senior executives of each major department, such as billing, clinical, human resources, audit, and operations). The Compliance Officer shall chair the Compliance Committee and the Committee shall support the Compliance Officer in fulfilling his/her responsibilities.

B. Written Standards

1. *Code of Conduct.* Within ninety (90) days of the effective date of this CIA, [*Provider*] shall establish a Code of Conduct. The Code of Conduct shall be distributed to all employees within ninety (90) days of the effective date of this CIA. [*Provider*] shall make the promotion of, and adherence to, the Code of Conduct an element in evaluating the performance of managers, supervisors, and all other employees. The Code of Conduct shall, at a minimum, set forth:

   a. [*Provider's*] commitment to full compliance with all statutes, regulations, and guidelines applicable to Federal health care programs, including its commitment to prepare and submit accurate billings consistent with Federal health care program regulations and procedures or instructions otherwise communicated by the Health Care Financing Administration ("HCFA") (or other appropriate regulatory agencies) and/or its agents;

   b. [*Provider's*] requirement that all of its employees shall be expected to comply with all statutes, regulations, and guidelines applicable to Federal health care programs and with [*Provider's*] own policies and procedures (including the requirements of this CIA);

   c. the requirement that all of [*Provider's*] employees shall be expected to report suspected violations of any statute, regulation, or guideline applicable to Federal health care programs or with [*Provider's*] own policies and procedures;

   d. the possible consequences to both [*Provider*] and to any employee of failure to comply with all statutes, regulations, and guidelines applicable to Federal health care programs and with [*Provider's*] own policies and procedures or of failure to report such non-compliance; and

   e. the right of all employees to use the confidential disclosure program, as well as [*Provider's*] commitment to confidentiality and non-retaliation with respect to disclosures.

   Within ninety (90) days of the effective date of the CIA, each employee shall certify, in writing, that he or she has received, read, understands, and will abide by [*Provider's*] Code of Conduct. New employees shall receive the Code of Conduct and shall complete the required certification within two (2) weeks after the commencement of their employment or within ninety (90) days of the effective date of the CIA, whichever is later.

   [*Provider*] will annually review the Code of Conduct and will make any necessary revisions. These revisions shall be distributed within thirty (30) days of initiating such a change. Employees shall certify on an annual basis that they have received, read, understand and will abide by the Code of Conduct.

2. *Policies and Procedures.* Within ninety (90) days of the effective date of this CIA, [*Provider*] shall develop and initiate implementation of written Policies and Procedures regarding the operation of [*Provider's*] compliance program and its compliance with all federal and state health care statutes, regulations, and guidelines, including the requirements of the Federal health care programs. At a minimum, the Policies and Procedures shall specifically address [*insert language relevant to allegations in the case*]. In addition, the Policies and Procedures shall include disciplinary guidelines and methods for employees to make disclosures or otherwise report on compliance issues to [*Provider*] management through the Confidential Disclosure Program required by section III.E. [*Provider*] shall assess and update as necessary the Policies and Procedures at least annually and more frequently, as appropriate. A summary of the Policies and Procedures will be provided to OIG in the Implementation Report. The Policies and Procedures will be available to OIG upon request.

   Within ninety (90) days of the effective date of the CIA, the relevant portions of the Policies and Procedures shall be distributed to all appropriate employees. Compliance staff or supervisors should be available to explain any and all policies and procedures.

C. *Training and Education*

1. *General Training.* Within ninety (90) days of the effective date of this CIA, [*Provider*] shall provide at least two (2) hours of training to each employee. This general training shall explain [*Provider's*]:
   - *a.* Corporate Integrity Agreement requirements;
   - *b.* Compliance Program (including the Policies and Procedures as they pertain to general compliance issues); and
   - *c.* Code of Conduct.

   These training materials shall be made available to the OIG, upon request.

   New employees shall receive the general training described above within thirty (30) days of the beginning of their employment or within ninety (90) days after the effective date of this CIA, whichever is later. Each year, every employee shall receive such general training on an annual basis.

2. *Specific Training.* Within ninety (90) days of the effective date of this CIA, each employee who is involved directly or indirectly in the delivery of patient care and/or in the preparation or submission of claims for reimbursement for such care (including, but not limited to, coding and billing) for any Federal health care programs shall receive at least [*insert number of training hours*] hours of training in addition to the general training required above. This training shall include a discussion of:
   - *a.* the submission of accurate bills for services rendered to Medicare and/or Medicaid patients;
   - *b.* policies, procedures and other requirements applicable to the documentation of medical records;
   - *c.* the personal obligation of each individual involved in the billing process to ensure that such billings are accurate;

d. applicable reimbursement rules and statutes;

e. the legal sanctions for improper billings; and

f. examples of proper and improper billing practices.

These training materials shall be made available to OIG, upon request. Persons providing the training must be knowledgeable about the subject area.

Affected new employees shall receive this training within thirty (30) days of the beginning of their employment or within ninety (90) days of the effective date of this CIA, whichever is later. If a new employee has any responsibility for the delivery of patient care, the preparation or submission of claims and/or the assignment of procedure codes prior to completing this specific training, a [*Provider*] employee who has completed the substantive training shall review all of the untrained person's work regarding the assignment of billing codes.

Each year, every employee shall receive such specific training on an annual basis.

3. *Certification.* Each employee shall certify, in writing, that he or she has attended the required training. The certification shall specify the type of training received and the date received. The Compliance Officer shall retain the certifications, along with specific course materials. These shall be made available to OIG upon request.

D. Review Procedures

[*Provider*] shall retain an entity, such as an accounting, auditing or consulting firm (hereinafter "Independent Review Organization"), to perform review procedures to assist [*Provider*] in assessing the adequacy of its billing and compliance practices pursuant to this CIA. This shall be an annual requirement and shall cover a twelve (12) month period. The Independent Review Organization must have expertise in the billing, coding, reporting and other requirements of the Federal health care programs from which [*Provider*] seeks reimbursement. The Independent Review Organization must be retained to conduct the assessment of the first year within ninety (90) days of the effective date of this CIA. For purposes of complying with this review procedures requirement, the OIG at its discretion, may permit the [*Provider*] to utilize internal auditors to perform the review(s). In such case, the [*Provider*] will engage the Independent Review Organization to verify the propriety of the internal auditors' methods and accuracy of their results. The [*Provider*] will request the Independent Review Organization to produce a report on its findings which report shall be included in the Annual Report to the OIG.

The Independent Review Organization (or the [*Provider*], if permitted by the OIG, as set forth above) will conduct two separate engagements. One will be an analysis of [*Provider's*] billing to the Federal health care programs to assist the [*Provider*] and OIG in determining compliance with all applicable statutes, regulations, and directives/guidance ("billing engagement"). The second engagement will assist the [*Provider*] and OIG in determining whether [*Provider*] is in compliance with this CIA ("compliance engagement").

1. *Billing Engagement.* The billing engagement shall consist of a review of a statistically valid sample of claims for the relevant period. The sample size shall be determined through the use of a probe sample.[1] At a minimum, the full sample must be within a ninety (90) percent confidence level and a precision of twenty-five (25) percent. The probe sample must contain at least thirty (30) sample units and cannot be used as part of the full sample. Both the probe sample and the sample must be selected through random numbers. [*Provider*] shall use OIG's Office of Audit Services Statistical Sampling Software, also known as "RAT-STATS", which is available through the Internet at www.hhs.gov/progorg/ratstat.html.

   Each annual billing engagement analysis shall include the following components in its methodology:

   a. Billing Engagement Objective: Provide a statement stating clearly the objective intended to be achieved by the billing engagement and the procedure or combination of procedures that will be applied to achieve the objective.

   b. Billing Engagement Population: Identify the population, which is the group about which information is needed. Explain the methodology used to develop the population and provide the basis for this determination.

   c. Sources of Data: Provide a full description of the source of the information upon which the billing engagement conclusions will be based, including the legal or other standards applied, documents relied upon, payment data, and/or any contractual obligations.

   d. Sampling Unit: Define the sampling unit, which is any of the designated elements that comprise the population of interest.

   e. Sampling Frame: Identify the sampling frame, which is the totality of the sampling units from which the sample will be selected.

   As part of the billing engagement:

   a. Inquire of management as to the procedures and controls affecting the billing process subject to the annual assessment as specified in the CIA. Document that aspect of the billing process (e.g., flow of documents, processing activities), and those controls that will be tested in the sample. The documentation may consist of flow charts, excerpts from policies and procedures manuals, control questionnaires, etc.

   b. Report the sample results, including the overall error rate and the nature of the errors found (e.g., no documentation, inadequate documentation, assignment of incorrect code).

   c. Document findings related to [*Provider's*] procedures to correct inaccurate billings and codings to the Federal health care programs and findings regarding the steps

[1] Probe sample is defined as a small, random preliminary sample.

[*Provider*] is taking to bring its operations into compliance or to correct problems identified by the audit.

2. *Agreed-upon Procedures or Compliance Engagement.* An Independent Review Organization (or the [*Provider*], if permitted by the OIG) shall also conduct an agreed-upon procedures or compliance engagement, which shall assist the users in determining whether [*Provider's*] program, policies, procedures, and operations comply with the terms of this CIA. This engagement shall include a section by section analysis of the requirements of this CIA.

   A complete copy of the Independent Review Organization's billing and agreed-upon procedures or compliance engagement shall be included in each of [*Provider's*] Annual Reports to OIG.

3. *Disclosure of Overpayments and Material Deficiencies.* If, as a result of these engagements, [*Provider*] or the Independent Review Organization identifies any billing, coding or other policies, procedures and/or practices that result in an overpayment, [*Provider*] shall notify the payor (e.g., Medicare fiscal intermediary or carrier) within 30 days of discovering the deficiency or overpayment and take remedial steps within 60 days of discovery (or such additional time as may be agreed to by the payor) to correct the problem, including preventing the deficiency from recurring. The notice to the payor shall include:

   a. a statement that the refund is being made pursuant to this CIA;

   b. a description of the complete circumstances surrounding the overpayment;

   c. the methodology by which the overpayment was determined;

   d. the amount of the overpayment;

   e. any claim-specific information used to determine the overpayment (e.g., beneficiary health insurance number, claim number, service date, and payment date);

   f. the cost reporting period; and

   g. the provider identification number under which the repayment is being made.

   If [*Provider*] determines an overpayment represents a material deficiency, contemporaneous with [*Provider's*] notification to the payor as provided above, [*Provider*] shall also notify OIG of:

   a. a complete description of the material deficiency;

   b. amount of overpayment due to the material deficiency;

   c. [*Provider's*] action(s) to correct and prevent such material deficiency from recurring;

   d. the payor's name, address, and contact person where the overpayment was sent;

   e. the date of the check and identification number (or electronic transaction number) on which the overpayment was repaid.

For purposes of this CIA, an "overpayment" shall mean the amount of money the provider has received in excess of the amount due and payable under the Federal health care programs' statutes, regulations or program directives, including carrier and intermediary instructions.

For purposes of this CIA, a "material deficiency" shall mean anything that involves: (i) a substantial overpayment or improper payment relating to the Medicare and/or Medicaid programs; (ii) conduct or policies that clearly violate the Medicare and/or Medicaid statute, regulations or directives issued by HCFA and/or its agents; or (iii) serious quality of care implications for federal health care beneficiaries or recipients. A material deficiency may be the result of an isolated event or a series of occurrences.

4. *Verification / Validation.* In the event that the OIG determines that it is necessary to conduct an independent review to determine whether or the extent to which [*Provider*] is complying with its obligations under this CIA, [*Provider*] agrees to pay for the reasonable cost of any such review or engagement by the OIG or any of its designated agents.

E. Confidential Disclosure Program

Within ninety (90) days after the effective date of this CIA, [*Provider*] shall establish a Confidential Disclosure Program, which must include measures (e.g., a toll-free compliance telephone line) to enable employees, contractors, agents or other individuals to disclose, to the Compliance Officer or some other person who is not in the reporting individual's chain of command, any identified issues or questions associated with [*Provider's*] policies, practices or procedures with respect to the Federal health care program, believed by the individual to be inappropriate. [*Provider*] shall publicize the existence of the hotline (e.g., e-mail to employees or post hotline number in prominent common areas).

The Confidential Disclosure Program shall emphasize a non-retribution, non-retaliation policy, and shall include a reporting mechanism for anonymous, confidential communication. Upon receipt of a complaint, the Compliance Officer (or designee) shall gather the information in such a way as to elicit all relevant information from the individual reporting the alleged misconduct. The Compliance Officer (or designee) shall make a preliminary good faith inquiry into the allegations set forth in every disclosure to ensure that he or she has obtained all of the information necessary to determine whether a further review should be conducted. For any disclosure that is sufficiently specific so that it reasonably: (1) permits a determination of the appropriateness of the alleged improper practice, and (2) provides an opportunity for taking corrective action, [*Provider*] shall conduct an internal review of the allegations set forth in such a disclosure and ensure that proper follow-up is conducted.

The Compliance Officer shall maintain a confidential disclosure log, which shall include a record and summary of each allegation received, the status of the respective investigations, and any corrective action taken in response to the investigation.

F. *Ineligible Persons*

[*Provider*] shall not hire or engage as contractors any "Ineligible Person." For purposes of this CIA, an "Ineligible Person" shall be any individual or entity who: (i) is currently excluded, suspended, debarred or otherwise ineligible to participate in the Federal health care programs; or (ii) has been convicted of a criminal offense related to the provision of health care items or services and has not been reinstated in the Federal health care programs after a period of exclusion, suspension, debarment, or ineligibility.

Within ninety (90) days of the effective date of this CIA, [*Provider*] will review its list of current employees and contractors against the General Services Administration's List of Parties Excluded from Federal Programs (available through the Internet at http://www.arnet.gov/epls) and the HHS/OIG Cumulative Sanction Report (available through the Internet at http://www.dhhs.gov/progorg/oig) to ensure that it is not currently employing or contracting with any Ineligible Person. Thereafter, [*Provider*] will review the list once semiannually to ensure that no current employees or contractors are or have become Ineligible Persons.

To prevent hiring or contracting with any Ineligible Person, [*Provider*] shall screen all prospective employees and prospective contractors prior to engaging their services by (i) requiring applicants to disclose whether they are Ineligible Persons, and (ii) reviewing the General Services Administration's List of Parties Excluded from Federal Programs (available through the Internet at http://www.arnet.gov/epls) and the HHS/OIG Cumulative Sanction Report (available through the Internet at http://www.dhhs.gov/progorg/oig).

If [*Provider*] has notice that an employee or agent is charged with a criminal offense related to any Federal health care program, or is suspended or proposed for exclusion during his or her employment or contract with [*Provider*], within 10 days of receiving such notice [*Provider*] will remove such employee from responsibility for, or involvement with, [*Provider's*] business operations related to the Federal health care programs until the resolution of such criminal action, suspension, or proposed exclusion. If [*Provider*] has notice that an employee or agent has become an Ineligible Person, [*Provider*] will remove such person from responsibility for, or involvement with, [*Provider's*] business operations related to the Federal health care programs and shall remove such person from any position for which the person's salary or the items or services rendered, ordered, or prescribed by the person are paid in whole or in part, directly or indirectly, by Federal health care programs or otherwise with Federal funds at least until such time as the person is reinstated into participation in the Federal health care programs.

G. *Notification of Proceedings*

Within thirty (30) days of discovery, [*Provider*] shall notify OIG, in writing, of any ongoing investigation or legal proceeding conducted or brought by a governmental entity or its agents involving an allegation that [*Provider*] has committed a crime or has engaged in fraudulent activities or any other knowing misconduct. This notification shall include a description of the allegation, the identity of the investigating or prosecuting agency, and the status of such investigation or legal proceeding. [*Provider*] shall also provide written notice to OIG within thirty (30) days of the resolution of the matter, and shall provide OIG with a description of the findings and/or results of the proceedings, if any.

H. Reporting

1. *Credible evidence of misconduct.* If [*Provider*] discovers credible evidence of misconduct from any source and, after reasonable inquiry, has reason to believe that the misconduct may violate criminal, civil, or administrative law concerning [*Provider's*] practices relating to the Federal health care programs, then [*Provider*] shall promptly report the probable violation of law to OIG. Defendants shall make this disclosure as soon as practicable, but, not later than thirty (30) days after becoming aware of the existence of the probable violation. The [*Provider's*] report to OIG shall include:
   a. the findings concerning the probable violation, including the nature and extent of the probable violation;
   b. [*Provider's*] actions to correct such probable violation; and
   c. any further steps it plans to take to address such probable violation and prevent it from recurring.

   To the extent the misconduct involves an overpayment, the report shall include the information listed in section III.D.3 regarding material deficiencies.
2. *Inappropriate Billing.* If [*Provider*] discovers inappropriate or incorrect billing through means other than the Independent Review Organization's engagement, the provider shall follow procedures in section III.D.3 regarding overpayments and material deficiencies.

IV. New Locations

In the event that [*Provider*] purchases or establishes new business units after the effective date of this CIA, [*Provider*] shall notify OIG of this fact within thirty (30) days of the date of purchase or establishment. This notification shall include the location of the new operation(s), phone number, fax number, Federal health care program provider number(s) (if any), and the corresponding payor(s) (contractor specific) that has issued each provider number. All employees at such locations shall be subject to the requirements in this CIA that apply to new employees (e.g., completing certifications and undergoing training).

V. Implementation and Annual Reports

A. Implementation Report

Within one hundred and twenty (120) days after the effective date of this CIA, [*Provider*] shall submit a written report to OIG summarizing the status of its implementation of the requirements of this CIA. This Implementation Report shall include:

1. the name, address, phone number and position description of the Compliance Officer required by section III.A;
2. the names and positions of the members of the Compliance Committee required by section III.A;
3. a copy of [*Provider's*] Code of Conduct required by section III.B.1;

4. the summary of the Policies and Procedures required by section III.B.2;
5. a description of the training programs required by section III.C including a description of the targeted audiences and a schedule of when the training sessions were held;
6. a certification by the Compliance Officer that:
   a. the Policies and Procedures required by section III.B have been developed, are being implemented, and have been distributed to all pertinent employees;
   b. all employees have completed the Code of Conduct certification required by section III.B.1; and
   c. all employees have completed the training and executed the certification required by section III.C;
7. a description of the confidential disclosure program required by section III.E;
8. the identity of the Independent Review Organization(s) and the proposed start and completion date of the first audit; and
9. a summary of personnel actions taken pursuant to section III.F.

B. Annual Reports

[*Provider*] shall submit to OIG an Annual Report with respect to the status and findings of [*Provider's*] compliance activities. The Annual Reports shall include:

1. any change in the identity or position description of the Compliance Officer and/or members of the Compliance Committee described in section III.A;
2. a certification by the Compliance Officer that:
   a. all employees have completed the annual Code of Conduct certification required by section III.B.1; and
   b. all employees have completed the training and executed the certification required by section III.C;
3. notification of any changes or amendments to the Policies and Procedures required by section III.B and the reasons for such changes (e.g., change in contractor policy);
4. a complete copy of the report prepared pursuant to the Independent Review Organization's billing and compliance engagement, including a copy of the methodology used;
5. [*Provider's*] response/corrective action plan to any issues raised by the Independent Review Organization;
6. a summary of material deficiencies reported throughout the course of the previous twelve (12) months pursuant to III.D.3 and III.H;
7. a report of the aggregate overpayments that have been returned to the Federal health care programs that were discovered as a direct or indirect result of implementing

this CIA. Overpayment amounts should be broken down into the following categories: Medicare, Medicaid (report each applicable state separately) and other Federal health care programs;

8. a copy of the confidential disclosure log required by section III.E;
9. a description of any personnel action (other than hiring) taken by [*Provider*] as a result of the obligations in section III.F;
10. a summary describing any ongoing investigation or legal proceeding conducted or brought by a government entity involving an allegation that [*Provider*] has committed a crime or has engaged in fraudulent activities, which have been reported pursuant to section III.G. The statement shall include a description of the allegation, the identity of the investigating or prosecuting agency, and the status of such investigation, legal proceeding or requests for information;
11. a corrective action plan to address the probable violations of law identified in section III.H; and
12. a listing of all of the [*Provider's*] locations (including locations and mailing addresses), the corresponding name under which each location is doing business, the corresponding phone numbers and fax numbers, each location's Federal health care program provider identification number(s) and the payor (specific contractor) that issued each provider identification number.

The first Annual Report shall be received by the OIG no later than one year and thirty (30) days after the effective date of this CIA. Subsequent Annual Reports shall be submitted no later than the anniversary date of the due date of the first Annual Report.

C. Certifications

The Implementation Report and Annual Reports shall include a certification by the Compliance Officer under penalty of perjury, that: (1) [*Provider*] is in compliance with all of the requirements of this CIA, to the best of his or her knowledge; and (2) the Compliance Officer has reviewed the Report and has made reasonable inquiry regarding its content and believes that, upon such inquiry, the information is accurate and truthful.

VI. Notifications and Submission of Reports

Unless otherwise stated in writing subsequent to the effective date of this CIA, all notifications and reports required under this CIA shall be submitted to the entities listed below:

OIG:

Civil Recoveries Branch—Compliance Unit
Office of Counsel to the Inspector General
Office of Inspector General
U.S. Department of Health and Human Services
Cohen Building, Room 5527

330 Independence Avenue, SW
Washington, DC 20201
Phone 202-619-2078; Fax 202-205-0604

[*Provider*]:
[*Address and Telephone number of Provider's Compliance Contact*]

VII. OIG Inspection, Audit and Review Rights

In addition to any other rights OIG may have by statute, regulation, or contract, OIG or its duly authorized representative(s), may examine [*Provider's*] books, records, and other documents and supporting materials for the purpose of verifying and evaluating: (*a*) [*Provider's*] compliance with the terms of this CIA; and (*b*) [*Provider's*] compliance with the requirements of the Federal health care programs in which it participates. The documentation described above shall be made available by [*Provider*] to OIG or its duly authorized representative(s) at all reasonable times for inspection, audit or reproduction. Furthermore, for purposes of this provision, OIG or its duly authorized representative(s) may interview any of [*Provider*'s] employees who consent to be interviewed at the employee's place of business during normal business hours or at such other place and time as may be mutually agreed upon between the employee and OIG. [*Provider*] agrees to assist OIG in contacting and arranging interviews with such employees upon OIG's request. [*Provider's*] employees may elect to be interviewed with or without a representative of [*Provider*] present.

VIII. Document and Record Retention

[*Provider*] shall maintain for inspection all documents and records relating to reimbursement from the Federal health care programs or to compliance with this CIA one year longer than the term of this CIA (or longer if otherwise required by law).

IX. Disclosures

Subject to HHS's Freedom of Information Act ("FOIA") procedures, set forth in 45 C.F.R. Part 5, the OIG shall make a reasonable effort to notify [*Provider*] prior to any release by OIG of information submitted by [*Provider*] pursuant to its obligations under this CIA and identified upon submission by [*Provider*] as trade secrets, commercial or financial information and privileged and confidential under the FOIA rules. [*Provider*] shall refrain from identifying any information as trade secrets, commercial or financial information and privileged and confidential that does not meet the criteria for exemption from disclosure under FOIA.

X. Breach and Default Provisions

[*Provider*] is expected to fully and timely comply with all of the obligations herein throughout the term of this CIA or other time frames herein agreed to.

A. Stipulated Penalties for Failure to Comply with Certain Obligations

As a contractual remedy, [*Provider*] and OIG hereby agree that failure to comply with certain obligations set forth in this CIA may lead to the imposition of the following monetary penalties (hereinafter referred to as "Stipulated Penalties") in accordance with the following provisions.

1. A Stipulated Penalty of $2,500 (which shall begin to accrue on the day after the date the obligation became due) for each day, beginning 120 days after the effective date of

this CIA and concluding at the end of the term of this CIA, [*Provider*] fails to have in place any of the following:

a. a Compliance Officer;

b. a Compliance Committee;

c. a written Code of Conduct;

d. written Policies and Procedures;

e. a training program; and

f. a Confidential Disclosure Program;

2. A Stipulated Penalty of $2,500 (which shall begin to accrue on the day after the date the obligation became due) for each day [*Provider*] fails to meet any of the deadlines to submit the Implementation Report or the Annual Reports to the OIG.

3. A Stipulated Penalty of $2,000 (which shall begin to accrue on the date the failure to comply began) for each day [*Provider*]:

   a. hires or contracts with an Ineligible Person after that person has been listed by a federal agency as excluded, debarred, suspended or otherwise ineligible for participation in the Medicare, Medicaid or any other Federal health care program (as defined in 42 U.S.C. 1320a7b(f)). This Stipulated Penalty shall not be demanded for any time period if [*Provider*] can demonstrate that it did not discover the person's exclusion or other ineligibility after making a reasonable inquiry (as described in section III.F) as to the status of the person;

   b. employs or contracts with an Ineligible Person and that person: (i) has responsibility for, or involvement with, [*Provider's*] business operations related to the Federal health care programs or (ii) is in a position for which the person's salary or the items or services rendered, ordered, or prescribed by the person are paid in whole or in part, directly or indirectly, by the Federal health care programs or otherwise with Federal funds (this Stipulated Penalty shall not be demanded for any time period during which [*Provider*] can demonstrate that it did not discover the person's exclusion or other ineligibility after making a reasonable inquiry (as described in III.F) as to the status of the person);

   c. employs or contracts with a person who: (i) has been charged with a criminal offense related to any Federal health care program, or (ii) is suspended or proposed for exclusion, and that person has responsibility for, or involvement with, [*Provider's*] business operations related to the Federal health care programs (this Stipulated

Penalty shall not be demanded for any time period before 10 days after [*Provider*] received notice of the relevant matter or after the resolution of the matter).

4. A Stipulated Penalty of $1,500 (which shall begin to accrue on the date the [*Provider*] fails to grant access) for each day [*Provider*] fails to grant access to the information or documentation as required in section V of this CIA.

5. A Stipulated Penalty of $1,000 (which shall begin to accrue ten (10) days after the date that OIG provides notice to [*Provider*] of the failure to comply) for each day [*Provider*] fails to comply fully and adequately with any obligation of this CIA. In its notice to [*Provider*], the OIG shall state the specific grounds for its determination that the [Provider] has failed to comply fully and adequately with the CIA obligation(s) at issue.

B. Payment of Stipulated Penalties

1. *Demand Letter.* Upon a finding that [*Provider*] has failed to comply with any of the obligations described in section X.A and determining that Stipulated Penalties are appropriate, OIG shall notify [*Provider*] by personal service or certified mail of (*a*) [*Provider's*] failure to comply; and (*b*) the OIG's exercise of its contractual right to demand payment of the Stipulated Penalties (this notification is hereinafter referred to as the "Demand Letter").

   Within fifteen (15) days of the date of the Demand Letter, [*Provider*] shall either (*a*) cure the breach to the OIG's satisfaction and pay the applicable stipulated penalties, or (*b*) request a hearing before an HHS administrative law judge ("ALJ") to dispute the OIG's determination of noncompliance, pursuant to the agreed-upon provisions set forth below in section X.D. In the event [*Provider*] elects to request an ALJ hearing, the Stipulated Penalties shall continue to accrue until [*Provider*] cures, to the OIG's satisfaction, the alleged breach in dispute. Failure to respond to the Demand Letter in one of these two manners within the allowed time period shall be considered a material breach of this CIA and shall be grounds for exclusion under section X.C.

2. *Timely Written Requests for Extensions.* [*Provider*] may submit a timely written request for an extension of time to perform any act or file any notification or report required by this CIA. Notwithstanding any other provision in this section, if OIG grants the timely written request with respect to an act, notification, or report, Stipulated Penalties for failure to perform the act or file the notification or report shall not begin to accrue until one day after [*Provider*] fails to meet the revised deadline as agreed to by the OIG-approved extension. Notwithstanding any other provision in this section, if OIG denies such a timely written request, Stipulated Penalties for failure to perform the act or *file* the notification or report shall not begin to accrue until two (2) business days after [*Provider*] receives OIG's written denial of such request. A "timely

written request" is defined as a request in writing received by OIG at least five (5) business days prior to the date by which any act is due to be performed or any notification or report is due to be filed.

3. *Form of Payment.* Payment of the Stipulated Penalties shall be made by certified or cashier's check, payable to "Secretary of the Department of Health and Human Services," and submitted to OIG at the address set forth in section VI.

4. *Independence from Material Breach Determination.* Except as otherwise noted, these provisions for payment of Stipulated Penalties shall not affect or otherwise set a standard for the OIG's determination that [*Provider*] has materially breached this CIA, which decision shall be made at the OIG's discretion and governed by the provisions in section X.C, below.

C. Exclusion for Material Breach of this CIA

1. *Notice of Material Breach and Intent to Exclude.* The parties agree that a material breach of this CIA by [*Provider*] constitutes an independent basis for [*Provider's*] exclusion from participation in the Federal health care programs (as defined in 42 U.S.C. 1320a7b(f)). Upon a determination by OIG that [*Provider*] has materially breached this CIA and that exclusion should be imposed, the OIG shall notify [Provider] by certified mail of (*a*) [*Provider's*] material breach; and (*b*) OIG's intent to exercise its contractual right to impose exclusion (this notification is hereinafter referred to as the "Notice of Material Breach and Intent to Exclude").

2. *Opportunity to Cure.* [*Provider*] shall have thirty-five (35) days from the date of the Notice of Material Breach and Intent to Exclude Letter to demonstrate to the OIG's satisfaction that:

   a. [*Provider*] is in *full* compliance with this CIA;

   b. the alleged material breach has been cured; or

   c. the alleged material breach cannot be cured within the 35-day period, but that: (i) [*Provider*] has begun to take action to cure the material breach, (ii) [*Provider*] is pursuing such action with due diligence, and (iii) [*Provider*] has provided to OIG a reasonable timetable for curing the material breach.

3. *Exclusion Letter.* If at the conclusion of the thirty-five (35) day period, [*Provider*] fails to satisfy the requirements of section X.C.2, OIG may exclude [*Provider*] from participation in the Federal health care programs. OIG will notify [*Provider*] in writing of its determination to exclude [*Provider*] (this letter shall be referred to hereinafter as the "Exclusion Letter"). Subject to the Dispute Resolution provisions in section X.D, below, the exclusion shall go into effect thirty (30) days after the date of the Exclusion Letter. The exclusion shall have national effect and will also apply to all other federal procurement and non-procurement programs. If [*Provider*] is excluded under the provisions of this CIA, [*Provider*] may seek reinstatement pursuant to the provisions at 42 C.F.R. §§1001.3001–.3004.

4. *Material Breach.* A material breach of this CIA means:

    a. a failure by [*Provider*] to report a material deficiency, take corrective action and pay the appropriate refunds, as provided in section III.D;

    b. repeated or flagrant violations of the obligations under this CIA, including, but not limited to, the obligations addressed in section X.A of this CIA;

    c. a failure to respond to a Demand Letter concerning the payment of Stipulated Penalties in accordance with section X.B above; or

    d. a failure to retain and use an Independent Review Organization for review purposes in accordance with section III.D.

D. Dispute Resolution

1. *Review Rights.* Upon the OIG's delivery to [*Provider*] of its Demand Letter or of its Exclusion Letter, and as an agreed-upon contractual remedy for the resolution of disputes arising under the obligation of this CIA, [*Provider*] shall be afforded certain review rights comparable to the ones that are provided in 42 U.S.C. §§1320a7(f) and 42 C.F.R. §1005 as if they applied to the Stipulated Penalties or exclusion sought pursuant to this CIA. Specifically, the OIG's determination to demand payment of Stipulated Penalties or to seek exclusion shall be subject to review by an ALJ and, in the event of an appeal, the Departmental Appeals Board ("DAB"), in a manner consistent with the provisions in 42 C.F.R. §§1005.2–.21. Notwithstanding the language in 42 C.F.R. §1005.2(c), the request for a hearing involving stipulated penalties shall be made within fifteen (15) days of the date of the Demand Letter and the request for a hearing involving exclusion shall be made within thirty (30) days of the date of the Exclusion Letter.

2. *Stipulated Penalties Review.* Notwithstanding any provision of Title 42 of the United States Code or Chapter 42 of the Code of Federal Regulations, the only issues in a proceeding for stipulated penalties under this CIA shall be (*a*) whether [*Provider*] was in full and timely compliance with the obligations of this CIA for which the OIG demands payment; and (*b*) the period of noncompliance. [*Provider*] shall have the burden of proving its full and timely compliance and the steps taken to cure the noncompliance, if any. If the ALJ finds for the OIG with regard to a finding of a breach of this CIA and orders [*Provider*] to pay Stipulated Penalties, such Stipulated Penalties shall become due and payable twenty (20) days after the ALJ issues such a decision notwithstanding that [*Provider*] may request review of the ALJ decision by the DAB.

3. *Exclusion Review.* Notwithstanding any provision of Title 42 of the United States Code or Chapter 42 of the Code of Federal Regulations, the only issues in a proceeding for exclusion based on a material breach of this CIA shall be (*a*) whether [*Provider*] was in material breach of this CIA; (*b*) whether such breach was continuing on the date of the Exclusion Letter; and (*c*) the alleged

material breach cannot be cured within the 35-day period, but that (i) [*Provider*] has begun to take action to cure the material breach, (ii) [*Provider*] is pursuing such action with due diligence, and (iii) [*Provider*] has provided to OIG a reasonable timetable for curing the material breach.

For purposes of the exclusion herein, exclusion shall take effect only after an ALJ decision that is favorable to the OIG. [*Provider's*] election of its contractual right to appeal to the DAB shall not abrogate the OIG's authority to exclude [*Provider*] upon the issuance of the ALJ's decision. If the ALJ sustains the determination of the OIG and determines that exclusion is authorized, such exclusion shall take effect twenty (20) days after the ALJ issues such a decision, notwithstanding that [*Provider*] may request review of the ALJ decision by the DAB.

4. *Finality of Decision.* The review by an ALJ or DAB provided for above shall not be considered to be an appeal right arising under any statutes or regulations. Consequently, the parties to this CIA agree that the DAB's decision (or the ALJ's decision if not appealed) shall be considered final for all purposes under this CIA and [*Provider*] agrees to waive any right it may have to appeal the decision administratively, judicially or otherwise seek review by any court or other adjudicative forum.

XI. Effective and Binding Agreement

Consistent with the provisions in the Settlement Agreement pursuant to which this CIA is entered, and into which this CIA is incorporated, [*Provider*] and OIG agree as follows:

a. This CIA shall be binding on the successors, assigns and transferees of [*Provider*];

b. This CIA shall become final and binding on the date the final signature is obtained on the CIA;

c. Any modifications to this CIA shall be made with the prior written consent of the parties to this CIA; and

d. The undersigned [*Provider*] signatories represent and warrant that they are authorized to execute this CIA. The undersigned OIG signatory represents that he is signing this CIA in his official capacity and that he is authorized to execute this CIA.

On Behalf of [*Provider*]

__________________ __________________
Date

__________________ __________________
Date

__________________ __________________
Date

[*Please identify all signatories*]

ON BEHALF OF THE OFFICE OF INSPECTOR GENERAL OF THE DEPARTMENT OF HEALTH AND HUMAN SERVICES

______________________________	______________________________
Lewis Morris	*[Date]*

Assistant Inspector General for Legal Affairs
Office of Inspector General
U.S. Department of Health and Human Services

.33

Appendix B

Sample Statement of Management's Assertions

[*Date*]

In connection with the Corporate Integrity Agreement (CIA) entered into with the Office of the Inspector General of the United States Department of Health and Human Services dated [*date*], we make the following assertions, which are true to the best of our knowledge and belief.

Governance

Within 90 days of the date of the CIA, we—

1. Established a Compliance Committee, which meets at least monthly and requires a quorum to meet.
2. Appointed to our Compliance Committee members who include at a minimum those individuals specified in the CIA.
3. Delegated to the Compliance Committee the authority to implement and monitor the CIA, as evidenced by the organization chart or the Compliance Committee's charter.
4. Appointed a compliance officer, who reports directly to the individual specified in the CIA.

We appointed a compliance officer who—

1. Has sufficient staff and resources to carry out his or her responsibilities.
2. Actively participates in compliance training.
3. Has authority to conduct full and complete internal investigations without restriction.
4. Periodically revises the compliance program to meet changing circumstances and risks.

Billing Practices, Policies, and Procedures

Although no system of internal controls can provide absolute assurance that all bills comply in all respects with Medicare, Medicaid, and other federal health care program guidelines, we are not aware of any material weaknesses in our billing practices, policies, and procedures. Billings to third-party payors comply in all material respects with applicable coding principles and laws and regulations (including those dealing with Medicare and Medicaid antifraud and abuse) and only reflect charges for goods and services that were medically necessary, properly approved by regulatory bodies (e.g., the Food and Drug Administration), if required and properly rendered. [*Insert other assertions as necessary to address matters covered in the CIA.*] Any Medicare, Medicaid, and other federal health program billing deficiencies that we identified have been properly reported to the applicable payor within 60 days of discovery of the deficiency.

Corporate Integrity Policy

1. Our policy was developed and implemented within [*number*] days of execution of the CIA.
2. The policy addresses the Company's commitment to preparation and submission of accurate billings consistent with the standards

set forth in federal health care program statutes, regulations, procedures and guidelines or as otherwise communicated by Health Care Financing Administration (HCFA), its agents or any other agency engaged in the administration of the applicable federal health care program.

3. The policy addressed the specific issues that gave rise to the settlement, as well as other risk areas identified by the OIG in published Fraud Alerts issued through [*date*].
4. Further details on the development and implementation of our policy were provided to the OIG in our letter dated [*date*].
5. Our policy was distributed to all employees, physicians and independent contractors involved in submitting or preparing requests for reimbursement.
6. We have prominently displayed a copy of our policy on the Company's premises.

Information and Education Program

As discussed more fully in our letter to the OIG dated [*date*], we conducted an Information and Education Program within [*number*] days of the CIA. The Information and Education Program requires that each officer, employee, agent and contractor charged with administering federal health care programs (including, but not limited to billers, coders, nurses, physicians, medical records, hospital administration and other individuals directly involved in billing federal health care programs) receive at least [*number*] hours of training.

The training provided to employees involved in billing, coding, and/or charge capture consisted of instructions on submitting accurate bills, the personal obligations of each individual to ensure billings are accurate, the nature of company-imposed disciplinary actions on individuals who violate company policies and/or laws and regulations, applicable federal health care program rules, legal sanctions against the company for submission of false or fraudulent information, and how to report potential abuses or fraud. The training material addresses those issues underlying our settlement with the OIG.

The experience of the trainers is consistent with the topics presented.

Confidential Disclosure Program

Our Confidential Disclosure Program—

1. Was established within [*number*] days of the CIA.
2. Enables any employee to disclose any practices or billing procedures relating to federal health care programs.
3. Provides a toll-free telephone line maintained by the Company, which Company representatives have indicated is maintained twenty-four hours a day, seven days a week, for the purpose of making any disclosures regarding compliance with the Company's Compliance Program, the obligations in the CIA, and Company's overall compliance with federal and state standards.
4. Includes policies requiring the review of any disclosures to permit a determination of the appropriateness of the billing practice alleged to be involved and any corrective action to be taken to ensure that proper follow-up is conducted.
5. A detailed summary of the communications (including the number of disclosures by employees and the dates of such disclosures)

concerning billing practices reported as, and found to be, inappropriate under the Confidential Disclosure Program, and the results of any internal review and the follow-up on such disclosures are summarized in Attachment [*title*] to our Annual Report.

Excluded Individuals or Entities

Company policy—

1. Prohibits the employment of or contracting with an individual or entity that is listed by a federal agency as convicted of abuse or excluded, suspended or otherwise ineligible for participation in federal health care programs.
2. Includes a process to make an inquiry into the status of any potential employee or independent contractor.
3. Provides for an annual review of the status of all existing employees and contractors to verify whether any individual had been suspended or excluded or charged with a criminal offense relating to the provision of federal health care services.

We are not aware of any individuals employed in contravention of the prohibitions in the CIA.

Record Retention

Our record retention policy is consistent with the requirements of the CIA.

Signed by:

____

[*Chief Executive Officer*]

____

[*Chief Financial Officer*]

____

[*Corporate Compliance Officer*]

.34

Appendix C

Sample Engagement Letter

The following is an illustration of a sample engagement letter that may be used for this kind of engagement.

[*CPA Firm Letterhead*]

[*Client's Name and Address*]

Dear ______________:

This will confirm our understanding of the arrangements for our performance of certain agreed-upon procedures in connection with management's compliance with the terms of the Corporate Integrity Agreement (CIA) with the Office of Inspector General (OIG) of the U.S. Department of Health and Human Services (HHS) dated [*date of CIA*] for the period ending [*date*].

We will perform those procedures enumerated in the attachment to this letter. Our responsibility is to carry out these procedures and report our findings. We will conduct our engagement in accordance with standards established by the American Institute of Certified Public Accountants. Our planned procedures were agreed to by management and will be communicated to the OIG for its review and are based on the terms specified in the CIA. The sufficiency of these procedures is solely the responsibility of the specified parties to the report. Consequently, it is understood that we make no representation regarding the sufficiency of the procedures described in the attachment for the purpose for which this report has been requested or for any other purpose.

Management is responsible for the Company's compliance with all applicable laws, regulations, and contracts and agreements, including the CIA. Management also is responsible for the design, implementation, and monitoring of the policies and procedures upon which compliance is based.

Our engagement to perform agreed-upon procedures is substantially less in scope than an examination, the objective of which is the expression of an opinion on management's compliance with the CIA. Accordingly, we will not express such an opinion or any other form of assurance thereon.[1]

Working papers that are prepared in connection with this engagement are the property of the independent accountant. The working papers are prepared for the purpose of providing the principal support for the independent accountant's report. At the completion of our work, we expect to issue an agreed-upon procedures report in the attached form.

---

[1] The independent accountant may wish to include an understanding with the client about any limitation or other arrangements regarding liability of the practitioner or the client in the engagement letter. For example, the following might be included in the letter:

> Our maximum liability relating to services rendered under this letter (regardless of form of action, whether in contract, negligence or otherwise) shall be limited to the charges paid to us for the portion of the services or work products giving rise to liability. We will not be liable for consequential or punitive damages (including lost profits or savings) even if aware of their possible existence.
>
> You will indemnify us against any damage or expense that may result from any third-party claim relating to our services or any use by you of any work product, and you will reimburse us for all expenses (including counsel fees) as incurred by us in connection with any such claim, except to the extent such claim (i) is finally determined to have resulted from our gross negligence or willful misconduct or (ii) is covered by any of the preceding indemnities.

If, however, we are not able to complete all of the specified procedures, we will so advise you. At that time, we will discuss with you the form of communication, if any, that you desire for our findings. We will ask you to confirm your request in writing at that time. If you request that we delay issuance of our report until corrective action is taken that will result in compliance with all aspects of the CIA, we will do so only at your written request. Our working papers will be retained in accordance with our firm's working paper retention policy.

The distribution of the independent accountant's report will be restricted to the governing board and management of the Company and the OIG.

Our fees will be billed as work progresses and are based on the amount of time required at various levels of responsibility plus actual out-of-pocket expenses. Invoices are payable upon presentation. We will notify you immediately of any circumstances we encounter that could significantly affect our initial estimate of total fees.

We agree that to the extent required by law, we will allow the Comptroller General of the United States, HHS, and their duly authorized representatives to have access to this engagement letter and our documents and records to the extent necessary to verify the nature and amount of costs of the services provided to the Company, until the expiration of four years after we have concluded providing services to the Company that are performed pursuant to this Engagement Letter. In the event the Comptroller General, HHS, or their duly authorized representatives request such records, we agree to notify the Company of such request as soon as practicable.

In the event we are requested or authorized by the Company or are required by government regulation, subpoena, or other legal process to produce our documents or our personnel as witnesses with respect to our engagements for the Company, the Company will, so long as we are not a party to the proceeding in which the information is sought, reimburse us for our professional time and expenses, as well as the fees and expenses of our counsel, incurred in responding to such requests.

If this letter correctly expresses your understanding of this engagement, please sign the enclosed copy where indicated and return it to us. We appreciate the opportunity to serve you.

Sincerely,________________
[*Partner's Signature*]
[*Firm Name or Firm Representative*]

Accepted and agreed to:________________
[*Client Representative's Signature*]

[*Title*]________________

[*Date*]________________

[Revised, June 2009, to reflect conforming changes necessary due to the issuance of recent authoritative literature.]

.35

Appendix D

Sample Procedures

Procedure	*Findings*

Governance

1. We read the Company's corporate minutes and organization chart and ascertained that, within [*number*] days of the date of the Corporate Integrity Agreement (CIA), the Company—

   a. Established a Compliance Committee, which is to meet meets at least monthly and requires a quorum to meet.

   b. Appointed to its Compliance Committee members who include, at a minimum, those individuals specified in the CIA.

   c. Delegated to the Compliance Committee the authority to implement and monitor the CIA, as evidenced by the organization chart or the Compliance Committee's charter.

   d. Appointed a compliance officer who reports directly to the individual specified in the CIA.

2. We interviewed the compliance officer and were informed that, in his or her opinion, the Compliance Officer—

   a. Has sufficient staff and resources to carry out his or her responsibilities.

   b. Actively participates in compliance training.

   c. Has the authority to conduct full and complete internal investigations without restriction.

   d. Periodically revises the compliance program to meet changing circumstances and risks.

3. We read the OIG notification letter as specified in the CIA and noted that the appropriate official signed the letter, that it was addressed to the OIG, that it covered items (*a*) through (*d*) in Step 1, and that it was dated within [*number of*] days of the execution of the CIA.

Billing Practices, Policies, and Procedures

The practitioner might be engaged to provide consulting services in connection with the evaluation of the company's billing practices, policies, and procedures. If so, generally no agreed-upon procedures would be performed relating to this area.
Alternatively, if the procedures relating to the Company's billing practices, policies, and procedures are performed by others such as the Company's internal audit staff, the practitioner performs Steps 4 through 9.

Procedure	*Findings*

4. We read the compliance work plan and noted the following:

a. The work plan's stated objectives include the determination that billings are accurate and complete, for services rendered that have been deemed by medical specialists as being necessary, and are submitted in accordance with federal program guidelines.

b. The work plan sampling methodology sets confidence levels consistent with those defined in the CIA.

c. The work plan identifies risk areas, as defined in the CIA (if applicable), and specifies testing procedures by risk area.

d. The work plan specifies that samples are taken in risk areas (if applicable) identified by the CIA.

e. The work plan includes testing procedures, which the practitioner should modify as required by the CIA, for the following risks areas (if applicable) identified in the CIA:

(1) Clinical documentation, as follows:

(i) No documentation of service

(ii) Insufficient documentation of service

(iii) Improper diagnosis or treatment plan giving rise to the provision of a medically unnecessary service or treatment

(iv) Service or treatment does not conform medically with the documented diagnosis or treatment plan

(v) Services incorrectly coded

(2) Billing and coding, as follows:

(i) Noncovered or unallowable service

(ii) Duplicate payment

(iii) DRG window error

(iv) Unbundling

(v) Utilization

(vi) Medicare credit balances

[*Note to Practitioner:* Modify the preceding list as required by the CIA.]

5. We selected [*quantity*] probe samples performed by the independent review organization for the following risk areas [*list risk areas tested*]. For the probe samples selected, we noted that the—

a. Sample patient billing files were randomly selected.

(continued)

Procedure	*Findings*

b. Sample size reflected confidence levels specified in the CIA.

c. Sample plan describes how missing items (if any) would be treated.

d. Patient billing files tested were pulled per the listing of random numbers and all patient billing files were accounted for in the working papers.

e. Work plans for the specific sample described the risk areas (if applicable) being tested and the testing approach/procedures.

f. Working papers noted the completion of each work plan step.

g. Working papers contained a summary of findings for the sample.

6. We reperformed the work plan steps [*list of specific steps performed*] for the sample patient billing files. The reperformance of work plan steps related to the medical review of the sample patient billing files was performed by the following individuals [*note the professional qualifications of individuals without listing names*]. Any exceptions between our findings and the Company's are summarized in the Attachment to this report.

7. We read the summary findings of all internal compliance reviews that the Company's Internal Audit department indicated it had performed for the Company and noted that all material billing deficiencies [*specify material threshold as defined by the Company*] noted therein were discussed in written communications addressed to the appropriate payor (for example, Medicare Part B carrier) and were dated within 60 days from the time the deficiency occurred.[1]

8. We inquired of [*individual*] as to whether the Company took remedial steps within [*number of*] days (or such additional time as agreed to by the payor) to correct all material billing deficiencies noted in Step 7. We were informed that such remedial steps had been taken.

9. By reading applicable correspondence, we noted that any material billing deficiencies noted in Step 7 were communicated to the OIG, including specific findings relative to the deficiency, the Company's actions taken to correct the deficiency, and any further steps the Company plans to take to prevent any similar deficiencies from recurring.

[1] The CIA provides its own legal definition of a "material deficiency." Determination of whether a billing or other act meets this definition is normally beyond the auditor's professional competence and may have to await final determination by a court of law. Accordingly, to avoid confusion, a working definition different from that provided in the CIA (e.g., a specified dollar threshold) may be necessary.

Procedure	*Findings*

Corporate Integrity Policy

10. We read the Company's Corporate Integrity Policy and noted the following.

a. The policy was developed and implemented within [*number of*] days of execution of the CIA.

b. The policy addressed the Company's commitment to preparation and submission of accurate billings consistent with the standards set forth in federal health care program statutes, regulations, procedures, and guidelines or as otherwise communicated by HCFA, its agents, or any other agency engaged in the administration of the applicable federal health care program.

c. The policy addressed the specific issues that gave rise to the settlement, as well as other risk areas identified by the OIG in published Fraud Alerts issued through [*agency*].

d. Correspondence addressed to the OIG covered the development and implementation of the policy.

e. Documentation indicating that the policy was distributed to all employees, physicians, and independent contractors involved in submitting or preparing requests for reimbursement.

f. The prominent display of a copy of the policy on the Company's premises.

11. We selected a sample of ten employees (involved in submitting and preparing requests for reimbursement) and examined written confirmation in the employee's personnel file indicating receipt of a copy of the Corporate Integrity Policy.

Information and Education Program

12. We read the Company's Information and Education Program and noted the following.

a. The Information and Education Program agenda was dated within [*number of*] days of execution of the CIA.

b. Correspondence covering the development and implementation of the Information and Education Program was addressed to the OIG.

c. The Information and Education Program requires that each officer, employee, agent, and contractor charged with administering federal health care programs (including, but not limited to billers, coders, nurses, physicians, medical records, hospital administration and other individuals directly involved in billing federal health care programs) receive at least [*number of*] hours of training.

(continued)

Procedure	Findings
13. We selected a sample of ten employees involved in billing, coding and/or charge capture and examined sign-in logs of the training classes and noted that each had signed indicating that they had received at least *[number of]* hours of training as specified in the Information and Education Program. We also reviewed tests and surveys completed by each of the ten trained employees noting evidence that they were completed.	
14. We inquired as to the training of individuals not present during the regularly scheduled training programs and were informed that each such individual is trained either individually or in a separate make-up session. We inquired as to the names of individuals not initially present and selected one such individual and examined that individual's post-training test and survey for completion.	
15. We read the course agenda and noted that the training provided to employees involved in billing, coding, and/or charge capture consisted of instructions on submitting accurate bills, the personal obligations of each individual to ensure billings are accurate, the nature of company-imposed disciplinary actions on individuals who violate company policies and/or laws and regulations applicable to federal health care program rules, legal sanctions against the company for submission of false or fraudulent information, and how to report potential abuses or fraud. We also noted that the training material addressed the following issues which gave rise to the settlement [*practitioner list*].	
16. We inquired of the Corporate Compliance Officer as to the qualifications and experience of the trainers and were informed that, in the Corporate Compliance Officer's opinion, they were consistent with the topics presented.	
17. We noted that the Company's draft Annual Report to the OIG dated [*date*] addresses certification of training.	
Confidential Disclosure Program	
18. We read documentation of the Company's Confidential Disclosure Program and noted that it—	
a. Includes the printed effective date that was within [*number of*] days of execution of the CIA.	
b. Consists of a confidential disclosure program enabling any employee to disclose any practices or billing procedures relating to federal health care programs.	
c. Provides a toll-free telephone line maintained by the Company, which Company representatives have indicated is maintained twenty-four hours a day, seven days a week, for the purpose of making any disclosures regarding compliance with the Company's Compliance Program, the obligations in the CIA, and Company's overall compliance with federal and state standards.	

Procedure	*Findings*

d. Includes policies requiring the review of any disclosures to permit a determination of the appropriateness of the billing practice alleged to be involved and any corrective action to be taken to ensure that proper follow-up is conducted.

19. We made five test calls to the toll free telephone line (hotline) and noted the following.

a. Each call was captured in the hotline logs and reported with all other incoming calls.

b. Anonymity is not discouraged.

20. We noted that the Company included in its draft Annual Report addressed to OIG dated [*date*] a detailed summary of the communications (including the number of disclosures by employees and the dates of such disclosures) concerning billing practices reported as, and found to be, inappropriate under the Confidential Disclosure Program, and the results of any internal review and the follow-up on such disclosures.

21. We observed the display of the Company's Confidential Disclosure Program, including notice of the availability of its hotline, on the Company's premises.

Excluded Individuals or Entities

22. We read the Company's written policy relating to dealing with excluded or convicted persons or entities and noted that the policy—

a. Prohibits the hiring of or contracting with an individual or entity that is listed by a federal agency as convicted of abuse or excluded, suspended, or otherwise ineligible for participation in federal health care programs.

b. Includes a process to make an inquiry into the status of any potential employee or independent contractor.

c. Provides for a semi-annual review of the status of all existing employees and contractors to verify whether any individual had been suspended or excluded or charged with a criminal offense relating to the provision of federal health care services.

23. We selected a sample of ten employees hired over the course of the test period as defined in the CIA and examined support in the employee's personnel file documenting inquiries made into the status of the employee, including documentation of comparison to the [*source specified in the CIA*].

24. We performed the following procedures related to the Company's semi-annual review of employee status.

(continued)

Procedure	*Findings*

a. Read documentation of the semi-annual review as evidence that a review was performed.

b. Selected and reviewed the lesser of ten or all exceptions and determined that such employees were removed from responsibility for or involvement with Provider business operations related to the Federal health care programs.

c. Examined a notification letter addressed to the OIG and dated within 30 days of the employee's removal from employment.

d. Inquired of [*officer*] as to whether he or she was aware of any individuals employed in contravention of the prohibitions in the CIA. If so, we further noted that [*indicate specific procedures*] to confirm that such situation was cured within 30 days by [*indicate how situation was cured*].

Annual Report

25. We read the Company's draft Annual Report dated [*date*] and determined that it included the following items, to be modified as appropriate, by the practitioner:

a. Compliance Program Charter and organization chart

b. Amendments to policies

c. Detailed descriptions of reviews and audits

d. Summary of hotline communications

e. Summary of annual review of employees

f. Cross-referencing to items noted in the CIA

Record Retention

26. We read the Company's record retention policy and noted that it was consistent with the requirements as outlined in the CIA.

.36

Appendix E

Sample Report

Independent Accountant's Report

[*Date*]

[*Sample Health Care Provider*]
Office of Inspector General of the U.S. Department of Health and Human Services

We have performed the procedures enumerated in the Attachment, which were agreed to by Sample Health Care Provider (Company) and the Office of Inspector General (OIG) of the U.S. Department of Health and Human Services, solely to assist the users in evaluating management's assertion about [*name of entity's*] compliance with the Corporate Integrity Agreement (CIA) with the OIG dated [*date of CIA*] for the [*period*] ending [*date*], which is included as Attachment A to this report. This agreed-upon procedures engagement was performed in accordance with standards established by the American Institute of Certified Public Accountants. The sufficiency of these procedures is solely the responsibility of the specified users of the report. Consequently, we make no representation regarding the sufficiency of the procedures described in Attachment B either for the purpose for which this report has been requested or for any other purpose.

We were not engaged to and did not perform an examination, the objective of which would be the expression of an opinion on management's compliance with the CIA. Accordingly, we do not express such an opinion. Had we performed additional procedures, other matters might have come to our attention that would have been reported to you.

This report is intended solely for the information and use of the Compliance Committee and management of the Company and the OIG, and is not intended to be and should not be used by anyone other than those specified parties.

[*Include as Attachments the CIA and the summary that enumerates procedures and findings.*]

[*Signature*]

Auditing Standards Board 1998

DEBORAH D. LAMBERT, *Chair*
JAMES S. GERSON, *Vice Chair*
JOHN T. BARNUM
ANDREW J. CAPELLI
ROBERT F. DACEY
RICHARD DIETER
SALLY L. HOFFMAN
STEPHEN D. HOLTON
J. MICHAEL INZINA
CHARLES E. LANDES
KEITH O. NEWTON
ALAN ROSENTHAL
R.C. STEINER
GEORGE H. TUCKER III
OLIVER R. WHITTINGTON

Health Care Pilot Task Force 1998

WILLIAM R. TITERA, *Chair*
DIANE CORNWELL
WILLIAM T. CUPPETT
DENNIS J. DUQUETTE
ERIC HOLZBERG
MARY R. MACBAIN
JOSEPH N. STEAKLEY

SOP Task Force

WILLIAM R. TITERA, *Chair*
ROBERT D. BEARD
GARY BREUER
DENNIS J. DUQUETTE
MARK EDDY
WILLIAM HORNBY
LEWIS MORRIS
JOSEPH N. STEAKLEY

AICPA Staff

BARBARA VIGILANTE
Technical Manager
PCPS/MAP

KARYN WALLER
Technical Manager
Industry and Management Accounting

JANE MANCINO
Technical Manager
Audit and Attest Standards

Appendix B

Statement of Position 00-1, Auditing Health Care Third-Party Revenues and Related Receivables

March 10, 2000

NOTE

This Statement of Position (SOP) is an interpretive publication and represents the recommendations of the AICPA Health Care Third-Party Revenue Recognition Task Force of the Auditing Standards Board (ASB) with regard to auditing financial statement assertions about third-party revenues and related receivables of health care entities. The ASB has found the recommendations in this SOP to be consistent with existing standards covered by Rule 202, *Compliance With Standards*, (AICPA, *Professional Standards*, vol. 2, ET sec. 202 par. .01) of the AICPA Code of Professional Conduct.

Interpretive publications are not as authoritative as pronouncements of the ASB; however, if an auditor does not apply the guidance included in this SOP, the auditor should be prepared to explain how he or she complied with the provisions of Statements on Auditing Standards addressed by this SOP.

TABLE OF CONTENTS

Summary

This Statement of Position (SOP) provides guidance to auditors regarding uncertainties inherent in health care third-party revenue recognition. It discusses auditing matters related to testing third-party revenues and related receivables, and provides guidance regarding the sufficiency and appropriateness of audit evidence and reporting on financial statements of health care entities exposed to material uncertainties. [Revised, June 2009, to reflect conforming changes necessary due to the issuance of recent authoritative literature.]

Introduction and Background

.01 Most health care providers participate in payment programs that pay less than full charges for services rendered. For example, some cost-based programs retrospectively determine the final amounts reimbursable for services rendered to their beneficiaries based on allowable costs. With increasing frequency, even non-cost-based programs (such as the Medicare Prospective Payment System) have become subject to retrospective adjustments (for example, billing denials and coding changes). Often, such adjustments are not known for a considerable period of time after the related services were rendered.

.02 The lengthy period of time between rendering services and reaching final settlement, compounded further by the complexities and ambiguities of reimbursement regulations, makes it difficult to estimate the net patient service revenue associated with these programs. This situation has been compounded due to the frequency of changes in federal program guidelines.

.03 Financial Accounting Standards Board (FASB) *Accounting Standards Codification*™ (ASC) 954-605-45-2 states, in part, that "service revenue shall be reported net of contractual and other adjustments in the statement of operations, including patient service revenue." As a result, patient receivables, including amounts due from third-party payors, are also reported net of expected contractual and other adjustments. However, amounts ultimately realizable will not be known until some future date, which may be several years after the period in which the services were rendered. [Revised, June 2009, to reflect conforming changes necessary due to the issuance of recent authoritative literature.]

.04 This SOP provides guidance to auditors regarding uncertainties inherent in health care third-party revenue recognition. It discusses auditing matters related to testing third-party revenue and related receivables, including the effects of settlements (both cost-based and non-cost-based third-party payment programs), and provides guidance regarding the sufficiency and appropriateness of audit evidence and reporting on financial statements of health care entities exposed to material uncertainties. [Revised, June 2009, to reflect conforming changes necessary due to the issuance of recent authoritative literature.]

Scope and Applicability

.05 This SOP applies to audits of health care entities falling within the scope of the AICPA Audit and Accounting Guide *Health Care Entities* (the guide). Its provisions are effective for audits of periods ending on or after June 30, 2000. Early application of the provisions of this SOP is permitted.

Third-Party Revenues and Related Receivables—Inherent Uncertainties

.06 Health care entities need to estimate amounts that ultimately will be realizable in order for revenues to be fairly stated in accordance with generally accepted accounting principles (GAAP). The basis for such estimates may range from relatively straightforward calculations using information that is readily available to highly complex judgments based on assumptions about future decisions.

.07 Entities doing business with governmental payors (for example, Medicare and Medicaid) are subject to risks unique to the government-contracting environment that are hard to anticipate and quantify and that may vary from entity to entity. For example—

- A health care entity's revenues may be subject to adjustment as a result of examination by government agencies or contractors. The audit process and the resolution of significant related matters (including disputes based on differing interpretations of the regulations) often are not finalized until several years after the services were rendered.
- Different fiscal intermediaries (entities that contract with the federal government to assist in the administration of the Medicare program) may interpret governmental regulations differently.
- Differing opinions on a patient's principal medical diagnosis, including the appropriate sequencing of codes used to submit claims for payment, can have a significant effect on the payment amount.[1]
- Otherwise valid claims may be determined to be nonallowable after the fact due to differing opinions on medical necessity.
- Claims for services rendered may be nonallowable if they are later determined to have been based on inappropriate referrals.[2]
- Governmental agencies may make changes in program interpretations, requirements, or "conditions of participation," some of which may have implications for amounts previously estimated.

.08 Such factors often result in retrospective adjustments to interim payments. Reasonable estimates of such adjustments are central to the third-party revenue recognition process in health care, in order to avoid recognizing revenue that the provider will not ultimately realize. The delay between rendering services and reaching final settlement, as well as the complexities and ambiguities of billing and reimbursement regulations, makes it difficult to estimate net realizable third-party revenues.

Management's Responsibilities

.09 Management is responsible for the fair presentation of its financial statements in conformity with GAAP. Management also is responsible for adopting sound accounting policies and for establishing and maintaining internal control that will, among other things, enable the entity to initiate, authorize, record, process, and report transactions (as well as events and conditions) consistent with management's assertions embodied in the financial statements. Despite the inherent uncertainties, management is responsible for estimating

---

[1] Historically, the Health Care Financing Administration (HCFA) contracted with Peer Review Organizations (PROs) to validate the appropriateness of admissions and the clinical coding from which reimbursement was determined. Such reviews were typically performed within ninety days of the claim submission date. However, the government has modified its policies with respect to such reviews and now analyzes coding errors through other means, including in conjunction with investigations conducted by the Office of the Inspector General (OIG) of the U. S. Department of Health and Human Services.

[2] Effective January 1, 1995, the Limitation on Certain Physician Referrals law prohibited physicians from referring Medicare and Medicaid patients to health care entities with which they had a financial relationship for the furnishing of designated health services. Implementing regulations have not yet been adopted as of the date of this publication.

the amounts recorded in the financial statements and making the required disclosures in accordance with GAAP, based on management's analysis of existing conditions. [Revised, June 2009, to reflect conforming changes necessary due to the issuance of recent authoritative literature.]

.10 Management's assertions regarding proper valuation of its revenues and receivables are embodied in the financial statements. Management is responsible for recognizing revenues when their realization is reasonably assured. As a result, management makes a reasonable estimate of amounts that ultimately will be realized, considering—among other things—adjustments associated with regulatory reviews, audits, billing reviews, investigations, or other proceedings. Estimates that are significant to management's assertions about revenue include the provision for third-party payor contractual adjustments and allowances. [Revised, June 2009, to reflect conforming changes necessary due to the issuance of recent authoritative literature.]

.11 Management also is responsible for preparing and certifying cost reports submitted to federal and state government agencies in support of claims for payment for services rendered to government program beneficiaries.

The Auditor's Responsibilities

.12 The auditor's responsibility is to express an opinion on the financial statements taken as a whole. In reaching this opinion, the auditor should conclude whether sufficient appropriate evidence has been obtained to reduce to an appropriately low level the risks of material misstatement in the financial statements. In developing an opinion, the auditor should consider all relevant audit evidence, including

- the evidence in support of recorded amounts.
- the reasonableness of management's estimates in the present circumstances,
- the fairness of the presentation and adequacy of the disclosures made by management,

[Revised, June 2009, to reflect conforming changes necessary due to the issuance of recent authoritative literature.]

.13 Current industry conditions, as well as specific matters affecting the entity.[3] provide relevant information when planning the audit. Among a number of procedures, the auditor's procedures may include an analysis of historical results (for example, prior fiscal intermediary audit adjustments and comparisons with industry benchmarks and norms) that enable the auditor to better assess the risk of material misstatements in the current period. When there are heightened risks, the auditor should perform audit procedures that respond to those risks, for example, more extensive tests covering the current period. Exhibit 5-1 of the guide includes examples of procedures auditors may perform. [Revised, June 2009, to reflect conforming changes necessary due to the issuance of recent authoritative literature.]

.14 With respect to auditing third-party revenues, a relevant consideration in addition to the usual revenue recognition considerations, is whether ultimately realizable amounts are known or will be presently known, or whether

---

[3] Risk factors, including ones related to legislative and regulatory matters, are discussed annually in the AICPA Audit Risk Alert *Health Care Industry Developments*.

those amounts are uncertain because they are dependent on some other future, prospective actions or confirming events. For example, under a typical fee-for-service contract with a commercial payor, if the provider has performed a service for a covered individual, the revenue to which the provider is entitled should be determinable at the time the service is rendered. On the other hand, if the service was provided under a cost-based government contract, the revenue ultimately collectible may not be known until certain future events occur (for example, a cost report has been submitted and finalized after desk review or audit). In this case, management estimates the effect of such potential future adjustments. [Revised, June 2009, to reflect conforming changes necessary due to the issuance of recent authoritative literature.]

.15 As stated previously, management is responsible for preparing the estimates contained in the financial statements. The auditor should evaluate the sufficiency and appropriateness of the evidence supporting those estimates, including the facts supporting management's judgments, and the judgments made based on conditions existing at the time of the audit. The fact that net revenues recorded at the time services are rendered differ materially from amounts that ultimately are realized does not necessarily mean the audit was not properly planned or carried out. Similarly, the fact that future events may differ materially from management's assumptions or estimates does not necessarily mean that management's estimates were not valid or the auditor did not follow generally accepted auditing standards (GAAS) as described in this SOP with respect to auditing estimates. [Revised, June 2009, to reflect conforming changes necessary due to the issuance of recent authoritative literature.]

Audit Evidence

.16 The measurement of estimates is inherently uncertain and depends on the outcome of future events. AU section 342, *Auditing Accounting Estimates*, and AU section 508, *Reports on Audited Financial Statements* (AICPA, *Professional Standards*), provide guidance to the auditor when the valuation of revenues is uncertain, pending the outcome of future events. In the current health care environment, conclusive evidence concerning amounts ultimately realizable cannot be expected to exist at the time of the financial statement audit because the uncertainty associated with future program audits, administrative re-views, billing reviews, regulatory investigations, or other actions will not be resolved until sometime in the future. [Revised, June 2009, to reflect conforming changes necessary due to the issuance of recent authoritative literature.]

.17 The fact that information related to the effects of future program audits, administrative reviews, regulatory investigations, or other actions does not exist does not lead to a conclusion that the evidence supporting management's assertions is not sufficient to support management's estimates. Rather, the auditor's judgment regarding the sufficiency and appropriateness of the evidence is based on the evidence that is available or can reasonably be expected to be available in the circumstances. If, after considering the existing conditions and available evidence, the auditor concludes that the evidence is sufficient and appropriate and supports management's assertions about the valuation of revenues and receivables, and their presentation and disclosure in the financial statements, an unqualified opinion ordinarily is appropriate. [Revised, June 2009, to reflect conforming changes necessary due to the issuance of recent authoritative literature.]

.18 The inability to obtain relevant evidence that the auditor needs may require the auditor to express a qualified opinion or to disclaim an opinion because of a scope limitation. For example, if an entity has conducted an internal evaluation (for example, of coding or other billing matters) under attorney–client privilege and management and its legal counsel refuse to respond to the auditor's inquiries and the auditor determines the information is necessary, ordinarily the auditor would qualify his or her opinion for a scope limitation. [Revised, June 2009, to reflect conforming changes necessary due to the issuance of recent authoritative literature.]

.19 The accuracy of management's assumptions will not be known until future events occur. In evaluating the accuracy of those assumptions, the auditor normally should consider the entity's historical experience in making past estimates and the auditor's experience in the industry. For certain matters, the best evidence available to the auditor (particularly as it relates to clinical and legal interpretations) may be the representations of management and its legal counsel, as well as information obtained through reviewing correspondence from regulatory agencies. [Revised, June 2009, to reflect conforming changes necessary due to the issuance of recent authoritative literature.]

.20 Pursuant to AU sec. 333, *Management Representations* (AICPA, *Professional Standards*), the auditor should obtain written representations from management concerning the absence of violations or possible violations of laws or regulations whose effects should be considered for disclosure in the financial statements or as a basis for recording a loss contingency. Examples of specific representations include the following:

- Receivables
  - — Adequate consideration has been given to, and appropriate provision made for, estimated adjustments to revenue, such as for denied claims and changes to diagnosis-related group (DRG) assignments.
  - — Recorded valuation allowances are necessary, appropriate, and properly supported.
  - — All peer review organizations, fiscal intermediary, and third-party payor reports and information have been made available.
- Cost reports filed with third parties
  - — All required Medicare, Medicaid, and similar reports have been properly filed.
  - — Management is responsible for the accuracy and propriety of all cost reports filed.
  - — All costs reflected on such reports are appropriate and allowable under applicable reimbursement rules and regulations and are patient-related and properly allocated to applicable payors.
  - — The reimbursement methodologies and principles employed are in accordance with applicable rules and regulations.

- — Adequate consideration has been given to, and appropriate provision made for, audit adjustments by intermediaries, third-party payors, or other regulatory agencies.
- — All items required to be disclosed, including disputed costs that are being claimed to establish a basis for a subsequent appeal, have been fully disclosed in the cost report.
- — Recorded third-party settlements include differences between filed (and to be filed) cost reports and calculated settlements, which are necessary based on historical experience or new or ambiguous regulations that may be subject to differing interpretations. While management believes the entity is entitled to all amounts claimed on the cost reports, management also believes the amounts of these differences are appropriate.

- Contingencies
  - — There are no violations or possible violations of laws or regulations, such as those related to the Medicare and Medicaid antifraud and abuse statutes, including but not limited to the Medicare and Medicaid Anti-Kickback Statute, Limitations on Certain Physician Referrals (the Stark law), and the False Claims Act, in any jurisdiction, whose effects should be considered for disclosure in the financial statements or as a basis for recording a loss contingency other than those disclosed or accrued in the financial statements.
  - — Billings to third-party payors comply in all material respects with applicable coding guidelines (for example, ICD-9-CM and CPT-4) and laws and regulations (including those dealing with Medicare and Medicaid antifraud and abuse), and billings reflect only charges for goods and services that were medically necessary; properly approved by regulatory bodies (for example, the Food and Drug Administration), if required; and properly rendered.
  - — There have been no communications (oral or written) from regulatory agencies, governmental representatives, employees, or others concerning investigations or allegations of noncompliance with laws and regulations in any jurisdiction (including those related to the Medicare and Medicaid antifraud and abuse statutes), deficiencies in financial reporting practices, or other matters that could have a material adverse effect on the financial statements.

.21 Management's refusal to furnish written representations constitutes a limitation on the scope of the audit sufficient to preclude an unqualified opinion and is ordinarily sufficient to cause an auditor to disclaim an opinion or withdraw from the engagement. However, based on the nature of the representations not obtained or the circumstances of the refusal, the auditor may conclude that a qualified opinion is appropriate.

Potential Departures From GAAP Related to Estimates and Uncertainties

.22 The auditor also is responsible for determining whether financial statement assertions and disclosures related to accounting estimates have been presented in conformity with GAAP. Departures from GAAP related to accounting estimates generally fall into one of the following categories:

- Unreasonable accounting estimates
- Inappropriate accounting principles
- Inadequate disclosure

Therefore, in order to render an opinion, the auditor's responsibility is to evaluate the reasonableness of management's estimates based on present circumstances and to determine that estimates are reported in accordance with GAAP and adequately disclosed. [Revised, June 2009, to reflect conforming changes necessary due to the issuance of recent authoritative literature.]

.23 As discussed in AU section 326, *Audit Evidence* (AICPA, *Professional Standards*), the auditor's objective is to obtain sufficient appropriate audit evidence to provide him or her with a reasonable basis for forming an opinion. As discussed previously, Exhibit 5-1 of the guide provides a number of sample procedures that the auditor may perform in auditing an entity's patient revenues and accounts receivable, including those derived from third-party payors. For example, the guide notes that the auditor might "test the reasonableness of settlement amounts, including specific and unallocated reserves, in light of the payors involved, the nature of the payment mechanism, the risks associated with future audits, and other relevant factors."[4] [Revised, September 2008, to reflect conforming changes necessary due to the issuance of Statement on Auditing Standards No. 105. Revised, June 2009, to reflect conforming changes necessary due to the issuance of recent authoritative literature.]

Unreasonable Accounting Estimates

.24 The basis for management's assumptions regarding the nature of future adjustments and calculations as to the effects of such adjustments are relevant factors when evaluating the reasonableness of management's estimates.[5] The auditor cannot determine with certainty whether such estimates are right or wrong, because the accuracy of management's assumptions cannot be confirmed until future events occur. [Revised, June 2009, to reflect conforming changes necessary due to the issuance of recent authoritative literature.]

.25 Though difficult to predict, it is reasonable for the auditor to expect that management has made certain assumptions (either in detail or in the aggregate) in developing its estimates regarding conditions likely to result in adjustments (for example, consistency with historical experience and basis of management's underlying assumptions). In evaluating reasonableness, the auditor should obtain an understanding of how management developed the estimate. Based on that understanding, the auditor should use one or a combination of the following approaches:

---

[4] See paragraphs .25–.28.

[5] The lack of such analyses may call into question the reasonableness of recorded amounts.

a. Review and test the process used by management to develop the estimate.

b. Develop an independent expectation of the estimate to corroborate the reasonableness of management's estimates.

c. Review subsequent events or transactions occurring prior to completion of fieldwork (AU sec. 342.10).

[Revised, June 2009, to reflect conforming changes necessary due to the issuance of recent authoritative literature.]

.26 Because no one accounting estimate can be considered accurate with certainty, the auditor may determine that a difference between an estimated amount best supported by the audit evidence and the estimated amount included in the financial statements may be significant and such difference would not be considered to be a likely misstatement. However, if the auditor believes the estimated amount included in the financial statements is unreasonable, he or she should treat the difference between that estimate and the closest reasonable estimate as a likely misstatement. (Paragraph .56 of AU section 312, *Audit Risk and Materiality in Conducting an Audit* [AICPA, *Professional Standards*]). The auditor also should consider whether the difference between estimates best supported by the audit evidence and the estimates included in the financial statements, which are individually reasonable, indicate a possible bias on the part of the entity's management. For example, if each accounting estimate included in the financial statements was individually reasonable, but the effect of the difference between each estimate and the estimate best supported by the audit evidence was to increase income, the auditor should reconsider the reasonableness of the estimates taken as a whole (Paragraph .58 of AU section 312 [AICPA, *Professional Standards*]). [Revised, June 2009, to reflect conforming changes necessary due to the issuance of recent authoritative literature.]

.27 Approaches and estimates will vary from entity to entity. Some entities with significant prior experience may attempt to quantify the effects of individual potential intermediary or other governmental (for example, the Office of Inspector General and the Department of Justice) or private payor adjustments, basing their estimates on very detailed calculations and assumptions regarding potential future adjustments. Some may prepare cost report[6] analyses to estimate the effect of potential adjustments. Others may base their estimates on an analysis of potential adjustments in the aggregate, in light of the payors involved; the nature of the payment mechanism; the risks associated with future audits; and other relevant factors. [Revised, June 2009, to reflect conforming changes necessary due to the issuance of recent authoritative literature.]

.28 One of the key factors in evaluating the estimate is the historical experience of the entity (for example, the aggregate amount of prior cost-report

[6] Medicare cost reimbursement is based on the application of highly complex technical rules, some of which are ambiguous and subject to different interpretations even among Medicare's fiscal intermediaries. It is not uncommon for fiscal intermediaries to reduce claims for reimbursement that were based on management's good faith interpretations of pertinent laws and regulations. Additionally, the Provider Reimbursement Review Board (PRRB) or the courts may be required to resolve controversies regarding the application of certain rules. To avoid recognizing revenues before their realization is reasonably assured, providers estimate the effects of such potential adjustments. This is occasionally done by preparing a cost report based on alternative assumptions to help estimate contractual allowances required by generally accepted accounting principles. The existence of reserves or a reserve cost report does not by itself mean that a cost report was incorrectly or fraudulently filed.

adjustments and previous regulatory settlements) as well as the risk of potential future adjustments. The fact that an entity currently is not subject to a governmental investigation does not mean that a recorded valuation allowance for potential billing adjustments is not warranted. Nor do these emerging industry trends necessarily indicate that an accrual for a specific entity is warranted. [Revised, June 2009, to reflect conforming changes necessary due to the issuance of recent authoritative literature.]

.29 In evaluating valuation allowances, the auditor may consider the entity's historical experience and potential future adjustments in the aggregate. For example, assume that over the past few years after final cost report audits were completed, a hospital's adjustments averaged 3 percent to 5 percent of total filed reimbursable costs. Additionally, the hospital is subject to potential billing adjustments, including errors (for example, violations of the three-day window, discharge and transfer issues, and coding errors). Even though specific incidents are not known, it may be reasonable for the hospital to estimate and accrue a valuation allowance for such potential future retrospective adjustments, both cost-based and non-cost-based. Based on this and other information obtained, the auditor may conclude that a valuation allowance for the year under audit of 3 percent to 5 percent of reimbursable costs plus additional amounts for potential non-cost-based program billing errors is reasonable.

.30 Amounts that ultimately will be realized by an entity are dependent on a number of factors, many of which may be unknown at the time the estimate is first made. Further, even if two entities had exactly the same clinical and coding experience, amounts that each might realize could vary materially due to factors outside of their control (for example, differing application of payment rules by fiscal intermediaries, legal interpretations of courts, local enforcement initiatives, timeliness of reviews, and quality of documentation). As a result, because estimates are a matter of judgment and their ultimate accuracy depends on the outcome of future events, different entities in seemingly similar circumstances may develop materially different estimates. The auditor may conclude that both estimates are reasonable in light of the differing assumptions.

Inappropriate Accounting Principles

.31 As previously stated, the auditor also is responsible for determining whether financial statement assertions and disclosures related to accounting estimates are presented in accordance with GAAP. When the financial statements are materially affected by a departure from GAAP, the auditor should expresses a qualified or adverse opinion. [Revised, June 2009, to reflect conforming changes necessary due to the issuance of recent authoritative literature.]

.32 Valuation allowances should be recorded so that revenues are not recognized until the revenues are realizable. Valuation allowances are not established based on the provisions of FASB ASC 450, *Contingencies*. [Revised, June 2009, to reflect conforming changes necessary due to the issuance of recent authoritative literature.]

.33 Indicators of possible measurement bias related to valuation allowances include

- valuation allowances that are not associated with any particular program, issue, or time period (for example, cost-report year or year the service was rendered).
- distorted earnings trends over time (for example, building up specific or unallocated valuation allowances in profitable years and drawing them down in unprofitable years).

[Revised, June 2009, to reflect conforming changes necessary due to the issuance of recent authoritative literature.]

Inadequate Disclosure

.34 If the auditor concludes that a matter involving a risk or an uncertainty is not adequately disclosed in the financial statements in conformity with GAAP, the auditor should express a qualified or adverse opinion. FASB ASC 275-10-50 provides guidance on the information that reporting entities should disclose regarding risks and uncertainties existing as of the date of the financial statements. [Revised, June 2009, to reflect conforming changes necessary due to the issuance of recent authoritative literature.]

.35 In the health care environment, it is almost always at least reasonably possible that estimates regarding third-party payments could change in the near term as a result of one or more future confirming events (for example, regulatory actions reflecting local or national audit or enforcement initiatives). For most entities with significant third-party revenues, the effect of the change could be material to the financial statements. Where material exposure exists, the uncertainty regarding revenue realization should be disclosed in the notes to the financial statements. Because representations from legal counsel are often key audit evidence in evaluating the reasonableness of management's estimates of potential future adjustments, the inability of an attorney to form an opinion on matters about which he or she has been consulted may be indicative of an uncertainty that should be specifically disclosed in the financial statements. [Revised, June 2009, to reflect conforming changes necessary due to the issuance of recent authoritative literature.]

.36 Differences between original estimates and subsequent revisions might arise due to final settlements, ongoing audits and investigations, or passage of time in relation to the statute of limitations. FASB ASC 954-605 requires that these differences be included in the statement of operations in the period in which the revisions are made and disclosed. Such differences are not treated as prior period adjustments unless they meet the criteria for prior period adjustments as set forth in FASB ASC 250-10-45. [Revised, June 2009, to reflect conforming changes necessary due to the issuance of recent authoritative literature.]

.37 Disclosures such as the following may be appropriate:

General Hospital (the Hospital) is a (not-for-profit, for-profit, or governmental hospital or health care system) located in (City, State). The Hospital provides health care services primarily to residents of the region.

Net patient service revenue is reported at estimated net realizable amounts from patients, third-party payors, and others for services rendered and includes estimated retroactive revenue adjustments due to future audits, reviews, and investigations. Retroactive adjustments are considered in the recognition of revenue on an estimated basis in the period the related services are rendered, and such amounts are adjusted in future periods as adjustments become known or as years are no longer subject to such audits, reviews, and investigations.

Revenue from the Medicare and Medicaid programs accounted for approximately 40 percent and 10 percent, respectively, of the Hospital's net patient revenue for the year ended 1999. Laws and regulations governing the Medicare and Medicaid programs are extremely complex and subject to interpretation. As a result, there is at least a reasonable possibility that recorded estimates will change by a material amount in the near term. The 1999 net patient service revenue increased approximately $10,000,000 due to removal of allowances previously estimated that are no longer necessary as a result of final settlements and years that are no longer subject to audits, reviews, and investigations. The 1998 net patient service revenue decreased approximately $8,000,000 due to prior-year retroactive adjustments in excess of amounts previously estimated.

.38

Appendix

Other Considerations Related to Government Investigations

In recent years, the federal government and many states have aggressively increased enforcement efforts under Medicare and Medicaid anti-fraud and abuse legislation. Broadening regulatory and legal interpretations have significantly increased the risk of penalties for providers; for example, broad interpretations of "false claims" laws are exposing ordinary billing mistakes to scrutiny and penalty consideration. In such circumstances, evaluating the adequacy of accruals for or disclosure of the potential effects of illegal acts in the financial statements of health care entities is a matter that is likely to require a high level of professional judgment.

As previously discussed in this SOP, the far-reaching nature of alleged fraud and abuse violations creates an uncertainty with respect to the valuation of revenues, because future allegations of illegal acts could, if proven, result in a subsequent reduction of revenues. In addition, management makes provisions in the financial statements and disclosures for any contingent liabilities associated with fines and penalties due to violations of such laws. FASB ASC 450, *Contingencies*, provides guidance in evaluating contingent liabilities, such as fines and penalties under applicable laws and regulations. Estimates of potential fines and penalties are not accrued unless their payment is probable and reasonably estimable.

The auditor's expertise is in accounting and auditing matters rather than operational, clinical, or legal matters. Accordingly, the auditor's procedures focus on areas that normally are subject to internal controls relevant to financial reporting. However, the further that potential illegal acts are removed from the events and transactions ordinarily reflected in the financial statements, the less likely the auditor is to become aware of the act, to recognize its possible illegality, and to evaluate the effect on the financial statements. For example, determining whether a service was medically necessary, obtained through a legally appropriate referral, properly performed (including using only approved devices, rendered in a quality manner), adequately supervised, accurately documented and classified, or rendered and billed by nonsanctioned individuals typically is not within the auditor's professional expertise. As a result, an audit in accordance with generally accepted auditing standards (GAAS) is not designed to detect such matters.

Further, an audit conducted in accordance with GAAS does not include rendering an opinion or any form of assurance on an entity's compliance with laws and regulations.[1]

Nor does an audit under GAAS include providing any assurance on an entity's billings or cost report. In fact, cost reports typically are not prepared and submitted until after the financial statement audit has been completed.

Certain audit procedures, although not specifically designed to detect illegal acts, may bring possible illegal acts to an auditor's attention. When a potentially illegal act is detected, the auditor's responsibilities are addressed in AU

---

[1] Even when auditors undertake a special engagement designed to attest to compliance with certain provisions of laws, regulations, contracts, and grants (for example, an audit in accordance with OMB Circular A-133), the auditor's procedures do not extend to testing compliance with laws and regulations related to Medicare and Medicaid fraud and abuse.

sec. 317, *Illegal Acts by Clients* (AICPA, *Professional Standards*). Disclosure of an illegal act to parties other than the client's senior management and its audit committee or board of directors is not ordinarily part of the auditor's responsibility, and such disclosure would be precluded by the auditor's ethical or legal obligation of confidentiality, unless the matter affects the auditor's opinion on the financial statements.[2] [Revised, June 2009, to reflect conforming changes necessary due to the issuance of recent authoritative literature.]

---

[2] Statement on Auditing Standards No. 54, *Illegal Acts by Clients* (AICPA, *Professional Standards*, AU sec. 317.23) discusses circumstances in which a duty to notify parties outside the client of detected illegal acts may exist.

Auditing Standards Board

DEBORAH D. LAMBERT, *Chair*
JAMES S. GERSON, *Vice Chair*
JOHN BARNUM
ANDREW J. CAPELLI
LINDA K. CHEATHAM
ROBERT F. DACEY
RICHARD DIETER
SALLY L. HOFFMAN
J. MICHAEL INZINA
CHARLES E. LANDES
W. SCOTT MCDONALD
KEITH O. NEWTON
ROBERT C. STEINER
GEORGE H. TUCKER
O. RAY WHITTINGTON

AICPA Health Care Third-Party Revenue Recognition Task Force

WILLIAM R. TITERA, *Chair*
MARTHA GARNER
ROBERT A. WRIGHT

AICPA Health Care Committee

ROBERT A. WRIGHT, *Chair*
THOMAS J. AARON
PHILLIP J. BRUMMEL
A. JAMES BUDZINSKI
RICK R. CORCORAN
MICHAEL T. DEFREECE
ROBERT E. MAZER
CHARLES V. ROBB
PEGGY B. SCOTT
ALAN A. SCHACHTER
GORDON J. VETSCH
JONATHAN G. WEAVER
AUDREY L. WENT

AICPA Staff

THOMAS RAY
Director
Audit and Attest Standards

ANNETTE SCHUMACHER BARR
Technical Manager
Professional Standards & Services

Appendix C

Information Sources

Further information on matters addressed in this guide is available through various publications and services listed in the table that follows. Many non-government and some government publications and services involve a charge or membership requirement.

Fax services allow users to follow voice cues and request that selected documents be sent by fax machine. Some fax services require the user to call from the handset of the fax machine; others allow the user to call from any phone. Most fax services offer an index document, which lists titles and other information describing available documents.

Recorded announcements allow users to listen to announcements about a variety of recent or scheduled actions or meetings.

All listed telephone numbers are voice lines, unless otherwise designated as fax (f) or data (d) lines.

Information Sources

Organization	*General Information*	*Fax Services*	*Available Publications*
American Association of Homes and Services for the Aging (AAHSA)	AAHSA Publications Dept. 5119 Washington, DC 20061-5119 202.783.2242 www.AAHSA.org		*Continuing Care Retirement Communities: An Industry in Action*
American Hospital Association	*Order Department* P.O. Box 92683 Chicago, IL 60675-2683 800.AHA.2626	Fax-on-Demand 312.422.2020	*Hospital Statistics* *National Hospital Panel Survey Report*
American Medical Association	*Order Department* 515 N. State Street Chicago, IL 60610-4325 800.621.8335	Information-on-Request Fax Line 800.621.8335	"Socioeconomic Resources in Medicine: Review of the Literature"
Center for Health Care Industry Performance Studies	*Order Department* 1550 Old Henderson Road Suite S277 Columbus, OH 43220-3626 800.859.2447		*Almanac of Hospital Financial and Operating Indicators*

(continued)

Organization	*General Information*	*Fax Services*	*Available Publications*
Healthcare Financial Management Association	*Order Department* 2 Westbrook Corporate Center Suite 700 Westchester, IL 60154 800.252.4362		*hfm* magazine Issue Analysis 98-1, *Compliance with Laws and Regulations for Healthcare Organizations*
HealthLeaders-InterStudy	*Order Department* One Vantage Way B-300 Nashville, TN 37228 800.643.7600	Fax-on-Demand 615.385.4979	*Competitive Edge: The HMO Industry Report*
Medical Group Management Association	*Order Department* P.O. Box 17603 Denver, CO 80217-0603 877.275.6462	Fax-on-Demand 303.784.6110	*Cost Survey Practice Management: Academic Practice*

Organization	*General Information*	*Fax Services*	*Website Address*	*Recorded Announce-ments*
American Institute of Certified Public Accountants	*Order Department* 220 Leigh Farm Road Durham, NC 27707-8110 888.777.7077 If outside of the United States, call 919.402.2317	*24 Hour Fax Hotline* 800.362.5066	www.aicpa.org	
Financial Accounting Standards Board	*Order Department* 401 Merritt 7 P.O. Box 5116 Norwalk, CT 06856-5116 203.847.0700, ext. 10 800.748.0659		www.fasb.org	*Action Alert Telephone Line* 203.847.0700, ext. 444

Organization	*General Information*	*Fax Services*	*Website Address*	*Recorded Announce-ments*
Governmental Accounting Standards Board	*Order Department* 401 Merritt 7 P.O. Box 5116 Norwalk, CT 06856-5116 203.847.0700 ext. 10 800.748.0659		www.gasb.org	
Government Accountability Office	441 G Street, NW Washington, DC 20548		www.gao.gov	
Government Printing Office	732 N. Capitol Street, NW Washington, DC 20401-0001		www.gpo.gov www.gpoaccess .gov	
Office of Management and Budget	725 17th Street, NW Washington, DC 20503 202.395.3080		www.omb.gov	
Securities and Exchange Commission (SEC)	100 F Street, NE Washington, DC 20549 *Publications Unit* 202.551.4040 *SEC Public Reference* 202.551.8090 *Information Line* 202.942.8088, ext. 4 TTY 202.551.6020		www.sec.gov	

Appendix D

References to AICPA Technical Practice Aids

The following nonauthoritative questions and answers, commonly referred to as Technical Questions and Answers (TISs), have been prepared by the AICPA staff and are included in *Technical Practice Aids*. The questions and answers have not been approved, disapproved, or otherwise acted upon by the Financial Reporting Executive Committee or any other senior technical committee of the AICPA. They are not sources of established accounting principles[1] nor are they sources of authoritative generally accepted auditing standards. The AICPA staff believes that the questions and answers listed subsequently may be useful and relevant for users of this guide. In addition to the following questions and answers, not-for-profit health care entities may find the questions and answers listed in TIS section 6140, "Not-for-Profit Entities" (AICPA, *Technical Practice Aids*), useful. Other questions and answers may also be useful and relevant to users of this guide, depending on the facts and circumstances.

TIS Section	*Title*
5250.15	"Application of Certain FASB Interpretation No. 48 (codified in FASB ASC 740-10) Disclosure Requirements to Nonpublic Entities That Do Not Have Uncertain Tax Positions"
6140.23	"Changing Net Asset Classifications Reported in a Prior Year"
6400.04	"Hospital as Collecting Agent for Physicians [Amended]"
6400.12	"General Obligation Bonds Issued for Current Use by City Owned Hospital [Amended]"
6400.17	"Elimination of Profit on Intercompany Sales"
6400.19	"Offsetting of Limited Use Assets"
6400.20	"Format of Combined or Consolidated Financial Statements"
6400.25	"Accounting for Transfer of Assets From Not-for-Profit to For-Profit Entities"
6400.26	"Transfer of Assets From Subsidiary For-Profit Entity to Not-for-Profit Stockholder Parent"
6400.29	"Timing of Recording Transfers Between Related Entities"
6400.30	"Accounting for Transactions Involving Medicaid Voluntary Contribution or Taxation Programs [Amended]"
6400.33	"Accounting for a Joint Operating Agreement"
6400.34	"Accounting for Computer Systems Costs Incurred in Connection With the Health Insurance Portability and Accountability Act of 1996 (HIPAA)"

(continued)

[1] See chapter 1, "Overview and Unique Considerations of Health Care Entities," of this guide for additional information regarding the hierarchy of generally accounting principles for nongovernmental health care entities.

TIS Section	*Title*
6400.35	"Note to Sections 6400.36–.42—Implementation of FASB ASC 958—Classification of a Beneficiary's Interest in the Net Assets of a Financially Interrelated Fund-Raising Foundation (in the Beneficiary's Financial Statements)"
6400.36	"Application of FASB ASC 958—Classification of a Beneficiary's Interest in the Net Assets of a Financially Interrelated Fund-Raising Foundation (The beneficiary can influence the operating and financial decisions of the foundation to such an extent that the beneficiary can determine the timing and amount of distributions from the foundation.)"
6400.37	"Application of FASB ASC 958—Classification of a Beneficiary's Interest in the Net Assets of a Financially Interrelated Fund-Raising Foundation (The beneficiary cannot influence the operating and financial decisions of the foundation to such an extent that the beneficiary can determine the timing and amount of distributions from the foundation.)"
6400.38	"Application of FASB ASC 958—Classification of a Beneficiary's Interest in the Net Assets of a Financially Interrelated Fund-Raising Foundation—Does Common Control Lead to the Conclusion That the Beneficiary Can Determine the Timing and Amount of Distributions from the Recipient?"
6400.39	"Application of FASB ASC 958—Classification of a Beneficiary's Interest in the Net Assets of a Financially Interrelated Fund-Raising Foundation (More Than One Beneficiary—Some Contributions Are Designated)"
6400.40	"Application of FASB ASC 958—Classification of a Beneficiary's Interest in the Net Assets of a Financially Interrelated Fund-Raising Foundation (The beneficiary makes an expenditure that meets a purpose restriction on net assets held for its benefit by the recipient entity—The beneficiary can influence the operating and financial decisions of the recipient to such an extent that the beneficiary can determine the timing and amount of distributions from the recipient.)"
6400.41	"Application of FASB ASC 958—Classification of a Beneficiary's Interest in the Net Assets of a Financially Interrelated Fund-Raising Foundation (The beneficiary makes an expenditure that is consistent with a purpose restriction on net assets held for its benefit by the recipient entity—The beneficiary cannot influence the operating and financial decisions of the recipient to such an extent that the beneficiary can determine the timing and amount of distributions from the recipient.)"

TIS Section	*Title*
6400.42	"Application of FASB ASC 958—Classification of a Beneficiary's Interest in the Net Assets of a Financially Interrelated Fund-Raising Foundation (Recipient Entity)—Accounting for Unrealized Gains and Losses on Investments Held by the Foundation"
6400.43	"Application of FASB ASC 958—Classification of Distributions From a Financially Interrelated Fund-Raising Foundation (Recipient Entity) to a Health Care Beneficiary"
6400.45	"Applicability of FASB ASC 460—Accounting and Disclosure Requirements for Guarantees, Including Indirect Guarantees of Indebtedness of Others"
6400.46	"Applicability of FASB ASC 460—Guarantor's Accounting and Disclosure Requirements for Guarantees, Including Indirect Guarantees of Indebtedness of Others—Mortgage Guarantees"
8700.03	"Auditor's Responsibilities for Subsequent Events Relative to a Conduit Debt Obligor"
9110.15	"Reporting on Medicaid/Medicare Cost Reports"

Appendix E

Other Information, Supplementary Information, and Required Supplementary Information

In February 2010, the Auditing Standards Board issued Statement on Auditing Standards (SAS) No. 118, *Other Information in Documents Containing Audited Financial Statements*; No. 119, *Supplementary Information in Relation to the Financial Statements as a Whole*; and No. 120, *Required Supplementary Information* (AICPA, *Professional Standards*, AU sec. 550, 551, 558). These standards collectively supersede AU section 550A, *Other Information in Documents Containing Audited Financial Statements*; 551A, *Reporting on Information Accompanying the Basic Financial Statements in Auditor-Submitted Documents*; and 558A, *Required Supplementary Information* (AICPA, *Professional Standards*), respectively, and are effective for audits of financial statements for periods beginning on or after December 15, 2010, with early application permitted.

Collectively, these statements address the auditor's responsibilities with respect to information that is required by a designated standard setter (the Financial Accounting Standards Board, the Governmental Accounting Standards Board [GASB], the Federal Accounting Standards Advisory Board, or the International Accounting Standards Board) to accompany an entity's basic financial statements and supplementary and other information that is presented outside the basic financial statements. Because the effective date for these standards is for periods ending after the date of this guide, the information in the various chapters in this guide is not updated for the requirements of these standards. The purpose of this appendix is to provide information on the requirements of SAS Nos. 118–120, as well as implementation guidance and examples.

SAS No. 118, *Other Information in Documents Containing Audited Financial Statements*

SAS No. 118, which is effective for audits of financial statements for periods beginning on or after December 15, 2010, addresses the auditor's responsibility in relation to other information (OI) in documents containing audited financial statements and the auditor's report thereon. In the absence of any separate requirement in the particular circumstances of the engagement, the auditor's opinion on the financial statements does not cover OI, and the auditor has no responsibility for determining whether such information is properly stated. The objective of the auditor with respect to OI is to respond appropriately when the auditor becomes aware that documents containing audited financial statements and the auditor's report thereon include OI that could undermine the credibility of those financial statements and the auditor's report.

SAS No. 118 defines *OI* as financial and nonfinancial information, other than the financial statements and auditor's report thereon, that is included in a document containing audited financial statements and the auditor's report thereon, excluding required supplementary information (RSI). In the context of this guide, OI includes information included with municipal securities filings (see chapter 7, "Municipal Bond Financing," of this guide).

Although OI is not a part of the basic financial statements nor required as supplementary information (SI) by a designated standard setter, auditors are required to perform certain procedures on unaudited OI.[1] The auditor should apply the following limited procedures to the OI, as required by paragraphs .06–.17 of SAS No. 118:

- Read the OI of which the auditor is aware in order to identify material inconsistencies, if any, with the audited financial statements.
- Make appropriate arrangements with management or those charged with governance to obtain the OI prior to the report release date. If it is not possible to obtain all of the OI prior to the report release date, the auditor should read such OI as soon as practicable.
- Communicate with those charged with governance the auditor's responsibility with respect to the OI, any procedures performed relating to the OI, and the results.
- If, on reading the OI, the auditor identifies a material inconsistency, the auditor should determine whether the audited financial statements or OI needs to be revised and should consider the following:
  - If a material inconsistency that requires revision of the audited financial statements is identified by the auditor prior to the report release date, and management refuses to make the revision, the auditor should modify the auditor's opinion, in accordance with AU section 508, *Reports on Audited Financial Statements* (AICPA, *Professional Standards*).
  - When a material inconsistency that requires revision of the OI is identified by the auditor prior to the report release date, and management refuses to make the revision, the auditor should communicate with those charged with governance and (*a*) include an explanatory paragraph in the auditor's report describing the material inconsistency, in accordance with paragraph .11 of AU section 508; (*b*) withhold the auditor's report; or (*c*) withdraw from the engagement if withdrawal is possible under applicable law or regulation.[2]

---

[1] *Unaudited other information (OI)* is financial and nonfinancial information (other than the financial statements and auditor's report thereon) that is included in a document containing audited financial statements and the auditor's report thereon, excluding required supplementary information (RSI) on which the auditor is not engaged to express an opinion whether it is fairly presented in conformity with generally accepted accounting principles (GAAP). Unless the auditor is engaged to audit the OI, this guide refers to the information as unaudited, even though generally accepted auditing standards (GAAS) require the auditor to perform specific procedures.

[2] In audits of governmental entities, withdrawal from the engagement or withholding the auditor's report may not be options (see paragraph .A8 of AU section 550, *Other Information in Documents Containing Audited Financial Statements* [AICPA, *Professional Standards*]). In such cases, the auditor may issue a report to those charged with governance and the appropriate statutory body, if applicable, giving details of the inconsistency.

- If a material inconsistency that requires revision of the audited financial statements is identified by the auditor subsequent to the report release date, the auditor should apply the relevant requirements in AU section 561, *Subsequent Discovery of Facts Existing at the Date of the Auditor's Report* (AICPA, *Professional Standards*).
- When a material inconsistency that requires revision of the OI is identified by the auditor subsequent to the report release date, and management agrees to make the revision to the OI, the auditor should carry out the procedures necessary under the circumstances.
- When a material inconsistency that requires revision of the OI is identified by the auditor subsequent to the report release date, and management refuses to make the revision to the OI, the auditor should notify those charged with governance of the auditor's concerns regarding the OI and take any further appropriate action.

- If, on reading the OI for the purpose of identifying material inconsistencies, the auditor becomes aware of an apparent material misstatement of fact, the auditor should discuss the matter with management. After such discussions, if the auditor still believes that an apparent material misstatement of fact exists, the auditor should request management consult with a qualified third party, such as legal counsel; consider the advice received by the entity in determining whether such matter is a material misstatement of fact; and consider the following:
  - When the auditor concludes that the OI contains a material misstatement of fact that management refuses to correct, the auditor should notify those charged with governance of the auditor's concerns regarding the OI and take any further appropriate action (for example, obtaining advice from the auditor's legal counsel, withholding the auditor's report if not yet released, or withdrawing from the engagement).

SAS No. 119, *Supplementary Information in Relation to the Financial Statements as a Whole*

SAS No. 119, which is effective for audits of financial statements for periods beginning on or after December 15, 2010, addresses the auditor's responsibility when engaged to report on whether supplementary information (SI) is fairly stated, in all material respects, in relation to the financial statements as a whole. Paragraph .04 of SAS No. 119 defines *SI* as information presented outside the basic financial statements, excluding RSI, that is not considered necessary for the financial statements to be fairly presented in accordance with the applicable financial reporting framework. SI may be presented in a document containing the audited financial statements or separate from the financial statements. For purposes of this appendix, the auditor's responsibilities related to SI that is presented in a document containing the audited financial statements will be discussed. Information related to the auditor's responsibilities for SI that is presented separate from the financial statements is discussed in paragraphs .10 and .A16 of SAS No. 119.

In order to opine on whether SI is fairly stated, in all material respects, in relation to the financial statements as a whole, the auditor should determine that all of the following conditions are met, as required by paragraph .05 of SAS No. 119:

- The SI was derived from, and relates directly to, the underlying accounting and other records used to prepare the financial statements.
- The SI relates to the same period as the financial statements.
- The financial statements were audited, and the auditor served as the principal auditor in that engagement.
- Neither an adverse opinion nor a disclaimer of opinion was issued on the financial statements.
- The SI will accompany the entity's audited financial statements, or such audited financial statements will be made readily available[3] by the entity.

The auditor's responsibilities with regard to unaudited SI[4] are provided in SAS No. 119. The auditor should apply the following limited procedures to the SI, as required by paragraphs .06–.07 of SAS No. 119:

- Obtain the agreement of management that it acknowledges and understands its responsibility
    - — for the preparation of the SI in accordance with the applicable criteria;
    - — to provide the auditor with written representations
        - that it acknowledges its responsibility for the presentation of the SI in accordance with the applicable criteria;
        - that it believes the SI, including its form and content, is fairly presented in accordance with the applicable criteria;
        - that the methods of measurement or presentation have not changed from those used in the prior period or, if the methods of measurement or presentation have changed, the reasons for such changes;
        - about any significant assumptions or interpretations underlying the measurement or presentation of the SI; and

---

[3] Audited financial statements are deemed to be readily available if a third-party user can obtain the audited financial statements without any further action by the entity, such as posted on the entity's website but not being available upon request.

[4] *Unaudited supplementary information (SI)* is information that accompanies the basic financial statements on which the auditor is not engaged to express an opinion whether it is fairly presented, in all material respects, in conformity with GAAP. Unless the auditor is engaged to audit the SI, this appendix refers to the information as unaudited, even though GAAS requires the auditor to perform specific procedures.

  - that when the SI is not presented with the audited financial statements, management will make the audited financial statements readily available to the intended users of the SI no later than the date of issuance by the entity of the SI and the auditor's report thereon;

- — to include in any document containing the SI the auditor's report on the SI that indicates the auditor reported on such SI; and
- — to present the SI with the audited financial statements or, if the SI will not be presented with the audited financial statements, to make the audited financial statements readily available to the intended users of the SI no later than the date of issuance by the entity of the SI and the auditor's report thereon.

- In addition to the procedures performed during the audit of the financial statements, in order to opine on whether the SI is fairly stated, in all material respects, in relation to the financial statements as a whole, the auditor should perform the following procedures, using the same materiality level used in the audit of the financial statements:[5]

  - — Inquire of management about the purpose of the SI and the criteria used by management to prepare the SI, such as an applicable financial reporting framework, criteria established by a regulator, a contractual agreement, or other requirements.
  - — Determine whether the form and content of the SI complies with the applicable criteria.
  - — Compare and reconcile the SI to the underlying accounting and other records used in preparing the financial statements or to the financial statements themselves.
  - — Obtain an understanding about the methods of preparing the SI, and determine whether the methods of preparing the SI have changed from those used in the prior period and, if the methods have changed, the reasons for such changes.
  - — Inquire of management about any significant assumptions or interpretations underlying the measurement or presentation of the SI.
  - — Evaluate the appropriateness and completeness of the SI, considering the results of the performed procedures and other knowledge obtained during the audit of the financial statements.

---

[5] If the auditor's report on the financial statements of a governmental entity includes multiple opinions, and materiality is considered by the auditor for each opinion unit, the auditor's opinion on the SI is in relation to the financial statements as a whole and considered at a level that represents the entire entity, as discussed in paragraph .A15 of AU section 551, *Other Information in Relation to the Financial Statements as a Whole* (AICPA, *Professional Standards*).

- Obtain the previously-noted representations from management.

The date of the auditor's report on SI in relation to the financial statements as a whole should not be dated earlier than the date on which the auditor completed the procedures required in paragraph .07 of SAS No. 119. When reporting on SI that is presented with the entity's financial statements, the auditor should report on SI in either (*a*) an explanatory paragraph following the opinion paragraph in the auditor's report on the financial statements or (*b*) a separate report on SI. The contents of the explanatory paragraph are discussed in paragraph .09 of SAS No. 120 and are as follows.

- A statement that the
  - — audit was conducted for the purpose of forming opinions on the financial statements that collectively comprise the government's basic financial statements
  - — SI is presented for purposes of additional analysis and is not a required part of the basic financial statements
  - — SI is the responsibility of management and was derived from, and relates directly to, the underlying accounting and other records used to prepare the basic financial statements
  - — SI has been subjected to the auditing procedures applied in the audit of the basic financial statements and certain additional procedures, including comparing and reconciling such information directly to the underlying accounting and other records used to prepare the financial statements or to the financial statements themselves, in accordance with GAAS
- If the auditor issues an unqualified opinion on the basic financial statements, and the auditor has concluded that the SI is fairly stated, in all material respects, in relation to the basic financial statements as a whole, a statement that in the auditor's opinion, the SI is fairly stated, in all material respects, in relation to the basic financial statements as a whole
- If the auditor issues a qualified opinion on the basic financial statements, and the qualification has an effect on the SI, a statement that in the auditor's opinion, except for the effects on the SI of [*refer to the paragraph in the auditor's report explaining the qualification*], such information is fairly stated, in all material respects, in relation to the basic financial statements as a whole

When the auditor's report on the audited basic financial statements contains an adverse opinion or a disclaimer of opinion, and the auditor has been engaged to report on whether SI is fairly stated, in all material respects, in relation to such financial statements as a whole, the auditor is precluded from expressing an opinion on the SI. When permitted by law or regulation, the auditor may withdraw from the engagement to report on the SI. If the auditor does not withdraw, the auditor's report on the SI should state that because of the significance of the matter disclosed in the auditor's report, it is inappropriate to, and the auditor does not, express an opinion on the SI.

If the auditor concludes, on the basis of the performed procedures, that the SI is materially misstated in relation to the basic financial statements as a whole, the auditor should discuss the matter with management and propose appropriate revisions of the SI. If management does not revise the SI, the auditor should either

- modify the auditor's opinion on the SI and describe the misstatement in the auditor's report or
- withhold the auditor's report on the SI in the case of issuing a separate report on the SI.

The auditor has no responsibility for the consideration of subsequent events with respect to the SI. However, if information comes to the auditor's attention prior to the release of the auditor's report on the financial statements regarding subsequent events that affect the financial statements, the auditor should apply the relevant requirements of AU section 560, *Subsequent Events* (AICPA, *Professional Standards*). In the event that information comes to the auditor's attention subsequent to the release of the auditor's report on the financial statements regarding facts that may have existed at that date, which might have affected the report had the auditor been aware of such facts, the relevant requirements of AU section 561 should be applied.

SAS No. 120, *Required Supplementary Information*

SAS No. 120, which is effective for audits of financial statements for periods beginning on or after December 15, 2010, addresses the auditor's responsibility with respect to information that a designated accounting standard setter requires to accompany an entity's basic financial statements (RSI). In the context of this guide, the designated accounting standard setter is GASB, and the most commonly required RSI applicable to governmental health care entities consists of management's discussion and analysis (MD&A) and certain information related to employer-sponsored benefit plans. In the absence of any separate requirement in the particular circumstances of the engagement, the auditor's opinion on the basic financial statements does not cover RSI.

When GAAP designates information as RSI, the designated accounting standard setter considers the information to be an essential part of financial reporting for placing the basic financial statements in an appropriate operational, economic, or historical context. Therefore, the omission of RSI or presentation of RSI in a manner that does not meet the prescribed guidelines does not affect the auditor's conclusion regarding the fair presentation of the basic financial statements. In the prescribed guidelines for RSI, GAAP often requires notes to RSI and specifies the placement of RSI in relation to the basic financial statements. Those note and placement requirements are part of the prescribed guidelines. RSI is normally presented separately from SI and OI, which are discussed earlier in this appendix. The auditor should consider whether RSI is sufficiently segregated from SI and OI. Except in specific situations, professional standards do not address whether RSI should be labeled as unaudited; thus, it may or may not be so labeled.

Only the information that a designated standard setter (for example, GASB in the context of governmental health care entities) requires to accompany an entity's basic financial statements can be considered RSI. All other information is considered SI or OI, even though law, regulation, or resource contributors may require that such information accompany the basic financial statements.

Although RSI is not a part of the basic financial statements, auditors are required to perform certain procedures on unaudited RSI.[6] If the auditor is not engaged to audit RSI, the auditor should apply the following limited procedures to RSI, as required by paragraph .05 of SAS No. 120:

- Inquire of management about the methods of preparing the information, including whether (*a*) it is measured and presented in accordance with prescribed guidelines, (*b*) methods of measurement or presentation have been changed from those used in the prior period and the reasons for any such changes, and (*c*) there were any significant assumptions or interpretations underlying the measurement or presentation of the information.
- Compare the information for consistency with (*a*) management's responses to the foregoing inquiries, (*b*) the basic financial statements, and (*c*) other knowledge obtained during the audit of the basic financial statements.
- Obtain written representations from management (*a*) that it acknowledges its responsibility for RSI; (*b*) about whether RSI is measured and presented in accordance with prescribed guidelines; (*c*) about whether the methods of measurement or presentation have changed from those used in the prior period and, if so, the reasons for such changes; and (*d*) about any significant assumptions or interpretations underlying the measurement or presentation of RSI. See AU section 333, *Management Representations* (AICPA, *Professional Standards*), for additional requirements and guidance.

If the auditor is unable to complete these procedures, the auditor should consider whether management contributed to the auditor's inability to complete the procedures. If the auditor concludes that the inability to complete the procedures is due to significant difficulties encountered in dealing with management, the auditor should inform those charged with governance.

Paragraph .07 of SAS No. 120 states that the auditor should include an explanatory paragraph after the opinion paragraph in the auditor's report on the financial statements to refer to RSI. The explanatory paragraph should include language to explain the following circumstances, as applicable:

- RSI is included, and the auditor has applied certain limited procedures (that is, the procedures are specifically delineated in the explanatory paragraph and are those required by paragraph .05 of SAS No. 120).
- RSI is omitted.
- Some RSI is missing, and some is presented in accordance with the prescribed guidelines.
- The auditor has identified material departures from the prescribed guidelines.
- The auditor is unable to complete the prescribed procedures.

---

[6] *Unaudited RSI* is information that accompanies the basic financial statements on which the auditor is not engaged to express an opinion whether it is fairly presented in conformity with GAAP. Unless the auditor is engaged to audit RSI, this appendix refers to the information as unaudited, even though GAAS requires the auditor to perform specific procedures.

- The auditor has unresolved doubts about whether RSI is presented in accordance with prescribed guidelines.

Paragraph .08 of SAS No. 120 discusses the auditor's reporting responsibilities when all or some RSI is presented. In such circumstances, the auditor should include the following additional elements in the auditor's explanatory paragraph, as applicable:

- A statement that GAAP requires RSI to be presented to supplement the basic financial statements.
- A statement that such information, although not a part of the basic financial statements, is required by [*designated standard setter*], who considers it to be an essential part of financial reporting for placing the basic financial statements in an appropriate operational, economic, or historical context.
- If the auditor is able to complete the procedures required in paragraph .05 of SAS No. 120, a statement that the auditor
    - — has applied certain limited procedures to RSI, in accordance with GAAS, which consisted of inquiries of management about the methods of preparing the information and comparing the information for consistency with management's responses to the auditor's inquiries, the basic financial statements, and other knowledge that the auditor obtained during the audit of the basic financial statements.
    - — does not express an opinion or provide any assurance on the information because the limited procedures do not provide him or her with sufficient evidence to express an opinion or provide any assurance.
- If the auditor is unable to complete the procedures required by paragraph .05 of SAS No. 120 a statement that the auditor
    - — was unable to apply certain limited procedures to RSI, in accordance with GAAS, and the reasons.
    - — does not express an opinion or provide any assurance on the information.
- If some RSI is omitted, a statement that
    - — management has omitted the [*describe the missing RSI*], which is required by GAAP to be presented to supplement the basic financial statements.
    - — such missing information, although not a part of the basic financial statements, is required by [*designated standard setter*], who considers it to be an essential part of financial reporting for placing the basic financial statements in an appropriate operational, economic, or historical context.
    - — the auditor's opinion on the basic financial statements is not affected by the missing information.
- If the measurement or presentation of RSI materially departs from the prescribed guidelines, a statement that although the auditor's opinion on the basic financial statements is not affected,

material departures from prescribed guidelines exist. Describe the material departures from GAAP.

- If the auditor has unresolved doubts about whether RSI is measured or presented in accordance with prescribed guidelines, a statement that although the auditor's opinion on the basic financial statements is not affected, the results of the limited procedures have raised doubts about whether material modifications should be made to RSI for it to be presented in accordance with guidelines established by GASB.

Paragraph .09 of SAS No. 120 discusses the auditor's reporting responsibilities when RSI is omitted. In such circumstances, the auditor should include the following additional statements in the auditor's explanatory paragraph:

- Management has omitted the [*describe the missing RSI*], which GAAP requires to be presented to supplement the basic financial statements.
- Such missing information, although not a part of the basic financial statements, is required by [*designated standard setter*], who considers it to be an essential part of financial reporting for placing the basic financial statements in an appropriate operational, economic, or historical context.
- The auditor's opinion on the basic financial statements is not affected by the missing information.

The exhibit of SAS No. 120 provides the following examples for explanatory paragraphs for various scenarios related to RSI:

The Required Supplementary Information Is Included, the Auditor Has Applied the Specified Procedures, and No Material Departures From Prescribed Guidelines Have Been Identified

[*Identify the applicable financial reporting framework (for example, accounting principles generally accepted in the United States of America)*] require that the [*identify the required supplementary information*] on page XX be presented to supplement the basic financial statements. Such information, although not a part of the basic financial statements, is required by [*identify designated accounting standard setter*] who considers it to be an essential part of financial reporting for placing the basic financial statements in an appropriate operational, economic, or historical context. We have applied certain limited procedures to the required supplementary information in accordance with auditing standards generally accepted in the United States of America, which consisted of inquiries of management about the methods of preparing the information and comparing the information for consistency with management's responses to our inquiries, the basic financial statements, and other knowledge we obtained during our audit of the basic financial statements. We do not express an opinion or provide any assurance on the information because the limited procedures do not provide us with sufficient evidence to express an opinion or provide any assurance.

All Required Supplementary Information Omitted

Management has omitted [*describe the missing required supplementary information*] that [*identify the applicable financial reporting framework (for example, accounting principles generally accepted in the United States of America)*] require to be presented to supplement the basic financial statements. Such missing information, although not a part of the basic financial statements, is required by [*identify designated accounting standard setter*] who considers it to be an essential part of financial reporting for placing the basic financial statements in an appropriate operational, economic, or historical context. Our opinion on the basic financial statements is not affected by this missing information.

Some Required Supplementary Information Is Omitted and Some Is Presented in Accordance With the Prescribed Guidelines

[*Identify the applicable financial reporting framework (for example, accounting principles generally accepted in the United States of America)*] require that [*identify the included required supplementary information*] be presented to supplement the basic financial statements. Such information, although not a part of the basic financial statements, is required by [*identify designated accounting standard setter*] who considers it to be an essential part of financial reporting for placing the basic financial statements in an appropriate operational, economic, or historical context. We have applied certain limited procedures to the required supplementary information in accordance with auditing standards generally accepted in the United States of America, which consisted of inquiries of management about the methods of preparing the information and comparing the information for consistency with management's responses to our inquiries, the basic financial statements, and other knowledge we obtained during our audit of the basic financial statements. We do not express an opinion or provide any assurance on the information because the limited procedures do not provide us with evidence sufficient to express an opinion or provide any assurance.

Management has omitted [*describe the missing required supplementary information*] that [*identify the applicable financial reporting framework*] require to be presented to supplement the basic financial statements. Such missing information, although not a part of the basic financial statements, is required by [*identify designated accounting standard* setter] who considers it to be an essential part of financial reporting for placing the basic financial statements in an appropriate operational, economic, or historical context. Our opinion on the basic financial statements is not affected by this missing information.

Material Departures From Prescribed Guidelines Identified

[*Identify the applicable financial reporting framework (for example, accounting principles generally accepted in the United States of America)*] require that the [*identify the required supplementary information*] on page XX be presented to supplement the basic financial statements. Such information, although not a part of the basic financial statements, is required by [*identify designated accounting standard setter*] who considers it to be an essential part of financial reporting for placing the basic financial statements in an appropriate operational, economic, or historical context. We have applied certain limited procedures to the required supplementary information in accordance with auditing standards generally accepted in the United States of America, which consisted of inquiries of management about the methods of preparing the information and comparing the information for consistency with management's responses to our inquiries, the basic financial statements, and other knowledge we obtained during our audit of the basic financial statements. Although our opinion on the basic financial statements is not affected, the following material departures from the prescribed guidelines exist [*identify the required supplementary information and describe the material departures from the prescribed guidelines*]. We do not express an opinion or provide any assurance on the information.

Specified Procedures Not Completed

[*Identify the applicable financial reporting framework (for example, accounting principles generally accepted in the United States of America)*] require that the [*identify the required supplementary information*] on page XX be presented to supplement the basic financial statements. Such information, although not a part of the basic financial statements, is required by [*identify designated accounting standard setter*] who considers it to be an essential part of financial reporting for placing the basic financial statements in an appropriate operational, economic, or historical context. We were unable to apply certain limited procedures to the required supplementary information in accordance with auditing standards generally accepted in the United States of America because [*state the reasons*]. We do not express an opinion or provide any assurance on the information.

Illustrative Auditor's Reports

Example E-1

Unqualified Opinion on Comparative Basic Financial Statements of a Governmental Hospital (Special-Purpose Government) That Has a Single Opinion Unit and for Which the Auditor Has Not Been Engaged to Examine and Express an Opinion on RSI

Independent Auditor's Report

To the Board of Trustees

Sample Governmental Hospital Authority

We have audited the accompanying statements of net assets of the Sample Governmental Hospital Authority (the Authority)[, a component unit of Feeling County, State of Union,][7] as of December 31, 20X1 and 20X0, and the related statements of revenues, expenses, and changes in net assets and statements of cash flows for the years then ended. These financial statements are the responsibility of the Authority's management. Our responsibility is to express an opinion on these financial statements based on our audits.[8]

We conducted our audits[9] in accordance with auditing standards generally accepted in the United States of America. Those standards require that we plan and perform the audit to obtain reasonable assurance about whether the financial statements are free of material misstatement. An audit includes examining, on a test basis, evidence supporting the amounts and disclosures in the financial statements. An audit also includes assessing the accounting principles used and significant estimates made by management, as well as evaluating the overall financial statement presentation. We believe that our audits[10] provide a reasonable basis for our opinion.

In our opinion, the financial statements referred to above present fairly, in all material respects, the financial position of the Authority as of December 31, 20X1 and 20X0, and the changes in its financial position and its cash flows for the years then ended in conformity with accounting principles generally accepted in the United States of America.

Those accounting principles require that the management's discussion and analysis on pages XX through XX be presented to supplement the basic financial statements. Such information, although not a part of the basic financial statements, is required by the Governmental Accounting Standards Board, who considers it to be an essential part of financial reporting for placing the basic financial statements in an appropriate operational, economic, or historical context. We have applied certain limited procedures to the required supplementary information in accordance with auditing standards generally accepted in the United States of America, which consisted of inquiries of management about the methods of preparing the information and comparing the information for consistency with management's responses to our inquiries, the basic financial

---

[7] *If the entity being reported on is a component unit of a larger financial reporting entity, the auditor's report should disclose that fact, as discussed in the paragraph 14.45 of the Audit and Accounting Guide* State and Local Governments.

[8] Because the report is covering audits for two years, the reference is to *audits*, rather than *audit*.

[9] See footnote 8.

[10] See footnote 8.

statements, and other knowledge we obtained during our audit of the basic financial statements. We do not express an opinion or provide any assurance on the information because the limited procedures do not provide us with sufficient evidence to express an opinion or provide any assurance.

[*Signature*]

[*Date*]

Example E-2

Unqualified Opinions on Single-Year Basic Financial Statements of a Governmental Hospital That Has One Opinion Unit for the Primary Government and Another Opinion Unit for Its Discretely-Presented Component Unit and for Which the Auditor Has Not Been Engaged to Examine and Express an Opinion on RSI

Independent Auditor's Report

To the Board of Trustees

University Hospital

We have audited the accompanying statements of net assets and the related statements of revenues, expenses and changes in net assets and statements of cash flows[11] of the University Hospital [*, a component unit of University, Any City and Any State,*][12] and of its discretely presented component unit as of and for the year ended December 31, 20XY, which collectively comprise the Hospital's basic financial statements. These financial statements are the responsibility of the Hospital's management. Our responsibility is to express opinions[13] on these financial statements based on our audit.[14]

[*Same second paragraph as in Example E-1*]

In our opinion, the financial statements referred to above present fairly, in all material respects, the respective financial position of the University Hospital and of its discretely presented component unit as of December 31, 20XY, and the respective changes in financial position and cash flows thereof for the year then ended in conformity with accounting principles generally accepted in the United States of America.

[*Same disclaimer on MD&A as in Example E-1*]

[*Signature*]

[*Date*]

---

[11] Presentation of a statement of cash flows for the discretely-presented component unit is not required.

[12] See footnote 7.

[13] Because two opinion units exist, the auditor is rendering two opinions (one on the Hospital and one on the discretely-presented component unit), and the report should refer to *opinions,* rather than *opinion*.

[14] The opinion on a set of single-year statements refers to one audit. Even though the auditor may be expressing multiple opinions, the auditor is conducting only one audit of the opinion units.

Glossary

The following terms can be found in the Financial Accounting Standards Board (FASB) *Accounting Standards Codification* (ASC) glossary:

acquiree. The business or businesses that the acquirer obtains control of in a business combination. This term also includes a nonprofit activity or business that a not-for-profit acquirer obtains control of in an acquisition by a not-for-profit entity.

acquirer. The entity that obtains control of the acquiree. However, in a business combination in which a variable interest entity is acquired, the primary beneficiary of that entity always is the acquirer.

acquisition by a not-for-profit entity. A transaction or other event in which a not-for-profit acquirer obtains control of one or more nonprofit activities or businesses and initially recognizes their assets and liabilities in the acquirer's financial statements. When applicable guidance in FASB ASC 805, *Business Combinations*, is applied by a not-for-profit entity (NFP), the term business combination has the same meaning as this term has for an NFP. Likewise, a reference to business combinations in guidance that links to FASB ASC 805 has the same meaning as a reference to acquisitions by NFPs.

acquisition date. The date on which the acquirer obtains control of the acquiree.

advance refunding. A transaction involving the issuance of new debt to replace existing debt with the proceeds from the new debt placed in trust or otherwise restricted to retire the existing debt at a determinable future date or dates.

affiliate. A party that, directly or indirectly through one or more intermediaries, controls, is controlled by, or is under common control with an entity.

agent. An entity that acts for and on behalf of another. Although the term *agency* has a legal definition, the term is used broadly to encompass not only legal agency, but also the relationships described in FASB ASC 958, *Not-for-Profit Entities*. A recipient entity acts as an agent for and on behalf of a donor if it receives assets from the donor and agrees to use those assets on behalf of or transfer those assets, the return on investment of those assets, or both to a specified beneficiary. A recipient entity acts as an agent for and on behalf of a beneficiary if it agrees to solicit assets from potential donors specifically for the beneficiary's use and to distribute those assets to the beneficiary. A recipient entity also acts as an agent if a beneficiary can compel the recipient entity to make distributions to it or on its behalf.

business. An integrated set of activities and assets that is capable of being conducted and managed for the purpose of providing a return in the form of dividends, lower costs, or other economic benefits directly to investors or other owners, members, or participants. Additional guidance on what a business consists of is presented in paragraphs 4–9 of FASB ASC 805-10-55.

business combination. A transaction or other event in which an acquirer obtains control of one or more businesses. Transactions sometimes referred to as true mergers or mergers of equals also are business combinations. See also [**business** and] **acquisition by a not-for-profit entity**.

capitation fee. A fixed amount per individual that is paid periodically (usually monthly) to a provider as compensation for providing comprehensive health care services for the period. The fee is set by contract between a prepaid health care plan and the provider. These contracts are generally with medical groups, independent practice associations, hospitals, and other similar providers. Capitation fees may be determined actuarially or negotiated based on expected costs to be incurred.

cash flow hedge. A hedge of the exposure to variability in the cash flows of a recognized asset or liability, or of a forecasted transaction, that is attributable to a particular risk.

charity care. Charity care represents health care services that are provided but are never expected to result in cash flows. Charity care is provided to a patient with demonstrated inability to pay. Each entity establishes its own criteria for charity care consistent with its mission statement and financial ability.

claim adjustment expenses. Expenses incurred in the course of investigating and settling claims [(further industry-specific information is provided in the following list of terms)].

collaborative arrangement. A contractual arrangement that involves a joint operating activity (see FASB ASC 808-10-15-7). These arrangements involve two (or more) parties that meet both of the following requirements:

a. They are active participants in the activity (see paragraphs 8–9 of FASB ASC 808-10-15).

b. They are exposed to significant risks and rewards dependent on the commercial success of the activity (see paragraphs 10–13 of FASB ASC 808-10-15).

compensation. Reciprocal transfers of cash or other assets in exchange for services performed.

conditional promise to give. A promise to give that depends on the occurrence of a specified future and uncertain event to bind the promisor.

conduit debt securities. Certain limited-obligation revenue bonds, certificates of participation, or similar debt instruments issued by a state or local governmental entity for the express purpose of providing financing for a specific third party (the conduit bond obligor) that is not a part of the state or local government's financial reporting entity. Although conduit debt securities bear the name of the governmental entity that issues them, the governmental entity often has no obligation for such debt beyond the resources provided by a lease or loan agreement with the third party on whose behalf the securities are issued. Further, the conduit bond obligor is responsible for any future financial reporting requirements.

contribution. An unconditional transfer of cash or other assets to an entity or a settlement or cancellation of its liabilities in a voluntary nonreciprocal transfer by another entity acting other than as an owner. Those characteristics distinguish contributions from exchange transactions, which are reciprocal transfers in which each party receives and sacrifices approximately equal value; from investments by owners and distributions to owners, which are nonreciprocal transfers between an entity and its owners; and from other nonreciprocal transfers, such as impositions of taxes or legal judgments, fines, and thefts, which are not voluntary transfers. In a contribution transaction, the value, if any, returned to the resource provider is incidental to potential public benefits. In an exchange transaction, the potential public benefits are secondary to the potential proprietary benefits to the resource provider. The term *contribution revenue* is used to apply to transactions that are part of the entity's ongoing major or central activities (revenues), or are peripheral or incidental to the entity (gains). See also **inherent contribution**.

control. The direct or indirect ability to determine the direction of management and policies through ownership, contract, or otherwise.

diagnosis-related group. A patient classification scheme that categorizes patients who are related medically with respect to primary and secondary diagnosis, age, or complications [(further industry-specific information is provided in the following list of terms)].

donor-imposed condition. A donor stipulation that specifies a future and uncertain event whose occurrence or failure to occur gives the promisor a right of return of the assets it has transferred or releases the promisor from its obligation to transfer its assets.

donor-imposed restriction. A donor stipulation that specifies a use for a contributed asset that is more specific than broad limits resulting from the following:

a. The nature of the not-for-profit entity (NFP)

b. The environment in which it operates

c. The purposes specified in its articles of incorporation or bylaws or comparable documents for an unincorporated association.

A donor-imposed restriction on an NFP's use of the asset contributed may be temporary or permanent. Some donor-imposed restrictions impose limits that are permanent, for example, stipulating that resources be invested in perpetuity (not used up). Others are temporary, for example, stipulating that resources may be used only after a specified date, for particular programs or services, or to acquire buildings and equipment.

economic interest. A not-for-profit entity's (NFP's) interest in another entity that exists if any of the following criteria are met:

a. The other entity holds or utilizes significant resources that must be used for the unrestricted or restricted purposes of the NFP, either directly or indirectly by producing income or providing services.

b. The NFP is responsible for the liabilities of the other entity.

See FASB ASC 958-810-55-6 for examples of economic interests.

endowment fund. An established fund of cash, securities, or other assets used to provide income for the maintenance of a not-for-profit entity (NFP). The use of the assets of the fund may be permanently restricted, temporarily restricted, or unrestricted. Endowment funds generally are established by donor-restricted gifts and bequests to provide either of the following:

a. A permanent endowment, which is to provide a permanent source of income *b.* A term endowment, which is to provide income for a specific period.

Alternatively, an NFP's governing board may earmark a portion of its unrestricted net assets as a board-designated endowment fund.

equity transfer. An equity transfer is nonreciprocal. An equity transfer is a transaction directly between a transferor and a transferee. Equity transfers are similar to ownership transactions between a for-profit parent and its owned subsidiary (for example, additional paid-in capital or dividends). However, equity transfers can occur only between related not-for-profit entities if one controls the other or both are under common control. An equity transfer embodies no expectation of repayment, nor does the transferor receive anything of immediate economic value (such as a financial interest or ownership).

financially interrelated entities. A recipient entity and a specified beneficiary are financially interrelated entities if the relationship between them has both of the following characteristics:

a. One of the entities has the ability to influence the operating and financial decisions of the other.

b. One of the entities has an ongoing economic interest in the net assets of the other.

functional classification. A method of grouping expenses according to the purpose for which costs are incurred. The primary functional classifications are program services and supporting activities.

fundraising activities. Activities undertaken to induce potential donors to contribute money, securities, services, materials, facilities, other assets, or time.

health maintenance organization (HMO). A generic group of medical care entities organized to provide defined health care services to members in return for fixed, periodic premiums (usually paid monthly) that are paid in advance.

incurred but not reported claims. Claims relating to insured events that have incurred but have not yet been reported to the insurer or reinsurer as of the date of the financial statements [(further industry-specific information is provided in the following list of terms)].

inherent contribution. A contribution that results if an entity voluntarily transfers assets (or net assets) or performs services for another entity in exchange for either no assets or for assets of substantially lower value and unstated rights or privileges of a commensurate value are not involved.

in-substance defeasance. Placement by the debtor of amounts equal to the principal, interest, and prepayment penalties related to a debt instrument in an irrevocable trust established for the benefit of the creditor [(further industry-specific information is provided in the following list of terms)].

intermediary. Although in general usage the term intermediary encompasses a broad range of situations in which an entity acts between two or more other parties, in this usage, it refers to situations in which a recipient entity acts as a facilitator for the transfer of assets between a potential donor and a potential beneficiary (donee) but is neither an agent or trustee nor a donee and donor.

legal entity. Any legal structure used to conduct activities or to hold assets. Some examples of such structures are corporations, partnerships, limited liability companies, grantor trusts, and other trusts.

maintenance costs. Costs associated with maintaining records relating to insurance contracts and with the processing of premium collections and commissions [(further industry-specific information is provided in the following list of terms)].

management and general activities. Activities that are not identifiable with a single program, fundraising activity, or membership-development activity but that are indispensable to the conduct of those activities and to an entity's existence.

membership development activities. Membership development activities include soliciting for prospective members and membership dues, membership relations, and similar activities. However, if there are no significant benefits or duties connected with membership, the substance of membership development activities may, in fact, be fundraising.

merger date. The date on which the merger becomes effective.

merger of not-for-profit entities. A transaction or other event in which the governing bodies of two or more not-for-profit entities (NFPS) cede control of those entities to create a new NFP.

natural expense classification. A method of grouping expenses according to the kinds of economic benefits received in incurring those expenses. Examples of natural expense classifications include salaries and wages, employee benefits, supplies, rent, and utilities.

net assets. The excess or deficiency of assets over liabilities of a not-for-profit entity, which is classified into three mutually exclusive classes according to the existence of absence of donor-imposed restrictions. See also **unrestricted net assets**, **temporarily restricted net assets**, and **permanently restricted net assets**.

nonfinancial assets. An asset that is not a financial asset. Nonfinancial assets include land, buildings, use of facilities or utilities, materials and supplies, intangible assets, or services.

nonprofit activity. An integrated set of activities and assets that is capable of being conducted and managed for the purpose of providing benefits, other than goods or services at a profit or profit equivalent, as a fulfillment of an entity's purpose or mission (for example, goods or services to beneficiaries, customers, or members). As with a not-for-profit entity, a nonprofit activity possesses characteristics that distinguish it from a business or a for-profit business entity.

not-for-profit entity. An entity that possesses the following characteristics, in varying degrees, that distinguish it from a business entity:

a. Contributions of significant amounts of resources from resource providers who do not expect commensurate or proportionate pecuniary return

b. Operating purposes other than to provide goods or services at a profit

c. Absence of ownership interests like those of business entities

Entities that clearly fall outside this definition include the following:

a. All investor-owned enterprises

b. Entities that provide dividends, lower costs, or other economic benefits directly and proportionately to their owners, members, or participants, such as mutual insurance entities, credit unions, farm and rural electric cooperatives, and employee benefit plans

performance indicator. A performance indicator reports results of operations. A performance indicator and the income from continuing operations reported by for-profit health care entities generally are consistent, except for transactions that clearly are not applicable to one kind of entity (for example, for-profit health care entities typically would not receive contributions, and not-for-profit health care entities would not award stock compensation). That is, a performance indicator is analogous to income from continuing operations of a for-profit entity.

permanently restricted net assets. The part of the net assets of a not-for-profit entity (NFP) resulting from the following:

a. Contributions and other inflows of assets whose use by the NFP is limited by donor-imposed stipulations that neither expire by the passage of time nor can be fulfilled or otherwise removed by the actions of the NFP.

b. Other asset enhancements and diminishments subject to the same kinds of stipulations.

c. Reclassification from or to other classes of net assets as a consequence of donor-imposed stipulations.

permanent restriction. A donor-imposed restriction that stipulates that resources be maintained permanently but permits the not-for-profit entity to use up or expend part or all of the income or other economic benefits derived from the donated assets.

prepaid health care plan. A plan in which the provider is compensated in advance by the sponsoring entity. The sponsoring entity pays or compensates the provider based on either a fixed sum or a per-enrollee amount. Prepaid health care plans include health maintenance organizations, preferred provider organizations, eye care plans, dental care plans, and similar plans. Under such plans, the financial risk of delivering the health care is transferred to the provider of services.

prepaid health care services. Any form of health care service provided to a member in exchange for a scheduled payment (or payments) established before care is provided, regardless of the level of service subsequently provided.

prepaid health care services providers. Entities that provide or arrange for the delivery of health care services in accordance with the terms and provisions of a prepaid health care plan. Providers assume the financial risk of the cost of delivering health care services in excess of preestablished fixed premiums. However, some or all of the financial risk may be contractually transferred to other providers (affiliated entities) or by purchasing stop-loss insurance. Other providers of prepaid health care services may include comprehensive medical plans, physicians groups (for example, independent practice associations), and hospitals.

program services. The activities that result in goods and services being distributed to beneficiaries, customers, or members that fulfill the purposes or mission for which the not-for-profit entity (NFP) exists. Those services are the major purpose for and the major output of the NFP and often relate to several major programs.

prospective rate setting. Prospective rate setting is a method used to set payment rates in advance of the delivery of health care services. Such payment rates determine what third parties will pay for health care services during the rate period (generally one year). Prospective rate setting may result from a contractual agreement with a third party, such as a Blue Cross plan, or it may be mandated through legislation. The intent of prospective rate setting is to establish payment rates before the period to which they will apply and that are not subject to change.

reinsurance. A transaction in which a reinsurer (assuming entity), for a consideration (premium), assumes all or part of a risk undertaken originally by another insurer (ceding entity). For indemnity reinsurance, the legal rights of the insured are not affected by the reinsurance transaction and the insurance entity issuing the insurance contract remains liable to the insured for payment of policy benefits. Assumption or novation reinsurance contracts that are legal replacements of one insurer by another extinguish the ceding entity's liability to the policyholder [(further industry-specific information is provided in the following list of terms)].

retrospective rate setting. Under retrospective rate setting, third parties usually determine an interim payment rate and, during the rate period (generally one year), pay the health care entity for services rendered using that rate. After the rate period has ended, a final settlement is made in accordance with federal or state regulations or contractual agreements. Under a retrospective system, an entity may be entitled to receive additional payments or may be required to refund amounts received in excess of amounts earned under the system. Although final settlements are not made until a subsequent period, they are usually subject to reasonable estimations and are reported in the financial statements in the period in which services are rendered.

stop-loss insurance. A contract in which an entity agrees to indemnify providers for certain health care costs incurred by members.

tail coverage. Insurance designed to cover malpractice claims incurred before, but reported after, cancellation or expiration of a claims-made insurance policy.

temporarily restricted net assets. The part of the net assets of a not-for-profit entity (NFP) resulting from the following:

a. Contributions and other inflows of assets whose use by the NFP is limited by donor-imposed stipulations that either expire by passage of time or can be fulfilled and removed by actions of the NFP pursuant to those stipulations

b. Other asset enhancements and diminishments subject to the same kinds of stipulations

c. Reclassification from or to other classes of net assets as a consequence of donor-imposed stipulations, their expiration by passage of time, or their fulfillment and removal by actions of the NFP pursuant to those stipulations

trading securities. Securities that are bought and held principally for the purpose of selling them in the near term and therefore held for only a short period of time. Trading generally reflects active and frequent buying and selling, and trading securities are generally used with the objective of generating profits on short-term differences in price.

trustee. An entity that has a duty to hold and manage assets for the benefit of a specified beneficiary in accordance with a charitable trust agreement. In some states, not-for-profit entities (NFPs) are organized under trust law rather than as corporations. Those NFPs are not trustees as defined because, under those statutes, they hold assets in trust for the community or some other broadly described group, rather than for a specific beneficiary.

unrestricted net assets. The part of net assets of a not-for-profit entity (NFP) that is neither permanently restricted nor temporarily restricted by donor-imposed stipulations. The only limits on the use of unrestricted net assets are the broad limits resulting from the following:

a. The nature of the NFP

b. The environment in which the NFP operates

c. The purposes specified in the NFP's articles of incorporation or bylaws

d. Limits resulting from contractual agreements with suppliers, creditors, and others entered into by the NFP in the course of its business

Unrestricted net assets generally result from revenues from providing services, producing and delivering goods, receiving unrestricted contributions, and receiving dividends or interest from investing in income-producing assets, less expenses incurred in providing services, producing and delivering goods, raising contributions, and performing administrative functions.

variable interest entity. A legal entity subject to consolidation according to the provisions of the "Variable Interest Entities" subsections of FASB ASC 810-10.

voluntary health and welfare entity. A not-for-profit entity (NFP) that is formed for the purpose of performing voluntary services for various segments of society and that is tax exempt (organized for the benefit of the public), supported by the public, and operated on a not-for-profit basis. Most voluntary health and welfare entities concentrate their efforts and expend their resources in an attempt to solve health and welfare problems of society and, in many cases, those of specific individuals. As a group, voluntary health and welfare entities include those NFPs that derive their revenue primarily from voluntary contributions from the general public to be used for general or specific purposes connected with health, welfare, or community services. For purposes of this definition, the general public excludes government entities when determining whether an NFP is a voluntary health and welfare entity.

The following is a list of additional terms that have been used in this guide and further information on select terms defined in the FASB ASC glossary:

acquisition costs. Marketing costs that are (*a*) directly related to the acquisition of specific subscriber contracts and member enrollment and (*b*) incremental to general marketing activities.

acute care. Inpatient general routine care provided to patients who are in a phase of illness that does not require the concentrated and continuous observation and treatment provided in intensive-care units.

administrative services only (ASO). A contract between a third-party company and self-funded plan in which the third-party company performs administrative services only and does not assume any risks. The employer is at risk for the cost of provided health care services. Services normally include claims processing but may include other services, such as actuarial analysis, utilization review, data reporting, and stop-loss coverage. This is a common arrangement when an employer sponsors a self-funded health care program.

advance fee. A payment required to be made by a continuing care retirement community (CCRC) resident prior to, or at the time of, admission to the CCRC for future services and the use of facilities specified in a contract that remains in effect for as long as the resident resides in the CCRC.

allocated loss adjustment expense. Claim expense that can be assigned to individual claims (for example, attorney's fees, claim adjusting service fees, or court costs).

allowable costs. Costs that are allowable under the principles of reimbursement of Medicare and Medicaid or contractual agreements with their payors, such as Blue Cross and Blue Shield.

allowance. The difference between gross patient service revenues charged at established rates for services rendered and amounts received or to be received from patients or third-party payors. Allowances are to be distinguished from uncollectible losses. The types of allowances are as follows:

- *Charity allowances.* The difference between charges at established rates and amounts received from indigent patients, voluntary agencies, or governmental units on behalf of specific indigent patients. Charity allowances are subtracted from gross charges to compute gross patient service revenue.
- *Contractual allowances.* The difference between charges at established rates and amounts received from third-party payors under contractual agreement. Contractual allowances are subtracted from gross patient service revenue to compute net patient service revenue.
- *Courtesy allowances.* The difference between charges at established rates and amounts received from doctors, clergymen, employees, and employees' dependents. Also called policy discounts. Courtesy allowances are subtracted from gross patient service revenue to compute net patient service revenue.

ambulatory care. Provision of health care services to outpatients and other patients who do not require admission to the hospital as inpatients. Any type of medical care provided to a patient who is not hospitalized.

ambulatory care organization. A partnership, association, corporation, or other legal entity organized to deliver health care services to patients that come or are brought to a health care facility for a purpose other than admission as an inpatient (for example, emergency room services, clinic services, or outpatient surgery).

ambulatory payment classifications (APC). The Medicare reimbursement mechanism that sets the prospectively established rate for outpatient reimbursement, which is similar to the diagnosis-related group (DRG) system that is used for inpatient reimbursement. APCs are based upon procedure versus diagnosis (as is used for DRGs) or encounter.

ancillary services. Services performed for diagnostic or therapeutic purposes. Ancillary services generally are those special services for which charges in addition to routine charges customarily are made (for example, laboratory, radiology, surgical, or other services).

anticipated revenues. Amounts including third-party payments (for example, those from Blue Cross and Blue Shield); contractually- or statutorily-committed investment income from sources related to the activities of a continuing care retirement community (CCRC); contributions pledged by donors to support CCRC activities; periodic fees expected to be collected; or the balance of deferred nonrefundable advance fees.

asserted claim. A claim made against a health care entity by or on behalf of a patient alleging improper professional service.

assets limited as to use. Assets that are segregated and limited regarding how the assets may be used either by the board or management (for example, designated for expenditure in the acquisition of property and equipment or for the liquidation of long-term debt) or by outside third parties other than a donor or grantor (for example, funds under bond agreements or malpractice arrangements).

associated entity. An individual practice association, hospital, medical group, or similar health care entity that contracts with a prepaid health care provider to provide health care services.

bad-debt expense. The current period charge for actual or expected doubtful accounts resulting from the extension of credit.

benchmark. The process of comparing an entity's operations and financial data with that of other entities, particularly comparing one entity with the entity considered the best in the industry. Quantitative benchmarks are used to establish performance objectives. Among physicians, it is often the standard for quality medical care and can be applied to any condition or procedure.

best-efforts remarketing agreement. A financing agreement in which the agent agrees to buy only those securities that it is able to sell to others; if the agent is unable to remarket the debt, the issuer is obligated to pay off the debt.

board-designated funds. Unrestricted resources set aside by the governing board for specific purposes or projects or for investment to produce income as if they were endowment funds.

capitation arrangement. An arrangement in which certain medical and other defined health care services are provided by third-party health care providers to a specified population under contractual arrangement with payors. In a capitation arrangement, the primary entity retains responsibility for the quality and performance of the provided services.

case mix. Grouping of patients possessing similar clinical attributes and output utilization patterns, primarily for purposes of cost accounting and reimbursement. The classifications or categories of patients treated by a hospital. Case mix directly influences the length of stays and intensity, cost, and scope of services provided by a hospital. Also defined as a weighting of a patient's acuity in which the average acuity is one.

census, average daily. The average number of inpatients, excluding newborns, in the hospital or facility each day for a given period of time. Average daily census for any classification is computed by taking the total number of patient days of care for that classification throughout the period and dividing those days by the total number of days in that period.

Centers for Medicare & Medicaid Services (CMS). The federal agency responsible for Medicare and Medicaid programs.

claim adjustment expenses. Claim adjustment expenses include any legal fees and the costs of paying claims and all related expenses (defined in the FASB ASC glossary, as presented in the first section of this glossary).

claims-made insurance policy. A policy that covers only malpractice claims reported to the insurance carrier during the policy term, regardless of the date of the incident giving rise to the claim.

clinic. A freestanding facility or part of another health care entity used for diagnosis and treatment of outpatients.

coinsurance. A percentage that the insured member pays after the plan's deductible is exceeded and until the policy's stop-loss provision is reached. Sometimes used synonymously with copayment, but a *copayment* is a flat fee. See also **copayment**.

commercial paper. Short-term, unsecured promissory notes that represent a flexible and low-cost form of short-term financing. Taxable commercial paper is sold on a discount basis, rather than an interest-bearing basis, with the discount determined by the maturity of the notes, the creditworthiness of the issuer or its credit support, and general market demand. The primary risk is the variable interest rate exposure. Issuance often requires some form of credit enhancement or liquidity support.

community rating. The rating methodology required of federally-qualified health maintenance organizations (HMOs); HMOs under the laws of many states; and, occasionally, indemnity plans under certain circumstances. The HMO must obtain the same amount of money per member for all members in the plan. Community rating does allow for variability by allowing the HMO to factor in differences for age, sex, mix (average contract size), and industry factors; however, not all factors are necessarily allowed under state laws.

component unit. Component units are legally separate organizations for which the elected officials of the primary government are financially accountable. In addition, component units can be other organizations for which the nature and significance of their relationship with a primary government are such that exclusion would cause the reporting entity's financial statements to be misleading or incomplete. A component unit may be a governmental organization, except those that meet the definition of a *primary government*, *nonprofit corporation*, or *for-profit corporation*.

conduit financing. A financing arrangement involving a government or other qualified agency using its name in an issuance of fixed income securities, generally for financing a not-for-profit entity's capital project. See also **conduit debt securities** in the FASB ASC glossary, as presented in the first section of this glossary.

continuing-care contract. An agreement between a resident and continuing care retirement community (CCRC) specifying the services and facilities to be provided by the CCRC to a resident over an established period of time, usually the remaining life of the resident.

continuing care retirement community (CCRC). A legal entity sponsoring or guaranteeing residential facilities, meals, and health care services for a community of retired persons who may reside in apartments; other living units; or, in some cases, a nursing center. Also called a residential care facility or life-care retirement community.

contract period. The period (typically one year) for which premium rates are fixed by contract.

contractual adjustments. The differences between revenue at established rates and the amounts realizable from third-party payors under contractual agreements.

copayment. That portion of a claim or medical expense that a member must pay out of pocket. Typical copayments are fixed or variable flat amounts for physician office visits, prescriptions, or hospital services. Sometimes used synonymously with coinsurance, but *coinsurance* is a percentage payment. See also **coinsurance**.

cost-plus. A third-party administrator contract in which the employer pays the administrator a fee based on paid claims, such as a percentage of paid claims. The administrator funds the payment of claims and, therefore, is liable for unpaid claims if the employer is unable to pay the claims.

costs of acquiring initial continuing-care contracts. Costs incurred to originate a contract that result from, and are essential to, the acquisition of the initial contracts and are incurred through the date of substantial occupancy but no later than one year from the date of completion of construction. These costs include the following:

- The costs of processing the contract, such as evaluating the prospective resident's financial condition; evaluating and recording guarantees, collateral, and other security arrangements; negotiating contract terms; preparing and processing contract documents; and closing the transaction
- The costs from activities in connection with soliciting potential initial residents, such as model units and their furnishings, sales brochures, semipermanent signs, tours, grand openings, and sales salaries. These costs do not include advertising, interest, administrative costs, rent, depreciation, or any other occupancy or equipment costs
- The portion of an employee's compensation and benefits that relates to the initial contract acquisitions

courtesy and policy discounts. The differences between revenue recorded at established rates and amounts realizable for services provided to specific individuals, such as employees, medical staff, and clergy. See also **allowance**.

covered charges. The charges incurred by a patient that are covered under the contractual agreements with third-party payors.

common procedural terminology (CPT) coding. A coding structure used to code surgical procedures for statistical analysis and billing purposes. CPT coding was copyrighted by the American Medical Association, and the Centers for Medicare & Medicaid Services mandates the use of these codes for Medicare billing.

credibility. A measure of the statistical significance of a provider's own data, dependent on its stability and volume in relation to the stability and volume of the industry data. Actuaries use credibility to blend an estimate from a provider's own experience with a broader estimate based on the experience of similar institutions. A provider's own experience may be assigned a credibility weight less than 100 percent due to year-to-year volatility. Such volatility is often a function of the size of the provider. Large providers generally have less volatility than small providers. In such an instance, a broader and more stable body of experience of similar providers would be used to supplement the specific provider's experience.

credit enhancement. Typically, a bank letter of credit that guarantees investors will receive principal and interest in the event of an issuer default. A line of credit provides liquidity support to an issuer but does not provide a guarantee of the repayment of principal and interest in the event of issuer default. The liquidity support provides a loan to issuers in the event that the issuer is unable to place large amounts of maturing commercial paper with investors.

crossover refunding. A type of advance refunding in which the old debt is not immediately replaced. The proceeds from the new debt; additional cash deposits, if any; and the income earned on the related investments are sufficient to pay the principal and any call premium of the old debt and interest on the new debt until the date of crossover. Until the crossover, the proceeds from the new debt serve as collateral for that debt. The old debt is serviced by the entity until the date of crossover, at which time the proceeds from the new debt are used to retire the old debt, and the entity becomes obligated to service the new debt. The old debt remains as a liability on the issuer's books until the crossover, when it is called in accordance with the call provisions of its indenture. Also called a delayed defeasance.

debt reserve funds. The amount of funds or cash that needs to be set aside to fund debt repayment.

deductible. The portion of a member's health care expenses that must be paid out of pocket before any insurance coverage applies. Deductibles are common in indemnity insurance plans and preferred provider organizations, or PPOs, but uncommon in health maintenance organizations, or (HMOs).

defeasance. Legal satisfaction of refunded debt without the debt necessarily being retired.

diagnosis-related group (DRG). A statistical system of classifying any inpatient stay into groups for purposes of payment. DRGs may be primary or secondary, and an outlier classification also exists. This is the form of reimbursement that the Centers for Medicare & Medicaid Services uses to pay hospitals for Medicare recipients. Also used by a few states for all payors and by some private health plans for contracting purposes (defined in the FASB ASC glossary, as presented in the first section of this glossary).

donated services. Services of personnel who receive no monetary compensation or partial compensation. The term is usually applied to services rendered by members of religious orders, societies, or similar groups to institutions operated by, or affiliated with, such institutions.

durable medical equipment (DME). Medical equipment that is not disposable (that is, used repeatedly) and is only related to care for a medical condition. Examples would include wheelchairs and home hospital beds. An area of increasing expense, particularly in conjunction with case management.

Emergency Medical Treatment and Labor Act (EMTALA). A federal law governing assessment and transfer of patients seeking emergency care. Sometimes called Emergency Medical Treatment and Active Labor Act.

enrollee. An individual who is a subscriber or an eligible dependent of a subscriber in a prepaid health care plan.

enterprise fund. In governmental accounting, an enterprise fund may be used to report any activity for which a fee is charged to external users for goods or services. An enterprise fund is a proprietary fund that is generally used to account for governmental activities that are similar to activities that may be performed by a commercial enterprise.

estimated costs of future services. Amounts that are expected to be incurred to provide services and the use of facilities to individuals over their remaining lives under continuing-care contracts. Examples include resident care, dietary, health care, facility, general and administrative, interest, depreciation, and amortization costs.

excess levels. The level of insurance coverage that applies to that portion of a loss or damage that exceeds a specified amount.

exposure. The amount of potential claim risk. The basis for reflecting differences in the claim potential among providers' bases for charging insurance premiums or allocating member contributions to a captive. Exposure bases for hospital professional liability include the number of occupied beds, outpatient visits, emergency room visits, and the number of residents by specialty.

Federal Employee Health Benefits Program. The program that provides health benefits to federal employees.

fee-for-service system. The traditional health care payment system under which providers receive a fee for each delivered service. Under the fee-for-service system, the total bill will increase not only if the fees increase but also if more units of service are rendered.

fee schedule. A comprehensive listing of fee maximums used to reimburse a provider on a fee-for-service basis. May also be referred to as fee maximums or a fee allowance schedule. A listing of the maximum fee that a health plan will pay for a certain service based on common procedural terminology billing codes.

final settlement. The ultimate liability of the health care entity to the third-party payor or the amount due to the health care entity from the payor as a result of determining the final total allowable cost for the reporting period and comparing that number with the amount that has been received from the payor for the reporting period.

floating rate note (FRN). A debt instrument that allows issuers to borrow at a floating short-term rate with a long-term stated maturity without some of the risks traditionally associated with commercial paper. The investor is subject to principal risk to the degree that the issuer's credit deteriorates or investor demand for FRNs decreases. Most health care issuers of FRNs require credit enhancement and a bank liquidity facility in conjunction with an FRN program.

full medical risk. The risk from uncertainties about the frequency, severity, and health care costs of rendered medical services.

fund. A self-contained accounting entity set up to account for a specific activity or project.

gross charges. The total charges at established rates for services rendered to a patient.

gross service revenues. Gross charges less charity allowances (charity care at established rates).

health care costs. For managed care services, health care costs include costs incurred to provide benefits to members under risk arrangements, such as costs of capitation, wellness, network management, utilization management, quality assurance, and other health care services. Health care costs generally exclude general and administrative, selling, maintenance, marketing, and interest costs.

health care services. Services provided to individuals related to the diagnosis or treatment of physical or mental illness.

Health Insurance Portability and Accountability Act (HIPAA) of 1996. Enacted by the federal government to improve patient security and confidentiality and also to standardize the formatting of electronic transactions.

home care. This level of care involves visits by health care workers to the home of the patient.

home health agency. An agency organized to provide health and supportive services in a person's home. These services may include nursing; nutritional; and therapeutic aid, such as physical therapy and dialysis, and the rental, as well as sale, of medical equipment.

hospital. A health care institution with an organized medical and professional staff and permanent facilities that include inpatient beds and provide medical, nursing, and other health-related services to patients (each state has its own definition of *hospital* for accreditation purposes).

incremental costs. Costs that vary with, and are directly attributable to, changes in business, such as an additional employer or health maintenance organization, or HMO, contract. Fixed costs, such as building depreciation or general overhead, that do not change with the addition or loss of a contract are not incremental costs.

incurred but not reported (IBNR). Costs associated with health care services incurred during a financial reporting period but not reported to the health care entity until after the financial reporting date. IBNR is also defined as potential claims for incidents associated with professional service that have occurred but have not yet been reported to the health care entity (defined in the FASB ASC glossary, as presented in the first section of this glossary).

indenture. An agreement between two or more persons specifying the reciprocal rights and duties of the parties under a contract, such as a lease, mortgage, or contract between bondholders and the issuer of the bond.

individual practice association (IPA). A partnership, association, corporation, or other legal entity organized to provide or arrange for the delivery of health care services to members of a prepaid health care plan and nonmember patients. In return, the IPA receives either a capitation fee or specified fee for rendered services.

inpatient. Under most circumstances, a patient who is provided with room, board, and general nursing service and is expected to remain in the health care facility at least overnight and occupy a bed.

in-substance defeasance. A form of advance refunding in which the debtor places into an irrevocable trust an amount of assets estimated to be sufficient to satisfy all future principal and interest payments of a specific obligation. In such cases, the debtor is not legally released from being the primary obligor (defined in the FASB ASC glossary, as presented in the first section of this glossary).

integrated delivery system. A provider or group of providers that is organized to deliver and finance acute and preventive health care services. An integrated delivery system generally will provide or arrange to provide a complete continuum of health care services (for example, inpatient acute care; ambulatory care; outpatient surgery; and home health care, including long-term care) to an enrolled population, generally for fixed, prepaid fees called premiums.

interest rate swaps. An agreement to exchange interest payments without actually exchanging the underlying principal. The two parties each agree to make interest payments based on the calculation formula for the other's debt. Swaps can be used for a variety of purposes, such as to reduce the overall cost of borrowing, lock in forward rates, reduce interest rate risk, or adjust the ratio of variable- and fixed-rate debt liabilities. Interest rate swaps do not change the amount or type of outstanding debt, but they do affect the issuer's debt portfolio and risk profile.

intermediate care facility (ICF). A facility that provides care to individuals whose mental or physical conditions require services that are above the level of room and board and that can be made available only through institutional facilities. The care provided at an ICF does not require hospitals or skilled nursing facilities. See also **nursing center**.

lag analysis. A report that tells managers the age of the claims that are being processed and the amount paid out each month (both for that month and any earlier months) and that compares those numbers with the amount of money that was accrued for expenses each month. A powerful tool used to determine whether the plan's reserves are adequate to meet all expenses. Plans that fail to properly perform lag studies may find themselves staring into the abyss.

length of stay (LOS). Number of calendar days that elapse between an inpatient's admission and discharge.

length of stay (average). A statistical measure of patient turnover determined by dividing the total number of patient days of care in a given period of time by the total number of inpatients who were discharged during that period.

London Interbank Offered Rate (LIBOR). A daily reference rate based on the interest rates at which banks offer to lend unsecured funds to other banks in the London wholesale money market.

long-term care. Provision of health, social, or personal care services on a recurring or continuous basis to persons with chronic physical or mental conditions who live in environments ranging from institutions to their own homes. This level of care is also called custodial care.

maintenance costs. Costs associated with maintaining enrollment records and processing premium collections and payments (defined in the FASB ASC glossary, as presented in the first section of this glossary).

managed care. A system of providing health care services to enrolled members in a plan through a defined network of health care providers who are given the responsibility to provide quality medical care while controlling the utilization of resources, use of expensive technologies, and access to specialists. Managed care can include a spectrum of systems, ranging from managed indemnity to preferred provider organizations, or, point of service, and open- and closed-panel health maintenance organizations, or HMOs.

managed care entities. A generic term applied to a managed care plan. These plans usually integrate the financing and delivery of health care services to an enrolled population. Managed care organizations contract with an organized provider network that either shares financial risks or has some incentive to deliver quality, cost-effective services. Also called managed care organizations.

mandatory tender. The requirement that a holder of a security surrender the security to the issuer or its agent (for example, a tender agent) for purchase. The tender date may be established under the bond contract or specified by the issuer upon the occurrence of an event specified in the bond contract. The purchase price typically is at par. Also called a mandatory put.

margin for risk of adverse deviation. Actuarially-determined estimate of the additional funding requirement to obtain a specific confidence level that losses will not exceed the amount paid into the self-insurance fund. Margins are determined using statistical simulation techniques.

Medicaid. Federal program created by Title XIX, "Medical Assistance," of the 1965 amendment to the Social Security Act of 1935 that provides health care benefits to indigent and medically-indigent persons (called Medi-Cal in California). Funded by the federal and state governments and administered by the states.

medical group. An association of physicians and other licensed health care professionals organized on a group basis to practice medicine.

Medicare. Federal program created by Title XVIII, "Health Insurance for the Aged," of the 1965 amendment to the Social Security Act of 1935 that provides health insurance benefits primarily to persons over the age of 65 and others eligible for Social Security benefits.

Medicare Administrative Contractors (MAC). A term used to describe those entities that are agents of the government in the application and provision of Medicare services. Previously referred to as a Medicare fiscal intermediary.

Medicare Part A. The portion of the Medicare program applicable to the reimbursement of inpatient hospital stays, critical access hospital services, certain care in a skilled nursing facility, hospice care, and some home health care.

Medicare Part B. The portion of the Medicare program applicable to the reimbursement of physician services, outpatient hospital care, durable medical equipment, and some medical services that are not covered by Medicare Part A.

Medicare Part C. The portion of the Medicare program created under the Balanced Budget Act of 1997 that includes the Medicare Advantage plans (formerly called Medicare+Choice) through which beneficiaries can enroll in additional types of health plans, including managed care plans.

Medicare Part D. The portion of the Medicare program created under the Medicare Modernization Act of 2003 featuring a voluntary outpatient prescription drug benefit, along with an interim prescription drug discount card and transitional assistance programs.

medium-term notes. An intermediate-term security offered on a continuous basis providing flexibility for an issuer to vary the amount of outstanding notes as its funding requirements change. The broad range of possible maturities enables an issuer to borrow at the most attractive yield at the time of each issuance. They can be issued domestically or abroad.

member. An individual who is enrolled as a subscriber or an eligible dependent of a subscriber in a prepaid health care plan.

minimum premium contract. A third-party administrator contract in which the administrator provides stop-loss insurance. A minimum fee is paid by an obligated entity, such as an employer, to a third-party administrator, such as an insurance company, in exchange for the third party administering the payment of claims up to a specified amount. Typically, the obligated entity is responsible for claims up to a certain limit, such as a percentage of total claims or specified amount, and uses the third party to pay the claims on its behalf, usually out of an employer-owned bank account. However, the third-party administrator is responsible for all payments above the predetermined limit.

multiprovider captive. An insurance entity owned by two or more health care entities that underwrites malpractice insurance for its owners.

Municipal Swap Index. The Securities Industry and Financial Markets Association Municipal Swap Index, which is a commonly used underlying for interest rate swaps that are used as hedges of interest rate risk associated with variable-rate tax-exempt debt. Also called the SIFMA Index.

net advance refunding. A type of advance refunding in which the proceeds from the new debt; additional cash deposits, if any; and the income earned on the related investments are sufficient to pay the interest, principal, and call premium on the old debt. After the advance refunding, the old debt is serviced by the investments in trust, and the new debt is serviced by the entity.

net service revenue. Gross service revenue less provisions for contractual adjustments with third-party payors, courtesy and policy discounts, or other adjustments and deductions, excluding charity care.

nonexchange transaction. As used in governmental financial accounting standards, an external transaction in which a government gives or receives value without directly receiving or giving equal value in exchange.

nursing center. A facility that provides nursing care to residents with a variety of needs or medical conditions. A nursing center may be a component of a continuing care retirement community. Also called a health center, skilled-nursing facility, intermediate-care facility, continuing-care facility, or basic-care home.

nursing home. Institution with an organized professional staff and permanent facilities, including inpatient beds, that provides continuous nursing and other health-related, psycho-social, and personal services to patients who are not in an acute phase of illness but who primarily require continued care on an inpatient basis.

occurrence-basis policy. A policy that covers claims resulting from incidents that occur during the policy term, regardless of when the claims are reported to the insurance carrier.

official statement (OS). The common term used for the offering document or offering circular prepared in connection with a new issue of municipal securities. Although functionally equivalent to the prospectus used in connection with registered securities, an official statement for municipal securities is exempt from the prospectus requirements of the Securities Act of 1933.

outliers. In referring to the Medicare Prospective Payment System, additional payments that are made for cases that have either unusually long lengths of stay or charges in excess of the cost outlier threshold.

outpatient. A patient who is not confined overnight in a health care institution. An ambulatory patient who visits the hospital for services but is not admitted to a hospital bed.

patient day. A common statistical measurement of hospital and inpatient activity. It represents one patient in the hospital or other facility overnight when the official patient census is taken. Many hospitals and providers follow the procedure of charging patients for fractional parts of a day or the day of discharge if the patient leaves after a particular hour referred to as the check-out time.

per diem reimbursement. Reimbursement of a health care entity based on a set rate per day, rather than charges. Per diem reimbursement can be varied by service (for example, medical or surgical, obstetrics, mental health, and intensive care) or uniform regardless of intensity of services.

periodic fees. Amounts paid to a continuing care retirement community by a resident at periodic intervals for continuing-care services. Such fees may be fixed or adjustable. Also called maintenance fees or monthly fees.

preferred provider organization (PPO). A plan that contracts with independent providers at a discount for services. The panel is limited in size and usually has some type of utilization review system associated with it. A PPO may be risk bearing, such as an insurance company, or nonrisk bearing, such as a physician-sponsored PPO that markets itself to insurance companies or self-insured companies via an access fee.

premium. The consideration paid for providing contract coverage. Also called a subscriber fee.

premium period. The period to which a premium payment applies (generally one month) that entitles a member to health care services according to the contract provisions.

prevailing charge. A charge that falls within the range of charges most frequently used in a locality for a particular service or procedure.

primary care. Care that is rendered in an ambulatory fashion, such as in an emergency room, outpatient clinic, or other outpatient department.

primary government. The foundation of a primary government is a separately elected governing body that is elected by the citizens in a general, popular election. As the nucleus of the financial reporting entity, the primary government generally is the focal point for the users of the financial statements. A primary government is any state government or general-purpose local government, municipality, or county. A primary government is also a special-purpose government (for example, a hospital district) that meets all of the following criteria:

a. It has a separately elected governing body.

b. It is legally separate.

c. It is fiscally independent of other state and local governments.

prospective payment system (PPS). Medicare payment made at a predetermined, specific rate for each Medicare discharge, based on the patient's diagnosis. Each discharge is classified according to a series of diagnosis-related groups. Prospective rate setting is used to set provider rates under a PPS. See also **diagnosis-related group**.

protected health information (PHI). As defined by the Health Insurance Portability and Accountability Act of 1996 regulations, health information that is created or received by a health care provider and relates to the past, present, or future physical or mental health or condition of an individual.

provider. A person or entity that undertakes to provide health care services.

rate setting. Process of establishing rates for providers of health care services by taking into account the financial needs of the provider. See also **prospective rate setting** and **retrospective rate setting** (defined in the FASB ASC glossary, as presented in the first section of this glossary).

refundable advance fees. The portion of an advance fee that is payable to a resident of a continuing care retirement community or the resident's estate.

refunded debt. Debt for which payment at a specified future date has been provided by the issuance of refunding debt.

refunding debt. Debt issued to provide funds to pay for refunded debt at a specified future date.

rehabilitation facility. Facility that provides medical, health-related, social, or vocational services to disabled persons to help them attain their maximum functional capacity.

reimbursement, cost-based. Payment by a third-party payor to a hospital of all allowable costs covered by the contract that are incurred by the hospital in the provision of services to patients.

reimbursement, prospective. Method of third-party payment by which costs to be incurred by an institution in providing services to patients are based not on actual costs but estimates made at the beginning of a fiscal period.

reimbursement, retroactive. Additional payment by a third-party payor to an institution for services not identified at the time of initial reimbursement.

reimbursement, retrospective. Method of third-party payment by which costs incurred by a hospital in providing services to covered patients are based on actual costs determined at the end of a fiscal period.

reinsurance. Reinsurance includes insurance purchased by a health plan to protect it against extremely high cost cases. It is a type of protection purchased by health maintenance organizations (HMOs) from insurance companies specializing in underwriting specific risks for a stipulated premium. Typical reinsurance risk coverages are individual stop-loss, aggregate stop-loss, out-of-area, and insolvency protection. As HMOs grow in membership, they usually reduce their reinsurance coverage and related direct costs as they reach a financial position to assume such risks themselves (defined in the FASB ASC glossary, as presented in the first section of this glossary).

resource-based relative value scales (RBRVS). A system to determine how much money medical providers should be paid. It is currently used by Medicare and many health maintenance organizations, or HMOs.

Resource Utilization Group (RUG). A system that categorizes skilled nursing facilities' patients into similar medical diagnoses for purposes of Medicare reimbursement.

retrospectively-rated insurance policy. An insurance policy with a premium that is adjustable based on the experience of the insured health care entity or group of health care entities during the policy term.

risk contract. A contract between a provider of health care services and a prepaid health care plan that exposes the provider to the uncertainty of financial gain or loss by obligating the provider to provide specified health care services to enrollees of the plan for a negotiated price, which may be an amount per case, service, or day. The price may vary based on the volume of services furnished during the contract period.

risk pool. A risk pool accumulates all the monies received from the capitation agreement and all the costs associated with providing patient services. At the end of the period, the excess of capitation payments over claims payments is distributed to the risk pool participants based upon the risk-sharing arrangement. See also **capitation arrangement**.

secondary care. Care that is rendered to inpatients in hospitals that offer short-term, acute-care services of either a general or specialized nature.

self-insurance. That portion of risk or loss assumed by a health care entity when no external insurance coverage exists.

self-insured obligation. The obligation for that portion of risk or loss assumed by a health care entity when no external insurance coverage exists.

self-insured plan or self-funded plan. A health plan in which the risk for medical cost is assumed by the company, rather than an insurance company or a managed care plan. Under the Employee Income Retirement Security Act of 1974, self-funded plans are exempt from state laws and regulations, such as premium taxes and mandatory benefits. Self-funded plans often contract with insurance companies or third-party administrators to administer the benefits.

sinking fund. A sinking fund is a means of repaying debt whereby the issuer makes periodic payments to a trustee who retires part of the issue, often by purchasing bonds on the open market.

skilled nursing facilities (SNF). These facilities provide services on a daily, inpatient basis. The services provided by an SNF are ordered by a physician and require the skilled services of technical or professional personnel.

subscriber. The person who is responsible for the payment of premiums or whose employment is the basis for eligibility for membership in a prepaid health care plan.

tender option. A provision in a bond contract under which the investor has the right to surrender the securities to the issuer or someone acting on the issuer's behalf, such as a tender agent, at the predetermined price (usually par) and on specified dates after the required notification. Also called an optional tender or put option.

tertiary care. Care that is rendered in hospitals that possess the personnel, equipment, and expertise to handle complex cases.

third-party administrator (TPA). A party unrelated to a plan who contracts to be responsible for plan administration.

third-party payor. Any entity, such as Blue Cross and Blue Shield, Medicare, or a commercial insurance entity, that contracts with health care entities and patients to pay for the care of covered patients.

trust fund. A fund established with an outside entity to be used for a specific purpose, such as to pay malpractice claims and related expenses as they arise.

ultimate cost. Total claims payments, including costs associated with litigating or setting claims.

unasserted claim. A medical malpractice claim that has not been formally asserted against a health care provider by, or on behalf of, a patient alleging improper professional service. It may relate to either reported or unreported incidents.

unrelated business. An activity that is a trade or business, regularly carried on, and not substantially related to furthering the exempt purpose of the not-for-profit entity. An unrelated business is subject to unrelated business income tax.

unreported incident. An occurrence in which improper professional service may have been administered by a health care provider, which may result in a malpractice claim of which the provider is not yet aware.

utilization (third party). The ratio of hospital services provided to third-party beneficiaries in relation to services provided to all patients of the hospital. This is usually based upon days, charges, or costs.

variable-rate demand notes (VRDN). Issuers may call the notes on any monthly interest payment date, which provides issuers the opportunity to refinance short-term obligations with long-term bonds if market conditions make this alternative attractive.

wholly-owned captive. An insurance entity subsidiary of a health care entity that provides malpractice insurance primarily to its parent entity.

Index

C

D

E

H

N

O

P

R

U

V